IRELAND

THE ROUGH GUIDE

KU-250-891

THE ROUGH GUIDES

OTHER AVAILABLE ROUGH GUIDES
**AMSTERDAM • BARCELONA • BERLIN • BRAZIL
BRITTANY & NORMANDY • BULGARIA • CALIFORNIA & WEST COAST USA
CANADA • CRETE • CZECH & SLOVAK REPUBLICS • CYPRUS • EGYPT
EUROPE • FLORIDA • FRANCE • GERMANY • GREECE • GUATEMALA & BELIZE
HOLLAND, BELGIUM & LUXEMBOURG • HONG KONG • HUNGARY • IRELAND
ISRAEL • ITALY • KENYA • MEDITERRANEAN WILDLIFE • MEXICO • MOROCCO
NEPAL • NEW YORK • NOTHING VENTURED • PARIS • PERU • POLAND
PORTUGAL • PRAGUE • PROVENCE • PYRENEES • ST PETERSBURG
SAN FRANCISCO • SCANDINAVIA • SICILY • SPAIN • THAILAND • TUNISIA
TURKEY • TUSCANY & UMBRIA • USA • VENICE • WEST AFRICA
WOMEN TRAVEL • ZIMBABWE & BOTSWANA**

FORTHCOMING
AUSTRALIA • CORSICA • ENGLAND • SCOTLAND • WALES

ROUGH GUIDE CREDITS

Series Editor: Mark Ellingham
Editorial: Martin Dunford, John Fisher, Jack Holland, Greg Ward,
  Jonathan Buckley, Richard Trillo
Production: Susanne Hillen, Kate Berens, Andy Hilliard, Gail Jammy

Many thanks to all the regional and local offices of the **Irish Tourist Board** and the **Northern Irish Tourist Board** who helped with the research of this book: in particular Mark Rowlette (London), Ellen Redmond (Dublin) and Anne Moore (Belfast), and to Naudi O'Sullivan of Shannon Development.

Thanks also to the **Youth Hostel Association of Northern Ireland**, **An Óige**, **Budget Hostels** and to Vary Knivett and Phil Kelly of the **Independent Hostel Owners** co-op.

For their invaluable help, encouragement and advice: Brian Trench, Ian Hill, Jo O'Donoghue, Killian Robinson, Luke Dodd, Chris O'Kane, Frank and Rosemarie Kennan, Tom Joyce, Charles and Geraldine O'Kane, Clare Coyle, Marleen, Jenny and Brian Nuttall, German Pump, Eamonn and Pauline Keenan, Pádraig Sugrue, Mary Hughes, Sara Hillen, Catherine Mulvenna, Michael O'Sullivan, Veronica O'Driscoll, Anne and Frank Greenwood, Ben Greenwood, Colin Hardwick, Niall Shanahan (lately), Maire Molloy, Charles Hueston, Juliana MacGregor, Mick and Nuala O'Driscoll, Ian McNicholl, Jack and Fidelis, Alice and John and Ben, Mary Hillen, George Gavan Duffy, Sean of Derrylahan, Elke and Karsten, Jean and Michael, Cillian Rodgers and family, Mike Gerrard, Jessica and to Mark Ellingham.

Thanks also to all those readers – too numerous to name here – whose letters were an enormous help in the production of the second edition, to Carol Gardiner for proofreading, and to the *Rough Guides* crew: Wendy Ferguson, Mick Sinclair, Jack Holland, Kate Berens, Dan Richardson, Jules Brown and John Gawthrop – and especially to the indefatigable trio of Jonathan Buckley, Greg Ward and Susanne Hillen.

And, of course, to the unflappable John Fisher.

Originally published by Harrap Columbus 1990 and 1992. Reprinted 1990, twice in 1991.
Reprinted by Rough Guides Ltd, 1 Mercer Street, London WC2H 9QJ, September 1992 and July 1993.
Distributed by Penguin Books, 27 Wrights Lane, London W8 5TZ.
Typeset in Linotron Univers and Century Old Style to an original design by Andrew Oliver.
Printed in the UK by Cox & Wyman, Reading, Berks.

Illustrations in Part One and Part Three by Ed Briant; Basics illustration by Gila.
Contexts illustration by Andrea McMordie.

608pp
includes index

British Library Cataloguing in Publication Data
A catalogue record for this book is available from the British Library.
ISBN 1-85828-051-6 (previously published by Harrap Columbus under ISBN 0-7471-0278-3).

IRELAND

THE ROUGH GUIDE

written and researched by

**SEÁN DORAN, MARGARET GREENWOOD
and HILDI HAWKINS**

With additional contributions by
Joe O'Connor, Luke Dodd, Killian Robinson, Paul Blaney,
Lin Coghlan, Tom Joyce and Richard Nairn

Contributing Editors
Susanne Hillen, Greg Ward, Jules Brown,
Wendy Ferguson and John Gawthrop

Edited by
JOHN FISHER and JONATHAN BUCKLEY

THE ROUGH GUIDES

CONTENTS

INTRODUCTION

L andscape and people are what bring most visitors to Ireland – South and North. And once there, few are disappointed by the reality of the stock Irish images: the green, rain-hazed loughs and wild, bluff coastlines, the inspired talent for talk and conversation, the easy pace and rhythms of life. What is perhaps more of a surprise is how much variety this very small land packs into its countryside. The limestone terraces of the stark, eerie Burren seem separated from the fertile flatlands of Tipperary by hundreds rather than tens of miles, and the primitive beauty of the West Coast, with its cliffs, coves and strands, seems to belong in another country altogether from the rolling plains of the central cattle-rearing counties.

The greatest attractions of the place are, with a few fine exceptions, rural. Ireland is becoming increasingly integrated with the industrial economies of western Europe, yet the modernisation of the country has to date made few marks: the countryside appears startlingly unspoilt and unpopulated if you have come over from England. It's a place to explore slowly, roaming through agricultural landscapes scattered with farmhouses, or along the endlessly indented coastline, where the crash of the sea against the cliffs and myriad islands is often the only sound. It is perfect if you want space to walk, bike or (with a bit of bravado) swim; if you want to fish, sail, or spend a week on inland waterways. In town, too, the pleasures are unhurried: evenings over a Guinness or two in the snug of a pub, listening to the chat around a blood-orange turf fire.

This said, there are sights enough. In every corner of the island are traces of a culture established long before the coming of Christianity: sites such as **Newgrange** in County Meath or the clifftop fortress of **Dún Aengus** are among the most stupendous Neolithic remains in Europe, while in some areas of Sligo almost every hill is capped by an ancient cairn. In the depths of the so-called Dark Ages the Christian communities of Ireland were great centres of learning, and the ruins of **Clonmacnoise**, the **Rock of Cashel** and a score of other **monasteries** are evocative of a time when Ireland won its reputation as a land of saints and scholars. Fortifications raised by the chieftains of the Celtic clans and the Anglo-Norman barons bear witness to a period of later turbulence, while the ascendancy of the Protestant settlers has left its mark in the form of vast mansions and estates.

But the richness of Irish **culture** is not a matter of monuments. Especially in the Irish-speaking *Gaeltacht* areas, you'll be aware of the strength and continuity of the island's oral and musical traditions. **Myth-making** is for the Irish people their most ancient and fascinating entertainment. The ancient classics are full of extraordinary stories – Cúchulainn the unbeatable hero in war, Medb the insatiable heroine in bed, or Fionn Mac Cumhaíl (Finn Mac Cool) chasing Diarmuid and Gráinne up and down the country – and tall tales, superstition-stirring and "mouthing off" (boasting) play as large a part in day-to-day life as they did in the era of the *Táin Bó Cuailnge*, Europe's oldest vernacular epic. As a guileless foreigner enquiring about anything from a beautiful lake to a pound of butter, you're ideally placed to trigger the most colourful responses. And the speech of the country – moulded by the rhythms of the ancient tongue – has fired such twentieth-century greats as Yeats, Joyce and Beckett.

Music has always been at the centre of Irish community life. You'll find **traditional** music sessions all around the touristed coasts and in the cities, too – some of it might be of dubious pedigree, but the *Gaeltacht* areas, and others, can be counted on to provide authentic renditions. Side by side with the traditional circuit is a romping **rock** scene, largely Dublin-based, that has spawned the Undertones, "Saint" Bob's Boomtown Rats, U2, and more recently Sinead O'Connor. And ever-present are the country and western performers, fathoming and feeding the old Irish dreams of courting, emigrating and striking it lucky; there's hardly a dry eye in the house when the guitars are packed away.

The lakes and rivers of Ireland make it an angler's dream, but the **sports** that raise the greatest enthusiasm amongst the Irish themselves are speedier and more dangerous. Horse racing in Ireland has none of the socially divisive connotations present on the other side of the Irish Sea, and the country has bred some of the world's finest thoroughbreds. Hurling, the oldest team game played in Ireland, requires the most delicate of ball-skills and the sturdiest of bones. Gaelic football, which commands a larger following, bears a superficial resemblance to the English version, but allows a wider range of violent contact. And, in Sean Kelly and Stephen Roche, Ireland has produced two of the supermen of professional cycling, the cruellest of endurance tests.

No introduction can cope with the complexities of Ireland's **politics**, which permeate every aspect of daily life, most conspicuously in the North. However, throughout the guide we have addressed the issues wherever they arise, and at the end of the book, in the *Contexts* section, we have included pieces that give a general overview of the current situation. Suffice it to say that, regardless of partisan politics, Irish hospitality is as warm as the brochures say, on both sides of the border.

Where to go

The area that draws most visitors is the **west coast**, where the demonically daunting peninsulas of the northern reaches are immediately contrasted a little inland by the mystical lakes of the **Donegal highlands**. The **midwest coastline** is just as strangely attractive, combining vertiginous cliffs, boulder-strewn wastes, and violent mountains of granite and quartz. In the **south**, the melodramatic peaks of the **Ring of Kerry** fall to lake-pools and seductive seascapes. Less talked about, but no less rewarding in their way, are the gentle sandy coves that **Cork** and **Kerry** share.

In the **north** of the island, the principal draw is the weird basalt geometry of the **Giant's Causeway**, not far from the lush **Glens of Antrim**. To the south of Belfast lies the beautiful walking territory of the softly contoured **Mountains of Mourne**, divided by **Carlingford Lough** from the myth-drenched **Cooley Mountains**.

The **interior** is nowhere as spectacular as the fringes of the island, but the southern heartlands of pastures and low wooded hills, and the wide peat bogs of the very centre are the classic landscapes of Ireland. Of the **inland waterways**, the most alluring are the island-studded **Lough Erne** complex of Fermanagh, and the **River Shannon**, with its string of huge lakes.

Some of the country's wildest scenery lies just offshore: west-coast **Aran** is the best known of the islands, but equally compelling are storm-battered **Tory Island**, to the far northwest, the savage **Skelligs**, off the southwest coast, and the sequestered **Scattery**, in the mouth of the Shannon.

For anyone with strictly limited time, one of the best options must be to combine a visit to **Dublin** with the mountains and monastic ruins of **County Wicklow**. Dublin is an extraordinary combination of youthfulness and tradition, a human-scale capital of decaying Georgian squares and vibrant pubs. **Belfast**, victim of a perennial bad press, vies with Dublin in the vitality of its nightlife, while the cities of **Cork, Waterford** and, above all, **Galway** have a new-found energy that makes them a pleasure to visit.

When to go

Ireland's **climate**, determined by the pressure-systems of the Atlantic, is notoriously variable, and cannot be relied upon at any time of the year. Each year produces weeks of beautiful weather – the problem lies in predicting when they are likely to arrive. In recent years **late spring** and **early autumn** have proved the sunniest, with May and September as the pleasantest months.

Geographically, the **southeast** is the driest and sunniest part of the country, and the **northwest** is the wettest. But regional variations are not particularly pronounced, the overall climate being characterised by its mildness in comparison with that of Britain, which doesn't benefit so much from the Gulf Stream. Even in the wetter zones, mornings of rain are frequently followed by afternoons of blue sky and sun – and besides, a downpour on a windswept headland can be exhilarating, and provides as good a pretext as any for a warming shot of whiskey.

PART ONE

THE
BASICS

GETTING THERE FROM BRITAIN

Since deregulation of Ireland's air transport and the opening up of a number of regional airports, there has been a proliferation of cheap flights to all parts of Ireland and, unless you need to take a car, flying is often the best-value way of getting there. The only problem is that at peak times some of the cheaper fares may not apply, or all the cheap seats may be booked. In that case it's worth looking at some of the combined rail/ferry or bus/ferry options, which are generally better value than making your own way to the port.

FLIGHTS

Flight time from London to the Republic is between an hour (to Dublin) and ninety minutes and, with *Aer Lingus* flying from ten British airports, and its main Irish competitor, *Ryanair*, from seven, it's a quick and easy way of travelling.

In general, there isn't much in the way of seasonal variations, although the astonishingly complex **fare structures** are constantly changing, so it's always a good idea to check the latest offers direct with the airlines or with your local travel agent. The main differences in price come from how much you're prepared to tie yourself down in advance in terms of travel dates, and on the particular days you want to travel; airline staff are generally very good at letting you know if leaving a day or two earlier or later is likely to save you a lot of money.

Fares from **London to Dublin** vary considerably: *British Midland's* cheapest single Heathrow–

Dublin fare costs £65; *Aer Lingus's* Saver ticket costs £77 from Heathrow; *Ryanair's* cheapest single fare from Stansted at £90 is in fact dearer than their Superapex return flight.

All the airlines also offer the standard range of APEX and **budget return fares**, and some are very cheap indeed. A Superapex flight (booked 14 days in advance, must include a Saturday night in Ireland and is non-refundable) with *Aer Lingus, Ryanair* or *British Midland* costs £79. Flights to regional airports are also well worth considering: *Aer Lingus's* Superapex return from London to Cork or Shannon costs £99; *Ryanair's* London–Galway Saver ticket costs £116.

Flying **from outside London** can be extremely cheap too. *Aer Lingus* serve all the main regional airports: a Superapex Manchester–Dublin return can cost as little as £49; Leeds–Dublin return costs £88; the short hop from Liverpool to Dublin with *Ryanair* costs £65 return on a Saver ticket. *Loganair* offer a flight from Manchester to Knock (£85 single, APEX return £121) and from Glasgow to Carrickfinn, Co. Donegal (£60 single, £85 APEX return).

FLYING TO NORTHERN IRELAND

Your fare to Northern Ireland is really going to be determined by where you want to fly from. Most cheap return fares involve spending at least one Saturday night away and many will only give a percentage refund if you need to cancel or alter your journey – some give no refund at all, so make sure you check the restrictions on your ticket carefully before you buy it.

If you are travelling from **Scotland** *Loganair* fly from Edinburgh to Belfast and from Glasgow to Belfast or Derry for £40–44 each way.

From the **north of England** *Loganair* fly from Manchester to Derry and Belfast (both routes £45 single, £90 return). From Newcastle you can fly with *Gill Air* to Belfast (single £49, Superapex return £94). The cheapest flight from Liverpool to Belfast is *Manx Airlines* £35 single, which must be booked either the day before or on the actual day of flight. Otherwise the cheapest single costs £48, return £76. From Leeds/Bradford Airport *Air UK* have a skylink single fare to Belfast for £50 which can be booked after 3pm the day before departure; other than this their cheapest single costs £66, return £98.

Flights from **the midlands** are quite pricey with *Jersey European* and *Birmingham European* both having flights from Birmingham to Belfast for £95 single, £99 return. *British Midland* fly from East Midlands Airport to Belfast (single £81, return £106).

Flights to Belfast from **Bristol and Exeter** with *Jersey European* are similarly expensive

with singles at £119 and £130 and returns at £129 and £146 respectively.

In the **southeast** *Britannia Airways* fly from Luton to Belfast for £35 single, £70 return. *British Airways* has a standby from Heathrow to Belfast for £61, a bookable single for £66; their cheapest return ticket is an APEX fare at £108. *British Midland* fly the same route with similar fares.

TRAVEL OPERATORS TO IRELAND

AIRLINES

Aer Lingus, 223 Regent Street, London W1 (☎081/899 4747).

Air UK, Stansted House, Stansted Airport, Essex (☎0345/666777).

Birmingham European, Birmingham International Airport, Coventry Road, Birmingham B26 3QB (☎021/782 0711).

Britannia Airways, Luton Airport, Luton, Beds LU2 9ND (☎0582/424155).

British Airways, 156 Regent Street, London W1 (☎081/897 4000).

British Midland, Donington Hall, Castle Donington, Derby DE7 2SB (☎0332/810 552).

Gill Air, Newcastle International Airport, Newcastle-upon-Tyne NE13 8BT (☎091/286 2222).

Jersey European, Exeter Airport, Exeter, Devon EX5 2BD (☎0345/078400).

Loganair, Trident House, Renfrew Road, Paisley (☎041/889 3181).

Ryanair, (☎071/435 7101).

Manx Airlines, Ronald's Way Airport, Ballasalla, Isle of Man (☎0264/824313, ☎071/493 0803, ☎051/486 3333).

FERRY COMPANIES

Brittany Ferries, 42 Grand Parade, Cork (☎021/277801).

B & I Line, Reliance House, Water Street, Liverpool L2 8TP (☎051/227 3131; ☎071/734 4681, 7512); Holyhead ☎0407/760222; Dublin ☎01/797977; Rosslare ☎053/33311. After-hours information lines; England ☎061/236 3936; Ireland ☎01/606666.

Irish Ferries, 2/4 Merrion Row, Dublin 2 (☎01/610511); Rosslare ☎053/33158.

North Irish Ferries, Victoria Terminal 2, West Bank Road, Belfast, BT3 9JN (☎0232/779090).

P & O European Ferries, Cairnryan, Stranraer, Wigtownshire DG9 8RF (☎05812/276). Central reservations ☎0304/203388; Larne ☎0574/74321

Sealink British Ferries, Charter House, Park Street, Ashford, Kent TN24 8EX (☎0233/647047); Fishguard ☎0348/872881; Dublin ☎01/808844; Dun Laoghaire ☎01/774206; Rosslare ☎053/33115.

Swansea–Cork Ferries, King's Dock, Swansea, W. Glamorgan (☎0792/456116).

STUDENT/YOUTH OPERATORS, TRAINS AND BUS COMPANIES

British Rail, Northern Ireland and services via Holyhead ☎071/387 7070. Services via Fishguard ☎071/262 6767.

Campus Travel, *London Student Travel*, 52 Grosvenor Gardens, London SW1W 0AG (☎071/730 3402). Other *Campus Travel/USIT* offices throughout Britain and Ireland.

Eurotrain, 52 Grosvenor Gardens, London SW1W 0AG (☎071/730 3402).

National Express Eurolines, 164 Buckingham Palace Road, London SW1 (☎071/730 0202).

Slattery's Bus Service, 162 Kentish Town Road, London NW5 (☎071/485 2778).

STA Travel, 86 Old Brompton Road, London SW7 (☎071/937 9921). Other offices throughout Britain.

Wasteels, 121 Wilton Road, London SW1V 1JZ (☎071/834 7066).

YOUTH AND STUDENT FARES

Under 25s can buy youth fares direct from airlines; a passport or driving licence are sufficient proof of age. Tickets are subject to availability; on *Aer Lingus* they can only be booked the day before travel and are left open for the return journey – which means you may not be able to come home when you want to during busy periods. For single journeys youth fares can be good value; if you are looking for a return regular APEX or Saver ticket might be a better option. Both *Aer Lingus* and *Ryanair* have a London–Dublin youth fare for £43 single; returns are double that. *Aer Lingus* offer a London–Galway youth fare of £69 single.

If you are a **student** or **under 26** it's also worth checking fares through a specialist agency like *STA Travel* or *Campus Travel* (see box for addresses), or any *Campus Travel* office around the country. A London–Dublin return (valid for 3 months) can cost as little as £68. You will need a *Youthcard* or a *Travelsave Stamp* for your *International Student Identity Card (ISIC)* to be eligible for discount fares: both can be bought for £6 when you book your ticket. If you are travelling with *Loganair*, student fares are available from the airline directly.

FERRIES

Taking the **boat** is the traditional way of getting to Ireland, but it's rapidly being outclassed by cheap air travel. With *Sealink* pulling out of the popular overnight Liverpool–Dublin crossing, where you could sleep on the boat, going by ferry has become that bit grimmer. Now, you either waste a day by doing the 3hr 30min **Holyhead–Dublin** journey during the daytime, or arrive exhausted because you've done it at night. **Pembroke** and **Fishguard to Rosslare**, at 4hr 15min and 3hr 15min respectively, are no better. Still, if you need a car when you get to Ireland, you don't have much choice (car hire in Ireland is among the most expensive in Europe – see under "Getting Around"). It's worth booking in advance in summer – almost all the sailings in June, July and August are "controlled", which means that you have to book in advance, or risk not being let on the boat, even if there's room.

Student reductions on ferries can be considerable – *B&I* give a 25 percent reduction to holders of an *ISIC* card, and a 50 percent reduction if the card has a *Travelsave* stamp. On *Sealink*, *InterRail* ticket holders get a 30 percent reduction

and both *Sealink* and *B&I* offer a reduction of 25 percent to *International Youth Hostel Association* card holders.

As an indication of **costs** a return ticket for a car and four passengers on both of *B&I's* routes (Pembroke–Rosslare and Holyhead–Dublin) costs between £100 and £340 depending on the time of year; *Sealink* prices are the same, though on their ticket the car can take up to five passengers. Fares for individual foot passengers start at around £32, rising to £46 high season; combined bus/ferry or train/ferry tickets (see below) are generally better value. Bear in mind that you will have to pay IR£5 **departure tax** on any ticket bought in the Republic.

Just one ferry service still operates out of **Liverpool**, *North Irish Ferries'* service to Belfast. At the moment it doesn't take foot passengers; a single ticket for a car and driver costs £100, and has to be booked in advance (see box).

Making the short crossing – 2hr 20min – from **Stranraer or Cairnryan to Larne** (near Belfast) is surprisingly expensive, whether you use *Sealink* or *P&O*. A typical fare is £60–90 each way for an average car, plus £16 single for passengers. Foot passengers pay £32–36 return. In high season there are slight reductions for night travel.

There's a ten-hour sailing between **Swansea and Cork** operated by *Swansea-Cork Ferries*. Connections from **Rosslare to Le Havre and Cherbourg**, and **Cork to Le Havre**, are operated by *Irish Ferries*; *Brittany Ferries* operates a summer crossing from **Cork to Roscoff** once a week (depart Sat 3.30pm; £47–58 one way; the crossing takes 14 hours).

TRAINS

Prices of combined rail/sea return tickets vary greatly according to the time of year: from London **to Dublin** costs £61–89; from Manchester the fare is £51–69. London **to Belfast** is £73–101 return; Birmingham to Belfast is £69–90 return. Simply book at your local station. Once in Ireland, north or south, you can pick up a *Rambler* ticket for either the rail system, the buses, or rail and bus combined (see "Getting Around").

Anyone **under 26** can get cut-price *BIJ* rail tickets from *Eurotrain*, *Wasteels* or direct from *British Rail*; their prices vary, but are around £56–81 return London to Dublin, from £64 return all the way to the west coast. An **InterRail** pass (available from *British Rail*, currently at £180 for under-26s) buys a month's travel on European – including Irish – railways, plus discounts on the ferries. If you buy it in the UK, however, it doesn't include British trains, so you'd have to have to be planning on a great deal of rail travel to make it worthwhile. InterRail passes for people over 26 cost £260 a month, £180 for fifteen days, and don't include ferry crossings, so are still less likely to be worth buying.

You must have been resident in Europe for at least six months to qualify for *InterRail*; if you're coming from **North America**, the equivalent **Eurail** passes are much less good value – and certainly not likely to pay for themselves if you travel only in Ireland. There are five different kinds of pass, valid for 15 days ($430), 21 days ($550), or one ($680), two ($920) or three months ($1150). There is also the **Eurail Youth Pass**, valid for those under 26, good for one or two months and costing $470 and $640 respectively, and the **Eurail Saverpass**, allowing 15 days of unlimited first-class travel for two people for $340 each between March and October (you need 3 people to qualify between April & Sept). The **Eurail Flexipass** is more flexible, in that you choose the number of days you want to travel: 5 days' first-class travel within 15 consecutive days costs $280; 9 days within 21 days costs $450; 14 days within one month costs $610; the **Eurail Youth Flexipass**, again for under-26s, is valid for 15 days within two months ($420).

BUSES

Getting to Ireland by bus is a slog, but it's very cheap. *Slattery*'s offers an off-peak **London to Dublin** return for £39, rising to £55 high season – the ticket takes you as far as the dock and then you have to make your own way into the city centre by bus which costs around £1.10. *Slattery's* operate direct services to Ireland from several English cities: Leeds, Bradford, Birmingham, Manchester, Liverpool, Chester and Holyhead. The outward journey is gruelling: you arrive at Holyhead in the small hours to wait around the ferry terminal until 4am; the return is less of an ordeal as coaches connect with the ferry.

If you're heading for the **west coast** it's worth buying a direct ticket. London–Galway for example costs £51–65 return, and they also offer services to Cork, Limerick and Tralee, with stops at major towns en route. *National Express*'s *Eurolines* fares also start at £39 from London to Dublin city centre, and they have departures from the same cities as *Slattery's*, along with services from Sheffield, and in summer from Bristol and Cardiff. Book these at your local *National Express* coach station, or through virtually any travel agent.

Getting **to the North** by coach is more expensive: London to Belfast £55 return with *Scottish Citylink*; Birmingham to Belfast £52.

GETTING THERE FROM THE USA AND CANADA

Ireland is easily accessible from the USA by a number of airlines that offer direct flights to either Dublin or Shannon, the country's two major gateways. If cost is your main concern, the proliferation of cheap flights from the British Isles, together with the number of rail/ferry and bus/ferry options, may also make flying via London worth consideration. Ferries and cheap flights also make Ireland easily accessible as part of a wider European travel itinerary.

FROM EASTERN AND CENTRAL USA

Aer Lingus, 122 E 42nd St, New York, NY 10166 (☎212/557-1110 or 800/223-6537), the national airline of Ireland, flies out of **Boston**, **New York**, and **Chicago** (Sunday only) to **Dublin** and **Shannon**. The fares from New York and Boston to Dublin are the same: the APEX ticket, requiring a fourteen-day advance purchase and permitting a maximum stay of six months, starts at around $475 in the low season, rising to $700 in the high, with fares to Shannon approximately $30 less. **From Chicago** the fares are around $700 in the low season and $800 in the high. A cheaper option are the promotional fares *Aer Lingus* offers throughout the year, including such offers as a Tuesday-to-Tuesday round-trip fare from New York for under $400. These are liable to change, so it's well worth inquiring about the latest promotion when calling.

Of the US airlines that fly direct to Ireland, *Delta* (☎800/221-1212) flies from Atlanta to both Shannon and Dublin. Their APEX fares range from $650 low season to $900 in the high, with a mid-season return costing around $750. If you are connecting from another US city, however, fares can be a good deal more reasonable.

Travelling **via London**, there are lots of options from most of the eastern hub cities, though the best deals are generally out of New York and Chicago. The lowest off-peak fare to London from New York with the major carriers – *British Airways*, *American*, *United* and *Virgin Atlantic* – is around $330, though peak season prices are likely to at least double this. If you're content to travel to London, *Virgin Atlantic* offer by far the best value for money, with excellent in-flight service and entertainment. To give an idea of the alternatives, *United* fly from Chicago to London for $460 off-peak, over $1000 in summer.

TRAVEL CUTS IN CANADA

Head Office: 187 College St, Toronto, Ontario M5T 1P7; ☎416/979-2406

ALBERTA
MacEwan Hall Student Centre, Univ. of Calgary, Calgary T2N 1N4; ☎403/282-7687. 10424A 118th Ave., Edmonton T6G 0P7; ☎403/471-8054

BRITISH COLUMBIA
Room 326, T.C., Student Rotunda, Simon Fraser University, Burnaby, British Columbia V5A 1S6; ☎604/291-1204. 1516 Duranleau St, Granville Island, Vancouver V6H 3S4; ☎604/687-6033. Student Union Building, University of British Columbia, Vancouver V6T 1W5; ☎604/228-6890 Student Union Building, University of Victoria, Victoria V8W 2Y2; ☎604/721-8352

MANITOBA
University Centre, University of Manitoba, Winnipeg R3T 2N2; ☎204/269-9530

NOVA SCOTIA
Student Union Building, Dalhousie University, Halifax B3H 4J2; ☎902/424-2054. 6139 South St, Halifax B3H 4J2; ☎902/494-7027

ONTARIO
University Centre, University of Guelph, Guelph N1G 2W1; ☎519/763-1660. Fourth Level Unicentre, Carleton University, Ottawa, K1S5B6; ☎613/238-5493. 60 Laurier Ave E, Ottawa K1N 6N4; ☎613/238-8222. Student Street, Room G27, Laurentian University, Sudbury P3E 2C6; ☎705/673-1401. 96 Gerrard St E, Toronto M5B 1G7; ☎(416) 977-0441. University Shops Plaza, 170 University Ave W, Waterloo N2L 3E9; ☎519/886-0400.

QUÉBEC (known as *Voyages CUTS*)
Université McGill, 3480 rue McTavish, Montréal H3A 1X9; ☎514/398-0647. 1613 rue St Denis, Montréal H2X 3K3; ☎514/843-8511. Université Concordia, Edifice Hall, Suite 643, S.G.W. Campus, 1455 bd de Maisonneuve Ouest, Montréal H3G 1M8; ☎514/288-1130. 19 rue Ste Ursule, Québec G1R 4E1; ☎418/692-3971

SASKATCHEWAN
Place Riel Campus Centre, University of Saskatchewan, Saskatoon S7N 0W0; ☎306/975-3722

NOUVELLES FRONTIÈRES

In the United States

NEW YORK 12 East 33rd St, New York, NY 10016 ☎212/779-0600

LOS ANGELES 6363 Wilshire Blvd, Suite 200, Los Angeles, CA 90048; ☎213/658-8955

SAN FRANCISCO 209 Post St, Suite 1121, San Francisco, CA 94108; ☎415/781-4480

In Canada

MONTREAL 800 East Blvd de Maison Neuve, Montréal, Quebec (☎514/288-9942)

QUEBEC 176 Grande Allée Ouest, Québec, P.Q. G1R 2G9; ☎418/525-5255

COUNCIL TRAVEL IN THE US

Head Office: 205 E. 42nd St, New York, NY 10017; ☎212/661-1450

CALIFORNIA
2486 Channing Way, Berkeley, CA 94704; ☎415/848-8604
UCSD Price Center, Q-076, La Jolla, CA 92093; ☎619/452-0630
1818 Palo Verde Ave, Suite E, Long Beach, CA 90815; ☎213/598-3338
1093 Broxton Ave, Suite 220, Los Angeles, CA 90024; ☎213/208-3551
4429 Cass St, San Diego, CA 92109; ☎619/270-6401
312 Sutter St, Suite 407, San Francisco, CA 94108; ☎415/421-3473
919 Irving St, Suite 102, San Francisco, CA 94122; ☎415/566-6222
14515 Ventura Blvd, Suite 250, Sherman Oaks, CA 91403; ☎818/905-5777

COLORADO
1138 13th St, Boulder, CO 80302; ☎818/905-5777

CONNECTICUT
Yale Co-op East, 77 Broadway, New Haven, CT 06520; ☎203/562-5335

DISTRICT OF COLUMBIA
1210 Potomac St, NW Washington, DC 20007; ☎202/337-6464

GEORGIA
12 Park Place South, Atlanta, GA 30303; ☎404/577-1678

ILLINOIS
1153 N. Dearborn St, Chicago, IL 60610; ☎312/951-0585
831 Foster St, Evanston, IL 60201; ☎708/475-5070

LOUISIANA
8141 Maple St, New Orleans, LA 70118; ☎504/866-1767

MASSACHUSETTS
79 South Pleasant St, 2nd Floor, Amherst, MA 01002; ☎413/256-1261
729 Boylston St, Suite 201, Boston, MA 02116; ☎617/266-1926
1384 Massachusetts Ave, Suite 206, Cambridge, MA 02138; ☎617/497-1497
Stratton Student Center MIT, W20-024, 84 Massachusetts Ave, Cambridge, MA 02139; ☎617/497-1497

MINNESOTA
1501 University Ave SE, Room 300, Minneapolis, MN 55414; ☎612/379-2323

NEW YORK
35 W. 8th St, New York, NY 10011; ☎212/254-2525
Student Center, 356 West 34th St, New York, NY 10001; ☎212/643-1365

NORTH CAROLINA
703 Ninth St, Suite B-2, Durham, NC 27705; ☎919/286-4664

OREGON
715SW Morrison, Suite 600, Portland, OR 97205; ☎503/228-1900

RHODE ISLAND
171 Angell St, Suite 212, Providence, RI 02906; ☎401/331-5810

TEXAS
2000 Guadalupe St, Suite 6, Austin, TX 78705; ☎512/472-4931
Exec. Tower Office Center, 3300 W. Mockingbird, Suite 101, Dallas, TX 75235; ☎214/350-6166

WASHINGTON
1314 Northeast 43rd St, Suite 210, Seattle, WA 98105; ☎206/632-2448

WISCONSIN
2615 North Hackett Avenue, Milwaukee, WI; ☎414/332-4740

STA IN THE US

BOSTON
273 Newbury St, Boston, MA 02116; ☎617/266-6014

HONOLULU
1831 S. King St, Suite 202, Honolulu, HI 96826; ☎808/942-7755

LOS ANGELES
920 Westwood Blvd, Los Angeles, CA 90024; ☎213/824-1574
7204 Melrose Ave, Los Angeles, CA 90046; ☎213/934-8722

2500 Wilshire Blvd, Los Angeles, CA 90057; ☎213/380-2184

NEW YORK
17 E. 45th St, Suite 805, New York, NY 10017; ☎212/986-9470; ☎800/777-0112

SAN DIEGO
6447 El Cajon Blvd, San Diego, CA 92115; ☎619/286-1322

SAN FRANCISCO
166 Geary St, Suite 702, San Francisco, CA 94108; ☎415/391-8407

FROM THE WEST COAST

From the **West Coast** there's less choice direct to Ireland: *Aer Lingus* APEX fares from **Los Angeles** are around $750 low season, rising to $900 in the high. Getting to London is again far easier: the big airlines fly at least three times a week (sometimes daily) from Los Angeles, San Francisco and Seattle. *British Airways* have plenty of flights and are competitive, with fares starting at $700 to London

DISCOUNT FLIGHTS

There is a good variety of **discount flights** available to Ireland. *STA* for example has a high-season fare of around $550 from New York, with cheap connections from other US cities, or more economically, *Council Travel* offers low-season round trips starting at about $400. Among the range of other discount companies worth checking out are *Nouvelles Frontières* (☎212/779-0600), *Access International* (☎800/333-7280), *McTravel* (☎800/333-3335), *International Travel Specialists* (☎800/444-6064), *Travel Cuts* in Canada, or any similar companies advertising in the travel sections of the Sunday papers.

Airhitch (☎212/864-2000) sells last-minute standbys to Europe from several US cities for one low price ($160 from New York, $229 from Los Angeles). However, precise dates and destinations cannot be guaranteed. Instead you tell them what range of days you want to fly on, and where you want to fly to, and a few days prior to the time you want to leave you will be offered a choice of flights. Naturally this form of travel is very unpredictable, and while you are almost sure to leave at the time you specified, it is not certain you will fly to the exact place you wanted to.

GROUP/STUDENT TRAVEL

A variety of short excursions and specialised tours to Ireland are available from a variety of organisations, including *Aer Lingus*, which offer a range of **fly-drive packages**. Other special interest operators in this field include *Forum Travel International* and *Backroads*, who both offer a range of bicycling tours, and *Equitours*, who lead horseback-riding trips. *CIE Tours International*, 108 Ridgedale Ave, Morristown, NJ 07690 (☎201/292-3438, ☎800/522-5258) are a good general operator to Ireland and also sell a variety of rail passes.

For students, programmes combining work and study with travel to a variety of destinations including Ireland are available from: *The Council on International Education Exchange*, 205 East 42nd Street, New York, NY 10017 (☎212/661-1414); *The Humanities Institute*, PO Box 18B, Belmont, MS 02178 (☎800/327-1657), and *The American Institute of Foreign Study*, College Summer Division, 102 Greenwich Avenue, Greenwich, CT 06830. For general information and publications about studying abroad, try contacting the *Institute of International Education*, 809 U.N. Plaza, New York, NY 10017 (☎212/883-8200).

RED TAPE AND VISAS

British nationals born in the UK do not need a passport to enter the Republic or the North, but it is useful to carry one in case you use the medical services, and for cashing travellers' cheques. If you don't take a passport, be sure to have some other form of convincing ID. UK passport holders *not* born in Great Britain or Northern Ireland must have a valid passport or national identity document. If you are a British national of Indian, Pakistani, Bangladeshi, Chinese or African descent, it is advisable to take your passport along, in spite of the fact that technically speaking you don't need one.

Other EC nationals, travellers from the USA, Canada, Australia, New Zealand simply need a passport and can stay for up to three months. After this you'll need to apply to the Department of Justice in Dublin (39 Anne's Lane, Dublin 2; ☎01/714811) to stay longer: there's no limit on the length of stay for British nationals. Travellers from Commonwealth countries should check with the Irish Embassy beforehand since regulations vary: if you are from India, Pakistan and certain African countries you will need a visa. In the North, British regulations of course apply. This means that EC nationals and travellers from most English-speaking and Commonwealth countries usually need only a passport to stay for up to six months.

IRISH CONSULATES ABROAD

Britain, 17 Grosvenor Place, London SW1X 7HR (☎071/235 2171).

Australia, 20 Arkana Street, Yarrulumla, Canberra 2600 A.C.T. (☎062/733-022).

Belgium, 19 Rue du Luxembourg, B 1040 Brussels (☎02/513-66-33).

Canada, 170 Metcalfe Street, Ottawa K2P 1P3, Ontario (☎613/745-8624)

Denmark, Ostbanegade 21, I.T.H., DK-2100 Copenhagen (☎045/423-233).

Germany, Godesberger Allee 119, 5300 Bonn 2 (☎0228/37-69-37, 38, 39).

Netherlands, 9 Dr Kuperstraat, 2514 BA The Hague (☎070/363/0993 194).

Sweden, Östermalmsgatan 97 (1V), 114 59 Stockholm (☎08/661-8005, 661-7409, 661-3241).

United States, Embassy, 2234 Massachusetts Avenue N.W., Washington DC 20008 (☎202/462-3939, 40, 41, 42). Consulates in New York, Boston, San Francisco and Chicago.

COSTS, MONEY AND BANKS

It may come as a surprise to find that Ireland is not a cheap place to travel. If anything, food, drink and transport work out more expensive than in Britain, while accommodation is not much less. The least expensive bed, in a hostel, will rarely be less than £4 a night, while Bed and Breakfast generally works out at £9–12 per person. Reckon on about £4 for a basic, filling meal, and on spending more than you expect on drink, partly because it's expensive (around IR£1.50–1.60 a pint) and partly because so much social life and entertainment revolves around the pubs.

In short you're likely to spend a minimum of £15 a day even if you're being very careful, and it's easy to find yourself getting through £25 or more if you plan to live it up at all. As always, if you're travelling in a group you may be able to save some money by sharing rooms and food.

The **currency** in the **Republic** is the Irish pound, also known as the *punt*, which is divided into 100 pence as in Britain. There is a myth (which Irish traders will do nothing to explode) that there is no need to change your cash if you are coming from Britain since the Irish will helpfully accept pounds sterling. This is not surprising since £1 sterling is equivalent to about IR£1.06. For the best rates change your money either in banks or in bureaux de change, located in major cities and the larger tourist offices.

Travellers' cheques, which you can buy at any bank or branch of *Thomas Cook*, or a **Eurocheque** book and card – apply to your bank – are the easiest ways to carry large amounts of money.

Banks in the Republic are open Mon–Fri 10am–12.30pm and 1.30–3pm; most are also open until 5pm on Thursdays. It makes sense to change your money while in the cities since many small country towns are served by sub-offices open only certain days of the week.

Foreign exchange counters are open at all main **airports**: Dublin daily summer 6.45am–10pm, winter 7.30am–8.30pm; Shannon summer daily to service all incoming flights; Cork Mon–Fri 10am–3pm; Knock International open all year to service all scheduled flights (located in the tourist office).

Credit cards are accepted in large department stores, petrol stations, hotels and up-market restaurants. *Visa* cards can be used to withdraw cash from branches of the *Allied Irish Bank*.

There are no limits to the amount of money you can take into the Republic, but you are only allowed to take out Irish notes up to the value of IR£150, and any foreign currency notes to a total not exceeding IR£1200.

THE NORTH

In the North currency is pounds sterling, and you will find all the major British **banks**. Main banks in large towns are open Mon–Fri 10am–3.30pm, with late opening till 5pm on Thursday in certain city branches. In very small villages the bank may open on only two or three days a week – so, as in the Republic, aim to get your cash in the bigger centres.

There are a couple of places in Belfast where you can change money outside banking hours: *Thomas Cook*, 11 Donegall Place; and the Post Office, 7 Shaftesbury Square. Large hotels may also change money, although the exchange rate is generally poor.

Access/Mastercard and *Visa/Barclaycard* are the most commonly accepted **credit cards**, and can be used, as in the Republic, in upmarket restaurants and hotels, petrol stations and large department stores. *Diners' Club* and *American Express* are not widely accepted.

HEALTH AND INSURANCE

There are no inoculations required for travellers to Ireland, nor any particular health hazards to beware of beyond those of taking care when travelling in an unknown place.

Certainly you're unlikely to suffer sunstroke. The water is safe and delicious almost everywhere, and if you're suspicious of it there's always Guinness. Still, you're as likely to fall ill or have an accident here as anywhere else, so it's as well to make sure you're covered by adequate travel insurance.

HEALTH CARE

Visitors from EC countries are entitled to medical treatment in the **Republic** under the EC Reciprocal Medical Treatment arrangement. EC visitors should collect a form E111 from their own Social Security office (or in Britain from any Post Office before entering the country – take your National Insurance number along and you can complete the form and get it stamped on the spot). Although an E111 is technically not a requirement for people from the UK, in reality it's essential to get the entitlement to free treatment and prescribed medicines. The Irish health service is being squeezed, and if you haven't the documents you will be charged for everything. Armed with your E111, check that the doctor or dentist you use is registered with the Health Board Panel, and make it clear you want to be treated under the European Community's social security arrangements. Similarly if you are admitted to hospital, make it clear you want to be treated within the EC Reciprocal Treatment scheme. The only other real problem is that in rural areas you may find yourself miles from the nearest doctor or hospital, and possibly even further from one prepared to treat you under the reciprocal arrangements.

British citizens need no documentation to be treated in the **North**; for non-British travellers, the requirements are the same as for the Republic.

Citizens of non-EC countries may enjoy a similar reciprocal agreement. Check before you leave. And remember that whatever your legal rights, the local doctor may not necessarily know anything about them.

INSURANCE

What all the above boils down to is that you'll have to worry a great deal less about medical treatment if you take out **travel insurance**. A decent policy will cover not just medical costs but also loss or theft of baggage or money; and in real trouble it should get you home. For the peace of mind it offers, it's well worth having.

Among **British** insurers, *Endsleigh* are about the cheapest, offering a month's cover for around £20. Their policies are available from most youth/student travel specialists or direct from their offices at 97–107 Southampton Row, London WC1 (☎071/436 4451). Travel insurance is also available from just about any travel agent, but do read the small print to make sure that the cover is adequate and appropriate. You must make sure you keep all medical bills, and, if you have anything stolen, get a copy of the police report when you report the incident – otherwise you won't be able to claim.

In the **US and Canada** you should check the insurance policies you already have carefully before taking out a new one. You may discover that you're covered already for medical and other losses while abroad. Canadians especially are usually covered by their provincial health plans, and holders of ISIC and other academic cards are entitled to $3000-worth of accident coverage and sixty days of in-patient benefits for the period the card is valid. Students may also find their health coverage extends during vacations, and many bank and charge accounts include some form of travel cover; insurance is also sometimes included if you pay for your trip with a credit card (though this is likely to be limited).

If you do want a specific travel insurance policy, there are numerous kinds to choose from: short-term combination policies covering everything from baggage loss to broken legs are the best bet and cost around $25 for ten days, plus $1 a day for trips of 75 days or more. One thing to bear in mind is that none of the currently available policies covers theft; they only cover loss while in the custody of an identifiable person – though even then you must make a report to the police and get their written statement. Again, most travel agents will be able to arrange insurance: otherwise two companies to try are *Travel Guard*, 110 Centerpoint Drive, Steven Point, WI 54480 (☎715/345-0505 or 800/826-1300), or *Access America International*, 600 Third Ave, New York, NY 10163 (☎212/949-5960 or 800/284-8300).

MAPS AND INFORMATION

There's no shortage of information published on Ireland, much of it free, and before you leave it's worth contacting the local office of the Irish Tourist Board (Bord Fáilte), and/or the Northern Ireland Tourist Board.

Bord Fáilte and NITB offices outside Ireland are listed below. Once **in Ireland**, you'll find some kind of tourist office almost anywhere that has a reasonable amount of tourists passing through: either a branch of *Bord Fáilte* or the NITB, or a locally-run information centre, many of which open only for the summer. Most of these are listed in the relevant sections of the guide, and again most are extremely helpful – with local maps and leaflets, as well as advice on where to stay. It has to be said, though, that they only give information on services which they have approved, so excluding many excellent hostels, campsites and private bus services. A Bord Fáilte recommendation implies a certain standard of service, so if you don't think your approved B&B comes up to scratch, they are the people you should complain to.

MAPS

There is a great variety of **road maps** of Ireland, any of which are adequate for driving, but none of which is particularly good beyond that; one of the clearest is the *Michelin* 4km=1cm map, which is detailed enough for cycling (but doesn't give you much idea of hills). The four Ireland Holiday Maps – North, West, East and South – at a scale of one quarter inch to 1 mile give more contour details and are probably the best general, all-purpose maps on offer. These and others are widely available in Ireland.

For more detail, and for **walking**, the Ordnance Survey half-inch maps are generally the best option, but be warned: they were surveyed in the nineteenth century and can be inaccurate over 1000 feet, so a certain amount of caution is advisable; revised editions are in preparation. The old Ordnance Survey maps also cover Northern Ireland, and there are also 1:50,000 and 1:25,000 versions available. However for really serious walking you should always check locally, as tourist boards or bookshops may have something better on offer. If you're doing any serious walking in Connemara or the Burren, for example, the only really safe, reliable maps are locally-produced by *Folding Landscapes*, available at the Galway tourist office. And for the Ulster Way the route guides published by the *Sports Council for Northern Ireland* (House of Sport, Upper Malone Road, Belfast BT9 5LA; four sections) are useful.

In **Britain**, the best selections of maps are at *Stanfords* (12–14 Long Acre, London WC2; ☎071/836 1321) and by mail order from *Cordee* (3a, DeMontfort Street, Leicester, England LE1 7HD; ☎0533/543579). In the **US**, a rather less wide range should be available from specialists like *The Complete Traveler* (199 Madison Av, New York NY 10016; ☎212/685-9007), *Rand McNally Mapstore* (150 East 52nd St, New York NY 10022; ☎212/758-7488), or *Map Link* (529 State St, Santa Barbara, CA 93101; ☎805/963-4438).

BORD FAILTE OFFICES ABROAD

Britain, 150 New Bond Street, London W1Y 0AQ (☎071/493 3201).

Australia, MLC Centre, 38th Level, Martin Place, Sydney NSW 2000 (☎02/232 7177).

Belgium, av de Beaulieu 25, 1160 Bruxelles (☎02/673 9940).

Canada, 160 Bloor Street East, Suite 934, Toronto, Ontario M4W 1B9 (☎416/929 2777).

Denmark, Box 104, 1004 Kobenhavn K (☎033/15 8045).

France, 33 rue de Miromesnil, 75008 Paris (☎01/47.42.03.36).

Netherlands, Leidsestraat 32, 1017 PB Amsterdam (☎020/622 31 01).

Sweden, Box 5292, 102 46 Stockholm (☎08/662 8510).

USA, 757 Third Avenue, New York NY 10017 (☎212/418 0800).

GETTING AROUND

Travel between major centres in the Republic is generally straightforward, with reliable – albeit infrequent and slow – public transport operated by the state-supported train and bus companies *Iarnród Éireann* (*Irish Rail*) and *Bus Éireann*. There are, however, glaring anomalies, and you should never assume that two major, local towns are necessarily going to be connected. It pays to think and plan ahead. Once off the main routes this becomes particularly important since it's quite usual for small towns and villages to be served by a couple of buses a week and no more. It can be a time-consuming and frustrating business, so don't expect swift efficiency. Here, it seems, there's no such thing as a hurry, and the only way to handle it is to slow down to the local pace.

Transport in the North is similarly infrequent in rural areas: Ulsterbus is generally regular and dependable, as is the (limited) train network.

TRAINS

In the **Republic** Irish Rail (Iarnród Éireann) operates **trains** to many major cities, and towns en route; on direct lines it's by far the fastest way of covering long distances, but the network is by no means comprehensive – Donegal, for instance, has no service at all. In general, rail lines fan out from Dublin, with few routes running north–south across the country. So although you can get to the west easily by train, you can't sensibly use the railways to explore the west coast.

Train travel is by no means cheap either. For example, a Dublin–Galway return ticket will cost £24.50 (four-day return), £32.50 over a weekly return. As always, there's a complex system of peak and off-peak **fares**, and the time and day on which you travel can significantly affect the cost of the ticket. It's always worth asking about any special fares that may be on offer.

If you're looking for a **rail pass**, Irish Rail's Rambler Ticket buys unlimited rail travel on any eight days out of fifteen for £60; a fifteen-day ticket valid over thirty days costs £90. To take a bicycle along on either of these tickets will cost an extra £22. An Irish Overlander, valid in the North as well, costs £70 for eight days, £100 for fifteen. For **unlimited rail and bus travel** in the Republic and the North, an Emerald Card costs £105 for eight days, £180 for fifteen (available in Northern Ireland for around £161 sterling). Bear in mind, though, that the nature of travel in Ireland is such that you very rarely stick to your carefully drawn itinerary – you may not get the value from your pass that you hope.

If you are a **student** in possession of an ISIC card, you can buy a Travelsave stamp (£6 from any USIT office in Britain or Ireland – Dublin, Cork, Galway, Limerick, Maynooth, Waterford,

Belfast, Coleraine, Jordanstown and Derry) which entitles you to discounts of 50 percent off Bus Éireann and Irish Rail tickets. The cost of taking **bikes** on trains varies between £2 and £6 per single journey.

The only service **between the Republic and the North** is the Dublin–Belfast express (six each way daily, 2hr; £12.40 single, £18.60 return). Once **in the North** you'll find only three short rail routes, but these are efficient and reasonably cheap: a Belfast–Derry ticket will cost you £8 single, £11 return. If you are looking for a **rail pass** a Runaround ticket is valid on all Northern Irish trains for one month and costs around £25; an Irish Rover ticket is valid on trains in the North and the Republic, valid for 7 days out of 15, and costs around £55.

Taking a **bike** on a train in Northern Ireland costs a quarter of the single fare. If you are a student with an ISIC card and have bought a Travelsave stamp, you'll get savings of up to 50 percent on the standard fares.

BUSES

Bus Éireann operate throughout the **Republic**, and their services are reliable, if infrequent. It's possible to travel by bus between all major towns, but routings can be complex, involving several connections, and hence very slow. Fares are generally far lower than the train, especially in midweek – a single ticket bought on Tuesday, Wednesday or Thursday gives you the return journey free (if you travel again Tues–Thurs). This system operates on short local journeys too, so it's always worth hanging on to your midweek bus tickets, even if you don't think you'll use them – they remain valid for a month. Occasional special fare offers are also worth looking out for.

A Rover ticket (around £24 for any 3 days out of 8) and Rambler tickets (£60 for any 8 days out of 15; £90 for 15 days out of 30) all give unlimited bus travel throughout the Republic; **students** can get small reductions on standard fares (rarely more than £1.50 off a journey) if they have a Travelsave stamp (see under "Trains"), but there are often less expensive alternative offers available. If you are going to be using buses a lot it makes sense to buy a **timetable** from any major bus station (around 50p), or at least to pick up the relevant information for the area you intend to explore before you leave; remote villages may only have a couple of buses a week, so knowing when they are is essential.

IRISH TRAINS

0 ___ 25 miles

To Stranraer & Cairnryan

Coleraine

Derry

Larne

Antrim

To Liverpool

Bangor

Belfast

Lisburn
Lurgan
Portadown

Sligo
Collooney
Ballymote
Boyle
Carrick-on-Shannon
Dromod

Ballina

Castlebar

Westport

Ballyhaunis
Castlerea

Claremorris

Roscommon

Longford

Mullingar

Dundalk

Drogheda
Mosney
Skerries
Rush & Lusk

Laytown
Balbriggan

Dublin Connolly

Athlone
Moate

Galway

Woodlawn

Ballinasloe

Atherry

Clara
Tullamore
Portarlington
Portlaoise

Newbridge
Kildare

Dublin Pearse
Dun Laoghaire

Dublin Heuston

Bray
Greystones
Wicklow
Rathdrum

To Holyhead

Roscrea

Athy

Cloughjordan

Nenagh

Birdhill

Ballybrophy

Templemore

Carlow

Arklow

Gorey

Limerick

Kilkenny

Thurles

Muine Bheag

Thomastown

Enniscorthy

Limerick Junction

Tipperary

Rathluirc

Cahir

Carrick-on-Suir

Campile

Wexford

Rosslare Strand

Tralee

Banteer

Mallow

Clonmel

Waterford

Ballycullane

Bridgetown
Wellington Bridge

Rosslare Harbour
Rosslare Harbour (Pier)

To Fishguard

Farranfore

Millstreet

Killarney
Rathmore

Cobh Junction
Cobh

Cork

To Pembroke

To Swansea

To Roscoff

To Le Havre & Cherbourg

Carrying a **bike** on a bus will cost you £4.50 single regardless of length of journey, though the driver is under no obligation to take them and you can be turned away at very busy times.

Private buses, which operate on many major routes, are often cheaper than *Bus Éireann*, and sometimes faster. Companies, timetables and pick-up points are listed in "Travel Details" at the end of chapters. They're very busy at weekends, so it makes sense to book ahead if you can; during the week you can usually pay on the bus. Prices for parts of their journeys are often negotiable, and bikes can be carried if booked with your seat. Some of these companies are unlicensed and have no insurance, so that in the event of an accident you would not be covered: if this bothers you, ask when you reserve your ticket.

In the **North** *Ulsterbus* run regular and reliable services throughout the six counties, particularly to those towns not served by the rail network. A *Freedom of Northern Ireland Ticket*, for daily (around £9) or weekly (£22) unlimited travel on all scheduled *Ulsterbus* services, is available at the main bus station in Belfast. An *Emerald Card* (see "Trains" above) can be bought in Northern Ireland for around £161.

DRIVING

Uncongested roads in the **Republic** make driving a very relaxing option – if you can afford the 70p (IR) per litre for petrol. As in Britain you drive on the left, and most of the road signs and markings are similar. The national speed limit is 55mph/88kph, except where posted otherwise. Front seat occupants must wear seat belts, and motor cyclists and their passengers must wear helmets. In remote areas wandering cattle, unmarked junctions, and appallingly pot-holed minor roads are all potential dangers, particularly for motorbikes. Other hazards to watch out for include drunk drivers late at night; despite high accident rates, the police have a lax attitude, and little seems to be done about the problem.

Ireland is very slowly converting to metric measures, and on the main roads the new (green) signs are in **kilometres**. In rural areas, however, you'll find mostly the old black and white fingerpost signs in miles. Most people continue to think and talk in miles too. There is also such a thing as an "Irish mile" – shorter than the standard imperial measure – though this is rare and found only on very old signposts.

Unleaded petrol is available just about everywhere. In all large towns a **disc parking** system is in operation: discs can be bought in newsagents and have to be displayed on the vehicle when parked in a designated area. The *Automobile Association* has offices in Dublin (☎01/779481), and in Cork (☎021/276922), and they're the people to call for any motoring queries.

CAR RENTAL

Large international **car hire** companies such as *Hertz* and *Europcar* have outlets in all major cities, airports and ferry terminals: they're expensive at around IR£340 a week, although if you book in advance all sorts of special offers apply which can come close to halving this price. Booking a fly-drive or a rail-sail-drive package is one of the cheapest ways to arrange car-hire, or if you don't want to be so tied down try an **agency** such as *Holiday Autos* (☎071/491 1111), who will arrange advance booking through a local agent and can usually undercut the big companies considerably.

If you haven't booked, then the smaller local firms can almost always offer better deals than the well-known names. You must produce a full valid driving licence (which you must have held without endorsement for at least two years); most companies will only rent cars to people over 23 years of age, though you might find some that will rent to drivers over 21; it will generally be dearer if they do. It's advisable to take out a collision damage waiver with your car hire – otherwise expect to be liable for around £1000 damages in the event of an accident. If you intend to drive **across the border**, you should inform your hire company beforehand to check you are fully insured.

If you do cross the border, note that there are twenty **approved border crossing points**, marked on all recent road maps. Although it is possible to drive across in other places, you are strongly advised to use these.

THE NORTH

Roads in the **North** are in general notably superior to those in the Republic. Driving is on the left and rules of the road are as in mainland Britain. Cars bearing large red "R" (Restricted) plates identify drivers who have passed their driving test within the past 12 months and are meant to keep to low speeds. Most towns have "**control zones**" in the centre, indicated by prominent yellow signs: "Control zone – no unattended parking". These are to prevent car-bombs being left in busy commercial and populated areas. A parked car in a control zone is considered a security risk (and likely to be blown up) unless someone is sitting in it.

Petrol prices in the North are much the same as in mainland Britain – far cheaper than in the Republic at around 50p a litre.

Hiring a car in the North involves much the same cost and age restrictions as in the Republic. There are fewer outlets, but hire is available in all major cities and at Belfast airport. Again, the cheapest deals are booked ahead, and here too you must inform the car-hire company if you plan to cross the border.

HITCHING

In the **Republic** hitching is commonplace; for locals it's almost as much a normal part of getting around as using the buses and trains, and for the visitor the human contact makes it one of the best ways to get to know the country.

Knowing the shortcomings of public transport, many drivers readily give lifts, and it's not unusual to see single women with babies and the shopping or whole families waiting for a ride. This said, it has to be borne in mind that local people experience no problems in getting lifts since they usually know everybody on the road; visitors can have a less easy time.

The chief problem if you plan to hitch extensively is lack of traffic, especially off the main roads, and if you are travelling around one of the tourist-swamped areas of the west, you may find there's a reluctance to pick up foreigners. That said, without transport of your own you are probably going to *have* to hitch if you want to see the best of Ireland's wild, remote places. Just be sure to leave yourself plenty of time.

Though it's probably safer than just about anywhere else in Europe, **women** shouldn't be lulled into naive notions of security. The Irish women you see hitching alone know what cars they should and should not get into. Chances are you'll get lifts easily and be subjected to nothing worse than some reactionary discussion about marriage and divorce, but it should go without saying, no hitching is entirely risk-free, and you can be unlucky anywhere. If you're travelling alone (though it's best not to), it's almost inevitable that you'll end up hitching some of the time. If this worries you, simply remember that you don't have to get in a car just because it stops for you.

The best way to hitch in the **North** is to make sure you look like a tourist, preferably an American or Australian female tourist. And even then, it's never easy. Men travelling alone or in pairs will be viewed with suspicion, and may find it impossible to get a lift. Men and women travelling together are at least in with a chance. Once in the car, you can expect conversation at some time to come round to the Troubles; most people want to know how their situation is viewed from outside the country. It makes sense to be cautious in your response – and if you are Irish or English this can be particularly tricky; even if you think you have managed to ascertain where the owner of the car stands on the subject, as with all social encounters in the North, you can never be sure who you are talking to. Someone else's car is the last place you want to get into a political argument. It's best to listen rather than talk. Getting a lift across **the border** can be very diffi-

cult since it's risky for both hitcher and driver. There is the possibility of taking a lift from someone who is under military observation – which could bring you under surveillance throughout your stay.

CYCLING

If you are lucky enough to get decent weather, cycling is one of the most enjoyable ways to see Ireland, ensuring you're continually in touch with the landscape. Roads are generally empty, though very poor surfaces may slow you down.

Most airlines carry **bicycles** free as long as you don't exceed your weight allowance; but be sure to check the regulations in advance (charters may be less obliging), and let them know when you are booking your ticket that you plan to carry a bike. Always deflate the tyres to avoid explosions in the unpressurised hold.

If you don't want to cycle long distances, it's easy and relatively cheap to **hire a bike** in most towns in the **Republic**, and at a limited number of places in the **North** (many outlets are listed in the text); you can't take a hired bike across the border. *Raleigh*, who operate a national hire scheme, and a choice of drop-off options, are the biggest distributors (£7 per day, £30 per week plus around £40 deposit; collection and delivery service £6–10; in the North £6.50 a day, £27 a week); but local dealers (including some hostels) are often less expensive. Wherever you hire your bike, it makes sense quickly to check the tyres and brakes, and demand a pump and repair kit before you set off. You should also consider the terrain: if you plan on mountain riding, make sure your machine has enough gears to cope. *Raleigh* may rent out **cycle helmets** by summer 1992, but if you want to be certain of wearing one, bring your own along.

In tourist spots at high season it's best to collect a bike early in the day (or book it the day before) as supplies frequently run out. If you arrive with your own bike, it's easy enough to carry it across long distances by train or bus. Finally, a problem you may encounter – for some reason particularly in the west – is that of farmers' dogs chasing and snarling at your wheels. Should you be fortunate enough to be heading downhill at the time, freewheeling silently past cottages and farm entrances is perhaps the only humane way of minimising the risk of savaged wheels.

SLEEPING

The cheapest way to sleep in Ireland, as anywhere, is to camp, though here the distinct possibility of continual rain somewhat detracts from its appeal. You'll also find that some of the terrain is very tricky – especially the areas of bog and rock in Clare, Galway, Mayo and Donegal. Next on the list, in terms of price, come hostels. These vary a lot, but all offer the essential basics of a bed and somewhere to wash and to cook, and some are very good indeed. Above these, in more or less the following order, come bed and breakfasts, guesthouses, town houses, country houses, and hotels, all officially graded by the tourist boards on a set formula which, most of the time, gives a fair idea of what to expect. Prices quoted throughout this book, and in the official tourist board guides, are per person sharing a twin or double room, or in hostels in a dormitory: single rates will generally be slightly higher in B&Bs and hotels.

Whatever your budget, remember that in **July and August** the big tourist centres get booked up well in advance, and during **festivals** things get even more hectic. For the really big festivals – like the *Fleadh Cheoil* and the *Cork Jazz Festival* – there's often an extra accommodation office trying to cope with the overload, but you may still end up sleeping in a different town, or perhaps just revelling your way through to morning. The less famous festivals can be equally difficult for the spontaneous traveller. Since festivals take place all over Ireland throughout the summer, it's worth checking out where and when they are before you head off – simply pick up an events calendar at any major tourist office.

CAMPING

The cost of staying on **organised campsites** varies – from about £1–6 a night depending on the facilities offered, the number of people sharing etc. – but really, unless you're after washing facilities, shops and the like, there is rarely any need to use them. There's usually absolutely no problem if you ask to camp in a field, and in out-of-the-way places nobody minds where you pitch a tent (the only place you definitely can't camp is in a state forest – but these are usually dark pine woods anyhow). You may find that the farmer will ask you for a pound or two if his field happens to be in a heavily touristed region such as Kerry, and if there's an organised site nearby you'll probably be directed to it, but other than this, expect to camp for free. Should you want a site, they're included in the Guide, and it's worth bearing in mind that most of the hostels will let you camp on their land for £2.50–3 a night, and the price may well include the use of kitchen facilities and showers.

HOSTELS

Until recently staying in hostels in Ireland meant – as it does almost anywhere else – subjecting yourself to the rather strictly disciplined regime of **An Óige** (the official Irish Youth Hostel Association) or the **Youth Hostel Association of Northern Ireland**. In recent years, however, the growth in the Republic of the **Independent Hostel Owners** group and **Budget Hostels**, both run along far more relaxed lines, has opened up cheap and attractive alternatives. As well as having traditional dormitory accommodation, an increasing number of these hostels have private double and family rooms. You can hire a sheet sleeping bag at most hostels, for 50p–£1, but it makes sense to take your own.

In the **Republic**, Independent and Budget hostels have the best of the cheap accommodation. **Independent hostels** are all privately owned, and they're all different, each reflecting the character and interests of its owner. Some are on organic farms, some are tucked away in such beautiful countryside that they're worth staying in for the setting alone. Very often the atmosphere is cosy and informal: you can stay in all day if you want and there are no curfews or chores. On the downside, such is their popularity that some hostels cram people in to the point of discomfort. July and August are particularly bad, especially in the major cities and on the west coast, as are festival times. If you're relying on them it's worth ringing ahead to check what the situation is; most won't let you book over the phone, but some may reserve you a bed up to a certain time in the early evening. Some hostels offer **bike hire**, some **food**: details are given in the text. Expect to pay around £.4.50–5 for a dormitory bed; £6–8 per person for private rooms where available.

Similarly informal are the **Budget hostels**, comfortable and efficiently run; again, there are no membership requirements, no chores and no curfews. Expect to pay similar prices.

An Óige hostels are run like youth hostels throughout Europe, with "duties" shared out, hostels closed during the daytime, and evening curfews. At least officially. In fact, thanks to the competition from alternative hostels, you'll find many far more flexible than the rule book would suggest, particularly in out-of-the-way places. Once again, some are worth visiting simply for the location; others, especially in the mountains, may be the only places you *can* stay. International Youth Hostel Association Membership (also valid for YHANI membership in the North) is required at most hostels, costing £4.70 if you are between 18–21 years, £8.90 if you are over 21. To join in Britain before you leave, contact the *YHA* at 14 Southampton St, London WC2 (☎071/836 1036). It is worth remembering that if you buy membership before leaving home you can get discounts of 25 percent on *Irish Ferries, B&I Line* and *Sealink*.

If you turn up at an *An Óige* hostel as a non-member, you will be charged a nightly supplement of £1.25, which accumulates so that after paying six such supplements you become a full member. Hostels are graded according to the quality of facilities and prices vary accordingly: category 1 £4.50–5.90, category 2 £3.80–5.50, and category 3 £3.50–4.50. Dublin hostels charge £7 Oct–May, £9 June–Sept, and Rosslare hostel also has higher prices. *An Óige* also offer special accommodation and travel deals, which you should check out on arrival, for instance their "one night stopover" combined hostel and rail ticket is often very good value.

In the **North** charges for an overnight stay include linen and are generally more expensive: £5–6.50 low season, from £5.50–7.50 high season.

B&B, GUESTHOUSES AND HOTELS

Bed and breakfast accommodation, available throughout Ireland, is the next most affordable option. B&Bs vary enormously, but most are welcoming, warm and clean, with huge breakfasts including cereal, massive fry-ups of bacon, egg, sausage and tomato, and toast and tea. Afternoon tea can usually be arranged, and can be delicious, with home-made scones and soda bread – it will cost you around £3 or £4. *Bord Fáilte* registered and approved B&Bs are generally pretty good, though it's not an absolute guarantee. Don't assume that non-registered places will be less good – inclusion in the official guide is voluntary, and a fair few simply choose not to bother.

You can expect to pay from around £10–12 per person sharing (from £8 for non-registered houses) and out of season you may be able to negotiate the price somewhat. **Bookings** for registered B&Bs can be made through tourist offices (£1 for local, £2 long distance), or you can do it yourself. Many phone numbers and addresses are given in the text of this guide, but if you want the complete list then buy *Bord Fáilte*'s *Guest Accommodation* book (£4), which has comprehensive, graded lists of B&Bs, hotels and campsites, or just for B&B they produce a guide that costs £1.50. Alternatively, finding accommodation is simple enough in just about any town or touristed village – simply go into a pub and ask.

If you want to stay in a **farmhouse**, or in a cottage, these can be arranged through the tourist board; for all their simple rooms and turf fires, almost all "Rent-an-Irish-Cottage" cottages cluster in tiny tourist villages, so it's worth checking out exactly what the set-up is if you're after real solitude.

Hotels are generally dearer but not always. Certainly if you get stuck in a small village it's always worth checking out any local hotels, which may be surprisingly inexpensive, and may well be an important social focus. Virtually all hotels have bars and provide meals to residents and non-residents alike.

Bed and breakfast accommodation is far less prominent in the **North**, and you will need to ring ahead if you want to guarantee somewhere to stay during the summer months. Addresses and phone numbers for B&Bs in all of the main centres are given in the Guide, while the Northern Ireland Tourist Board's *All the Places to Stay* gives extensive, highly detailed lists.

EATING

One thing you won't be going to Ireland for is a wonderful gastronomic experience. The country has no real tradition of eating out, and the food you'll find as a traveller will tend to be (at best) simple and hearty. Often the best bet is to fill up with a hearty breakfast and/or a good pub lunch in the middle of the day, and concentrate on drinking in the evening – few pubs serve food at night.

MEAT AND POTATOES

Irish food is generally highly meat-orientated, and you don't have to be a vegetarian to find this becomes wearing after a while. For carnivores, there's nothing wrong with Irish meat – steaks, in particular, are excellent – but after a while you begin to long for some variety in your diet, and for something which hasn't been fried.

If you're staying in B&Bs, it's almost impossible to avoid the "traditional" Irish **breakfast** of sausages, bacon and eggs, which usually comes accompanied by generous quantities of delicious soda bread. Pub **lunch** staples are usually meat and two veg, with plenty of gravy, although you can usually get freshly made sandwiches (sometimes excellent, but often sliced white bread and processed cheese – and if toasted served in a grill-crisped cellophane wrapper); homemade soups can be very good too.

Most larger towns have good, simple **cafés** (open daytimes only) where you can get soup, sandwiches, cakes and the ubiquitous apple pie as well as slightly more ambitious and filling dishes – in the North, in particular, they all seem to serve enormous portions of meat and thoroughly overcooked vegetables that will ground you for the rest of the afternoon. It's worth remembering that **hotels** are obliged to offer food to all comers – so you can always find a sandwich and a cup of coffee, at any reasonable hour; you can generally order a plate of sandwiches and a pot of tea in pubs, too.

Many traditional Irish dishes are based on the **potato** and, all jokes aside (like the one that describes an Irish five-course meal; four pints of Guinness and a potato), you do get an awful lot of them – often served up in several different forms in the same meal. Potato cakes can be magnificent – a flour and potato dough fried in butter – as can potato soup. **Irish stew** of varying qualities will be available almost everywhere; and **colcannon**, cooked potatoes fried in butter with onions and cabbage, or leeks, can also be very good. Colcannon is a traditional dish for Hallowe'en, as is **barm brack**, a sweet yeast bread with spices and dried fruits in which a gold ring is traditionally concealed; the person who finds the ring in their slice of barm brack will be the next to marry.

RESTAURANTS AND ALTERNATIVES

Much is made of Ireland's recent **gastronomic revolution**, but in practice you're likely to find that its effects are restricted to the more expensive restaurants. Far more noticeable is the **fast-food** revolution, which has brought kebabs and burgers to every town of any size – old-fashioned fish and chips are always a safer bet. For the occasional binge, however, there are some very good **seafood restaurants**, particularly along the west coast, serving freshly caught seafood and, often, home-grown vegetables. Irish **oysters** are famous; the season opens with an oyster festival at Clarinbridge on Galway Bay. **Salmon** and trout can also be fabulous, but be warned that they may not be all they seem, especially away from the coast: fish-farming is becoming big business in Ireland, and your fish may have spent all its life in cages and be pumped full of hormones.

Some **guesthouses**, particularly if they're historic buildings, serve very good food, in what can be very grand surroundings. **Wholefood** restaurants or cafés are very thin on the ground outside Dublin, Belfast and some of the more tourist-influenced areas in the west; some of the hostels here have very good, locally-grown food. We've included them in the Guide, where they exist. And of course if you are staying in hostels you can cook for yourself.

Cooking for yourself, at least some of the time, may in fact be the best option. Produce available in Ireland is limited in range – aside from in the cities and some touristy towns on the west coast, you won't find exotic fruit or vegetables, for instance – but usually fresh and excellent. Irish potatoes, cabbages and carrots are delicious, though surprisingly hard to buy in rural areas, where the population may be too small to support even a grocer's shop. Meat is very good; bread and scones are wonderful; and if you're travelling around the coast, you can often buy seafood very cheaply direct from the fishermen. Sometimes you'll be able to find more unusual things in this way – spider crabs and monkfish, for example – that you would never find in local fish shops; it's all exported. In many places you can gather your own mussels from the rocks too – but be sure to check locally in case there's a sewage outlet nearby.

Dairy products, especially cheese, can also be excellent. The past decade has seen a revolution in the Irish cheese business, which now produces delicious, often unpasteurised cheeses such as Cashel Blue. There's no need to go to a smart restaurant to taste these – you can often find them in grocer's shops, alongside freshly baked soda bread. Fill up with this, and you're unlikely to need to eat again for at least half a day. **Cream** is also served everywhere, with everything.

PUBS

To travel through Ireland without visiting a **pub** would be to miss out on a huge chunk of Irish life, some would say the most important. Especially in rural areas, the pub is far more than just a place to drink. It's the social and conversational heart of any Irish village, and often the political and cultural centre too. If you're after food, advice or company, the pub is almost always the place to head for; and very often they'll be the venues for local entertainment too, especially traditional and not so traditional music (see "Festivals and Entertainment", following).

Along with Mass and market day, the pub is the centre of Irish social activity: a cultural cliché, perhaps, but one that wears very well. Talking is an important business here, and drink is the great lubricant of social discourse. Having said all this, it doesn't pay to arrive with too romantic a notion of what this actually means. Away from the cities and the touristed west coast, there are plenty of miserable, dingy bars where the only spark of conviviality is the dull glow of the TV. But in major cities you'll find bars heaving with life (they're actually very similar to English pubs), and out in remote country villages it can be great fun drinking among the fig rolls and trifle sponges of the ancient grocery shops-cum-bars you'll find dotted around.

While women will always be treated with genuine (unreconstructed) civility, it's true to say that most bars are a predominantly male preserve. In the evening, especially, women travellers can expect occasional unwanted attention, though this rarely amounts to anything too unpleasant. Should your first encounters be bad ones, persist – the good nights will come, and will probably rank amongst the most memorable experiences of your trip.

In the Republic, **opening hours** are Mon–Sat 10.30am–11pm (11.30pm in summer, 12.30–2pm & 4–11pm on Sunday); some pubs, especially in the cities, may close for a couple of hours in the afternoon ("holy hour") while illegal lock-ins remain something of an after-hours institution in rural parts. In the **North** pubs are open Monday to Saturday 11am–11pm, 10am–2.30pm and 7–10pm on Sundays.

DRINKS

The classic Irish drink is of course **Guinness** ("a Guinness" is a pint; if you want a half of any beer, ask for "a glass") which, as anybody will tell you, is simply not the same as the drink marketed as Guinness outside Ireland. For one thing, good Guinness has to be kept properly, something non-Irish pubs abroad tend not to do; it has to be poured gradually (you don't pour a pint, you build one – the ultimate gaffe in a pub is to ask them to hurry this process); and even across Ireland you'll taste differences – it's best in Dublin where it's brewed. A proper pint of Irish Guinness is a dream, far less heavy than you may be used to, though still a considerable, filling drink. Other local stouts, like *Beamish* and *Murphy's* (a Cork stout, far sweeter and creamier), make for interesting comparison: they all have their faithful adherents.

If you want a pint of English-style **bitter**, then try *Smithwicks*, which is not so different from what you'd get in an English pub. As everywhere, of course, **lager** is also increasingly popular: mostly *Harp* (made by Guinness) or *Heineken*. Whatever your tipple, you're likely to find drinking in Ireland an expensive business at around IR£1.50 –£1.60 a pint.

Irish **whiskeys** – try *Paddy's*, *Powers* or, from the North, *Bushmills* – also seem expensive, but in fact the measures (in the Republic) are far larger than those you'll get in Britain. If you've come in from the cold you can have your whiskey served warm with cloves and lemon. Asking for Scotch in an Irish pub is asking for trouble, and in any case anyone here will tell you that the Irish version is infinitely superior.

Non-alcoholic drinks are limited to an uninspiring array of the usual fizzy drinks and bottled fruit juices, but, unless the bar is extremely busy, you can always get **coffee** (served with a dollop of full cream) or **tea**. You can usually get **Irish coffee** too (with whiskey and cream), which is delicious if not very traditional – it was invented at Shannon airport.

COMMUNICATIONS: POST, PHONES AND MEDIA

Ireland may not look far away, but it can sometimes seem it when you're trying to get in touch with home. Post from the Republic, especially, is notoriously unreliable; if you have anything important or urgent to say, best do it by phone.

PHONES

In towns throughout Ireland you'll find fully automatic **payphones** in kiosks; instructions for use are on display, and internal and international calls can easily be made. A local call costs 20p minimum but, as you might imagine, long-distance daytime calls are expensive. International calls are cheapest if dialled direct

after 6pm. New **cardphones**, found in towns all over the country, are by far the most convenient way of making long-distance calls, avoiding the chugging of coins interrupting your call; phone cards can be bought at newsagents and post offices. In rural areas in the Republic you may well come across the old-style "button A" telephones. To operate these insert a minimum of 20p and dial the number: when you get a reply, press button A – this will cause the machine to swallow the coins; if you can't get through, press button B and the coin will be returned. These phones only accept 5p and 10p pieces, and are fairly useless for international calls. If you make calls from a hotel or the like, expect a hefty premium charged on top of the normal price.

Dialling the Republic from the North is, peculiarly, not the same as dialling the Republic from mainland Britain, and you'll have to check in the local phonebook or call Directory Enquiries.

MAIL

Post to or from the Republic is slow and unreliable, and parcels sent to the country seem to have little better than a 50 percent chance of reaching their destination. If it's something important, it's worth spending the extra for recorded or registered mail. To send a letter within Ireland and to all EC countries costs 30p – postcards are 26p; to the US 40p and 34p. Main post offices are open Monday to Friday 9am–5.30pm, Saturday 9am–

OPERATOR SERVICES

In the Republic:
Operator ☎10
Directory Enquiries ☎190
Long Distance Calls ☎10
International Calls ☎114
Telegrams ☎115

In the North:
Operator ☎100
Directory Enquires ☎192
Long Distance Calls ☎100
International Calls ☎155
Telegrams ☎190/193

1pm. Post from the North is more efficient. Letters and postcards travel anywhere in the EC for 24p, between 32p and 39p for the rest of the world.

MASS MEDIA

The most widely read **papers** in the Republic are the *Irish Times*, the *Irish Press* and the *Irish Independent* – good, but remarkably slim, they really bring home just how small (and conservative) the population is. There are also lots of local and regional papers which can be useful for checking on what's happening in your area. British newspapers are generally available the same day in Dublin and other cities. In the North, all the British papers are sold: based in Belfast are also the *Belfast Telegraph*, the biggest selling evening paper in the North, which attempts to steer a middle course in terms of Northern Irish politics. The morning papers are the *Irish News*, read by the Nationalist community, and the loyalist tabloid *News Letter*.

In the Republic, *RTE* (*Radio Telefís Éireann*) runs two state-sponsored **television** channels and two radio stations: both services are imaginatively known as RTE1 and RTE2. Programming on all of them is, for the most part, fairly dull. In the north and east you can also pick up programmes from Britain (or the North). You'll find rather more interesting fare on local radio stations around the country (including all-Gaelic stations in Connemara and tiny Ring, County Waterford) – worth tuning in for the traditional music and for insights into local issues. In the North you get the BBC and *Ulster Television*, and you can also pick up plenty of broadcasts from the South.

FESTIVALS AND ENTERTAINMENT

A festival in Ireland is never a half-hearted affair. Whatever the pretext for the celebration, it's always also an excuse for serious partying. Well established ones like the Cork Jazz Festival and the Wexford Opera Festival are big international events, and getting tickets for top performances can be well nigh impossible without advance planning – but if you fail to get into the concert you came for, chances are you'll stumble across wild merriment in some poky bar roundabout. The very word festival seems to act as a magnet for all sorts of musicians, and many events are wonderfully overwhelming – no matter what the size of the town, there's rarely enough room for all that's going on, with music and dancing bursting out of the official venues into surrounding streets and bars. The biggest of the annual events are listed here, but pick up a calendar of events at any major tourist office and you'll soon get a picture of the huge range of celebration.

MUSIC

The most enjoyable aspect of Irish festivals – sheer exuberance apart – is probably the **traditional music**. Many festivals (known as *Fleadh* – pronounced *fla*) are devoted almost exclusively to this: the biggest of them is the *Fleadh Cheoil na hÉireann* (see box), which includes the finals of the All Ireland music and dance contests.

However, you don't have to go to a festival to experience this; music in Irish **pubs** is similarly legendary, and again there's a huge range to experience, only a relatively small proportion of it "traditional". **Country and Western**, for example, is extremely popular, and there are a frightening number of middle-of-the-road pop bands lurking in country areas, with regular country and western nights at pubs across Ireland. **Ballads** are another well-developed Irish music form. The term "ballad" is a bit of a catch-all, and open to countless interpretations – it's generally some form of dull crooning, and essentially middle-aged in spirit. Brace yourself for the worst, and from time to time you'll be very pleasantly surprised.

The best of pub music, however, has to be the **traditional folk sessions** of fiddles, accordions, *bodhrán* (a drum) and singing. Interest from abroad and the tourist industry have a lot to do with the resurgence of this musical culture – but this hardly matters, since the music can be phenomenal. The west coast (especially around Clare and Galway) has the best of the traditional scene, but you'll find something almost anywhere. Pointers as to where to find sessions are given in the text, but the locations of the best are hard to pin down for long. The thing to do is to ask around and keep your ears open for local tips.

Traditionally Sunday evening was the night for sessions, and in rural areas this is still often the case (a throwback to restrictions on holy days that meant partying on Saturdays had to stop at midnight), but increasingly Friday and Saturday are becoming equally important – and you may find something happening any night of the week. Things generally don't get going till late, and a bar that's still empty at 10pm may be a riot of music by half-past. While it's all extremely convivial and relaxed, if you're a musician yourself and want to join in, then do so tactfully. The first thing to do is sit and listen for a while – to make sure you can play to a high enough standard – and then work out who the leader is and ask. If you're not playing, don't crowd the musicians; the empty seats around them are for others who may join in.

Comhaltas Ceoltóiri Éireann is an organisation that exists purely to promote traditional music and culture, and evenings organised by them (not always in bars), though by their nature not spontaneous, are well worth looking out for. Run by real enthusiasts, the standard of playing is usually pretty high.

MAJOR ANNUAL FESTIVALS AND EVENTS

Saint Patrick's Day (March 17): celebrations in all the big cities for several days roundabout.

Irish Grand National (April): horseracing at Fairyhouse (Meath).

Cork International Choral Festival (April/May): one of the big ones.

Festival of Music in Great Irish Houses (June): just what it says, at venues around the country.

Irish Derby (June): and other important race meets at the Curragh (Kildare).

Galway Arts Festival (July): festival of music, theatre and general partying; one of the best.

Galway Races (July/August) Another important race meeting, very popular.

Rose of Tralee International Festival (August): another big one, with a beauty contest as its (rotten) heart.

Fleadh Cheoil na hÉireann (July): the most important of all the traditional music festivals, held in a different town every year; in 1992 it will be in Clonmel.

Kilkenny International Arts Week (August): includes recitals, poetry readings, art exhibitions.

Lisdoonvarna Matchmaking Festival (September): plenty of traditional entertainment accompanies the lonely hearts side.

All Ireland Hurling Final (September): the biggest event of the hurling year, in Dublin.

Cork Film and Jazz Festivals (October): actually two separate events, but they often run into one another. The jazz especially is enormously popular.

Wexford Opera Festival (October/November): another really big one, of international renown.

SPORT

One thing that attracts many people to Ireland is the **fishing**, and there really are superb opportunities for virtually every form, from seasonal salmon and trout angling on the rivers, to coarse fishing in the Loughs and sea-fishing all year round. Both *Bord Fáilte* and the NITB publish detailed leaflets on fishing, including the best times and places and how and where to apply for permits; alternatively just ask a local hotel or tackle shop, it's easy enough to buy a licence locally.

Other big participatory sports are also mostly water-based (unless you count **pony-trekking**, easily arranged in most of the bigger tourist centres). Sailing, and especially **windsurfing**, are both increasingly popular. Small dinghies can very occasionally be hired in at seaside resorts; windsurfing is much more readily available at new centres all around the coast.

As for watching, **horseracing** is a national obsession, constantly on the TV and enormously popular live too. The biggest races are mostly at courses around Dublin – in counties Kildare and Meath – during the summer; it's worth going for the atmosphere as much as the race itself. Even more fun, perhaps, are local events at festivals, where both horses and riders may be amateurs: races along the beach, for example.

Other traditional sports – **hurling** and **Gaelic football** – also remain tremendously well-supported. Even if you don't understand a thing to begin with, the atmosphere of the big games is again at least as much an attraction as the sports themselves. Irish **rugby** is in something of a decline at the moment, though still wholeheartedly physical, while **football** is on the up and up, inspired by unprecedented success under new Eire team manager Jack Charlton.

OPENING HOURS AND HOLIDAYS

Business and shop **opening hours**, both North and South, are very similar to Britain's: approximately 9am to 5.30pm, Monday to Saturday, with a smattering of late openings (usually Thursday or Friday), and half days.

In the South, however, particularly away from the bigger towns, hours are more approximate, with later opening and closing times. In rural areas you can generally find someone to sell you groceries at any reasonable hour, even if they have to open their shop to do it – and very often the village shop doubles as the local pub. For banking hours see "Costs, Money and Banks" on p.000. On the main **public holidays** (see box), virtually everything will be closed except the pubs.

There's no pattern to the opening and closing of **museums**, **archaeological sites** and the like, though most close altogether for at least one day a week. Wherever possible, hours and prices are listed in the guide. The bigger attractions will normally be open throughout the day, while smaller places may open only in the afternoon. Many sites away from the main tourist trails – especially houses or castles which are also private homes – are open only during the peak summer months.

Churches, at least if they're still in use, are almost always open, and if they're locked there's usually someone living nearby (often the priest himself) who will have the keys; otherwise, opening times will follow religious activity fairly closely.

PUBLIC HOLIDAYS

IN THE REPUBLIC:
New Year's Day
St Patrick's Day, March 17
Good Friday
Easter Monday
First Monday in June
First Monday in August
Last Monday in October
Christmas Day
St Stephen's Day, December 26

IN THE NORTH:
New Year's Day
St Patrick's Day, March 17
May 1
Last Monday in May
Orange Day, July 12
Last Monday in August
Christmas Day
December 26.

SECURITY AND THE POLICE

The Republic has to be one of the safest countries in Europe in which to travel. Limerick is not a pleasant city after dark, and you might be robbed in the street in Dublin – the capital has a big heroin problem and a lot of poverty – but beyond this nothing much is likely to happen to you. This said, don't let the friendliness of people as a whole lull you into a general carelessness; like anywhere else visitors are seen as easy targets for petty thieves. In the North, of course, the problems are very different, and security is an ever-present awareness. You need to be careful of where you go, and when. But personal security, and crimes against the individual, are less of a problem. You're probably less likely to be robbed or mugged here than in most of Britain.

POLICE

In the Republic, people generally have a healthy indifference to law and red tape, perhaps in part a vestige of pre-Independence days, when any dealings with the police smacked of collusion with the British. The **police** – known as **Garda** or **Gardai** (pronounced "gar-dee") – accordingly have a low profile. In rural areas the low level of crime is such that policing is minimal and, should you need them, you might spend an entire afternoon waiting for the Garda to arrive. If you have any dealings with the Garda at all, the chances are you'll find them affable enough.

In the **North** the **Royal Ulster Constabulary** (RUC) deal with all general civic policing, and are the people you should go to if in difficulties. Security at police stations is tight and they're generally covered in barbed wire. The North is subject to British law and heavily policed, with several "emergency measures" permanently in effect that seriously restrict personal freedom.

You may well find yourself being quizzed about where you are going, what you are doing, and so forth, especially in border areas. Be cooperative and polite and you should have no difficulties. Again, whatever their reputation, you'll find that the RUC are helpful enough in matters of everyday police activity. The emergency number in both North and South is ☎999.

SECURITY AND THE NORTH

If you are British or Irish it's likely you'll have a strong response to the sight of **British troops**, tanks and weaponry on the streets in the North. Like the police, armed soldiers may stop and question you. Whatever your thoughts on the presence of the army, it really isn't a good idea to share them with the soldier on the street. Travellers from the Republic may experience more troublesome dealings with both the RUC and the army, as anyone with a Southern Irish accent will tell you. All you are obliged to tell the army is your name, address, date of birth and where you're going: the more open you are with them, of course, the less likely you are to have trouble; but in certain areas you may want to weigh against this the fact that appearing to be on good terms with the army will not endear you to the local population.

Road checks are common – tedious, but nothing to worry about. **Crossing the border** into the Republic, you *must* use official border crossing points, marked on all up-to-date maps, and clearly signposted. Security is such that there are no public places to leave luggage anywhere in the North, and you should never leave baggage unattended. All towns and cities, and even some small villages, have **security zones**, areas in which it is illegal to leave an unattended parked car. It is illegal to take **photographs** of police barracks and army installations.

SEXUAL HARASSMENT, PREJUDICE AND RACISM

For women Ireland is wonderfully relaxing: the outlandish sexism of Irish society manifests itself in a male courtesy that can range from the genuine and delightful to the downright insufferable, but you are unlikely to experience any really threatening behaviour. Most uncomfortable situations can be defused by a straightforward, firm response.

This said, don't believe the general view that *nothing* can happen to you. Talk to men and they will tell you that serious sexual assaults never happen; talk to women and you'll realise they do.

It is worth remembering that outside the cities, communities are very small, and local women you see hitching alone do so in safety because they know and are known by just about everybody on the road. Foreign travellers don't have that added security, and, though it is very unlikely, you could be unlucky. In the case of serious assault, if possible contact a Rape Crisis Centre before going to the police (telephone numbers are given in chapter listings). Attacks are rare and, though well-meaning, the Garda have little experience of handling distressed women.

Black travellers may have a less easy time of it. The Republic of Ireland, and, to an extent, the rural North, are fiercely conservative and shamefully intolerant of minority groups. If you are black you may well experience a peculiarly naive brand of ignorant racism. Open comment on the colour of a person's skin isn't uncommon outside the major cities, where people simply aren't used to seeing black people. This said, there's no need to anticipate any real malice.

The **gay** community is both the biggest and least visible minority in Ireland. Although nominally part of the UK, Northern Ireland was excluded from the 1967 Act that legalised homosexuality for consenting adults in Britain. This led one individual to take his case to the European Court of Human Rights in 1982, which brought the legal status of gays in Northern Ireland into line with the rest of the UK. In the Republic, homosexuality is still illegal, denying over 250,000 Irish citizens the most basic rights to a full emotional and social life. Encouraged by the success of the Northern Irish gay community, activists are hopeful that similar legislation for the Republic is not far off. Meanwhile, be aware that intolerance is not just a product of the legislators: public displays of affection are out of the question.

OTHER THINGS

BAGGAGE In the North, because of the security situation, there are no left luggage facilities anywhere, and you should never leave your bags unattended. In the Republic, most big city bus and train stations will have lockers or a left luggage office.

BRING Most things you really need you'll be able to buy. Remember, though, to take warm clothes and rain gear; a torch is useful for exploring dingy churches and archaeological sites, as is a compass if you plan to do any serious walking;

a sheet sleeping bag is pretty essential if you're using a lot of hostels; and film is relatively expensive in the Republic.

CONTRACEPTIVES Throughout Ireland anyone over 18 can buy condoms at chemist shops (though in the Republic, where legal contraception was only recently introduced, you may still find places which don't sell them – or don't approve); the pill is available on prescription only.

DEPARTURE TAX A £5 departure tax is payable on leaving the Republic if you buy your ticket in Ireland – it's normally paid when you buy your ticket.

ELECTRICITY In the Republic, electricity is 220V AC, in the North 240V AC. Plugs everywhere are British-style three square pins (just occasionally you may still find old round ones). In other words British appliances will work everywhere; North American ones will need both a transformer and a plug adapter.

EMERGENCIES For police or ambulance ☎999 throughout Ireland.

HERITAGE CARD If you are planning on visiting a lot of **historic monuments** it may be worth buying a *Heritage Card* (£10, student £4) which gives you unlimited admittance to sites cared for by the *Office of Public Works* for one year from the date of purchase. Cards can be bought from the first *OPW* site you visit, or in advance from their main office at 51 St Stephen's Green, Dublin 2 (☎01/613111 ext 2386). Monuments for which the card is valid are indicated in the Guide.

KIDS Large families are still the norm in much of Ireland, and consequently it's relatively easy to travel with kids, even if there are few places actually designed to cater for them. Baby supplies are sold everywhere, and children are generally welcome at B&Bs (though few have cots or special facilities), in pubs during the daytime, and almost anywhere else.

LAUNDERETTES You'll find launderettes only in the bigger towns and on large caravan/ campsites; hostels, though, will often have a washing machine for residents' use, and at many B&Bs they'll do your washing for you. Elsewhere it's worth taking along a tube of *Travel Wash* – designed to be used in hotel washbasins – which makes a lot less mess than powder.

TAX In the North VAT at 15 percent will be added to all your bills: in the Republic VAT rates vary for different goods – up to a hefty 23 percent. If you're buying a lot of souvenirs to take home, you can claim this back (so long as you leave the country within 2 months of purchase): either have the shop send the goods out of the country for you (in which case no tax is paid); or ask for a special VAT receipt when you buy, take this and have it stamped by customs on your way out of the country, and send the receipt they give you back to the shop for your refund (less commission).

TOILETS Public toilets are reasonably common in all the big towns, and generally acceptably clean, if no more. Or you can pop into the local pub, and stop for a drink while there. The Gaelic labels to look out for are *Fír* (Men) and *Mna* (Women).

WORK Although EC citizens are legally allowed to live and work in Ireland, local unemployment is extremely high, and your chances of finding a decent job slim. The best opportunities for travellers are in seasonal work in resorts; poorly paid cleaning and waiting jobs, or perhaps helping out in a hostel in return for board and pocket money. You'll need to search locally.

PART TWO

THE

GUIDE

DONEGAL

ANTRIM AND DERRY

FERMANAGH & TYRONE

BELFAST

DOWN AND ARMAGH

SLIGO AND LEITRIM

MONAGHAN & CAVAN

GALWAY, MAYO AND ROSCOMMON

MEATH, LOUTH, WESTMEATH AND LONGFORD

DUBLIN AND AROUND

LAOIS & OFFALY

WICKLOW & KILDARE

CLARE

WATERFORD, TIPPERARY & LIMERICK

WEXFORD, CARLOW & KILKENNY

KERRY

CORK

0   50 km

CHAPTER ONE

DUBLIN AND AROUND

Dublin, however much its inhabitants may complain about the city's provincialism, is emphatically Ireland's capital, a splendidly monumental city clustered on the banks of the River Liffey. Approaching by sea, you'll have an opportunity to appreciate the magnificent physical setting before you're plunged into the reality of the urban sprawl, with the fine sweep of Dublin Bay, and the Wicklow Mountains providing an exhilarating backdrop to the south. The moment of actual arrival is generally less dramatic – whether you're coming from the harbours of Dún Laoghaire or Dublin Port to the east, or from the airport to the north, the first thing you're likely to see are less-than-exciting suburbs.

The city's **vitality** springs from its contradictions: elegance and wealth against glaring poverty, youthful energy against bleak economics and leaden traditionalism. In pubs and cafés, eloquent Dubliners spin deeds and characters into legends, woven into the fabric of a city whose human story is clearly marked on every street. Look at some of the flyblown Georgian tenements that still remain around Connolly Station on the north side of the Liffey, and you'll understand why not all Dubliners were sad to see so much of the old city torn down. Then look at the modern office blocks that replaced Georgian streets on the south side, where humane civic planning gave way to corporate exhibitionism. On a human level, beggars and bag ladies walk the streets, refusing to hide themselves; a happier manifestation of Dubliners' assertiveness comes across in buying and selling – whether in the markets in Henry Street or The Liberties, or in the flamboyant malls that sprang up in the heady days of the 1980s, when a combination of Euromoney and a service economy seemed set to make shopping a national pastime.

Despite the decanting of people from the grim tenements of the North and South Sides to the suburbs during the 1960s and 1970s, the focus of the city is still very much in the centre, and perhaps that's one of the reasons why it feels so vibrant. Dublin is also a **young** city. Of roughly one million people in the immediate city area, and another half million in greater Dublin, about half are under 25, and many more – the baby boomers – under 40. With the drift of population from the country to the capital continuing, Dublin is bulging at the seams. Membership of the European Community has infused money into the city, and you'll see new building everywhere, but you'll also witness inner-city deprivation as bad as any in Europe. It's the collision of all these factors that makes Dublin the pulsating, reactionary, progressive, cosmopolitan, parochial, aggravating, energetic place it is.

The urban sprawl is in sharp contrast to the countryside around – commuter trains make access easy to the whole sweep of **Dublin Bay**, from the fishing port of Howth to the north, through Sandycove with its James Joyce connections, Dalkey made famous by Flann O'Brien, to the sprawling suburban resort of Bray in the south. Further afield – and covered in following chapters – the **Wicklow Mountains** form a barrier to the south. Here you'll find some of the wildest countryside in Ireland, along with much beautiful architecture – from the Celtic ruins of Glendalough to the Georgian splendour of Russborough House. Northwards, the **Boyne valley**, with its spectacular prehistoric remains, is in equally easy reach.

DUBLIN

Arriving in **DUBLIN** it can be hard, at first, to see the attraction. Certainly it is not as immediately beautiful or welcoming as much of Ireland. But it doesn't take long to be drawn in: despite the uneasy mix of magnificent architecture and elaborate new shopping developments with obvious deprivation, it's an easy place in which to feel at home. Above all, it's a city of great good humour, with a street and pub life of vibrant, disorganised energy. That it is such an enjoyable place is largely due to the people, and you'd be well advised to spend much of your time here getting to know them, and the pubs where they seem to spend much of their time.

Some History

Dublin celebrated its millennium in 1988, and though there was much argument as to whether the anniversary really meant anything, it does give an indication of the city's antiquity. Although the first indication of a settlement beside the Liffey is in Ptolemy's celebrated map of 140 AD, which shows a place called *Eblana*, it's as a **Viking settlement** that Dublin's history really begins. The Viking raiders sailed up the Liffey and, destroying a small Celtic township, set up a trading post on the south bank of the river, at the ford where the royal road from the Hill of Tara in the north crossed the Liffey on its way to Wicklow. The Vikings adopted the Irish name, **Dubh Linn** or Dark Pool, for their settlement, which soon amalgamated with another Celtic settlement, **Baile Átha Cliath** ("town of the hurdles", pronounced *Ballya-aw-kleea*, and still the Gaelic name for Dublin), on the north bank.

The next wave of invaders were the **Anglo-Normans**, whose involvement in Ireland began in the twelfth century with the support of the opportunistic Strongbow and a band of Welsh knights and soldiers of the beleaguered king, Dermot McMurrough. Henry II, concerned that Strongbow and his Welsh adventurers were becoming too powerful, set up a court at Dublin, thereby establishing the city as the centre of British influence in Ireland and setting the precedent for the annual social and political **Season**, which was to shape Dublin's role and character for the next seven centuries.

Because most of the early city was built of wood, only the two cathedrals, part of the Castle and one or two churches have survived from before the seventeenth century. What you see today, in both plan and buildings, dates essentially from the **Georgian** period. By this time, soldiers who had been rewarded with confiscated land had begun to derive income from their new estates, had replaced the original fortified houses with something more fashionable, and wished to participate in the country's growing economic and political life which was centred on Dublin. Their town houses (along with those of the growing business and professional classes), and the grandeur of the public buildings erected during this period, embodied the new confidence of the British ruling class: a group that was, however, starting to regard itself not as British, but as Irish.

In the second half of the eighteenth century the wealth of this Anglo-Irish class was reflected in a rich cultural life – Handel's *Messiah*, for instance, was first performed in Ireland, and the legacy of architecture, furniture and silverware, though now much diminished, speaks for itself. Growing political freedom was to culminate in the **parliament** of 1782 in which Henry Grattan made a famous Declaration of Rights, modelled on the recent American example, which came very close to declaring Irish (by which he meant Protestant Anglo-Irish) independence. A severely limited and precarious enterprise, the Irish bid for independence was to collapse very soon, with the abortive uprisings of 1798 and the Act of Union which followed in 1801.

The **Act of Union** may have shorn Dublin of its independent political power, but the city remained the centre of British administration, in the shape of the Vice Regent, and the Seasons which formed the basis of the social and political life of the Anglo-Irish continued to revolve around the Vice-Regal Lodge (now the President's Residence) in Phoenix Park. Along with the rest of Ireland, Dublin entered a long economic decline; but it was also the focus of much of the agitation that eventually led to independence. In 1829 the Catholic lawyer (and Kerryman) **Daniel O'Connell** secured an important advance by achieving limited Catholic emancipation, allowing Catholics to play some part in the administration and politics of their capital city and, in a signal victory, was elected Lord Mayor of Dublin. Dublin was also the centre of the **Gaelic League**, which, founded by Douglas Hyde in 1893, encouraged the formation of an Irish national consciousness through efforts to restore the native language and culture. This paved the way for the Celtic literary revival under W. B. Yeats and Lady Gregory, and the establishment, in 1904, of the Abbey Theatre.

Dublin in the Twentieth Century

Poverty and violence were the other side of the political coin, and the early years of the **twentieth century** saw the struggle for the establishment of trade unionism in Ireland. In 1913 this came to a head in the Great Lock-out, when forcibly unemployed workers and their families died of hunger and cold. Open violence hit the streets during Easter Week of 1916 in the uprising that was the main event in the long **struggle for Irish independence**. The main battles were fought in and around the centre of Dublin, and the insurgents made the General Post Office their headquarters.

The history of Dublin **since independence** has been the history of the capital of a young-old nation endeavouring to leave behind its colonial past. It's to this, as well as the appalling condition of many of the old tenements, that the destruction of much of the Georgian city can be attributed. Today the inner city remains fractured and decaying, despite corporation plans to attract investment and to build housing there rather than in the inadequately planned suburban estates that were seen as the answer to the problem between the 1950s and the 1970s. High-rise building in the city centre is the one evil of town planning that Dublin has managed to avoid – when the Central Bank in Dame Street, for instance, deliberately exceeded its height limit, the builders were forced to take twenty feet off the top (although it remains slightly over the statutory limit), and the city centre really has, so far, only one tall building, the repulsive Liberty Hall, headquarters of the Irish Transport and General Workers' Union; although plans for a financial sector further down the Liffey may soon change all that. For all its sufferings, however, the centre remains very much the focus of the city.

Orientation: arriving and getting around

Central Dublin is not big, and it's easy to find your way around. One obvious axis is formed by the river, the **Liffey**, running from west to east and dividing the city into two regions of very distinct character – the North and South Sides – each of which has a strong allegiance among its inhabitants. The other main axis is the north–south one formed by Grafton and Westmoreland streets south of the river, running into O'Connell Street in the north.

The **South Side** includes most of what is left of Georgian Dublin (although the earliest Georgian squares are to the north), and certainly all that is best preserved: Fitzwilliam and Merrion squares, Harcourt Street and Trinity College, as well as the upmarket shopping district around Grafton Street, and the famous St Stephen's Green, central Dublin's largest open space. Further west are the few significant relics of pre-Georgian Dublin: Dublin Castle (started in 1205, but remodelled in the eighteenth century), Christchurch (1172) and St Patrick's

Cathedral (1190). West again, you pass through The Liberties, full of bargain shops and bustle, to the gem-like seventeenth-century Kilmainham Hospital, recently restored and now the home of the new Irish Museum of Modern Art and, close by, the grim bastion of Kilmainham Jail.

On the **North Side**, the huge expanse of Phoenix Park, Dublin's major open space and pleasure ground, begins directly across the Liffey from Kilmainham. Working eastwards back along the river, you come to St Michan's Church, set back a little from the quays; the Four Courts, one of the grandest of Georgian Dublin's public buildings; and then back to the rough north–south axis, O'Connell Street, now full of shops and fast-food outlets but scene of some of the bitterest fighting in the Easter Uprising of 1916. The immediate area is dominated by Liberty Hall and, a little further west, the monumental Custom House, another of the grand monuments of the Georgian period.

The phone code for Dublin is ☎01

Arrivals and departures

Buses from out of town, the airport included, will drop you at or close by the Central Bus Station, or **Busáras**. Right by the river, this is dead central for almost anywhere in the city. Coming in from the **airport**, six miles north of the centre, you can take the official airport bus for £3, or a scheduled city bus, #41, will do the same job for 95p. Either takes around half an hour to reach the bus station. (A taxi will cost you around £19.) If you arrive by **ferry**, you'll come in at one of two harbours: **Dún Laoghaire** (pronounced *Leary*; for *Sealink* services), six miles out, is on the efficient DART (Dublin Area Rapid Transit) city train network, which will whisk you into town in about twenty minutes; **Dublin Port** (*B&I*), nearer in, is served by local bus #53.

Leaving Dublin, the #41 bus to the **airport** sets off from Eden Quay (not all of them go into the airport compound, so check with the driver), or there's a service that goes round all the major hotels collecting airport passengers (check times with Dublin Buses – see number below). For the **ferries**, take the DART service to Dún Laoghaire; or a bus to Dublin Port from Eden Quay. **Buses** to all parts of the country (*Bus Éireann*) leave from the *Busáras* or the streets immediately around (Eden Quay/Abbey Street/Talbot Street); ☎366111 for information. Officially approved **private buses** are generally cheaper: ask to see the bus information file at the tourist office or go to *Funtrek*, 32 Bachelor's Walk by O'Connell Bridge (☎733633/733244). Unofficial buses may be cheaper still; they leave from various points around the city, especially on Friday and Sunday evenings. Check the *Evening Press* for advertisements – weekend buses generally need advance booking.

Trains to the limited parts of Ireland served by the national rail system leave from **Heuston Station** on the South Side (Cork, Waterford, Limerick, Killarney, Tralee, Athlone, Galway, Westport, Ballina, Claremorris) or **Connolly Station** on the North Side (Belfast, Derry, Portadown, Dundalk, Sligo, Arklow, Wexford, Rosslare Harbour). Mainline commuter trains serving coastal towns north and south of Dublin call at Connolly, Tara Street and Pearse Street stations. For train information call ☎787777.

To Ashbourne, Slane & Derry

To The Airport

To the Airport, Balbriggan, Drogheda, Dundalk & Belfast

To Trim, Kells & Navan

DRUMCONDRA

DRUMCONDRA ROAD

FINGLAS ROAD

MARINO

NAVAN ROAD

CABRA

Royal Canal

PHIBSBOROUGH

CLONLIFFE ROAD

ANGLESEY PARKWAY

CABRA ROAD

PHIBSBOROUGH ROAD

Mountjoy Prison

NORTH CIRCULAR ROAD

NORTH

NORTH ROAD

PORTLAND ROW

NORTH STRAND ROAD

Phoenix Park

NORTH CIRCULAR ROAD

NORTH RING

DORSET ST

Zoo

CHURCH ST

KING ST

Cathedral (Pro.)

Connolly Station

Bus Station

CUSTOM HOUSE QUAY

To Mullingar, Athlone, Galway, Sligo and Westport

G.P.O.

EDEN Q.

NORTH WALL QUAY

CONYNGHAM ROAD

PARKGATE ST.

WOLFE TONE ST.

ELLIS Q.

ARRAN Q.

INNS Q.

UPR. ORMOND Q.

BACHE. Q.

CUSTOM HOUSE QUAY

CHAPELIZOD ROAD

Heuston Station

VICTORIA QUAY

USHERS ISL.

MERCHANTS Q.

LWR. ORMOND Q.

WELLING Q.

ASTON Q.

BURGH Q.

GEORGE Q.

CITY QUAY

River Liffey

LINK ROAD

Kilmainham Jail

Guinness Brewery

Christ Church Cathedral

Dublin Castle

PEARSE STREET

Trinity College

Pearse Station

ISLANDBRIDGE

Kilmainham Hospital

KILMAINHAM

St. Patrick's Cathedral

ST. PATRICK'S ST.

NEW ST.

St. Stephen's Green

MOUNT ST.

HADDINGTON ROAD

SHELBOURNE RD.

INCHICORE

Black Horse Inn

Grand Canal

DOLPHIN RD.

DOLPHIN'S BARN

CLANBRASSIL ST.

SOUTH RING

GRAND PAR.

MESPIL ROAD

BALLSBRIDGE

TYRCONNELL ROAD

SOUTH RING

PARNELL ROAD

GROVE ROAD

CANAL ROAD

LEESON ST.

UPR. MOREHAMPTON RD.

To Naas, Kilkenny, Waterford, Limerick, Cork & Killarney

HAROLDS CROSS ROAD

CRUMLIN

RATHMINES

DONNYBROOK

ST. PETER'S ROAD

MILLTOWN

TERENURE

RATHGAR

University College

GREENTREES ROAD

DODDER PARK ROAD

BRAEMORE ROAD

TEMPLEVILLE ROAD

SPRINGFIELD AVENUE

RATHFARNHAM

CHURCHTOWN ROAD

MT. ANN

TANEY ROAD

MAIN ST.

SANDYFORD ROAD

DUNDRU

To Blessington

To Dublin Mts.

DUBLIN AREA

Malahide

DOLLYMOUNT

CLONTARF

Dollymount Strand

ST ALEXANDRA ROAD

Car Ferry
Terminal

H STREET

STRAND ROAD

Dublin Bay

ROCK
ROAD

BOOTERSTOWN

BLACKROCK

NEWTOWN

FOSTERS AVENUE

MT. MERRION AVENUE

SEAPOINT AVENUE

TEMPLE ROAD

MONKSTOWN ROAD

Car Ferry
Terminal

DUNLEARY RD

LWR GEORGES ST

DUN
LAOGHAIRE

STILLORGAN ROAD

STRADBROOK ROAD

DEANS GRANGE ROAD

GLENAGEARY RD

Joyce's
Tower

To Bray, Wicklow
Wexford & Rosslare

City transport

It's customary to say that the way to get to know Dublin is to walk. It's true that the city's size makes this a practical possibility, but equally true that walking the city streets can quickly become a tiring slog. Luckily the city has an extensive, and reasonably priced, **local bus network** that makes it easy to hop on a bus whenever you need to. Buses start running between 6 and 6.30am, and the last city-centre buses leave town around 11.30pm. Maximum **fare** on the bus (and DART) system is 95p. A one-day bus-only **pass** costs £2.20; a bus and rail pass (including DART) £3; a four-day version of the latter (explorer ticket) is still better value at £7; or a weekly bus-only pass costs £8.80. Passes are available from most newsagents. Finding your way round the bus system may prove more of a problem, although most stops do now have timetables and routes for the buses that stop there. If you don't know which stop to go to in the first place, though, either ask a bus inspector – there usually seems to be one around, dispensing directions – or invest in a bus timetable (50p from newsagents) which includes a Dublin bus map. Or you can do what most locals seem to, pop into the nearest newsagent when you're lost, look up the route, and put the book back on the shelf.

The other useful city transportation service is the **DART**, the *Dublin Area Rapid Transport* system, which links Howth to the north of the city with Bray to the south, via such places as Sandycove, where you'll find the James Joyce Martello Tower. The DART is quick, efficient and easy to use, and the stretch that runs along Dublin Bay from Dalkey to Killiney, in particular, gives you such an amazing view that it's worth taking the train just to see it. It's not expensive – maximum single fare is 95p – but if you're considering taking more than one or two trips, it's worth buying a Day Rambler ticket for £3.00 (again, from most newsagents or any station). The DART runs from 6.55am to 11.30pm.

Although, if you're lucky, you may be able to flag one down, **taxis** in Dublin don't generally cruise the streets. Instead they wait at ranks in central locations, such as outside the *Shelbourne Hotel* on St Stephen's Green, or close to *Jury's Hotel* in Ballsbridge. If you want to order a cab by phone, try ☎772222.

Information

The obvious first stop for information is Dublin's main **tourist information office** at 14 Upper O'Connell Street (Mon–Fri 9am–5pm; ☎747733): other branches are at Dublin Airport (☎376387), and the port at Dún Laoghaire (☎806984). The main office is always incredibly busy, but it's big, has much of the most frequently needed information posted on the walls, and has a vast collection of literature and maps (not all of it free). There's a **room booking service**, which costs 50p for accommodation in Dublin and £1.50 for anywhere else. Since the staff aren't allowed to make recommendations all you're paying for is a phone call: if you're planning to stay in bed and breakfasts or hotels most of the time – and you find you need more information than we supply – you can buy one of their **accommodation guides** and do the phoning yourself.

More practical, but always in a state of total chaos, is the **USIT office** on Aston Quay, just opposite O'Connell Bridge (Mon–Fri 9am–5.30pm, Sat 10am–1pm; ☎778117). *USIT* not only books bed and breakfasts during the summer, but also has its own hostel and a travel agency offering student discounts on ferries and flights. Go here for *Travelsave* stamps, *ISIC* cards, and information on everything that's going on in Dublin.

For **listings of Dublin events**, the best source is the fortnightly magazine *In Dublin*, which you can pick up from any newsagent for £1.50. An inferior alternative is the *Dublin Event Guide*, free from the tourist office.

Accommodation

As you'd expect, Dublin has plenty of accommodation in all price ranges, from hostels to five-star hotels, so finding somewhere to stay really shouldn't be a problem. Central **B&Bs** tend to be grimy or overpriced: if you're determined to be right at the heart of the action, various well-organised official and private **youth hostels** offer the cheapest rooms in the centre, though you may have to share your room. **Hotels** are generally expensive, and often no more comfortable than good guesthouses, but if you're travelling out of season it's worth checking reductions, which can be considerable. The **tourist office** in O'Connell Street has lists of everything available, and should know where there are vacancies at peak times.

Bed and Breakfast

Bed and breakfast places abound, with the cheapest dives clustered around Connolly Station on the North Side. In the south there are more salubrious – and more expensive – guesthouses in the Ballsbridge area, still within easy walking distance of the centre. The best balance between price and quality, though, generally involves staying further out, in the suburbs. Given the relatively small scale of the city and the excellent public transport, these places are definitely the better option.

Centre and Ballsbridge
If you're determined on something central, start from the tourist office and head north towards Mountjoy Square. Most of these are pretty seedy, however, and hostels usually offer a better deal. Directly south of the centre, but still within walking distance, Ballsbridge is on bus routes #5, #6, #6A or #7.

Leitrim House, 34 Blessington Street (☎308728). Perhaps the best value in the centre. £9.00.

Avondale Guest House, 40 Lower Gardiner Street (☎745200), more expensive at £16 for a single room (£13 per person sharing), but including a good breakfast.

Mrs O'Donoghue's, 41 Northumberland Road, Ballsbridge (☎681105). A large Victorian house, comfortable and friendly, with quite a few non-tourist guests; expensive, though, at £18.

Miss V. McNamara's, 73 Anglesea Road, Ballsbridge (☎689032). One of the cheapest here, at £14.

Sandymount
Sandymount – buses #1, #2, #3 or #6 – is further out again, but the attraction here is that you're near the sea; it's also handy for the ferry.

Mrs E. Trehy's, 110 Ringsend Park (☎689850). One of the cheapest, at £10.50 plus 75p for a shower.

Mrs R. Casey, Villa Jude, 2 Church Avenue (☎684982). Quiet rooms and an excellent breakfast. £12.

Northwest

Glasnevin, Phibsboro and Cabra, on the northern fringes of Phoenix Park, are all reasonable places to stay, and here you won't feel too far away from the action.

Mrs M. Lambert, 8 Ballymun Road (☎376125). Little over two miles from the centre. £12, showers 50p extra.

Mrs M. Cummins, Renwell House, 33 Finglas Road, Harts Corner (☎302061). £12.

Mrs E. Delahunty, Marymount, 137 New Cabra Road (☎303024). £13.50.

Cassidy's Guest House, 4 Ardmore Avenue (☎388846). Friendly and convenient. £18.

Northeast

Northeast, towards Drumcondra and Clontarf, you're into suburbia again, but you'll be close to the sea. Here rates are generally reasonable, with lots of places to choose from, particularly along the Clontarf Road, which runs right by the seafront. Drumcondra itself is less convenient.

Mrs E Byrne-Poole, Sea Front, 278 Clontarf Road (☎336118). Nice position. £12.50.

Carmel Geoghegan, The White House, 125 Clontarf Road (☎333196). Close to Dublin Bay and on the #30 bus route. £14.

Mrs C. Kehoe, 13 St Patricks Road, off Whitworth Road (☎306934). £9.50.

Hotels

Shelbourne, St Stephen's Green (☎766471). Widely acknowledged to be Dublin's best hotel. Be prepared to pay, though: full rates are £70–100 per person.

Gresham, Upper O'Connell Street (☎746881). Runs the Shelbourne a close second. Similar rates.

The Georgian House, 20–21 Lower Baggott Street (☎618832). One of the few period buildings in Dublin where you can actually stay, five minutes' walk from St Stephen's Green, with a good seafood restaurant. £30–50.

Central Hotel, 1–5 Exchequer Street (☎6797302). Recently refurbished and centrally located close to the lively Temple Bar area. Bright pink walls and modern Irish art save it from overpowering yuppie-tastefulness; excellent breakfasts and a good restaurant serving some organically grown food. £45.

Clarence Hotel, Wellington Quay (☎776178). Lively and centrally situated, overlooking the Liffey and close to Dublin Castle and Temple Bar, with the dubious distinction of hosting the Elvis fan club and sundry ballroom dancing events. £25–35.

Wynn's Hotel, Lower Abbey Street (☎745131). On the North Side, an old-fashioned, dusty establishment whose downstairs bar is the scene of dedicated, if subdued, drinking by locals. Close to the Abbey Theatre and very much a part of city life. £25–32.

Othello House, 74 Lower Gardiner Street (☎743460). A good budget option, just off O'Connell Street – a small hotel with 16 rooms. £20–22.

Maple Hotel, 75 Lower Gardiner Street (☎745239). Similarly comfortable small, central hotel. £18–25.

Hostels

As well as the official *An Óige* hostel, Dublin has a variety of less formal and often more enjoyable independent hostels

Dublin International Youth Hostel, 61 Mountjoy Street (☎301766). This modern hostel is extremely well set-up and open all year; a supplementary hostel, *Scóil Lorcáin*, opens for July and August at Eaton Square, Monkstown, four miles from the centre (☎801948; bus #7, #7A or #8, or DART to Seapoint). You'll need an *An Óige* or IYHF membership card to use either, and they charge £7–9.

YWCA hostel, just out of town at Radcliff Hall, St John's Road, Sandymount (☎694521). £12.

Isaac's, 2–5 Frenchman's Lane, just round the corner from Busáras (☎749321, 363877). Otherwise known as the *Dublin Tourist Hostel*, *Isaac's* is housed in an eighteenth-century wine warehouse. It offers a mix of accommodation, from basic dormitory bunks to single and double rooms, plus kitchen and good restaurant with plenty of choice for vegetarians, music some evenings and jazz on Sundays. Room lockout 11am–5pm; no curfew. Bed £4.75, blankets 25p, sheets 75p.

The Young Traveller, St Mary's Place, just north of Parnell Square (☎305000). More luxurious and sociable accommodation in small, four-bed rooms in what used to be a school run by the Christian Brothers. It also has a restaurant and washing machine. No curfew or daytime lockout. £7.50 including continental breakfast.

Cardijn House, 15 Talbot Street, above Tiffany's Shoe Shop (☎741720). Also known as *Goin' My Way*. Closes from 10am to 5pm, although the coffee bar stays open; midnight curfew. £4 including breakfast and sheet rental.

Kinlay House, 2–12 Lord Edward Street (☎6796644). The *USIT* hostel, close to Christchurch Cathedral. Relaxed, friendly place – no curfew – with 4-to-6-bedrooms, some doubles, laundry and kitchen facilities. £7–16, depending on size of room. Breakfast included.

North Strand Hostel, 49 North Strand Road, about fifteen minutes' walk from the centre (☎364716). Small rooms rather than dormitories, an open fire and a bicycle lock-up. £4 plus £1 key deposit; sheets and sleeping bags available; closed for Christmas period.

Dunsinea House, Ashtown, Dublin 15 (☎383252; bus #37, #38 or #39 from Abbey Street to the *Halfway House* pub nearby). Again some way out, but welcoming and open all year round. £5.

Trinity Hall, Dartry Road, Rathmines (☎971772). In the summer holidays (mid-June to Sept) students in possession of an ISIC card can stay in student accommodation here. £9.50.

Camping

There are several campsites around Dublin, including two at Ballybrack village, south of Dún Laoghaire, but none particularly close in.

Donabate, on the North Side, a few miles beyond Swords (☎8450038; bus #33B from Eden Quay). Fairly basic site with only limited space for tents, so phone in advance. £4 per tent.

Cromlech, Three miles south of Dún Laoghaire, close to the pretty seaside village of Dalkey, on the DART line (☎826882/824783; bus #46 from Dublin or #46A from Dún Laoghaire). Relatively luxurious caravan and camping site; open mid-April to mid-Sept. £4 per tent, 50p per person.

Shankill, close to the DART stop at Shankill, or take bus #45, #45A, #46 or #84. (☎820011). South of Dún Laoghaire by the sea, within reach of secluded beaches; open Easter to October. £4–5 per tent, plus 50p per person.

The City

It's difficult to say exactly where the **centre of Dublin** is. Visitors will generally locate it south of the Liffey, around Grafton Street, the main pedestrianised shopping street, which links St Stephen's Green with Trinity College. Dubliners, on the other hand, are more likely to shop in the maze of streets that lead off O'Connell Street, north of the river; and the fact that almost all Dublin's cinemas, plus two of its most important theatres, the Gate and the Abbey, are on the North Side, also implies that that's where downtown Dublin really is. Nonetheless, the majority of the city's historic monuments, including its ancient centre, are south of the river; and College Green is as good a place as any to start.

CENTRAL DUBLIN

College Green and Trinity College

In some ways the topography of Dublin has stayed remarkably constant since the city was founded, when the Vikings sited their *Haugen* or *Thengmote*, the central meeting place and burial ground, on what is now **College Green**. Formerly known as Hoggen Green, it remained the centre of administrative power in Ireland until the Act of Union.

The Bank of Ireland

Although Trinity College is the most famous landmark, the massive **Bank of Ireland**, which faces it obliquely across the busy traffic interchange, has played an even more central role in the history of Anglo-Irish ascendancy. When originally begun in 1729 by Sir Edward Lovett Pearce, it was envisaged as a suitably grand setting for the parliament of a nation, as the Anglo-Irish were coming to regard themselves. Their efforts to achieve self-government culminated in the famous Grattan parliament of 1782 in which **Henry Grattan** – whose gesturing statue stands outside on College Green – uttered the celebrated phrase, "Ireland is now a nation". The Protestant, Anglo-Irish parliament endorsed the country's independence unanimously.

However, this rebellious spirit was short-lived; with the passing of the Act of Union Ireland lost both its independence as a nation and its parliament (which acquiesced to the extent of voting itself obediently out of existence). With its original function gone, the building was sold to the Bank of Ireland for £40,000 in 1803. Though not exactly geared up for coach parties, the bank does admit sightseers during normal banking hours (Mon–Fri 10am–12.30pm & 1.30–5pm). Its **interior** is magnificently old-fashioned – you are shown around by ushers wearing costumes seemingly unchanged since the nineteenth century, and in winter, coal fires glow in the entrance hall's massive grates. In the atmospheric former **House of Lords**, with its coffered ceiling and eighteenth-century Waterford glass chandelier, you can see the mace from the old House of Commons.

Trinity College

In comparison to the mighty facade of the Bank, the modest portico of **Trinity College** seems almost domestic in scale. Founded in 1591 by Queen Elizabeth I, it played a major role in the development of an Anglo-Irish tradition, with leading families often sending their sons to be educated here rather than in England. The statues outside represent Edmund Burke and Oliver Goldsmith, two of Trinity's most famous graduates. The philosopher and statesman Burke (1729–97) adopted an interesting position, simultaneously defending Ireland's independence and insisting on its role as an integral part of the British empire; Goldsmith (1728–94) was a noted wit and poet. Other illustrious alumni include Jonathan Swift (1667–1745) and Wolfe Tone (1763–98), as well as Bram Stoker (1847–1912), J. M. Synge (1871–1909) and the playwright Samuel Beckett (1906–1991).

Until recently, Trinity's Anglo-Irish connections gave it a strong **Protestant** bias. At its foundation, the college offered free education to Catholics who were prepared to change their religion, and right up to 1966 – long after the rule on religion had been dropped by the college itself – Catholics had to get a special dispensation to study at Trinity, or risk excommunication. Nowadays, roughly seventy percent of the student population is Catholic, and Trinity is just one of Dublin's universities. University College Dublin is based near Stillorgan in the

suburb of Belfield, and forms part of the National University of Ireland; Dublin City University is in Glasnevin.

Simply as an architectural set piece, Trinity takes some beating. It served as an English university in the film *Educating Rita* – bizarre, but understandable, given that it looks the way a great university should. Its stern grey college buildings are ranged around cobbled quadrangles in a grander version of the arrangement at Oxford and Cambridge (the cobbles apparently have to be relaid every seven years as the land, reclaimed from the sea, subsides).

Just inside the entrance, the **Chapel** is reflected on the right by the **Theatre** or examination hall, whose elegant, stuccoed interior is sometimes used for concerts (check the notice boards in the main entrance). Both were designed by Sir William Chambers, a Scottish Neoclassical architect who never visited Ireland. Beyond the chapel on the left is the **Dining Hall**, also used for exams, built by the German architect Richard Cassels in 1743. The bell tower, or **Campanile**, in the middle of the square, was put up in 1853 and is believed to mark the site of the priory which long predated the university. A startling element of colour is introduced by the red brick of the **Rubrics**, student accommodation dating from 1712, and one of Trinity's oldest surviving buildings.

The Library and the Book of Kells

The other early survivor is the famous **Library** (Mon–Fri 9.30am–4.45pm, Sat 9.30am–12.45pm; £1.75, under 18s free), which is meant to receive a free copy of every book published in Britain and Ireland and also contains a famous collection of priceless Irish manuscripts, above all the celebrated Book of Kells. Some 200,000 of the total collection of three million books are held here in the old Library: the rest is stored off site, where over half a mile of new shelving is needed every year to accommodate new volumes. It's a long – 209 feet in all – tall, aristocratic room, flooded with light, with books housed on two storeys of shelves. The library originally had just one floor, but in 1859 the roof was raised and the upper bookcases were added.

Trinity's **illuminated manuscripts** are derived from the tradition of Saint Columba, which embraced not only Ireland but also Scotland and the north of England and had a strong influence on the European monastic tradition. There's still some debate over whether the most famous of the manuscripts, the eighth-century **Book of Kells**, was really copied and illuminated in Ireland at all; the location may have been Scotland – maybe Iona, Saint Columba's first Scottish port of call – or even Lindisfarne in northern England. Totalling 680 pages, the Book of Kells was rebound in the 1950s into four separate volumes, of which two are on show at any one time, one open at a completely illuminated page, the other at a text page, itself not exactly unadorned, with patterns and fantastic animals intertwined with the capitals.

Famous as the Book of Kells is, the **Book of Durrow** is in many ways equally interesting. It is the first of the great Irish illuminated manuscripts, dating from between 650 and 680, and has, unusually, a whole page (known as the carpet page, for obvious reasons) given over to ornament. It's noticeable in all these early manuscripts that the depictions of the human form make no attempt at realism – Saint Matthew in the Book of Durrow, for instance, is apparently wrapped in a poncho, with no hands. The important thing is the pattern, which is derived from metalwork (as in the amazing Ardagh Chalice and Tara Brooch, which you can see in the National Museum close by). The characteristic spirals are always

slightly asymmetrical – apparently another trick to ensure that the eye doesn't tire – and it's believed that the ornamentation in general had a symbolic meaning, although its full meaning is now unknown.

At the far end of the library are two early Irish **harps**, one of them traditionally known as Brian Boru's harp, although it's been dated to the fifteenth century, some four centuries after Boru. There's also an original copy of the 1916 **Proclamation of Independence**.

The Dublin Experience

Unfortunately, you are unlikely to be left in peace to drink in the library's scholarly atmosphere. A new multi-media show, **The Dublin Experience**, has put Trinity firmly on the tourist trail, and each day sees a steady stream of busloads deposited at the gates. Using a combination of archive and new material, the show traces Dublin's history and gives some guide to the main events of Irish history. It's unlikely that it will give, as it claims, a "complete orientation to the city", but if you're footsore and still have money in your pocket, tickets for the shows, every hour from 10am to 5pm, are £2.75, or £4.25 if combined with admission to the Library.

The old parts of Trinity, although they're all very much in use, tend to have the look of a museum exhibit. For contact with student life, it's best to head for the **arts and social sciences block**, an award-winning piece of Sixties concrete brutalism by the side entrance in Nassau Street. There's a theatre and coffee bar here and plenty of information, in term-time, on what's going on. The **Douglas Hyde Gallery of Modern Art**, housed in the same complex, is one of the city's few experimental art venues and always worth checking out (it also has a good bookshop).

South to Saint Stephen's Green

The streets that surround pedestrianised Grafton Street frame Dublin's quality shopping area. Boasting no less than two shopping malls – the converted Georgian *Powerscourt Town House*, and an extraordinary Eighties confection on the corner of St Stephen's Green, exhibiting a confusion of cultural references that have been variously described as French, Indian, Renaissance and Georgian – it's a totally different Dublin from that which you'll find on the North Side: chic, sophisticated and expensive.

Grafton Street

Grafton Street itself has long since been swamped by the rush to commercialism, but it's a pleasant enough place to while away some time. As well as simply wandering in and out of its retail palaces – Dublin's two leading **department stores**, *Switzers* and the more old-fashioned and upmarket *Brown Thomas*, are here, and *Powerscourt Town House* is set back a little on Clarendon Street – you can take in the **street life**: since its pedestrianisation, Grafton Street has become the centre of Dublin's burgeoning street theatre, and this is one of the few places where you'll find buskers – including a poetry busker who claims to be able to recite any (Irish) poem on request, and often throws in works of his own too – and clowns entertaining passers-by.

The unmissable stop on Grafton Street is **Bewley's coffee house**. In its dark wood and marble-tabled interior, Bewley's does all-day tea, coffee and food ranging from meals to cakes and sticky buns, along with the best potato soup in the universe. It's an extraordinary atmosphere and unbeatable value – a great place to sit and watch people, read a book or write your novel (no one will try to hurry you, even if you've only bought a cup of tea). A testament to the vigour of the café tradition in Dublin, *Bewley's* is a place where everyone goes, and you'll see a range of people from students and old ladies to high-powered businessmen.

The Grafton Street *Bewley's* has a small **museum** on the top floor tracing the history of this Dublin institution. Founded in the 1840s by the Quaker Bewley family, it has been a meeting place for all levels of Dublin society ever since. Becoming a workers' co-operative in 1971, it almost folded in 1986 and provoked a national crisis in which the government stepped in to offer help before a buyer was eventually found. There are two other central branches of *Bewley's*, each with a slightly different character; in Westmoreland Street (wonderful Art Nouveau fireplaces; open Mon–Sat 7.30am–6pm), and South Great George's Street (open until 2am Wed–Sat).

Dawson Street

Dawson Street is altogether quieter than Grafton Street, and home of some of Dublin's better bookshops (see "Listings") as well as a number of august institutions. Chief among these is the **Mansion House**, a really delightful Queen Anne building of 1710 weighed down by heavy Victorian wrought iron. This has been the official residence of the Lord Mayor since 1715 and was also where the *Dáil Éireann*, the Irish parliament, met in 1919 to ratify the Declaration of Independence. The Mansion House isn't generally open to the public, but in any case there's not a great deal to be seen inside.

Next door, the decorous red-brick house containing the **Royal Irish Academy** is also closed to the public. One of the great learned institutions of Europe, it publishes books of Irish interest and has a weighty collection of Irish manuscripts. Next door again, **St Anne's** (Church of Ireland) church has an amazingly ornate Italianate facade which is a real surprise when you catch sight of it along Anne Street. Inside, behind the altar, are wooden shelves that were originally designed to take loaves of bread for distribution among the poor of the parish as the result of a 1720s bequest. On Thursday lunchtimes, St Anne's hosts a series of recitals and other cultural activities – check *In Dublin* for details.

Kildare Street: Leinster House

Kildare Street is the really monumental section of the Grafton, Dawson, Kildare trio, and it also marks the point where what's left of the Georgian city gets going. The most imposing building is undoubtedly **Leinster House**, built in 1745 as the Duke of Leinster's town house. At that time, the fashionable area of Dublin was north of the river, and there were those who mocked him for building a town house in the south on what was then a green-field site. The Kildare Street facade, facing the town, is built to look like a town house; the other side, looking out on to what is now Merrion Square, looks like a country house.

Nowadays, this is one of the most important buildings in Dublin, housing the Irish parliament – the **Dáil Éireann**, or House of Representatives, and the **Seanad Éireann**, or Senate (open, when parliament isn't in session, Tues–Sat 10am–5pm, Sun 2–5pm) – as well as the National Museum and National Library. The Dáil (pronounced "Doil") has 166 representatives – *Teachtaí Dála*, usually shortened to TDs – elected by direct proportional vote, representing 41 constituencies. The Senate is proposed on a vocational basis, with six members elected by the universities and eleven nominated by the *Taoiseach* (pronounced "Tee-shuck"), or Prime Minister. General elections take place at least every five years; presidential elections, which are also direct, are held every seven years. Mary Robinson, elected in 1990 as Ireland's first woman president, has breathed welcome new life into this formerly symbolic role by speaking out for women and the political left in a country whose politics are still essentially delineated by the battle lines of the civil war.

National Library and National Museum

Whether or not the massive twin rotundas, housing the entrances of the National Library on the left and the National Museum on the right, do anything to complement the Georgian elegance of Leinster House is debatable; they were added in 1890. The **National Library** (Mon–Thurs 10am–9pm, Fri 10am–5pm, Sat 10am–1pm; free) is, however, worth visiting for its associations alone: it seems that every major Irish writer from Joyce onwards used it at some time, and the Reading Room is also the scene of the great literary debate in *Ulysses*. The Library has a good collection of first editions and works of Irish writers, including Swift, Goldsmith, Yeats, Shaw, Joyce and Beckett. It's also often used for temporary exhibitions on Irish books and authors.

The **National Museum** (Tues–Sat 10am–5pm, Sun 9am–5pm) is the place to go to see the treasures of ancient Ireland. If you've arrived in Dublin after travelling elsewhere in Ireland, names like the Tara Brooch and the Ardagh Chalice will probably speak for themselves; indeed it's sometimes infuriating that all the major finds seem to have been taken to Dublin, so take the chance to see them while you can. Entrance to the museum is free, and the one part not to miss is the **Treasury**, housing all the real goodies.

The Ardagh Chalice and Tara Brooch, both eighth-century, along with the so-called St Patrick's Bell and the Cross of Cong, twelfth-century, are among the earliest exhibits in the Treasury. The **Tara Brooch** is regarded as perhaps the greatest piece of Irish metalwork, and it's thought that the patterns of manuscript illuminations such as the Book of Kells, which you can see in Trinity College Library, may be derived from this rich craft tradition. Remarkably, the Tara Brooch is decorated both on the front and the back, where the intricate filigree work could be seen only by the wearer – the brooch is displayed above a mirror so that you can see both sides.

One of the more recent finds is the **Derrynaflan Hoard**, a testament to the Irish enthusiasm for metal-detecting. This collection of eighth- and ninth-century silver objects was discovered in February 1980 in County Tipperary by amateur treasure-hunters using a metal detector that one of them had got for Christmas.

To discover more about the Viking tradition, go round the corner into Merrion Row (past the *Shelbourne Hotel*) for the **National Museum Annexe**, which exhibits the results of digs at the Christchurch Place, Winetavern and Wood Quay sites, around Christchurch, carried out between 1962 and 1981. The complexity of the culture is on show in artefacts like eleventh-century combs and carrying cases carved from bones and antlers, scales for weighing precious metals together with accurate lead weights, and iron swords.

Right at the top of Kildare Street, at the point where it intersects with Nassau Street, the fussy, Venetian-inspired red-brick building on the corner used to house one of the major institutions of Anglo-Irish Dublin, the **Kildare Street Club**.

Saint Stephen's Green

Walk to the bottom of any of these streets and you'll emerge on the north side of **St Stephen's Green**, the focus of central Dublin's city planning. It's an oddly decorous open space, neat and tidy with little bandstands and pergolas, laid out as a public park in 1880 by Lord Ardilaun (Sir Arthur Edward Guinness). An open common until 1663, the final buildings ringing it went up in the eighteenth century; unfortunately, very few of these have survived, and their replacements speak eloquently of the failure of Sixties planning regulations.

The **gardens**, with their ornamental pond, can be a pleasant place to while away some time on a sunny day, but in terms of architecture, or even city life, there's not a lot to see. The statue in memory of Wolfe Tone, backed by slabs of granite, is known locally as "Tone-henge".

The north side of the square – known in the eighteenth century as the "Beaux Walk" for the dandies and glitterati who used to promenade there – is dominated by the **Shelbourne Hotel**. Fittingly, the Shelbourne – which boasts that it has "the best address in Dublin" – continues to be a focus for the upper echelons of the city's social life. It's worth bearing in mind that, as with all Irish hotels, you can wander in for a drink and something to eat in the lobby at any time of day, even if you're not staying. The Shelbourne's afternoon teas (from 3pm) are wonderful; but the airy, chandeliered lobby and the *Horseshoe* bar come into their own in the early evening when the hotel is a great place for both celebrity spotting and watching the parade of young Dubliners who are there to be seen. The Shelbourne is too well-bred to pass comment on jeans and trainers in the lobby, but you'll feel out of place if you penetrate to the excellent (but expensive) restaurant (see "Eating") unless you dress up a bit.

Linked to the east side of the Green by Hume Street is **Ely Place**, where you can see some of the best-preserved Georgian domestic buildings in Dublin and get a real feel of what the street atmosphere must once have been like. The sober exteriors conceal some extraordinary flights of fancy: no. 8, for instance, has an amazing staircase with elaborate stucco work telling the story of the labours of Hercules. Unfortunately it isn't open to the public.

The Catholic University of Ireland: Newman House

University College, Dublin's second-oldest university (after Trinity), is now housed at a new campus at Belfield in the suburb of Donnybrook, but the original premises of its predecessor, the **Catholic University of Ireland**, are at nos. 85–86 on the south side of the Green, and are now being restored to something approaching their original appearance. The original aim was to provide a Catholic answer to the great academic traditions of Oxford and Cambridge but, despite the appointment of John Henry Newman (who had famously converted from high-church Anglicanism) as its rector, the new university was, initially, denied official recognition in Britain. Eventually, in 1853, it was successfully established as a University College. The poet and Jesuit priest Gerard Manley Hopkins (1844–89) taught as a professor; Pádraig Pearse, Éamon de Valera and James Joyce are among its more famous graduates.

The original university premises, collectively known as **Newman House** (May–Oct, Tues–Fri 10am–4pm, Sat 2–4.30pm, Sun 11am–2pm; £1), are still in the midst of restoration, but already provide an unparalleled opportunity to get a taste of what the Georgian town-houses of St Stephen's Green must originally have been like. No. 85 is a small, early Georgian villa built about 1738 for Hugh Montgomery, a wealthy Ulster landowner and member of parliament for County Fermanagh. This was one of the first town houses built by Richard Castle, or Cassels, the fashionable German country-house architect (who also designed Castletown, just outside Dublin, and later the Dining Hall at Trinity College), and shows his mastery of the more intimate scale of urban building.

Inside, one of Dublin's most remarkable interiors is worth visiting just to see the **Apollo room**, with its stucco reliefs of the nine muses made by the brilliant Swiss *stuccadores* Paolo and Filippo Lanfranchine. Upstairs on the first floor, a fine double-cube room with ceiling reliefs celebrating the subjects of good government and prudent economy awaits restoration. The Lanfranchinis boasted that their work was so good that it didn't need colour, so the ghastly 1940s colour scheme is all wrong, and destroys the delicacy of the mouldings (compare the simple grey of the restored Apollo room); but you can easily make out the extraordinarily ham-fisted additions made by the nineteenth century Jesuits, who decided that the ceiling showed far too many naked female bodies and helpfully added what look like fur suits to protect the morals of their students.

In 1765 the small villa was joined by a bigger town house, which also forms part of the phased restoration (due for completion in 1999). The original house was then extended with an additional room at the back which became the **physics theatre**, where James Joyce lectured to the "L & H" (the "Literary and Historical Soceity") and which features in his *Portrait of the Artist as a Young Man*. The new house was built by Richard "Burnchapel" Whaley, a virulent anti-Catholic who swore never to let a Papist across his threshold and earned his sobriquet by burning chapels in County Wicklow. His son, "Jerusalem" Whaley, was a founder of the Hellfire Club. Legend tells that he threw a crucifix through the front window on Maundy Thursday, and ever afterwards on the same day its image is still to be seen there. The **newer house** is characterised by lighter, airier plasterwork (the main staircase, decorated with musical instruments and flowers, is particularly beautiful), and is to be restored to its mid nineteenth-century appearance, with some of the interventions made by the university prelates.

Next door, **University Church** is an amazingly prolix Byzantine fantasy, with an interior decorated with coloured marble – more familiar from the cloud-burst patterns on country bungalows – quarried in Armagh, Offaly and Kilkenny as well as at the better-known quarries of the far west, Mayo and Connemara.

West of the Green

Harcourt Street, leading off from the southwest corner of St Stephen's Green, is a graceful Georgian street that has survived relatively unscathed. There's nothing much to do here (though there is a good Celtic bookshop) but it's worth strolling down a little way to admire the graceful proportions and elegant town planning.

On the west side of the Green is the **Royal College of Surgeons**, which during the events of Easter week in 1916 was held by the Irish Citizen Army with Constance Markiewicz as second-in-command. The most recent interruption to the skyline of St Stephen's Green is the shopping mall on the corner with Grafton Street, its white wrought-iron detailing intended, presumably, to echo the Georgian balconies of Merrion and Fitzwilliam squares. In the few years since it was built, its flashy architecture has made its peace extraordinarily well with its surroundings, something that may not be too surprising, given that the famous good taste of Georgian building conceals much the same kind of boom-time, get-rich-quick expansionism.

Merrion Square and Georgian Dublin

Merrion Square, Fitzwilliam Square and the streets immediately around them form the heart of what's left of **Georgian Dublin**. Representing the latest of the city's Georgian architecture – decrepit Mountjoy Square and Parnell Square, north of the river, are almost all that's left of the earlier Georgian city – their worn red-brick facades are a brilliant example of confident, relaxed urban planning. The overall layout, in terms of squares and linking streets, may be formal, but there's a huge variation of detail. Height, windows, wrought-iron balconies, ornate doorways, are all different, but the result is a graceful meeting of form and function that's immensely beguiling.

Merrion Square has the feeling of grandeur and repose of much of the Georgian area, and it comes as no surprise that it's been the home of a lot of well-known people – Daniel O'Connell, the Wildes, W. B. Yeats. It hasn't always been simply an area devoted to gracious living, however: during the famine years, between 1845 and 1847, the park in the centre of the square was the site of soup kitchens to which the starving and the destitute flocked. Nowadays the park railings are used on Saturdays and Sundays by artists flogging their wares; the area is also a centre for most of Dublin's private galleries (see "Listings").

Looking along the south side of the square, you experience one of the set pieces of Dublin's architecture: the hard outlines – pepperpot tower, Ionic columns and pediment – of **St Stephen's Church** (1825). If you want to know more about Ireland's architectural heritage, and its Georgian architecture in particular, call at the **Irish Architectural Archive** at no. 63 (Mon–Fri 10am–1pm & 2–5pm; ☎763430). The house is a particularly tatty one but it will give you some idea of what the interiors of these elegant buildings are like.

The National Gallery

Alongside the back of Leinster House – its country house facade – is Ireland's **National Gallery** (Mon–Sat 10am–6pm, Sun 2–5pm, late opening until 9pm on Thurs; free). It's a place that has a real feeling of activity, mainly because of all the people dropping in to eat at the excellent restaurant (see "Eating and Drinking"), and as a gallery it's also a delight. The collection is not huge, though there are over 2000 paintings on show, but the intimacy of its scale gives it a particular charm. The displays include seventeenth-century French, Italian and Spanish paintings, Dutch masters – some good Rembrandts – English watercolourists and French Impressionists; but it's the Irish paintings that are the real draw.

Inevitably, the **Irish section** is heavy on the art of the Anglo-Irish, and in the paintings you can trace the pattern of their history from the formal portraits of the early seventeenth century to the beginnings of interest in the life of ordinary people, which is to say the native Irish. Some of these pictures seem shockingly sentimental – one, by Edwin Hayes, is a calmly beautiful depiction of an emigrant ship at sunset in Dublin Harbour. Exotica, in the shape of such subjects as Indians and Mandarins, also make their appearance, presumably through the involvement of the Anglo-Irish in British military and trading activities. Later paintings include Jack B. Yeats' walls of chaotic colour. If the Irish paintings seem to stop short at the modern period, it's because the late nineteenth and twentieth centuries are well represented in the Municipal Art Gallery in Parnell Square and at the new Museum of Modern Art in Kilmainham.

For anyone who's travelled around Ireland before arriving in Dublin, some of the most fascinating items have to be the gallery's **topographical paintings**. Landscape paintings of estates, commissioned by their owners, these show more than what the estates looked like: they're aspirational portraits of how their owners wanted them to be. There are amazingly evocative paintings of the estates at Lucan in County Dublin, and Ballinrobe in County Mayo – a place that, though it exudes a sense of past glory, gives no indication of the pleasure gardens depicted in these paintings.

Georgian Life?

At the other side of Merrion Square, at no. 29 Lower Fitzwilliam Street, is what's billed as a "faithfully **recreated Georgian family home**" (Tues–Sat 10am–5pm, Sun 2–5pm; admission currently free; ☎765831). Recreated is the word – the house fell down, and has been rebuilt brick by brick by the Electricity Board, whose offices adjoin it at the back. If you want a postmodern experience of the Georgian, this is it, furnished in a notional style of between 1790 and 1820. Visiting the house is an extraordinary experience, a bit like being a Martian on a visit to earth: there's no feeling that you might have anything in common with the people who once lived here: rather you're told that the creatures who lived here "only drank wine and beer", or that the women "did nothing but write letters to themselves". Georgian life is turned into a cabinet of curiosities, a weird kind of sideshow which does, admittedly, have its fascination. For an idea of "real" eighteenth-century Dublin life, Newman House (see above) is far superior; but if you have a taste for kitsch, "Number 29" can certainly be fun.

Eastwards – Baggot Street and the Grand Canal

Baggot Street – with its multitude of lively pubs – starts out Georgian, but the street plan is pretty soon broken by the great black metal-and-glass bulk of the Bank of Ireland building, enlivened only by a few brightly coloured metal constructivist sculptures. Just afterwards, you reach the Grand Canal, one of Dublin's two man-made waterways: the Royal Canal runs through the north of the city.

The **Grand Canal** was the earlier and more successful of the two: started in 1756 and reaching the Shannon by 1803 (the Royal Canal was begun in 1790), it carried passengers and freight between Dublin, the midland towns and the Shannon right up to the 1960s. You can see just how slow these epic journeys across Ireland were in timetables from the late eighteenth and early nineteenth centuries exhibited in the tiny **Civic Museum** in South William Street, off Grafton Street (Tues–Sat 10am–6pm, Sun 11am–2pm). True Dubliners, or Jackeens, are said to be those born between the canals – like the business about true Cockneys being born within the sound of Bow Bells; however, there may be a bit of leeway in interpretation. The best stretch to see the Grand Canal on its journey through Dublin city is in the south, between Leeson Street Bridge and Huband Bridge.

Just over Baggot Street Bridge, **Parson's bookshop** is a ramshackle old store worth visiting for its serious Irish-interest books and complete lack of trendiness, as well as for writer spotting. It was a haunt of Patrick Kavanagh and Brendan Behan, among others; Kavanagh lived in a flat nearby in Pembroke Road and produced a newspaper, *Kavanagh's Weekly*, "a journal of literature and politics", almost entirely written by the poet himself (with contributions from Behan and Myles na Gopaleen, among others). It ran to a grand total of 13 issues before it folded. The complete edition has been reprinted (Goldsmith Press, 1981) and is to be found in the bigger bookshops. There are pieces about almost everything – professional marriage makers, visits to the bookies, weeks when nothing happens – as well as some useful straight-talking about Irish myth-making, including Dublin theatre: on the rebuilding of the Abbey Theatre in 1952, Kavanagh commented, "The Abbey Theatre is the opposite of what it set out to be. The Abbey Theatre was never much good. The life it portrayed was not Irish, nor any other life, but a convention invented by Synge mainly."

Ballsbridge

Further out, you come to the respectable suburb of Ballsbridge, where you'll find some of the pleasanter guesthouses (see "Accommodation") as well as many of the foreign embassies and smarter hotels. The **showgrounds** of the *Royal Dublin Society* – the first of its kind in Europe, founded over 250 years ago to promote improvements in agriculture, stock breeding and animal medicine – are also here. If you're in town for the Spring Show in May or, even more so, the Dublin Horse Show (usually in August), don't pass them by.

The **Chester Beatty Library and Gallery of Oriental Art** (Tues–Fri 10am–5pm, Sat 2–5pm; ☎692386), in Shrewsbury Road, is a collection of biblical papyruses, Persian and Turkish paintings, Korans, Chinese jade books and Japanese and European wood-block prints, some of them going back 4500 years. It's a testament to one man's tenacity: Chester Beatty, who began his career mining in the Wild West, made his first million at forty and developed a fascination with exotic art through spending his winters in Africa to ease the symptoms of silicosis. He settled in Dublin in 1950 and bequeathed this collection to the Irish nation, along with some important paintings of the Barbizon school which are shown in the National Gallery.

West of College Green: Temple Bar

Staying south of the river, the main thoroughfare leading west from College Green is Dame Street. Immediately north, the area between the modern Central Bank and the Liffey is known as **Temple Bar**. Bought up by *CIE* (formerly the state transport company), who wanted to build a new central bus terminal to replace the one on the other side of the river, it has suffered from a benign sort of planning blight: although the bus station idea has been abandoned, shops, studios and offices in the area have been rented out on short leases, the streets are full of cheap restaurants, second-hand bookshops and bric-a-brac stores, plus the admirable *Project Arts Centre*. The place is often compared with Covent Garden in London or Les Halles in Paris, which is pushing it a bit – there hasn't been the money that has been poured into either of those projects, although there is some creeping gentrification in the form of cobbling and olde-worlde street lights, and Temple Bar certainly doesn't have anything like Covent Garden's relentless commercialism – but it's still one of the liveliest and most interesting parts of town, and a place worth spending some time, especially in the evenings.

The **Project Arts Centre**, in East Sussex Street, is where you're most likely to find experimental or politically sensitive theatre. They also run late-night music spots at weekends, and there's a gallery space which runs temporary exhibitions; check out what's on in *In Dublin*. Also worth a visit is the **Dublin Resource Centre** in Crow Street, a bookshop with plenty of material to provide an alternative, radical view of Irish politics and history, attached to an old-fashioned (Sixties/Seventies style) vegetarian co-operative, the *Well-Fed Restaurant*. Just off the other side of Dame Street, the **Andrews Lane Theatre** is a leading place for new Irish writing.

Dame Street itself, focus of Dublin's banking and business, rapidly leads you out of the prosperous centre. Soon the city plan begins to fragment into haphazardly built housing and shops, and you begin to see the other side of Dublin life – bag ladies, drunks and beggars. It's ironic that this part of the city, with many of Dublin's sights, also draws big tourist crowds: Dublin Castle, St Patrick's Cathedral, Christchurch and, the other side of the area known as The Liberties, Kilmainham Hospital and Kilmainham Jail, are all close by.

Dublin Castle

Dublin Castle (Mon–Fri 10am–12.15pm & 2–5pm, weekends 2–5pm; £1, children 50p, heritage card; ☎777129) is just a short walk along Dame Street. Outside its gates, the lime-green headquarters of the *Sick and Indigent Roomkeepers Society*, founded in 1790, still seems to be going strong. Once inside, you're confronted with a real pig's breakfast of architectural styles: an ugly modern tax office stands to your left, an over-precise gothic fantasy of a church of 1803 adorns the ridge straight ahead, and to your right is the worn red brick of the castle itself.

Given the castle's age – it dates from King John's first Dublin court of 1207 – it's a surprise to find that in its present state it's a gracious eighteenth-century building, with only the massive stone **Record Tower** giving the game away. Originally there were four such towers (the base of the Bermingham tower, to the southwest, also survives), and the castle was a real fortified building; but it later became more an administrative than a military centre. As the heart of British power – it continued as the Viceroy's seat after the Act of Union – it stands as a symbol of 700 years of British influence on Ireland.

The Castle hosted the **European Parliament** on one of its peregrinations in 1990, and massive amounts of EC funds were spent on refurbishing it in honour of the occasion. Excavations for the new conference centre revealed part of the original moat, plus the base of another tower; and part of the old city wall, and the steps that used to lead down to the Liffey, are now on view.

The **State Apartments** are now used by the president to entertain foreign dignitaries (so at times they will be closed to visitors), and there's a great deal of pomp and circumstance: the grandeur of the furnishings takes a bit of adjusting to. All the rooms have Donegal hand-tufted carpets that mirror the eighteenth-century stucco-work, for instance; superb examples of craftsmanship but really quite revolting. The simplicity of the **inner courtyard**, all warm old red brick and stone facing, with a little clock tower on one side, manages to be far more evocative.

Wood Quay

Directly down towards the Liffey from the Castle is **Wood Quay**, site of the Viking and Norman settlements which have yielded amazing quantities of archaeological finds (on show in the National Museum Annexe). The excavations were never completed and there's undoubtedly more to be discovered on the site, but despite a lot of argument the corporation of Dublin was able to go ahead and put up two massive Civic Offices, known to everyone as "The Bunkers", destroying what may have been the most important early Viking archaeological site in Europe.

Saint Patrick's Cathedral

Werburgh Street (left as you come out of the Castle, and then left again) is home of *Burdock's* legendary fish and chip shop as well as **St Werburgh's Church**. Reputedly, by origin, the oldest church in Dublin, its plain exterior – peeling paint in motley shades of grey – conceals a flamboyant interior which is well worth seeing. Unfortunately, as with a lot of Dublin's Church of Ireland churches, you'd better resign yourself to the fact that it nearly always seems to be closed (this one does open by arrangement, Mon–Fri 10am–4pm; ☎783710). John Field, the early nineteenth-century Irish composer and pianist who is credited with having invented the nocturne, later developed by Chopin, was baptised here.

This part of Dublin is remarkable for its strange combination of urban desolation, urban renewal – generous tax concessions are ensuring that there's plenty of new building – and the massive, over-restored grey bulks of not one, but two **cathedrals**. Both date originally from the twelfth century – Christchurch from 1172 and St Patrick's, designed to supersede it, from 1190. The reason why both have survived appears to be that one (Christchurch) stood inside the city walls, the other outside.

St Patrick's Cathedral (Mon–Fri 9am–6pm, Sat 9am–4pm, Sun 10–11am and 12.45–3pm) is now the national cathedral of the Church of Ireland (Christchurch is also C of I; the Catholic Pro-Cathedral off O'Connell Street is a subdued building dating from the days when it was expedient for Catholic churches not to advertise their presence too strongly). Once inside, it's a much more elegant place than the tank-like grey exterior leads you to expect.

Jonathan Swift

The presence of **Jonathan Swift** (1667–1745), who was dean of the cathedral from 1713 to 1745, is everywhere in St Patrick's. Immediately to the right of the entrance are memorials to both him and Esther Johnson, the "Stella" with whom he had a passionate though apparently Platonic relationship. Swift's epitaph, which he wrote himself and which appears in simple gold lettering on a plain black slab, translates:

> *Where fierce indignation can no longer*
> *Rend the heart*
> *Go, traveller, and imitate, if you can*
> *This earnest and dedicated*
> *Champion of liberty.*

Elsewhere in the church there's a tribute from the sharp-quilled English poet Alexander Pope. The two men were good friends and used to plan sharing a home in retirement (the correspondence is an interesting one, particularly for the gentle light it casts on the often vitriolic Pope, and well worth reading):

Let Ireland tell how Wit upheld her cause,
Her Trade supported and supplied her Laws
And leave on Swift this grateful verse engraved
"The rights a Court attack'd a Poet sav'd."

The **north pulpit** contains Swift's writing table, chair, portrait and death mask. Best known for his satires – *Gulliver's Travels*, *A Tale of a Tub* and the truly outrageous *A Modest Proposal*, in which he suggested that the poor in Ireland could solve their problems by selling their babies to the English for food – he was also highly active in contemporary Irish politics. He died at 78, the victim of a disease, unidentified at the time, whose symptoms – giddiness and deafness – terrified him with the possibility of madness. He left money to build a hospital for the insane – **Swift's Hospital**, close to Kilmainham Hospital – which, opening in 1757, was one of the first psychiatric institutions in the world. When Sir William Wilde, father of Oscar, exhumed and examined Swift's skull in 1853, he diagnosed the disease to have been nothing more dangerous than a disorder of the inner ear called Ménière's Syndrome.

Other memorials

At the west end of the church is an old **wooden door** with a roughly hewn aperture, formerly the chapter door of the south transept. Anecdote claims this to have brought a new phrase into the English language when, in 1492, the feuding Earls of Kildare and Ormonde met here. Ormonde's supporters were barricaded inside the cathedral; Kildare, eager to end the struggle, cut the hole in the door and put his arm through it, inviting Ormonde to shake hands. He did, peace was restored, and the phrase "chancing your arm" was born.

There are plenty of interesting tombs and memorials in the cathedral. One of the most elaborate, at the west end of the church, is a seventeenth-century **monument to the Boyle family**, teeming with painted figures of family members. Robert (who, as the only son, has pride of place in a niche of his own in the centre of the lowest tier) went on to become a scientist who proved the important relationship between the pressure, volume and temperature of a gas ($PV=RT$), known as Boyle's Law.

At the east end of the church a series of three **Elizabethan brasses** tell the plaintive stories of some of the early settlers in Ireland. There's a small, plain monument in the north transept to one Alexander McGeek, a servant of Swift, erected by the Dean in what was clearly an unusual gesture – all the other tablets are to people of property. An inscription to William Taylour interestingly reverses the usual sentiments:

As You are, so were Wee
And as Wee are, so shall You be.

Finally, near the entrance, it comes as a surprise, among all the relics of the Anglo-Irish, to find an inscription in Gaelic: to Douglas Hyde, founder of the Gaelic League, first president of Ireland, and son of a Church of Ireland clergyman.

Archbishop Marsh's Library

Just outside the main entrance is a compact Georgian building, faced in brick at the front but, tactfully, in the same unrelenting grey stone as the cathedral on the side that faces the church. This is Archbishop Marsh's Library (Mon & Wed–Fri

10am–12.45pm & 2–5pm, Sat 10.30am–12.45pm), the first public library in Ireland, built in 1701 and given to the city by the wonderfully named Archbishop Narcissus Marsh. Inside, the tiny reading cubicles and the dark carved bookcases carrying huge leather-bound tomes – some 25,000 of them in all, most dating from the sixteenth to the eighteenth century – can hardly have changed since the library was built. The chains that once protected the books from theft are long gone, but three cages for locking readers in with rare books survive, although modern readers sit in the main office under the watchful eye of the librarian. There's no admission charge, but there is a "voluntary" donation of £1.

Christchurch Cathedral and around

Christchurch (May–Sept Mon–Sat 9.30am–5pm; Oct–April Tues–Fri 9.30am–12.45pm & 2–5pm, Sat 9.30am–12.45pm), at the other end of Patrick Street, stands isolated by the traffic system. Like St Patrick's, Christchurch suffered at the hands of Victorian restorers, but it remains a resonant historic site. Dublin's first (wooden) cathedral was founded here by Sitric Silkenbeard, first Christian king of the Dublin Norsemen, in 1038; that church was demolished by the Norman Richard de Clare – Strongbow – who built the new, stone cathedral in 1172. As such the building is a monument to that first serious British incursion into Ireland. Strongbow himself is buried here (or part of him, most likely his bowels), underneath an effigy which quite possibly depicts an Earl of Drogheda. Vague though the connection is, this is one of the places where you find yourself asking how things would have gone had his ambition, and that of his Welsh knights, not led him to intervene in Irish affairs.

Close by, the augustly monumental **St Audoen's Church** was transformed into a slice of walk-in history for Dublin's millennium celebrations in 1988. Two separate shows, one dealing with Norse Dublin, the other with pre-Christian Ireland, have proved so popular that, for the time being at any rate, they continue. The **Viking Experience**, in the crypt, is the more spectacular of the two. At £2.45 it's not cheap, but unless there's a massive queue it's worth going to: there's a reconstruction of the original Viking village complete with smells, and real live Vikings in the shape of actors who you can annoy by asking awkward questions. Upstairs, for another entrance fee, the pre-Christian period is dealt with in an altogether tamer audio-visual show entitled **The Flame on the Hill**.

For all its air of authenticity, the pub opposite, **Mother Redcap's**, is a modern creation amid the open spaces left by the clearance of the inner-city slums. Opposite, however, the **Tailors' Guild Hall** (1706) is the city's last surviving guildhall, with an assembly room that includes an eighteenth-century musicians' gallery where Wolfe Tone and Napper Tandy spoke to the revolutionary "Back Lane Parliament" in the run-up to the 1798 uprising. Tailors' Hall is now the headquarters of *An Táisce* (pronounced "*On Tashka*"), one of Ireland's few building conservation organisations. Its restoration was carried out in conjunction with the Irish Georgian Society, and the two groups are currently lobbying the government to set up an umbrella organisation along the lines of the English and Scottish National Trusts to look after Ireland's architectural heritage. With the setting up of a National Heritage Committee in 1988, funded from the National Lottery, that aim came one step closer to fulfilment; there are even hopes that in the future there may be grants for the restoration of historic buildings.

The Guinness Brewery and The Liberties

Heading westwards along High Street you'll enter **The Liberties**, an area once outside the legal jurisdiction of the city, and settled by French Huguenot refugees. Not that this is anywhere apparent: The Liberties are now just a series of busy streets full of barrows and bargain- and betting-shops.

The whole area immediately to the west of Christchurch, interspersed with grim corporate housing and deserted factories, is dominated by the **Guinness brewery** – a setting out of Fritz Lang's *Metropolis*, with huge dark chimneys belching smoke, tiny figures hurrying along grimy balconies, and the smell of malt heavy on the air. For all the seediness of its surroundings, Guinness is one of Ireland's biggest commercial successes. Founded in 1759, the brewery covers 64 acres, and has the distinction of being the world's largest single beer-exporting company, exporting some 300 million pints a year. Although unfortunately you can't go round the brewery, the former Guinness Hop Store in Crane Street houses an exhibition centre (Mon–Fri 10am–3pm; admission £2, children 50p; ☎536700). You may feel ripped off at having to pay for what is essentially a souvenir shop, but you can at least taste what is arguably the best Guinness in Dublin (arguably, because the honours traditionally went to *Mulligan's* in Poolbeg Street, which still has its supporters). In addition, the upper floors of the airy, four-storey building are given over to exhibitions of contemporary art, and offer fine views over Dublin.

Kilmainham

Plenty of buses (including the #21A, #23, #78, #78B, #79 and #90, most of which leave from outside the Virgin megastore opposite O'Connell bridge) ply the road out to **Kilmainham** and its beautiful, precise Hospital, which now houses the Irish Museum of Modern Art. If you get off where Bow Lane joins James's Street (a sign to the right points to Kilmainham Hospital), you'll walk past Swift's Hospital, now known as St Patrick's.

Kilmainham Hospital and the Museum of Modern Art

Kilmainham Hospital was extensively and well restored between 1980 and 1984, and the result is that Ireland's first classical building – its date is 1680 – is a joy to look at, from the outside at least. The name doesn't imply a medical institution of any kind: it was built as a home for wounded army pensioners, like Chelsea Hospital in London or Les Invalides in Paris. The plan is simple: a colonnaded building around a central courtyard, built with cool restraint so that the sober stone arcading creates a lovely, unadorned rhythm.

The use of the Hospital to house the **Irish Museum of Modern Art** (Tues–Sun 11am–6pm; free; ☎718666), which opened in the summer of 1991, has caused a great deal of controversy, not least because the re-conversion has eaten up funds that might have been better used elsewhere. Almost half the inside has been depersonalised and painted white to provide gallery space of the correct, "modern" kind in a conversion which has led one commentator to quote the Flann O'Brien story about a man born at the age of 25 with a consciousness but no history: the clean white spaces, and the art hung in them, certainly make little reference to the Hospital's past.

More critically, the Museum has been seen as an effort on behalf of the Irish government – and, behind it, the figure of the prime minister, Charles Haughey, who some feel cuts an unlikely figure as a patron of the arts – to "buy into" the modernist tradition in art. In early exhibitions, Irish works of art have been hung alongside European examples to suggest a participation in mainstream modernism that many critics have felt is not warranted. However, the record of the director, Declan McGonagle, in commissioning and exhibiting radical and interesting art at the Orchard Gallery in Derry (see p.473), does make him someone to watch. There is no permanent exhibition in the Museum, which so far owns few works of its own, but instead a regularly changing collection of works mainly borrowed from European collections, hung alongside Irish ones. Whatever else, it is always stimulating.

Kilmainham Jail

Outside the Hospital, a small formal garden runs down to the Liffey, and a long, tree-lined avenue leads out to the front gates, beyond which looms the grim mass of **Kilmainham Jail** (June–Sept daily 11am–6pm; Oct–May Wed & Sun 2–6pm; adults £1.50, students/children 60p, heritage card; ☎535984). Built in 1792, the jail was completed just in time to hold a succession of nationalist agitators, from the United Irishmen of 1798, through Young Irelanders, Fenians and Land Leaguers (including Parnell and Davitt) in 1883, to the leading insurgents of the Easter Uprising of 1916; Pádraig Pearse and James Connolly were executed in the prison yard. Eamon de Valera, subsequently three times prime minister and later president, was the very last prisoner to be incarcerated here; he was released in July 1924.

The complex is a grim monument to the darker side of the independence struggle, with tiny cells, covered walkways, and stone exercise yards. Not all the prisoners were political: an indication of the severity of punishments is given by a document recording a sentence of seven years' transportation for stealing a piece of printed calico. The guided tours (included in admission price) give an emotionally coloured impression of the place, climaxing in the low lighting of the chapel, where, on May 4, 1916, Joseph Plunkett, one of the leaders of the Easter Uprising, was married by candlelight to Grace Gifford while twenty British soldiers stood to attention, bayonets fixed. They were married at 1.30am; he was executed at 3.30, and they were allowed precisely ten minutes in each others' company.

North of the Liffey

O'Connell Street and the shopping streets leading off it represent, for most Dubliners, the centre of the city. It's certainly a lively area – almost all the cinemas, plus the Gate and Abbey theatres, as well as the central bus station and a rash of fast-food restaurants are here – but it's hardly the most beautiful part of town. You wouldn't guess it now, but it was on the North Side that the Georgian development of Dublin began. Two battered squares, named after Parnell and Mountjoy, and dozens of mouldering, uncared-for tenements are the only surviving evidence.

The **North Side** has its points of interest culturally – the Custom House, the Four Courts (two of Georgian Dublin's most important monuments), and the ancient St Michan's Church with its weirdly preserved mummies – but to get to them you'll find yourself walking through areas of urban neglect far worse than anything south of the river. There's street life all right, but it's hardly picturesque: an old man in a battered overcoat bending to pick up scraps of firewood from the gutter, children with white, pinched faces and skin breaking out in sores. These are the things that can make you wonder what you're doing in Dublin as a visitor; and quite how the tourist coachloads can accommodate such contrasts.

O'Connell Street

O'Connell Street needs no introduction: at some time or another you're bound to find yourself here, changing buses, grabbing something to eat, or using the services of the **Irish Tourist Board** office at 14 Upper O'Connell Street.

Most things of historical interest have long since been submerged under the tide of neon and plate glass, but one major exception is the **General Post Office**, which stands at the corner of Henry Street and O'Connell Street. Built in 1816, its fame stems from the fact that a century later it became the rebel headquarters in the battle for Irish independence. It was from the Post Office steps that Pádraig Pearse first read the **proclamation of the Irish Republic**, on Easter Monday, 1916. The entire building, with the exception of the facade, was destroyed in the fighting; it was later restored, and reopened in 1929. From the street you can still see the scars left by bullets: inside (Mon–Sat 8am–8pm, Sun 10.30am–6.30pm) the reconstructed marbled halls are also worth a look.

O'Connell Street itself is reputedly one of Europe's widest, and there's a paved stretch down the middle with a series of **statues**. Until 1966 one of them, directly in front of the GPO, depicted Nelson on top of a column; it was blown up by IRA sympathisers in March 1966 (you can inspect the statue's head in the Civic Museum). Millennium year saw a notoriously expensive new addition to the gallery: an angular recumbent woman bathed by a fountain, quickly nicknamed "the floozie in the jacuzzi", or "the whore in the sewer" (this rhymes, which says something about the Dublin accent).

Beside the Post Office, Henry Street leads to **Moore Street Market**, where you'll find some of the disappearing street life that people are apt to get misty-eyed about. Truth is that the same activities continue to flourish in the less romantic settings of the Ilac shopping centre, round the corner, or in the new mall on St Stephen's Green; but that doesn't alter the fact that Moore Street's brightly coloured stalls and banter are a lot of fun.

The final statue at the top of O'Connell Street commemorates **Parnell**, quoting his famous words, "no man has a right to fix the boundary to the march of a nation". It's a fine irony, in fast-growing Dublin, that his statue is pointing towards the **Rotunda Maternity Hospital**, dated 1752, and the very first purpose-built maternity hospital in Europe. The barber-surgeon Dr Bartholomew Mosse funded the hospital by organising events including fancy dress balls, recitals and concerts – one of these was the first performance of Handel's *Messiah*, which took place on April 15, 1742. There's a superb chapel with a stucco ceiling by Bartholomew Cramillion. The Rotunda Room itself found use as a cinema until quite recently, and is now used for occasional exhibitions: part of the remainder of the building is still a maternity hospital; another section houses the Gate Theatre.

Parnell Square

Behind the Rotunda, the **Gate Theatre** occupies the Assembly Rooms built by Dr Mosse to finance his hospital, and behind that, bordering on Parnell Square, is all that remains of the pleasure gardens, another fund-raising venture. This little open space is now a **Garden of Remembrance** for all those who died in the struggle for Irish independence.

Parnell Square, originally called Rutland Square, was one of the first of Dublin's Georgian squares, and still has its plain, bright red-brick houses, broken by the grey stone mass of the **Hugh Lane Municipal Art Gallery** (Tues–Sat 9.30am–6.00pm, Sun 11am–5pm Sunday; free; buses passing include #10, #11, #12, #13, #14, #16 and #22). This was originally the town house of the Earl of Charlemont, built for him by the Scottish architect Sir William Chambers in 1762 and the focus of fashionable Dublin before the city centre moved south of the river. Chambers was also the architect of the delightful Casino, built to embellish the aesthetic Lord Charlemont's country house a few miles away at Marino (see p.77).

The house works well in its new role as an art gallery, with plenty of good lighting and an intimate scale that complements the pictures. The gallery was set up in 1908 with funds donated by Sir Hugh Lane (nephew of Lady Gregory of Abbey Theatre fame) who died when the *Lusitania* was torpedoed in 1915. He left his collection – centred round the French Impressionists – to "the nation", and with Ireland's independence the problem arose of which of the two nations he might have meant. In 1960 the two governments agreed to exchange halves of the collection every five years, but in 1982 the British government put in a claim for the lot; the matter still isn't settled. All the same, it makes an interesting collection, with work from the pre-Raphaelites onwards added to by more modern Irish painters such as Jack B. Yeats and Paul Henry. There are sometimes free recitals on Sunday lunchtimes (check *In Dublin* for details), and downstairs there's a good value café/restaurant.

Two doors down, at numbers 18 to 19, a pair of modest Georgian houses is the home of the new **Dublin Writers' Museum** (Mon–Sat 10am–5pm, Sun 2–6pm; £2, students £1, children 50p; ☎722077) a sometimes uneasy combination of tourist crowd-puller and serious literary venue that opened in autumn 1991. There's plenty of material to draw on: apart from its three Nobel laureates – George Bernard Shaw, W. B. Yeats and Samuel Beckett – Dublin nurtured a host of other writers including Joseph Sheridan le Fanu, Jonathan Swift, Sean O'Casey, Brendan Behan and, of course, James Joyce. The museum has a predictable range of memorabilia – including Brendan Behan's typewriter – and a first-floor gallery of first editions, but is also worth checking out for the planned programme of literary lectures and seminars. See *In Dublin* or call the museum for details of these. In the same complex is a bookshop, coffee shop and bar/restaurant (*Chapter One*), while next door is the Living Writers' Centre, with work rooms, a couple of apartments and a lecture room.

Mountjoy Square

Heading towards Mountjoy Square, the streets are full of rotting Georgian and Victorian tenements (lots of cheap dives here – see "Accommodation"). Appropriately enough given the presence of the new Writers' Museum, the area also has plenty of **literary associations**: Belvedere College in Gardiner Row is where James Joyce went to school; Sean O'Casey wrote all his plays for the Abbey Theatre – *The Shadow of a Gunman*, *Juno and the Paycock*, *The Plough and the Stars* and *The Silver Tassie* – at 422 North Circular Road; and Brendan Behan grew up at 14 Russell Street.

Mountjoy Square itself is Dublin's earliest Georgian square, now in an advanced state of decay. Although there are some signs of revitalisation, there's little left of the elegance described by Thomas Cromwell in his *Excursions through Ireland* in 1820: "Taste and opulence have united to embellish; the streets in the vicinity are all built on a regular plan; the houses are lofty and elegant; and neither hotels, shops, nor warehouses, obtruding upon the scene, the whole possesses an air of dignified retirement – the tranquillity of ease, affluence and leisure. The inhabitants of this parish are indeed almost exclusively of the upper ranks . . . ."

The King's Inns and Four Courts

Leaving Parnell Square at the northwest, you come to the **Black Church** in St Mary's Place, a sinister, brooding building with spiky finials, next to the excellent *Young Traveller* hostel (see "Accommodation"). Legend has it that St Mary's and other similar massive Protestant churches built during the 1820s were designed so that they could be turned into defensive positions should the Catholics attack. Dublin's – indeed, the nation's – **Wax Museum** (Mon–Sat 10am–5pm, Sun 1–5.30pm; £2.50, children £1.50) is nearby at the corner of Granby Row and Dorset Street, if you like that sort of thing.

As you walk down Dorset Street and into Bolton Street, everything speaks of urban deprivation: rubbish blowing in the gutters, broken glass, barred shop windows. **Henrietta Street**, dowdy as it's become, comes as a surprise: one of the first sites of really big houses in Dublin, it has two (nos. 9 and 10, at the far end) by Sir Edward Lovett Pearce. These adjoin the impressive **King's Inns**, designed by James Gandon, architect of the Four Courts and the Custom House, but sadly not open to the public.

The Four Courts

Making your way from the King's Inns to the Four Courts, you're assailed by more blighted urban landscapes. **Capel Street**, once one of Dublin's most fashionable addresses, shows few signs of it now – it's full of cut-price furniture stores and pawnbrokers. More streets full of rubbish and rotting vegetables from the early-morning fruit and vegetable market in Mary's Lane do nothing to prepare you for a solid example of Georgian architecture and urban planning: the **Four Courts** (Mon–Fri 9.30am–5pm), designed by James Gandon between 1786 and 1802 as the seat of the High Court of Justice of Ireland and a sort of chambers for barristers.

From the outside the Four Courts have a grim perfection. Inside, the four courts – Exchequer, Common Pleas, King's Bench and Chancery – radiate from a circular central hall. The building was completely gutted during the Civil War, but has been thoroughly restored.

Saint Michan's Church

Though it doesn't look much now – only the tower and a few other fragments are original – **St Michan's Church** (Mon–Fri 10am–12.45pm & 2–4.45pm, Sat

10am–12.45pm; £1), founded in 1095, is the oldest building on the North Side. Turn right up Church Street a block beyond the Four Courts, and you'll find the church a short walk along at the junction with St Mary's Lane. The reason it's on the tourist trail is that the crypt's combination of dry air and constant temperature, together with methane gas secreted by rotting vegetation beneath the church, keeps corpses in a state of unnatural, mummified preservation: some of the "best" are on display, with skin, fingernails and hair all clearly identifiable, sometimes after 300 years. St Michan's also boasts an early-eighteenth-century organ, still with its original gilding, which Handel played on and admired during a visit to Dublin.

Towards Phoenix Park

As you head west towards Phoenix Park, the street scene remains desolate. A large area is taken up by the decaying remains of Jameson's distillery, closed in 1972: enormous walls with weeds growing from the top, and gaping, broken windows. The **Irish Whiskey Corner** is an unexpected patch of neatness – a well-kept little courtyard leads to a whiskey museum converted from an old warehouse. There's an audiovisual show on the history and manufacture of Irish whiskey, working models of the distilling process and artefacts associated with it and, best of all, at the end of the tour you're invited to conduct a comparative tasting of five different kinds of Irish whiskey with Scotch and bourbon. Open by appointment only; ☎725566.

Smithfield Horse Sales and Collins Barracks

The cobbled expanse of **Smithfield** seems like an opening without a purpose unless you're there on the first Sunday of a month, when it's the scene of **horse sales**. There's nothing remotely glamorous about it, but the event does possess a certain fascination. Apparently an entirely male activity, it consists of a load of horse trailers carrying filthy ponies, and deals being struck through the ritual of spitting into the palm and clapping the hands together. Many of the buyers and sellers are travellers, once known as itinerants, and before that gypsies: people who speak their own secret language, *shelta*. In fact, *shelta* has nothing to do with Romany (the most common theory is that the travellers are of purely Irish origin, and took to the roads at the time of the Famine), but the travellers do share with gypsies an impressive knowledge of horses. After the sales you'll see ragged ponies being ridden away bareback towards the grim northern suburbs, where impromptu pony races are held.

West of Smithfield stand **Collins Barracks**, a series of imposing grey stone buildings formerly known as the Royal Barracks. Founded in 1704, their chief claim to fame is as the oldest continuously occupied purpose-built barracks in the world.

The Park

Having walked through the urban confusion of the North Side, the open spaces of **Phoenix Park**, Dublin's playground, come as a welcome relief. A series of pillars stand across the road and suddenly you're surrounded by grand clipped hedges and tended flowerbeds. The name is a corruption of the Gaelic *fionn uisge*, or clear water; the park originated as priory lands, seized after the Reformation in the seventeenth century and made into a royal deer park. The Viceroy's Lodge is here as well as a 205-foot obelisk erected in 1817 in tribute to the **Duke of Wellington**. Wellington was born in Dublin, but was less than proud of his roots – when reminded that he was Irish by birth, the Duke replied tersely, "Being born in a stable doesn't make one a horse".

The park was also the scene of two politically significant **murders** in the late spring of 1882, when two officials of the British parliament, Lord Frederick Cavendish, the chief secretary, and T.H. Burke, the under-secretary, were killed by an obscure organisation known as "The Invincibles". At first it seemed that the motivation for the crime – long standing bitterness over the landlord and tenant relationship in post-Famine Ireland – was directly connected with Parnell's ongoing agitation for reform on behalf of the Irish tenancy. It seemed to Parnell that he would have to withdraw from public life due to the implication – however ill-founded – that he was connected with these murders, but his obvious sincerity in denouncing them, and the effect that the event had on British policy regarding the tenancy issue, was in fact to make his position in Ireland stronger than ever.

Phoenix Park also contains Dublin's **zoo**, where the MGM lion was bred; the old duelling grounds, or **Fifteen Acres**, now the venue for gaelic football, cricket, soccer and, occasionally, polo; the **President's Residence**, *Aras an Uachtaráin*, formerly the British Vice-Regal Lodge; and a racecourse where there's a flea market every Sunday from noon.

Across the river

If you cross to the south bank of the Liffey on your way back into town, you can see the Four Courts as they're meant to be seen, across the water, and you could also stop off at the **Brazen Head** pub, at 20 Lower Bridge Street. Reputedly the oldest bar in the city, there's been an inn here since 1198; the current building dates from the seventeenth century. It has recently gone through a period of refurbishment, but since the walls have been painted a shade that seems to have come ready coated with forty years' worth of nicotine, you're none the wiser. A group of United Irishmen were arrested here during the 1798 rebellion.

The elegant, arching pedestrian bridge before O'Connell Bridge is known as the **Halfpenny Bridge**, from the toll which was charged until early this century. Close by, on the north side of the river, is *The Winding Stair* (40 Lower Ormond Quay), an excellent second-hand bookshop with plenty of good remaindered paperbacks, and a café where you can sit and stare peacefully through the grimy windows while the Liffey oozes past the Halfpenny Bridge.

The Custom House

It's easy enough to overlook the **Custom House**, lying in the shadow of the metal railway viaduct that runs parallel to O'Connell Bridge, east along the river. But, as the third of the great Georgian masterpieces built by James Gandon, it's well worth seeing. It is principally Gandon's public buildings that put Dublin ahead of other great, and better-preserved, Georgian cities such as Bath and Edinburgh. The Custom House was the first of them, completed in 1791 (the Four Courts, although started in 1786, were not completed until 1802, and the King's Inns were designed in 1795). It burned for five days after it was set alight by Republicans in 1921, but was thoroughly restored (and is currently being refurbished again) and now houses government offices.

The best **view** of the building is from the other side of Matt Talbot Bridge, from where you can admire the long, regular loggia, portico and dome, all reflected in the muddy waters of the Liffey. This elegance conceals a story of personal ambition and dirty tricks. The building was originally planned by John Beresford, chief commissioner of revenue, and his friend Luke Gardiner. A large stone in the bed of the Liffey was preventing certain craft from reaching the old customs point, further upstream, and this was ostensibly the argument for building a new one; but Beresford and Gardiner's prime reason for backing the scheme was that it served their own purposes to shift the commercial centre of the city east from Capel Street to the area where O'Connell Street now stands. Their plans were opposed through parliamentary petitions, personal complaints, even violence, and the hostile party were delighted to discover that the site for the new building was the muddy banks of the Liffey where, they thought, it would be impossible to build foundations. Gandon, however, confounded the scheme's critics by building the foundations on a layer of pine planks, which seem to have done the job.

Eating

Dublin may not be the gastronomic capital of the world, but there's plenty of choice for both lunchtime and evening eating. Cheapest **fast-food** outlets are centred around O'Connell Street, but are generally – with one or two exceptions such as *Beshoff Ocean Foods* – pretty unpleasant. At lunchtime, Dublin's many **pubs** generally offer the best value: you can usually get soup and sandwiches and often much more substantial, traditional meals. Central Dublin also has plenty of **cafés** and cheap restaurants catering for its office workers. In the evening there's no shortage of **restaurants** either, some cheap, some very expensive; cheaper, livelier places tend to be concentrated around the **Temple Bar** area, between Dame Street and the Liffey.

South Side

The area **around Grafton Street** is, as you'd expect, full of restaurants of all price ranges. At least once, you really must experience one of *Bewley's* coffee houses, the most central of which are located in Grafton Street, Westmoreland Street and South Great George's Street. All of them serve tea, coffee and everything from a full meal to a sticky bun, as well as deservedly famous potato soup, Monday to Saturday from 7.30am to 6pm. Try the waitress-service section on the second floor of the Grafton Street branch for elegance and potted palms at much the same prices. (South Great George's Street *Bewley's* is currently open until 2am Wednesday to Saturday.)

Cheap

Bad Ass Café (Crown Alley, Temple Bar; ☎712596). Still the hippest of Dublin's pizza joints. Sinead O'Connor was waitressing here when she cut her first disc with Ton Ton Macoute.

Cornucopia Wholefoods (21 Wicklow Street; ☎777583). Vegetarian shop and café, open only until 9pm. For anyone who has pigged out on one traditional Irish breakfast too many, Cornucopia offers a vegetarian alternative, including vegetarian sausages, between 8 and 11am.

Leo Burdock's (2 Werburgh Street; ☎540366). Dublin's legendary fish and chip shop, now modestly wondering whether its fish and chips are the best not only in Dublin, but maybe in the world. Best to book for dinner, or you may find yourself spending most of the evening in the *Barley Mow* pub next door waiting for a table. Mon, Wed & Fri 5–10.45pm, Thurs & Sat 5.30–10.45pm. Closed Tues and Sun.

Well Fed Café (Dublin Resource Centre, Crow Street, Temple Bar). Truly excellent old-fashioned radical vegetarian cooking, run by a workers' co-operative, seasoned with the almost forgotten smell (for Sixties/Seventies survivors) of patchouli oil. Good, small book-shop in the front of the restaurant has a fine selection of alternative/feminist/politically radi-cal books. 10am–6pm only.

Fat Freddy's Pizza Warehouse (Crow Street/Temple Lane; ☎796769). One of the best of many pizza parlours and cheap eating places in the Temple Bar area, grossly decorated but cheap and filling.

Pasta Fresca (Chatham Street; ☎792402). Ireland's first fresh pasta shop. Its restaurant consists of a few tables and chairs in the window, always well patronised at lunchtime, so aim to get there early. Closes at 7pm.

Captain America's (top end of Grafton Street, on the first floor on the left-hand side as you head towards St Stephen's Green; ☎715266; open till 1am daily). Dublin's original American-style burger restaurant, still going strong, with plenty of loud music (Chris de Burgh started out playing guitar here), and Tex-Mex and vegetarian dishes as well as regular burgers. There's an offshoot, *Captain America's West*, in the Dún Laoghaire shopping centre should you find yourself marooned there (☎804688).

Bananas (15 Upper Stephen Street). Good vegetarian dishes.

Fitzers (the National Gallery Restaurant, Merrion Square, daytime only; ☎686481). Good self-service restaurant where wine is very reasonable by Dublin standards.

Kilkenny Kitchen (Nassau Street, on the first floor of the *Kilkenny Design Centre*). Great place for lunch but always packed, so be prepared to queue.

The Buttery (Trinity College). Just inside the College gates on the left, handy for a good, cheap lunch, with a wide selection of salads.

Moderate

Rudyard's (15–16 Crown Alley; ☎710846). Busy restaurant and wine bar on three floors; excellent spinach pancakes at lunchtime, jazz on Saturday nights.

Coffee Bean/Capers (4 Nassau Street; ☎684626). *Coffee Bean* by day, *Capers* at night (when it also becomes more expensive), this is above the *Runner Bean*, a vegetable shop which is doing pioneering work selling exotica such as chillies, avocadoes and garlic in a country of cabbage, carrots and potatoes. Decor is Seventies ethnic, with wicker chairs and Chinese paper lampshades, which makes you expect dull but worthy wholefoods, but in fact the cook-ing is subtle and excellent, making good use of the vegetables downstairs, with a selection of vegetarian dishes as well as plenty of choice for serious carnivores. There's a good panorama over the wall into Trinity College.

Judge Roy Bean's (45 Nassau Street; ☎6797539). Tex-Mex style and food.

Wildebeest (7 Johnson's Court, a narrow lane off Grafton Street close to *Bewley's*; ☎712276). An elegant self-service restaurant – oil-cloth on the tables, plenty of newspapers to read – which does salads and hot dishes (vegetarian included) at lunch and dinner. Live music Wed–Sat.

Trocadero (Andrew Street; ☎775545,. 792385). Looks like an obnoxiously rich sort of trat-toria, but in fact is pleasant, friendly and has excellent food. It's one of Dublin's oldest Italian restaurants, and the walls are hung with plaudits in the form of signed photographs of visit-ing showbiz luminaries.

Elephant and Castle (18 Temple Bar; ☎6791399). Cross between a diner and a brasserie: busy and elegant place – would be equally at home in London, or New York – to pop in for anything from a drink to dinner. Unpretentious; ketchup bottles on the tables.

Gallagher's Boxty House (20 Temple Bar; ☎772762). A boxty is an Irish potato pancake cooked on a griddle, offered with a variety of meat and vegetable stuffings. Filling, if bland, food in a pleasant and friendly atmosphere.

Le Restaurant Casablanca (22 Temple Bar; ☎6799996). Excellent Moroccan food – couscous, tahini, grilled fresh sardines – though with a Dublin flavour: ask for your merguez with couscous, and you'll find them served with couscous and chips.

Little Lisbon (Temple Lane; ☎711274). Cooking from Portugal, Goa and the Cape Verde islands. Early evening "happy hour".

Tante Zoe's (1 Crow Street; ☎6794407). New Cajun restaurant with good food at decent prices. Very popular, so book.

The Cedar Tree (11 St Andrew's Street; ☎772121). Good Lebanese restaurant.

Expensive

Shay Beano (37 Stephen Street; ☎776384). Its reputation for good cheap French cuisine is not altogether deserved: the set-menu dinner is pricey, although reputedly extremely good. Rather chi-chi, full of smartly dressed couples, and not the sort of place where you're likely to feel comfortable either alone or wearing jeans.

Shelbourne Hotel (St Stephen's Green; ☎766471). Prime location and loads of cachet. You can have a drink in the lobby even if you're not staying, and the Aisling restaurant (which, like the lobby, faces out on to St Stephen's Green) is excellent, though decidedly not cheap. Still, it's good value by international standards, with classily presented, French-inspired cuisine. The menu includes vegetarian dishes.

The Unicorn (off Merrion Row in an unpromising little courtyard that leads off to the right a few paces down from St Stephen's Green; ☎762182). Plain, no-nonsense interior and an extensive Italian menu including pasta and pizzas as well as the standard meat-and-sauce dishes. With Doheny and Nesbitt's pub, across Baggot Street, it forms a focus for the more intellectual side of Dublin life, frequented by journalists, economists, campaigners and musicians.

La Fiesta (Camden Street, towards The Liberties; ☎753109). Depsite the Spanish name, serves North African and West Indian food.

King Sitric Fish Restaurant (East Pier, Howth; ☎335235). Situated at Howth Head (see below), the rocky knob of land that terminates Dublin Bay to the north. Howth is also a day-trip destination for Dubliners, with the bracing air of a seaside resort (get there on the #31 bus from the centre of town, or on the DART). It's also a working fishing port, hence the King Sitric's magnificent seafood. You could also take in the *Abbey Tavern*, a bare, stone-walled pub with turf fires and gas lighting that strains a bit to achieve its air of authenticity, but is worth visiting for traditional music sessions in the evenings.

North Side

O'Connell Street is full of fast-food chain restaurants – everything from *Pizzaland* and *Wimpy* to cheap Chinese and the ubiquitous kebab houses that seem to be the latest in fast food to hit Dublin. While you will never be short of somewhere to fill your stomach, places where you'll want to spend any time are thin on the ground. As ever, there are plenty of pubs which make a good alternative.

Cafe Kylemore (O'Connell Street at the junction with North Earl Street). A cross between *Bewley's* and a Parisian brasserie, all brass and bentwood chairs, this serves good, plain basics – chips with almost everything – and has a drinks licence.

Beshoff Ocean Foods (14 Westmoreland Street and 7 Upper O'Connell Street). Superior fish and chips, with bistro-type decor.

Midday's (self-service restaurant in the Peacock Theatre, Lower Abbey Street; 10am–5pm). A pioneer of vegetarian/wholefood cooking in Dublin.

Gresham Hotel (O'Connell Street). Dublin's second-best hotel serves drinks and excellent sandwiches in the elegant lobby.

Entertainment

What to do in the evenings is never much of a problem in Dublin, even if the answer is almost inevitably just to head for the nearest pub. However much some Dubliners moan about the provinciality of the city's cultural life, there's plenty to keep you amused – as long as you don't depend on nights out at the opera or classical concerts, both of which are, admittedly, in short supply.

Pubs and music

Pubs are an integral part of Dublin's social life, and an essential part of any visit. You certainly won't get much of a feel for Dublin unless you spend plenty of your time in the pub. Guidebooks are apt to write as if there's some great mystery about them, or as if they're somehow dangerous places where you shouldn't venture alone, and certainly not without a recommendation from this or that guide; neither is true, and the charm of most Dublin pubs derives from the fact that they're simple, no-nonsense places, the better ones unchanged for decades, where you can get a good pint of Guinness and the people are friendly. There are around 800 pubs in Dublin, so what follows doesn't try to be anything like a comprehensive, or even a representative, guide. Instead it's a small – and very personal – selection of Dublin drinking places, with some indication of where you're likely to find music and other entertainment.

The **music scene** is volatile, though, so if you're after something in particular – jazz, folk, traditional – the best place to check is yet again the listings magazine *In Dublin*. *Hot Press*, the national music paper, is also worth checking out. For traditional music, contact the traditional music society, *Comhaltas Ceoltóirí Éireann* (also known as *Cultúrlann*) at 32 Belgrave Square, Monkstown (☎800295). Their offices are, in any case, worth a visit almost any night for their programmes of traditional music and theatre.

Two general points of etiquette: pubs in Dublin tend to be fairly **male** preserves, but if you're a woman don't let that put you off – you're unlikely to be made to feel uncomfortable, even if you're alone. And many Dublin pubs have **snugs**, or small private rooms, which can be the cosiest places to drink if there's a group of you. There's nothing exclusive about these – just go in and stake your claim if you find one empty – and drinks cost the same as in the main bar.

Traditional bars

Neary's (1 Chatham Street; ☎777391). *Neary's* announces its presence with a pair of arms in flowing sleeves holding lighted glass orbs. Inside the place is no less exalted in tone: plenty of bevelled glass and shiny wood, plus Liberty print curtains to demonstrate a sense of style to suit the stars from the Gaiety Theatre, opposite, who like to frequent it after shows.

McDaid's (3 Harry Street; ☎6794395). A literary pub very nearby, this is where Brendan Behan used to drown his talent in Guinness – there's a photograph of him with a tiny typewriter wedged between two glasses of the black stuff, one full, one empty.

Davy Byrne's (21 Duke Street, off Grafton Street; ☎775217). Here, in *Ulysses*, Leopold Bloom stopped to eat a gorgonzola sandwich and quaff a glass of burgundy; and here, on Bloomsday (16 June) every year, numerous pilgrims stop to do exactly the same thing. Now decked out in tasteful shades of lemon and grey, *Davy Byrne's* no longer looks exactly Joycean.

The Bailey (2 Duke Street; ☎770600). Another stop on the *Ulysses* trail (in the book it appears under its old name and identity as *Burton's*, a hotel and billiard room), *The Bailey* has a distinguished facade decorated with eight horse's heads. A literary venue between the

Forties and the Sixties, *The Bailey* is now the meeting point for Dublin's Literary Pub Crawls (7.30pm Tuesday to Thursday during the summer; ☎540228 for details), as well as a gay meeting place.

Mulligan's (8 Poolbeg Street; ☎775582). Mulligan's traditionally served the best Guinness in Dublin; many people now acknowledge that honour to have passed to Guinness's own visitor centre, but Mulligan's still has its partisans, among them journalists from the nearby *Irish Press* offices.

Kehoe's (South Anne Street, off Grafton Street). Wonderful snugs if you want to curl up in comparative privacy to sip your pint.

Flannery's (44 Temple Bar). Gathering place of the Temple Bar crowd, young, friendly and unhurried.

Ryan's (Parkgate Street, across the river from Heuston Station). Another pub famous for its cosy, wood-lined snugs; considered the finest Victorian pub in Dublin.

Stag's Head (1 Dame Court, a tiny turning off Dame Street almost opposite the Central Bank; ☎6793701). Hard to find – a mosaic set in the pavement on Dame Street alerts you to the tiny alleyway it's located in – but worth it when you get there: inside it's all mahogany, stained glass and mirrors. Good pub lunches too, and friendly atmosphere.

Doheny and Nesbitt (5 Lower Baggot Street; ☎762945). Archetypal Dublin pub – the tiny, atmospheric, smoke-filled room looks as if it has hardly changed since the beginning of the century. Always packed, cosy snugs. Upstairs is a slightly less hectic lounge if you can't stand the pace. Much frequented by *Irish Times* hacks.

Toners Victorian Bar (139 Lower Baggot Street; ☎763090). Dark, cosy pub with a refreshingly plain interior. Snugs, with glazed partitions, for making and breaking confidences.

Music pubs

International Bar (23 Wicklow Street; ☎779250). Very spacious, if smoky; a Dublin institution. Good music pub, mostly rock bands. Comedy club upstairs on Wednesday nights.

Mother Redcap's Tavern (Back Lane, off High Street; ☎538306). Traditional and country music – Ireland's other folk tradition – in an old shoe factory in one of the oldest parts of Dublin. A pint of Guinness here, fried fish and a poke of chips from *Leo Burdock's* famous fish and chip shop around the corner (see "Restaurants"), and your Friday night's made.

O'Donoghue's (Merrion Row). The place where the Dubliners began their career; very popular and packed.

Bad Bob's Backstage Bar (East Essex Street; ☎775842). Still Dublin's central late night music venue; in Temple Bar. Three floors – live bands downstairs, quieter lounge in the middle, and a disco upstairs.

Corbett's (Werburgh Street, near The Liberties). From time to time new singing clubs are set up; one of the latest, *Songs of Struggle*, takes place here on the first Saturday of every month. It's devoted to songs about the struggle for justice and bars sexist and racist songs, thereby ruling out most of the folk repertoire.

The Brazen Head (20 Lower Bridge Street; ☎6795156). Claims to be the oldest bar in the city – there's been an inn here since 1198, although the present building dates from the seventeenth century. A recent refurbishment has apparently left the ancient strata of nicotine on the anaglypta totally untouched. Traditional music every night.

The Merchant (Lower Bridge Street, opposite the Brazen Head). Traditional music.

Slattery's (129 Capel Street; ☎727971). Dublin's best-known venue for traditional music, with set dancing and ballads as regular features.

Hughes's (Chancery Street, North Side). Traditional music.

Wexford Inn (Wexford Street). Traditional music.

An Béal Bocht (Charlemont Street). Traditional music.

Baggot Inn (143 Baggot Street; ☎761430). Rock venue handy for the Baggot Street pubs.

Dublin Underground (55 Dame Street). Rock pub. Worth checking out for new and established groups.

Theatre

As seems fitting for a city with Dublin's rich literary past, **theatre** flourishes. The traditional diet of Irish classics at the "establishment" theatres is now spiced by experimental or fringe programmes at newer, smaller venues, and by pub drama and comedy; tickets are cheap – averaging £7–8 – and drama is accessible, and popular. You'll find details of all theatre performances in the fortnightly listings magazine, *In Dublin*.

Abbey Theatre (Lower Abbey Street, just off O'Connell Street; ☎787222). The grim concrete building housing the famous Abbey Theatre gives little away about its illustrious past. Founded in 1904 by W. B. Yeats and Lady Gregory, the theatre had its golden era in the days when writers like Yeats, J.M. Synge, and later Sean O'Casey, were its house playwrights. It's still known for its productions of older Irish plays, but does encourage younger writers, while the new artistic director, Gary Hynes, has managed to inject a much-needed touch of fresh magic. In addition to the main auditorium, the building houses the smaller **Peacock Theatre**, which sometimes has more experimental shows.

Andrews Lane Theatre (Andrews Lane; ☎6795720). Theatre and studio just off Dame Street in what appears to be the middle of a car park, concentrating on new Irish writing. One of Dublin's new performance spaces, under the same management as the remarkable **New Eblana Theatre**, in the basement of Busáras, which tends to concentrate on slightly more "popular" billings.

Gate Theatre (Parnell Square, next to the Rotunda; ☎744045/746042). Another of Dublin's literary institutions; a bare, rectangular room, it stages more modern Irish plays and can be lively and atmospheric.

Gaiety Theatre (South King Street; ☎771717). Dublin's oldest theatre stages a mix of musical comedy, revues, occasional opera, and, every now and then, something really worth seeing.

Olympia Theatre (Dame Street; ☎778962/778147). Formerly *Dan Lowry's Music Hall*, and that's exactly how it looks: raffish, down-at-heel, with an air of faded, once tinselly glamour. It now puts on (no surprises) vaudeville, comedy, ballet and drama, sometimes packing in two completely different shows in one evening with a late-night music spot to round things off.

Project Arts Centre (East Sussex Street in the Temple Bar Area; ☎712321). This is where you're most likely to find experimental or politically sensitive work. There's also a gallery space which runs temporary exhibitions which are well worth checking out, and occasional late-night music sessions.

Cinema

Dublin doesn't have an art film house as such, but it does have a large number of cinemas – almost all of them on and around O'Connell Street – showing mainstream films, which may be worth checking out. The peculiarities of the film distribution system mean that new movies are often released earlier in Ireland than in Britain. Details of all of them are in *In Dublin*.

Nightlife

Dublin **nightlife** has traditionally been fairly thin on the ground, with the best entertainment to be found in the pubs. Over the past few years, however, there's been a sea-change, with many pubs offering comedy programmes or drama (see Pubs), and a lively music scene. **Leeson Street** is the place to head late at night, with a string of basement clubs busy after everything else has shut. Most have no entry fee but very expensive drinks – they're at their best Thursday to Sunday from around 1am till dawn.

A couple of central **music venues** worth checking out are given below – try also Bad Bob's Backstage Bar (see Pubs). **Nightclubs** as such remain mostly pretty dull, and often directed single-mindedly at the tourist or business trade.

Music

The Waterfront (Sir John Rogerson's Quay; ☎778466). Just along the Liffey from Windmill Lane and the famous U2 wall, the Waterfront is a music venue and restaurant run by promoter Pat Egan, filled with rock memorabilia (U2's gold disc, the Emmy Sinead O'Connor wouldn't accept).

The Olympia (74 Dame Street: ☎778962). When the evening performance ends in this tinselly ex-music hall on Friday and Saturday nights, the theatre closes down for half an hour; at 11.30 the doors open and the late night music spot, *Midnight at the Olympia*, begins. As a music venue it's a strange place – you sit in plush theatre seats, and dance in the aisles – but it's unbeatable for its line-up of both up-and-coming and established performers. Bar stays open until 2am.

Clubs and discos

Sides (Dame Lane). Well-designed space with wine and food bar, one of the larger dance floors, and a fair variety of music – soul, disco, hi-energy – and people; fashion types, students and gays. Sunday night is cabaret night.

Pink Elephant (South Frederick Street; ☎775876). Full bar coupled with a lively clientele of models, A&R men, hairdressers and execs. If you get through the door, then it can be a lot of fun. £5 entrance. Closed briefly in July.

Risk (off South Anne Street). Tiny, and fun crowd – but may change under new management.

Cathedral Club (top of Dame Street). Interesting space in old Synod Hall with large dance floor. Entertains get-rich-quick kids. Tuesday night is the *Green Linnet Club* with traditional music.

Hirschfeld (Fownes Street). Large gay club on three floors.

Night Train (Mount Street, below O'Dwyers pub). Live music and disco – friendly, young crowd.

Gay Life

Although Ireland's celebrated gays include Oscar Wilde, Somerville and Ross, Eva Gore-Booth and Brendan Behan, prejudice remains considerable. In 1988 the European Court of Human Rights decreed that Ireland's anti-gay laws contravened the European Convention on Human Rights, but nothing has been done about them as yet.

Nevertheless, Dublin has a lively gay scene. *Gay Switchboard L blin* is on ☎721055, 8–10pm Mon–Fri, 3–6pm Sat, 7–9pm Sun. Gay and mixed meeting places include *The Bailey* pub and *Bewley's* in Grafton Street; more specifically gay places include:

The Parliament (27 Parliament Street). Central Dublin's main meeting place for gays and/ lesbians, a relaxed pub on three floors.

The George/The Loft (South Great George's Street). Long-established, down-at-heel pub, predominantly gay in the evenings.

Hooray Henry's (Powerscourt Townhouse Centre, South William Street). Nightclub located in Georgian house turned shopping mall in central Dublin. Free admission, but with drinks prices to match the august surroundings.

The Grotto at SIDES (Dame Lane). This popular night club runs a gay night on Sundays. Free admission, reasonably priced drinks.

Listings

Airlines *Aer Lingus*, 20 Upper O'Connell Street and 42 Grafton Street (☎370011); *British Airways*, 60 Dawson Street (☎610666); *British Midland*, 54 Grafton Street (☎798733); *Capital*, Dublin Airport (☎774422); *Dan Air*, Dublin Airport (☎379900 ext 4040); *Ryanair*, 3 Dawson Street (☎774422).

Airport Six miles north of the city centre: take bus #41A or #41C from Eden Quay, 90p; the official airport bus picks up passengers from the main hotels and takes them to the airport for £2.50; ☎746301 for information.

Banks Banking hours are Mon–Sat 10am–12.30pm and 1.30–5pm. Branches throughout the city centre. Best exchange rates are given by banks; *Thomas Cook*, 118 Grafton Street, will also give a fair rate.

Bike hire *USIT* (58 Lower Gardiner Street; ☎725399/725931; Mon–Sat 9am–6pm) rent bikes for £3 per day, £18 per week, or will sell you a bike at the beginning of the summer for around £150 and guarantee to buy it back from you for around £90. They also do repairs. *Square Wheel Cycleworks* (Crow Street above *Well Fed Café*) is a workers' co-operative cyclists' information centre.

Buses The central bus station (Busáras; ☎366111) is in Store Street, behind the Custom House. Expressway and provincial buses all leave from here. Private buses run from the Quays.

Car hire *Dan Dooley Rent-a-Car*, 5 Lyon House, Cathal Brugha Street (☎720777); *Kenning Car Hire*, 42 Westland Row (☎772723); *Budget*, 29 Lower Abbey Street (☎787814/747816); plus all the usual desks at the airport.

Chemist *O'Connell's*, 55 Lower O'Connell Street (☎730427), is open till 10pm daily.

City tours *Dublin Buses* ☎734222, or ask at Busáras. *Dublin Buses* also run cheap tours outside Dublin, to places the regular services don't visit, so it's worth enquiring about these.

Counselling *Samaritans*, 112 Marlborough Street (☎727700); *Open Line Counselling Centre*, 3 Belvedere Place (☎787160); *Well Woman's Centre*, 73 Lower Leeson Street (☎610083); *Rape Crisis Centre*, 70 Lower Leeson Street (☎614564/614911).

Embassies UK, 31–33 Merrion Road (☎695211); US, 42 Elgin Road, Ballsbridge (☎688777); Australia, Fitzwilton House, Wilton Terrace (☎761517); Canada, 65 St Stephen's Green (☎781988); Denmark, 121 St Stephen's Green (☎756404); France, 36 Ailesbury Road (☎694777); Netherlands, 160 Merrion Row (☎693444); Norway, Hainault House, 69 St Stephen's Green (☎783133); Sweden, Sun Alliance House, Dawson Street (☎715822).

Ferry companies *B&I*, 16 Westmoreland Street (☎724711); *Sealink*, 15 Westmoreland Street (☎808844).

Gay Switchboard *Gay Switchboard Dublin* is on ☎721055 (Mon–Fri 8–10pm, Sat 3–6pm, Sun 7–9pm; *Tel-A-Friend*, 10 Fownes Street (☎710608; Sun–Fri 8am–10pm, Sat 3.30–6pm; Thurs women only). For gay health information try *Gay Health Action* (☎710895).

Hospital Jervis Street; ☎723355.

Launderettes Nothing very central. *Powder Launderette*, 42a South Richmond Street (☎782655); *Exel Launderette*, 12 Main Street, Donnybrook (☎697172); *Shirley's*, 141 Rathmines Road (☎962228).

Left luggage There are left luggage offices at Busáras (Mon–Sat 8am–8pm, Sun 10am–6pm), Heuston Station (Mon–Sat 7.15am–8.35pm, Sun 8am–3pm & 5–9pm) and Connolly Station (Mon–Sat 7.40am–9.30pm, Sun 9.15am–1pm & 5–9pm).

Legal advice Free Legal Advice Centre, administration office, 49 South William Street; ☎794239.

Lost property ☎721311.

Phones International pay phones are available in the General Post Office.

Police The main metropolitan *Gardai* station is in Harcourt Street, just off St Stephen's Green (☎732222). In an emergency dial ☎999.

Post Office General Post Office, O'Connell Street (☎728888). Mon–Sat 8am–8pm, Sun 10.30am–6.30pm.

Shopping in Dublin centres round Grafton Street and O'Connell Street. The O'Connell Street area represents the more ordinary, high-street end of the market, with cut-price shops and chain stores. *Clery's* august department store in Upper O'Connell Street and *Eason's* bookshop at 40–42 Lower O'Connell Street (beside the GPO) are two of the highlights. The smarter stores, and the tourist shops, are all south of the river. Pedestrianised Grafton Street contains Dublin's two swankiest department stores, *Switzer's* and the more old-fashioned and posher *Brown Thomas*. Just off Grafton Street, the 200-year-old Powerscourt Town House has been converted into a covered mall, with plenty of expensive clothes shops including the *Irish Fashion Design Centre*, with a changing range of stalls by young designers. Round the corner in Nassau Street is the excellent *Kilkenny Design Centre*, set up by the government but now privately run, stocking high-quality Irish design. Bookshops are concentrated in the same area: *Fred Hanna's* at 27 Nassau Street (good second-hand stock), *Waterstone's* around the corner in Kildare Street and *Hodges Figgis*, across the road. *Books Upstairs*, just outside the gates of Trinity College, is still Dublin's major radical bookshop, and has a good selection including feminist fiction, women's studies, poetry and cinema, and magazines and reviews. For camping equipment, try *The Great Outdoors* in Chatham Street, where there's a ten percent discount for students and youth hostellers. The Temple Bar area has more quirky stores: three enjoyable, mostly second-hand clothes shops in Upper Fownes Street are *The Real McCoy*, *Flip Flip* and *Los Desperados*.

Taxis There are taxi ranks throughout central Dublin. *National Radio Cabs* can be booked on ☎772222, 24 hours a day.

Tourist information Dublin's main tourist information office is at 14 Upper O'Connell Street (Mon–Fri 9am–5pm; ☎747733). Others are at the airport (☎376387) and Dún Laoghaire (☎806984). There's a Northern Ireland Tourist Information office in *Clery's* department store on O'Connell Street (☎786055).

Trains Heuston Station on the South Side (still sometimes known by its old name of Kingsbridge) serves the south and west; Connolly Station on the North Side (aka Amiens Street Station) serves the east coast and the north. Commuter trains call at Connolly, Tara Street and Pearse Street stations. ☎787777 for information.

Transport information Enquiries about provincial and Dublin buses, Expressway, DART and mainline rail are all handled at the information office located at 59 Upper O'Connell Street, opposite the main tourist information office (Mon–Fri 9am–5pm, Sat 9am–1pm; ☎787777).

Travel Agents *USIT*, 7 Anglesea Street (☎778117/778112) are experts in student/youth travel; *Thomas Cook*, 118 Grafton Street (☎771721) offers good general services; *CIE Tours*, 35 Lower Abbey Street (☎300777) is the biggest internal tour operator, if you want a coach trip around Ireland.

OUTSIDE DUBLIN

Even without going as far as the Wicklow Mountains, whose unlikely outlines you encounter every time you look to the south, there are a number of **trips beyond the centre** which are well worth making time for. The best of these are out along Dublin Bay, using the frequent DART services. These trains will take you southwards to **Sandycove** and the James Joyce Tower; to the pretty village of **Dalkey**, with its incongruously continental atmosphere; and to the magnificent views across **Dublin Bay** between Dalkey and Killiney. They will also take you up to the northern terminus, the rugged hill of **Howth** at the northern end of Dublin Bay; **Malahide**, further out, is accessible by both commuter train and bus.

South: Sandycove

Taking the DART south out of Dublin, you very quickly have the happy feeling that you're leaving the grime of the city far behind. Almost immediately, the track starts to run along the coast, past **Booterstown Marsh**, a designated bird sanctuary now threatened with a motorway development, and out to **DÚN LAOGHAIRE**, where the *Sealink* car ferries come in from Britain. At this distance, Dún Laoghaire manages to retain some of its flavour as a superior kind of Victorian resort, full of wide, tree-lined avenues, promenades and wedding-cake architecture. Its port is still the base for Irish lightships and the biggest Irish centre for yachting.

SANDYCOVE's main claim to fame – the Martello Tower in which James Joyce spent a week in 1904 with his friend Oliver St John Gogarty, whom he later transformed into Buck Mulligan in *Ulysses* – is for some reason not signposted from the station. But it's not hard to find. Turn right down the street into what appears to be the centre of this sleepy suburb, then left at the lights for the seafront. You'll see the tower, next to an extraordinary bit of 1930s modern seaside building, on your right.

The James Joyce Tower

The reason the **Martello Tower** has become a place of pilgrimage for Joyce fans is not so much the association with the writer's life – the 22-year-old writer spent barely a week here in August of 1904, a month before he left the country with Nora Barnacle – as the fact that it features so prominently in the opening chapter of *Ulysses*. Joyce's stay wasn't a particularly happy one: Gogarty's other guest was one Samuel Chenevix Trench who, on their sixth night, had a nightmare, grabbed a gun and let off some shots into the fireplace of the room they were all sleeping in. Gogarty then seized the gun and shot a row of saucepans that were hanging above Joyce's head, shouting, "Leave him to me!" Joyce left the following morning.

The tower (April–Oct Mon–Sat 10am–1pm & 2–5pm, Sun 2–6pm; erratic the rest of the year – phone ☎809265, the museum, or ☎808571, the Dún Laoghaire tourist office, to check; admission £1.20, students 90p, children 60p) was opened as a **museum** in 1962 by Sylvia Beech, who first published *Ulysses*. The exhibits inside amount to little more than a collection of memorabilia – the author's guitar, cigar case and cane are on display – which, with one or two exceptions, offer no great insights into his life. Perhaps most interesting are the letters, including a plaintive note to Nora Barnacle on September 10, 1904 accusing her of "treating me as if I were simply a casual comrade in lust". But it's the atmosphere of the place that really makes it worthwhile, particularly when you climb up the narrow staircase to the open top of the tower where stately, plump Buck Mulligan performs his ablutions at the beginning of *Ulysses*.

On the seaward side of the tower is the **Forty Foot Pool** (named, not for its size, but because the 40th Regiment of Foot used to be stationed in a battery above it), for many years a men-only swimming hole where nude bathing was the rule. Now that women are allowed – although you seldom see them – it's strictly "togs required – by order", as the notice says. The hardier swimmers use this rocky, natural swimming pool all year round. Sandycove is also good for canoeing, wind-surfing and water-skiing.

Dalkey and Killiney

Further south along the coast lies the little town of **DALKEY**. Immortalised, if that's the word, in Flann O'Brien's satirical *The Dalkey Archive*, Dalkey (pronounced "Dawkey") is nowadays a charming little seaside town, and nothing much besides. Its origins as a walled medieval settlement and important landing place for travellers from England are evident, though, especially in the massive Archibold's Castle which dominates the main street. There are narrow lanes with fine, bourgeois residences and, back in the main street, a really excellent new and second-hand bookshop, with plenty of recent review copies. John Dowland, the melancholy Elizabethan lutenist and composer, may have been born here, and George Bernard Shaw certainly lived at Torca Cottage on Dalkey Hill: he later claimed to be "a product of Dalkey's outlook". When the sun is shining, Dalkey has an almost Mediterranean holiday atmosphere, and it's thoroughly pleasant just to stroll about and drink it all in.

In the summer you can hire a boat to take you out to **Dalkey Island**, where you'll find a bird sanctuary, another in the series of Martello towers that were built to defend the coast from Napoleonic attack, and the ruins of the early Irish St Begnet's Church. A curious ritual involving the "King of Dalkey", complete with crown and sword, is still occasionally enacted here: originating in the eighteenth century, it started out as a student joke, but became increasingly political until it was stamped out by Lord Clare in 1797.

Dublin Bay, views and fishing

From Dalkey Hill a ridge leads to the public park laid out atop **KILLINEY HILL** (pronounced "Kill-eye-nee"), with terrific views of Dublin Bay and the Wicklow Mountains. The stretch south from Dalkey Head is as beautiful a piece of scenery as you'll come across anywhere. As good a way as any to see it is from the DART line (if you walk, you're restricted to the road until you round Sorrento Point, so you're probably better off taking the train to Killiney): as you come out of Dalkey hilltop tunnel you're overwhelmed by the sweep of the bay, the blue sea on one side and on the other the weird bulk of the Sugarloaf mountain.

The entire coastline from Dún Laoghaire to Bray is good for **fishing**. Off Dalkey Island the dominant catches are conger, tope, pollock, skate and coalfish; further out, on the Burford and Kish banks, turbot, brill, dab and plaice are common. Fishing from the rocks and piers at Dún Laoghaire is free, and you can hire boats at Bray, Bullock and Coliemore harbours.

North around the bay

The journey north on the DART is nothing like as spectacular as the southward trip: once the industrial city ends, it gives way to suburbia and it's only when you get as far as **Sutton** (a much sought-after address) that you even see the sea. For a couple of worthwhile stops closer in to the city, it's easier to take the bus.

Dollymount Strand

Immediately north of Dublin Harbour, **Dollymount Strand**, or Bull Island, is one of the seaside areas most readily accessible to Dubliners. Designated, like

Booterstown Marsh, a UNESCO Biosphere Reserve (though with the plans to build a motorway next to Booterstown, it's doubtful what protection that really affords), Dollymount Strand is a spit of low sand dunes linked to the shore by a turn-of-the-century wooden bridge. Apart from holidaying Dubliners, it's host to thousands of overwintering wildfowl and wading birds, and provides a stopping-off point for Arctic migrants. Birds are not the only interesting wildlife of Dollymount Strand: just a couple of miles from the centre of Dublin, there are foxes, shrews, badgers and rabbits, as well as a wide range of grass and plant species. You can find out more at the new **interpretative centre**, where the causeway road meets the island. Bus #30 will take you out here, up the Clontarf Road.

Howth

HOWTH (the name derives from the Danish *hoved*, or head, and is pronounced to rhyme with "both") lies at the northernmost point of both Dublin Bay and the DART line. Arriving in Howth, turn right out of the DART station for the castle, left for the village, abbey and cliff walks. You can also get here on the #31 bus, which passes not far from Marino on its way out.

Howth Head is a natural vantage point giving views right across Dublin Bay to the Wicklow Mountains and at times, so they claim, even as far as the distant Mountains of Mourne in the north and those of Wales across the Irish Sea. Not surprisingly, it has been a strategic military point for centuries and its history involves a long line of fearful incumbents on the lookout for raiders. The legendary copper-mining Parthalons and Firbolg were the first to come, later conquered by the Gaelic chieftain Criomthain, whose grave is reputedly marked by a cairn on the summit. The Gaels, in turn, were ousted by the Vikings in the eighth century, and they were overthrown by the technologically and strategically superior Normans, led by Sir Almeric Tristram. His descendants, bearing the surname St Lawrence, continue to live at Howth Castle today.

Howth itself is a popular day-trip destination for Dubliners, and it has the happy and bracing air of a seaside resort, even off-season. There's a **harbour** on the north side, close to the DART station, dating from the days when Howth, rather than Dún Laoghaire, was the main packet station for Dublin. At the jetty at the end of the West Pier you can see the footprint of King George IV, who landed here in 1821 instead of at Dún Laoghaire (which was expecting to rename itself Kingstown in honour of the event; he made up for it later by going home via Dún Laoghaire). It was here, in July 1914, that the Irish Volunteers succeeded in landing 900 rifles and 25,000 rounds of ammunition from Erskine Childers's yacht *Asgard*. The harbour, full of working boats, is nowadays sited alongside a marina crowded with less practical craft. You can fish from the harbour pier; and, if you're in Howth on a Thursday evening, it's worth staying to see the spectacle when the herring boats come in. (Michael Wright, on the quay, sells freshly caught fish from his shop all week.)

Opposite the harbour, the rock-encrusted island is **Ireland's Eye**, an uninhabited expanse of scrub grass and ferns sporting yet another Martello tower and the ruins of a sixth-century monastic church. It's also a bird sanctuary, and you can cross by boat to visit it in summer.

Much of the interior of Howth Head is built up, but a **footpath** runs all the way round the coast. There are impressive cliffs and amazing views – south past the mouth of the Liffey to the Wicklow Mountains and beyond, north to the flatlands of the Boyne. To get to the cliffs, either carry straight on along the shore road, or take the #31B bus up to the summit and cut down from there.

Howth village itself is a sleepy, suburban place full of steep streets and sudden views. Its one monument, on a quiet site overlooking Ireland's Eye, is the ruined **Howth Abbey**, the first church founded by Sigtrygg, Norse king of Dublin in 1042. In one of the later phases of a chequered history, it was used by smugglers for storing contraband. The abbey is kept locked, but you can get the keys from Mrs McBride at 20 Church Street, opposite: inside you'll see the fifteenth-century tomb of Christopher St Lawrence and his wife.

Just below the abbey is the **Abbey Tavern**; bare, stone-walled, with stark wood furniture, turf fires and gas lighting. The air of authenticity can seem overdone, but it's worth visiting, as long as you don't mind the tourist coach trip approach to Irish wit and music. There's a restaurant, specialising in fish (best to book; ☎390307), and music in the evenings from around 9pm, for which there's a £3 cover charge. The other good eating place, if you've money to burn, is the excellent *King Sitric's Tavern* (see "Restaurants", above). Again, it's worth booking. For a budget alternative, try the *Royal Howth* on Main Street (open only to 8.30pm).

To get to **Howth Castle**, back-track a few hundred yards along the road to Dublin and turn left. The castle itself isn't open to the public, but you pass it on the way to the *Deer Park Hotel* and there's a small transport museum (daily 2–6pm; ☎8475623 to check). It's an impressive building, even from the outside – a true, battlemented castle, partly ruined, partly inhabited – and one that architects from Francis Bindon to Edwin Lutyens have had a hand in restoring. The gardens are famous for their azaleas and rhododendrons in May and June.

Malahide

The easiest way to get to **MALAHIDE** from the centre of town is to take the suburban train service from Connolly Station (you can also take the #42 bus from Talbot Street; or the #47 bus from Marino Casino will take you there). Either way, **Malahide Castle** (April–Oct Mon–Fri 10am–5pm, Sat 11am–6pm, Sun 2–6pm; Nov–March Mon–Fri 10am–5pm, Sat & Sun 2–5pm; good recorded guided tour available; adults £2.15, students £1.75; ☎8452655) is well worth seeing. When the last Lord Talbot died in 1973, his family home was taken over by the state. Much of the grounds have since been given over to playing fields but, unpromising as these look, the castle itself is terrific.

Dating in parts from 1174, when a marauding Norman, Richard Talbot, seized the lands and made it his fortress, the castle has been added to haphazardly over the ensuing centuries to make it look just how you think a castle ought to: turrets, Gothic windows, battlements and all. As well as being satisfyingly picturesque, what's fascinating about Malahide Castle is that you can follow its progress from a simple defensive tower – the first room you see inside, with amazing black carved panelling, is within the original square tower – to the addition of embellishments such as battlemented walls and turrets and, later still, its transformation into a country house, all fortifications now strictly decorative, with a mock-Gothic entrance.

Inside, a remarkably successful attempt has been made to show the best Irish furniture and pictures in good period settings: much of what you see is on loan from the National Portrait Gallery of Ireland. In case you're in need of refreshment, there's also an excellent **tea room**. It's indicative of the complex history of the Anglo-Irish that the rich and powerful Anglo-Norman Talbot family didn't actually turn Protestant until the eighteenth century. The castle even passed out of the hands of the family for ten years during the Cromwellian wars; but they managed to get it back. In the dining room is a large picture of the Battle of the Boyne; it comes as some surprise that the Talbots fought, not for Prince William, but on the losing side. It's said that of the fourteen members of the family who sat down to breakfast in the dining room before setting out to fight, all were killed.

Malahide village, which must once have been little more than a crossroads at the gates of the castle, has long since outgrown its estate village status. It's a delight, one of those places where there's nothing much to write about, but which for some reason is really pleasant to be in: just a few grandish houses, some more modest colour-washed ones, the most spick-and-span railway station you've ever seen, and quiet streets sloping gently down to the sea.

Marino Casino

For a short trip closer into town, but not actually on the coast, it's well worth hopping on the #20A or #24 bus from Eden Quay to **MARINO**, just off the Malahide Road three miles north of the centre, to visit the eighteenth-century Casino, one of the most delightful pieces of Neoclassical lightheartedness you could hope to see anywhere. The bus will let you off next to some playing fields, from where the Casino, exuberantly decorated with urns and swags of carved drapery, is clearly visible to the left.

Needless to say, the **Casino** (mid-June–Sept daily 10am–6.30pm; £1, children/students 40p, heritage card; ☎331618) has nothing to do with gambling. Commissioned by Lord Charlemont (whose town house in Parnell Square is now the home of the Municipal Art Gallery), it was designed by Sir William Chambers, the leading Neoclassical architect of the day, to accompany a villa which would in turn house some of the priceless works of art he had brought home from his grand tour of Europe. Marino House – the building of which spared no expense, and is said to have crippled Lord Charlemont's estate – was demolished long ago, but the Casino, restored in 1984, survives in perfect condition, crowded with witty and unlikely architectural features: the urns, for example, conceal chimneys.

As you go back into town, try to sit upstairs on the left-hand side of the bus. As it turns from the Malahide Road into Fairview, you can see Marino Crescent, which was once nicknamed "Ffolliot's revenge" after a painter who built it out of spite to block the view from Marino House to the sea. Ffolliot's final twist of the knife in the flesh of the aesthetic Lord Charlemont was to make the backs of the houses, which faced Marino House, an unsightly jumble of chimneys, ill-placed windows and sheds.

travel details

Trains

From Dublin Connolly to Belfast (6 daily; 2hr 15min); from Heuston to Galway (4; 3hr); from Connolly to Sligo (3; 3hr 15min); from Heuston to Waterford (4; 2hr 30min); from Heuston to Cork (8; 3hr); from Heuston to Limerick Junction (11; 1hr 50min); from Connolly to Rosslare (3 daily; 2hr 50min).

Dublin Buses

From Dublin to Derry (2; 4hr 25min); Waterford (2; 3hr 30min); Donegal (3; 5hr); Galway (2; 3hr 45min); Cork (1; 6hr 20min).

Private buses

Scores of private companies connect Dublin with the rest of the country. Routes are too numerous to detail here – we've listed the most useful under the "travel details" section of the relevant chapters. Major companies include *Funtrek*, 32 Bachelors Walk, O'Connell Bridge, Dublin (☎730852).

CHAPTER TWO

WICKLOW AND KILDARE

To Mullingar

Royal Canal

River Boyne

Ballynadrumny

Innfield

Maynooth
Leixlip

Castletown
House

Celbridge

Edenderry

Bog of Allen

River Liffey

Prosperous

Rathcoole

DUBLIN

To Liverpool
& Holyhead

Dún Laoghaire

Grand Canal

K I L D A R E

Naas

Droichead Nua
(Newbridge)

Killbride

Bray

Powerscourt
Enniskerry

Greystones

Kildare

Russborough
House

Blessington

Sally
Gap

Wicklow Way

Monasterevin

The Curragh

Wicklow
Mountains

Lough
Tay

Great
Sugar Loaf

To
Portlaoise

Fontstown

Dunlavin

Lough
Dan

Roundwood

Ballitore

Donard

Glendalough

River Avoca

Laragh

Rathnew

Wicklow

Athy

Moone

W I C K L O W

Wicklow
Head

Baltinglass

Lugnaquillia
Mountain

Rathdrum

Castledermot

Brittas Bay

Meeting of
the Waters

Mizen Head

Carlow

Avoca

Johnstown

Tinahely

Rathgall
Stone Fort

Arklow

Shillelagh

0   5 miles

River Barrow

River Barrow

To Wexford

Kildare and Wicklow, both easily accessible from Dublin, provide a welcome respite from the capital's urban blight. As central counties of the Pale, each is heavily resonant with the presence of the Anglo-Irish, yet scenically they are in complete contrast to one another. **County Wicklow**

has some of the wildest, most spectacular mountain scenery in Ireland, as well as some impressive monuments – the early Celtic monastery of **Glendalough** and the Neoclassical splendours of the great houses of **Russborough** and **Powerscourt** (now ruined) above all. **County Kildare**'s charms are more understated: a gently undulating landscape of farming land punctuated only by the great horse-racing plain of the **Curragh**, where the National Stud and Japanese Gardens are well worth making time to see. Here, too, there are signs of the shifting patterns of settlement and land ownership – a pedimented building here, a Celtic high cross there – written into the landscape for you to read as you travel around.

Their proximity to Dublin makes **transport** very easy in both counties. The Dublin inner city railway network, or DART, will take you southwards as far as the dull seaside resort of Bray on the Wicklow coast; the main line continues to the much more enticing towns of Wicklow and Arklow. The main tourist locations inland in County Wicklow are well served by buses. In County Kildare the major N7 road and the railway line to Limerick offer ready access to most sites. The scenic beauties of Wicklow attract a lot of visitors, principally Dubliners, and the positive spin-off is that **accommodation** is no problem – there are plenty of youth hostels and cheap B&Bs. Kildare is less visited, and here you'll find yourself relying on the B&B trade.

COUNTY WICKLOW

Get on a bus in central Dublin and in half an hour or so you can be deep into **County Wicklow**, high in the mountains among gorse, heather, bracken and benty grass, breathing in clear air with no one in sight. It's great **walking** and **cycling** country – particularly challenging for mountain bikers, and with the **Wicklow Way** as an obvious focus for hiking – with plenty of golden sandy **beaches**, too (and some rather stuffy **resort towns** closer to Dublin, best avoided). On a short trip to Ireland, you could do a lot worse than simply combine Dublin with a few days in the wilds of Wicklow. It's also a place to get to grips with two of the dominant themes of Irish history, sometimes strangely superimposed: the **monastic tradition** in the shape of one of its most important and charismatic sites, Glendalough; and that of the **Anglo-Irish**, at the great demesnes of Russborough and Powerscourt.

Wherever you go, apart from a few obvious centres like Wicklow town and Arklow, you're struck by the **sparseness of population**. It's the same old story as everywhere else in Ireland, and Wicklow is far from being the most painful sufferer: first the famine, and then the gradual drift of the rural population to the towns. In 1841 the population of Wicklow was 126,431; the county suffered comparatively little from the Famine, which reduced it to 100,000, but steady seepage of population brought it to a low of 58,473 by 1961. Since then it has recovered to around 90,000, partly through the development of commuter towns, as first the railway, then the suburban DART service, have penetrated further into the county.

Heading out from Dublin you could follow the **coast**, but a far more attractive option is to head straight for the hills, where **Enniskerry** and **Powerscourt** make an obvious first stop.

The Wicklow Mountains

The **Wicklow Mountains**, so clearly viewed from Dublin, are really round-topped hills, ground down by the Ice Ages, with the occasional freakish shape like the Great Sugarloaf mountain, where a granite layer has arrested the weathering. Despite their relatively modest height (Lugnaquilla, the highest peak, only just tops 3000 feet), they're wild and uninhabited, with little traffic even at the main passes. Given this, and their proximity to Dublin, it's hardly surprising that the Wicklow Mountains were traditionally bandit territory, and that the last insurgents of the land agitation that spread all over Ireland following the French invasion of County Mayo in 1798 hid out here. The mountains were virtually inaccessible until after the 1798 uprisings, when the army built a road to enable them to patrol effectively. This you can still follow, from Rathfarnham in the Dublin suburbs to Aghavannagh, high in the mountains: the **Wicklow Way** partly follows the road, too.

Powerscourt House and Enniskerry

ENNISKERRY, the estate village of Powerscourt House, is famously picturesque, and there are people who travel to Ireland just to see it, and go no further. That's just about understandable, for it is indeed picture-book pretty, with a sloping triangular "square" and plenty of day-trippers from Dublin always in attendance to admire it. But what's more interesting is that its *raison d'être* is its relationship with the adjoining great house – it was here, in the heart of the Pale, that the Anglo-Irish were at their most confident and relaxed. It's a bold statement of a theme repeated all over Ireland: big houses with adjoining tied villages. In Powerscourt's case, the estate stands as a sort of metaphor for the passing of the power of the Ascendancy.

An estate without a heart, **Powerscourt** is the shell of a house designed in 1740 by the German architect Richard Cassels (later anglicised to Castle), and burnt out in 1974 on the eve of a big party to celebrate the completion of an extensive programme of renovation. Although the Irish Georgian Society has announced plans to restore it, the house remains a ruin, surrounded by magnificently showy gardens. Typical of the scale that Powerscourt is built on, the avenue leading up to the house is nearly a mile long – the estate itself covers some 14,000 acres.

The **gardens** (Easter to October, daily 10am–5.30pm; £2, students £1; waterfall open daily 10.30am–7pm, dusk in winter; £1) are essentially mid-Victorian in character, and, if you enjoy the municipal park-like formal school of gardening, well worth seeing. The Wicklow mountains to the south and east give shelter from the wind and rain, and there are some rare plants, and curiosities including a pets' cemetery and the obligatory Japanese garden. The Edwardian craze for Japanese gardening had a major impact on Ireland, perhaps because the mild climate was highly suited to growing the right kind of plants. It is also visible at Russborough, close by in County Wicklow, and in its most unbridled and eccentric form at the National Stud not far away in County Kildare (see pp.91–2).

The really spectacular aspect of the **landscaping** is the view across a massive 250-yard terrace to the unlikely cones of the Great and Little Sugarloaf Mountains; one of many instances in Ireland where landscape and landscaping are miraculously blended. At Powerscourt, the designer of the upper terraces was one Daniel Roberton, an all too human individual with a relaxed approach to his job. Roberton had himself wheeled about in a barrow, clutching a bottle of sherry; when this was exhausted his creative powers waned, and he finished work for the day. A four-mile walk (signposted) through the grounds will bring you to the **waterfall**, at 400 feet the highest in Ireland or Britain, and another place where the landscape seems almost too good to be true.

To get to Enniskerry and Powerscourt, take the #44 bus from the Quays in Dublin (every 25 min) or the #85 from Bray, every forty minutes.

Glencree

Enniskerry lies at the foot of **GLENCREE**, which leads up into the Wicklow mountains with good access to the Wicklow Way. There's a **youth hostel** at Knockree, halfway up the valley close to Powerscourt, but it's many degrees less prepossessing than the one right up at the head (both are *An Óige*, and it's wise to book in summer through the main office in Mountjoy Square in Dublin, ☎01/363111; local numbers are ☎01/864036, Knockree, and ☎01/864037, Glencree; £4.50, £3.00 under 18). Glencree youth hostel is a solid, pedimented stone building dating from the construction of the military road in 1798 (the barrack buildings opposite now house the *Glencree Reconciliation Centre*, which attempts to promote dialogue between young people of the north and south). Both hostels are open all year round.

Glencree was once famous for its **oak woods**, but the small one behind the hostel was actually planted in 1988, in sad commemoration of the fact that broadleaved woodlands now cover barely one percent of the country. Further down the valley a dense conifer plantation has been designated a place for walks, with the misleading name of Old Boley Wood.

Above the youth hostel, dark, sinister terrain ascends to one of the two main mountain passes, the **Sally Gap**. Close to the source of the Liffey, it has been heavily cut up by Dubliners seeking peat; a further depredation inflicted upon the landscape. The most spectacular route on from here is the military road down from the Sally Gap to Glendalough, which runs over rough country until it joins the Glenmacnass River – an extraordinary, extended waterfall. The other road takes you past Lough Tay and Lough Dan as it winds its way down to Sraghmore.

Dramatic, inaccessible **Lough Tay** – whose scree sides plunge straight into the water – is owned by Garech a'Brún, a member of the Guinness family who is also the man behind Claddagh Records. Although **Lough Dan** has gentler woodlands, visitors are made to feel unwelcome by numerous signs warning against trespassing on private land, and barring access to the lake. Even avoiding such areas, though, there's still plenty of good, boggy walking, and some spectacular views.

Roundwood

Coming down to Glendalough, you pass through **ROUNDWOOD** (one of the stops for the *St Kevin's* bus service, see below), which doesn't seem to have anything much to recommend it, although people reputedly go there for their holidays. A café here claims to be the highest café in Ireland and has a sign assuring it's been passed for food hygiene – both are no doubt true, but no claims are made as to the quality of the food. Roundwood's one enticement, apart from its setting, is its good independent **hostel**, *Little Flower* (June–Sept; £4; bicycle hire available; ☎01/818145). All the same, the best bet is probably to head on down to the crossroads at Laragh, where any of the three directions lead on to more impressively lonely scenery.

The Wicklow Way

Glencree is one of the better places to pick up the **Wicklow Way**, Ireland's first officially designated long-distance walk. Following a series of sheep tracks, forest firebreaks and bog roads, above 1600 feet for most of the way, it leads from Marlay Park in Dublin's suburbs up into the Dublin Mountains; skirts the end of Glencree; cuts across the bleak, boggy hillside below Djouce Mountain, and pushes on to Glendalough and Aghavannagh, ending up 82 miles later at CLONEGAL on the Wexford border. It's not particularly well organised – one of its chief attractions for many hikers – but the whole route can be walked comfortably in ten to twelve days.

If you want to do this, **Marlay Park** is accessible via the #47B or #48A bus from Dublin city centre. If you're short of time, the best part to walk is probably the section between Enniskerry and Glendalough, where the path reaches its highest point at White Hill (2073 feet), from which you can get a view of the mountains of North Wales on a fine day. For this section (three days), take the #44 bus from Dublin Quays to Enniskerry, and pick up *St Kevin's* bus service at Glendalough.

Low as they are, the Wicklow Mountains are notoriously treacherous, and even if you're planning on spending no more than a day **walking**, you should make sure you have the Ordnance Survey's Wicklow Way map, plus the tourist board's information sheet on the Wicklow Way (number 30). Bad weather can close in rapidly, making the going dangerous and frightening if you're far from a road or house. All the customary warnings about mountain walking apply; and if you don't have any great experience of map reading, you'd do best to follow the yellow way-marking arrows. Trail walking – and indeed the whole idea of walking for pleasure – is fairly new in Ireland; consequently, the paths are far less crowded than their counterparts in, say, Britain.

There are three *An Óige* **hostels** along the way, plus plenty of places to stay around Glendalough (see below), so accommodation shouldn't be a problem, although it may be wise to book ahead in high summer. By a stroke of great imagination, two of the hostels – Glencree (see above) and Aghavannagh – are housed in the great stone barracks complexes built to serve the military road built after 1798, so you can pick up the resonances of those grim times. The middle stop is at **Glenmalure**, itself a forbidding, shadowy valley (see below). The youth hostel here (open July–Aug & Sat nights throughout the year; book ahead through *An Óige*'s Dublin office, ☎01/363111; £4.50), with no phone, electricity or running water, stands at the head of the valley just above the point where the river rushes over a weir. With no other buildings in sight, it must be one of the best settings imaginable for somewhere to stay. At **Aghavannagh**, the hostel (open all year; ☎0402/36102, book through head office, ☎01/363111; £4.50) is in a massively grand and remote barracks building on a hill with views all round.

Glendalough

GLENDALOUGH – the valley of the two lakes – is one of the standard tours out of Dublin, and its popularity with coach parties may persuade you to give it a miss. Don't. Besides being one of the most important monastic sites in Ireland, it has an amazing, quite tangible quality of peace and spirituality. **Transport** to Glendalough from Dublin is easy – use the *St Kevin's Bus Service* (£4 one-way, £7 return; ☎01/818119), which leaves from the Royal College of Surgeons on St Stephen's Green at 11.30am every day (with a second service at 6pm Mon–Sat, 7pm Sun), and comes back at 4.15pm Mon–Sat, 5.30pm on Sundays. The bus passes through Bray, where you can pick up the railway if you're heading south.

Glendalough is amply equipped to receive its many sightseers, with acres of car parking and a huge, modern **visitors' centre** (mid-June to mid-Sept daily 10am–7pm; mid-May to mid-June and rest of Sept daily 10am–6pm; mid-March–mid-May & Oct daily 10am–5pm; Nov to mid-March Tues–Sun 10am–4.30pm; ☎0404/45325; £1, students 40p; heritage card). This is genuinely helpful, with an excellent exhibition and a video show that sets Glendalough in the context of the monastic ruins elsewhere in Ireland; worth seeing, particularly if you're not visiting any others. The admission charge includes the video show, exhibition and the guided tour of the site itself.

The monastery

The **monastery** at Glendalough was founded by Saint Kevin, a member of the royal house of Leinster, during the sixth century. As a centre of the Celtic church, it became famous throughout Europe for its learning, and despite being sacked by the Vikings in the ninth and tenth centuries and by the English in the fourteenth century, it was patiently restored each time, and monastic life continued tenaciously until the sixteenth century.

The **cathedral**, dating from the early ninth century, has an impressively ornamental east window, while **St Kevin's Cross** is a massive slab of granite, carved around 1150, in the Celtic form of a cross superimposed on a wheel. It may have been left unfinished, since the "halo" formed by the wheel has not been pierced. In the **round tower**, the doorway is ten feet above the ground. The traditional explanation, and the one that the guide will undoubtedly tell you, is that this design was adopted so that in times of trouble monks could pull up the ladder and turn the tower into an inaccessible treasury and refuge; however, more recent thinking suggests that the reason may be structural. The twelfth-century **Priest's House**, partially reconstructed 700 years later, got its name from being used as a burial place for local priests during the suppression of Catholicism. The carving above the door, so worn as to be indecipherable, possibly shows Saint Kevin between two ecclesiastical figures.

Glendalough's most famous building is **St Kevin's Church**, a solid, barrel-vaulted stone oratory, also known as St Kevin's Kitchen. Although it may well date from Saint Kevin's time, the round-tower belfry is an eleventh-century addition, and the structure has clearly been altered many times.

The lakes and surrounding attractions

All these buildings are clustered between the visitors' centre and the **lower lake**, and you'll be shown all of them unless it's raining hard, in which case the tour gets truncated. But the real delights of Glendalough lie beyond what you get to see on the tour. As you climb above the monastery complex, landscape and architecture combine in a particularly magical way, and you could spend days walking the footpaths that criss-cross the upper valley, drinking it all in. The scenery is at its most spectacular at the secretive **upper lake**, where wooded cliffs and a waterfall plunge vertically into the water. Also here is the Wicklow Mountains National Park **Information Point** (mid-June to mid-Sept daily 10am–6.30pm), where you can get details of some of the many local walks.

There are plenty more antiquities connected with the monastic life among the cliffs around the upper lake, many of them formerly pilgrim shrines. The site of Saint Kevin's original church, the **Temple-na-Skellig**, is on a platform approached by a flight of stone steps, accessible only by boat. **St Kevin's Bed** is a rocky ledge high up the cliff, where it's said the holy man used to sleep in an attempt to escape from the unwelcome advances of a young girl. Eventually she found his hiding place and, waking up one morning to find her beside him, he reacted with the misogyny characteristic of the early church fathers – and pushed her into the lake.

Practicalities

Accommodation is no problem. If you want to stay right in the middle of this amazing landscape, the *Luganure* bed and breakfast actually overlooks the Upper Lake. There are also plenty of B&Bs between Laragh and Roundwood, although the countryside here is decidedly less attractive. Otherwise, you've a choice between the *An Óige* **hostel**, right by the lower lake (£5.50; ☎0404/45342; book through head office ☎01/363111; full of school parties in the summer holidays) and the independent *Old Mill Hostel* (£5.50; ☎0404/45156; open all year) half a mile out of Laragh, over the bridge on the right, on the Rathdrum/Wexford road. A comfortable stone building complete with craft shop and pine kitchen, it makes a good base for exploring the area. The *Wicklow Heather Restaurant* in Laragh serves good **meals** with fresh ingredients including local trout for under £5 for a main course.

Finally, if you need guidance on how to exploit the **sporting opportunities** of the area, you could check out the rock-climbing, mountaineering, canoeing and kayaking courses offered by the *Tiglin Adventure Centre* (☎0404/40169).

Glenmalure and the Glen of Imail

Northwest of Glendalough, the main road takes you over the **Wicklow Gap**, whence there's a tolerably tough climb up to the top of Tonelagee (2677ft). South and west, the country rises, becoming wilder and more desolate, dominated by **Lugnaquilla**, the highest mountain in the Wicklow range. In this direction you can head southwest along the military road towards AGHAVANNAGH and stay in the *An Óige* hostel (see "The Wicklow Way"), or experienced walkers and map-readers have the option of trekking to the head of Glendalough, and down into the next glen.

Either way, you'll arrive in dark and lonely **GLENMALURE**, half of which is off limits as an army firing range. Perhaps appropriately, Glenmalure was the scene of a decisive victory by the Wicklow Irish under Fiach MacHugh O'Byrne over the English under Elizabeth I. One of the 1798 barracks, now ruined, stands at the point where the military road hits the valley. It's a symbol of decay that somehow sets the tone for the entire valley, with its enclosed, mysterious feeling and steep scree sides which scarcely afford a foothold to the heather. The road eventually peters out in a car park, but a track continues past a weir up to the **youth hostel** (see "The Wicklow Way"). Past the hostel, the trail forks right for Glendalough, and left, over the Table Mountain, for the Glen of Imail.

By comparison with Glenmalure, the **Glen of Imail** is almost inviting. Again, it's dominated by the impressive head of Lugnaquilla, and likewise, half of it is reserved as an army shooting range. Altogether, it's as wild and desolate as you could wish for, though more open and lighter than Glenmalure. There's an *An Óige* **youth hostel** at BALLINCLEA (£4.50; ☎045/54657, book through head office, ☎01/363111; open all year).

At **DERRYNAMUCK**, on the southeast side of the valley, stands a cottage where Michael O'Dwyer, one of the last insurgents of 1798, took refuge when trapped by the British, and escaped because Samuel McAllister drew the enemy's fire and died in his place. Now run as a **folk museum**, the cottage is unmarked on most maps, the exception being the Ordnance Survey Kildare-Wicklow sheet.

Russborough

The west of County Wicklow, away from the mountains, is less spectacular than the rest, and the main reason for coming here is to visit the third of Wicklow's great cultural landmarks, **Russborough House** (Easter–Oct Wed, Sat & Sun 2.30–6.30pm; last admission 5.30pm) and its impressive art collection. Getting to Russborough is no problem – BLESSINGTON, the pleasant coaching town it adjoins, is forty minutes from central Dublin on the Waterford **bus**, and has several places to stay should you wish to do so. There's an *An Óige* **youth hostel** in a tranquil location on the peninsula almost opposite Russborough (£4.50; open all year; ☎045/67266, book through the main office in Dublin, ☎01/363111).

Designed, like Powerscourt, by Richard Castle (with the assistance of Francis Bindon), Russborough is one of the jewels of the Pale. A classic Palladian structure whose central block is linked to two wings with curving arms, its design was subsequently repeated throughout Ireland, as a result of Castle's influence and its own suitability as a kind of glorified farmhouse.

In Russborough's case, it's very glorified indeed. The house was constructed for Joseph Leeson, son of a rich Dublin brewer and MP for Rathcormack in the days of the semi-independent Irish parliament: he was created **Lord Russborough** in 1756, and later an earl. Russborough epitomises the great flowering of Anglo-Irish confidence before the Act of Union deprived Ireland of its parliament, much of its trade and its high society (thereafter, the rich Anglo-Irish spent much of the year in London). No expense was spared. Not only were the fashionable architects of the day employed; the plasterers, the Francini brothers, were also of the best. The plaster ovals in the drawing room, for instance, were made to order to fit the four Joseph Vernet marine paintings that still occupy them, and the over-the-top plasterwork on the stairs has been described as representing the ravings of a lunatic, and an Irish lunatic at that.

The **lake** in front of Russborough provides the house with an idiomatically eighteenth-century prospect. The impression is a false one, however – it's actually a thoroughly twentieth-century reservoir, created by damming the Liffey, which provides Dublin with twenty million gallons of water a day.

The art collection

Impressive though it is, the chief reason why Russborough is so firmly on the tourist trail is its collection of **paintings**. The German entrepreneur Alfred Beit (1853–1906) was a co-founder with Cecil Rhodes of the De Beer Diamond Mining Company, and he poured the fortune he derived from that enterprise into amassing works of art. His nephew, Sir Alfred Beit, acquired Russborough in 1952, which explains why such an extraordinary collection of famous pictures is kept in this obscure corner of County Wicklow. Whatever you may feel about their irrelevance to the site, or the source of the wealth that made the acquisitions possible, there are some marvellous paintings by Goya, Murillo, Velazquez, Gainsborough, Rubens and Frans Hals, to name but a few.

Russborough has been burgled twice: in 1974, when Bridget Rose Dugdale stole sixteen paintings to raise money for the IRA (although her booty, worth £18 million, was recovered undamaged from a farmhouse in County Cork a week later); and in May 1986. The paintings taken in the second heist are still missing and the thieves remain unknown. Nowadays security is tight, and visitors are herded around the house in groups, with little chance to study the paintings – or anything else – in detail. You could take a second tour, but a better way to get a more leisurely look would be to visit Russborough during the **Festival of Irish Music in Great Irish Houses** in June; phone ☎045/65239 for information about this.

Along the coast

Unless you're heading south to County Wexford, in which case the train runs right down the coast to Wicklow town, the coastal route is probably not the best one out of Dublin – it's commuter land for a depressingly long way.

BRAY, the first conurbation along the coast, is connected to Dublin by the DART suburban railway, so it's very much a dormitory suburb. Originally a Victorian resort, developed when the railway was extended south of Dún Laoghaire in the 1850s, it provides a grotty welcome for the hordes of visitors from Dublin at the weekends. With a seafront full of dingy hotels, video arcades, B&Bs and fast-food shops, Bray has little charm: its chief claim to fame is that James Joyce lived here from 1889 to 1891. Perhaps the best thing to do here is to walk round **Bray Head**, a knob of rock pushing into the sea, where a massive cross erected to mark the holy year of 1950 serves as a reminder that you are now in Catholic Europe. There are a few secluded coves in the shadow of the Head where you can swim.

Though impressive enough in an oddly genteel sort of way, this is hardly what most people come to Ireland to see, and even Wicklow town, a few miles further on down the coast, is more dramatic and rewarding. Like most places, Bray improves if you stick with it (the **tourist office** in the town hall, open June–Aug, ☎01/2867128, may help persuade you of its attractions), but not much. On the whole it's better to push on down the coast – scrubby and unremarkable for the most part – through Greystones and on to Wicklow, the county town.

Wicklow

There's nothing much to **WICKLOW**, and no great reason to come, but it is the first place that wholly escapes the influence of Dublin as you go down the coast and, should you find yourself with time on your hands, it's an oddly pleasant, ramshackle town with plenty of entertainment, good, cheap places to eat, and walking and swimming too. It has none of the presence you might expect of a county town, and comes across as a happily disorganised kind of place, full of people chatting on pavements, cars cheerfully park d on double yellow lines and solidly built little houses in bright marine pastels.

B&Bs are in reasonable supply – try, for example, Mrs Crennan's *Seacrest House*, Ashtown Lane (☎0404/67772; £14), Mrs Gorman's *Thomond House*, St Patrick's Road Upper (☎0404/67940; £13.50), or for a bit more comfort in the centre of town the *Bayview Hotel* in the Mall (☎0404/67383; £17.50) – and there's **camping** on the beach at Silver Strand, a little over two miles south of town (☎0404/67615). The nearest **hostel** is the *An Óige* one at Tiglin, six miles away near Ashford (£4.50; ☎0404/40259, book through head office, ☎01/363111; open all year). For **food and drink** there are plenty of pubs – try *The Boathouse* on Main Street for music – and, unusually, there's also a cheap pizza/steak restaurant, the *Pizza del Forno*, also on Main Street, which stays open until midnight, and two Chinese restaurants. You can rent **bikes** from *Harris's* on Main Street (☎0404/67247; £4 per day, £20 per week). More information from the **tourist office** on Fitzwilliam Street (☎0404/69117; open year-round).

Just outside town on the seaward side, a knoll encrusted with some knobbly piles of stone constitutes all that's left of **Black Castle**, one of the fortifications built by the Fitzgeralds in return for lands granted them by Strongbow after the Anglo-Norman invasion of 1169. **Wicklow Head**, unlike Bray, really is spectacular, and you can walk all the way round (there are two tiny swimming beaches, sunny in the mornings) accompanied by exhilarating views of the open sea and, northwards, the weird silhouettes of the Great and Little Sugarloaf Mountains.

Moving on: Brittas Bay and Mount Usher Gardens

Heading south **towards Arklow** there's a string of white sand **beaches**. The one at **Brittas Bay**, just north of Mizen Head, is particularly good – don't be put off by the caravan site; and in summer, you can buy great seafood there, particularly crab. To get to Arklow you can either take the train down the coast, or jump on the Dublin to Wexford bus, which will take you on a scenic detour via the heavily wooded Vale of Avoca (see below). The journey takes just under an hour, and buses leave Wicklow at 10.30am and 7pm.

Horticultural enthusiasts should also know about **Mount Usher Gardens** (mid-March to Oct Mon–Sat 10.30am–6pm, Sun 11am–6pm; £2.00, students £1.50; ☎0404/40116), a few miles inland near Ashford, where rare trees, shrubs and flowers grow in profusion in a narrow strip next to the road. For others, the gardens' main attraction may be the miniature suspension bridges where you can see engineering principles at work as they sway and bounce under your weight. Close by, up a side road, *Hunter's Hotel* at Rathnew (☎0404/40106; B&B from £30) is a good, old-fashioned hostelry where Parnell used to stay. It's well worth a splurge if you've money to burn, or, if you haven't, a drink in the bar and a stroll in the gardens that slope down to the river Vartry.

Arklow

ARKLOW has all the vitality you might have expected to find in Wicklow. Built on a site sloping gently towards the sea at the mouth of the Avoca river, it has a long and prosperous history, based on fishing, shipbuilding and the export of copper ore, pyrites and even gold, mined further up the valley. Evidence of continued riches in relatively recent times can be seen in the elegant Art Deco cinema at the top of the main street.

Arklow is no longer a major port, but shipbuilding continues to be a dominant factor – *Gypsy Moth IV*, Sir Francis Chichester's prize-winning transatlantic yacht, was built at John Tyrrell's yard here. So, for a grip on the past, it's worth stopping off at the **Maritime Museum** (top of the main street and turn left). A happily haphazard collection of local finds, it claims a history for Arklow going back to Ptolemy's celebrated second-century map. It also emerges that Arklow was a major centre for arms-smuggling during the upheavals of 1798. The museum houses such curiosities as a whale's tooth and eardrum, and a model ship made with 10,700 matchsticks.

Accommodation should be easy enough to find, with plenty of B&Bs – try Mrs Crotty's *Vale View*, Coolgreany Road (☎0402/32622; £12.50) or Mrs Hayes' *Tara*, Gorey Road (☎0402/39333; £13) – and hotels, such as *Hoyne's* on Main Street (☎0402/32167; £15). There are lots of **pubs** too – an ID system operates at all of them so be prepared for trouble if you look under 18 – most of which seem to have some kind of entertainment on offer, albeit slightly bizarre. Afternoon dances, demure discos and pub quizzes all seem unnaturally popular here.

Avondale and the Vale of Avoca

Heading back up towards Glendalough via Woodenbridge – the bus from Wexford to Dublin does the journey twice a day, leaving Arklow at 8am and 1pm, and continuing through Wicklow – you pass through the **Vale of Avoca**, one of those places designated "scenic" which are a sure draw for coach parties. It is beautiful, to be sure, once you leave the fertiliser plant behind: thickly wooded slopes on either side of the river, culminating in the **Meeting of the Waters**, the confluence of the Avonmore and Avonbeg rivers.

Apart from the Meeting of the Waters, the main attraction is the handweaving at **AVOCA**, a pleasantly unassuming village on the river. The weavers are housed in a group of whitewashed buildings with steep grey roofs, where the fly-shuttle looms that caused mass unemployment when they were introduced in 1723 are presented as picturesquely traditional. You might not like Avoca's products – cloaks, kilts and deerstalker hats in bright, heathery pinks and purples, with plenty of models for the fuller figure – but there's a good, cheap lunch room selling sandwiches, soup and cakes. Numerous small B&Bs offer **accommodation** should you want to stay.

A few miles upriver towards Rathdrum is the **Avondale Forest Park**, where you can see Parnell's house at **AVONDALE**. The effects of the Famine in Wicklow – though less severe than in other parts of the country – led Charles Stewart Parnell to start his campaign for land reform. Twelve years after his death in 1891, the first Wyndham Land Act enabled tenant farmers to use government grants to buy the land they had leased, and thus marked the beginning of the end of the long heyday of the Anglo-Irish.

COUNTY KILDARE

County Kildare, in the heart of the Pale, forms part of the hinterland of Dublin. Although it lacks the spectacle of Wicklow to the capital's south, or the extraordinary range of ancient monuments of the lush Boyne valley to the north, it has a quiet charm of its own. The **landscape** is a calm one of rolling farmland for the most part, with open grasslands and rough pasturage, just touching the dreary stretches of the monotonous Bog of Allen in the northwest. This is ancient country, marked by a string of **Celtic crosses** at Moone, Old Kilcullen and Castledermot; but you're also constantly made aware that you're in Pale country – with big stone estate walls bordering many of the fields and Georgian proportions in the buildings noticeable features of the landscape, as well as more obvious attractions such as the magnificent **Castletown House** with its model village at Celbridge, the **Grand Canal**, which traverses the county and has a walkable towpath, or the pin-neat **National Stud** at Kildare and its extraordinarily extravagant Japanese Garden.

Because of its proximity to Dublin, there's no problem about transport in County Kildare. The main **buses** to Limerick ply up and down the N7 trunk road, with the **rail** line running close beside it for most of the way. **Accommodation** is less easy – you're reliant on B&Bs, many of them the more expensive kind, catering for business travellers rather than individual tourists.

Out from Dublin

All you see of Kildare if you're headed for the far west, as most people are, is the view from the N7, the main Dublin–Limerick road, now motorway as far as **NAAS** (pronounced *Nace*). It's an unpromising introduction to the county: a motorway sign advertises Naas as "a nice place to shop", and there's probably not a great deal more to be said. *Nás na Rí* (Naas of the Kings), once the centre of the extensive kingdom of the Uí Dunlainge and their successors, the Uí Faelain, now seems little more than a battered parade of shops. Its one great attraction is **Punchestown Racecourse**, whose main meeting is the three-day steeplechasing festival in late April, when the racecourse itself is greatly celebrated for its flowering gorse.

NEWBRIDGE, a nineteenth-century town which grew up around the British barracks there (now re-Gaelicised as Droichead Nua) is similarly unmemorable, except for its traffic jams. But after Newbridge the road heads over the grassy, unfenced stretches of the Curragh, and you're into racing country proper.

Kildare and the Curragh

KILDARE town is delightful: a solid, respectable little place around a sloping triangular square, with none of that feeling of depopulation that becomes so familiar in other parts of Ireland. The town is dominated by the massive, squat Church of Ireland **cathedral of St Brigid**, who founded a religious house here in 490. The present structure dates originally from the thirteenth century, though the north transept and choir were burned to the ground in the Confederate War of 1641, and the Victorian reconstruction in 1875 is pseudo-medieval. Its round tower, probably twelfth-century, has a particularly elaborate doorway twelve feet up, and it's hoped that the bizarre nineteenth-century battlements that have been removed can be replaced with something more in sympathy with the original style.

Accommodation in Kildare is limited to B&Bs, which are themselves a bit thin on the ground. Try Mrs O'Connell's *Freemont*, Tully Road (☎045/21604; £12); the Brontes at *Emdale*, Newtown Cross (☎045/22060; £12); or contact the **tourist office** (summer only) which operates out of a caravan located in the car park on the Dublin side of town. There's the usual range of **pubs** plus, in the old cinema, a chi-chi steak bar that wouldn't be out of place in the metropolis, named after Silken Thomas, a member of the ruling Fitzgerald family, whom the growing powers of the Tudor monarchy provoked into rebellion in 1536. The uprising was unsuccessful, and a bloody massacre followed at Maynooth; later known, ironically, as "the pardon of Maynooth".

The real reason for spending time in Kildare, however, is **racing. The Curragh** is the centre of the Irish racing world, with two racecourses – the Curragh itself, and Punchestown, three miles southeast of Naas – plus dozens of studs. In early morning you can see strings of slim racehorses exercising on the 6000 acres of grassland. Breeding and training them is one of Ireland's major money-spinners, and much of it is centred on the Curragh. For an idea of the scale of the operation, Goff's Kildare Paddocks at KILL, which sells over half of all Irish-bred horses, has an annual turnover of around £IR20 million.

The National Stud

The best place to see the perfectionism that attends the breeding and training of these valuable pieces of horseflesh is the **National Stud** (Easter–Oct Mon–Sat 10.30am–12.30pm & 2–5pm, Sun 2–5.30pm), just outside Kildare. You can easily walk out from the town, though the entrance is not the obvious one through the main gates that you pass on the road from Dublin – instead follow the signs from the centre for the Stud and the Japanese gardens. You can pay to see just the Stud, or buy a joint ticket including the Japanese gardens. This is well worth it even if you're not interested in horticulture: far more than a collection of rare plants, it's also an extraordinary legacy of Anglo-Irish eccentricity.

The National Stud itself consists of neat white buildings set in green lawns as close-cropped and well-groomed as a Derby-winner's coat: a spick-and-span monument to the greater glory and perfectability of horses. Established in 1900 by Colonel William Hall Walker, who believed that horoscopes affected horses' form, the stud enjoyed an extraordinary record of success, and in 1915 was bequeathed to the British Crown, which rewarded Walker by creating him Lord Wavertree. When transferred to the Irish state in 1943, it became the National Stud.

Colonel Hall Walker's belief in the stars is reflected in the **stallion boxes**, built in the 1960s according to his astrological principles, with lantern roofs allowing moon and stars to exert their influence on the occupants. There's a brass plaque on each door giving the stallion's name and details of his racing career. The National Stud's **museum** is an enjoyably chaotic account of the history of horses and horse-racing which contains, among other bizarre exhibits, the skeleton of the 1960s champion racehorse, Arkle. Outside is a calming **Zen garden of meditation**.

The Japanese gardens

The bizarre **Japanese gardens** were laid out on drained bog (between 1906 and 1910) by Colonel Hall Walker and two Japanese gardeners. Part of the Edwardian craze for all things Japanese, they're planned to represent the "life of man". Man, emphatically, it has to be said, rather than woman. In a weird kind of enumerated metaphysical joyride, you're led from birth to death via the Tunnel of Ignorance (no. 3) and the Parting of Ways (no. 6), where you're invited to choose between a life of philandering bachelorhood or marriage. In fact the choice is illusory: choosing marriage, you step across stepping stones to the Island of Joy and Wonder (no. 7) and meet your wife at the engagement bridge (no. 8; easily confused with the Red Bridge of Life, no. 17) and so on. Finally you pass through the Gateway to Eternity (no. 20), and it's time to go.

A day at the races

You don't have to know anything about horses to enjoy **a day at the races**. Irish race-going is quite unlike its English counterpart: there's none of the snobbery attached to who's who or who's allowed in the enclosure, and it's not as expensive. It's also different in that there's just as much excitement attached to steeplechasing as flat racing – steeplechasing, in fact, despite its smaller prize money, is often regarded as the better sport.

The major Irish **classic meets** are all held at the Curragh: the Airlie/Coolmore 1000 Guineas and Goffs Irish 1000 Guineas in May; the Budweiser Irish Derby in June; the Kildangan Irish Oaks in July, and the Irish St Leger in September. Punchestown is also famous for a three-day jump race meeting in late April. **Details of race meetings** can be found in all the daily papers or in the specialist press: *Irish Field* (published Saturday morning) and the *Racing Post* (daily). *Bord Fáilte* publishes an annual information sheet with the dates of the current year's meetings; you should also be able to get schedules from local tourist offices.

If you are interested in **getting to the Curragh**, there are special bus and train services scheduled to fit in with all major meetings; ring Busáras in Dublin (☎01/366111) for details.

Maynooth and Castletown House

Both Maynooth – due west of Dublin on the N6 – and Celbridge (for Castletown House) are firmly on the one-day tourist trip trail from Dublin, so you're unlikely to be on your own here. There really isn't all that much to detain you in **MAYNOOTH** (pronounced *Ma-nooth*, with the stress on the second syllable), pretty though it is. Its main claim to fame is its seminary, **St Patrick's College**, which in addition to training priests now houses two universities. For fans of Victoriana, the square is by Pugin in Gothic revival style. The ruins beside the entrance to the college are those of the thirteenth-century **Maynooth Castle**, one of the two main strongholds of the Anglo-Norman Fitzgerald family, who ruled Kildare and, effectively, most of Ireland, from the thirteenth century until the coming of the Tudor monarchs (their other castle is at Kilkea, in the south of the county). Maynooth's formal town planning is made sense of by Carton House, a Georgian gem by Richard Castle which lies at the other end of the main street;

however, although its grand avenue looks promising, you can't visit the house at present (although its new owner – the house was sold in 1991 – plans a luxury hotel and golf course, so this may change).

Castletown House

Few places give a better impression of the immense scale on which the Anglo-Irish imagination was able to work than **Castletown House**, designed in 1722 for the Speaker of the Irish House of Commons, William Conolly, by the Italian Alessandro Galilei. You enter the grounds through the village of CELBRIDGE, planned to lend importance to the house itself. This exhibits the strictest classicism: the front facade, facing out over the Liffey, gives little away except for a rigidly repeated succession of windows. It's the only thing about the house that is restrained, though, for Castletown, from the very beginning, was built for show.

William Conolly, who commissioned it, was a publican's son from Donegal who – like many others – owed his success to the changed conditions after the Battle of the Boyne, and made his fortune by dealing in forfeited estates. Member for Donegal in the Irish Parliament since 1692, he was a staunch supporter of the Hanoverian cause, and was unanimously elected Speaker of the Irish House of Commons in 1715. In 1717 the Ambassador at Florence noted Conolly's intention to bring to Ireland "the best architect in Europe", a move of some significance to national self-esteem. A letter to the famous metaphysician Bishop Berkeley states: "I am glad for the honour of my country that Mr Conolly has undertaken so magnificent a pile of building . . . . Since this house will be the finest Ireland ever saw, and by your description fit for a Prince, I would have it as it were the epitome of the Kingdom, and all the natural rarities she affords should have a place there." Although plans for the house were magnificent, work proceeded in a haphazard way. The cellar vaults, begun before the design of the house was finalised, still bear little relation to what's above ground; and the house interior remained unfinished – lacking, for instance, a main staircase – until the end of the long life of William's wife, who preferred building **follies**.

The fruits of old Mrs Conolly's imagination are most obvious in the **grounds**, where one folly closes the vista to the north, 140 feet of what appears to be a monument to chimney-sweeping, while the **Wonderful Barn** forms a focus for the view to the east. Both projects were set up to provide relief work for estate workers hard hit by the famine-ridden winter of 1739, and Mrs Conolly's sister, for one, disapproved: "My sister is building an obleix to answer a vistow from the bake of Castletown house," she wrote of the folly; "It will cost her three or four hundred pounds at least, but I believe more. I really wonder how she can dow so much and live as she duse". Incidentally, it seems that the ground on which the obelisk stands did not belong to Castletown, not that this bothered Mrs Conolly.

The **interior** decoration was the inspiration of Lady Louisa Lennox, who married into the Conolly family in 1759 at the age of fifteen. The newly-weds might have lived in London (Louisa's brother-in-law described her as wanting "to buy every house she sees"), but the fact that Louisa's elder sister, Lady Emily Kildare, had settled at Carton, close by at Maynooth, decided matters. It was Louisa who commissioned the Francini brothers to produce the extraordinary plasterwork in the halls and ordered the long gallery at the back of the house, which she considered "the most comfortable room you ever saw, and quite warm; supper at one end, the company at the other, and I am writing in one of the piers at a distance from them all". Apparently, she ordered the magnificent Murano glass chandeliers on a journey to Venice, but when they arrived they were found to clash with the room's blue, Pompeiian-style decor.

The Irish Georgian Society

Given this personal, idiosyncratic stamp on Castletown, it seems a shame that no one lives here any more. In 1967 the house was bought by Desmond Guinness, a founder of the **Irish Georgian Society**. Established in 1958 with the aim of preserving Ireland's magnificent Georgian heritage, the society is regarded with suspicion or amusement in some quarters. It has strong Anglo-Irish leanings and shows some degree of eccentricity (the English chapter teams up with the Silver Ghost Club to cruise around the countryside in antique Rolls Royces), but it's done sterling work in, for example, providing small but vital grants that have enabled buildings to be saved. Enquiries to the *Irish Georgian Society*, Leixlip Castle, Leixlip, County Kildare (☎01/8244211).

Accommodation with a suitably Georgian flavour is to be found for a reasonable price close by at *Ringwood*, Newcastle, an eighteenth-century house surrounded by 65 acres of rolling farmland (☎01/6288220, £16.50; open May–Oct).

Canal country

Monuments to eighteenth-century confidence in Irish trade, which was to be dashed by the Act of Union, the **Royal and Grand Canals** flow from Dublin through County Kildare and on into the Irish heartland. While Ireland had experienced a minor industrial revolution in the mid- to late eighteenth century, when mines, mills, workshops and canals were created, the Act of Union precluded further development. By walking along the **towpaths**, or cruising on the Grand Canal, you can see how industrialisation affected – and failed to affect – the eighteenth-century landscape. **Grand Canal cruises** are based at Tullamore in County Offaly (*Celtic Canal Cruisers*; ☎0506/21861); from here you can head on to the Shannon, or join the River Barrow, which meets the Grand Canal at Robertsbridge and is navigable all the way down to Waterford.

The **Grand Canal** was a truly ambitious project, running from Dublin to Robertstown, where it forks. The southern branch joins the River Barrow at Athy, effectively extending the waterway as far south as Waterford; while the western branch runs up to Tullamore in County Offaly, and on to join the great natural waterway of the Shannon at Shannon Harbour. As late as 1837 the Grand Canal was carrying over 100,000 passengers a year; and it continued to be used for freight right up to 1959. The **Royal Canal** runs past Maynooth and Mullingar before joining the Shannon, many tortuous meanderings later, at Cloondara, north of Lough Rea, for access to the northwest.

Robertstown and Monasterevin

Two locations are particularly evocative of canal life. **ROBERTSTOWN**, due north of Kildare, where the ways divide, is no more than a village, yet it boasts a canal stop complete with a grand, pedimented canalside hotel (now pebbledashed and painted bright orange). This is occasionally used for candlelit dinners and is also a centre for canoe training and canal barge trips; for more information call ☎01/8452655 (all year) or ☎045/60020 (May–Sept).

THE CANAL SYSTEM

GRAND CANAL SYSTEM

SHANNON RIVER NAVIGATION

RIVER BARROW NAVIGATION

Lough Allen
Lough Key
Carrick-on-Shannon
Drumsna
Lough Boderg
Roosky
Longford
River Shannon
Lanesboro
Lecarrow
Lough Ree
Athlone
Clonmacnois
Tullamore
Robertstown
DUBLIN
Shannon Bridge
Monasterevin
Kildare
Naas
Shannon Harbour
Portumna
Lough Derg
Athy
Mountshannon
Carlow
Garrykennedy
Killaloe
Borris
Limerick
R. Shannon
Graiguenamanagh
Inistioge
St. Mullins
R. Nore
New Ross
R. Suir
Waterford

------- Paths
~~~ Navigable waterways

0   25 miles

At **MONASTEREVIN**, west of Kildare along the N7, there's a truly magnificent example of eighteenth-century state-of-the-art technology. Here the Grand Canal crosses the River Barrow on an aqueduct (in eighteenth-century terms, the equivalent of a motorway flyover), with superseding technologies upstream (a railway bridge) and downstream (the N7 Dublin–Limerick trunk road). Otherwise, Monasterevin follows the set pattern of an Irish Pale town: a big house, in this case **Moore Abbey** (once the home of the Irish tenor John McCormack, famous for his syrupy renditions of Irish folk songs), a church, and the town itself: a street of eighteenth-century houses on one side of the road only, their gardens sloping down to the River Barrow on the other. The houses get steadily grander going towards the canal; almost at the end of the terrace, *Carlow House* is a fine **bed and breakfast**.

South Kildare: ancient remains

It's a mistake to think of County Kildare as a relatively modern landscape, seeing in it only the legacies of the Anglo-Normans and Anglo-Irish. South of Naas on the Carlow road, three **high crosses** set in the green, rolling farmland attest that settlements and cultural history here are much, much older. **OLD KILCULLEN**, off the road in a field, is the site of an early Celtic monastery with the remains of eighth-century crosses, and an evocative round tower damaged during the 1798 rebellion. The small village of **MOONE**, just south of Timolin, once formed a link in the chain of monasteries founded by Saint Columba, and the garden of Moone Abbey contains the ruins of a fourteenth-century Franciscan friary and a ninth-century cross. At **CASTLEDERMOT** there's more to see: two tenth-century granite high crosses, plus a bizarre twelfth-century Romanesque doorway standing by itself in front of an ugly modern church and a truncated round tower. Castledermot also has a thirteenth-century Augustinian abbey, an early example of how the European monastic orders muscled in on the indigenous Irish church. Its substantial remains give a completely different feel to what might otherwise be merely a roadside stop; get the keys from the caretaker, who lives next door.

Kilkea Castle, the Fitzgeralds' second Kildare stronghold (after Maynooth), stands a couple of miles up the Athy road from Castledermot. It's impressive looking, though largely a sham – originally built in 1180, it was modified in the seventeenth century and most of it is a mid-nineteenth-century restoration. Recently it has been used as a luxury hotel, and a further large-scale refurbishment looks set to take it still further away from its roots.

Ballitore

Almost exactly halfway between Naas and Carlow is **BALLITORE**, an old Quaker village where the eighteenth-century Anglo-Irish political philosopher **Edmund Burke** was educated, and a good example of the religious toleration that it sometimes seems the British government was prepared to grant anyone but the Catholics. A **museum** (open afternoons) above the village library gives a vivid picture of what life was like: the industrious Quakers each plied a trade and their sober, businesslike approach made Ballitore a model village by comparison to the general squalor and poverty of surrounding places. But the dominant impression given by the copperplate handwritten letters on show is the sheer boredom of life in a place where any stranger was cause for excitement. The *Cottage Biography* of one of Ballitore's nineteenth-century residents, Mary Leadbeater (on sale at the museum) preserves more of the same stultifying atmosphere. Up towards the main road is the walled **Quaker graveyard**, whose plain, dignified tombstones seem worthy monuments to the deceased.

Athy

On the border with County Laois sits **ATHY** (emphasis on the second syllable), one of those places where a bucketful of imagination is required to envisage it as it once was: prosperity has turned a formerly handsome Georgian town with a fine main square into something much more ramshackle. A massive riverside factory sits oddly with the Georgian fanlights and a quite repulsive new church: the latter is apparently supposed to make reference to a dolmen, although the Sydney Opera House seems a stronger influence. By the riverside stands the square tower of a fifteenth-century **castle** built to protect the ford, nowadays a private house.

travel details

Trains

From Kildare to Dublin Heuston (20 daily; 30min).

From Bray to Dublin Connolly (DART, 4 daily; 25min)

From Wicklow to Dublin (4 daily; 50min)

From Arklow to Dublin (4 daily; 1hr 20min).

Bus Éireann

From Kildare to Dublin (15 daily; 1hr 20min).

CHAPTER THREE

LAOIS AND OFFALY

f you've come to Ireland for the scenery, or the wild remote places, or the
romance of the far west, then the central counties of **Laois** and **Offaly** probably don't hold a great deal to entice you. But this quiet and unremarkable part
of the country between Dublin and the Shannon is an excellent place to get to
know another Ireland, one not hyped by the tourist authorities. It's gentle, green
farming land bearing the marks of a complex pattern of settlement: the Celtic
church, Viking invaders, the arrival of the Anglo-Normans and, very strongly in
these twin counties, the planted settlements with which the British sought to
keep their base in the Pale secure. It's a subtle, detailed landscape, which the
destruction of Ireland's foreign trade by the Act of Union in 1801 ensured
remained virtually untouched by the industrial revolution.

Transport in Laois and Offaly is easy – the main N7 trunk road and the main railway line to Limerick slice straight through Laois, while the industrial centre of Tullamore makes an obvious transport centre, both road and rail, for Offaly. The major problem, as in much of central Ireland, is with **accommodation**. There are, simply, no hostels and very few official campsites, so you're restricted to B&Bs, or asking permission to camp in fields.

LAOIS

Laois, or Leix – neither spelling gives any useful clue as to its pronunciation: *Leash* – is in many ways Ireland's least known county. Most people know it only for the maximum security jail at Portlaoise, or as an ill-defined area you go through on the way to Limerick. While most Irish counties have a strong identity, Laois seems oddly accidental. To the east it's more or less bordered by the river Barrow; to the north, it forms part of the Slieve Bloom mountain range (though some of that is in county Offaly); but to the west and south there seems little sense in the borders.

Until the mid-sixteenth century, Laois remained under its **traditional chiefs**, the O'Mores, FitzPatricks, O'Dempseys and O'Dunnes, and posed an increasing threat to the British in the Pale. In 1556, a new county was carved out of these tribal lands, settled (or "planted", in the terminology of the time) and named Queen's County (to Offaly's King's County). A new town, **Maryborough**, named after Mary Tudor, was established at what is now Portlaoise. None of this quelled the O'Mores (in particular), but eventually transplantation succeeded where mere plantation had failed. The troublesome clans of Laois were exiled to County Kerry and Laois was left free for the colonisers. Because Laois came under British control so early, there are none of the huge estates that were later dished out, by Cromwell and Charles II, to loyal followers in the far west. Rather, there are smaller landholdings and planned towns, interspersed with some settlements of dissenting religious groups. Ironically, given the treatment Ireland's Catholics were getting at the time, these groups were able to find the freedom of worship they desired here. All this makes for an intimate – if unspectacular – landscape, epitomising a history of colonialism as much as anywhere else in the British empire.

Portlaoise and around

PORTLAOISE, unremarkable except for the top security **jail** which leaps into the news whenever there's an argument about extradition of a prisoner to the North, is a suitably grim place. It was founded in 1547, when the O'Mores held the fortress of Dunamase to the south, as a fortification under the name of Fort Protector. In 1556 the town was planted and renamed Maryborough. Today it's seedy and depressed; the main road by-passes it entirely and, unless you arrive by train and can't avoid it, you're probably well advised to do the same. It does, however, have a **tourist office** (☎0502/21178; May–Sept) which may be useful for information.

What is well worth seeing, though, is the **Rock of Dunamase**, two or three miles out on the Stradbally road. An extraordinary, knobbly mound encrusted with layer upon layer of fortifications, it's a great place for gazing out, beyond the flat surrounding countryside, to the Slieve Bloom mountains to the north and the Wicklow hills in the east. There are suggestions that Dunamase was known to Ptolemy under the name of *Dunum*, and Celtic *Dun Masc* was valuable enough to be plundered by the Vikings in 845. Today, the hill is crowned by a **ruined castle** of the twelfth-century king of Leinster, Dermot MacMurrough. He it was who invited Strongbow to Ireland, and married his daughter, Aoife, to him, including Dunamase in her dowry. Explicable only in terms of the complex history of the Anglo-Normans, Dunamase eventually passed from Strongbow – Henry II's right-hand man – to the Mortimers and the O'Mores, bitter opponents of the British. It was finally blown up by Cromwell's troops in 1650. The earthworks 500 yards to the east of the fortress are still known as Cromwell's lines.

STRADBALLY (literally "street-town"), a few miles further south, is notable chiefly for the **narrow-gauge railway** at Stradbally Hall. A nineteenth-century steam locomotive, formerly used in the Guinness brewery in Dublin, runs every weekend from March to October; there's also a **traction engine museum** in the town, and a **steam engine rally** on the first weekend in August.

The South: Abbeyleix and Durrow

The south of County Laois consists of lush farmland, dotted with estate towns and villages. The largest of these is **ABBEYLEIX**, named after a Cistercian abbey founded here by a member of the O'More family in 1183. In one of those periodic bursts of enthusiasm that seem to be a mark of the Ascendancy, Abbeyleix was entirely remodelled by Viscount de Vesci in the eighteenth century and relocated on the coach road away from the old village to the southwest.

Unfortunately, the attractive pedimented eighteenth-century **Abbeyleix House** (designed by James Wyatt) isn't open to the public, although the gardens sometimes are. In the village, *Morrissey's Bar* is an enormous grocer's shop and pub combined which probably hasn't changed in fifty years, with pew seats and a brazier, and old advertisements for beer and tobacco that seem to have been forgotten by time. It's a great place to sit and soak up the atmosphere. There are a couple of small **B&Bs** in Abbeyleix itself, or you can stay in a modest example of Georgian architecture at nearby BALLINAKILL, where *The Glebe* is run as a B&B by Mrs Dowling (☎0502/33368; £18).

DURROW, further south on the Kilkenny road, is yet another planned estate town, grouped around a green adjoining **Castle Durrow**, the first great Palladian house to be built in this area (1716). It's now a convent, but you can walk up the drive and see it. The town was owned by the Duke of Ormond, who for reasons of his own had it adopted by County Kilkenny; it took an act of parliament to get it returned to what was then Queen's County in 1834. The *Castle Arms* here has **rooms** (☎0502/36118; £20).

The very **southwest** corner of County Laois is quiet farming land punctuated by small villages such as CULLAHILL, RATHDOWNEY and ERILL. Although all you can do there is look at the neat colour-washed houses, visit the local pub or shop, and ponder the changing ways of the world, just being there is delightful, and these are good places to stop over if you're cycling.

Accommodation in these parts is almost non-existent, but Mrs Carroll does run a B&B at *River House* in Errill (it's best to phone ahead, ☎0505/44120; £11.50).

Slieve Bloom and North Laois

North Laois is dominated by the **Slieve Bloom Mountains** (pronounced *Schlieve Bloom*), which bring some welcome variation to this flat county. Although they scarcely reach 1200 feet – the Slieve Bloom mountaineering club is something of a standing joke with mountaineers from loftier parts of Ireland – they're ruggedly desolate enough to give a taste of real wilderness, even if you follow the **Slieve Bloom Way**. The Way, little over twenty miles in length, takes you across moorland, woods and bog, along part of one of the old high roads to Tara and through the bed of a pre-Ice Age river valley. Along the way dense coni-fer plantations attempt to survive, with a little help from the taxpayer, way above the natural tree line. If your time is limited and you have a car, the best place to start is probably **Glen Barrow** or the **Forelacka valley**, where standing stones and a tumulus evince ancient human settlement just across the border in County Offaly. Otherwise, you can catch the Dublin–Portumna **bus** at Birr or Portarlington and start walking at KINNITY, a really delightful upland village which has an excellent pub.

Unfortunately, **accommodation** is limited in this neck of the woods. The pub in COOLRAIN in the Slieve Bloom foothills – good for traditional music, too – has rooms (not tourist-board approved), or, if you feel like a real treat, there's **Roundwood House** just outside MOUNTRATH, a mid-eighteenth-century Palladian mansion nowadays run as a guesthouse. Originally built by a Quaker who had made his fortune in America, it's a doll's house of a building decorated in vibrantly authentic Georgian colours, with a double-height hall boasting a Chinese Chippendale-style staircase. The tourist board says Roundwood can't call itself a hotel (too few rooms) or a grade A guesthouse (no fitted carpets or curtains – period rugs and original shutters instead) so it functions as a B&B, with prices scaled accordingly (£29 a night; £18 for dinner; ☎0502/32120).

Mountmellick, Portarlington and Emo

Mountmellick and Portarlington are typical of the few little settlements that grew up independently of the great houses, and both were communities of outsiders. **MOUNTMELLICK**, almost encircled by the Owenmass river, was founded in the seventeenth century by Quakers, and still has a spacious eighteenth-century feel to it. You need some imagination to see the houses as the elegant buildings they must once have been, but Mountmellick in its heyday was undoubtedly both prosperous – it was famous for its embroidered white laceware – and cultured.

PORTARLINGTON was founded in 1667 by General Ruvigny, Earl of Galway, and settled by a group of Huguenot refugees, who built the elegant eighteenth-century houses with their spacious orchards and gardens, which once grew exotic fruit like peaches and apricots (particularly good examples are to be seen in Patrick Street). Some of the inscriptions on the tombstones of St Michael's Church, still known as the French Church, are in French.

One of the few really big estates in County Laois is **Emo Court**, just off the N7 at NEW INN. Designed by James Gandon for Lord Arlington around 1790 (but finished, not entirely according to Gandon's plans, only in the mid-nineteenth century), it's a massive, domed building which has been impressively restored by its present owner after years of neglect when it was run as a Jesuit seminary. The enormous **grounds** are open afternoons from the end of March to the end of October; the **house** only on Monday afternoons (other times by arrangement with the owner, ☎0502/26110). If the charms of Laois's quiet landscape take hold of you, you can find out more in John Feehan's excellent topographical survey, *Laois: an environmental history* – a good example of the new breed of local history which deals with both the natural and the man-made past.

OFFALY

From the Bog of Allen in the east to Boora Bog in the west, **County Offaly** is dominated by bog and peat. A low-lying region bounded to the northwest by the meandering Shannon and its flood plain, it's only in the south that the land rises at all into the foothills of the Slieve Bloom range. The **Bog of Allen**, vast, black and desolate, has been intensively exploited for peat; and only real bog freaks will find much of interest there. **Boora Bog** is entirely different – smaller and less unremittingly flat and bare. It's the site of an archaeological find that proves that there was human life here 9000 years ago; and of Clonmacnoise, the greatest monastery of early Celtic Ireland.

The Bog of Allen

The **Bog of Allen** only really becomes overpowering after EDENDERRY, traditionally on the edge of the Pale. But even here, after miles of dark bogland, it's a distinct relief to reach somewhere with lots of people and an air of prosperity. Pushing on along the Dublin–Portumna bus route towards Tullamore, you pass through DAINGEAN, formerly Philipstown, the provincial capital in the days when Offaly was known as King's County. Both county and capital were planted in Mary Tudor's reign and named after her husband, Philip II of Spain.

Tullamore

Coming from either direction, the Bog of Allen to the east or Boora Bog to the west, the bright lights and solid buildings of **TULLAMORE**, astride the Grand Canal, seem welcoming. Its Victorian ambience makes the town look more English than Irish, a result of moving the capital from Philipstown to Tullamore in 1834, following decades in which the British pushed the boundaries of King's County ever further westwards. Apart from the shops and a certain amount of nightlife, there are really only two reasons to come to Tullamore. One is **Irish Mist**, a truly delicious whiskey liqueur, samples of which might be available from the information centre on Bury Quay (a little way down the Rahan road and turn right; Mon–Fri 10am–5pm).

The other reason is **Charleville Forest**, an extraordinary Georgian-Gothic mansion ("perhaps the first deliberately formed asymmetrical house in Ireland", wrote Dan Cruickshank in the excellent *Guide to the Georgian Buildings of Britain and Ireland*), built in 1779 to the designs of Francis Johnston. It has recently changed hands, and the new owner (unlike his predecessor) isn't into receiving visitors, but it's worth checking at the **tourist office** in the middle of

ALL ABOUT BOGS

Ten thousand years ago, after the last Ice Age, the melting glaciers and ice sheets left central Ireland covered by shallow lakes. As time went by the lake and lakeside vegetation grew and died and partly decomposed, in a continuing cycle that changed these lakes to fens, and eventually into domed bogs. Ireland now has the finest range of peatlands in Europe.

At one time there were 311,000 hectares of raised bog in Ireland; by 1974 there were 65,000; and by 1985 there were just 20,000 hectares left. They continue to disappear at a rate of 3000 hectares per year. It is only recently that the Irish have awoken to the great natural importance of the boglands. Not only are they home to rare plants, from mosses to bilberries, but they provide a habitat for birds. The bog gases also act as preservatives, and the bogs of Ireland have yielded archaeological evidence of botanical and human history up to 9000 years ago in the form of pollens and plant remains, gold and silver artefacts, dug-out canoes and human bodies.

To see a raised bog of international importance, go to **Mongan Bog** in County Offaly. Part of the Clonmacnoise Heritage Zone, it's situated on the banks of the Shannon. And if the bog bug really bites, head for the **Peatland Information Centre** in Lullymore, County Kildare, where you can buy a copy of the Irish Peatland Conservation Council's *Guide to Irish Peatlands*.

town (by the bridge, June–Aug; ☎0506/52141) in case this attitude has changed. In any case the estate is open, and wonderfully spooky it is too. The Gothic element is highly suggestive of a horror movie: castellated turrets, shady trees and clinging ivy, while the house in the centre of the estate, surrounded by a second wall topped by urns, is a secretive place made for diabolical activities. With its splendid old trees, leafy walks and even a grotto, the estate has everything you could wish for. To get there, take the Birr road out of Tullamore: Charleville's gates are on the right as you leave the town – about ten minutes' walk – by the Offaly Historical Society's offices.

If you want to **stay**, there are numerous B&Bs roundabout, such as *Oakfield House*, Rahan Road (☎0506/21385; £15), as well as the comfortable *Phoenix Arms* on Bridge Street (☎0506/21066; £25) – also a good place to **eat**.

Durrow Abbey

Four miles north of Tullamore on the N52, by some handsome wrought-iron gates to the left of the road, a signpost marks the way to the site of **Durrow Abbey**, one of the monasteries founded by the energetic Saint Colmcille (better known as Saint Columba), and the place where the *Book of Durrow* – an illuminated late-seventh-century copy of the gospels, now exhibited in Trinity College Library, Dublin – was made.

A long avenue brings you to a typically Irish juxtaposition: a grand Georgian mansion next to a medieval church, which stands on the site of the monastery. A notice at the main gates gives directions to the high cross and tombstones; behind you is the formality of the avenue, ahead the well tended grounds of the house. Inside the church walls everything is different – the disused churchyard, the masonry strangled with ivy, gravestones leaning crazily on uneven ground as if the earth has opened and disgorged their contents . . . an eerie place, where Durrow's high cross and tombstones seem to represent sweet reason.

Western Offaly

Western Offaly is dominated by the bog and the **Shannon**, one virtually impassable, the other for centuries a means of communication; there's a huge range of ancient sites along the river. Exploring the *esker* ridges (raised paths above the bog) of this quiet, bog-and-water landscape has a certain appeal if you hit good weather. It's excellent cycling country, and while there's nothing specific to see much of the time, following roads that have for centuries been the only passages through the bog has a resonance of its own. The only problem is **accommodation**: generally you're restricted to B&Bs – and even these are few and far between – or camping in fields (ask permission first). For information on B&B availability, check with the **Clonmacnoise tourist office** (☎0905/74134, April–Oct).

Clonmacnoise

Of all the ancient sites along the Shannon, **CLONMACNOISE**, early Celtic Ireland's foremost monastery, in the northwest of the county is by far the most important. Approaching from Shannonbridge, the first evidence of its whereabouts is a stone wall leaning precariously towards the Shannon. This is actually a remnant of a thirteenth-century Norman **castle**, built to protect the river crossing, which has leaned ever since its wooden foundations were destroyed by fire, and has nothing whatever to do with the monastery.

When you first see the **monastic complex** itself (daily June–Sept 9am–7pm, mid-March to May & Sept–Oct 10am–6pm, Nov to mid-March 10am–5pm; ☎0905/74195; £1, students 40p, heritage card) – a huddle of wind- and rain-swept buildings on an open plain in a bend in the Shannon – it seems hard to believe that this was a settlement of any importance. Deep in the unfashionable, untouristed centre of Ireland, it's still remote enough not to receive huge numbers of visitors. Yet this was not just a monastery, but a **royal city** and a burial place for the kings of Connacht and Tara, including the last high king of Ireland, Rory O'Conor, buried here in 1198. As the bookshrines, croziers and other richly decorated artefacts on show in the National Museum in Dublin testify, it was also an artistic centre of the highest order; the twelfth-century *Book of the Dun Cow*, now in the Royal Irish Academy Library in Dublin, is only one of many treasures made here.

Founded by **Saint Kieran** around 548, the monastery was largely protected by its isolation: surrounded by bog, Clonmacnoise could only be reached by boat, or along a causeway atop an *esker* known as the **Pilgrims' Causeway**. Irish, Viking and Norman attacks it withstood, but in 1552 the English garrison at Athlone looted the monastery and left it beyond recovery. However, plenty remains: a cathedral, eight churches, two round towers, high crosses, grave slabs and a thirteenth-century ring fort.

The buildings

Seeing any significant differences between these small, gaunt, grey buildings takes a trained eye. The **cathedral**, scarcely bigger than its companions, was built in 904 by King Flann and Abbot Coman Conailleach, and rebuilt in the fourteenth century by Tomultach MacDermot; the sandstone pillars of the west doorway may have been incorporated from the earlier church. Not everything at Clonmacnoise, however, is as simple as it seems: to the right of the cathedral, **Teampall** (Temple) **Doolin** carries the elaborate coat of arms of Edmund

Dowling of Clondarane, who restored the building in 1689; **Teampall Hurpan**, adjacent, was actually added in its entirety in the seventeenth century. **Teampall Kieran**, on the other side of the cathedral, is the reputed burial place of the founding saint, as well as allegedly the place where he built the first church on the site; the ruined **Teampall Kelly** is probably twelfth century.

High crosses and outlying structures

Of the high crosses, the early tenth-century **Great Cross**, over twelve feet high, is said to commemorate King Flann and Abbot Coman; the carvings represent the monastery's foundation and scenes from the passion story. The **South Cross**, dating from the ninth century, is decorated with flower and animal motifs.

A little further from the main group of buildings is **O'Rourke's tower**, a round tower sixty feet high, erected just after the cathedral and blasted by lightning in 1134. On the outer boundary of the site, by the Shannon, are the **Teampall Finghin**, with another round tower dating from 1124, and the **Teampall Conor**, which was founded early in the eleventh century by Cathal O'Connor and used as a parish church from around 1790.

The **Church of the Nunnery**, away from the main enclosure, is signposted but difficult to find, and most people lose heart before they reach it. Follow the path across the site and bear left along the lane. The Church is a little further along on the right, two lovely Romanesque arches in a field by the Shannon, exuding a feeling of peace. It's hard to imagine Clonmacnoise ever feeling crowded, but if your arrival does happen to coincide with a coach party, this is the place to come.

Shannonbridge, Shannon Harbour and Banagher

From Clonmacnoise, the road to Shannonbridge skirts the Boora Bog. **SHANNONBRIDGE** has a set of traffic lights, but only because the sixteen-span bridge across the river is so narrow. Upstream, the wetlands of the Shannon open up; downstream a power station signifies the exploitation of the boglands. This is the point where Counties Offaly, Roscommon and Galway meet and the River Suck joins the Shannon: hence the strategically placed and massive artillery fortification dating from Napoleonic times. There's a music pub – *Killeen's Tavern* – on the main street and, should you find yourself spending a night here, a couple of **B&Bs** including Mrs Grennan's *The Bungalow*, River View (☎0905/74180; £12).

Further south, **SHANNON HARBOUR** – a few buildings and the ivy-covered *Grand Hotel* – is where the River Brosna and the Grand Canal meet the Shannon after their journey right across Ireland. As you walk down to the junction, there comes a magical point where the entire landscape seems to become water. **Clonony Castle**, a mile or two further inland, is a ruined sixteenth-century tower house with a nineteenth-century reconstructed barn, scene of a private colonisation attempt, in the seventeenth century, by an entrepreneurial German, Mathew de Renzi.

Another couple of miles downstream, **BANAGHER** is one long street sloping down to the Shannon, fortified on the Connacht side with a Martello tower. The *Shannon Hotel* and a house further up on the other side of the street show a local variant of classicism: pepperpot towers with elaborate doorways in which everything curves – doors, fanlights, pediments and all. Anthony Trollope wrote his first novels while stationed in Banagher as a post office surveyor from 1841. The *Brosna Lodge Hotel* (☎0902/51350; £20) has rooms overlooking the Shannon.

Birr

BIRR is a perfect example of a middling-sized town planned round a great house – in this case, Birr Castle, home of the Parsons family (Birr used to be known as Parsonstown), later elevated to the Earls of Rosse. Here, eighteenth-century urban planning has resulted in a truly delightful Georgian town, with wide, airy streets and finely detailed, fan-lit houses. Surprisingly, it's not a prissy place, but rather feels slightly seedy, down-at-heel and full of life. One of the many places to be billed as the centre point of Ireland, Birr makes a good base for exploring both the Slieve Bloom mountains and the wetlands of the Shannon.

The Earls of Rosse still live at **Birr Castle**, and their house isn't open to the public, except occasionally to very rich paying guests (contact *Elegant Ireland*, 15 Harcourt St, Dublin, ☎01/751665/751012). The **grounds**, however, are: laid out in the 1830s and 40s by the second Earl, they contain rare plants from all over the world as well as an enormous artificial lake and a really charming early example of a suspension bridge over the river. It's a pleasant place to while away a sunny day – the grounds are shut at lunchtime but the keepers are perfectly happy to lock you in.

Much more remarkable, and Birr's real claim to fame, is the shell of the **Rosse telescope**. In 1845 the third Earl built what was then, and remained for three-quarters of a century, the largest telescope in the world – a reflector with a diameter of 72 inches. The instrument was used by the fourth Earl (1840–1908) to make the first accurate measurement of the heat of the Moon, and to catalogue the spiral nebulae. The walls that held the telescope – at 16.5 metres long, it was too cumbersome to be rotated in more than one plane – are still in place, built in the same stone and battlemented style as the house; unfortunately the telescope itself has been dismantled. There's some information about the casting of the lens, no mean feat in those days, but on the whole the exhibition drastically underplays an extraordinary episode in the history of modern science.

Practicalities and an excursion

Accommodation is available at a couple of B&Bs (try Mrs Spain's *Ard na Greine*, Hillside, ☎0509/20256; or check with the **tourist office**, May–Oct, ☎0509/20110) or if you're feeling slightly richer, you could try *Dooly's Hotel* in Emmet Square, recently refurbished and extremely pleasant (☎0509/20032; £25). *Dooly's* is where the Galway Hunt acquired the nickname of the Galway Blazers after a hunt in 1809, when their over-enthusiastic celebrations resulted in the gutting of the building by fire.

Up another notch in comfort, and perfection for anyone with an expensive taste in interiors, is *Tullanisk*, Birr Castle's Dower House (☎0509/20572; £30). Set in its own parkland a couple of miles out of town on the Banagher road, *Tullanisk* dates from around 1790 and boasts a huge bay window in the drawing room through which you can contemplate the deer munching the grass.

Finally, a little excursion for ghostbusters. A few miles south of Clareen, as the land rises towards the Slieve Bloom mountains, the fifteenth-century **Leap Castle** fortifies the valley between Leinster and Munster. Before it was destroyed in 1922, it enjoyed the sinister reputation of being the most haunted house in Ireland, and was particularly famous for an unusual, smelly ghost, which was described both by Yeats and his contemporary Oliver St John Gogarty.

travel details

Trains
From Portlaoise to Dublin (8 daily; 1hr); Limerick Junction (13; 1hr); Cork (9; 2hr).

Bus Éireann
From Portlaoise to Dublin (6 daily; 2hr); Abbeyleix (2; 20min); Durrow (1; 30min).

Private buses
Pierce Kavanagh Coaches (☎056/31213, ☎01/734344) serve Durrow, Abbeyleix and Portlaoise on their daily Thurles–Dublin route.

CHAPTER FOUR

MEATH, LOUTH, WESTMEATH AND LONGFORD

S tretching from the borders of County Dublin to the frontier with the North, and from the coast to the heart of Ireland, these four counties at one and the same time epitomise green and rural Ireland and yet provide a total contrast with the west. It's a region neglected by most visitors, whose impression, if any, is one of monotonously similar countryside. Pass through at speed, as most people do, and you'll probably share that impression. But if you slow down, and target a small area for more detailed exploration, you'll discover far more. In the east there's a wealth of remains of an exceptionally long, rich history, and one or two great beaches on the coast. As you head west the interest gradually dwindles until by the time you reach Longford it has, frankly, died altogether. Nonetheless, the area as a whole repays exploration, and it's a very different Ireland to that you'll find in the west.

In practical terms, you'll find it easy enough to get about, with most of the sites conveniently strung along major roads well served by public transport. Accommodation is less easy, with only a handful of hostels throughout the four counties, and B&Bs only in the major centres. Still, if you base yourself strategically you'll find that a surprising amount can be seen in a short time.

Louth, the smallest of the 32 counties, stretches northwards along the coast. Here you'll find the only two towns of any real size in this chapter, **Drogheda** and **Dundalk**. Inland, hilly *drumlin* country hardens in the northeast to real mountains. Here, on the **Cooley Peninsula**, lies the most exciting part of the coast between Dublin and the border. The peninsula is also the setting of one of the richest and oldest legendary tales of Irish literature, the **Táin Bó Cuailnge** (Cattle Raid of Cooley).

Until the mid-sixteenth century **Meath** (*Midhe*, middle) was combined with Westmeath, making it Ireland's fifth and most powerful province. Although it does touch the coast (with a couple of excellent beaches), this is primarily an inland county, whose exceptionally rich farmland unfurls lazily around its major river, the **Boyne**, and its tributaries. To discover the place you simply follow these waterways – above all the Boyne itself and the **Blackwater** – as thousands of years of civilisation have done before. Along its rivers, Meath can boast by far the richest bounty of historical remains in Ireland. This history starts in the Stone Age, with some of the oldest buildings in the world at **Brú Na Bóinne** and **Sliabh Na Caillighe**, and other important Neolithic remains still being discovered. Celtic Ireland was ruled from **Tara**, in Meath, and from Uisneach in Westmeath. Christian Ireland has left a wealth of early monastic remains, magnificent tenth-century **High Crosses**, and the celebrated illuminated manuscript known as **The Book of Kells**. The largest Norman fortress in Ireland can be seen at **Trim**, and later castles and mansions – from the Plantation period when the county was wholly confiscated and extensively developed – are everywhere, though only a few (notably **Dunsany Castle**) are open to the public.

Westmeath is characterised by its lakes – **Lough Sheelin**, **Lough Lene**, **Lough Derravaragh**, **Lough Owel** and **Lough Ennel** cut down through its heart – which go a long way to compensate for the falling off in historical or scenic splendour. In the south it becomes increasingly flat, easing into the bogland of northern Offaly, while in the west the border is defined by **Lough Ree** and the **River Shannon**. The Shannon also forms the western border of **Longford**, which is about all the county has going for it. There's nothing wrong with the place in a dull and placid sort of way, but placid and dull is what it is, and you're unlikely to want to stay long.

UP THE COAST: LOUTH

The main N1 Dublin to Belfast road, and the railway, provide rapid access to Drogheda, and on to Dundalk and the North. Here on the coast, Meath is barely more than ten miles across and you can cross over into Louth hardly noticing you've passed through. If you have any time, though, there are some delightful old-fashioned resorts on the coast, and a couple of fine sandy beaches. Biggest of them is **Bettystown**, where there's plenty of dark sand, a campsite and various B&Bs. Pleasant as it is, however, it's certainly not somewhere you should spend a lot of time if you're going to be seeing the west coast too.

Pressing on, Drogheda lies immediately across the county border, straddling the River Boyne.

Drogheda

Aside from its obvious advantages as a base for visiting sites like Monasterboice, Mellifont, Newgrange and, slightly further afield, the beaches on the Meath coast, **DROGHEDA**, tightly contained between two hills, is an enjoyable place in its own right: easily accessible and surprisingly unused to tourism. The architectural legacy of successive civilisations forms the main attraction. The ancient **Millmount mound** and the Boyne itself echo the early habitation you'll see further upstream, but the history of Drogheda as a town really began with the **Vikings**, who arrived in 911 AD and founded a separate settlement on each bank. By bridging the ford between these two, the Danes gave the place its name – *Droichead Atha*, the Bridge of the Ford. By the fourteenth century, the walled town was one of the most important in the country, where the parliament would meet from time to time: remnants of **medieval** walls and abbeys lie like splinters throughout the town. As ever, though, most of what you see is from the **eighteenth century** or later, reflecting the sober style of the Protestant bourgeoisie (after the horrific slaughter of Drogheda's defenders and inhabitants by Cromwell).

DROGHEDA

The important surviving buildings of this age, the Tholsel, the Courthouse and St Peter's Church, have mellowed romantically, and stand now among the **nineteenth-century** flowering of triumphal churches celebrating the relaxation of the persecuting stranglehold on Catholicism, and the riverside warehouses and huge rail viaduct that welcomed the boom years of the industrial era. More recent development, with riverside laneways and suburban housing estates, has affected the flavour of the place very little: the past somehow seems stronger here than the present.

Millmount

The Meath side of town, south of the Boyne, is probably the best place to start exploring Drogheda. Atop the southern hill, **Millmount**'s Martello tower offers an excellent overview of the town, both in a literal sense and through the excellent display in the local museum sited here. The tower (key from the museum) was severely damaged by bombardment during the 1922 Civil War (there's a large picture of the attack in the museum), but in any event it is the earthen mound on which it stands that gives the place its real importance. The strategic value of the site was recognised from the earliest times: in mythology the mound is the burial place of **Amergin**, the poet warrior, one of the sons of **Mil** of the

Milesians who are reckoned to be the ancestors of the Gaels. He arrived in Ireland from northern Spain around 1498 BC and later defeated the *Tuatha Dé Danann* at Tailtiu (Telltown). Another belief is that the mound houses a passage grave. However, the tumulus has never been excavated to find out which story – if either – is true. Not surprisingly the Normans chose the same strategic eminence for their motte in the twelfth century, and later a castle was built, standing until 1808 when it was replaced by the tower and military barracks you see today. The quickest way up here on foot is via the narrow flight of steps by *Dina's* corner shop, directly opposite **St Mary's Bridge**. This is near enough the spot where the original bridge was built by the Danes.

Millmount Museum

The eighteenth-century houses in the barrack square now shelter various arts and crafts enterprises, and above all **Millmount Museum** (Tues–Sun 3–6pm), one of Ireland's finest town museums. Within a glass cabinet in the **foyer** hangs a topographical quilt showing much of Ireland's east coast – note the two thousand (or thereabouts) grains of French knots that depict the sandy shores. Next to this is a quilted cummerbund of the Georgian houses in Fair Street, very pleasing and precise in its eighteenth-century detail. When you get out into the town you'll find that the area depicted (Fair Street, along with William, Lower and Upper Magdalene streets and Rope Walk) is still rich in period buildings and architectural detail.

The **Guilds Room** follows, hung with three large drapes (the only surviving Guilds' banners left in the country) celebrating the **broguemakers'**, **carpenters'** and **weavers'** trades. The broguemakers' banner – in effect an early advertisement – is particularly wonderful. It depicts Saint Patrick, who in myth rid the country of snakes, standing with his foot on a serpent: even the saint needs some protection, however, so he is sturdily shod in a pair of good Irish brogues. King Charles II also has a bit part, hiding up an oak tree to symbolise both the use of oak for tanning the leather and the security offered by a good pair of shoes (Charles escaped from Cromwell's troops in 1651 by hiding in an oak tree). The carpenters' and weavers' banners are more straightforward, the former depicting compasses and blades, the latter with shuttles clasped in leopards' mouths. In the next room there's a similar theme, with the **trade banners** of the fishermen, labourers and bricklayers. The bricklayers' shows the **barbican at St Lawrence Gate** as their proudest achievement. This, again, is something worth seeing once you get out into the town, still standing, perfectly preserved, with two round towers flanking a portcullis entry and retaining wall. It is much the most significant part of the town walls to have survived (part of the West Gate also exists, and a buttress and embrasure can be seen just south of the gate), and arguably the finest such survival anywhere in Ireland.

Heading down the museum stairs you come to a series of displays of a more domestic nature. Halfway down are some fourteenth-century **Chester floor tiles** found at the Magdalene tower and some pristine examples of rotary and saddle quernstones (used for grinding corn). At the foot of the staircase is a **Boyne Coracle**, a recent example of the type of circular fishing boat in use from prehistoric times right up to the middle of this century. This one has a framework of hazel twigs and a leather hide taken from a prize bull in 1943. To one side is an old photograph of the **Newgrange** monument, taken before it was restored. This is worth noting if you're planning a visit to Newgrange, especially as it shows the original position of the enscrolled kerbstone placed at the entrance to ward off trespassers. This has now been moved out of the way to avoid damage by visitors.

In the museum **basement** is a fully-equipped period kitchen, pantry and scullery. Among the artefacts displayed are an 1860 **vacuum cleaner** (a man would wind the suction mechanism from outside the house), a tailor's **hen and goose irons** (clothes irons named for their various shapes and sizes) which would be heated in the fire (hence the phrase "too many irons in the fire"), a **seddle bed** (preferred by the Irish peasant because it would be next to the warmth of the dying embers and could sleep two adults lengthways and four or five children acrossways) and a vast array of other everyday miscellany. On the **top floor** is a small picture gallery, and various exhibits on historical and industrial Drogheda – in general, the least exciting part of the museum. Up here, too, are rooms devoted to the Foresters and Hibernian societies, both nineteenth-century benevolent institutions set up to provide sickness benefits, burial expenses and the like for the poor.

The rest of town: an overview

Standing on the Millmount hill, you can enjoy an unimpeded **panorama** of Drogheda, with the bulk of the town climbing up the northern hill-slope opposite. From this standpoint it's clearly apparent how the tight-fitting street pattern of the medieval town gave scant breathing space for the overcrowding of succeeding centuries. The backs of the houses stagger down to the Boyne river in a colourless wash of daubed mortar, their windows staring blankly back at you. On top of the hill opposite, the fifteenth-century **Magdalene Tower** was once the belfry tower of an extensive Dominican friary, founded in 1224 by Lucas De Netterville, Archbishop of Armagh. The tower rises above a Gothic arch where the transept and nave would have met; inside, a spiral staircase reaches up into its two storeys, but since it is railed off from public access it's probably seen to best advantage from a distance. In March 1395 **Richard II**, king of England, received within the priory the submission of the Ulster Chiefs; and later Thomas, Earl of Desmond, a former Lord Chief Justice, was found guilty of treason and beheaded here in 1467 (with him went his Act of Parliament for a university in Drogheda).

Lower down, the spire that leaps out from the centre of town belongs to the heavily Gothic-styled nineteenth-century **St Peter's Roman Catholic Church** on West Street, the town's main thoroughfare. It's an imposing building (not to be confused with the eighteenth-century Church of Ireland St Peter's on Magdalene Street) with a grand double flight of steps, but it's the presence of a martyr's head, on view in a tabernacle-like box that forms part of a small shrine down the left-hand aisle, that transforms the place into a centre of pilgrimage. The severed head is a searing reminder of the days of religious persecution. It once belonged to **Oliver Plunkett**, Archbishop of Armagh and Primate of all Ireland in the seventeenth century when Drogheda was the traditional seat for that role. On July 1, 1681, Plunkett was executed in London for treason: as the Lord Chief Justice of England explained "the bottom of your treason was your setting up your false religion, than which there is not anything more displeasing to God". His head and mutilated members were snatched from the fire but were not brought back to Ireland until 1721, a time when the persecution had subsided somewhat. Plunkett was canonised a saint in 1975, after miracles were performed in his name in southern Italy.

East of the church, towards the docks, the back alleys and stone warehouses are relics of the short-lived Industrial Revolution and of the local brewing and milling trades. A few are being done up by a new breed of entrepreneur, but as many are empty and crumbling. The docks themselves seem mostly lifeless and deserted too, and the Boyne's funereal pace does little to enliven a depleted commercial shipping fleet where once sixty Viking ships are said to have rested at anchor. There is, however, one very bright spot down here in the form of **Mrs Carbery's pub**, as appealing as any in Ireland. This has been a local, family-run institution for over a century and in the evening or early morning (it opens at 7.30am to cater for the dockers and the men off the boats) the faint orange glow from the lanterns or fire inside makes a welcome landmark and sign of life.

Out of town: Beaulieu House

Further downstream, the **viaduct** carrying trains on the Dublin–Belfast line spans what is effectively a 200-foot deep gorge. It's an impressive feat of nineteenth-century engineering (by Sir John MacNeill) that you can examine at closer quarters if you feel like extending your visit to *Carbery's* into a country stroll out along the Baltray road. Beyond the viaduct and cement works you reach some pleasant woodland. Part of this belongs to **Beaulieu House**, a private domain that claims to have been Ireland's first unfortified mansion (1660–65), built after Cromwell's departure when the land was confiscated from Oliver Plunkett and given to Sir Henry Tichbourne, whose descendants reside there today. The house has a hipped roof in the artisan style and an almost perfectly preserved interior. Most rewarding of all is a mouth-wateringly indulgent **picture gallery** with a collection ranging from contemporary portraits of William and Mary on tall canvases by the court painter Van der Wyck to an intense collection of early twentieth-century Irish art, and much else besides. Unfortunately the house is strictly private, but the owners do open their doors to tours by the Drogheda Historical Society, so it's worth checking (at the museum) to see if your visit coincides with one of these.

Practicalities

Drogheda is a pretty easy place to find your way around. The **Bus Éireann** depot is on New Street, on the south bank of the river, and the **train** station is also on the south side, a short way east of town just off the Dublin Road. **Taxis** line up on Lawrence Street. The town is small enough not to need them for local trips, but you could arrange a lightning **tour** around the sights of Newgrange, Mellifont and Monasterboice for around £25 – though you'd have to be in a real hurry to want to see it all this way. A cheaper way to do this would be with the bus operated by the *Harpur House Hostel*, which offers regular half-day tours of the Boyne Valley (£10), worthwhile if you can only spare a few hours.

If you want to **stay**, *Harpur House Tourist Hostel* on William Street (☎041/ 32736; £6, or £8 in double room; no curfew) is probably your best bet, with some forty hostel beds. **B&B** is also available: try *Ivy House*, a very nice Georgian home next door (£11), or the more upmarket *Walker's Hotel* on West Street (☎041/ 31017; £20). There's a **tourist information office** open in the summer (June– Aug; ☎041/37070) if you need further help with accommodation; they'll also have details of other local tours. If you want to **hire a bike** to explore on your own try P.J. Carolan, 77 Trinity Street (£8 a day, £32 a week, £40 deposit; ☎041/38242).

Pubs, food and entertainment

As far as entertainment goes, check out the **pubs**, many of which are rich in character. *Carbery's* on the North Strand is probably the best known gathering place on this part of the east coast, especially for the traditional sessions on Tuesday nights (from 9pm) and Sunday lunchtimes (12.30–2.30pm). To get a seat on Sunday make sure you're there by noon. *Clarkes*, on the corner of Fair and Peter streets, is quiet and old-fashioned during the week, popular with the local literary set, but on Saturday nights is a fashionable meeting place. *Peter Matthews* on Lawrence Street (known locally as *McPhail's*) is also very popular (with a younger crowd) with lots of toffee-brown woodwork, partitions and cubicles and a back room for music. *McHugh's*, just up from here on Lawrence Street, is a friendly place with traditional music on Thursday nights. *Walker's Hotel* (West Street) has music Wednesday, Friday and Sunday nights. Less traditional venues include *Reds* on Dominick Street, formerly the *Horse and Hounds*, now a disco-bar, and *Branagan's* on Lower Magdalene Street (hot snacks 12.30–2.30pm and 5–11pm).

Weavers on Dominick Street is an excellent pub for a cheap lunch, always crowded, and *Snackmasters Restaurant*, a few doors down, serves similar **food**, similarly good value (Mon & Tues noon–3pm & 6pm–1am, Wed & Thurs noon–3pm & 6pm–3am, Fri and Sat noon–4am, Sun noon–3am). *Walker's Hotel* also offers a good value three-course lunch special. The *Buttergate Restaurant* in Millmount Square (Tues–Sun 12.30–2.30pm, also Thurs–Sat 7–11pm; ☎041/37407) is much more expensive, but not bad value for good French cuisine. At the other end of the scale, *King's Cafe* (popular with truckers), a short way out on the Collon Road will serve up four courses for around £3.50 and a full tea for under a fiver. *Fortune Peking* in Narrow West Street is a good Chinese restaurant, with cheap takeaway and sit-down meals.

Entertainment outside the pubs is limited. The best bet is to check out what's happening at the *Droichead Arts Centre* in Bellscourt Lane off West Street, which regularly hosts plays, poetry readings and exhibitions. There are also two **theatres**, both amateur and neither very exciting (*Duke Theatre*, Duke Street, ☎041/36122, and the *Parochial Theatre*) and a couple of **cinemas** (in the Abbey and Boyne shopping centres). There's also an occasional **disco** at *Lucianos* in the *Boyne Valley Hotel* (☎041/37737) and at *The Place* in the *Rosnaree Hotel*, each a couple of miles out of town.

Mellifont and Monasterboice

Not far from Drogheda, in the south of County Louth, lie two of the great historical sites which characterise this part of the country: the monasteries of Mellifont and Monasterboice. Both are easily reached from Drogheda, and can be visited on your way to or from the sites of the lower Boyne valley.

To get to Mellifont from Drogheda (about five miles), turn off the road to Collon at MONLEEK CROSS; alternatively turn off the Slane–Collon road at the signpost. There are two **buses** a day from Drogheda (Mon–Fri 9.15am & 6.15pm, Sat 2.15pm & 6.15pm), and two from Dublin via Slane (*McConnans*, 5.15pm, return 9.20am; £2.50). Monasterboice can be reached from the main N1 Dublin–Belfast road, or by continuing up the Drogheda–Collon road and following the signs to the right.

Mellifont Abbey

Mellifont (May to mid-June Tues–Sat 9.30am–1pm & 2–5.30pm, Sun 2–5.30pm; mid-June to mid-Sept daily 9.30am–6.30pm; 80p, students 30p, heritage card; ☎041/26459) was, in medieval times, one of the most important monasteries in Ireland, the Motherhouse of the Cistercian movement and a building of exceptional beauty and grandeur. The ruins you see today in no way do justice to this former glory, but they're pretty impressive even so.

At its foundation in 1142 – the inspiration of Saint Malachy, Archbishop of Armagh, who did much to bring the early Irish church closer to Rome – Mellifont was the first **Cistercian monastery** in Ireland. Malachy's friend Saint Bernard, then abbot of the Cistercian monastery at Clairvaux, did much to inspire the work, and sent nine of his own monks to form the basis of the new community. The Abbey took fifteen years to build, and you can gauge something of its original size and former glory by imagining the gargantuan pillars that once rose, finishing high among a riotous sprouting of arches and vaulted ceilings, from the broad stumps remaining today. For nearly 400 years Mellifont flourished, at its peak presiding over as many as 38 other Cistercian monasteries throughout the country, until in 1539 all of them were suppressed by Henry VIII.

One hundred and fifty monks fled from Mellifont, and the buildings were handed over to Edward Moore, ancestor of the Earls of Drogheda, who converted the place into a fortified mansion. In 1603 the last of the great Irish chieftains, **Hugh O'Neill**, was starved into submission here before eventually escaping to the continent in the Flight of the Earls. Mellifont, meanwhile, went into gradual decline. It was attacked by Cromwellian forces, and then used as William's headquarters during the Battle of the Boyne, before eventually falling so far as to be pressed into service as a pigsty in the nineteenth century.

The ruins

Today the remains rarely rise above shoulder height, with the striking exception of the Romanesque octagonal **Lavabo**, built around 1200, whose basins and water jets provided washing facilities for the monks.

The rest of the ruins can be easily identified on the map provided, their ground plan almost perfectly intact. You enter through the **North Transept**, which originally had five chapels, three in its eastern and two in its western aisle. Two of the three on the eastern side had apsidal ends, an unusual feature in medieval Ireland, seen here presumably because of the French influence on the builders. The chancel area, or **Presbytery**, has the remains of an ornate arch and a **sedilia** where the celebrants of the Mass would sit. The entire nave would have been paved in red and blue tiles, some inscribed with the words "Ave Maria" and others decorated with the *fleur-de-lis* emblem; the **pillars**, too, would originally have been painted in brilliant colours and topped with flowery capitals. At the river end of the nave is a **crypt** – an unusual position which in this case served to level the site on which the church was built. The **Chapter House**, beyond the South Transept, was once the venue for the daily meetings of the monks. It now houses a collection of medieval **glazed tiles**, moved here from around the site for safety.

Behind the Lavabo is the **South Range**, where the Refectory would have been, and back towards the road you'll find the **Gatehouse**, the only surviving part of a high defensive wall that once completely ringed the monastic buildings. Also within the grounds are another ruined church up on the slope (converted to a Protestant place of worship in 1542) and a building that was converted by *An Óige* into a **youth hostel**. This has been closed indefinitely, a shame since the setting is delightful, with the River Mattock gliding through gently wooded country, and it used to make a great base from which to move out to the other places of interest nearby – Monasterboice and the Brú Na Bóinne complex. If you want to check on plans to reopen the place, try phoning the *An Óige* head office (☎01/ 363111).

Monasterboice: high crosses

Monasterboice (*Mainistir Buite* or Buite's monastery) is a tiny enclosure, but it contains two of the finest High Crosses (both dating from the tenth century) and one of the best round towers in the country – the site is open to all during daylight hours. As you enter, the squat cross nearer to you is reckoned the finer of the two, and certainly its high-relief carving has worn the centuries better. It is known as **Muiredach's Cross** after the inscription in Gaelic at the base of the stem – *Or do Muiredach i Chros*, "A prayer for Muiredach by whom this cross was made". The boldly ornate stone picture panels retell biblical stories and were designed to educate and inspire the largely illiterate populace. Some of the subjects are ambivalent and open to a certain amount of conjecture (William Wilde, father of Oscar, argued that many relate as strongly to events associated with Monasterboice as with the Bible), but most have been fairly convincingly identified.

The story begins at the bottom of the **east face** of the cross, nearest the wall, with **Eve tempting Adam** on the left and **Cain slaying Abel** on the right. Above this, **David and Goliath** share a panel with King Saul and David's son Jonathan. The next panel up shows **Moses striking the rock** with his staff to conjure water whilst the Israelites wait with parched throats, and above this, the **Wise Men** bear gifts to the Virgin Mary and baby Jesus. The centrepiece of the wheel is the scene of the **Last Judgment**, with the multitudes risen from the dead begging for entry to Heaven, their hands holding one another in good will and the trumpets playing loudly. Below Christ's foot the Archangel Michael is seen driving a staff through Satan's head after weighing the balance of good and evil in one individual's favour. At the very top, saints Anthony and Paul are seen breaking bread.

The **west face** of the cross is largely devoted to the **life of Christ**. At the bottom is his arrest in the Garden of Gethsemane, with Roman soldiers and the treacherous kiss of Judas. This is followed by three figures clutching books – thought to represent the dispelling of the **doubts of Saint Thomas**. The third panel shows the **Risen Christ** returned to meet Saint Peter and Saint Paul, their faces bowed in shame at ever having doubted the truth. The hub of the wheel shows the **Crucifixion**, with soldiers below, angels above and evil humanity to the sides. This is surmounted by **Moses** descending from Mount Sinai with the ten commandments. The flanks of the cross are also decorated. On the **north side** are Saints Anthony and Paul again, Christ's scourging at the pillar, and the **Hand of God** (under the arm of the cross) warning mankind. On the **south side** is the Flight of the Israelites from Egypt and also possibly Pontius Pilate washing his hands. All this is capped at the top as if under the roof of the church and surrounded with abstract or uninterpreted embellishment.

The West Cross

The **taller cross** (the West Cross) is made up of three separate stone sections, all of them much more worn. The east face shows **David** killing the lion, then **Abraham** ready to sacrifice his son Isaac, with the ram which became the last-minute substitute. Above this is the worship of the **golden calf**, with Moses coming down from the mount to catch his people red-handed in idolatry. The panel shows their trembling for forgiveness. The other three panels, before Christ seated in Heaven at the end of the world in the centre of the wheel, are hard to identify, though on the right arm of the wheel you can see the upside-down Satan being speared again by Saint Michael. The **west face** begins with the **Resurrection**, and the **Baptism of Christ** is shown on the second panel. The four three-figure panels before the wheel are once again difficult to identify, although the central figure looks a strong candidate for Christ. Once again the **Crucifixion** dominates the wheel, with Christ tied to the Cross by rope; the left arm shows him being blindfolded and ridiculed whilst the right arm has Judas's kiss of betrayal.

The Round Tower and two churches

Behind the West Cross stands possibly the tallest **round tower** in Ireland, 110 feet even without its conical peak. Round towers were adopted between the ninth and eleventh centuries by monks throughout the country as a defence against constant Viking attack. They needed no key stone that enemies could pull out for speedy demolition; their height created a perfect look-out post; and the entrance would be several feet from the ground, allowing a ladder to be drawn in when under attack. The only drawback was that if a lighted arrow were to pierce the inner floorboards the whole column would act as a chimney, guaranteeing a blazing inferno. Sadly you can't actually go into the tower, which has been closed for safety reasons.

Finally within the enclosure are two thirteenth-century **churches**, the north and the south church. They probably had no real connection with the monastic settlement, which had almost certainly ceased to function by then, and there's little of great interest within their ruined walls.

North to Dundalk

The main reason to head northwards into County Louth, apart from reaching the border, is to get to the mountains of the **Cooley Peninsula**. You have three routes to choose from. The main Drogheda to Belfast road, the N1, is the fastest, speeding directly towards the border and passing **Monasterboice** early on, but with little other reason to stop. An alternative inland route to take is to head towards COLLON, taking in **Mellifont Abbey**, and from there continue to Ardee and Louth town (for **St Mochta's House**) and ultimately on to Dundalk or into County Monaghan. Both these routes give excellent, unhindered cross-country views of County Louth, especially of the drumlins rising inland towards counties Cavan and Monaghan.

Termonfeckin

The third option, to take the bay road out of Drogheda and **follow the coast** north, is the most scenic, and the one to choose if you want to dawdle along the way or if you're cycling. In the early stages, there's little point diverting into BALTRAY: instead, carry straight on for **TERMONFECKIN**, a placid country village lying in a wooded dip half a mile from the shore. The village has a small tower house **castle** and a tenth-century **High Cross** in the graveyard of St Feckin's Church. The castle (keys from Patrick Duff in the bungalow across the cul-de-sac) dates basically from the fifteenth and sixteenth centuries and has as its most unusual feature a corbelled roof – notably less well-constructed than the 4000-year-older one at Newgrange. You can get good **food** here at *The Triple House* restaurant, whose Italian/French menu offers five courses for £9.95 before 7.30pm, £18 thereafter (four-course Sunday lunch £8.50 from 12.30 to 2.30pm, otherwise open 6.30–9.30pm except Mon; ☎041/22616). If you're neither hungry nor in a hurry to push ahead, then take a stroll into the reception area anyhow to see three highly individual computer-print collages by the Irish artist Robert Ballagh – *The Ambidextrous Paradigm*, *The Global Embrace* and *The Plough and the Stars*.

Clogherhead and Castlebellingham

CLOGHERHEAD is a far busier place, a bustling holiday village for the Irish, with plenty of bars aimed squarely at the holiday trade – their briny names, *The Lobster Inn* for example, give the game away. From here the road to **PORT ORIEL** takes you to **Clogher Head** (one mile) and a tiny fishing harbour tucked hard into the coast's rockface – good mackerel fishing off the pier in summer. It's only beyond here, as you approach **ANNAGASSAN**, that the signposts designating the scenic route begin to earn their keep, with the mountains of Cooley and Mourne, one range south of the border, the other north, spectacularly silhouetted against the sky. It's an enthrallingly unimpeded view of the best that lies ahead in counties Louth and Down. *The Glyde Inn* in Annagassan has food (of sorts) and is a nice reclusive spot to take time out for "a small drop of medicine". There's little else to see around the village, although local archaeological explorations are provoking controversy as they lay bare what is claimed to have been the first permanent Norse settlement in Ireland, predating even Dublin. Continuing north-wards across the hump-backed stone bridge, you've a watercolourist's idyll of rowing boats laid out along the bulging ramparts of the canalised river as it meets the sea.

Only a couple of miles further on, you'll rejoin the N1 at **CASTLEBELLINGHAM**. Despite the main Dublin–Belfast road blundering right through the middle, Castlebellingham remains one of the prettiest villages around (albeit in a consciously olde-worlde way). It's a strange clash of ancient and modern, from which you can take refuge down by the mill, now converted into a restaurant. This has a turning gable-end water wheel and a run of several man-made weirs on the river Glyde up the back through woodland alongside a sugary, castellated hotel (good two-course bar lunches £4; *Castle Special* four-course dinner £9); contrived, but pretty nevertheless. Moving northwards again the next significant turning off the N1 (right) takes you to **BLACKROCK** and later allows you to bypass most of Dundalk. Blackrock itself (the *Claremount Arms* has good Saturday night traditional sessions involving the uilleann pipes) is an over-stretched ribbon of Victorian seaside villas along a mudflat beach. It does, though, offer a handsomely crystalline view across **Dundalk Bay** and on to the Cooley Peninsula, by now looming really close.

Ardee and inland

The inland route is far less travelled, and there's less to see along it. Without transport of your own you'll have difficulty getting anywhere, unless you're prepared for some very leisurely hitching. Nonetheless it has its rewards, mostly in just this lack of traffic or population; a rural tranquillity unrivalled even in the west. Almost exactly halfway between Drogheda and Dundalk, **ARDEE** (*Baile Átha Fhirdhia* or Ferdia's Ford) recalls the tragic legendary duel between Cúchulain the defender of Ulster and his foster-brother Ferdia, a battle brought about through the trickery of Medb, Queen of Connacht*.

> Ferdia: *"Attack then if we must.*
> *Before sunset and nightfall*
> *I'll fight you at Bairche*
> *in bloody battle.*
> *Men of Ulster will cry out:*
> *'Death has seized you!'*
> *The terrible sight*
> *will pierce you through."*
>
> Cúchulainn: *"You have reached your doom,*
> *your hour is come*
> *My sword will slash*
> *and not softly.*
> *When we meet you will fall*
> *at a hero's hands.*
> *Never again*
> *will you lead men."*

These taunting jibes laid down the gauntlet for their fight to the death, in which eventually Ferdia was fatally wounded by the *gae bolga*, a weapon summoned from the *Tuatha Dé Danann*, God Lug, by Cúchulainn during the fight in the stream. Ardee is named after the ford where this great battle was fought.

Today, Ardee reeks far more strongly of the Plantation era, with fortified buildings along the main street and a memorial **statue** to a landlord erected by his thankful tenants in 1861. The thirteenth-century **castle** on the main street (key in the house on the right) is now used as a courthouse, and inside bears no intimation of its original purpose. It stands here mainly because the town was at the northern edge of the Pale, and from here the Anglo-Irish made forays into Ulster, or were themselves periodically forced onto the defensive.

An interesting short diversion from Ardee takes you to the so-called **Jumping Church** at KILDEMOCK. To get there head east from the junction at the southern end of Ardee's main street and turn right after about quarter of a mile – the small, ruined church lies a further mile down this road. It gets its name from its

---

*Although Medb (pronounced *Maeve*) is always referred to as queen, she was more likely a goddess of Tara. The duel is only one episode of Europe's earliest vernacular epic, the *Táin Bó Cuailnge* or Cattle Raid of Cooley, but makes a glorious thirty-eight pages of reading in Thomas Kinsella's translation, *The Táin*, published in Ireland by the Dolmen Press and well worth getting hold of.

end wall having shifted three feet from its foundations, which, according to local lore, it did to exclude the grave of an excommunicated person. Less romantic accounts tell of a severe storm taking place in 1715 at around the time the wall jumped, but either way it's a remarkable sight, with the wall shorn clear of its foundations yet still standing (albeit at a 35-degree angle). In the graveyard are simple, foot-high stone markers, some of the earliest graveslabs for the poor.

Louth village

Ardee is a major road junction, and moving on you could head northeast to Dundalk, northwest to Carrickmacross, or west to Kells. If you want to go on heading north, however, a more interesting route is along the minor roads to **LOUTH** village: keep on the left fork at the northern end of Ardee and take an immediate right towards TALLANSTOWN, where you'll need to turn right again for Louth. It's not much in itself (and certainly doesn't seem to deserve sharing a name with the county) but it does have one thing well worth seeing in **St Mochta's Church** – turn left towards Carrickmacross and immediately right onto the Inniskeen road.

According to legend the church was built in a night to give shelter to its founder, **Saint Mochta**, who died in 534. Originally part of a monastery, and dating probably from the late twelfth century, it has a high, vaulted roof, beautifully crafted, reached by a constricted stairway. In its early years it was plundered many times; these days they obviously feel safer, since the church is left open to any passing visitor. The fifteenth-century **Louth Abbey** is accessible through the graveyard back up the road, from where, if you look west, you'll notice a *motte* on the nearby hill.

Dundalk

DUNDALK you should avoid. It's a true border town in the wild west tradition – dead when not deadly. Starting life in legendary prehistory as a fort guarding a gap in the mountains to the north (*Dún Dealgan*, the Fortress of Dealga), it became in turn a Celtic, Norse, Anglo-Norman, Jacobean and finally Williamite stronghold. This hard tradition seems still to hang over the town, and it never seems a place where you – or for that matter the locals – can feel fully at ease.

Having said that, there are, as ever, some good **pubs**. *Mark's Bar* on Crowe Street is a sawdust on flagstone hide-out where the men have what looks like designer stubble but which here is probably for real: there are good traditional sessions every Thursday, Friday and Saturday. *McManus's* pub near the library in Seatown is self-described "simply a great pub" – there are old-fashioned snugs to drink in, excellent value soup and sandwiches, guitar folk music on a Sunday night and more bluesy stuff on Monday. *McArdles* on Anne Street hosts *Ceolteóirí* every Thursday night, or if rock is more to your taste, try the *Tara* on Park Street.

As far as sights go, the outstanding one is the nineteenth-century Neoclassical **Courthouse**, whose open Doric portico leads into an airy, classically proportioned interior. In the plaza outside, the Guardian Angel or motherland statue is unequivocally dedicated to "the martyrs in the cause of liberty who fought and died in the struggle against English Tyranny and foreign rule in Ireland" – a far cry from the monument of gratitude in Ardee. **St Patrick's Cathedral** in Francis Street is also worth a look while you're here: its cornucopia of embellished towers, turrets and crenellated walls is a reasonably successful imitation of King's College Chapel, Cambridge. Inside are some rich mosaics using gold pieces in abundance to depict biblical stories.

Eating well and cheaply is not a Dundalk speciality, but there are plenty of fast-food places around the centre of town which will do if you're starving. Slightly better fare can be had at the *Michael Rice Pub* on Clanbrassil Street (opposite the *Café de Paris*) or, more upmarket, at *Caspars* on the corner opposite the court-house (lunch £9, 12.30–2.30pm; dinner £17, 6–9.30pm; local bands play Wed, Thurs, Fri & Sun 9pm). **Bikes** can be hired at the *Cycle Centre*, opposite the shop-ping complex (£4 per day; £20 per week; 9am–6pm, open till 9pm Thurs & Fri; ☎042/37159). The regional **tourist information office**, which also hosts touring art exhibitions, is in the market square opposite the courthouse (June–Sept Mon–Fri 9am–6pm, Sat 10am–1pm & 2–6pm; Oct–May Mon–Fri 9.30am–1pm & 2–5.30pm; ☎042/35484); they can provide information on **B&Bs**, of which there are plenty should you need to stay.

Towards the border: Faughert

From Dundalk, **the border** lies just eight miles on up the N1, and Newry only five miles beyond that. Just a couple of miles out of Dundalk, though, is the turn-off for the Cooley peninsula. Opposite, a lesser road leads a short distance inland to **FAUGHERT**. A small place of little modern interest, Faughert nevertheless has several interesting associations worth mentioning as you pass. **Cúchulainn** was born at Castletown Hill on the edge of the plain of *Muirthemne*, which stretches away towards Armagh in the north, and in the legendary account he was sent a false offer of peace by Medb asking him to meet her at Faughert. Instead, fourteen of Medb's most skillful followers awaited him: fourteen javelins were hurled at him simultaneously but Cúchulainn guarded himself so that his skin, and even his armour, was untouched. Then he turned on them and killed every one of the "Fourteen at Focherd".

Faughert is also said to be the birthplace of **Saint Brigid**, Patroness of Ireland, whose four-armed rush-cross is so common on the walls of rural Irish house-holds. In the local churchyard you can see her holy well and pillar-stone, as well as the grave of **Edward Bruce**, who was defeated here in 1318 after being sent to Ireland by his brother (Robert the Bruce) to divert the English away from the Anglo-Scottish border. There is a stone nearby which in legend was used to decapitate him.

The Cooley Peninsula

You come to **Cooley** for the raw beauty of its mountains, to walk, and to experi-ence a life where the twentieth century intrudes only rarely. Indeed, when you get up among the bare hilltops the peninsula's links with legend seem at least as strong as its grip on modern reality. For above all this is country associated with the **Táin Bó Cuailgne**, and in the mountains many of the episodes of the great epic were played out. Its plot (set around the first century AD) concerns the Brown Bull of Cooley (*Donn Cuailgne*) which is coveted by Medb, Queen of Connacht, in her envy of her husband Ailill's White Bull (*Finnbenach*). In their efforts to capture the bull, Medb and Ailill, who come from the west, effectively declare war on the east in general, and Ulster in particular. All the men of Ulster

– save one, Cúchulainn – are struck by a curse which immobilises them through most of the tale, leaving our hero to face the might of Medb's troops alone. The action consists largely of his (often gory) feats, but the text is also rich in topography and place names, many of them still clearly identifiable.

A single road runs around the peninsula, leaving the N1 to trace the southern slopes of the Cooley mountains and then cutting across country to Greenore and Carlingford on the north shore. It is here, facing the Mountains of Mourne across **Carlingford Lough**, that the most beautiful scenes lie, with forested slopes plunging steeply toward the Lough. The southern slopes are gentler and lazier, making a far more sedate progress to the water's edge. Among the more extraordinary sights looking north over Carlingford Lough are the patrolling British Army helicopters: look at the map and you'll see what seems a fairly random dotted line dividing the water in two; look up and you'll see it traced out with uncanny precision in the air in front of you.

Before you reach any of this, however, only about a mile down the peninsula road, there's a short detour well worth taking. From the back of the *Ballymascanlon Hotel*, a footpath leads to the **Proleek Dolmen**, whose massive capstone balances with far more elegance than its 46 tons ought to allow. If you see smaller stones on top they're recent additions, flung there by visitors who hope to have a wish granted. On the path just before the dolmen, a Bronze Age wedge-shaped **gallery grave** can be seen: both of these monuments may become harder to visit if, as local rumour has it, they are incorporated into holes five and six of a new golf course.

Bases for hill walking: Omeath

Aside from being the more scenic, the peninsula's north shore is also the best place to base yourself for hill walking, and the easiest for finding food and a bed. In **OMEATH**, right up towards the border, there's an *An Óige* **hostel** a mile or so south of town, a few metres off the main road behind the *Ranch Pub and Restaurant* (open all year; £4.50; ☎042/75142). The youth hostel has two separate houses, one for lounging and eating, the other divided into dormitories with some basic washing facilities (no hot water or central heating as yet). As ever you can't officially check in before 5pm, but the sitting area is always open to drop off your stuff and shelter, if it's raining. At Omeath the Lough has narrowed dramatically, so that the sedate towns of WARRENPOINT and ROSTREVOR on the Mourne Mountain slopes across the border seem only a handshake away. In summer there's a handy passenger **ferry service**, which also takes bikes, between Omeath and Warrenpoint (July & Aug Mon–Sat 1–5pm, Sun 1–7pm; £1 return; 5min). Staying in the Republic, you can hire **jaunting cars** for short trips out of town; they run mostly to the open-air **stations of the cross** at the Rosminian Fathers' School down the road.

As a village, Omeath, with its widely scattered dwellings, is far from typical of the east coast – it was until recent years the last remaining *Gaeltacht* village of any significance in this part of the country. Around the crossroads which mark the centre of town are grouped a few **grocery stores** and **pubs**, the only facilities apart from the hostel that the place offers. One of Ireland's best young flautists, Des Wilkinson, lives in Omeath, so look out for his regular Friday-night sessions in one or other of the pubs. *Davey's Lounge*, a few miles up the road towards the border, is another pub worth checking out.

Carlingford

CARLINGFORD, a former fishing village five miles or so back down the Lough, makes a considerable contrast to Omeath, both for its neatly ordered network of narrow, whitewashed, terraced streets, often with naive murals, at the foot of the Sliabh Foye Mountain, and in its development as an upmarket resort. The latter has been remarkably successful, and the place retains real charm as well as some excellent places to eat and drink. There's an **oyster festival** here around the middle of August, though it's now over-run by lager-swilling bus tours from the North, and – one of the less brilliant ideas to encourage tourists – a **leprechaun hunt** for a prize of £500 (£10 entry fee) on Easter Monday.

Carlingford is also an historic place. Saint Patrick is said to have landed here briefly on his way to introduce Christianity to Ireland (he finally ended his journey further north, in County Down) and the settlement is ancient enough to have been raided by the Vikings. But the oldest visible remain is the D-shaped ruin of **King John's castle**, down by the main road on the water's edge. King John is said to have visited in 1210, and the Anglo-Norman castle, guarding the entrance to the Lough, may be even older than that. It has its counterpart across the Lough at Greencastle. The village in general retains a distinctly medieval feel, and there are a couple of solid fifteenth-century buildings: the **Mint**, in a narrow street off the square, is a fortified town house with an impressive gate tower; **Taaffe's Castle**, which stood on the shore when it was built but is now some way from it, is impressively crenellated and fortified but sadly not open to the public. The best and safest **beaches** in the area are at GYLES QUAY and SHELLING HILL.

Jordans pub-cum-bistro, in the first street above the main road, parallel to it, is probably the best of the places to **eat and drink** in Carlingford. They may try a little too hard – the menu includes such exotica as Louisiana alligator and Annalong (County Down) quail – but the food, especially the fish, is good and excellent value (dinner £11; gourmet dinner £16; lunch £4–6; open year-round 12.30–2.30pm and 7–10.30pm; you'll need to book, weekends especially, on ☎042/73223). There's a small room at the back of the pub which sometimes acts as a pre-dinner theatre. *O'Hare's* (aka *PJ's*), on the corner near the Mint, is an old grocery store and bar, and the most entertaining place to drink – its publican has a considerable local reputation as a raconteur of tall tales. They also serve pub grub, and oysters in season, which here seems to mean most of the year round. The *Village Hotel*, nearby in the Market Square, serves more substantial food (four-course lunch £9, 12.45–2.15pm; Innkeeper's special £12, 6.30–8pm). *Ghan House*, a fine Georgian mansion down near the crab-clawed pier, is yet another place where you can get a meal and a drop to drink.

If you want to **stay**, try *Viewpoint* on Omeath Road, whose modern, motel-like flatlets enjoy good views from a little way up the hill (B&B £14; ☎042/73149); the *Village Hotel*, Market Square (£24; ☎042/73116), for a little more luxury; or the *Carlingford Holiday Hostel*, Tholsel Street (☎042/73100; £4.90 in 6- or 8-bed room, £5.90 in 4-bed room; £7 in double room; £1 extra in July or Aug; meals available). This is part of the new **Carlingford Adventure Centre**, in converted warehouses around the Mint, where they also organise group tours and adventure holidays in the likes of canoeing, windsurfing and hill-walking: there may be something you can join in, or you can **hire bikes** (£8 a day), canoes and windsurfers (around £12 for 2 hours).

Legendary walks

You can walk almost anywhere in the mountains behind Carlingford and Omeath, and once you're up there the heather-tuffeted ground on top offers some of the most beautiful hill walking imaginable, stained with episodes from the *Táin Bó Culainge*. It's at its best in the afternoon, with the light bringing out the colours of the Mourne Mountains across the water – in the morning the sun tends to get in your eyes. The road up behind the youth hostel in Omeath offers the best approach, switchbacking its way into the hills with the climb ever increasing the drama of the fjord below. At about 1200 feet there's a car park where a map table marks out the major sights and there's a long spiel on the formation of the Lough: a valley gouged out by a glacier which was flooded at the end of the Ice Age.

With a little imagination, it's not hard to translate the gaps, boulders and fording points of rivers up here into the scenes of Cúchulainn's epic battles. And some of the places are clearly identified. From **Trumpet Hill** (*Ochaine*) he slew a hundred men of Medb's army with his sling on three successive nights as they rested in a plain to the west. This forced Ailill, fearing that his entire force would be destroyed, to offer up champions in single combat. Between Ochaine and the sea Cúchulainn slew the first of these warriors, **Nadcranntail**, by letting his spear fly high into the air so that it dropped down onto Nadcranntail's skull and pinned him to the ground. Then he sprang onto the rim of Nadcranntail's shield and struck his head off and then struck again through the neck right down to the navel so that he fell in four sections to the ground.

From **Slievenaglogh** (*Sliab Cuinciu*) Cúchulainn swore to hurl a sling stone at Medb's head – no easy task as she never moved without her army in front holding a barrel-shaped shelter of shields over their heads. Then one of Medb's bondmaids, Lochu, went to fetch water and, thinking it was Medb herself, he loosed two stones, killing her on the plain in the place known as *Réid Locha*, Lochu's level ground. In fact, when he had the chance, Cúchulainn couldn't bring himself to kill Medb. During the final battle a deliberately salacious episode is inserted when Medb suddenly gets a gush of blood that makes her need to urinate. Fergus, her chief warrior and lover, is furious at her bad timing and takes his place in the army of shields raised to protect her while she relieves herself, creating three great channels known as *Fual Medba*, Medb's foul place. Finding her in this delicate position, Cúchulainn was too honourable to kill her from behind (though he seems happy enough to kill everyone else whenever and wherever he can).

Fual Medba is not clearly identified, but you can find the scene of an earlier episode, the **Black Cauldron** (*Dubchoire*), where Medb divides her armies to search for the bull, which has last been seen here: it's a recess north of the Glenngat valley (the valley above Ballymackellet). When the spoils are brought back and the cattle have to be driven over the mountain at the source of the Big River (the River Cronn), Fergus decides that they will have to cut a gap in the hills to get the cattle. This is the *Bernas Bo Ulad*, today known as **Windy Gap**. It's also the point in the story where Fergus and Medb hang back behind the army to make love, and where Ailill, aware of their trysts, sent a spy to take Fergus's sword, thus acquiring proof of his unguarded weakness and the basis of a phallic joke which recurs throughout the story.

Windy Gap is also the setting of a far later tale, the tragic legend behind the **Long Woman's Grave**, marked by a pile of stones at the roadside. The story concerns two sons at their father's deathbed: the elder promised to give his younger brother a fair share of the estate, saying he would take him up to a high place in the mountains and give him all he could see. He kept his word, but the place where they stood was Windy Gap, where if you look around you see nothing but the immediate hills rising on all sides. The younger son instead became a trader, and on one trip wooed a Spanish beauty to whom he gave the same promise, tempting her hand in marriage. When he brought her home and took her up to the Windy Gap to show her his estate she dropped dead on the spot from shock. Thus the Long Woman's Grave for the tall Spanish beauty is explained.

INLAND: MEATH AND THE RIVER BOYNE

The River Boyne has a name resonant of Irish history, for it was on its banks that one of the battles which shaped the nation's destiny was fought. As you travel up the river, however, this is not what most occupies your attention. For in the early stages, following the N51 to Navan, is the area known as the **Brú Na Bóinne** complex, with some of Europe's finest prehistoric remains. The whole Boyne valley, in fact, has been heavily populated from the earliest times, and traces of virtually every period of Irish history can be found here.

Oldgrange: The Battle of the Boyne

For all the significance attached to it now – there are big Protestant celebrations in the North on July 12 – the **Battle of the Boyne** was just one skirmish, and arguably not the decisive one, in the "War of the Kings". It took place at OLDGRANGE, less than five miles from Drogheda, on July 1, 1690 (the change of date came with the switch to the Gregorian calendar in the eighteenth century). The deposed James II, retreating southwards, took up defensive positions on the south bank of the river, with some 25,000 men (including 7000 well-equipped French troops, but largely Irish irregulars) holding the last major line of defence on the road to Dublin. William's forces – around 36,000 – occupied a rise on the north bank from where they forced a crossing of the river and put their enemies to flight. In terms of losses, the battle was a minor one – some 1500 Jacobites and 500 of William's men – and James's forces were to regroup and fight on for another year. But in political terms it was highly significant and can legitimately be seen as a turning point. In the complexities of European struggle, the Protestant William was supported by the pope and the Catholic king of Spain, both fearful of the burgeoning power of James's ally, the French King Louis XIV. Although the victory on the battlefield was small, the news gave heart to William's supporters in Europe while making Louis fearful of extending further aid to the Jacobite cause. At the same time, it gave William a breathing space to establish his control back home: in the long run, Protestant ascendancy was assured.

The location of the battlefield is directly opposite the turn-off from the N51 to TULLYALLEN. Here a stepped path leads to a viewing point on the site occupied by William's troops before the battle. It's only a slight elevation, but it nevertheless commands a broad swath of the valley and it's not too hard to conjure up a picture of the armies battling it out in front of you. A panoramic plan marks out the various positions of the opposing forces.

Brú Na Bóinne

The area known as **Brú Na Bóinne** comprises a group of forty or so related prehistoric monuments caught within a curve of the river between Tullyallen and Slane. The three most important of them, Dowth, Knowth and Newgrange, are what is known as **passage graves** – high round mounds raised over stone burial chambers. They predate the pyramids by several centuries, and although there's no comparison in terms of size or architecture, there are certain parallels. Just as the fertility of the Nile helped create the great Egyptian culture, so the River Boyne and its watershed have been proved to have had some of the richest soil in Europe (and considerably higher temperatures than today) around 3000 BC. On the banks flourished what seems to have been the most advanced Neolithic civilisation in Europe. Physically, the tombs' size and solidity are what impress most. Beyond the massive, bare stones there's not much to be seen, but there's plenty of scope to try and disentangle the various theories about these structures, to work out who built them, where they came from and where they went.

Dowth

Dowth is the first of the great sites if you're heading upstream, reached by taking the first left off the N51 after the battlesite, a minor road which trails the north bank of the river. Just before you reach the cairn you'll see the tower of **Dowth Castle** on the left, adjoining a rambling red-brick Victorian mansion, now converted into a Buddhist centre. John Boyle O'Reilly, a Fenian patriot transported to Australia, who later became editor and part-owner of the *Boston Pilot*, was born in the castle in 1844. At the back of the neighbouring ruined church there's a monument to him that forms the heart of a small **commemorative festival** every year on the Sunday closest to August 10.

The **Dowth mound** itself – roughly fifty feet high and 200 feet in diameter – is not open to visitors, but you can wander about and see the outside. The signs of earlier excavations and of pillaging (in the nineteenth century, some of the stones were removed for road-making) are immediately apparent, having left a crater in the top of the mound and a large chunk burrowed out of the side. Around 100 **kerbstones**, perhaps half of which can be seen today, originally marked the edge of the tumulus. Inside are two **passage tombs** and an early Christian chamber. The passages are similar in construction to those at Newgrange (see below) as is the decoration of the standing stones which form the walls of the passage, and the ten-foot-high corbelled roof. One distinction between the two sites, however, are the **sill stones** placed across the passage floor and at the entrance to the chamber.

The name Dowth derives from the Irish for "darkness", and the main chamber faces west to the setting sun (the minor chamber looks southwest, directly towards Newgrange). In myth, the site was built when the Druid *Bresal*, attempting to build a tower that would reach heaven, contracted all the men of Erin for a single day. His sister worked a spell so that the sun would not set until the mound was built, but the two then committed incest, destroying the magic and causing the sun to set: thereafter the sister declared "Dubad (darkness) shall be the name of that place forever". Today, as the sun sets on the winter solstice, its rays enter the tomb (at about 3pm), lighting up the tall stone slab at the back and then moving across to illuminate a recess in which is a decorated stone precisely angled to catch this moment, before finally sinking below the horizon.

Newgrange

The second of the tombs, **Newgrange** (June to mid-Sept daily 10am–7pm; mid-March to May & mid-Sept to Oct daily 10am–1pm & 2–5pm; Nov to mid-March Tues–Sun 10am–1pm & 2–4.30pm; £1.50, children and students 60p, family and group reductions, heritage card; ☎041/24488), is far more visited, so much so in fact that long queues can build up at peak times. To get there follow the road directly on from Dowth and take a left at the T-junction. You're led around the monument in a guided tour about 25 minutes long (the closing times above are the *end* of the last tour), and if you want to avoid a long wait and a large group you should try not to come between noon and 4pm at peak times or especially on Sunday during the holidays. One or two of the most popular dates are booked up months in advance, above all the winter solstice when you've no chance at all of getting in to see the phenomenon described below (it is effectively reserved for local dignitaries). You may be lucky, though, if you come a couple of days before or after the solstice, when the effect is almost as good – cloud cover permitting. To book ahead, which is essential for large groups at any time, call the Newgrange office (☎041/24488), or write to The Director, Office of Public Works, National Parks and Monuments Branch, 51 St Stephen's Green, Dublin 2.

At the entrance to the site there's a **museum and interpretative centre** where aspects of Newgrange and other nearby prehistoric sites are more fully explored, and there's also a seasonal **tourist office** (April–Oct; ☎041/24274). In the farmhouse just down from the entrance is a welcome **coffee shop** (open Easter–Sept; ☎041/24119).

The site

The **Newgrange tumulus** has an average diameter of around 338 feet and is some thirty feet high at its centre point. It has been so completely restored that at first sight it reminds you of a grounded Fifties sci-fi flying saucer. But once you get over the initial shock, the sparklingly new appearance of it all serves only to heighten the wonder. The quartzite retaining wall is glisteningly white, and gives some hint (not revealed at other sites where everything is grey and moss-covered) of the power this particular stone must have had for the builders. The nearest natural source is in the Wicklow Mountains, south of Dublin. You'll notice that the wall is bossed with small, round granite stones, the purpose of which no one knows. Speculation is not helped by the fact that they are probably not in their original positions: during the most extensive of the renovations (1962–75) the original photographs were lost and their placement was therefore a matter of educated guess. Other non-original features worth noting are that the front and most ornate kerbstone was originally placed by the entrance tunnel (it was moved to prevent damage by visitors); that the entrance tunnel itself was closed by a standing slab; and that the concave wall at the entrance is designed to accommodate 100,000-odd tourists each year – originally the wall would have continued directly up to the sides of the spirally decorated kerbstone. It is also believed that an obelisk once stood at the top of the mound, to mark it out from afar.

The outer ring of **standing stones**, of which only twelve uprights now remain, was a feature unique among passage grave tombs, and it may have been the addition of a later civilisation. None of the standing stones is decorated, and many show signs of being eroded by water, which suggests that they may have been hauled up here from the river. There is an inner ring of 97 **kerbstones** all placed on their sides and touching each other, engineered one supposes as a support to the layers of sod, loose stones, shale and boulder clay (20,000 tons of it) that were laid over the chambers.

Perhaps the most important feature of Newgrange – again unique – is the **roof-box** several feet in from the tunnel mouth. This contains a slit through which, at the **winter solstice**, the light of the rising sun begins to penetrate as soon as its full disc appears above the horizon. The rays edge their way slowly up the passage tunnel and, narrowed into a single shaft, eventually find the back of the cruciform chamber. In minutes the chamber becomes radiant with a glow of orange light which fades as suddenly as it has blazed. The sun actually rises at about 8.20am above a hill known as the Red Mountain: it reaches the chamber a couple of minutes before 9am, and by 9.15 the whole thing is over. The guided tour includes a "recreation" of the phenomenon which involves a flash of orange electric light: if you prefer to rely on your imagination, keep your eyes shut through this performance.

The rest you'll be effectively guided through on the tour. The entry passage, about three feet wide, leads into the **central chamber** where the finest of the work is. Its corbelled roof creates a space some twenty feet high, and on the stones everywhere are carved superbly intricate decorations, apparently abstract but perhaps (see below) with some more precise meaning. On the way out, beware of the last roof-slab – on which most tall people will graze their heads even after this warning.

Myth and theory

The name Newgrange derives from "new granary", simply because that was its function at one stage in its history. This hardly seems an adequate description for one of the most important Stone Age sites in Europe, however, and an alternative derivation ("the Cave of Gráinne") is considerably more satisfying, if less accurate. The site has many **associations with myth**. First among these concern the *Tuatha Dé Danann*, the first Irish gods who descended from the sky and inhabited the land before the Celts. Dagda (the Irish Zeus, chief of the gods) gained possession of the mound by making love to Boand (the white cow goddess who later knowingly drowned herself at the source of the Boyne so as to invest the river with her divinity), first tricking her husband Elcmar by sending him on an errand for a day which took him nine months. From their union **Oengus** was born and called *ac ind Oc* (The Youthful Son). In ancient literature Newgrange is *Brugh Mac ind Oc*, the Brugh of Oengus. Oengus also appears later in the **Fenian Cycle** as the succourer of Diarmuid and Gráinne, carrying the fatally wounded body of Diarmuid to Newgrange "to put aerial life into him so that he will talk to me every day". Other legends make the local mounds the burial tombs of the Kings of Tara; radio-carbon dating (to the third millennium BC) however disproves this fairly convincingly.

What does emerge is just how little concrete information there is on the people who created Newgrange. Perhaps the most tempting of the more off-beat **theories** regarding the meaning of the monuments is that of the American Martin Brennan in his book *Stars and Stones* (Thames and Hudson, 1983). He claims that the scrollwork, lozenges and lines on the stones, which most archaeologists see as abstract decoration, perhaps with religious significance, are in fact all part of a single incredibly involved **astronomical chart** which includes not only Newgrange itself, but the rest of the Brú Na Bóinne complex and even sites as far-flung as Loughcrew (see pp.138–9), and those in the Curlew Mountains in south Sligo. In his book he claims that the scrollwork all relates to a calibration system based on the diameter of the earth. Brennan insists that the Newgrange monument is not only the largest but also the oldest such system in the world: predating and far outranking in sophistication the instruments of the Greek astronomers. It is not a theory you are likely to find espoused by your guide, but it does have its convincing aspects. In the end, though, you have to ask why, if they were so sophisticated, is this the only evidence that survives ?

Knowth

To reach **Knowth**, carry on west from Newgrange, take a sharp right and then left at the next junction, whereupon you'll see a makeshift wooden watchtower overlooking the site. Major excavations have been going on here since 1962, but recently about a third of the complex has been opened to the public (May–Oct 9.30am–6.30pm; £1, students 40p, heritage card). Though there's less to see for visitors, the discoveries at Knowth have already surpassed what was excavated at Newgrange, perhaps because the place lay undisturbed until modern times, and consequently archaeologists have been able to explore far more methodically than they have elsewhere. It's well worthwhile if you can find the time for a visit.

Several periods of occupation by different civilisations have been identified, from the original Neolithic passage tombs (3000–2000 BC), through occupation by the **Beaker** people (2000–1800 BC; so called because of a distinctive beaker left with each of their dead), a late **Celtic** settlement in the early centuries AD, early **Christian** occupation (eighth to twelfth centuries) and finally **Norman** usage (twelfth and thirteenth centuries) that brought an extensive settlement and a glut of *souterrains* (underground passages and chambers), some bored into the Neolithic mound itself. The main passage tomb is about twice the size of that at Newgrange – with a tunnel over 100 feet long leading to the central chamber – and even more richly decorated. At Knowth there is also, so far uniquely, a second, smaller passage tomb within the main tumulus, and up to twenty **satellite tumuli.** Both main tombs are aligned east–west. In construction the mound is basically the same as Newgrange, with a cruciform chamber, high corbelled roof and richly decorated stones, but here there is also evidence of settlement around the mound. Probably the two were created by two distinct communities of the same culture: a supposition backed by carbon dating that places the Knowth mound some 500 years earlier than Newgrange. At Knowth alone about 250 decorated stones have been found – over half of all known Irish passage grave art.

South of the Boyne: Donore and Duleek

Across the other side of the Boyne River at this point are two secondary diversions, Donore and Duleek. Unfortunately you can't simply pop across, as there's no river crossing between Drogheda and Slane, but either is easily reached from Drogheda itself, or they're a minor diversion if you're heading up the N2 from Dublin towards Slane. **DONORE**'s chief interest, apart from having been James's base at the time of the Battle of the Boyne, lies in its **ten pound castle**. In 1429 Henry VI promised a grant of £10 to every one of his subjects who, in the next ten years, built a castle twenty feet long, sixteen feet wide and forty feet high within the counties of Meath, Louth, Kildare and Dublin, the area known as the **Pale**. The three-storey castle here is built almost exactly to these measurements, though unfortunately it seems to be permanently locked up.

DULEEK (*An Damh Liag*, the stone church), on the river Nanny, is an historic little place of considerably more interest. The south of the Boyne equivalent of Kells, it was founded by Saint Patrick who settled Saint Cianán here to build the first stone church in Ireland and found a monastic settlement; it was also an early bishopric. Much later, the Jacobite forces withdrew to Duleek after the Battle of the Boyne and spent the night here, while James himself fled to Dublin and then on to France. The ruined **St Mary's Priory** you see today was probably founded in the twelfth century, and was abandoned after Henry VIII's dissolution of the monasteries: there are some fine tombs in the roofless building, and nearby a squat, tenth-century **High Cross**. In the town square is a **wayside cross** of a different nature, erected by Genet de Bathe in 1601 as a memorial to William, one of her husbands – one of the finest examples of a type of cross that crops up all over the place.

If you want to **stay** in this area there's good, reasonably priced accommodation and home-produced food at the historic house of *Annesbrook*, a short way out of town (follow the signs; B&B £17, dinner £14; May–Sept; contact Mrs Kate McElveen, ☎041/23293). William Thackeray in his *Irish Sketchbook* (1842) wrote uninspiringly about Annesbrook, but its most striking asset, the Ionic pedimented portico, has an interesting tale attached. The stately entrance is said to have been hastily affixed onto the box-shaped house when its owner was told to expect a visit from George IV, the first king to arrive from England after the departure of William and James. The portico was felt a necessary addition to bring the house up to the standards expected by royalty.

The Francis Ledwidge Museum

Continuing on the north side of the river, Slane is still less than nine miles from Drogheda, straight down the N51. If you're coming from Knowth, carry straight on and you'll emerge on the main road once again. A short way east of this junction, *The Tourists' Bar* is a handy stopover for tea and snacks; a short way west, just a mile out of Slane, you'll pass the **Francis Ledwidge Museum** (irregular guided tours in summer, Sat–Thurs, otherwise get the key from the small printing firm further down the road on the left-hand side). This stone-built labourer's cottage was the birthplace, in 1887, of the local poet Francis Ledwidge, who died on a battlefield in Flanders on July 31, 1917. Ledwidge was untypically pastoral for an Irish poet, and perhaps for this reason comparatively little known. Rather his poems were written on the small scale, and the museum reflects this: a modest, almost spartan, house with the poetry daintily hung in miniature picture frames. The lines inscribed on a stone plaque outside the cottage were written when Ledwidge heard of the death of his Irish poet friend Thomas MacDonagh, who was executed by the British for his involvement with the Easter Rising of 1916: it's an echo of MacDonagh's own poetic translation of Cathal Buidhe's *Mac Giolla Ghunna* (The Yellow Bittern).

> *He shall not hear the bittern cry*
> *In the wild sky, where he is lain,*
> *Nor voices of the sweeter birds*
> *Above the wailing of the rain*

There's a fine parallel to this in the modern poet Seamus Heaney's *In Memoriam Francis Ledwidge*:

> *I think of you in your Tommy's uniform,*
> *A haunted Catholic face, pallid and brave,*
> *Ghosting the trenches with a bloom of hawthorn*
> *Or silence cored from a Boyne passage-grave.*

Slane

SLANE itself, set on a steep hillside running down to the Boyne, is a beautiful little place which packs a surprising amount of interest. The scene is set at the village centre, where four three-storey eighteenth-century houses stand at the four corners of a crossroads, each virtually identical (with arched entrance courtyards to the side) and composed of a lovely, rough-cut, grey limestone. There's a good yarn about these, concerning the four spinster sisters said to have built them, which may be recounted to you locally. It's not true, but you can't help feeling it ought to be.

Down by the river, the Georgian theme is continued in the fine **Mill** (1766), across the road from which stands a large Gothic gate to Slane Castle, whose lands stretch out westward along the river. There's a **Transport Museum** (daily June–Sept) on the river bank as well, with around fifty cars on display.

Slane Castle, although it has a nightclub and expensive restaurant, is not generally open to the public. Approximately once a year, however, it does open its gates to half of young Ireland for massive, open-air rock concerts promoted by the entrepreneurial Lord Henry Mountcharles. There are also guided tours (mid-March to Oct, Sun only 2–6pm; £1.60, students £1; ☎041/24207 for information) of a small number of the more interesting rooms – including one used by U2 in the recording of *The Joshua Tree*. On Friday and Saturday nights the tiny castle **nightclub** opens up in the basement (£5; 10.30pm–2.30am; arrive early to get in). On a more traditional level, the castle is the seat of the **Conyngham Family**, a classically proportioned mass of mock battlements and turrets with a neo-Gothic library. The best architects of the day – Wyatt, Johnston and Gandon – were involved in the design, and the grounds were laid out by Capability Brown. Inside, there's a substantial art collection and many mementoes of King George IV, who is said to have spent the last years of his life involved in a heady liaison with the Marchioness Conyngham: some claim that this relationship accounts for the exceptionally fast, straight road between Slane and Dublin. Further out in the castle grounds, and again not for public consumption beyond a glimpse from the river towpath, is **St Erc's Hermitage**.

The Hill of Slane

Walking north from the crossroads, uphill, you can climb to the top of the **Hill of Slane**, where **Saint Patrick** lit his Paschal Fire in 433 AD, announcing the arrival of Christianity. This was in direct defiance of Laoghaire, High King of Tara, who had ordered no fire-making until Tara's own hillside was set alight. Fortunately for Saint Patrick, Laoghaire was promptly converted, welcoming the new religion throughout the country. The summit commands magnificent views of the whole Boyne valley. Near the top, the ruined **Friary Church** (1512) and separate college building are worth investigating. The church has a well preserved **tower**, with a very narrow and steep flight of sixty-odd steps: if you make it up you're rewarded with a broad panorama of the eastern counties, though Slane itself is all but hidden from view. In the graveyard there is a very unusual early Christian tomb with gable-shaped end-slabs. This is supposed to be the final resting place of **Saint Erc**, Patrick's greatest friend and servant whom he made Bishop of Slane. The **college** was built to house the four priests, four lay-brothers and four choristers there to serve the church; assorted pieces of carved stonework can be found if you mooch round its ruins.

Eating and sleeping in Slane

If you're looking for somewhere to **stay** in Slane, the best option is probably a newly converted Georgian house by the canal walk, tucked in behind the mill, which offers both B&B and basic hostel-type accommodation; there's accommodation also at the *Conyngham Arms Hotel* (☎041/24155; £24) and a couple of other B&Bs including Mrs Fortune's at 2 Castle Hill (☎041/24696; £12). The **restaurant** at Slane castle is extremely good but also very pricey; *Bartles*, in one of the historic houses at the crossroads is also relatively expensive; you'll find cheaper eats at the *Conyngham Arms* (pub lunches and evening meals) or at the *Roadhouse restaurant* a few miles from Slane out on the Dublin Road (going south take the right turn just before *McKeever's Esso Garage*). There's a good **swimming** spot on the Boyne below the weir, but check first with locals as the river currents can be strong in places.

Upstream to Navan

In its course upstream to Navan the **Boyne** runs past the grounds of several great houses. You can't visit any of them, but if you follow the river – a distance of some eight miles from Slane to Navan – you get a real sense of an all but vanished world. The old towpath switches sides from time to time, with no obvious means of crossing: the solution to this apparent mystery is that the horse would step onto the barge and be poled across to the other side. It is just about possible to walk all the way if you're prepared to crash out your own path some of the time, but it's a great deal easier to walk as far as you can from this end, then travel to Navan by road and do the same from the other end. After Slane Castle itself, on the opposite side of the river, comes **Beauparc House**, the mid-eighteenth-century home of Lord Mountcharles (B&B available if you can spare £150-odd a night).

A little further on you pass the remains of **Dunmoe Castle** (signposted off the N51, but accessible from there only by a nightmarish potholed lane) high on the northern bank. All that remains are two sides of a four-storey castle which was square in shape with large rounded turrets at the four corners. Inside you can still see parts of the vaulted ceilings of the lower storeys. Better than the crumbling structure, though, are the views it commands: in the river a diagonally dividing weir breaks the water into a stretch of rapids and another of calm, while on the opposite bank there's a delightful red-brick mansion with a stretch of garden steps worthy of Versailles breaking through the wooded thickets to reach the river. Finally, shortly before Navan and right by the side of the main road, you pass the **Domhnach Mór** (Great Church), site of a superbly preserved round tower above whose arched doorway is carved a relief figure of Christ.

Navan

At **NAVAN** the **River Blackwater** meets the Boyne. It's an historic crossroads –
important in the days when the waterways were the chief means of transport –
and also a modern one: the N3 comes up from Dublin to follow the course of the
Blackwater on into County Cavan, the route to Kells and to the Loughcrew
Mountains in the northwestern corner of Meath; the N51 arrives from Drogheda
to continue into Westmeath, its interest diminishing rapidly as you go; and to the
south you can continue to follow the Boyne, along minor roads, to Bective Abbey,
Tara and Trim.

Although it offers access to a lot of places, however, Navan itself has little to
detain you. There's a **tourist information office** housed in the local *Bank of
Ireland*, but it never seems to be open. You'll find a good cheap **lunch** at *Bon
Appetit*, centrally placed in the Market Square at the corner of Ludlow Street, and
there's a nice quiet **pub** nearby, the *Bermingham Bar* opposite the cinema on
Ludlow Street. *Peter Kavanagh's* on Trimgate Street is another good, old-
fashioned pub, or there are **traditional music** sessions every Wednesday in the
Lantern, Watergate Street. There are a couple of hotels here and a number of
fairly simple B&Bs not far away should you wish to **stay**, such as *Tower View*, on
the Slane Road at Donaghmore (☎046/23358; £11; see below).

Around Navan: Athlumney Castle

One local sight worth going out of your way for is **Athlumney Castle**, about a
mile's walk from the centre of town – head over the bridge then turn first right
following the signs. Just as you come up to the ruin, veer right into **Loreto
Convent** (once the castle's outbuildings) where you can pick up the keys. In the
convent grounds you should immediately spot the twelfth-century motte (now
surrounded by a ring of trees) that would have had a *Bretesche*, or wooden tower,
built on it. This was purely defensive, and the owner would actually have lived
closer to the river.

The castle you see now is a fifteenth-century tower house to which a Jacobean
manor house was added in the early seventeenth century. The **Tower House** has
four floors in excellent condition, the first of which has a secret chamber down
the stairs in the wall. The last occupant of the mansion was Sir Lancelot Dowdall,
a Catholic who on hearing of the defeat of James II decided to set his home alight
rather than see it fall into the hands of William's army. According to the story, he
crossed the river and stood all night watching it burn before heading into permanent exile. The interior shows large gaping fireplaces and a horseshoe stone-oven
on the bottom floor which would have been the area of the kitchens (the heat
from which would rise to warm up the living quarters above). It once had a
gabled roof within which the servants were housed and it still has many impressive mullioned windows left as well as a magnificent oriel window overlooking the
modern road.

If you head back to the bridge you can take the steps down to the **ramparts**
and then follow the canalside all the way to STACKALLEN, although a
certain amount of building work may disrupt your way to begin with. Just a mile or so
northeast of Navan on the Slane road, there's a fine hundred-foot round tower at
DONAGHMORE. This stands on an early Christian site, reputedly founded by
Saint Patrick.

The Blackwater: Kells and northeast Meath

Following the Blackwater upstream from Navan, Kells is the obvious place to make for, ten miles up the N3 Dublin–Cavan road. En route, you'll pass the site of the **Tailteann games*** (on the hill above Teltown House), a little over halfway. Here games and ancient assemblies sacred to the god **Lugh** took place in the first days of August (the Gaelic for the month of August is *Lúnasa*, or *Lughnasa*). As late as the twelfth century the games were still being recorded, and right up to the eighteenth century a smaller celebration took place, in which locals rode their horses across the river for the benefit of the sacred qualities of its waters. Christianity eventually put paid to most of the rituals, but there is still talk of what was known as the **Teltown marriages**, where young couples would join hands through a hole in a wooden door, live together for a year and a day, and then be free to part if they so wished. Today only a very few earthworks remain, and certainly if you have visited Tara, or intend doing so, there 's little to be gained in stopping here.

Kells

KELLS itself (*Ceanannus Mór*) is a place of history and monastical antiquities – several High Crosses, an eleventh-century oratory, a round tower and an ancient square bell tower – but it is most famous for what is not here, the magnificent illuminated manuscript known as the **Book of Kells**, now housed in Trinity College, Dublin. The monastery was founded by **Saint Columba** in the sixth century, and from about 807 it became the leading Columban monastery in Ireland, when the monks from the original foundation on Iona fled here from repeated Viking raids. It is probable that the Book of Kells was actually made on Iona, and that they brought it with them when they moved. The new home was little safer than the original one, and was attacked time and again by Danes and later the Normans: in the twelfth century the monastic order's headquarters moved on to Derry, and by the time of the Dissolution there was little left to abolish. So most of what you actually see is eighteenth-century or later, and although the town's layout still etches out the concentric ridges of the early monastery's plan, it's a surprisingly characterless place. Nonetheless, the little that survives is well worth making the effort to see.

When you arrive, head for the spire of the **bell tower** that stands within the grounds of the modern church where most of the relics are to be seen. In the church itself (if it's not open the key can be got from the gate-lodge outside working hours, otherwise search for the priest) there's a facsimile copy of the Book of Kells, and up in the gallery you'll find a small exhibition of blown-up photos of some of its pages. The **Round Tower** in the churchyard is known to have been here before 1076, for in that year Murchadh Mac Flainn, who was claiming the High Kingship, was murdered within the tower. It's a little under 100 feet high, with five windows near the top, and missing only its roof.

Near the tower is the **South High Cross**, the best and probably the oldest of the crosses in Kells, carved as ever with scenes from the Bible. Here you'll see,

---

*Old Irish literature not untypically begs to differ, and describes the place rather as a pagan cemetery named after the goddess *Tailtiu*.

on the south face, Adam and Eve and Cain and Abel; then the Three Children in the Fiery Furnace; then Daniel in the Lions' Den. On the left arm of the wheel Abraham is about to sacrifice Isaac, and on the right are saints Paul and Anthony in the desert; at the top is David with his harp and the miracle of the loaves and fishes. There are two other complete crosses in the churchyard, and the stem of a fourth (behind the church back-entrance door) with the inscription *Oroit do Artgal*, A Prayer for Artgal. This again has several identifiable panels. The near side shows the Baptism of Christ, the Marriage Feast at Cana, David with his harp again, the Presentation in the Temple, and others too worn to make out. On the other side are a self-conscious Adam and Eve, Noah's Ark, and others hard to identify with any accuracy. There are also sculptured stones embedded in the walls of the bell tower.

Saint Columba's Oratory can be found just outside the churchyard walls at the north end – coming out of the main gates take a sharp left uphill, but first obtain the keys from the chocolate-brown house just after the Stop sign. It's a beautifully preserved building – thick-walled and high-roofed – and peculiarly in character with the terrace of nineteenth-century workers' houses alongside which it stands. In outer appearance it is not unlike St Kevin's Kitchen at Glendalough. A modern entrance has been broken in at ground level, when originally the door would have been about eight feet off the ground in the west wall (reached, for security, by a removable ladder); you can still see the intended way in round to the left from where you enter now. Inside is a space about 23 by 21 feet, where you emerge into a vaulted room that would have once had two levels (with the present ground floor as a basement). Above were three tiny attic rooms, reached now by a metal ladder, which were probably where the residents slept and also a hideout in times of trouble.

In the central **Market Square** there's another fine **High Cross**, discoloured by traffic fumes, said to have been placed here by Jonathan Swift. In 1798 it served as the gallows from which local rebels were hung. Yet again, it is liberally festooned with fine stone carving. The base shows horsemen and animals in a battle scene; on the west face are the Adoration of the Magi, the Marriage at Cana and the Miracle of the Loaves and Fishes, all surrounding the Crucifixion in the centre of the wheel; on the east are Christ in the tomb, Goliath, Adam and Eve, and Cain and Abel, with Daniel in the Lions' Den occupying centre-stage.

Staying in Kells

If you want to stay, the **tourist information** office, opposite the *Bank of Ireland* on the Dublin Road, is the best place to start for information: if they're shut try Mrs Anna Sweeney's **B&B** (☎046/41510; £10) next to the *Headfort Arms* hotel (☎046/40063; £25) at the beginning of the Dublin Road. **Buses** pick up outside *O'Rourke's* lounge in Castle Street. You'll get very tasty **food** during the day at *Robins*, a café/lunch room at the bottom end of Market Street (closes 6pm), but in the evenings there's not much choice outside the pubs. *R. O'Loughlin's* on Farrell Street serves fine snacks, but otherwise good **pubs** are surprisingly scarce too. One that's definitely worth a visit, however, is the *Inishfree* on Church Street (running along the bottom of the church plot) which has Irish ballads and old time music on Friday, Saturday and Sunday nights at 9pm. The song *The Isle of Inishfree* was actually written there by Deek Farley, the former owner who was also once superintendent at Dublin Castle.

The Castlekeeran Crosses

From Kells the N3 follows the Blackwater northwest into County Cavan. A considerably more interesting route takes the Oldcastle road (the one that passes alongside the round tower) towards the Loughcrew Cairns (*Sliabh Na Caillighe*). Only a mile out of Kells a very worthwhile short detour takes you up a winding road to the right that leads, after about another mile, to the **Castlekeeran Crosses**. Entry is signposted through the yard of a creamy-orange farmhouse and across a field which will take you into the old monastery enclosure.

Hardly anything of the monastery that was known as **Díseart Chiaráin**, the Hermitage of Ciaran, has survived, although you can pick out a partially earth-covered arch. The High Crosses here, three of them plus a fourth in the middle of the river, are older than those at Monasterboice and Kells and far simpler. But their greatest charm lies in the fact that you'll probably be quite alone as you contemplate their history. The only decoration on the crosses are some simple fringing patterns and boss protruberances in the "armpits" and tops and wheel centres. The story of the cross in the River Blackwater tells how Saint Columba was caught red-handed by Saint Ciaran as he carried the cross off to his own monastery. In his shame he dropped the cross where he stood and fled back to Kells.

There is also an **Early Christian grave slab** in the graveyard, and a very good example of an **ogham stone**. Ogham was an early Irish script which was widely used from around the fourth to the seventh century AD, after which it was very gradually replaced by Latin script. Even at the height of its popularity ogham co-existed with Latin writing: it was used primarily on stones and monuments such as this, while Latin script was found in manuscripts. It is thought that the script was once used for secret communication, part of a signalling or gesture system for magical or cryptic purposes; it can also be found in parts of Devon, Wales and Scotland. As late as the nineteenth century some isolated peasant communities still used ogham script if they needed to write anything down – it had the advantage that no one from outside would be able to interpret it. On stones like this, the edge is used to help define the characters. Five strokes above the line give you five letters; five below another five letters. Five strokes that cross the line make five more letters and five oblique strokes five more: to these a few less obvious symbols are added to make up the alphabet. The inscription here apparently reads *covagni maqi mucoi luguni*, but although the letters can be made out nobody seems to know what these words actually mean.

Sliabh Na Caillighe

Sliabh Na Caillighe, the Mountain of the Sorceress (910 feet), is the highest part of the **Loughcrew Mountains**, whose two-mile east–west stretch virtually cuts off the furthest tip of County Meath. From the top there's a wonderfully disparate view, with the Cavan lakelands in one direction and the undulating flow of earthy Meath in the other, blending in the far distance into the mountains of Wicklow and Slieve Bloom. Three major groupings of **Neolithic cairns** were constructed on these summits, no doubt chosen to be seen from afar. The first group (coming from the east) is known as the **Patrickstown Cairns** and has been so thoroughly despoiled, largely for building material in the nineteenth century, that no significant trace remains. The other two summits have one major cairn each: **Cairn T**

on **Carnbane East** and **Cairn L on Carnbane West**. Each of these has a handful of satellite mounds, though these represent only a fraction of what must once
have been here. The sites are not easy to get to – you'll need transport and still
face a hefty walk at the end – but they are well worth the effort. Little known as
they are, the Loughcrew Cairns are almost as impressive as the Newgrange
mounds (certainly when you take into account the sheer number) and you'll
almost certainly be free to explore them entirely alone, and with as much time as
you want. Bring a torch if you want to appreciate what lies inside.

The Oldcastle road runs beneath the northern flank of the mountains, and
about four-and-a-half miles before Oldcastle you'll see a broken signpost pointing
off to the left, to *Sliabh Na Caillighe*. Follow this road for a mile and then take the
right turn (signposted) that clearly heads towards the hill complex. In the first
bungalow on the right you will be able to get the loan of **keys** from Basil Balfe
(buy a leaflet plan off him for 20p, and to be sure of finding someone in – or if you
want to be there for sunrise – ring ahead to arrange to pick up the keys, ☎049/
41256). These open the iron grilles on the few major cairns on top of the hills; the
minor ones have either been deroofed or are left open.

Carnbane West

Half a mile up the road – a steep climb – you'll come to a small clearing where a
stile leads into a field: this path heads to the **Carnbane West** grouping. On your
way across you'll notice **Cairn M** off to your left on a high peak – except for its
astronomical involvement with Cairn L this hasn't much of interest, and it's not
really worth the hike. **Cairn L**, with its wide ring of kerbstones, should be obvious to you immediately. It was most recently explored by Martin Brennan (in
1980; his theories about Newgrange have already been mentioned) after years of
relative neglect by archaeologists. It is his astronomical theories which are in part
set out below: they are far from being generally accepted, but in the absence of
other explorations they do at least attempt to answer some of the questions about
the sites.

Cairn L has an asymmetrical chamber (unique among the Loughcrew cairns)
with a white **standing stone**, over six feet high, positioned at the back right. It is
probable that the mound was built as a majestic housing for this one special
stone. According to Brennan its function is found in the rising sun on the cross-
quarter days November 8 and February 4 (the days halfway between the solstices
and the equinoxes). On these days a flash of light enters the tomb from the rising
sun (at about 7.40am) and catches the top of the standing stone. The lower edge
of the light is formed by the shadow of Cairn M, and other standing slabs in L
further shape it so that the ray marks out only the standing stone. If you have a
torch, then study the decorated slab by the basin to the left of the stone, facing
away from the entrance. There are many designs carved into the various stones,
but at the bottom of this one, according to Brennan, you can see a pictorial representation of this astronomical event.

Cairn H Brennan sees as a warning of the November cross-quarter day. The
rising sun begins to penetrate its chamber from mid-October onwards with the
backstone being touched come November and then from about the third
onwards the sun leaves Cairn H and moves on to cairns M and L for November 8.
Cairn F, with several examples of decorative grooves, kicks off another align-
ment series. The sun begins to enter in late April, ready to mark another cross-
quarter day on May 6, when the rays of the setting sun centre on **Cairn S**. Cairn

S is also aligned for the final cross-quarter day, August 8. By August 16 they enter F again, and from there move on to **Cairn I** to warn of the autumn equinox. If Brennan's theories are correct (critics tend to claim that if you look long enough, and pick enough times and days, you can prove almost anything this way), then cairns I, T, F and S form the longest such sequence of alignments known.

Carnbane East

To get to **Carnbane East**, return to the hill road and carry on until you reach a large car-parking space where a path leads up the hill to the mounds. If you lose the path, which is vague at times, just keep climbing steeply, steering left if there's any doubt: towards the top follow the barbed wire round and enter by the kissing gate which will put you on the threshold of Cairn T. At Carnbane East Brennan sees three mounds functioning as solar dials. **Cairn T** deals with the spring and autumn equinoxes (March 23 and Sept 22). In its cruciform chamber is a large backstone liberally patterned with chevrons, ferns, petals, and moon and sun signs. At the spring equinox a shaped patch of light passes across a passage stone and various of the other designs to focus on the large radial sun sign in the centre of this stone. On the autumn equinox the sun makes a more leisurely progress, rising at about 7.11am and strikes the backstone just over half an hour later. Once again it crosses the sunwheel emblem. Of the satellite mounds, neither of which have roofs any more, **Cairn S** is said to mark the cross-quarter days on May 6 and August 8, while **Cairn U** is synchronised with Cairn L to mark November 8 and February 4. Cairn S has lots of sun emblems, while Cairn U has a variety of more unusual (and less identifiable) markings. Whatever you make of Brennan's theories in the end, he has at least opened an important new area of exploration; and in the undeniable light of Newgrange's connection with the equinox there are few people any more who would contend that these structures were simply tombs and nothing more.

Oldcastle

OLDCASTLE is a mild-natured eighteenth-century town, built around a crossroads which no longer seems to have much significance. The clock-tower that marks the centre of town stopped long ago, and that seems to just about sum up the place. It has the feel of an outpost in a long-forgotten conflict. You can eat and sleep here – there's a **B&B** (☎049/41437; £10) out on the main road, below the cairns, a good **lunch** in the *Manor Arms Hotel* in the square, traditional music at weekends in the *Céilí House Bar* – but there's not much else to do.

In terms of interest you're better off heading on to CASTLEPOLLARD, ten miles south in County Westmeath (p.150), from where you can explore the Fore Valley, Tullynally Castle and the sights around Lough Derravaragh.

Further up the Boyne: southern Meath

The River Boyne flows into Navan from the south, and some nine miles in this direction **Trim** marks the last real glory, a medieval one this time, to stand on its banks. History and a magnificent castle aside, it's not a terribly exciting place, but it does make a good base from which to explore the southern half of the county, and in particular **Bective Abbey**, **Dunsany Castle** and the **Hill of Tara**.

Bective Abbey

Bective Abbey lies about halfway from Navan to Trim between the main road and the river. A beautiful example of medieval architecture, it is also set in flawlessly idyllic surroundings by an old bridge over the river. The Abbey was once a considerable power in the land, and its abbot held a peer's seat in the English Parliament – one of only fifteen granted to the whole of the Pale. At this time the church as a whole owned as much as a third of the county of Meath. The buildings you see date from a variety of different periods, sometimes bewilderingly so, but its basics are clearly identifiable.

Of the original abbey, founded in 1146 by **Murcha O Maelechlainn**, king of Meath, nothing at all survives. In the late twelfth century the abbey, the first daughter house of Mellifont, was completely rebuilt, perhaps in time to accept the disinterred body of **Hugh de Lacy** in 1195. By 1228 it was decided that Bective should sever its ties with Mellifont and go under direct rule from Clairvaux in France. Of this second abbey you can still see the **chapter house** with central column, part of the **west range** and fragments of the cruciform **church**. In the fifteenth century this church was shortened on the west side, its aisles were removed, new south and west ranges were built inside the lines of the old cloister, and a smaller cloister erected. Both the south and west alleys of this latest cloister remain. The **tower** at the entrance over the porch is in excellent shape, and you can also see the layout of the fortified mansion that was built after the abbey's dissolution in 1543.

Trim

TRIM can boast the remains of the largest Anglo-Norman castle in Ireland, ruins of various abbeys and a host of other medieval remains. Yet it remains surprisingly little visited, and somewhat downbeat in atmosphere. Nonetheless it's worth a visit, with plenty to see in and around the town.

The obvious place to start exploring is the **castle** itself, right in the centre of town and approached either from the riverside walk or via the gate at the end of a modern causeway off Castle Street. Inside you're free to wander at will, but there's also a guided tour which (at less than £1) makes a handy introduction to what you'll see. The first castle on the site was a motte-and-bailey construction put up by **Hugh de Lacy** in 1173 after he had been granted the lordship of Meath by Henry II. Within a year this was attacked by Roderick O'Conner, king of Connacht, and destroyed. A new castle was begun in the late 1190s, too late for Hugh de Lacy who, in the meantime, had had his head severed with an axe by an Irish labourer in Durrow. It was this second attempt that eventually grew to become the finest, and largest, Anglo-Norman castle seen in Ireland.

The new castle became known as **King John's Castle** after John spent a day or two in Trim in 1210 – though in fact he didn't even lodge there – but it has stronger associations with Richard II, who incarcerated his ward Prince Henry of Lancaster (later Henry IV) here for a time. In look and feel this is very much an English medieval castle, with a 486-yard **curtain wall** enclosing some three acres, ten D-shaped **towers**, various **sally gates** (small openings in the wall for surprise sorties) and, most impressive of all, a massive, square, seventy-foot-high **castle keep** with its walls running at a thickness of a solid eleven feet. The keep is named after Geoffrey de Joinville who, along with Walter de Lacy, was responsible for its construction in 1220–25. De Joinville spent many years on the Crusades (his brother Jean was the companion and biographer of Saint Louis, King of France) and finally became a monk in the Dominican "Black Friary" which he built at the northern end of Trim (and which is currently undergoing excavation). One unusual, and not altogether successful, feature of the keep was the addition of a side chamber on each face (three out of four survive): an experiment not repeated elsewhere as it greatly increased the number of places which could be attacked, and hence which had to be defended. Here, though, it hardly mattered given the solidity of the outer wall. Hardly anything is left inside the keep, but you can make out the outlines of two great halls and, above these, the main bedrooms. The entrance door was in the east tower on the second floor.

Outside, the curtain wall runs round only three sides of the keep – on the fourth, the deep-running river was relied on as adequate cover. As you walk around, take in especially the **Dublin gate**, with its well preserved barbican and two drawbridges, and the impressive section of the wall between here and the river, near the end of which is an underground chamber thought to have been used as a **mint** in the fifteenth century.

Across the river

On the opposite bank of the river from the keep stands **Talbot's Castle**, a beautiful, three-storey fortified manor house. It was built in 1425 by the Lord Lieutenant of Ireland, Sir John Talbot, on the site of an Augustinian Abbey; remains of the earlier building are incorporated into the lower floors of the castle. Queen Elizabeth I formulated a plan to convert it into Ireland's first university, but instead it was established as a Latin school whose most famous scholar was Arthur Wesley, later (having changed his name to Wellesley) the Duke of Wellington. Wellington entered Parliament as MP for Trim and, despite his contempt for his Irish roots, was responsible as Prime Minister for passing the Act of Catholic Emancipation.

Behind Talbot's Castle rises the **Yellow Steeple**, so called because of the glint of its stone in the sunset. This is the only surviving part of **St Mary's Abbey**, and its ruined state owes more to Cromwell's attack in 1642 than the ravages of time. The abbey itself once housed **"Our Lady of Trim"**, an object of pilgrimage for the miraculous cures it performed. The wooden statue was burnt in front of Commander Croot, Cromwell's general, as he lay recuperating from wounds received in the attack on Trim. An artist's impression of this lost treasure can be seen at the roadside by the junction of the Dublin Road and New Dublin Road. Near the Yellow Steeple, **Sheep Gate** is the only remaining piece of the fourteenth-century town walls.

Also on this side of the river, and easiest reached from Trim Castle by heading out of Dublin Gate, along the Dublin Road, and across the river by the sign, are the ruins of thirteenth-century **Newtown Cathedral** and its cemetery. The cathedral burned down over five hundred years ago, but its remains preserve a surprising amount that is worth seeing, especially in the cloister. The wall also acts as a soundpost to create a natural echo that is eerily brilliant in its clarity and closeness. In the cemetery, look out for the famous tomb of the **Jealous Man and Woman**, Sir Lucas Dillon and his wife Lady Jane Bathe. Their stone effigies are in Elizabethan costume and a sword rests between them. The rusty pins you'll see left in the stone tresses are thanksgiving offerings to the rainwater caught here that is reckoned to cure warts.

Taking the next left turn off the Dublin Road will take you to the **Crutched Friary** (key from the tourist information office), yet another fine medieval ruin. This was a base of the Knights of St John of Jerusalem after the Crusades, and takes its name from the invalided Crusaders who settled here. Next to it is a gorgeous old **Norman bridge**, reckoned to be the second oldest in Ireland (*Marcy Regan's*, at the other end of the bridge, similarly claims to be the **second oldest pub** in the land!). In the 1950s the film *Captain Lightfoot* used the bridge as a location, and its star, Rock Hudson, is said to have spent much of his time in the pub.

Practicalities

The **tourist office** (June–Sept) is in a temporary hut next to the castle – in the centre of town on Castle Street. For **B&B** try *Brogans* in High Street (☎046/31237; £12) or Ms O'Brien (☎046/31745; £11). More upmarket accommodation can be found at the *Station House* (☎046/25239; £28), six miles or so to the east in KILMESSAN, which is almost equidistant from Tara, Bective and Dunsany. If you're hungry, you can get excellent wholefood snacks from the *Salad Bowl Delicatessen* on Market Street, or more substantial **meals** at *Badges* restaurant on Emmett Street (left off Market Street, away from the river). **Pubs** are as plentiful as ever, but one you should definitely sample is *Marcy Regan's* (see above), a tiny, ancient place: remember not to order a pint for the pub is too old to cope with draught.

Around Trim

A couple of miles south of Trim is **LARACOR**, the place where Jonathan Swift lived during his association with Stella Johnson and where he was rector (with very little rectitude) from 1699 to 1714. No trace of him, however, remains. Two miles further is **Dangan Castle**, the family home of the Duke of Wellington, now no more than a shell and again with little trace of its past. Ambrosio O'Higgins, father of Bernardo O'Higgins, liberator of Chile, was born here.

Perhaps a more interesting excursion is to the Gaelic-speaking community at **RATHCAIRN**, near ATHBOY, eight miles northwest of Trim, where traditional Gaelic entertainment may well be taking place. The community was uprooted from Connemara by the Land Commission between 1935 and 1940, and replanted here in Meath as a *Gaeltacht*. The population is about 350 and increasing, a unique statistic as most Gaelic-speaking peoples in their natural habitats are rapidly decreasing in numbers. Not far away, in a field beside the Athboy–Navan road, is the **Rathmore Church and Cross** (*An Ráth Mhór Teampall agus Cros*). The church was built by the Plunkett family in the fifteenth century and is full of interesting stone carvings which are worth leaving the road to take a look at. There's an octagonal shaft from a baptismal font, a violated Norman sarcophagus in the fortified tower, a decorated altar stone, the stalk of an ancient cross and other stonework. Note the corbelled roof in the other tower, now trapped as a pigeon-cote.

Tara

TARA, the home of the High Kings of Ireland and source of so many of the great tales, looks nowadays like nothing so much as a neatly kept nine-hole golf course; a gently undulating swath of green marked out by archaeological plaques. To recreate the palace, whose wood-and-wattle structures have entirely disappeared, leaving only scars in the earth, takes a fair degree of imagination. But it's an effort worth making, for this was a great royal residence, already thriving before the Trojan Wars and still flourishing as late as the tenth century AD. The origins of the site are lost in pre-history, but it probably originally had a religious significance, gradually growing from the base of a local priest-king to become the seat of the High Kings. Its heyday came in the years following the reign of the legendary Cormac Mac Art* in the third century AD – when five great highways converged here – and by the time of the confrontation of Saint Patrick with King Laoghaire in the fifth century, its power was already declining. The title of High King was not, on the whole, a hereditary one: rather the kings were chosen, or won power on the battlefield. So they were not necessarily local – or even permanently based here – but all evoked the spirit of Tara as the basis of their power.

In later history, there was a minor battle at the site during the 1798 revolution, and in the mid-nineteenth century **Daniel O'Connell** held a mass meeting – said to have attracted as many as a million people (a quarter of Ireland's population today) – as part of his campaign against Union with Britain.

You'll find **the site** signposted just off the Dublin to Navan road, about 25 miles from Dublin. From the car park it appears as a wild meadow on a table-top hill, no more than 300ft above the surrounding countryside (just beside the car park is the *Banquet Hall Café*, open daily 9.30am–6/7pm). There is a plan of the place near the entrance, which will help you to identify the various mounds. Once on top of what is actually very rich pasture, the power of the setting immediately becomes clear, with endless views that take in whole counties and their patchwork fields, and a huge sky.

The Banquet Hall

Teach Miodhchuarta – the Banquet Hall – is on the northern hill slope and consists of two parallel banks between which runs a long sunken corridor. Its length is about 750 feet and the breadth ninety feet. An account of it in the medieval book known as the *Dinnshenchas* reads:

> *The ruins of this house are situated thus: the lower part to the north and the higher part to the south; and walls are raised about it to the east and to the west. The northern side of it is enclosed and small; the lie of it is north and south. It is in the form of a long house, with twelve doors upon it, or fourteen, seven to the west, and seven to the east. It is said that it was here the* Feis Teamhrach *was held, which seems true; because as many men would fit in it as would form the choice part of the men of Ireland. And this was the great house of a thousand soldiers.*

The *Feis Teamhrach* was the great **Feast of Samhain** (a harvest fair if you like, but more probably Hallowe'en) and it's easy to imagine the five ancient highways thronged with people on their way to crowd the hall for the great *Feis* – bards,

---

*One of the more frequently recounted stories concerning Cormac is about his death. After years of heroism he died, the victim of a druid's curse, in a singularly unheroic manner, choking on a salmon bone (the salmon being the Celtic symbol of wisdom). The curse had been laid after he began proclaiming his belief in a new God who would soon be arriving in Ireland (a belief borne out by the arrival of Saint Patrick). In defiance of the king's stated wishes, his body was taken to be buried at Newgrange; when the funeral procession reached the Boyne, however, the tides came to the king's defence, and in the end his body had to be laid to rest on the south side of the river, at Ros Na Rí.

athletes, poets, princes, musicians, druids. The twelfth-century *Book of Leinster* and the fifteenth-century *Book of Lecan* enumerate the various grades of society in attendance and even the particular foods appropriate to each carouser (from ribs of beef for the nobility to pig shoulders for the musicians). Both medieval books also display ground plans and agree on the building being divided into five aisles with a central open space for scores of servants and cauldrons. Seán Ó Ríordáin, who excavated the site in the late 1950s, surmised that the roof timbers would have rested on the two side banks and that lengths of upright support posts would have created the aisles.

Gráinne's Fort and the Sloping Trenches

Northwest of the hall is a smaller group of earthworks, the first of which is **Ráth Gráinne** (Gráinne's Fort). It is surrounded by a fosse and bank and has a low mound at its centre, probably once a burial mound or maybe even a house site. From here the tragic love tale of the *Pursuit of Diarmuid and Gráinne* began its journey. Gráinne was the daughter of Cormac Mac Art, who had arranged to marry her to his aged commander-in-chief, Finn Mac Cool. Instead she fell in love with Diarmuid, one of Mac Cool's young warriors, and the two of them fled together, relentlessly pursued by Finn Mac Cool. Their various hiding places lie strewn throughout Ireland, marking practically every geological oddity in the country.

Further west lie the **Claoin-Fhearta**, or Sloping Trenches, created, according to the legend, when Cormac Mac Art as a youth in disguise corrected the judgements of the then king, Lugaid MacCon. (Mac Art was also something of an Irish Solomon figure.) The consequence of his justice was that half the house where the false judgements had been given slipped down the hill, creating the sloping trenches. The southern part of the trenches witnessed the murder of the princesses of Tara, some thirty of them in a massacre whose total casualties were said to have been 3000, by Dúnlaing, King of Leinster, in 222 AD.

The major mounds

South of the Banquet Hall lies the main group of mounds, and first of all the **Rath of the Synods**. This is so called because of the various church synods said to have been held here by saints Patrick, Brendan, Ruadhan and Adamnan, although little archaeological evidence has been found relating to this function. Two gold torques (flat strips of gold soldered and twisted together rope-like into a necklace) were found here in 1810. Much of the rath, however, which appears to have originally been a ring fort defended by three concentric banks, has been destroyed over the years: partly by the graveyard which encroaches on it, but more especially by a group of British Israelites who earlier this century rooted around trying to find the Ark of the Covenant. More serious archaeologists have discovered four stages in the rath's construction: in the centre was a flat-topped mound known locally as the **King's Chair**. There were timber palisades on the banks, and in the middle a house where five burnt bodies were found, along with Roman artefacts which suggest trading links between Tara and the Romans in Britain or Gaul.

The **Mound of the Hostages** (*Dumha na nGiall*) is the most prominent of the mounds and also the most ancient. It contained a passage grave to which entrance is now barred, though you can look in to see the markings on the upright slab at the threshold. About forty Bronze Age cremated burials were found inside, many in large urns which were then inverted over the remains. Eating vessels and knives were found with them, and an elaborate necklace of amber, jet, bronze and faience round the neck of a fifteen-year-old boy, the only body not cremated. A wealth of goods from the passage grave culture (carbon dated 2000 BC) were also discovered, making it the most comprehensive find rescued from any tumulus in Ireland. The mound, once again, is associated with Cormac Mac Art: here he is said to have imprisoned hostages taken from Connacht, who subsequently died within the chamber.

The **Ráth na Ríogh** (Royal Enclosure), immediately to the south, is a large area surrounded by a bank and ditch, within which are two earthworks, the **Forradh** (Royal Seat) and **Teach Cormaic** (Cormac's House). Both, though they're not contemporary, are typical ring forts, with a central raised area for a rectangular house – Cormac's has two protective fosses and banks, the Royal Seat only one. In the centre of Cormac's House are a grotesque, lichen-scabbed **statue of Saint Patrick**, entirely inappropriate to the site, and the **Lia Fáil** (Stone of Destiny), a standing stone moved from elsewhere on the site and re-erected here in memory of those who died in 1798. It is marked with a cross and the letters RIP. According to one tradition this stone was the original Jacob's Pillow, brought to Ireland by the Milesians from the Island of Fal. It is also said to be the stone used in the inauguration of the High Kings, which would roar three times to signify its approval of the coronation.

The final remaining Rath on the site is named after High King Laoghaire, who made the historic meeting with Patrick when he lit his challenging fire on the Hill of Slane.

Dunsany

Dunsany Castle is only a few miles south of Tara, just outside the village of DUNSANY. If you want to visit you'll need to arrange it beforehand, either with the tourist office in Trim (which will know about forthcoming planned tours) or well in advance at any other tourist office. This is still a private residence, owned by the Plunkett family (under the title Lord Dunsany) who have lived here since the sixteenth century. The Lord Dunsany who died in 1957 established an unlikely dual reputation as an author; he wrote witty sketches of London club-land, and also bizarre dream-fantasy tales that influenced such American writers as H.P. Lovecraft. It's worth going to the trouble of arranging a visit, for this is one of the finest, most thriving examples of an Irish castle you're likely to see, and packed with a wealth of art.

The castle was originally built in the twelfth century by Hugh de Lacy, another of his fortresses defending the Anglo-Norman possessions around Dublin. It has been much altered and added to since, but it's still a magnificent building, with grounds to match. Among the family relics kept here – and quite apart from the superb private art collection, and the furniture, that you'll see on the tour – are the ring and other reminders of Patrick Sarsfield, second-in-command of the Jacobite forces in Ireland and successful defender of Limerick for over a year, and possessions and a portrait of Saint Oliver Plunkett, who was hanged in London for treason (his offence: being Catholic). The Dunsanys, in fact, seem to have made a habit of being on the wrong side in Ireland's conflicts, and it's remarkable that they have held on here so long.

Neighbouring **Kilkeen Castle** belonged to another branch of the Plunkett family (when the estate was divided, the boundaries were supposedly set by a race; the wives of the inheritors ran from their castles, and the border was set where they met) and during the long years of Catholic suppression it was kept in trust for them by the (converted) Protestant Dunsanys.

In the grounds of Dunsany castle there's a fifteenth-century **church**, built by and for the family on the site of a still older one – again, you'll need permission to visit. There are some fine family tombs in here and, above all, a beautiful carved fifteenth-century font, with representations of the Twelve Apostles and the Crucifixion.

WESTMEATH AND LONGFORD

As you head west, leaving the Boyne Valley behind, historical interest diminishes rapidly. The attraction of Westmeath lies mainly in its lakes, although in the northeast, around **Castlepollard**, there is an area which deserves more exploration. **Athlone**, in the far west, is an important meeting of the ways near the very heart of Ireland, and a centre for Shannon cruising, but again it preserves little interest in itself. Longford, if you visit at all, you'll see only briefly as you pass through on your way to the northwest coast.

The main route into the counties is the N4, which follows the Royal Canal, and the border of counties Meath and Kildare, out from Dublin to **Mullingar** and then **Longford Town**. As the road enters Westmeath the N6 turns off, to cut across the south of the county to Athlone. If you're coming from Meath, roads from Navan and from Kells converge at DELVIN, to run on together towards Mullingar. Or if you're up by Oldcastle in northwestern Meath, you can cut directly across the border to the most interesting part of Westmeath, the Fore Valley and Castlepollard.

Cooksborough

Heading for Mullingar, though, the only thing that might tempt you to stop on any of the roads is **COOKSBOROUGH**, a hamlet of a few houses strung together about eight miles from Mullingar on the Delvin road. What you're looking for is a tomb in the shape of a beehive in the graveyard. Neither Cooksborough nor the tomb is signposted but you can find it by looking out for the sign to the *Bee Hive Nite Club*: about thirty yards past this, in the direction of Delvin, enter by an old gate and cross the field to a church and graveyard smothered in bramble, weed and grass. The tomb, which looks like a stone missile warhead poking out of its silo, is that of **Adolphus Cooke** and his nurse Mary Kelly. A famous local eccentric, Cooke was convinced that he would be reincarnated as a bee and he was making sure he was prepared for the event. During his life he was similarly convinced that one of the turkeys scratching around in his yard was his father reincarnated. He also had the windows of his house made into the shape of spoon-backed chairs, in order to reflect the furniture within. There's more information on Adolphus Cooke in the Market Hall Museum in Mullingar.

Mullingar

MULLINGAR, the chief town of Westmeath, is a raucous, wheeling-and-dealing provincial capital that pretty much sums up the things you don't come to Ireland for. The centre of a rich cattle-rearing area, its inhabitants are rural but the speed and noise of everything is continually wound up by its being a big trading centre on a short lead from Dublin. The first ever **Fleá Cheoil** (Festival of Music) was held in Mullingar in the late 1960s, but it fell so far short of local expectations that the town has never asked for it back. In short, you're unlikely to fall in love at first sight with Mullingar, but with perseverance you should be able to find a few positive moments before moving on – and there are a couple of good museums.

The first of these, on the corner of the main street at the turnoff to Tullamore, is the **Market Hall Museum** (May–Sept Mon–Sat 11.30am–1pm & 2–5pm; 50p). Run by local enthusiasts, it doesn't have any one item of outstanding interest (and if it had, it would no doubt be whipped off to the Dublin Museum), but it does have a modest charm in the peculiar wealth of local items on display. There's also the usual quota of Iron Age implements, quernstones and weaponry, together with a potted history of the celebrated local eccentric, Adolphus Cooke (see above).

A second museum is attached to Mullingar's **Cathedral**, an uninspiring Neoclassical structure whose tapering twin towers (which look like melting candles) you'll be able to spot in the south of town. Inside, behind the side altars of St Patrick and St Anne, are two well-known mosaics by the Russian artist Boris Anrep. To get into the **Ecclesiastical Museum** – whose contents include many wooden penal crosses and the vestments of Saint Oliver Plunkett – ask for the key at the parochial house, on the right.

The Military Museum

Best of all, however, is the **Military Museum** (Mon–Fri 9am–4.30pm; ☎044/48391; free) at the Columb Barracks; going southward, turn right after the bridge over the canal, then swing left and it's 200 yards up on the left, easily walkable. The collection, in the **Old Guard Room**, has a surprisingly broad range of interest. There's all the weaponry you'd expect, of course, with plenty of World War I and II firearms, and uniforms and flags from all over the world. But more intriguing are the sections devoted to the **old IRA**, with various local bands' uniforms and the tunic of Dan Hogan, Chief of Staff after 1929, who was shot by the FBI in 1941. There's also the uniform of Giles Vandeleur whose role in World War II was portrayed by Michael Caine in the film *A Bridge too Far* and a pistol said to be that of **Michael Collins**, who was Chief of Staff throughout the War of Independence and the Civil War – though it's well-known that Collins rarely carried a weapon.

More miscellaneous items on display include long, canoe-like boats of bog-blackened oak, that were dredged up from the surrounding lakelands. These were first thought to be of Viking origin, but carbon dating has placed them well into the first millennium AD. Similar boats are still being dredged up today, especially in Lough Derravaragh, but are as quickly being wrapped up again in peat and resunk in the middle of the lake. One of the stranger curios is the **military cycling handbook** that was in use until at least 1964. The book instructs the young cadet as to where to put his left foot and where his right and, with even more disciplinary stringency, orders him not to twist the handlebars without the officer's permission. All of this is arranged (or not arranged) amid a fair degree of chaos, though there's usually someone to show you around and attempt to make sense of it all.

Practicalities

If you want to **stay** in Mullingar, there are plenty of places to choose from: a good **B&B** is *Hilltop* (☎044/48958; £12), a mile or so out on the Delvin road; or you can **camp** at the *Lough Ennel Caravan and Camping Park* (£6 per person and tent; ☎044/48101), three miles out on the Tullamore Road. Good **food** is served in the *Greville Arms* on central Pearse Street (where they also offer slightly more luxurious accommodation; ☎044/48563; £26); a wax effigy of James Joyce stands in the foyer, a reminder of a mention of Mullingar somewhere in *Stephen Hero*.

Southern Westmeath: Lough Ennel and Belvedere House

South of Mullingar there's just one significant attraction, **Lough Ennel**. With its low-lying, rushy shoreline it's not an especially dramatic expanse of water, but it is an easy place to go bathing, boating or fishing, especially if you base yourself at the holiday camp, immediately outside Mullingar. If you do stay here, it's well worth making the short trip to **Belvedere House and Gardens** (April–Sept Mon–Fri noon–8pm, Sat & Sun noon–6.30pm; Oct–March Mon–Thurs noon–6pm; £1), also off the Tullamore road just before the turning to the campsite. You're not meant to cut across the fields from the campsite – the way lies across private land – but it does save a lot of walking.

The house was built by **Lord Belfield**, the first Earl of Belvedere, in 1740, and conceived by him as a fishing villa. Much of Belfield's life seems to have been spent feuding with his younger brothers, George and Arthur. In 1736 he married a sixteen-year-old bride, Mary Molesworth, daughter of the third Viscount Molesworth. Within a few years of building Belvedere House he accused her of having an affair with Arthur, and virtually imprisoned her for thirty-one years at another of his houses. She was eventually released by her son on his father's death in 1774, still protesting her innocence. Meanwhile Arthur had fled to Yorkshire but when he returned to Ireland in 1759 the Earl sued him for adultery and Arthur, unable to pay, spent the rest of his life in jail. An argument with his other brother was responsible for one of the first sights you'll come across in the gardens south of the house, the **Jealous Wall**. This folly is said to be Ireland's largest purpose-built ruin, and was built to block the view of Tudenham House, where George lived, from the Earl's own home. Considerable expense went into the construction, including the employment of an Italian architect to design the authentic-looking Gothic facade.

The interior of the **house** is still in the process of renovation, a job which short-age of funds looks certain to make a long one. However, the **rococo plasterwork** of the drawing and dining room ceilings is well worth ducking inside to snatch a look at for a few moments, as is the curved balustrade staircase in the entrance recess. Otherwise, the **gardens** are the main attraction. In front of the house three terraces run down to the lake's shore, and behind woodland stretches along the northeast shore of Lough Ennell. There's also the aforementioned Jealous Wall to see, and a **walled garden**, **gazebo**, **ice house** and **stables**. In the last of these is a **coffee shop** where you can stop for refreshments.

Northeast Westmeath

A good portion of the interest of Westmeath lies in the northeast, around the Fore Valley, Lough Lene and Lough Derravaragh. Certainly this is the most beautiful part of the county by some way. It's easily approached from Meath, from the area of Oldcastle and the Loughcrew Cairns, or from Mullingar. Coming from Mullingar you'll pass through **CROOKEDWOOD**, near the scenic lower end of **Lough Derravaragh**, set among steep wooded hills that stand out immediately in such flat country. There are two main attractions here, a **restaurant** which is far better than you would normally hope to find in such an obscure location (*Crookedwood House*; dinner Tues–Sat 7.30–10pm, Sun lunch 12.30–2.30pm; ☎044/72165), and **St Munna's Church**. This beautifully restored fifteenth-century tower-fortified church lies a mile and a half up the road which turns off to the right by the pub; fifty yards before is a butterscotch-coloured bungalow on the left belonging to Seamus O'Simon, who has the key. From the church you can spot a motte on the hill slope, behind which is the Georgian house whose rustic cellar contains the restaurant already mentioned.

THE CHILDREN OF LIR

You'll find continually throughout Ireland that physically atmospheric places are the setting for ancient tales or myths, and Lough Derravaragh is no exception. In this case the legend is that of the **Children of Lir** (*oidheadh cloinne Lir*), one of the most tragic of all Irish fables.

Lir had married the daughter of Bodb Derg, king of Connacht. Her name was Aebh and she bore him twins, Fionula and Aodh, and then two more children, Fiachra and Conn. Aebh died and Lir then married her sister, Aoife, who very quickly became jealous of Lir's love for her sister's children. She took them to Lough Derravaragh, and with the help of a druid changed them into swans, condemned to spend 300 years on Derravaragh, another 300 years on the Sea of Moyle, the waters between Ireland and Scotland, and a final 300 on Inis Glóire off Erris Head, County Mayo. In a last minute pang of remorse she granted them one mercy, that they could have human voices and make the most beautiful music for all humans to hear. When Lir learned of what had happened, in a rage he changed Aoife into an ugly grey vulture. Meanwhile the sons of Bodb Derg, Fergus and Aed, set out to search for the Children of Lir with a host of the Tuátha Dé Danann. They eventually found them suffering on the Sea of Moyle, but were helpless to save them from the spell. Left to their destiny the children flew towards Inis Glóire, stopping on the way to search for their father's palace on the plains of Armagh, but finding that only earth mounds remained as they were now 600 years on in their own lives. At the end of the allotted span they died, finally returning to a very aged human form for their last few breaths, and were buried at the onset of the Christian era on Inis Glóire.

Castlepollard and Tullynally Castle

Towards the northern end of Lough Derravaragh, **CASTLEPOLLARD** is the most convenient base from which to explore the whole area, handily placed right in the middle of all the attractions. It's not the most exciting of villages, but it is picturesque, with a vast triangular green surrounded by carefully tended eighteenth- and nineteenth-century dwellings. Many of the visitors are here for the fishing, and consequently there are a number of **B&Bs**, of which the *Castlepollard Arms* is probably the most attractive.

The biggest draw in the immediate vicinity is **Tullynally Castle** (35-min tours mid-July to mid-Aug, daily 2.30–5.30pm; £2 for castle tour, £1 entry to gardens alone; check for possible off-season tours on ☎044/61159), whose entrance can be found a half mile from Castlepollard down the road to GRANARD (alongside the gable of the *Derravaragh Inn*). From the gatehouse a drive leads across another half mile of rolling parkland, very English-looking, to the castle itself. The home of ten generations of the Anglo-Irish Pakenham family – the Earls of Longford – it's one of the largest and most romantic of castles in Ireland, a vast conglomeration of architectural styles (largely Gothic revival) with four towers and a long stretch of battlements.

Three hundred years ago the castle was no more than a tower house set amidst the ancient oakwoods which grow around Lough Derravaragh. The park was first laid out, very much along the lines you see today, in 1760 by the first Earl Longford. His wife founded the family **library** of over 8000 volumes, which will be one room on your tour. Their son returned from the French wars to greatly expand the castle to the Gothic designs of **Francis Johnston**, whose work crops up throughout Ireland. The second earl's other claim to fame is to have refused his daughter Kitty's hand in marriage to the young man later to become the Duke of Wellington – they eventually married regardless. One of Kitty's brothers, Edward, fought as Commander-in-Chief of the British Army in America in 1814, and died leading his troops in the attack on New Orleans. His body was sent home pickled in a barrel of rum. In 1840 the third earl added a further 600 feet of battlements, a servants hall for forty, and an immense **Victorian kitchen** which will also make up part of your tour. Later Pakenhams have been less militarily inclined than their forebears: one, Charles Pakenham, forsook the army in the nineteenth century to found the Irish Passionist order of monks; and the present Lord Longford is well known in Britain for his liberal writings and involvement in prison reform.

In the grounds in front of the castle, a **Garden Walk** leads to a spacious demesne on the left, and the flower garden, River Sham pond and walled gardens off to the right. Passing further to the right, between two stone sphinxes, is the **kitchen garden**, one of the largest in the country and still resplendent with its row of Irish yews. Slightly further afield, the most rewarding walk of all is a forest path which takes you around the perimeter of the spearhead-shaped demesne; with excellent views back onto the castle.

The Fore Valley

East of Castlepollard towards the Meath border, the **Fore Valley** is an area of exceptional natural beauty. It's easy hiking country with a wealth of small-scale interest, especially in the **Seven Wonders of Fore**. There are moves afoot to convert these into some kind of tourist trail; so far, however, there are few visitors, and the local tradition, strengthened by an early Christian legacy in stone, still seems close to the surface. The wonders are all based on ordinary things which you can find in the valley, and in this perhaps lies the lasting strength of their reputation. They are: the water that will not boil; the wood that will not burn; the monastery built on a quaking sod; the mill without a race; the miraculous emplacement of the lintel stone above the door of St Fechin's Church; the water that flows uphill; and the Anchorite's Cell in the Greville-Nugent family vault.

The village of **FORE** sits at the eastern end of the valley, and this is the best place to start, discovering the wonders as you walk west. There's a tiny ancient cross on the tiny village green, once part of a stations of the cross pattern, and a couple of pubs which are worth visiting. You'll need to pop into the *Seven Wonders* anyway, to pick up the key for the Anchorite's Cell: the *Abbey* next door has seven old murals depicting the wonders, worth contemplating over a pint. There's usually plenty of ready advice in here for anyone planning to head down the valley.

The Seven Wonders

On the valley plain you'll immediately spot the ruined Benedictine Priory built on reclaimed bogland (the third wonder), and en route to it you'll pass the first two. The **wood that will not burn** consists of a dead branch of a tree, landscaped into a viewing spot as part of the creation of the tourist trail (from the picture in the *Abbey* pub you'll remember it looking more lively than this); the idea of piercing its bark with coins is also a recent invention. The **well of unboilable water** is handily close by.

The **Priory** itself was founded by the De Lacys around 1200, and its remains are the most substantial reminder of the Benedictine order left in Ireland. It was fortified in the fifteenth century; the towers also served as living quarters. There's a plan in the cloister of the various periods' additions, and some subtly sensitive restoration has been undertaken so that although it's very much a ruin, there's a strong monastic feel to the walls and halls. If you intend to ascend the **tower** at the chancel end, beware that its spiral staircase seems to wind around the diameter of a dinner plate and above all that the steps finish in mid air; it should certainly not be attempted in poor light.

On the far hillside from here, the lower of the two buildings is the tenth-century **St Fechin's church**, which marks the site of the original monastery founded in 630 by Saint Fechin himself. At one time there were over 300 monks here. Notice the rare Greek cross on the massive **lintel stone** (which weighs over two tons and was only moved by the miraculous intervention of the saint, hence wonder five), resting on two boulder-sized jambs. Within the ruin is a very weatherbeaten font to your left, a cross slab pinned next to the wall in the chancel at the far end (the chancel was a thirteenth-century addition), and a few other stone slabs, the engravings on which are not clear. From here a ridged path takes you up to the tiny, fortified church known as the **Anchorite's Cell** (wonder seven), decoratively hugged by a low-lying, castellated perimeter wall. The most famous hermit to have lived here was Patrick Beaglan, who broke his neck trying to climb out of the window in 1616, thereby fulfilling his vow to stay in the cell till his death. The Romanesque doorway leads into a barrel-vaulted, sandstone interior.

The **water that flows uphill** (wonder six) refers to another of Saint Fechin's miracles; and the river flowing out of Lough Lene up at the head of the valley does indeed look as if it's flowing upwards. The **mill without a race** (wonder four) is not so easy to trace.

West to Athlone – the Heart of Ireland

As you head west from Mullingar towards Athlone on the R390, you're approaching the middle of Ireland, a spot traditionally identified as the **Hill of Uisneach**. About a mile before KILLARE (ten miles or so from Mullingar) there are two signposts pointing off the road up to the hill. Follow the second, more westerly one, climb the hill steeply, veering a little to the left, and after crossing a few fields you'll come to the **Catstone** (so-called because it resembles the poise of a pouncing cat). More historically known as the *Ail na Mearainn* (the Stone of Divisions), it's a massive boulder (now fragmented a little) set into a circular indentation of the hillside. The stone was said to mark the very **centre of Ireland** and the division of the five provinces of old. A further and longer walk up the slope will bring you to the summit of a flat-topped hill, barely 250 feet above the neighbouring land yet able, on a clear day, to command a view of parts of twenty of the thirty-two counties of Ireland.

Here, it is recorded, stood the palace of **King Tuathal Techtmar** in the second century AD, and here some claim that the High Kings of Ireland ruled for the two centuries preceding the arrival of Saint Patrick in 433 AD, when the seat moved back to Tara. On the hill there are two spurs with traces of earthworks, but these are neither easy to find nor to make out if you do, so it's probably easier to accept the history without evidence. Excavations were made here in the late 1920s, but came up with surprisingly little. No pottery was found, nor any significant trace of permanent occupation. Instead there were great **beds of ashes** which suggested that the place was used for elaborate feasts and ceremonials rather than for defence or peaceful habitation. This accords with the tales of the great pagan festival of *Bealtaine* (Bel's Fire), that was said to be held here in the opening days of the month of May, when vast fires were lit and cattle sacrificed. It was both a religious festival and a market, where traders from the Mediterranean would arrive with their silks and spices in exchange for Irish tools and materials. *Bealtaine*, incidentally, is now the Gaelic word for the month of May.

As you continue towards Athlone, look out for the tenth-century **Twyford Cross** on a hillside to the left about four miles before you arrive. It was re-erected here after being found sunk in a bog.

Athlone

The Hill of Uisneach may be the traditional centre of Ireland, but **ATHLONE** is a more convincing modern contender. Here, east meets west and north meets south at the mid-point of the Shannon River. This position is its greatest asset, with access by boat upstream to the islands and shores of **Lough Ree**, and downstream to the magnificent Early Christian site of **Clonmacnoise**. Either of these trips can easily be done in an afternoon: contact *Avon Ree* boats on the Strand (daily 2.30pm and 4pm for Lough Ree; less frequently to Clonmacnoise), or *Aloha Cruisers*, 5 Retreat Heights (☎0902/92849): or ask for details of other trips at the **tourist information** (April–Nov Mon–Sat 10am–1pm & 2–6pm; ☎0902/94630) at the foot of the castle in Market Square. Boats of all sizes can be hired locally, too. Much good rod **fishing** can also be done in Athlone, just past the weir, where you'll often see a line of anglers – hire rod and reel from the *Strand Tackle Shop* in the Strand (£2 a day). **Bike hire** from *Hardiman's*, 48 Connaught Street (☎0902/78669).

ATHLONE

To Mullingar

To Longford

G.A.A.

BALLYMAHON ROAD

LOVE LANE

Sports Complex

RETREAT ROAD

To Dublin

DUBLIN ROAD

BRIDESWELL STREET

CASTLEMAINE STREET

G.A.A. Park

ST MARY'S PLACE

S. COSTELLO STREET

UPPER IRISHTOWN

SOUTHERN STATION ROAD

BEECH PARK

C.I.E. Bus Depot and Railway Station

Old Wall of Athlone

The Bawn

GRIFFITH ST.

WOLFE TONE

Burgess Park

Fishing Spot

Hospital

Abbey Ruins

St Mary's (C.I.)

CHURCH STREET

Boats to Clonmacnoise & Lough Ree

THE STRAND

Weir

NORTHGATE STREET

ABBEY ROAD

Cinema

BRIDGE

Castle & Museum

Docks

Lock Gates

FRY PLACE

River Shannon

RIVER WALK

Library

St Peter & Paul's Church (R.C.)

Post Office

Garda Barracks

BARRACK ST.

PEARSE ST.

Temporary Tourist Office

MARKET PLACE

CASTLE STREET

MAIN ST.

CONNOLY ST.

HIGH STREET

ABBEY LANE

O'CONNELL ST.

To bathing place

To Galway & Roscommon

200 m

If you plan to stay in Athlone, there's good value **B&B** at the *Villa St John* (Roscommon Road; ☎0902/92490; £11), or try *Bogganfin House* (Roscommon Road; ☎0902/94255; £11) or *Cluain Inis* (Galway Road; ☎0902/94202; £11). Your best bet for reasonable and **cheap eating** is the *Gate Restaurant* on Northgate Street (open from breakfast till 9.30pm), and there's a Chinese restaurant a little further down that serves good-value lunches and is open very late. On Lloyd's Lane, leading off Church Street down to the Strand, is a takeaway kebab place and there's good lunchtime bar food at the *Anchor Bar*. This apart, the best pub is probably *Sean's Bar*, tucked in behind the castle and easily identified by its four Ionic columns. It has popular **traditional music** sessions on a Tuesday (pipes and violin), Thursday (violins) and Sunday. You'll find both the **post office** and a **launderette** on Pearse Street.

Athlone in legend and history

Not surprisingly, perhaps, given its position, Athlone has quite a history attached, and at least one important legend. The name *Áth Luain*, the **Ford of Luan**, came from (or may perhaps have inspired) the **Snám Dá Én** (Swim of Two Birds), a tale that tells of Estiu, wife of Nár. She had a lover called Buide who used to come and visit her in the form of a bird with his foster-brother Luan. The magic of their song lulled all around to sleep, allowing the lovers to enjoy their trysts undisturbed. Nár, however, questioned a druid about the coming of the birds and on learning the secret he set out for the place on the Shannon (near Clonmacnoise) where Buide and Luan could be found and shot both of them with one cast of his sling. Buide was killed instantly, but Luan managed to fly as far north as the ford that marks Athlone today, where he dropped dead from the sky. An alternative derivation of the name comes from the *Táin*, which describes how the remains of the white bull (*Finnbennach*) were deposited throughout the countryside as he died. His loins were left at a place that came to be known as *Áth Luain*, the Ford of the Loins.

In straight historical terms, this ford of the Shannon has always been strategically important. The first castle was erected in 1129 by Toirrdelbach Ua Conchobair, king of Connacht, and replaced in 1210 by the **Norman castle** which, in essence, still stands today. It saw action many times, above all in the seventeenth century in the Cromwellian Wars and the Jacobite invasion. The former put a swift end to the predominantly Catholic nature of the town, placing most of the land and political power in the hands of Protestants. The later battles of 1690–91 saw probably the most vicious fighting in the **War of the Kings**, as the Williamites captured first the Leinster part of town and, after 12,000 cannon-balls had reduced much of it to rubble, the Connacht side. In some ways Athlone has still to recover.

Athlone today

The few really distinguished old buildings that survive (the castle apart) can be found off Church Street in the **Court Devenish** area. Finest of them is **Court Devenish House**, a seventeenth-century Jacobean mansion now resting ruined in private grounds. Nearby the ruins of the **Abbey** (also seventeenth-century) offer perhaps the most peaceful spot in town. There's an intriguing corridor of tombstones leading off the Abbey Road into its graveyard.

The one place really worth visiting, if only briefly, is the **museum** in the **castle** by Market Square (June–Sept 11.30am–1pm & 3–6pm; £1), housed in the two storeys of the circular keep. On the upper storey is a section devoted to **Folk History**, an Aladdin's cave of rustic implements used in threshing, seeding, rope-making, harnessing, milking and the like. There's a beautiful article on milking, telling how a few squirts were always dropped first on the grass for the fairies and at the end the sign of the cross made on the teat to bless its consumption. You'll also come across a pair of pony boots that were used when rolling the lawn, to prevent any hoof marks.

Downstairs is a more regular collection on local history, and the ever-present Stone, Bronze and Iron Age finds. There are two **Sheila na Gig** sculptures, nude female figures generally represented face on with their legs splayed and hands placed behind the thighs, the fingers opening the vulva. The sculptures were thought to be either the symbol of a fertility cult or used to ward off the evil eye, though quite how they managed the latter is not explained. Most appear in the walls (usually near the main entrance door) of castles, and occasionally churches, built between 1200 and 1600. To a lesser extent they are also found in round towers and on standing stones, bridges etc. They are also known in other parts of the British Isles, and even France, but the majority of them by far are in Ireland.

On a quite different level there's an old 78rpm **gramophone** on which you can request your choice of the recordings of **John McCormack**. McCormack (1884–1945) was a native of Athlone and arguably one of the best lyric tenors the world has ever heard. The gramophone was McCormack's own, travelling all over the world with him so that he could use it to test out the quality of his new releases. He is said to have been born in the Bawn area, the old market quarter up behind Devenish Gate Street, and in 1928 he was rewarded for his work for Catholic charities by being made a Count of the Papal Court. The one song that even the youngest generations in Ireland are able to associate with his voice is his *Panis Angelicus* – the record may be among the pile. Before you leave, look out for an Early Christian grave slab with carvings as beautifully ornate as any high cross that you're likely to have seen.

Lough Ree

If you're taking a trip out to Lough Ree, the islands to ask for are **Inchclearaun** (although this may better be approached from a more northerly point on the lake) and **Inchbofin**. Both islands, especially Inchclearaun, have churches and Early Christian graveslabs. Inchclearaun (Inis Clothrand) took its name from Clothru, who was murdered by her sister Medb so that she could bed and wed Clothru's husband Ailill and rule Connacht from the island. Medb, goddess of war and fertility, is the most famous of all the legendary and historical characters and a source of continual argument as to which branch of study (legend or history) she truly belongs when Clothru's son Furbaide hurled a piece of cheese from his sling that entered Medb's forehead and struck her dead whilst she was bathing, thus avenging the murder of his mother.

North into Longford: Goldsmith Country

The N55 rushes north from Athlone into **Goldsmith Country**, so called after its geographical associations with the works of the eighteenth-century poet, playwright and novelist, Oliver Goldsmith. It's pretty enough countryside, gently rolling and ready-made for cycling through landscaped villages and along aromatic hedge-lined lanes that run off the N55 down to various small boating points on Lough Ree (Killinure, Kileenmore, Muckanagh). But it helps to keep Goldsmith's verse in mind if you really want to appreciate it. **GLASSAN** village – "the village of the roses" or "sweet auburn" of Goldsmith's *The Deserted Village* – is untypical with its orderly layout of creamy-grey pebbledash cottages, but has a good village inn and restaurant. **TUBERCLARE**, a mile up the road, offers one of the better panoramic views towards the east of the county. A little further (exactly eight miles from Ballymahon) is the site of the "never failing brook, the busy mill", nowadays no more than a bubbling rivulet, but still easy to identify. The original millstone is now said to be the lintel-stone at the *Three Jolly Pigeons* pub, a quarter of a mile up the road, where the school once stood.

Goldsmith Country seeps into **County Longford** through Ballymahon (where his mother lived) and across to PALLAS (near Abbeyshrule) where he was born. **BALLYMAHON** is a pretty dull village, but it's probably the best place to stay to explore this part of northern Lough Ree and Goldsmith Country. There's **B&B** at *Burd's* (☎0902/32294; £8, dinner £7); you can hire a bike very cheaply (£2 per day) at the cycle shop near the bridge; and there's even something which describes itself as a nightclub.

On the road from dull NEWTOWNCASHEL to BARLEY HARBOUR on Lough Ree you'll pass the workshop of the bogwood sculptor Michael Casey, whose raw material is timber many thousands of years old. The wood is dug out of the bog and left for a few years to dry out. On the road from Newtowncashel to Lanesborough stands **Rakish Paddy's Pub**, worth a visit above all on a Tuesday night for its traditional session: look in for a drink anytime, though, and you can see the three superb modern metal sculptures (by John Mahan) of a seated fiddler, boy and girl dancers, and a wooden-flute player obviously playing the well known reel called Rakish Paddy. **LANESBOROUGH** itself, at the head of Lough Ree, is another place to stop off for the boating or fishing (the last bungalow before the bridge has boats for hire) but for no other reason.

Longford Town and around

Inland, County Longford doesn't improve, and as far as tourism goes the county is a desert. Still, you might enjoy trying to prove us wrong. Along with large parts of southern Sligo and Leitrim, Longford has been hard hit by very recent emigration, leaving even the grandest looking houses and mansions deserted by the roadsides. However, if yours is an endlessly indulgent holiday and you have rapid transport of your own, then there are a few things you can catch on your way through. **LONGFORD** itself is a market town that has little to offer beyond convenience as a base: there are plenty of places to **stay**, including the *Longford Arms* on Main Street (☎043/46296; £19; good food too) and numerous B&Bs, especially on Dublin Road (such as Mrs O'Donnell's; ☎043/46898; £12.50). There's a **tourist office** open during the summer (☎043/46566) for local information, and if you've time to spare an **ecclesiastical museum** in nineteenth-century St Mel's Cathedral (Mon & Wed 11am–1pm, Sat 1–3pm, Sun 4–6pm). **Bicycle hire** is also available from the *Central Cycle Stores*, Sallymount Street (☎043/46345).

Carrigglas Manor

Chief of the surrounding attractions is **Carrigglas Manor** (June–Sept Mon, Tues & Fri noon–5pm, until 6pm in Aug, 40-min tours on the half-hour beginning 1.30pm; Sun 2–6pm, tours 2.30, 3.30 & 4.30pm; £1.50; B&B available at an indulgent £40, dinner £17.50). Situated just three miles out of Longford on the Ballinalee road, it's the seat of the descendants of the the Huguenot Lefroys. As you go up the avenue, the stables with their classically pedimented and rusticated archways (designed by James Gandon of O'Connell Bridge and Dublin Custom House repute) are on the left. They now house a **costume museum** and tearoom. The yard and buildings are being restored at the moment but you're free to wander around it and the parkland, within the hours listed above. The costumes in the museum date mainly from the mid-eighteenth century, and were found mouldering in trunks left behind at the castle. The castle's architecture is perhaps best described as Tudor-Gothic Revival, and extremely handsome it is too. It was built in 1837 by Chief Justice Thomas Lefroy, possibly the model for Darcy in *Pride and Prejudice*, as at one stage he enjoyed a romantic liaison with Jane Austen.

The **tour** of the building is directed by the present Lefroys who are attempting to restore the place to its former majesty. It should take in the Dining Room, with its set of 1825 Waterford glasses and original ironstone china; the Drawing Room with its Dutch furniture, one cabinet of which contains an original tea and break- fast set of 1799; a fastidiously well stocked Library; and family portraiture on virtu- ally every wall. All this is explained and expanded on in detail by the present occupier.

Granard and Edgeworthstown

Continuing on this same road you'll reach **GRANARD**, about fifteen miles from Longford. A famous **harp festival**, originating in 1784, took place here and was revived in 1981. Nowadays it spreads over the second weekend of August, start- ing on the Friday afternoon with competitions, street entertainment, *seisiúns* and *ceilidhs*. Lessons on the harp can be arranged on the spot and usually start on the Friday morning. Two **campsites** are set up for visitors, or you can stay (bed only) at *Finton Floods* on Market Street (behind the library). The biggest Norman **motte** in Ireland is sited at Granard, with yet another statue of Saint Patrick on top. The site is said to date back to 5 AD, and to Cairbre, eldest son of Niall of the Nine Hostages.

Finally, it's worth noting a couple of Longford's other literary connections, centred on MOSTRIM or **EDGEWORTHSTOWN**. It takes the latter name from Maria Edgeworth, one of 22 children of a local luminary, who in her day was an extremely famous author (*Castle Rackrent* is perhaps her best-known work) and said to have influenced both Sir Walter Scott and Turgenev. The family vault can be seen in the graveyard of St John's church, on the road out to Mullingar, and Oscar Wilde's sister Isola is also buried here. One of his most touching poems, *Requiescat*, was written in her memory:

> *Tread lightly, she is near*
> *Under the snow,*
> *Speak gently, she can hear*
> *The daisies grow.*
>
> *All her bright golden hair*
> *Tarnished with rust,*
> *She that was young and fair*
> *Fallen to dust.*

Lily-like, white as snow,
She hardly knew
She was a woman, so
Sweetly she grew.

Coffin-board, heavy stone,
Lie on her breast,
I vex my heart alone,
She is at rest.

Peace, peace, she cannot hear
Lyre or sonnet,
All my life's buried here,
Heap earth upon it.

travel details

Trains
From Athlone to Westport (3 daily; 2hr); Galway (1hr 10min); Dublin Heuston Stn (8 daily; 1hr 45min); **from Mullingar** to Sligo (4 daily; 2hr); Dublin Connolly (4 daily; 1hr 25min); **from Longford** to Sligo (3 daily; 1hr 20min); Dublin Connolly (4 daily; 2hr 10min).

Bus Éireann
From Athlone to Dublin (6 daily; 2hr 45min); **from Mullingar** to Dublin (2 daily; 1hr 30min); **from Longford** to Dublin (3 daily; 2hr 10min).

Private Buses
North Galway Club: Galway–Dublin service calls at Athlone. See Galway chapter "Travel Details".
Funtrek: Sligo–Dublin bus calls at Longford. See Sligo chapter "Travel Details".

CHAPTER FIVE

WEXFORD, CARLOW AND KILKENNY

f you are in the southeast at all, the chances are you've come to Ireland via Rosslare; it's not the most obvious of areas to visit, especially if this is your first time in the country. There are none of the wild wastes of rock, bog, and water, nor the accompanying abandoned cottages of famine, eviction and emigration that are so appealing to current romantic tastes. It is, however, Ireland's sunniest and driest corner, and what the region does have to offer – whether you're spending a couple of days passing through, or if you simply haven't the time for more distant wanderings – is worth savouring. On the whole the region's attractions are frustratingly widely scattered, but its medieval and Anglo-Norman history is richly concentrated in the ancient city of **Kilkenny** – the region's only heavily touristed town – and the lush countryside roundabout shelters some powerful medieval ruins. **Wexford** town's conviviality makes up for its disappointingly scant traces of a rigorous Viking and Norman past; **Carlow** town, sadly doesn't. While the extreme east is dull and low-lying, and the Blackstairs Mountains open and empty, overall the southeast is characterised by a quality of rich cultivation, as much to do with its history as its natural fertility.

Inland the region is shaped by three majestic **rivers**: the Nore, the Barrow, and the Slaney, and by the empty Blackstairs Mountains which form a rough natural boundary between counties Wexford and Carlow. The rivers roll through rich, lush pastures and pretty wooded valleys, past medieval Christian ruins and the little towns and villages whose history belongs to the trade these waterways brought inland. This landscape is at its prettiest in the hills and valleys of the Nore and Barrow, just north of New Ross, and south of Kilkenny: perfect countryside for leisurely **cycling** and easy **walking** – an option made all the more attractive by the newly opened hostels at Carlow, Kilkenny and New Ross. The signposted *South Leinster Way* meanders through the heart of this countryside to some of the choicest spots, before heading northeast to the less intimate country of Carlow and the Blackstairs Mountains.

Head for the **coast** and, to the east, superb sandy **beaches** stretch practically the entire length of County Wexford. While the south coast is less suitable for swimming, its sand banks, shallow lagoons and silted rivers offer great opportunities for **wildlife** enthusiasts: prime spots for birdwatching include the Wexford Slobs (around the town itself); the lakes of Lady's Island and Tacumshane; the Saltee Islands off Kilmore Quay; and the Hook Head peninsula. This low-lying southern coastal region also provides an excellent quick route west to Waterford, as there's a car ferry from Ballyhack across Waterford Harbour.

Some history

The settled, developed character of the region owes much to its **history** of invasion, settlement and trade. The Vikings wrought havoc, but they also built the port of Wexford, which developed steadily, all the while assimilating ideas and peoples from overseas, ensuring the continual cultural influence of Europe. The arrival of mercenaries from Wales, for instance, was common throughout the medieval period and after Henry II had consolidated the Anglo-Norman victories, Strongbow settled fellow Welshmen in the region: a dialect descended from these people, known as "*yola*", survived in the far southeast of County Wexford right into the nineteenth century.

But it was the power of the English Crown that was to have by far the greatest influence on the character of the region. The towns of Wexford, Carlow and Kilkenny still bear the marks of their **Anglo-Norman** past, in city walls and ruined castles; and the well-tended farmland of rich, surrounding countryside similarly reflects centuries of English settlement. The Anglo-Norman takeover of the southeast was swift and would have been total were it not for the fiercely Gaelic enclave of Counties Carlow and Wexford. There the MacMurrough Kavanaghs became the scourge of the English in Ireland, and continually thwarted the Crown's attempts to control the entire region. It was Art MacMurrough who defeated Richard II in battles which lost him not only control of Ireland, but his English throne too. Only after the arrival of Cromwell was the power of the MacMurroughs broken once and for all.

Colonisation was thereafter pursued vigorously: the proximity of the Pale (and of England itself) meant that the Crown's influence was always far stronger here than in the remote west. The English found the area easier to control and administer, and during the growing unrest of the eighteenth century the region remained relatively tranquil. Surprisingly then, by far the most significant uprisings of the **Insurrection of 1798** took place in counties Wexford and Carlow. For nationalists the bloodshed and heroics of that summer form the region's most fêted history and legend.

COUNTY WEXFORD AND COUNTY CARLOW

Though the ancient Viking town of **Wexford** bills itself as a tourist centre, you're unlikely to spend more than a couple of days here unless you have a car. Sadly, little evidence remains of the town's long and stormy history and the place is most enjoyable for its small but lively cultural scene. The wildfowl reserves of the North and South Slobs are easily accessible, and some marvellous beaches are to be found nearby, stretching the length of the county north to the popular resort of **Courtown**. Inland, historic towns like **New Ross**, **Enniscorthy** and **Ferns** merit a call if you're passing through. To see the best of the **south coast**, you'll need a bicycle at the very least, certainly if you want to get anything out of the intriguing **Hook Head peninsula**, isolated and still largely unspoilt.

County Carlow is less likely to feature on your itinerary, for the good reason that there's little to attract a stop. The *South Leinster Way* trudges at its most lonesome and desolate through the **Blackstairs Mountains**; the county is at its prettiest along the River Barrow, which for much of its length forms the boundary between Carlow and Kilkenny. **Carlow** itself, situated on the Dublin to Kilkenny train route, barely warrants attention.

Wexford Town

Apart from its narrow, quirky lanes (a Viking legacy) **WEXFORD** town retains few traces of its past, and only the quays suggest that it was once an important trading centre. The harbour, in business from the ninth century, has now silted up, and Wexford has lost its trade once and for all to its old rival Waterford. That's not to say, though, that the town's **history** stopped with the fall of the Vikings. Settled by the Normans in the twelfth century, it became an English garrison town, brutally taken by Cromwell in 1649, who had 1500 Wexford citizens put to death. In the 1798 Insurrection the town saw brave rebel fighting against the English Crown (backed by a mainly Protestant yeomanry), which was fearful that the port might be used as a landing place by the French. The rising lasted longer in Wexford than in most places but the rebels were finally put down and the Crown was quick to exact retribution. Wexford, though, plays down its contribution to Republicanism and has emerged as a positive, forward-looking place, proud of its ethnic and religious mix. It is internationally famous for its prestigious **Opera Festival**, while a more mainstream draw are the town's estimated 93 **bars**, reason enough to give Wexford at least a night.

Arrival and accommodation

If you're **arriving** by *Bus Éireann* or by train, you'll be dropped at the **train station**, at the north end of the quays and just past the bridge over the estuary – which, if you crossed, would take you out of town to the campsite (see below), the wildfowl reserve (see below), and the beaches of the county's east coast. The *Ardcavan Coach Company*'s **buses** to and from Dublin stop at The Crescent (see "Travel Details"). The **tourist office** is down by the quays (May–Sept Mon–Sat 9am–6pm; Oct–April Mon–Fri 9am–5.15pm; July & Aug also Sun 10am–5pm; ☎053/23111). And if you need to hire a **bicycle**, try *Hayes*, 108 South Main Street (☎053/22462), or *The Bike Shop*, 9 Selskar Street (☎053/22514).

There are a handful of **B&Bs** right in the town. Along Westgate is Mrs Allen's at *Westgate House* (☎053/24428; £12.50); other central alternatives include *Bilrene,* 91 John Street (☎053/24190; £12)and Mrs Kathleen Donnelly's *The Abbey,* 3 Lower George Street (☎053/22787, £12). There are others along North Main Street, and some bars along Commercial Quay also offer B&B accommodation, such as *The Wavecrest* at no. 17 (☎053/22849; £12). Best of the possibilities further out is the thirteenth-century *Killiane Castle* (☎053/58898; £12–16) on the Rosslare road, B&B with style. Bear in mind that rooms are at a premium during the Opera Festival (see below).

You can **camp** at the municipal site, immediately over the bridge from Commercial Quay (☎053/44378; Easter to mid-Sept; £3–6) – and there's a **swimming pool** next to the campsite. The nearest **hostel** is at Rosslare (see below); a day return ticket by bus or train costs around £3. *Pádraig's* **laundrette** is at 4 Peter Street.

The Town

Set on the south side of the broad, featureless Slaney estuary, Wexford town sits behind its **quays**, which drag on relentlessly. The only relief is **The Crescent** where a statue of John Barry, a local who founded the American Navy during their Wars of Independence, strides against the buffetting wind, cloak billowing. Parallel to the quays runs Wexford's lengthy **Main Street**, a narrow and winding route that gives some idea of the medieval town's layout. Once you've seen it there is little else left to explore. This is Wexford's problem: it's touted as a city proud of its history, but even the site of its most bloody and violent event – the **Bull Ring**, where Cromwell massacred all but 400 of the population – is a barely distinguishable interruption. Only a monument to the fighting of 1798 draws your attention.

A lane up behind *Macken's* off-licence on the Bull Ring, most famous as being both pub and undertakers, leads to the Cornmarket and the parallel streets of the small centre. The massive **Westgate**, built around 1300, is the sole survivor of the medieval walled city's five gates. Nearby, too, are the remains of **Selskar Abbey**, wrecked by Cromwell, where Henry II spent an entire Lent in penitence for the murder of Thomas à Becket in Canterbury cathedral. As indications of what has been lost, both the gate and the abbey add to the general air of disappointment. As far as the town goes, that's about it, though you might like to check out the modern Gothic **churches** of The Immaculate Conception and The Assumption. They are identical in design and, as if to hammer home the shortage of imagination, their foundation stones were both laid on the same day in 1851.

Food, drink and culture

There's no shortage of places to get a decent **meal** in Wexford, and some of the best cheap eating is to be found in pubs and bars. Of these, *The Wren's Nest*, Custom House Quay, offers reliable, reasonably priced pub meals, as does *The Centenary Stores*, Charlotte Street, while *Tim's Tavern*, 51 South Main Street, specialises in seafood and serves hot lunches at midday (Mon–Sat) and, between July and October, dinners in the evening, up to 8.30pm.

As for **restaurants** proper, *The Country Kitchen*, White's Hotel, North Main Street is a good daytime option for roast dinners for around £4 and *Michael's Restaurant*, 94 North Main Street (open noon–midnight), is just about the cheapest place for a decent meal in the evening; a little more expensive is *The Bohemian Girl*, North Main Street, serving steaks. For pizza and pasta, try *Robertino's*, 19 South Main Street (Mon–Sat 7.30pm–1am, Sun 6pm–1am). *Kate's Kitchen,* Henrietta Street, is open from 8.30am for breakfasts, and serves lunches, including a vegetarian dish (till 6pm, around £2–4); *Kelly's Deli*, 80 South Main Street, is a largely vegetarian café offering snacks and extravagant gateaux.

Alongside all of this the town has a vast selection of plain-drinking **pubs and bars**, many of which feature **live music** on one or more days of the week. Start your explorations at one of the following places. *The Goal Bar*, South Main Street, is *the* busiest place for music, having bands seven nights a week and sessions on Sunday that start at lunchtime and go on throughout the day: expect anything from country and western, rock and traditional Irish, to a frighteningly popular karaoke spot. *Kinsella's Bar*, 79 South Main Street, has traditional Irish music nightly during the summer and at weekends during the winter – the sign on the window reads *Stamp's Stores*, and inside it's full of wooden drawers labelled "Rice", "Soap", "Candles" and the like. *The Centenary Stores*, Charlotte Street, is a lively, young spot with traditional Irish music on Sunday mornings and Wednesday nights and local blues band on Sunday nights. *The Thomas Moore Tavern*, Cornmarket, is known for being a music pub, although sessions here are sporadic – frequent though irregular set dancing sessions are held here during the winter. *The Tower Bar*, North Main Street, has live music on Thursday and Sunday and you can find ballad and pop sessions at *Mooney's*, 12 Commercial Quay, every Friday night, and also in *The Talbot Hotel* bar every Friday and Saturday. *The Crown Bar*, Moncke Street, is an absolute must – the oldest pub in the city, it has been run by the family for the last 150 years and is chock full of ancient fire-arms. If you're looking for jazz, try *White's Hotel*, George's Street, on Sunday, also the venue for discos and pop bands on Friday and Saturday.

Opera and theatre

The annual Opera Festival in October is well worth catching, usually featuring rarely performed works by renowned composers; information on ticket availability and programmes from the festival office on High Street (☎053/22240). The festival attracts a range of other performers too, and you'll find traditional music, blues and jazz in the bars, along with poetry readings and exhibitions. Even out of festival time Wexford has a lively cultural life, largely generated by a couple of **theatre venues** – *The Theatre Royal* in High Street (☎053/22240, 22144) and *The Wexford Arts Centre* (☎053/23764), in Cornmarket, housed in an eighteenth-century market house and town hall. The latter has a healthy turnover of travelling modern exhibitions, and occasionally hosts performance artists, dance groups, drama and music.

Around Wexford Town

Within a few miles of Wexford are plenty of attractions to justify staying around for a few days. Some, like the **wildfowl reserves** at the endearingly named North and South Slobs are of specialist interest. Others, though, could claim anyone's time – not least the excellent **sandy beaches** as near as Curracloe five miles to the north, and also to the south at the resort town of **Rosslare**.

Birdwatching in the North and South Slobs

The mud flats sheltered behind the sea walls of the Slaney estuary, known as the **North and South Slobs**, are home to the **Wexford Wildfowl Reserve**. The Slobs are the main wintering grounds for half the world's population of Greenland white-fronted geese, Bewick's swans, pintails and blacktailed godwits; you can also see spotted redshanks, gulls and terns. At the reserve there's a wildfowl collection, a research station, hides, lookout towers and identification charts, all freely accessible.

To reach the North Slobs you take the Dublin road out of Wexford over the bridge, and it's signposted on the right after about two miles; for the South Slobs take the Rosslare road out of Wexford for two miles, turn left at the *Farmer's Kitchen* pub, and take the second turn on the left. Either of these is a considerable walk, but it's easy enough to hitch to the turn-offs, or a pleasant short bike ride.

Ferrycarrig and Johnstown Castle

Just two and a half miles inland from Wexford, the **Irish National Heritage Park** at FERRYCARRIG (summer daily 9am–7pm; winter daily 10am–4pm; £2.50, students £1.50) plots 9000 years of social change through full-scale models of settlements, homesteads and burial places from the Stone Age through to Norman times. It's a great place to clarify your knowledge of Ireland's ancient history, and helps make sense of the numerous archaeological remains that are littered throughout the country. The park is also being developed as a nature reserve, and the environment has been carefully nurtured to provide the appropriate settings. It works well, so that as you walk through the Mesolithic campsite, the shaggy lichen-covering on the hazel trees, the mud and the reeds all help evoke a primeval bog; while the Viking shipyard nestles convincingly on the estuary's banks. Public transport **access** is by once-daily *Bus Éireann* bus from Wexford train station; alternatively tours to Ferrycarrig leave Wexford tourist office twice daily during the summer (£4.50, including admission to the park).

Four miles southwest of Wexford, off the Rosslare road, the **Irish Agricultural Museum** (June–Aug Mon–Fri 9am–5pm, weekends 2–5pm; May & Sept–Oct Mon–Fri 9am–12.30pm & 1.30pm–5pm, weekends 2–5pm; Nov–April same hours but closed weekends; £1.50, students 75p) is set in the gardens of **Johnstown Castle**, a Gothic Revival castellated mansion. The museum, signposted *Research Centre*, has good, clear displays on all aspects of rural life: domestic objects, farming machinery, carts and carriages, reconstructed workshops, and much on dairy farming. In addition, the grounds are darkly wooded with mounds of rhododendrons, ornamental lakes, hot houses and walled gardens – all very spruce and well maintained. Tours to Johnstown Castle leave Wexford tourist office once daily (£4.50 ticket includes entrance to the park but not the museum).

The beaches

The southeast has more sunshine than any other part of Ireland, and as the entire coast of the county to the north of Wexford town is made up of safe and sandy **beaches**, the region is a popular spot in summer for families and caravanners.

From **CURRACLOE**, five miles northeast of town, superb, sandy dunes stretch away into the far distance, and though the little villages roundabout are overloaded in July and August, the sands themselves aren't. If you want to stay in the area, *O'Gorman's Caravan and Camping Park* (April–Sept; ☎053/37110, 37221) charges £4 in high season for hikers and cyclists, £3 in low season. Camping on the dunes is discouraged. If you're not mobile, then you'll have to rely on the *Bus Éireann* **buses** from Wexford to Curracloe, which run only on Monday and Saturday.

Roughly six miles southeast of Wexford is the huge sandy beach at **ROSSLARE**, the county's other main seaside resort, not to be confused with Rosslare Harbour, another five miles further south.

Rosslare Harbour

ROSSLARE HARBOUR is served by ferries from Cherbourg and Le Havre in France, and Fishguard and Pembroke Dock in South Wales. At Rosslare Harbour terminal there's a **tourist office** (☎053/33622), open for all incoming sailings during June, July and August, and in winter open for afternoon and evening sailings. The *An Óige* **hostel** in Goulding Street (☎053/33399; £6.50) is clearly signposted up the hill from the harbour. **Bike hire** is available at the hostel (£5 a day, £25 a week), and it is possible to hire here and drop the bike off in Dublin, Killarney, Cork or Limerick. The hostel also stays open for whatever time the boat comes in and there's a supermarket nearby. If you are **camping** and need to catch the morning ferry it is possible to pitch your tent in the dunes by the beach; alternatively head for *The Holiday Inn Caravan and Camping Park* at Kilrane (☎053/31168), three miles from the port. The nearest **B&Bs** to the port are Mr Shiel's *Ailsa Lodge* (☎053/33230; £12) and Mrs McDonald's *Laurel Lodge* (☎053/33291; £11.50), or you could try Mrs Barry's Glenville (☎053/33142; £11), on St Patrick's Road a good twenty minutes' walk away.

Moving on from Rosslare Harbour is fairly straightforward. Trains from the pier for Wexford and Dublin leave twice daily and for Waterford twice daily from Monday to Saturday. To get to Dublin, the daily private coach operated by *Ardcavan Coach Company* is more economical; it's also an easy hitch.

ROSSLARE HARBOUR TRAVEL INFORMATION

Ardcavan Coach Company (☎053/22561). Buses to Dublin.

B& I Line (☎053/33311) operate services to Pembroke Dock (summer Tues–Sun 2 daily, 1 on Mon; winter at least one daily; 4hr 30min); student reductions 25–50 percent; single fare £16.

Funtrek (☎01/730852). Buses to Dublin.

Irish Ferries (☎053/33158) operate services to Cherbourg (twice weekly; winter weekly; 18 hours) and Le Havre (5 weekly, winter twice weekly; 22 hours).

Irish Rail, Rosslare Harbour (☎053/33114).

Sealink (☎053/33115) operate sailings to Fishguard (twice daily all year, 3hr 30min). International Youth Hostel Card holders are eligible for reductions of 25 percent; Interail ticket holders get a 30 percent reduction; no student cards are accepted; bikes carried free. A single to Fishguard costs £16–22, boat and train to London £49.

Around County Wexford

Once out of Wexford town's environs, County Wexford splits into three main regions. To the **north**, Enniscorthy and Ferns have smatterings of historical interest, while the best of this coast's resorts is Courtown. In the **west** New Ross offers river trips that give you a different view of the county. Along the **south** coast, low-lying, flat land makes cycling easy. There are more sandy beaches here, and two scenic spots in particular are worth taking in – Kilmore Quay and the attractive Hook Head peninsula, both targets for birdwatchers.

Enniscorthy, Ferns and Courtown

Fourteen miles north of Wexford, at the likeable market town of **ENNISCORTHY**, is the **County Museum** (☎054/35926; June–Oct daily 10am–6pm; Nov & Feb–May daily 2–5.30pm; Dec & Jan Sun only 2–5pm; 80p). Focussing on the events of 1798 and 1916, the museum is housed in the Norman castle that dominates Enniscorthy, overlooking the Slaney. Across the river, covered in mustard and yellow gorse, lies **Vinegar Hill**, the site of the rebels' main encampment during the 1798 Insurrection – and the scene of their final slaughter by Crown forces. If you're around in summer, Enniscorthy has an enjoyable *Strawberry Fair*, usually held the first or second week in July.

The higher countryside to the north and west of Enniscorthy is bald and spartan. There's little in the way of sights on this side of the Blackstairs Mountains, though if you're heading north, **FERNS** – seven miles from Enniscorthy – would make a good lunch stop. One-time seat of the kings of Leinster, it's now a little scrap of a village, top-heavy with history: when Dermot MacMurrough was attacked here by Tiernán O'Rourke – whose wife he had abducted fourteen years earlier – MacMurrough sought help from Henry II in France. Henry lent him Richard Fitzherbert de Clare – **Strongbow** – and thus an adultery led to the Norman invasion of Ireland. An abbey was founded in Ferns in the sixth century, and you can see remains of this in **St Edan**'s churchyard and the adjacent field. Most impressive, though, are the ruins of the thirteenth-century **castle**, with its pair of towers – which you can climb – and two curtain walls. The *Buttle Arms* in the village does daily set meals.

Quite the nicest family seaside town hereabouts is **COURTOWN**, about 25 miles north of Wexford and plumb in the middle of another excellent, long stretch of sand. If you want to stay, there's a new independent **hostel**, *Anchorage Hostel*, at Poulshone, Courtown Harbour (☎055/25335; open May–Oct £5, private rooms £6), with a shop nearby and the beach just five minutes' walk away.

New Ross to Tintern Abbey

First impressions of **NEW ROSS**, 21 miles west of Wexford, are not encouraging: a glamourless old port of grubby wharf buildings and lacklustre shops. However, the place isn't without character, thanks mostly to the river, which provides New Ross with its livelihood and gives access to the heart of the Wexford and Kilkenny countryside. From the town, the *Galley Cruising Restaurant* runs **river trips** up the Barrow and Nore, as far as St Mullins and Inistioge (see p.177), and along the Suir to Waterford. Lunch (£11), afternoon tea (£5) or dinner (£17.20) is part of the package, and cruises operate from mid-May to the end of September; advance booking is advisable (☎051/21723, after 7pm ☎051/73752).

Should you find yourself with time to spare in New Ross, it's worth climbing the steep back alleys to the top of town for views over the river and hills. Any remaining time can be spent at **St Mary's Church**, alongside which are the ruins of New Ross's thirteenth-century **abbey**, with graceful early English windows, and some carved, medieval tombstones in the chancel. New Ross has a **tourist office** (mid-June to mid-Sept Mon–Sat 10am–1pm & 2pm–6pm; ☎051/21857) tucked in the back of *Foodrack Store* on the quay, while *Bus Éireann* **buses** to local towns and the Hook peninsula leave from the quays, outside *The Mariners Inn*. If you are looking to **eat**, *Katie Pat's* bar on the quays serves very good pub lunches all day. One of the best reasons to **stop over** is to stay at the very friendly *MacMurrough Farm Hostel* (☎051/21383; £4.50; open all year), a comfy cottage hostel in a beautiful setting. If you are cycling it makes a good base from which to explore the Nore and Barrow river valleys. It's a couple of miles out of town – ask for directions to *Kelly's* BP petrol station on the ring road; the hostel is signposted down the lane alongside. There are also a fair number of B&Bs roundabout, and the *New Ross Hotel*, 1 North Street (☎051/21457; £21), right in the centre of town.

Five miles south of New Ross, the **arboretum** known as the *J.F. Kennedy Memorial Park* (May–Aug 10am–8pm; April & Sept 10am–6.30pm; Oct–March 10am–5pm; admission car £3, pedestrian £1) contains a collection of around 5000 species of trees and shrubs. Kennedy's great-grandfather was born in DUNGANSTOWN, close by, so the place is often frequented by Americans in search of presidential roots. If you have transport, the road south of here will take you down to the coast and the Hook Head peninsula.

Dunbrody and Tintern abbeys

Approaching the Hook Head peninsula from this direction, a couple of brief diversion are well worth making. The magnificent ruin of **Dunbrody Abbey** stands open to all at the widening of the Barrow estuary. A thirteenth-century Cistercian foundation, it was altered in the sixteenth century after the Dissolution of the Monasteries, when the large central tower and adjacent buildings were added.

To the east, near the muddy Bannow Bay, scene of the first Norman landing in 1169, is **Tintern Abbey** (free access), built in 1200 by William Marshall, Earl of Pembroke. Another fine Cistercian edifice, it owes its existence in this unprepossessing spot to a vow made by the earl while he was caught in a storm off the south coast. Praying that he might be saved, he promised to build an abbey wherever his boat came ashore. The presbytery is based on that of the foundation's more famous namesake in Wales.

The South Coast: Kilmore Quay and Hook Head peninsula

In the southeast corner of Ireland the sea has made inroads into an otherwise flat region, forming small lagoons at **TACUMSHANE** (popular with windsurfers) and **LADY'S ISLAND**, both venues for bird enthusiasts. Lady's Island itself sits mid-lagoon at the end of a causeway, and has been a place of religious devotion for centuries: an annual pilgrimage is still made here on August 15. On the island are the remains of an Augustinian priory and a Norman castle, both built in the thirteenth century – but the spirit of the place has been destroyed by a large, modern church building that has been tacked onto the side. There are few amenities for travellers in the area, but the *Lobster Pot* bar and restaurant at **CARNE** is a great exception, serving delicious seafood meals. There are **campsites** at both Carne and Lady's Island, but nowhere else to stay.

Kilmore Quay and the Saltee Islands

KILMORE QUAY, at the offputtingly named Forlorn Point, comes as a real surprise after the largely dull countryside which precedes it. A small, unspoilt fishing and holiday village of thatched cottages and whitewashed walls, it's prettily situated around a stone harbour wall, looking out at the nearby Saltee Islands. Wexford's **Maritime Museum** is housed in an old lightship in the harbour (June–Sept daily 2pm–8pm; £1). There is a fine sandy beach, and you can **camp** among the dunes; about a mile outside the village the *Kilturk Independent Hostel* (☎053/29883; dorm £4, private room £7; bike hire and bureau de change) will open in 1992 – we have not yet visited it. There are also a couple of B&Bs – *Coral House*, Grange (☎053/29640; £14), and *Sarshill House*, Sarshill (☎053/29604; £12) – a little further out.

Kilmore Quay hosts a **seafood festival**, usually in the second week of July – check the dates with Wexford tourist office. A fine excuse to eat plenty of seafood (whatever your budget), the festival includes a trawler race around the Saltees in which anyone can take part – just pay around £4 to one of the fishermen involved. The village also has a handful of good **bars**, including *The Wooden House* which has traditional music several nights a week during the summer. The *Hotel Saltees* holds discos at the weekend.

Kilmore Quay is also point of departure for visiting the uninhabited **Saltee Islands**, one of Ireland's most important bird sanctuaries, especially for puffins, razorbills, cormorants, shags, gannets, kittiwakes and auks. In the nesting period of late spring and early summer, there are thousands of them; by the end of July they've all left – so time your trip carefully. Boat trips for groups are available during the summer; enquiries to Willie Bates, who lives opposite the church (☎053/29644).

The Hook Head Peninsula

Only when you reach the **Hook Head peninsula**, which forms the eastern side of Waterford Harbour, does the flat coastline begin to undulate and the scenery become more attractive. **ARTHURSTOWN**, on the estuary near the neck of the peninsula, has a tiny sandy spot you can swim from, a nice pub that serves seafood snacks, a post office, a shop and an *An Óige* **hostel** (closed Oct–April; no phone; grade C) in the old Coastguard Station at nos. 1, 2 and 4. Just a mile to the north is the village of **BALLYHACK** which has a useful year-round **car ferry** service running regularly across the harbour to PASSAGE EAST in County Waterford. The crossing takes just ten minutes (see p.193 for details). If you've got time to kill before you cross then **Ballyhack castle** is worth a look, a fine five-storey, sixteenth-century tower house. Ballyhack village also boasts a very good seafood **restaurant**, the *Neptune Restaurant* (☎051/89284).

Unfortunately, the pretty, wooded coastline from Ballyhack south, down the peninsula to Duncannon, is privately owned and you can't walk along it. **DUNCANNON** itself is a holiday town, pleasant enough, and with a rocky coast to the south that protects its big, sandy beach. There are minimal facilities here, though: a couple of bars do sandwiches and burgers, *Yvonne's* coffee shop does good light meals and the *Fort Conan Hotel* is the only place to get a more substantial meal. If you're going to **stay**, try the *Hook Trekking Centre* (☎051/89166), one mile from Duncannon on the Hook Road, which does B&B for £8. (The pony trekking itself operates only in June, July and August; £6 an hour, with reduced B&B rates for riders.) Back in Duncannon, there's also a caravan site, but better if you're **camping** is to sleep amidst the dunes, or ask to use a local field.

From Duncannon, you can walk wherever you like southwards. A bike is the ideal way to get down to the very **end of the peninsula**, as there's hardly any traffic. Little sandy bays lie concealed behind low cliffs, and there are lovely views across to the broad and beautiful Waterford coastline. Although the Hook peninsula promotes itself as a tourist area, the caravans and kids mostly keep to the areas around Duncannon and FETHARD, to the east, and there are plenty of isolated spots to be found. A couple of particularly fine, sandy beaches are **Booley Strand**, two miles south of Duncannon, and beyond that the smaller **Dollar Bay**.

Beyond these, six miles from Duncannon, **Loftus Hall** hotel sits at the end of a long drive behind an ostentatious gateway. It's said that the hall was built for a princess whom the owner was to bring home as his bride, and that the princess never arrived. There's something quite eerie about all this decorative splendour in such a desolate spot: the grandiose Italian staircase, for instance, is made up of 49 different shades of wood, and cost the monumental sum of £5000 in 1822. From Easter to September bar food is available all day at the hotel.

At the peninsula's tip the shoreline is rockier, the limestone rich with fossils, and the land, flat and desolate, just slips away into the sea. The extremity is marked by a **lighthouse** said to be the oldest in Europe – the first on this site was built in the twelfth century. You can take a tour of the lighthouse by arrangement (contact Mrs M.J. Wilson; ☎051/97179), or simply ask the keeper in charge if you can look around. This part of Hook Head is favoured by ornithologists who come to watch the bird migrations, and if you're lucky you can sometimes spot seals. Crashing spray and blow-holes make it a dangerous and dramatic place in a storm – and you certainly shouldn't swim here at any time. You can **camp** near the lighthouse, though be careful not to pitch your tent by the blow-holes on the other side of the lane. The nearest **shop** is three and a half miles away at the *Texaco* petrol station at the Fethard/Duncannon junction. *The Templars Inn* in TEMPLETOWN, about three miles from the tip, has a restaurant and bar food.

Tucked away on the east flank of the peninsula, the evocatively crumbling harbour of **SLADE** retains not even a single pub or shop, but it's worth going just to look at the place. Slade is quite simply beautiful: fishing boats cluster around its quays and slipways; stacked lobster pots lean against a fifteenth-century castellated castle; and the whole place is built from stone a nutty brown colour, rich, rusty and warm.

County Carlow

Northwest of Wexford, tiny **County Carlow** shares little of the appeal of its close neighbours. Much of the terrain is unenticing agricultural land, and none of the few small towns retain much of their history – though the county capital does sport a ruined Norman castle. The most attractive fringes of the county – along the River Barrow and in the Blackstairs Mountains – are covered in the "County Kilkenny" section below, being more approachable from that direction.

Carlow Town

For centuries, the town of **CARLOW** was an Anglo-Norman stronghold at the edge of an otherwise fiercely Gaelic county. As such, it has a bloody history, the most terrible battle coming during the Insurrection of 1798 when over 600 rebels were slaughtered. Today, there's nothing to suggest its former frontier status, and the small, busy town is distinguished only by a fine Classical courthouse with a portico modelled on the Parthenon. Even the remains of the once proud Norman **castle** now lie neglected within the grounds of *Corcoran & Co*; if you want to poke around, ask at the factory. Otherwise, there's plenty on local military, religious and folk history in the **museum**, housed in the Town Hall (May– Sept daily 11am–5.30pm).

You might be stopping in Carlow town to take advantage of the **hostel** in the centre of town: *Verona*, Pembroke Road (☎0503/31700; £4.50, camping £2 per tent; open May–Sept). This aside, Carlow tries hard to put you off staying. Even the town's favourite young person's **bar** – *Tully's* in Tullow Street, with jazz and blues at the weekend – shuts at 6pm during the week. There are other bars around though, like *Scragg's Alley* in Tullow Street, and *The Little Owl* in Dublin Street, both popular with a young crowd, while *The Royal Hotel* in Dublin Street, has occasional ballad sessions (as well as expensive rooms; ☎0503/31621; £35). If you need to **eat** plenty of pubs serve meals: try *Tully's, The Little Owl* or *Carpenters* in Barrack Street. **B&Bs** include Mrs Farrell's *Westlow*, Green Lane (☎0503/43964; £10) or the slightly more upmarket and central *Redsetter House*, 14 Dublin Street (☎0503/41848; £15).

You can get more local information from Carlow's **tourist office** (July and Aug Mon–Sat 10am–6pm; ☎0503/31554). There's a **train** link north to Kildare and Dublin, south to Kilkenny, Thomastown and Waterford. If you want to get around under your own steam, **bike hire** is available during the summer from *A.E. Coleman* in Dublin Street (☎0503/31273).

County Carlow's most impressive sight, the **Browneshill dolmen**, lies two miles out of town on the R726 road. It's enormous, possibly the largest of its type in Europe, but you'll have to ask the farmer for permission to view it.

COUNTY KILKENNY

County Kilkenny offers the finest of the southeast's countryside. Mostly it's rich farmland, intensely pretty especially around the confluence of two fine rivers, the Nore and the Barrow, just to the north of New Ross. Medieval ruins are spattered all over the county, but they reach their richest concentration in ancient **Kilkenny** city – a really bustling, quaint favourite. The delightful surroundings make it almost essential to hire a bike and explore the river valleys and their medieval ruins, most notably **Kells Priory** and **Jerpoint Abbey**. The **cycling** is easy: off the main roads there's little traffic, and the minor roads that stay close to the rivers are especially scenic. Alternatively, the heart of this rich, historical farmland can be crossed **on foot**. As they head south, the Nore and Barrow rivers flow through gentle valleys of mixed woodland: the **South Leinster Way** provides unstrenuous walking, passing through pretty riverside villages – **Inistioge, Graiguenamanagh**, and nearby **Borris** and **St Mullins** – before heading north towards the Blackstairs Mountains. Immediate access from Kilkenny is by local bus or by taking the train as far as Thomastown and walking. Or you could see this region from the **cruises** that operate from the river port of New Ross (see p.168).

Kilkenny

KILKENNY is Ireland's finest medieval city, its setting superb: above the broad sweep of the River Nore sits the castle, while a pretty, humpbacked stone bridge leads up into narrow, cheerful streets laced with carefully maintained buildings. Kilkenny's earliest settlement was a monastery founded by Saint Canice in the sixth century, but all that remains from those days is the Round Tower which stands alongside the Cathedral. The layout of Kilkenny today owes more to its medieval history. Following continual skirmishes between local clans, the arrival of the **Normans** in 1169 saw the building of a fort by Strongbow on the site of today's castle. His son-in-law, William Marshall, consolidated Norman power in Kilkenny, maintaining the fortified city and keeping the indigenous Irish in an area of less substantial housing beyond its walls – of which only the name "Irishtown" remains. In 1391 the Butler family acquired Kilkenny castle, and thus ensured the city's loyalty to the English Crown.

In the mid-seventeenth century, Kilkenny became virtually the capital of Ireland, with the founding of a parliament in 1641 known as the **Confederation of Kilkenny** (see "Historical Framework" in *Contexts*). This was an attempt to unite resistance to the English persecution of Catholics, and although powerful for a while, its effectiveness had greatly diminished by the time Cromwell arrived – in his usual destructive fashion – in 1650. Kilkenny never recovered its former prosperity and importance. The disgrace of the Butler family in 1715, coupled with English attacks upon the rights of Catholics through the Penal Laws, saw the city decline still further, though the towering mill buildings on the river banks are evidence of a considerable industrial history.

Enough medieval buildings remain to attest to Kilkenny's former importance, however, and in a place brimming with civic pride, there's been a tasteful push towards making the town a major tourist attraction. Kilkenny is sometimes known as "the marble city" because of the limestone mined locally, which when polished develops a deep black shine. Echoing this, the town's bar and shop signs all gleam with black and brown lacquer, the names cut in deeply bevelled, stout gold lettering.

Arriving and Accommodation

The **bus and train station** (☎056/22024) is on the north road out of the city, at the top of St John's Street: note that in Gaelic the city is called *Cill Chainnigh*, and this is what it says on the front of buses. The **tourist office** in Rose Inn Street (May–Sept Mon–Sat 9am–6pm, Sun 10am–7pm; Oct–April Tues–Sat 9am–12.45pm & 2pm–5.15pm; ☎056/21755) is a worthwhile first stop, with free maps of the city and plenty of other information.

Accommodation

Kilkenny is well served by **B&Bs**, although in the summer the city can get crowded and during festival week in August (see below) you'll need to book in advance. In the centre of town try: *The Pumphouse* bar, Parliament Street (☎056/63924; £10); Mrs Dempsey's at 26 James Street (☎056/21954; £12–13); Mrs O'Connell's, *St Mary's*, next door (☎056/22091; £10–12); or one of several along the Waterford Road – Mrs Flannery's at *Ashleigh* (☎056/22809; £11.50) or Mrs Flanagan's at *Burwood*, (☎056/62266; £11.50; June–Sept only) for example.

There's **camping** at Mrs Murphy's, 25 Upper Patrick Street (☎056/62973; £2.50 per person per night), a basic but friendly site with an excellent central location. The new *Kilkenny Tourist Hostel* is also in a great spot in the town centre – 35 Parliament Street (☎056/63541; £5).The *An Óige* **hostel**, *Foulksrath Castle*, Jenkinstown (☎056/67674; £4.50; closed Nov–Feb), is eight miles north of town along the N77, but the setting – a sixteenth-century fort in lush meadows – makes up for the inconvenience. *Buggy's* buses (☎056/41264) run from Kilkenny Castle to Jenkinstown Mon–Sat 11.30am and 5.30pm (and July & Aug Sun 2pm); for the return journey buses depart from the hostel to town Mon–Sat 8.25am and 3pm (and an extra bus at 10.15am during July & Aug). There is also an evening service into town during July and August departing from the hostel at 9pm, bringing you safely home at midnight.

The City

Kilkenny is focused on the hill and its castle. Climbing **Rose Inn Street** from the river brings you to the tourist office (see above) housed in the sixteenth-century **Shee Alms House**, one of the very few Tudor almshouses to be found in Ireland. A **walking tour** of the city leaves from here four times a day, costing £2. At the top of Mary Inn Street to the left is the broad stretch known as **The Parade**, which leads up to the castle. Formerly used for military and civic ceremonies, it now serves as a coach park in summer. To the right, the High Street soon becomes **Parliament Street**, the main thoroughfare busy with people. Crooked and intriguing, little medieval slips and alleyways duck off it, while there's more substantial interest in the eighteenth-century **Tholsel**, with its stone pillars and arches. This was once the centre of the city's financial dealings, and is now the town hall.

Of all the surviving buildings from the prosperous Tudor commercial period, **Rothe House** (April–Oct Mon–Sat 10.30am–5pm, Sun 3pm–5pm; Nov–March Sat & Sun 3pm–5pm; £1, students 60p) on Parliament Street is the finest. Home to the Kilkenny Archaeological Society **museum**, and a newly opened **costume gallery** of waistcoats, bonnets and gowns from the eighteenth century onwards, it's worth visiting as much for the structure as for the contents. Built in 1594, it's a unique example of an Irish Tudor merchant's home, comprising three separate houses linked by interconnecting courtyards. There is also a genealogical research centre here for those wanting to trace their roots locally.

Kilkenny Castle

It's the **castle** (April–May daily 10am–5pm; June–Sept daily 10am–7pm; Oct–March Mon–Sat 10.30am–5pm, Sun 11am–5pm; £1, children and students 40p, guided tours on request), an imposing building standing high and square over the river, that really defines Kilkenny. Dating originally from the twelfth century, it was much added to in the seventeenth and nineteenth centuries. While the furnishings and paintings suggest a civilised wealth and domesticity, the scale and grandeur of the rooms, with their deeply recessed windows and robust fireplaces, signify a much cruder political power. The biggest surprise is the flimsy wooden hammer-beam roof of the **picture gallery**, covered with folksy, pre-Raphaelite decoration – plenty of gold and burnt umber plant life smudging its way across the ceiling, the work of John Hungerford Pollen.

Also within the castle is the **Butler Gallery**, housing an exhibition of modern art. You can take a break in the **tearoom** (May–Oct only), once the castle's kitchen, and you may want to drop in here at other times too – you don't have to pay the castle entrance fee to visit either the Butler Gallery or the tearoom. While you're around, it's well worth taking a look at the eighteenth-century stables, opposite the castle, too. These have been converted into *The Design Centre*, an outlet for locally produced craft goods: quality is very high, but so are prices, geared towards the tourist market.

The Cathedral, Round Tower and other churches

The other must in Kilkenny is the magnificent hilltop **St Canice's Cathedral** (Mon–Sat 9am–1pm & 2–6pm, Sun 2–6pm). Built in the thirteenth century, the purity and unity of its architecture lends it a grandeur beyond its real size. Rich in carvings, it has an exemplary selection of sixteenth-century monuments, many in black Kilkenny marble, the most striking being effigies of the Butler family.

The **round tower** (50p, students 30p) next to the church is all that remains of the early monastic settlement reputedly founded by Saint Canice in the sixth century: there are superb views from the top – ask anyone working in the church or churchyard for access (if you want to climb the tower during June, July and August be there before 4.30pm; arrangements are more flexible at other times).

Kilkenny is littered with the remains of other medieval churches. The **Black Abbey**, founded by Dominicans in 1225, has been carefully restored and contains some unusual carvings and sepulchral slabs. On the other side of town, **St John's Priory** has only a roofless chancel, a fine seven-light window and a medieval tomb. Thirteenth-century **St Francis's Abbey** stands in ruins by the river.

Eating, drinking and music

There are plenty of good choices for **food** in Kilkenny, in a multitude of pubs and restaurants. *Flannery's Hotel* in John Street is perhaps the most popular place to eat, serving daily lunches from £3.50, evening meals for £4–8. *Shems*, also in John Street, serves good bar lunches for around £4, as do *Daniel Bollards* in St Kieran's Street and *The Caisléin Uícuain* next to the Allied Irish Bank in Patrick Street. For lighter meals, try the vegetarian quiches and salads in *The Design Centre*, opposite the castle (Mon–Sat 10am–5pm, Sun 11am–4.15pm). The tearoom in Kilkenny Castle (see above) is worth a visit for the setting and the cakes; while *Mike's*, upstairs in the High Street shopping arcade, is worth bearing in mind for good value snacks and basic meals, despite the unappealing location (daily 9am–6pm). In the evening *The Italian Connection*, Parliament Street, is a popular, cheap pizza place, while *Lautrec's*, just down the road, is a friendly place serving lasagnes, curries and steaks, with a bar open until 12.30am. Arguably the best **chip shop** in town is the one up beyond Mrs Murphy's campsite in Patrick Street.

Bars are as alluring in Kilkenny as anywhere in Ireland, and you won't be hard pushed to find **music** here either, though it will be a matter of luck as to what you get. The *Caisléin Uícuain* is one of the youngest and liveliest; *John Cleere's* bar in Parliament Street has traditional Irish and folk music on Mondays, plus a tiny theatre to the rear where they occasionally lay on drama and comedy; and *The Pumphouse*, Parliament Street again, has bands virtually every night during the summer and on Fridays and Saturdays during the winter – a mix of blues, rock, folk and traditional. During the winter *Flannery's Hotel*, John's Bridge, has regular jazz sessions in the bar at lunchtime on Sunday, and a traditional session Wednesday evenings. There are plenty more **traditional bars** around town: two favourites in High Street are *Jim Holland's* and *The Marble City Bar*. If you're looking for a **disco**, try the *Hotel Kilkenny*, College Road, at weekends. For the occasional big name **bands** and for a Friday punk/alternative night head for *The New Park Inn*, Castlecomer Road.

Entertainment – Arts Week
Other **entertainment** is fairly easy to come by in summer; *The Kilkenny People*, published on Thursday, lists what's on in the city and the surrounding villages. One event to try and coincide with would be the **Arts Week** festival, held one of the last two weeks in August. The emphasis is on classical music, but alongside this are literary readings, art exhibitions and jazz and folk sessions. All in all it's well worth catching, though you'll need to reserve accommodation some time in advance.

Listings

Bank *Allied Irish Bank*, 3 High Street.

Bike hire and repairs *J.J. Wall*, Maudlin Street (☎056/21236); £5 per day, £25 per week, £30 deposit; a *Raleigh* drop-off point.

Bookshops For Irish interest books, maps and guides, try *O.K. House*, High Street. Other shops worth visiting include *Cody Books*, Kieran Street, and *The Book Centre* in the High Street.

Camping Supplies *Kilkenny Camping and Watersports*, Kilkenny Arcade (upstairs), High Street (☎056/64025).

Chemist *Michael O'Connell*, High Street.

Launderette *Bretts*, Michael Street (☎056/63200).

Police ☎056/22222.

Post Office High Street (Mon–Sat 9am–5.30pm, Wed opens 9.30am).

Swimming Pool Michael Street (10am–11pm).

Travel Agent *Mannings Travel*, High Street (☎056/22950).

Near Kilkenny: the Dunmore caves

If you ask about places of interest, the tourist office will doubtless direct you to the **Dunmore Caves** (March–June Tues–Sat 10am–last admission 4.15pm, Sun 2pm–4.15pm; July–Sept daily 10am–6.15pm; rest of year Sat, Sun & bank holidays 10am–4.15pm – though it is wise to check the times with the tourist office before you set off; entrance £1, kids & OAPs 70p; ☎056/67726), situated seven miles north of Kilkenny on an isolated limestone outcrop of the Castlecomer plateau. In 1967 Viking coins and the skeletons of 46 women and children were found among the stalactites and stalagmites. It's supposed that the Vikings attacked the native Irish, and the women and children were put in the caves for protection. The plan obviously failed, but the fact that the skeletons showed no broken bones suggests that the victims starved to death, or got lost, or that the Vikings tried to smoke them out.

To reach the caves, hire a bike in Kilkenny, hitch out on the Castlecomer Road past the train station, or Monday to Friday take *Buggy's* coach from The Parade at 11.30am or 12.30pm, returning at 3.30pm; it's a one mile walk to the caves from where the bus stops.

The Nore and Barrow rivers

Two rivers, the Nore and the Barrow, flowing magnificently through the rich countryside, have long been of immense importance to the southeast. Formerly they were the chief means of communication, bringing prosperity to the heart of the region: the Nore brought trade to medieval Kilkenny, the Barrow to Carlow. Today they are treasured for their considerable beauty, and are a real treat for fishermen. The surrounding countryside is as pretty as you'll find anywhere, perfectly enjoyed by bike, or on foot – the *South Leinster Way* dips down into some of the choicest spots. Plan a leisurely route, and you can meander your way through picturesque ancient villages, and take in some exceptional medieval ruins.

The Nore

The **Nore valley** is deservedly renowned for its beauty, the river rolling through lush countryside, past old villages and some engaging ruins. It is perhaps at its finest as it broadens to the south of Kilkenny where, along the tributary King's River eight miles from the city, sits medieval **KELLS**. Set amidst lush pastureland, the tiny village is an unexpected sight. Its broad bridge is majestically out of scale; an ancient stone water mill stands on the river bank; and the encompassing deep hollow is flecked with mallows, marsh marigolds, docks and irises. Hard by, the magnificent ruin of **Kells Priory** – founded in 1193 – sits like a perfect scale model of a medieval walled city, a clean iron-grey against the surrounding green fields. The ruins consist of a complete curtain wall with square towers and fortified gatehouse, and the remnants of the fourteenth- and fifteenth-century church – one of the most impressive and largest medieval sites in Ireland. This has nothing to do with the Book of Kells, which is associated with Kells in County Meath, though ironically enough the remains at that far more famous site are considerably less exciting than these.

Signposted from Kells, two miles south, are **Kilkree Round Tower** – just one of the many round towers scattered around this part of the country – and the nearby **High Cross**, decorated with much-eroded Biblical carvings. Alternatively, you can take the Stonyford road out of Kells to reach placid **Jerpoint Abbey** (May to mid-June Tues–Sat 10am–1pm & 2pm–5pm; mid-June to Sept daily 9.30am–6.30pm; the rest of the year a key can be obtained from the caretaker at the fourth house down on the left; admission 80p), which follows a typical Cistercian-Gothic layout, built square around an elegant, cloistered garden. The abbey is built of warm, oat-coloured stone and is generally visited for its tombs and twelfth-century carvings – especially the animated figures in the cloister.

Thomastown and Inistioge

A mile north of Jerpoint is **THOMASTOWN**. Formerly a medieval walled town of some importance, it's now simply a picturesque country town on the Kilkenny–Waterford train line. Minimal ruins of the walls, a castle, and a thirteenth-century church (with some weathered effigies) remain, and in the Catholic church you'll find the high altar from Jerpoint. There are plenty of places doing pub lunches, and if you want to stop over in Thomastown, the *Bridge Brook Arms* (☎056/24152) does **B&B** for £12 – and has traditional Irish and ballad sessions at weekends and occasionally on Monday nights. For a little more you can stay in a restored medieval tower, *The Tower House* on Low Street (☎056/24500, 24234; £14.50–17). *Rapid Express Club Coaches* operate a cheap **bus** to Dublin and Waterford three times a day, picking up at *Barcoe's* shop (☎051/72149). If you're heading north from here, it's worth calling in at the ruined church at KILFANE (three miles away) to see the fourteenth-century **Cantwell Effigy**, an impressive piece of stone carving of a knight in full armour.

INISTIOGE, a few miles southeast of Thomastown, boasts a tree-lined square beside a fine stone bridge. The village is dotted with crumbling stonework, and little eighteenth- and nineteenth-century houses climb the steep lane that twists away from its centre. The grounds of the local estate, *Woodstock*, are open to the public if you fancy a stroll overlooking the neighbouring countryside, but the house itself was burnt down in 1922 after it had been occupied by the Black and

Tans. There's no pub grub available in the village but the *Old Schoolhouse Cafe* serves tea, homemade cakes and local salmon (Easter & June–Sept only, 11am–6.30pm daily), or *The Motte* restaurant offers a surprisingly adventurous menu (☎056/58655; main courses from £10; booking essential). You're not allowed to **camp** on the land by the river – ask at *The Three Stars* to use their field.

The Barrow

Northeast from Inistioge, the **South Leinster Way** heads to the little market town of **GRAIGUENAMANAGH**, a gorgeous spot beside the **River Barrow**, with herons fishing in the rushing weir. The town's great age is indicated by the central **Duiske Abbey** which dominates Graiguenamanagh. Founded in 1204, it was the largest Cistercian abbey in Ireland, and although much has been altered and added outside (including a nineteenth-century clock tower and pebble-dashed walls), the thirteenth-century interior has been lovingly preserved. Besides some original *fleur de lys* tiling and a fine effigy of a knight in chain mail, most impressive is the superb Romanesque processional doorway – heavily decorated, this is one of the best to have survived the Reformation (find it through a door to the right of the organ). In the churchyard, near the steps outside the south transept, stand a couple of ninth-century stone crosses; and a sixth-century font from Ullard stands outside the north wall of the chancel.

If you're walking the *South Leinster Way* Graiguenamanagh is one of the most appealing places to rest up. *O'Shea's* pub doubles as a grocery shop, while *The Anchor Bar* serves sandwiches, bar lunches and evening meals (Mon–Sat all day, Sun noon–2pm); they also do **B&B** (☎0503/24207; £12). There are a handful of good **bars**: *The Anglers Rest* is probably the best, with local jazz and blues bands playing on Saturdays; *The Tavern Bar* has M.O.R. pop bands (Wed & Thurs), traditional and ballads (Fri) and a jazz session (Sun lunchtime) and *The Globe* has similarly mainstream music on Saturday and Sunday, and also on Thursday during the summer.

St Mullins

Five miles south down the towpath, **ST MULLINS** is tucked away from the river, among wooded hills, with the open heights of the Blackstairs Mountains beyond. A stroll through the village takes you to the scant remains of the monastery, founded in AD 696 by Saint Moling, Bishop of Ferns and Glendalough, and along-side them in the churchyard are the base of a round tower and a very worn stone cross. Down beside the stream, at the back of the ruins, a path leads to St Moling's Well, while near the centre of the village stands a defensive earthwork, looking like a sturdy pudding just shaken from its bowl. You might want a break here, too: there's a **restaurant and café** down by the river (follow the steep lane down besides the church), and *Blanchfield's* **pub** does soup and sandwiches (all day Easter–Sept). For B&B phone Margaret Dwyer (☎051/24665; £14), or you can **camp** on the village green. The nearest shop is at GLYNN, one and a half miles away.

Borris – and Mount Leinster

Following the *South Leinster Way* north from Graiguenamanagh, along the Barrow, you'll reach the tiny roadside town of **BORRIS**, just over the border in County Carlow. Not especially attractive, it's nonetheless as good a place as any to stop overnight in the area. You can **camp** on the disused railway line, getting your Gaz and provisions from *O'Shea's* bar and shop. Mrs Susan Breen in Church Street does **B&B** (☎0503/73231; £12). *Kiernan's* petrol station (☎0503/73211) is open for cheap **bike hire** (Mon–Sat until 9pm; £3 a day, £15 a week).

Considering its size, there's a lot going on in Borris. Between *The Green Drake Inn*, *The White House Inn* and *The Step House* (where they also have rooms; ☎0503/73401; £20), you should be able to track down some live music most nights, singalongs and ballads mostly. And you're well off for **food** as well; good lunches and dinners in all of the above, particularly *The Step House Bistro* (daily noon to midnight; set dinners from £4), whose food is home-baked, wholesome, and often vegetarian.

East of Borris, the *South Leinster Way* leaves the the intimate landscape of the valleys, crossing the open farmland of south Carlow and eventually skirting the bleak height of **Mount Leinster**. The way finally descends to the lonely cluster of houses which is KILDAVIN, six miles or so from Mount Leinster on the main Carlow–Enniscorthy road.

travel details

Trains
From Kilkenny to Carlow (4 daily; 30min); Dublin (4; 1hr 40min).

From Wexford to Dublin (3; 2hr 30min); Rosslare Pier (3; 30min).

From Rosslare Harbour to Dublin (3 daily; 3hr 10mins)

Bus Éireann
From Wexford to Dublin (4; 3hr); Rosslare Harbour (peak seasons only 2 daily; 20min).

From Kilkenny to Dublin (3; 2–3hr). Wexford–Kilkenny buses run daily during the summer months only.

Private buses
Pierce Kavanagh Coaches (☎056/31213, ☎01/734344) serve **Urlingford** and **Johnstown** on their daily Thurles–Dublin route.

Waterford Travel Club (☎051/77177) serve **Thomastown**, **Gowran** and **Carlow** on their daily Waterford–Dublin route.

Funtrek (☎01/730852) run a daily service **from Wexford to Dublin**, leaving from The Crescent (Mon–Sat 8am, Sun 6.30pm and 8pm); also serving Arklow, Gorey and Rosslare. **Departs Rosslare** half an hour earlier.

Ardcavan Coach Company (☎053/22561) operate a service **from Rosslare**, outside the chapel, (Mon–Sat 7.30am, Sun 7.30pm) and **from Wexford to Dublin**, leaving from The Crescent, (Mon 6am and 8am,Tues–Sat 8am, Sun 8pm). Returns from Dublin daily (the *Gresham Hotel*, O'Connell St, Mon–Thurs & Sat 6pm; Kildare St, Fri 6pm; Sunday depart *BHS*, O'Connell Street at 9pm and 10pm; £5 day return, £8 monthly return).

Quantabus (☎01/729644 and 056/31534) depart George's Quay, Dublin for **Carlow**, **Bagenalstown**, **Borris**, **Graiguenamanagh** and **New Ross**.

CHAPTER SIX

WATERFORD, TIPPERARY AND LIMERICK

The route from Waterford through Tipperary to Limerick is the quickest way from the southeast, and the arrival points of the ferries, to the centre of western Ireland. Yet in this chapter it's the south, not the west, that has all the real appeal. Tipperary and Limerick, despite their resonant names, are far from the most attractive counties in Ireland, while Waterford, not necessarily the first place that springs to mind, can be a delight.

Waterford, whose coastline stretches west from the expanse of Waterford Harbour towards Cork, combines many of the attractions of the south. Rolling green hills spread down to a fine shore of cliffs interspersed with expansive bays and private, enclosed beaches. There's plenty of history here, both out in the county, where **Lismore**, inland, and **Ardmore**, on the coast, preserve extensive early Christian remains, and in **Waterford City** itself, which has been an important port since the Viking invasions. Nowadays the city preserves an ancient heart, but it's also a thriving, modern commercial centre, young and enjoyably lively to visit. Inland, rich farmland is contained by mountain ranges that offer excellent opportunities for easy, scenic walking – and occasionally for more challenging stuff. Above all there's the **Munster Way** in the northwest, by which you can cross to Tipperary. All of this is contained within a relatively small area, and if you wanted further confirmation that Waterford combines a little of everything, it even has its own tiny *Gaeltacht* area, around **Ring** (An Rinn).

Crossing into southern **Tipperary**, the mountains continue, and for a while there's equally attractive walking, especially in the **Knockmealdown** and **Galty** mountains, and the **Glen of Aherlow** beyond them. For the most part, though, the county consists of prosperous farming country. The Tipperary **Golden Vale** enriches its luckiest residents, but these farming towns have little to offer visitors. At the very heart of the county though, is a site of outstanding interest – the **Rock of Cashel**. A spectacular natural formation topped with Christian buildings from virtually every period, it's effectively a primer in the development of Irish ecclesiastical architecture.

In **Limerick** you've arrived in the west of Ireland, but the county still has relatively little to tempt you. **Limerick City** itself, the third in size in the Republic, looks on the map as if it ought to be good. But it isn't. Industrial and depressed, it has a strangely sour flavour, and certainly can't compare in terms of enjoyment with the other big towns of the south and west. Inland, the county continues the rich pasture of Tipperary, and perhaps its greatest attraction is the exceptional number of medieval **castles** and towers that dot the landscape; above all immaculately preserved **Castle Matrix** in the west, one of the finest anywhere. There's also an extremely important Neolithic site at **Lough Gur**, in the heart of the county, and at **Adare** a famously quaint village. In the end, though, Limerick is somewhere you go through to get to counties Clare or Kerry.

WATERFORD

Photographs rarely do justice to the beauty of **Waterford**. Its strengths lie in a broad grandeur of scale and richness of colour, dark greens and ruddy sandstone reds. In the **south**, grand hills rise gradually from coast and valley, their slopes cloaked with plantations of fir trees. The smoothly sculpted **coastline** is of bold proportions, low cliffs giving views over large, open bays. The mountains in the **north** lose the prettiness of their wooded valleys as they rise – not dramatically, but describing gradual, open heights, offering long walks with stupendous views over the plains of Tipperary. Central to the county, Waterford's **river valleys** are luxuriant and fertile, the finest being that of the **Blackwater**, which rolls through rich farmland with a real majesty. Here, it's obvious why the county was so attractive to foreign invaders – Viking, Norman and English. The influence of wealthy colonists is clear, their opulence reflected in remnants of stately and elegant estates.

The county and the **city** of Waterford developed quite separately. The city was initially a Viking settlement that became a Norman stronghold, and thrived as an independent city state, with a major share of Ireland's European trade. While the city prospered as a mercantile centre, its culture linked by trade to Europe, the surrounding county lived off farming and fishing, retaining much of its Celtic identity. The Vikings and Normans were not the first newcomers to leave their mark: the area of **Old Parish** around Ardmore gets its name as the arrival point of Saint Declan in the first half of the fifth century, supposedly the very first of Ireland's proselytising Christians, preceding Saint Patrick. The region's early Christian foundations became influential across the country, the most important being that at **Lismore**, founded in 636. It flourished first as a centre of ecclesiastical learning, and later as a secular power rivalling that of Waterford city itself.

Today the distinctions between urban and rural remain marked. Alongside thriving, modern Waterford city, pockets of ancient cultures and histories survive, such as the tiny Gaelic community of **Ring**, and the historic ecclesiastical foundations of **Ardmore** and Lismore. An air of prosperity pervades the county as a whole, in farmland enriched by centuries of cultivation, and in the renewed commercial importance of the historic port of Waterford city. The coast offers sandy beaches, a handful of quaint fishing harbours and some great seascapes. It's easily accessible too – notably good main roads serve city and county, good for long-distance cycling and hitching.

Waterford City

WATERFORD's appearance from the river is deceptively grim: the bare and open stretch of water with the ugly grey wharves and cranes of the working port holds no suggestion of the lively city pulsating behind its dull quays. This is the commercial capital of the southeast; and yet it retains buildings from Viking and Norman times, and from the eighteenth century, both periods of past eminence.

The web of narrow streets that grew up as the focus for commercial activity in the city's earliest days holds the modern city together in compact dynamism. While Waterford has had the modern infrastructure of an industrial, rather than a rural, centre for decades, the city has developed socially and economically even within the last ten years.

Waterford is basically a modern European port wrapped around an ancient Irish city. The **historic town** can happily be explored in a day or so, and the **nightlife** also warrants some sampling. One of the few buoyant commercial centres of any size in the Republic, a sign of Waterford's comparative prosperity is the number of young people the place now attracts (and sustains), in strong contrast to other parts of this country bled by emigration. Glad to be here and working, the youth have created an increasingly positive social life. Though a small city by European standards, Waterford has some excellent bars, a small but growing number of decent and imaginative places to eat, and the burgeoning youth/rock scene of an optimistic, albeit small-scale, urban environment. Alongside the city's vigorous modernity, though, there's plenty that's traditional, most obviously the place of the **pub** as a focal point of social activity, and the persistence of traditional **music**.

A further measure of Waterford's social and economic confidence is the town's attitude towards the large numbers of people known as "West Brits", a curiously affectionate term used to describe English people living here and a social peculiarity of the southeast. Either recently arrived, or, if remnants of the Anglo-Irish ascendancy, no longer representing a threat, they are accepted and have integrated, while keeping a separate identity.

History

The deep, navigable **River Suir** has been the source of the city's importance since the ninth century. Waterford has an excellent harbour; deep inland, and therefore easily defended, it's also perfectly positioned for the internal trading routes of the Barrow and the Nore rivers, reaching into the heart of the southeast's rich farmland. Reliable recorded history of the city starts with the **Viking** settlement founded in the tenth century. The layout of the city (so similar to that other Viking town, Wexford) retains its Viking roots, the very long quays and adjacent narrow lanes forming the trading centre. Waterford was the most important Viking settlement in Ireland, and its inhabitants were so feared that even the bellicose Celtic Deises had to pay them tribute – failure to pay *Airgead Sróine* (Nose Money) resulted in having your nose chopped off. Reginald's (originally Ranguald's) Tower dates from this time, as do some of the remains of the city walls. Nearby, two well-preserved stone arches inside the *Reginald Grill Bar* were in fact "sallyports", through which ships entered the fortified city from what is now The Mall but was then water.

The next wave of invaders to leave an imprint were the **Anglo-Normans** in the twelfth century. When the King of Leinster, Dermot MacMurrough, made his bid for the High Kingship of Ireland, he knew Waterford was strategically vital for control of the southwest. In 1170, he called on his Welsh Anglo-Norman allies to attack the city, the most important of these being the Earl of Pembroke – **Strongbow**. The city's walls and towers were formidably strong, but on the third day of attack, August 25, the Normans discovered a weak point, made a breach and flooded in, taking the city with scenes of bloodcurdling violence. Strongbow received his reward: Dermot MacMurrough's daughter Aoife's hand in marriage, and her inheritance. The wedding celebrations took place in Reginald's Tower; the marriage was the first such alliance between a Norman earl and an Irish king, a crucial and symbolic historical event.

The following year, surprised at the Welsh Norman lords' success, **Henry II** arrived with an awesome display of naval strength (400 ships) and gave the Waterford Normans a charter offering protection – his way of ensuring allegiance to the English crown. Subsequent English monarchs maintained this allegiance, and in 1210 King John arrived with a huge army and enlarged the city with new fortifications. The best preserved towers of these **Norman walls** are at Railway Square, Castle Street, Stephen Street and Jenkins Lane. During the thirteenth century, the city was the unspoken capital of Ireland. It reaped further royal favour through its part in bringing to ground two would-be usurpers threatening Henry VII; first Lambert Simnel in 1487, and then Perkin Warbeck ten years later.

Waterford flourished as an important European port into the sixteenth and seventeenth centuries, **trading** with France, Spain, Portugal and Newfoundland, as well as maintaining its inland commerce. It was the only city in Ireland to withstand **Cromwell**, though his forces returned under the command of General Ireton, who took the city without the usual scenes of carnage, giving its citizens honourable terms. The city's importance in trade continued into the eighteenth century, and there's plenty of architectural evidence, both ecclesiastical and secular, of this period's prosperity. The name Waterford is nowadays most famous for its **crystal**, first produced in 1783. The factory closed in 1851, but reopened in 1951, and is now one of the city's major employers.

Arriving and Accommodation

Roads from the north and the east converge on the river at the **railway and bus stations** (*Bus Éireann* information ☎051/79000; *Irish Rail* information ☎051/73401); the city lies over the bridge to the south. Regular daily **trains** connect Waterford to Clonmel, Tipperary, Limerick, Wexford, Kilkenny and Dublin. *Rapid Express Club Travel*, 32 Michael Street (☎051/72149; Mon–Sat 9.30am–6pm; see "travel details" at the end of this chapter), operates a **coach service** to Dublin and Tramore that's cheaper than *Bus Éireann* standard fares. You can pay on the coach, but advance booking is advisable, and at weekends essential. There are scheduled **flights** to London daily from **Waterford Regional Airport**, Killowen (☎051/75589). There's no bus to the airport: a taxi will cost you around £8.

The **tourist office** (May–Sept Mon–Sat 9am–6pm, Oct–April Mon–Fri 9am–12.45pm & 2–5.15pm; ☎051/75823) is at 41 Merchants Quay, roughly midway between the bridge and the nineteenth-century clock tower. It has comprehensive lists of recommended **hotels and B&Bs**. Otherwise, you'll find the cheaper B&Bs along Parnell Street, The Mall and O'Connell Street: some central possibilities are recommended below. In addition, there is a **private hostel**, *Bolton House* in Bolton Street (☎051/79870; £3.50), but the owner is a "character" whom some have found offensive: we would advise against a stay, particularly for women travellers. There's no **campsite** within walking distance of

Rooms

Portree Guest House, Mary Street (☎051/74574). Friendly, comfy and clean. £11.50–13.

O'Connell House, O'Connell Street (☎051/74175). Also welcoming and central. £12.

Saint Thomas's B&B, Thomas Street, off O'Connell Street (☎051/75058). £11–12.

Maryland House, The Mall (☎051/76162, 75000). Larger place with hotel status, and facilities including a bar. £16.

Derrynane House, 19 The Mall (☎051/75179). Good, plain B&B, open March–Nov. £13.

Mrs M Ryan, *Beechwood*, 7 Cathedral Square (☎051/76677). Again March–Nov only, simple, but attractive location. £12.

Mayors Walk House, 12 Mayors Walk (☎051/55427). £12.

Dooley's, 30 The Quay (☎051/73531). Fine central location for this more upmarket hotel. £25–30.

The Bridge Hotel, The Quay (☎051/77222). Sizeable hotel, where the bars can get rather rowdy. £28–35.

The City

Waterford is centred on a lovely wedge of Georgiana, between the eighteenth-century shops and houses of **O'Connell** and **George** streets, which run behind the modern quays, and the decaying splendour of **Parnell Street** and **The Mall** with their fine doorways and fanlights. These converge on **Reginald's Tower**, and the angle the two thoroughfares describe is arced by the extensive remains of Viking and Norman city walls. The area immediately behind the quays is still the city's commercial centre. Continue from **Barron Strand Street** through all its changes of name down to where **John Street** meets Parnell Street, and you find a great concentration of fast-food joints and bars. The area of lanes between The Mall and **Parade Quay** contain some of the city's nicest juxtapositions of medieval and eighteenth-century architecture.

Reginald's Tower and the French Church

Waterford's most historic building is **Reginald's Tower**, a large cylindrical Norman tower of 1003, its design similar to the Scottish *broch*, with a concealed stairway built within its massive wall. It houses the city's **museum** (Easter–Sept Mon–Fri 11am–1pm & 2–7pm, Sat 11am–2pm), which has an impressive collection of royal charters that make quite clear the central role Waterford's allegiance to the English crown played in the city's history. The collection includes the Charter Roll of Richard II (1399), a fabulous transcript of earlier charters.

Wander up Bailey's New Street just behind Reginald's Tower and you immediately come to Waterford's other important medieval building, the **French Church**, or Greyfriars. Founded by Franciscans in 1240, the church served as a hospital in the sixteenth century (thus escaping destruction at the suppression of the monasteries), and from 1693 to 1815 was used as a place of worship by French Huguenot refugees, whom the city sheltered in their exile from persecution at home. It's now a solid, roofless ruin with a complete tower and fine east triple-lancet window. Stones at the base of the outer windows have comic carved figures, and the church has some interesting carved slabs, including that of Sir Neal O'Neill, who accompanied James II in his flight from the Battle of the Boyne.

WATERFORD CITY

Heritage Centre and the cathedrals

Just off to the right of Bailey's New Street, in Greyfriars street, the **Waterford Heritage Centre** is housed in a small, old church (☎051/71227; Easter–Sept Mon–Fri 9am–7pm, Sat 11am–4pm; 50p). This is arguably Ireland's most exciting new museum: in 1987/88 extensive excavations of a large portion of the city's old Viking and Norman centre (prior to building development) resulted in finds of quite exceptional quality and variety, dating largely from the early eleventh century. The heritage centre displays the best of these, including leather foot-wear, antler combs, intricately wrought brooches, lathe–turned wooden bowls, weaponry and ceramic vessels. The collection should grow as conservation work continues, and even now it's all well worth seeing.

Further up Bailey's New Street, you enter Waterford's next significant period of church building at the Church of Ireland **Christ Church Cathedral** (May–Sept Mon–Fri 10.30am–1pm & 2–4pm, though this does vary). Rebuilt in the 1770s by John Roberts, who did much work in Waterford for both Catholics and Protestants, it's a nicely proportioned building in soothing cream and grey, with a fine steeple and a spacious interior. It's set in an equally pleasant square, the lanes around it showing yet more classical doorways and fanlights, some fine, some derelict. The monuments inside the cathedral are worth a look, in particular that of James Rice (1469), an effigy of a corpse in an advanced state of decay, with various creatures crawling in and out of the carcass.

Roberts was also responsible for **Holy Trinity Cathedral** in Barron Strand Street. Originally built in 1793, this was greatly altered during the nineteenth century to become the curving, heavy extravaganza it is today. It's a swirling exercise in decoration, hung with Waterford chandeliers and striving for maximum opulence: the fourteenth-century vestments on display were donated by the protestants of Christ Church.

City Hall, Georgian architecture and Waterford crystal

Christ Church apart, it's in the city's secular architecture that the best of the eighteenth century is realised. Christ Church Cathedral looks down over The Mall where the **City Hall** (1788, again by John Roberts) has a spacious entrance hall that was once used as a meeting place and merchants' exchange. It's now the council building, but if you are interested in Waterford crystal ask at the desk to see pieces from the original glassworks, including a huge **chandelier**. By far the finest eighteenth-century architectural detail in the city, though, is the oval staircase inside the lilac-coloured **Chamber of Commerce** in George Street (open office hours). Once again the work of John Roberts (1795), it's a beautiful cantilevered staircase with fine decorative stucco work. Georgian housing continues down O'Connell Street, where you'll also find the *Garter Lane Arts Centre*, at numbers 5 and 22a (see below).

If you want to follow up on **Waterford Crystal** (which is of course for sale all over town), the *Waterford Crystal Glass Factory* offers free **tours** (Mon–Fri at 10.15am, 11am, 11.45am, 1.45pm & 2.30pm) around its glass-cutting and blowing workshops. This is interesting if you've never seen the process before, and a fair way to work up an appetite on a wet day, but not the "absolute must" the publicity tends to suggest. Tours take about forty minutes and in high season it's advisable to book in advance; the tourist office will do this for you free of charge, or you can do it yourself on ☎051/73311. Buses to the factory leave from beside the clock tower on the quays: ask the driver to put you off at the factory.

River Cruises

If you want to escape the city for a while, *Galley River Cruises'* **trips to New Ross** offer a unique view of the countryside. The cruise includes either lunch, afternoon tea or evening meal (June–Aug, £5–17, book at tourist office or phone ☎051/21723/73752). Alternatively enquire at the tourist office about Viking Cruises.

Food and Entertainment

Finding something to **eat** is unlikely to prove a problem. There are plenty of **fast-food** joints down Michael Street and John Street, or for more substantial fare *Poppy's Restaurant*, 18 High Street, offers large helpings, lovingly prepared, with a vegetarian dish always available (☎051/70008; from £4 for lunch, around £10 in the evening). *Haricot's* on O'Connell Street (Mon–Fri 10am–last orders 8pm, Sat 10am–5.45pm) is a cosy and reasonably priced wholefood restaurant also catering well for vegetarians. **Pizza and pasta** is plentiful; *Gino's* (the Applemarket; daily noon–midnight) is cheery and serviceable with pizzas from £2.50, and home-made Italian ice-cream. *The Happy Garden*, Arundel Square, is the best **Chinese** restaurant in town; meals around £10.

For **pub food**, *Egans* (Broad Street; Mon–Sat noon–2.30pm) serves delicious home-made bread, soup, cooked lunches, and seafood during the summer, and hot specials daily from £4.50; *Geoff's* bar on John Street serves good sandwiches. The historic *Munster Bar*, on The Mall, produces generous helpings of simple dishes, freshly cooked on the premises and served at the bar (Mon–Fri 12.30–2.30pm): it also has a restaurant upstairs (dinner around £12), almost as popular for its fine nineteenth-century oak-carved interior as for the food.

Drinking and the music scene

Waterford has some wonderful **bars**, and there is a steadily growing **music scene** here. John Street has two of the city's favourite watering holes – *Geoff's* and *The Pulpit* – both lively, young places with a good social mix, and useful for keying into what's happening in the city. *The Olde Rogue*, across the street on Applemarket, has a good mixed crowd and is another useful place to check out what music is on locally. In Michael Street *The Old Stand* is another lively young bar, and *Bobby McGee's* has regular sessions on Thursdays – rock, blues, MOR or country. *Barrs* on Mayors Walk is also young and friendly, and a good bet for women who don't want to be hassled. This pub has occasional **blues/jazz** sessions on a Monday.

For **traditional music** there are a few regular spots: *T.H.Doolans*, George Street; *Mullanes*, Newgate Street, a singing pub; and *The Metropole*, Bridge Street. Out of town there's *Meade's Bar* (☎051/73187) at Halfwayhouse, three miles down the road to Cheekpoint, with very good sessions on Saturdays and occasional Wednesdays. There is not a great deal of **jazz** in Waterford, but you could try *The Reginald*, next to Reginald's Tower, or *The Trap* (3 The Manor, at the bottom of John Street). A good spot for bands (rock/punk/heavy metal) is *The Mansion*, Johnstown (opposite the hospital), either free or around £1; more when they have top Irish bands.

Clubs include *Snages*, behind *Egans* pub on Broad Street (Tues–Sun £4, Sat £5), and *Cheers* (O'Connell Street); both with discos and expensive drinks. As everywhere, most of the hotels have discos at weekends. *The Bridge Hotel* on The Quays is a bit of a meat market, probably at its best at weekends, but it's also where big name bands play.

Finally, Waterford's music scene would not be the same without the *Freewheelers*, a local bikers club. They may look like Hell's Angels, but they're more interested in their bikes than in violence. It's well worth checking out gigs organised by them – usually in *O'Shea's* out at TRAMORE, for which they arrange buses so people don't have to drink and drive. They also organise a **custom and classic bike** weekend at Whit, which involves lots of bands, bonfires and camping. For further information about any of their events, ask those who display *Freewheeler* posters on their premises.

Arts and Theatre

The *Garter Lane Arts Centre* (☎051/55038; Tues–Sat 11am–6pm), with two locations at 5 and 22a O'Connell Street, has painting and sculpture exhibitions, a theatre and a good current events notice board. It's the place to catch a performance by *Red Kettle Theatre Company* (☎051/79688), and by a varied programme of small touring companies. Waterford's other theatre is the *Theatre Royal*, on The Mall, which stages the city's **Light Opera Festival** in October. The *Regional Technical College* on the main Cork road is used for **classical music** recitals, generally advertised in the tourist office.

Listings

Bicycles *Wright's Cycle Depot*, Henrietta Street off Parade Quay (☎051/74411), for bike repairs and parts. There is nowhere to hire bikes in the city.

Dental emergencies South Eastern Health Board (☎051/76111; Mon–Fri 9am–5pm); ask to be put through to Newgate Street Dental Clinic.

Family Planning Clinic Michael Street, above *Tokens* boutique.

Hospital Ardkeen Regional Hospital, Dunmore Road (☎051/73321); for emergencies, and dental emergencies out of office hours.

Launderette *Washed Ashore*, The Quays (Mon–Fri 8am–9pm, Sat 8.30am–6.30pm).

Rape Crisis Centre ☎051/75248, 76124, 73362.

Shopping There's shopping until 9pm every Friday; the Applemarket is a general market held on Friday and Saturday. For committed junk enthusiasts, Waterford Auction Galleries (O'Connell Street; Tues–Sat) are compulsive.

Travel agents *USIT Youth and Student Travel Office*, 36/37 Georges Street (☎051/72601, 77166; Mon–Fri 9.30am–6pm, Sat 11am–4pm). *Harvey Travel Limited*, Gladstone Street (☎051/72048, 72784) is the agent for *Slattery* and *Funtrek*.

Youth Information and Advice Centre Parade Quay (Mon–Fri 9.30am–6pm, Sat 10am–5pm), is a general welfare and advice centre for young Irish citizens, but can give referral advice to people in difficulties.

Around the county

It's easy to get into the heart of Waterford county's rich farmland and empty mountains from Waterford city. Fast main roads offer good hitching inland, and the *Munster Way* just north of Lismore is as good a route as any from which to enjoy the Knockmealdown Mountains. The Blackwater River valley is the county's most impressive, while that of the Nire offers more intimate scenery, especially in the stretch above Ballymacarbery (about six miles south of Clonmel, Tipperary) as it flows down from the Comeragh mountains. Discovering Waterford's stunning and varied coast is slower and requires a narrower focus – it makes more sense to pick a small area, such as Ardmore, Helvick Head or Dunmore East, and explore it at a leisurely pace, than to try and see the whole coastline.

Inland: the Blackwater Valley

Typical of the outstanding beauty of the inland county is the stretch of the **Blackwater valley** around Cappoquin, where the river makes a sharp westward turn towards County Cork, describing as it goes the southerly limit of the Knockmealdown Mountains. **CAPPOQUIN** itself is prettily situated on a wooded hillside overlooking the river. Despite this beautiful location, the village seems strangely neglected, and there's little attempt to cater for visitors beyond a few B&Bs used mainly by a handful of fishermen at holiday times: if you want to stay Cathy Lynch's in Main Street is a good, central option (☎058/54642; £10). The only music you'll get will be a country and western/ballad mix on Friday and Saturday at *Fawlty's* bar, Mill Street, probably the best place for a weekday lunch, with a typical bacon-and-cabbage style menu.

Although there's little to detain you in the village, however, the surrounding countryside is lovely. Walk half a mile east, take the right fork by the statue of the Virgin, and you come to the **Glenshelane River walk**. This follows the river through its deep valley banked by pine trees and, after about three miles, brings you to **Mount Melleray**, a Cistercian monastery that welcomes visitors in search of solitude. The trail eventually opens out to more level country, affording great views of the Knockmealdowns and the Galtymore mountains of Tipperary. In all, the walk's a taster for the varied terrain of the major long-distance walk in this part of the country, the *Munster Way* (see below).

Lismore

Set in the lovely broad plain of the Blackwater valley three miles west of Cappoquin, **LISMORE** is a gem of ecclesiastical history. Roads approach the town between the river and gentle slopes of mixed woodland – especially beautiful in spring and autumn. The setting is dominated by the hugely romantic towers and battlements of **Lismore Castle**, whose pale, white-grey stone, set with mullioned windows, rises magnificently on the hill from glorious woodlands and sumptuous **gardens** (gardens open to the public during summer, Sun–Fri 1.45pm–4.45pm – though hardly worth the £1.50 to get in). The castle itself is a successful mid-nineteenth-century imitation of a Tudor castle, remodelled by Joseph Paxton (designer of the Crystal Palace) around the remains of the medieval fort that originally stood here. The castle's long occupation by the Anglo-Irish aristocracy (and less permanent colonists, including Sir Walter Raleigh) explains why so much of the layout of the parkland and farmland around here is reminiscent of wealthy English shires. The whole setting is strongly evocative of Lismore's former power and glory – even though this building in fact has nothing to do with that era.

Around 630 AD Saint Carthage founded a monastic complex for both monks and nuns in Lismore, and the place flourished as a centre of learning so much that in the next century, under the influence of great teachers such as Saint Colman, it became an important university city. This growth continued into the twelfth century, despite 300 years of sporadic pillage by first Vikings then Normans. Lismore held great political as well as religious power, and the rivalry between the Sees of Lismore and Waterford, which epitomises the split histories of Waterford city and county, was only resolved in 1363 when the two were united.

Invaders continued to attack the city, and in the late sixteenth century the medieval cathedral was almost totally destroyed by Queen Elizabeth's army. Its site is now occupied by **Saint Carthage's Church of Ireland Cathedral**. Although this was built in 1633, the overall look is early nineteenth-century neo-Gothic, the tower and ribbed spire having been added in 1827 by James Pain, and the windows of the nave reshaped at the same time. It's a lovely building, sitting in a cobbled churchyard of ancient yews and pollarded limes. Inside is some interesting stonework, including the McGrath family tomb (1548), which has almost comic carving around the base of the stone slab. The chunky carving of a bishop holding an open book set in the back wall is from the tenth-century monastic settlement. In the south transept, there's some striking stained glass by Burne-Jones, the English Pre-Raphaelite.

There's not much sign of this rich history in Lismore's current economically depressed existence, but it does somehow seem to preserve a quiet reverence about itself. It does little to raise its sleepy head for visitors, and the sporadic tourist buses that pull up, briefly disgorge, and head off again, only accentuate the feeling of being left in another age. Plans are afoot though to change all this: Lismore was recently designated a Heritage Town, and there are plans to turn the courthouse into an audio-visual centre, make the Cathedral library publicly accessible, open a tower of the castle as a viewing point, and generally spruce the place up. For the time being, though, it remains quietly charming.

Lismore practicalities

If you want to stay in Lismore, you'll find **B&B** in the centre of town at *Alana* in Chapel Street (just up behind the courthouse; £11), at *Ballyrafter House* (☎058/54002; £20), or at Mrs J Power's *Beechcroft*, Deerpark Road, half a mile out of town (☎058/54273; £11.50). There's an *An Óige* **youth hostel** three miles north of Lismore (☎058/54390; April & May £3.50, June–Sept £4.50). For free **camping** in town go down over the bridge and to the left through the gate; there's a fabulous spot beneath the castle.

Lismore has some fascinating ancient **bars** and grocery stores, a delight to explore in themselves, though there's not much beyond this trip into the past by way of food or entertainment. Options for **eating** are pretty limited: along the main street are *Eamonn's* (hot cooked lunch Mon–Sat midday), *The Red House*, with a great range of pub meals (all day and into the evening, 7 days), and *The Ballyrafter*, which serves excellent cheap, simple lunches. For **music** try *Rosie's West End Bar*, *Eamonn's* or *The Red House*, at any of which you might catch traditional, country and western and ballad sessions on summer weekends.

The Munster Way

The road north from Lismore to the youth hostel is typical of this area's gorgeous river valleys, stuffed with rhododendrons, bracken, beech trees and oaks, and dripping feathery pines. Spongy mosses cover walls, and young ferns spring out of them. The hostel marks the start of the long-distance hiking path, the **Munster Way**.

Immediately north of the hostel, you come to higher ground and more open spaces, scattered with sheep and fir trees. The path goes through the Knockmealdowns, round the huge peat-covered mound of Sugarloaf Hill, to a viewing spot known as **The Vee**, just five miles from the hostel. From its steep, heathery V-shaped sides there's a tremendous view of the perfectly flat vale below with its patches of fields, and the town of Cahir at the foot of the Galty Mountains. From here the Way descends to Clonmel in County Tipperary, around seventeen miles furhter, but if you don't want such a long walk you can follow the road down to CLOGHEEN and hitch to the independent **hostel** at Cahir, County Tipperary (see p.201), or the *An Óige* hostel of *Mountain Lodge*, Burncourt, Cahir (☎052/67277; March–May £3.50, June–Sept £4.50).

The *Munster Way* is clearly signposted all the way to, eventually, Carrick-on-Suir in Tipperary. The walk involves long distances rather than steep, dramatic inclines, and most of the way it's within a mile or so of habitation. Nevertheless solitary walkers should bear in mind that much of the route is out of sight of the lowlands, and distress signals won't be noticed. The relevant *Bord Fáilte* Information Sheet, giving route guidelines for this section of the way, is *Carrick-on-Suir–the Vee*, Information Sheet No. 26J.

The Coast

Waterford's coastline offers good sandy beaches, and some breathtaking coastal walks. The open grandeur of bays like Dungarvan is offset by the intimacy of hidden fishing ports, and pockets of ancient history at Ring and Ardmore. The best of the **beaches** are at Dunmore East, Tramore, Annestown, Bunmahon and Ardmore. Major seaside towns are connected to Waterford by regular bus services, but the choicest spots are best walked, cycled or slowly hitched to: using *Bus Éireann* to get to these involves a manipulation of the timetable verging on the miraculous.

Passage East and Ballyhack

Immediately east of Waterford city, at the neck of its long harbour, the pretty ferry village of **PASSAGE EAST** nestles under craggy hills, the estuary slopes aflame with wild gorse. The ferry here connects with **BALLYHACK** in County Wexford (*Passage East Car Ferry* ☎051/82488; continuous services Mon–Sat 7.30am–8pm & Sun 9.30am–8pm; in summer until 10pm; average crossing time ten minutes; car and passengers £3.50 single, £5.50 return, pedestrians £1 return) – a particularly useful route east for cyclists, especially if you're making for Rosslare, or want to stay with the coast. *The Farleigh Pub* in Passage East does a great range of **bar food** during the summer; sandwiches anytime of year. Across the water, less than a mile from Ballyhack, there's an *An Óige* **hostel** at ARTHURSTOWN (☎051/89186; March–May £3.80, June–Sept £5.50). Ballyhack should be as pretty as her Waterford counterpart but isn't, despite the fact that the village is dominated by a fine sixteenth-century tower house. It has one miserable bar and a very good seafood restaurant.

Dunmore East

Further around the Waterford coast, **DUNMORE EAST** settles snugly between small, chunky sandstone cliffs topped by masses of rambling golden gorse. The main street follows a higgledy-piggledy contour from the safe, sandy cove beside which the east village sits, towards a busy harbour full of the rippled reflections of brightly coloured fishing boats, and cradled by the crooked finger of the harbour wall. From here, the ruddy sandstone cliffs make bold ribs around the coast. This is still a very active fishing harbour, but has also cashed in on its undeniable picturesqueness, with self-consciously new thatched houses sneaking in alongside the originals.

Quaint as it is, Dunmore East has become very much a playground for affluent Waterford people, and there are three large **hotels** to cater for them – the best being the *Haven* (☎051/83150; £30). At least this means there are plenty of facilities. You can get decent **pub food** at *The Ocean Hotel* (☎051/83136; also rooms for around £30), and the conservative *Candlelight Inn* (☎051/83215; rooms around £27.50); both have very middle of the road singalongs by way of entertainment. *The Ship* restaurant and bar's customers are mostly sailors, visiting and local, and the food is excellent. The handiest reasonably priced **B&Bs** are Mrs Butler's *Church Villa* (☎051/83390; £12.50) and Mrs Rodgers' *Copper Beech*, Dock Road (☎051/83187; £12). For **camping**, there's *Dunmore East Caravan and*

Camping Park (☎051/83174; June to mid-Sept). The **supermarket** is on Dock Road, and there's an Allied Irish **Bank** with a Banklink machine always available. Dunmore East is the home of *Waterford Harbour Sailing Club* (☎051/83389, 83230), where an experienced sailor might get some crewing.

West to An Rinn

Nine miles west of Dunmore East, **TRAMORE** caters for a different type of holidaymaker, and a different kind of bank balance. It's a busy, popular seaside resort serving families from Waterford and Cork, and has plenty of amusements, caravans, B&Bs, and a huge sandy beach. *O'Shea's* is probably the liveliest bar in Tramore, very popular, with rock or blues every weekend; a good alternative watering-hole is the bar of *The Victoria Hotel*.

DUNGARVAN is the major coastal town of County Waterford, and its setting is magnificent. There's a wonderful view over the grand, broad bay as you descend to the town, the open heights around topped by pine forests that seem to have been poured on like thick syrup. The town itself is modern, with all the amenities that go along with that, as well as a fine beach; but of more interest and charm are the small communities along the coast to the west.

The An Rinn *Gaeltacht*

AN RINN, or RING, is a pocket of Irish tradition hidden away on the modern Waterford coast. It's a tiny **Gaelic-speaking community** of about 800 that has somehow survived in what is otherwise one of Ireland's more developed counties, all the more remarkable given the "West Brit" flavour of much of the county's coast. The language survives healthily as do other traditions, notably music and set dancing, and Ring has its own radio station.

It's quite tricky to find – signposts to An Rinn on the R674 (off the N25) are minimal – and hard to recognise when you do: like many *Gaeltacht* villages Ring consists of a community of farms and a handful of **bars** spread over a wide area, with no real centre. This can be frustrating if you don't have transport, as you have to rely on hitching to and from some of the best bars. A good place to get your bearings is *Tigh an Cheoil* (☎058/46209), a bar down by the pier with traditional sessions on Thursdays, Saturdays and Sundays throughout the year, and at other times during the summer. The owners have a field you can **camp** in, and will put you in touch with whatever's going on in the area. Other bars for **traditional music** are *Murrays*, just over a mile away at Helvick; *Mooneys*, on the way out of Ring towards Dungarvan; *The Marine Bar*, six miles west of Dungarvan on the N25; *Seanchaí*; and John Paul Walsh's bar, *Old Parish* – ask locally for directions.

Ring must have some of the cheapest **B&Bs** in the country. Breda Maher's *Aisling*, Gurtnadiha, Ring (☎058/46134; around £8), is welcoming and well run, in a fabulous spot overlooking Dungarvan Harbour, or call Liam and Breda Maher at *Helvick View*, Ring (☎058/46297).

There's nothing specific at Ring beyond the way of life. When the tide's out, you can walk a few miles along the shoreline west of Ring around **Helvick Head**. When the tide's in, a walk on this headland gives splendid views of sculpted cliffs along the coast, and of the mountains inland. Alternatively, local fishermen will take you out in their boats by arrangement.

Ardmore

ARDMORE is delightful, combining ancient history with a setting full of character. The sixth century saw the arrival here of Saint Declan, at least thirty years before Saint Patrick, and the surrounding area of **Old Parish** is so called because it's supposedly the oldest parish in Ireland. At Ardmore, a medieval **cathedral and round tower** stand on the site of the saint's original monastic foundation, commanding stunning views over Ardmore Bay. The long, low twelfth-century cathedral has massy buttresses, its stoutly rounded doors and windows confirming the proud – albeit roofless – Romanesque solidity of the building, while the slender round tower, tall and fine with a conical roof, stands alongside in poignant contrast. There are stones with early *ogham* inscriptions inside the cathedral, but the most exceptional carvings are on the west external wall. Romanesque arcading, originally from an earlier building, has been set here beneath the window, with boldly carved scenes showing The Weighing of Souls, The Fall of Man, The Judgement of Solomon and The Adoration of the Magi; truly impressive, and unique in quality and design. **Saint Declan's Oratory**, supposedly his burial site, also stands in the graveyard.

The village down below consists of a pleasant row of cottages, a few pubs, a shop and a couple of excellent sandy beaches. There's a **caravan and camping** site, a small **hotel** (*Cliff House*; ☎024/94106; £27) and a **B&B** (*Byron Lodge*; ☎024/94157; £13.50), and in the summer the place is busy with people. Myth has it that when Saint Declan arrived here from Wales, his bell and vestments were magically carried by the large stone that now sits on the beach. This would explain why the boulder is of a completely different geology from the surrounding land – though the Ice Age seems a more likely, if comparatively mundane, explanation. Another improbable tale is that crawling under the stone cures rheumatism. It looks unlikely that a fit person could squirm under it, let alone an invalid.

If you walk through the village to the east, up the hill and to the path past the *Cliff House Hotel*, you come to **Saint Declan's Well** and a steeply gabled **oratory**. Like many ancient wells, it's a moving spot, with fresh water springing beside three primitive stone crosses where pilgrims used to wash, and a stone chair. From here, there's a fine walk around the headland along rocky cliffs for five miles or so, as far as Whiting Bay.

TIPPERARY

Tipperary is the largest of Ireland's inland counties, and also the richest. The county's wealth comes from the central **Golden Vale**, a flat limestone plain shared with eastern Limerick that's prime beef and dairy cattle territory. This enormous stretch of farming land is abutted on most borders by crops of mountain ranges, the most beautiful of which are the **Comeragh** and **Galty** mountains and the **Glen of Aherlow**. These are all in the south of the county, and it's this area, without doubt, that packs in the most excitement. The curling course of the **Suir**, Tipperary's principal river, sweeps up most of what there is to see. But for many, Tipperary's attractions hang on one site alone. The **Rock of Cashel** is the county's most dramatic feature by far, its limestone sides rising cliff-like two hundred feet above the level ground, crowned with the high walls and towers of some splendid medieval ecclesiastical architecture.

Tipperary often has a vaguely familiar ring, thanks to the World War I marching song, *It's a long way to Tipperary*. The county was actually picked for the song simply for the rhythmic beat of its name, which dashes the romance somewhat. In fact Tipperary isn't particularly far from anywhere in southern Ireland, and this is probably its greatest advantage: you can catch the few worthwhile sights on your way through, and still be on the south or west coast within a few hours.

Carrick-on-Suir

Tucked in Tipperary's southeast corner, at the foot of the mountain slopes of neighbouring County Waterford, **CARRICK-ON-SUIR** may well be the first place you see in Tipperary, a slight country town raised a cut above the rest by what is perhaps Ireland's most beautiful **Elizabethan mansion**: similar examples abound in England but were always a rarity here. Set at the very eastern end of the main street, the mansion was built by Thomas, Earl of Ormond ("Black Tom"), in anticipation of a visit from Queen Elizabeth I – and tributes to her are incorporated in the decoration throughout: above all in a fresco over the entrance way and in the superb stucco work of the long gallery. A stunning mansion, with mullioned windows running the length of the building, it's the only major example of a completely unfortified dwelling to date from the fifteenth century. It adjoins an earlier castle built on the banks of the Suir in 1450, and a claim is still disputed among historians that Anne Boleyn was born here. The guided tour, available on request, is well worth taking (mid-May to mid-Oct daily 9.30am–6.30pm; 80p, students 30p, heritage card; ☎051/40787).

Regardless of the mansion's splendours, it's as the birthplace of the champion cyclist **Sean Kelly** that the town is most proud of itself – and the tiny main square at the very west end of the main street has been renamed in his honour. **Tourist information** (☎051/40726; May–Sept Mon–Sat 10am–6pm) can be found beneath the clock on the square.

The Park Inn on New Street is probably the best place for good **bar food** (available midday and evenings); for excellent steaks and chops try *The Carrick Inn* (on the corner as you enter town from the direction of Clonmel), or you can always get fast food from the *Europa Grill* on the main street. If you need to stay the most reasonably priced **B&B** is at *The Carrick Inn* (☎051/41186; £10); alternatively try *Orchard House* in Sean Kelly Square (☎051/41390; £13).

Ahenny

Five miles north of Carrick, **AHENNY** has two beautiful high crosses in its graveyard. They're thought to be eighth-century, and are excellent examples of the transition period between the Early Christian plain shaft crosses and the highly ornate didactic crosses of Monasterboice and Kells.

Clonmel

CLONMEL, thirteen miles upstream, is far and away Tipperary's prettiest centre. It's a strangely genteel kind of place and retains something of its flavour as an early coaching town. It was the birthplace in 1713 of Laurence Sterne, philosopher and literary comic genius of the age of the stage, and it's not at all difficult to imagine Tristram Shandy goings-on in the fine Georgian inns around about. A hundred years later Clonmel became the principle base for *Bianconi,* the most successful coach business in the country. Bianconi came from Lombardy in Italy and ran his so-called *Bians* from what is now *Hearn's Hotel* on Parnell Street.

The town is a beautiful place to breeze through: you can't miss Clonmel's finest building, the sorely delapidated **Main Guard** sagging at the eastern end of O'Connell Street. The oldest public Classical building in Ireland, predating Dublin's Royal Hospital, it's hoped that funds will soon be found to prevent it sinking further into decay. The facade visible today was built by James Butler, first Duke of Ormond, as a courthouse for the Palatinate of the County of Tipperary and bears two panels showing coats of arms dated 1675.

Off to the left of the Main Guard runs Gladstone Street; to the right Sarsfield Street runs down to the river, and it's worth wandering here through the town's preserved backstreets and quayside mills. Other examples of period architecture include the nineteenth-century **St Mary's Roman Catholic Church**, with ziggurat tower and portico, in Irishtown, out past the imitation West Gate; the Greek revival styled **Wesleyan Church** on Wolfe Tone Street; and the **Old St Mary's** Church of Ireland Church with its octagonal tower and tower house. All of these are impressive from the outside, none offer much if you venture in. The **museum** in Parnell Street (☎052/21399; Tues–Sat 10am–1pm & 2–5pm), records local history in a collection of maps, newspapers, postcards and Bianconi prints, and also has a small gallery of fine paintings.

Practicalities

Clonmel's tourist information point is at 56 Parnell Street (☎052/22960; June 17–Sept 7; it may move location). There are plenty of **B&Bs** in the area, but few in the centre of town: try *Jervis,* 3 Jervis Place, Parnell Street (☎052/25327; £10–20), *Larkins Guest House,* Gladstone Street (☎052/22005; £12) or the *New Quay Guest House,* on The Quays, down beside the river. The nearest **hostel** is *Powers the Pot* at Harneys Cross, not too far from town up the slopes of the Comeragh Mountains (☎052/23085; £5, private room £6; camping £2.50; May–Sept; breakfasts and excellent dinners available). At 1200 feet this claims to be the highest house in the country, and it's on the threshold of excellent hill-walking country. The owner will pick up hostellers from Clonmel by arrangement, otherwise follow the hostel's signpost leaving Clonmel over the bridge and up via the Golf Club Road (R678) for about six miles. The cosy bar at the hostel will probably be alluring enough once you have actually found the place, but if you are here for any period of time and crave variety there is plenty of traditional music to found in the pubs of the Nire valley: *Melody's* bar, seven miles away at BALLYMACARBERY, has regular session (Wed, Fri & Sun), and the owners of the hostel will be able to give you up to the minute information about what's on round about.

There's no shortage of places to **eat** in Clonmel: for good coffee, soups and wholefood lunches try *The Rainbow Restaurant* on Abbey Street. *Bagwell's,* Sarsfield Street (Mon–Sat 10am–7pm) is a quaint bistro serving very good, very cheap meals, along with wine at familiarly high Irish prices; the owners also run the *Café Marie* (Mon–Sat 9am–6pm), upstairs in the small shopping mall opposite the museum. The *Salad Bowl,* Gladstone Street, is another good choice, or for huge helpings of good **pub grub,** try *Tierney's* on O'Connell Street (Mon–Sat 10.30am–8.30pm). For evening eats *La Scala,* just off Gladstone Street, has an inspiring and reasonably priced Italian menu.

There's no shortage of decent pubs too: if you want **music** try *Kitty O'Donnell's* near the station, for occasional traditional sessions at weekends, *Larkins Lounge Bar*, Gladstone Street, for a regular singalong round the piano any time, or take pot-luck at *Tierney's*, O'Connell Street.

Clonmel is the capital of Irish **greyhound racing**, and you can see the sport on Monday and Thursday nights at the local stadium; the surrounding countryside is also famous for racehorse breeding. **Fishing** off the quay is free, otherwise you can get a day's trout licence (£3) from John Carroll at Powers the Pot (☎052/ 23085). The river is said to be very good for the late run of the salmon in early September. In 1992 the **Fleadh Cheoil** is held in Clonmel from August 28–30; expect accommodation to be impossible.

North via Fethard

Leaving Clonmel, you could either head southwest, to the plain between the Knockmealdown and Galty mountains (see below); or north for Cashel, in which case the route via **FETHARD** is the most rewarding. A touchingly plain place to travel through, and rarely sought out by tourists, Fethard has a number of forgotten medieval remains, set at the back of the town towards the river. One of these is a ruined **Templar's Castle**, access to which is through the *Castle Inn* – contact the publican, Mr Keogh. Other remains of old friaries and Iron Age raths can be found in the surrounding land. There's also a **Folk Farm and Transport Museum** at the beginning of the Cashel Road (May–Sept Mon–Sat 10am–6pm, Sun 1.30–6pm). If you want to eat, *P.J. Lonegan's* home-cooked **lunches** (around £4) are worth stopping off for.

The Knockmealdown and Galty mountains

Of the two mountain ranges in southern Tipperary, the **Galties** make up one of the most scenic inland ranges in the country and are well worth discovering. The **Knockmealdowns** are less interesting, but offer easier hill walking. The valley plain between the two, which runs for about ten miles east of Mitchelstown (itself over the border in County Cork), is not much in itself – but if you base yourself plumb in the centre, you're well-placed to walk either range. Starting from Clonmel you've a choice of two routes west: the main roads via Cahir, or the lesser R665, which cuts straight across to Mitchelstown.

On this minor route you pass through **ARDFINNAN**, where a beautiful fourteen-arched stone bridge crosses the Suir, and a private castle stands on the overlooking hillside. Follow along the foot of the Knockmealdowns for several miles, and you'll come to CLOGHEEN, where there's the best turn-off route into the mountains, towards the terrific scenic point known as the **Vee** (see p.192). Powerfully telescopic views over Waterford and Tipperary stretch out from beside the lough in the mountain gap, revealing how uncompromisingly flat Tipperary is, hemmed in by its opposing and distant sets of mountain ranges. Two shepherds' shelters are set up here, with half the back wall missing so that the shepherds could always keep an eye on the sheep on the hill behind.

Back on the R665, you'll come next to **BALLYPOREEN**, a wide-streeted crossroads turned ghost town, whose moment of glory came on June 3, 1984, when **Ronald Reagan** made a prodigal return – his great-grandfather was supposedly born here in 1810. You can read all about it and look at photos of the visit in a specially built centre at the crossroads; opposite the *Ronald Reagan* pub.

Hostels in the mountains

The best place by far for **hikers** is the *Farmhouse* **hostel** (☎052/41906; £5; open all year; groceries fresh from the farm), in a small farmhouse annexe just off the N8 Cahir–Mitchelstown road. It's about four miles from Cahir, up a small lane off to the left, round two right-angle bends and by the laneside on the right. For the hitcher it's the most accessible hostel in the south Tipperary area.

Two more **hostels**, both *An Óige*, are conveniently set in the Galty mountains and the Glen of Aherlow beyond, deliberately distanced a short day's trek apart. The intervening terrain has its fair share of tarns, cliffs and wooded forests. The *Mountain Lodge Hostel* (☎052/67277; June–Sept £4.50, March–May £3.50) is a spacious Alpine-like old shooting lodge, eight miles along the Mitchelstown road from Cahir, then up a right turn, climbing for a mile by the river into the mountain. The *Ballydavid Wood House Hostel* (☎062/54148; June–Sept £5.50, March–May & Oct–Nov £3.80) is in the Glen of Aherlow six miles out of Cahir. Try and arrive in daylight for this one, for although meticulously signposted, the route has enough twists and turns to get you lost.

The Mitchelstown Caves

Walking aside, the main attraction of this area is the **Mitchelstown Caves** (daily 10am–6pm; £2, students £1; ☎052/67246) a massive pre-glacial underworld that's well worth visiting. Located eight miles from Mitchelstown itself, the caves are signposted north from Ballyporeen (or south off the N8) down the interlacing lanes of the valley. They are by far the most extensive and complicated cave system in Ireland (a couple of miles in all) and have remained, considering their scale, very uncommercialised. The whole underground system was discovered in 1833, when a labourer lost his crowbar down a crevice, though there are records from much earlier of one cave being used as a hiding place, most famously to shelter the Earl of Desmond after his unsuccessful rebellion in 1601.

The opening to the system is a cleft in the hill behind the house of the curator, Jackie English, whose harnessing of legend and folklore to match every calcite formation makes for an imaginative **tour**. Oisín, Niamh of the long golden hair, the cave of the Tír Na nÓg, the Tower of Babel and even the Shroud of Turin are all visualised in a range of colours washed down from the minerals in the limestone above – brown from the iron oxide, blue from the copper sulphate, black from the manganese and grey from the lead and zinc. The caves were formed by the incessant action of rainwater on the limestone over millions of years, and the fantastical stone formations grew out of the calcium carbonate (dissolved limestone) deposited by the dripping water, hardening as it evaporated into gigantic encrustations of stalactites and stalagmites. The temperature in the caves is around 54°F – this can feel chilly in summer, so bring a sweater. The tours only take in a few of the major caves, but are nonetheless worth taking.

Cahir

You're unlikely to miss **CAHIR**. The town sits on a major crossroads, its rectangular-shaped central area radiating routes from each corner: to Clonmel, Cork,

Cashel and Tipperary itself. The **castle**, set on a rocky islet in the River Suir, beside the road to Cork, is Cahir's outstanding attraction (even the name Cahir means "Fort"). In essence the building is Anglo-Norman, dating originally from the thirteenth and fifteenth centuries, though the virgin appearance of the outer shell is deceptive, with a good deal of the brickwork going on into the eighteenth and nineteenth centuries. The Irish chieftain Conor O'Brien was the first to build a fortress on the rock; but it was the Anglo-Norman Butlers, the Earls of Ormond, who made this into one of the most powerful castles in the country. The Earl of Essex showered the castle with artillery fire in 1599; but it had a quiet time of the Cromwellian and Williamite invasions, and receded towards ruin until rejuvenated, along with other town buildings, by the Earl of Glengall in the mid-nineteenth century. In modern times, the interior has been uniformly white-washed, and spartanly furnished.

Entrance to the castle (mid-June–mid-Sept daily 9am–7.30pm; April to mid-June & mid-Sept to Oct daily 10am–6pm; Nov–March Mon–Sat 10am–4.30pm, Sun 2–4.30pm; £1, students 40p, heritage card; ☎052/41011) is along the side rampart, bringing you into the confined space of the **middle ward**, dominated by the three-storey thirteenth-century **keep**. The keep itself consists of vaulted chambers, a portcullis and a round tower containing a prison, accessible through a trap door. Down to the left, you pass through a gateway topped by machicolations, musket loops to either side, where sixteenth-century invaders could have been bombarded with missiles, or boiling oil. Beyond is the much larger **outer ward** and, at its far end, the cottage built by the Earl of Glengall. The cottage now houses a **video theatre** where a twenty-minute film enthuses rhapsodically on the antiquities of southern Tipperary.

In the the **inner ward**, two corner towers overlook the road to Cork. The larger was probably designed to be independently defensible once the keep had fallen, and dates from a mixture of periods – straight, thirteenth-century stone stairs; fifteenth to sixteenth-century stone vaulting over the ground-floor main room; and nineteenth-century renovation work in the Great Hall, whose stepped battlements reflect sixteenth-century style. The smaller, square tower at the other end of the ward and the curtain wall date from the nineteenth century, though with medieval bases. Just to the left of this second tower, steps lead to the bottom of the well tower, where the castle could safeguard its water supply during a siege. The informative **guided tour** of the castle is well worth taking.

One further building worth seeing is the **Swiss Cottage** (June–Sept Tues–Sun 10am–5.30pm; March–June & Oct–Nov Sat & Sun 10am–5.30pm; last admission 30mins earlier; £1, students 40p, heritage card; ☎052/41144), about a mile out of Cahir on the Clonmel road. This ornamental cottage, probably designed by John Nash, was built in 1810 to provide the Earls of Glengall with a lodge of romanticised – and fashionable – rustic simplicity from which to enjoy their hunting, shooting and fishing. With its thatched roof and ornate timberwork it certainly looks the part, and its status as a unique period piece makes it a popular attraction – in high season and at weekends it's advisable to book your visit, out of season you should also check, as the official hours are not wholly reliable.

Practicalities

From the castle you can see another castellated mansion on the hill further along the Cork road: this was once the town prison but now offers **B&B** for little more than many others around town (*Carrigeen Castle*; ☎052/41370; £12–15). There's a basic but adequate independent **hostel**, *Lisakyle Hostel*, a mile south of town (open all year; £4.50, camping £3; ☎052/41963): ring for a lift if you're without transport, or ask at the owner's shop in town (*Condons*, opposite the post office at the Dublin road exit of the main square). Alternatively the *Farmhouse Hostel*, mentioned above, four miles out of town, is better. *Bus Éireann* **buses** leave from outside the *Crock of Gold*, across from the castle; there's a timetable posted in the window. The **tourist information office** (☎052/41453; May–Sept) is in the car park beside the castle.

For **food**, the coffee shop above the *Crock of Gold* provides sandwiches, scones and lunches. *Roma's Café*, on the Dublin side of the square, has normal café fare, and the cheapest prices in town. For good pub lunches try the *Galtee Inn* on the square. **Traditional music** is minimal and not of a high standard but takes place ad hoc on a Friday night at *O'Looney's* pub, on the Dublin road just before the railway station. One of the more interesting **pubs** to pop into is *Black Toms* on the Tipperary road; sawdust floor and very macho (even rough), but animated, with ballad and rebel songs playing on the tape recorder.

Cashel

Just eleven miles north of Cahir en route to Dublin, **CASHEL** is an obvious next stop. The town has grown around, and is completely dominated by, the spectacular **Rock of Cashel**. No tourist coach will bypass the site – so an early-morning or late-afternoon visit will make an important difference to your first impressions.

Not the most adequate as a base for visiting the Rock – there are a couple of upmarket hotels and a handful of central **B&Bs**: try *Rockville House*, the Rock (☎062/61760; £11), *Abbey House*, 1 Dominic Street opposite St Dominic's Friary (☎062/61104; £11), *Ashmore Guest House*, John Street (☎062/61286; £12) or *Maryville*, Bankplace (☎062/61098; £14–17). If you want to **camp** in the shadow of the rock, head for the O'Brien's farmhouse, *Rock House*, on St Patrick's Road (☎062/61003); to find it walk to the south end of the main street, past the post office, and turn right at the junction following the Dundrum road – it's less than a mile. **Eating** in Cashel is surprisingly limited, though pub lunches are available at *Grant's Castle Hotel* on Main Street (also rooms and evening meals; ☎062/61044; £17) and at *O'Reilly's*, and there are several cafés – *Alice's Bistro* in Main Street and *The Coffee House* are probably the best options, though they close early (7pm and 7.30pm respectively). **Cycle** parts and repairs are available at *Burke's*, in the centre The **tourist information office** (☎062/61333; mid-March to Sept) sits in the market house in the middle of the main street.

To get to the Rock from here, take the left hand route, then first left past the **Folk Village** (a rather tacky reconstruction of "traditional" village life, with a newly tarmacked road). You pass St Dominic's Friary (see below), and the next left takes you up the rampart to the entrance to the Hall of Vicars.

The Rock of Cashel

Approached from the north or west, the **Rock of Cashel** (mid-June to Sept daily 9am–7.30pm; mid-March to mid-June daily 9.30am–5.30pm; Oct to mid-March daily 9.30am–4pm, Sun 2–5pm; £1.50, students 60p, heritage card; ☎062/61437) appears as a spectacular mirage of fairytale turrets, crenellations and walls rising bolt upright from the vast encircling plain. It's a tour operator's dream: on one piece of freak limestone outcrop stands the most beautiful and complete Romanesque church in the country, a gargantuan medieval cathedral, a castle tower house, an eleventh-century round tower, a unique early high cross and an exquisite fifteenth-century Hall of Vicars – medieval Irish architecture wrapped up in a morning's investigation. Two more medieval priories lie at its feet.

In **legend** the Rock was formed when the Devil, flying overhead with a large stone in his mouth, suddenly caught sight of Saint Patrick standing ready to found his new church on the site, and in his shock dropped the rock (in the northeast of the county, a striking gap in a mountain range is known as the *Devil's Bit*). The Rock is also the place where Saint Patrick is supposed to have picked a shamrock in order to explain the doctrine of the Trinity – God the Father, Christ the Son and the Holy Ghost as three beings of the one stem – since when the shamrock has of course become Ireland's unofficial emblem.

The Hall of the Vicars

Approaching the Rock from Cashel town, you come first to the **Hall of the Vicars**, built in the fifteenth century to cater for eight vicar *meistersingers*, who assisted in the cathedral services but were later dispensed with due to jealousy of the power and land their privileged office entailed. The upper floor of the building is divided between the main hall, with screens and a minstrels' gallery, and what would have been the dormitories. The ground floor, a vaulted undercroft, today contains the original **Saint Patrick's Cross**, a unique type of high cross. It once stood outside, where there's now a replica. Tradition has it that the cross's huge plinth was the coronation stone of the High Kings of Munster, the most famous of whom was Brian Boru, killed in his tent by a fleeing Viking at the Battle of Clontarf. The cross is simpler than other high crosses, with a carving of Christ on one side and Saint Patrick on the other. It has an upright supporting its left arm, and is without the usual ring-wheel in the centre. It may be that originally the upright and its missing counterpart represented the two thieves crucified with Jesus, and it is also possible that it was never intended as a freestanding cross in the first place, but for erection on a wall.

Cormac's Chapel

Cormac's Chapel (1127–34) is the earliest and most beautiful of Ireland's surviving Romanesque churches, and the intricacies of its decoration are as spectacular as they are unique. The architecture has clear continental influences – the twin square **towers**, for example, were probably engineered by monks sent from Regensburg, Germany. The **tympana**, or panels above the grandiloquent north door (more than likely the original entrance, now leading blindly into the flank of the cathedral) and south door (today's entrance), are also rare in Irish church architecture. Above the north door is depicted a curious carved scene of a large beast ensnaring a smaller beast, itself on the point of being speared by a very male centaur in a Norman helmet. The north door is set in six orders of pillars, creating a tunnel-vaulted **porch**, which in turn is sheltered by an outer stone roof porch. Each arch is crowned with capitals, human heads, fantastic beasts, flutings and scallops.

The small size of the chapel is particularly Irish, as are the lack of aisles and the steeply pitched stone roof – you'll find similar-looking buildings at Glendalough and Kells, though Cormac's Chapel is larger than these. Inside is a nave and a chancel with a small recess in the east wall. The wall opposite you as you walk in has a tall triple arcade, in the centre of which is a large round-headed **window** that would once have lit up the whole interior, illuminating all the painted colour – of which a little remains up at the altar and just above the chancel arch. The **sarcophagus** at the foot of this wall, although fragmented, has an exquisite Scandinavian *Urnes* design of interlacing serpents and ribbon decoration. It's said to have been the tomb of King Cormac, and certainly it's old enough for this to be true.

The Cathedral and round tower

The **Cathedral** was begun a century or so after Cormac's chapel. Although Anglo-Norman in conception, with its Gothic arches and lancet windows, it's a purely Irish-built endeavour, without help from abroad. A graceful limestone building, it features a series of tall, high-set lancet **windows**, and also some good examples of quatrefoil, or four-petalled, windows, especially above the lancets in the choir space. You'll notice that some of the lancets have been shortened – probably as a measure of fortification. The **choir** is longer than the nave and both are without aisles. The nave was shortened to make room for the **castle tower**, built most obviously for refuge, but also as an archepiscopal residence. A wooden-floored hall would once have been above the nave (the corbels are still apparent), accessible from the castle tower.

The **central tower**, at the meeting of the transepts, is also on a grand scale, and, typically, did not appear until the fourteenth century. It's supported by four Gothic arches rising from very wide piers, their shafts sweeping beautifully into the concave bottom. Access to the tower is by winding stairs from the south transept (this may not be open to the public, so ask). **Passages** also ran through the nave and choir walls, supposedly for the outcasts or lepers of the community, so that they could watch the holy ceremony without being seen themselves. The **transepts** have shallow chapel altars with some tomb and *piscina* niches. In the north transept some panels from sixteenth-century altar-tombs survive, one with an intricately carved retinue of saints and the others more broken but just as dextrously beautiful.

The **Round Tower** is the earliest building on the rock. Its tapering features have led to suggestions that it's as early as tenth-century, though the officially accepted date is early twelfth century. It's not a typical tower; the entrance door was originally twelve feet above the ground, and various levels of windows ensnare viewpoints in all directions.

Around the Rock

From the grounds of the Rock you can look down at **Hore Abbey** on the plain below, and it's an easy enough walk down, over the fields and jumping the road wall. But there's little to be gained in doing this, beyond escaping the sightseers – you can see just as well from the Rock. The thirteenth-century abbey was the last Cistercian daughter monastery of Mellifont to be completed before the Reformation, and was probably built by those working on the cathedral on the Rock. Originally a Benedictine foundation, it converted after its abbot had a wild dream that his Benedictine monks were plotting to cut his head off; he expelled them and donned the Cistercian habit in 1269. There's yet another abbey ruin, **Saint Dominic's**, down the south side of the Rock in the town, but this has even less to offer in terms of things to see.

A path known as the **Bishop's Walk** leads from the Rock's rampart entrance down through the back garden of the **Palace Hotel** (☎062/61411; £75). The walk is officially for patrons only, but anyone planning to have a bite or a drink in the luxury hotel's basement buttery and bar can use it. The *Palace* was built in Queen Anne style by Archbishop Theophilus Bolton in 1730 as a mansion for the Archbishops of Cashel (hence the Bishop's Walk to the Rock). It has a simple, redbrick front and a cut stone rear. Cashel owes much thanks to this particular archbishop; it was he who saw the value of Cormac's Chapel and put his wealth into its restoration at a time when the Rock's antiquities were degenerating rapidly towards irrevocable ruin. A further legacy is the **GPA Bolton library** (Mon–Sat 9.30am–5.30pm, Sun 2.30–5.30pm; £1, students 70p; ☎062/61944), out on the road opposite the hotel and set in the grounds of the slender-spired eight-eenth-century St John's Protestant Cathedral. Its manuscripts (from as early as the twelfth century), rare maps and wealth of literary treasures were principally his bequest when he died in 1744. A selection of the books and maps are on display, changing bi-monthly, and well worth viewing.

West to Tipperary town

Having seen the Rock of Cashel, most people head out of Tipperary for the West, and frankly this isn't a bad idea – the north of the county has little to distract you. Leaving Cashel on the N74, you come after a few miles to **GOLDEN**, where **Athassel Abbey** sits on the banks of the Suir. Once the largest medieval priory in Ireland, its ruins even today are fairly extensive – though not dramatic enough to seriously draw you off your route. The west door is the most impressive feature, and the peacefulness of the surroundings the most rewarding. The plain immediately encircling the abbey was once the site of the town; but it was razed to the ground twice during the fourteenth century – enough to obliterate it forever.

Tipperary

A few miles further on, twelve miles from Cashel and less than five from the border of Limerick, the county's honorary namesake, **TIPPERARY** town, is tucked by the northern side of the Glen of Aherlow. Like many of these name-sake county towns, Tipperary is much less important than it sounds. If you've already visited Clonmel, it will come as something of a shock – compared to Clonmel's yuppy prosperity, it feels out of another century altogether. The town has bold statues sculpted in granite here and there, most notably one to its liter-ary local son, Charles J Kickham, entitled *Poet, Novelist but above all Patriot.*

The one thing that might tempt you to stop over briefly is an intriguing small **museum**, hidden away in the foyer of the town swimming pool, by the Cashel road exit. A tiny store of memorabilia, it exhibits photos, letters and weaponry from the warring years of 1919–23, especially relating to the old IRA. Tipperary was a particular hot spot during the Anglo-Irish and Civil War strife, especially through its most remembered son, **Seán Tracey**, whose battalion fired the first shots of the Anglo-Irish war (1919–21). There are letters he wrote to his family from prison, some talking about the honour the British had bestowed on him by taking the trouble to get him captured, others of a more domestic nature. A violin belonging to **Joseph Mary Plunkett** (one of the poets executed in the 1916 uprising) hangs beside revolvers, pistols and land mines. Most striking of all, perhaps, are the photographs of the young officers shown clenching their revolvers, either posturing a rebel's stance of defiance or slightly abashed, with innocent-looking smiles.

Butler's Pantry, a basic café near the junction of the Cahir road, is the cheapest place to **eat** in town (£5.50 for four-course evening meal), the *Brown Trout* (☎062/51912) offers an excellent, inexpensive lunch, with all sorts of fish dishes; they also do **B&B** and there are numerous other small B&Bs, especially on Emly Road. The *Royal Hotel*, Bridge Street (☎062/51204; £20), is a slightly more upmarket alternative for food and accommodation.

North to Thurles: Holy Cross Abbey

Upstream from Cashel, both the Suir itself and the attractions along its banks wane. The river passes through the larger towns of Thurles and Templemore, though its source in the Devil's Bit Mountain falls short of the major town in the northeast, Roscrea. All three centres have railway connections.

THURLES is of very little interest in itself, but **Holy Cross Abbey**, just four miles south, sits beside a fat stretch of the Suir and is well worth a visit if you're passing by. Founded in 1180, restored significantly in the fifteenth century, and then left derelict for 400 years, the abbey was totally restored between 1971 and 1985, and is now a thriving parish church as well as a tourist attraction. You really need to see photographs of the period before restoration to appreciate its significance; these suggest that every other ruin you've seen could as easily be converted. Holy Cross always had singular importance as a centre of pilgrimage, claiming to possess a splinter of the wood from the **True Cross**, Christ's cross on Calvary. The splinter relic was reckoned to have been given to Murtagh O'Brien, King of Munster, by Pope Paschal II in 1110. At the turn of the seventeenth century both O'Donnell and O'Neill, the Ulster chiefs, stopped off to idolise this relic on their way to Kinsale to meet the French – no doubt hoping they'd be rewarded with a victory over Elizabeth I.

The **interior** of the church is fully restored, though here there's been no particular attempt at period accuracy; virtually every wall and pillar has been whitewashed, and all the pews have been varnished. The incongruities are, in a sense, inherent in the major fifteenth-century renovations that stripped the site of its medieval character and left a confused mix of revelation and awe for today. Nevertheless, it's rewarding to see the stone ribbing of the vaulted roofs and most particularly the undamaged fifteenth-century **sedilia** in the chancel area, the finest in the country. The sedilia, recessed stone seats for the celebrants of the Mass, is of a hard limestone shaped into cusped arches and crowned with crockets, showing decorative friezework as well as the English royal crest and the escutcheon of the Earls of Ormond. In the transept to the left of the nave, you'll find one of Ireland's rare medieval **frescoes**, this one showing a Norman hunting scene painted in browns, reds and greens. The exterior of the church has a startling full-length slate roof, which reaches down to the cloister pillars. There's a **tourist information centre**, a coffee shop and a religious goods store within the abbey complex.

Ballynahow Castle

If you're cycling or driving north towards Thurles you might also think of taking in **Ballynahow Castle**, a circular castle tower built by the Purcell family in the sixteenth century. To get there from Holy Cross, take the road directly opposite the Protestant church, not the Thurles route (even though the signpost says so). From Thurles itself, it's out on the Nenagh Road, right at the *Jet Petrol* station, and after another mile the castle stands next to a farmhouse (*Ballynahow Castle Farm*) where you can pick up the key (also **B&B** accommodation April–Oct; ☎0504/21297; £13). The castle is distinguished by its circular plan; inside, entering the lowest of its five storeys is like walking into an igloo, with the corbelled roof curving round almost to the floor. There are many little rooms hidden within the walls and, although undecorated and entirely bare (and quite dark), most of it is in an excellent state of preservation, and strongly atmospheric.

Templemore and Cranagh Castle

TEMPLEMORE is even less interesting than Thurles, but it does happen to be within easy reach of one of the more historical of listed hostels, **Cranagh Castle**, which on its own is worth a visit – though it's not particularly easy to get to, and hard to find even when you do get there. From Templemore, head first for TEMPLETUOHY, five miles away. Once there, turn right through the village and at the first bend on the other side of town head straight on, off the main road; the castle lies about a mile and a half further on, through a narrow gateway edged by two stone pillars, its rusty white gates peeled back. Coming up the Thurles-Templemore road from the south, take the turnoff for LOUGHMORE (signposted as "Loughmoe", a few miles before Templemore), where you'll find the ruin of a four-storeyed tower house. Head straight on from here in the direction of Templetuohy, and the gateway into *Cranagh Castle* is on the left-hand side. There's no sign on the gate.

The **hostel** (☎0504/53104; dorms £4, private room £6, camping £2.50; open all year) occupies parts of the eighteenth-century mansion house attached to the circular Purcell tower house – the family live in the basement. A wide wooden stairway leads to the dorm rooms on the second and third floors, which are extremely spacious, with single beds and left-over period furnishing. Outside, the yard is full of the sounds of an old-fashioned farm: geese, cocks, cows and the gallop of horses first thing in the morning. The produce here is all organic, and there's wonderful fresh milk and bread, though not at all cheap. If you're interested in the working of the farm, then ask about the courses on organic farming that are run off-season. It's a very relaxing place to take time out (though smokers are discouraged) – in low season their motto "hard to find and hard to leave" takes on an eerie twist once you've stayed here. If you're on a bike, the **Devil's Bit Mountain** is within easy reach, and is reckoned worth the climb for the views.

Roscrea

ROSCREA sits on a low hillock between the Slieve Bloom Mountains to the northeast and the Devil's Bit to the southwest. It's a charming place, with streets running down the hill slopes and a certain conscious lack of worldliness. However, where the rest of Ireland has secluded river sites and spacious countryside for its abbey ruins, Roscrea has the main Dublin–Limerick road running raucously through the middle of **St Cronan's Monastery**. On one side of the road is the round tower, with a garage shed built into the side of it and the top third removed by the British in 1798. Immediately opposite, virtually on the pavement, is the west gable of St Cronan's church, its yellow sandstone carved out in a twelfth-century Romanesque style reminiscent of Cormac's Chapel in Cashel. The rest of the church was pulled down in the nineteenth century, and the stone used as building material elsewhere. **Saint Cronan's Cross**, just to the right of the gable, must have been a beauty once, but now it's severely weatherbeaten and hacked. Up by the centre of the town is a large, sturdy-looking **Gate Tower Castle** from the thirteenth century backed by a polygonal curtain wall. An imposing eighteenth-century town house now used for office purposes stands at the centre of the medieval plot. As both of these are on the Dublin–Limerick route, you'd get a reasonable view staring out of a bus window in slow traffic.

Nenagh and Lough Derg

Once again, in comparison with the south of the county, the northwest lacks significant attractions. The remaining crumbs of interest rest on the shores of **Lough Derg**, not far from the sole town of any size, Nenagh. There are no hostels on this east side of the lake but there is one across the water at Mountshannon in County Clare (see p.289).

NENAGH is usually jam-packed with heavy traffic trying to plough its way through. It has one singular historical remain, a colossal round **castle keep** (a *donjon*) with walls twenty feet thick, its five storeys reaching a height of a hundred feet and topped with nineteenth-century castellations. Totally gutted within, the *donjon* (the final retreat tower) was originally one of five round towers which, linked by a curtain wall, formed a Norman stronghold. Founded by Theobald Walter, a cousin of Thomas à Becket, the tower was occupied by the Butlers, then captured in turn by the O'Carrols of Eile, Cromwell, went back to James II and then to and fro between Ginckel (William's chief general) and O'Carrol in the Williamite war. And there the fighting stopped until many centuries later a farmer, wanting to get rid of a nest of sparrows that were feeding on his crops, stuck some gunpowder in the walls of the donjon and blew another hole in the fortress. A few reinforced concrete steps help you to get near the top, but there's little to be seen.

Across the road from the donjon, the Nenagh **heritage centre** (£1, students 50p) is set in the old jail, now a Convent of Mercy school. Housed in the octagonal Governor's House, up the driveway, the museum has a display room that houses temporary exhibitions, a mock-up of an old schoolroom with a four-foot mannequin nun (very liberal with her mascara) and a mock-up of an old post office/bar/telephone exchange. In the basement are the usual agricultural items and a realistic but clinical-looking forge. Back at the entrance arch, the cells of the old jail have their original hefty iron cell doors, and you can also see the former exercise yard, tiny and cluttered.

Tourist information is available from an office on Connolly Street (☎067/31610; May 11 to Sept 12 Mon–Sat 9.30am–1pm & 2–5.30pm). There's a reasonably priced **B&B** (*Sun View*, Ciamaltha Road; ☎067/31064), quite close to the bus and railway stations, and you can get fairly good snack **food** at the *Foodhall* on the main street (Pearse Street). At the northern end of this road, the *JKC Shopping Arcade* provides more substantial lunch venues.

Lough Derg

Along the shores of **Lough Derg** are a number of small villages, none of them really worth making a special trip to visit (unless you're after the fishing), but which may be worth calling at if you're cruising on the lake. The first of them is **DROMINEER**, a small and picturesque yachting harbour, with a tiny castle ruin on its pier. There's food (and drink) at the *Whiskey Still Pub* and more expensively at the *Waterside Restaurant*. **KILGARVAN** has a good antiques shop next to the *Brocka-on-the-water* restaurant. **TERRYGLASS**, where *Paddy's Pub* has a nice interior and bar food, offers little else besides a crafts shop in the old church.

LIMERICK

To an even greater extent than Tipperary, everyone passes though **Limerick**, and hardly anyone stays. Once here, you're tantalisingly close to the much more rewarding counties of Cork, Kerry and Clare, and frankly you're not likely to linger. Still, what interest there is lies close to the roads to Cork, Killarney and Tralee, three main routes that run southwards from Limerick city in the northeastern corner. You should try to see at least one of two places; **Castle Matrix**, an authentic, lavishly restored and renovated tower house on the Killarney route, and **Lough Gur**, a Mesolithic to Neolithic lake and hill enclave of preternatural beauty. Both can be reached easily no matter what transport you're using.

For **cyclists**, Limerick's terrain is more variable than it's usually given credit for. In its western to southwestern corner, the upland bears a likeness to barren stretches of Donegal, whereas the northern estuary stretch is indeed only a slightly bumpy flatland. The centre and east bow in contour towards the eastern frontier of the Tipperary Golden Vale's rich dairy land; but not without gently rising mounds for hills, and broadish trickles for rivers. More so than any other county, the land in Limerick is dotted with an array of **tower castles**, some inhabited, but most in ruins or no more than stumps.

Historically, Limerick's most notable period arrived with the Norman strongholds, the most dominant family being the Fitzgeralds (or **Geraldines**), also known as the Earls of Desmond – virtually all of Limerick's significant ruins were once this clan's power bases. They quickly became Gaelicised and ruled as independent monarchs, pulling very much away from English rule. The inevitable confrontation with Britain came to a head at the end of the sixteenth century, when in 1571 the Geraldine uprising against Elizabeth I sparked off a savage war, which brought about their downfall and destroyed in its wake much of the province of Munster.

SPORT IN LIMERICK: THE GARRYOWEN

Even more than most of Ireland, Limerick seems obsessed with sport: horse racing, hurling, Gaelic football, soccer and rugby are all avidly followed, and hurling and rugby have particularly strong local traditions. In rugby, the region has passed into immortality with the invention of the **Garryowen** – named after the district of Limerick City which lent its name to one of Ireland's finest rugby clubs. The move, a high kick upfield pursued by a charging team who hope to hit the opposition as they catch the ball, the equivalent of Rugby League's "up-and-under", was supposedly invented here in the 1920s.

Limerick City

Squarely on the path of all the major routes across the country, and situated pretty much at the head of the Shannon estuary, **LIMERICK** seems a logical place to make for but actually, it's a disappointment. Though it's the Republic's third city, and heavily industrialised, it somehow falls significantly short of being a metropolis (where Cork succeeds) but lacks the attractions of a typically relaxed western seaboard town (where Galway succeeds). It's also probably the most Catholic of all Irish cities, its churches seemingly crowded every minute of the day.

Like Derry in the north, Limerick also seems tainted by 300-year-old wars, carrying a stigma that it has still to shrug off. Modern unemployment and economic hard times have also left their mark. It rarely feels a terribly friendly town, and at night certain areas can feel positively intimidating – its reputation in recent years as "stab city" will be a hard one to shift. Still, moves are underway to clean up Limerick's image, with new development and the renovation of the city's cathedral and castle, and along with this there are signs of an interesting emergent youth/music scene. Like it or not, this is an important crossroads, and you're likely to end up here at some time, if only to pass straight through.

The city you see now is predominantly Georgian, but nevertheless Limerick has three distinct historical sectors: **Englishtown**, the oldest part of the city, built on an island in the Shannon; **Irishtown**, which began to take shape in the thirteenth and fourteenth centuries; and **Newtown Perry**, the modern centre and the most distinct of the three, with beautiful avenues of Georgian streets and houses – it's here you'll probably spend most of your wanderings.

Some history

Limerick's history has to be spelt out. Even today, the town is only too aware of spectres from its past. This lowest fording point of the Shannon was first exploited by the **Vikings**, who in the tenth century sailed up the Shannon to *Inis Sibhton* (now Kingstown in Englishtown), an island by the eastern bank formed by a narrow by-pass from the main stream now known as Abbey River. Here they established a port, and for a hundred years war after war raged between them and the native Irish. The Vikings were frequently defeated, and were finally crushed nationally in 1014 at the Battle of Clontarf, at the hands of Brian Boru, the High King of Ireland. Limerick itself was attacked soon after, and burned to the ground. Most of the Vikings didn't actually leave, but from then on they were gradually assimilated into the Gaelic population. The fate of Limerick itself didn't improve much, however, as over the next hundred years the Irish fought amongst themselves, burning the town to the ground again and again.

Some kind of stability was established with the arrival of the **Normans** at the end of the twelfth century. They expanded and fortified the town; King John arriving in 1210 to inaugurate King John's Castle, one of his finest. High walls were built that were now to keep the Gaels out, and because of this exile the first suburb across the Abbey River began to grow into **Irishtown**. There was trouble again with the visits of Edward Bruce in the fourteenth century; but the real emasculation of the city began with the onslaught of Cromwell's forces under the command of his son-in-law, Ireton, in the late 1640s. It was concluded when the city rallied to the **Jacobite** cause in 1689.

A lost cause

Once James II had lost the Battle of the Boyne in 1690, most of his supporters surrendered quickly – except for the ones at Limerick. As the Williamites advanced, the Jacobite forces within Limerick castle resolved to fight it out under the command of their Irish champion **Patrick Sarsfield**, Earl of Lucan and second in overall command of the Jacobean army. Although the walls of a medieval castle had little hope of withstanding seventeenth-century artillery (one of James's French generals declared that they would not stand up to a bombardment of apples), Sarsfield gained time by sneaking out, with five hundred of his troops, for a surprise night attack on William's supply train. He succeeded in totally destroying the munitions, while William sat waiting for them in front of the castle walls. However, when the Williamites returned the following year, Sarsfield could finally hold out no longer, and he surrendered on October 3, 1691 to the terms of a **treaty** that's so sore an historical point that it's still stuck in the minds of most Limerick people today.

The treaty terms were divided into military and civil articles. Militarily, Jacobeans were allowed to sail to France, which most of them did, along with Sarsfield himself (he died on the battlefield at Landon, Belgium, two years later). The civil agreement promised Catholics the religious and property rights they'd once had under Charles II. Within a couple of months the English reneged on this part of the treaty, and instead enforced **anti-Catholic measures** extreme even by Irish standards. There followed civil unrest on such a scale that the city gates were locked every night for the next sixty years. The betrayal has never been forgotten – it alone may explain the roots of today's element of Republican support in the city. The concordat was supposedly signed upon the **Treaty Stone** that rests on a plinth at the western end of Thomond Bridge. For many years, although this was used as a stepping stone for mounting horses, small pieces continued to be gouged out as souvenirs; one fragment set into a ring is said to have fetched £1000 in the USA.

It was not a promising start for the modern city, and there are those who claim that festering resentment has stunted Limerick's growth ever since. Being also lumbered with a geographical setting that gives it the Irish name *luimneach* ("a barren spot of land") has not helped. One redeeming factor has to lie in its humour; how else could its corporate motto read *An ancient city well studied in the arts of war*.

Arriving and finding a place to stay

Limerick is the nearest big city to **Shannon Airport** (☎061/61444; see p.282) – ten miles away off the Ennis road. Airport buses (£4) run half-hourly in the morning, hourly in the afternoon, and irregularly after 6pm; a taxi costs around £14. The **railway and bus stations** are next door to each other on Parnell Street in Newtown Perry: for train information call ☎061/315555; for Bus Éireann ☎061/313333. This is a fairly unkempt area of the city, but the *Railway Hotel* (☎061/44250; £15–19), opposite, is comfortable and convenient. There's an *An Óige* **youth hostel** not far away in Perry Square on the far side of People's Park (☎061/314672; £5.90; strictly run); turn left from the stations to find People's Park. The *Limerick Holiday Hostel*, Barrington House, George's Quay (☎061/415222; £4.50), is an excellent, large independent hostel – further away, but a much more pleasant place to stay.

Most of the cheaper **B&Bs** are some way out, above all across the river on the Ennis Road where there seem to be dozens (*Parkview*, ☎061/51505; *Clifton House* ☎061/51166; *Trelawne House*, ☎061/54063; and *Shannonville*, ☎061/53690, for example; all around £13). Most of the big hotels are out on Ennis Road, too. A few rather more expensive places can also be found around Newtown Perry, particularly in and around Glentworth and Henry streets – head down Davis Street directly opposite the railway station, then right and left into Glentworth Street, which crosses first O'Connell Street (the main commercial thoroughfare) and then Henry Street further down towards the Shannon. Try, for example, *Harbour House* (☎061/410616), on Catherine Street off Glentworth Street, the *Glentworth Hotel* on Glentworth Street (☎061/43822; £20–25), or the *Royal George* on O'Connell Street (☎061/44566; £27). The handiest **campsite** is at Currahchase Forest Park, sixteen miles west (see p.214).

The new, well-informed **tourist information office** (☎061/317522; June–Aug Mon–Fri 9am–6.30pm, Sat 9.30am–5.30pm, Sun 11am–3pm; May & Sept Mon–Fri 9am–6pm, Sat 9.30am–5.30pm, Sun 11am–3pm; Oct–April Mon–Fri 9.30am–5.30pm, Sat 9.30am–1pm & 2–5.30pm) is at Arthur's Quay, near where the river branches merge and you cross over into Englishtown: easiest found by following O'Connell Street north to the Custom House. Their city map has much useful information and phone numbers, and you can buy **parking discs** – also from most local newsagents. **Walking tours** of the city are organised by the tourist office in summer. **Arthur's Quay** itself is a lively modern complex of shops and a civic park.

For **bike hire** try *Noel McMahon*, 25 Roaches Street (☎061/415202; £5 daily, £27 weekly, panniers included) or *Emerald Cycles*, 1 Patrick Street (☎061/416983; £7 daily, £30 weekly, panniers extra; cycles can be left in another town, £6 extra); both offer ten percent reductions to anyone with this guide – book in advance in the summer.

The City

The sometimes incongruous blend of old and new in Limerick is testimony to a city discovering itself after years of neglect. Renovations and new building programmes stand alongside buildings – and indeed whole districts – that seem barely touched by the last fifty years. The best **views** of the city are to be had walking along the banks of the Shannon, or alternatively from the top of King John's Castle or the spire of St Mary's Cathedral. Although virtually all the sights are in the old parts, Englishtown and Irishtown, the modern centre of the city – where the shops, pubs and restaurants congregate – is **Newtown Perry**, an area of broad parallel streets laid out in the eighteenth century and still scattered with fine Georgian buildings. O'Connell Street is the chief artery of this part of the city, and it's worth wandering down here, checking out the side streets with their characterful pubs and shops. Getting around the centre is easiest on foot.

Englishtown
Englishtown, which still has the narrow curving streets of its medieval origins, if few of the buildings, is the oldest part of the city, north of the modern centre. Crossing Matthew Bridge, the first thing you'll see is St Mary's Cathedral. Before you go in, though, look down to the right on the embankment near the Art College, and your eye should just catch two very fine but armless torsos, metal-

sculpted and set upon tall plinths facing one another some forty paces apart. This twentieth-century grotesquerie of war from within and without takes you by surprise – it's an unusually strong statement for Limerick.

St Mary's Cathedral (Church of Ireland; summer daily 9am–1pm & 2.30–5.30pm, winter daily 9am–1pm & 2.15–5pm; free; for tours call ☎061/43157) was built at the end of the twelfth century, but only the Romanesque doorway, the nave and parts of the transepts remain from this period. The chancel, windows and the rest of the transepts date from the fifteenth century. The cathedral's unique feature is its *misericords*, the only set in Ireland: these are choir seats of lovely black oak with reptilian animals – cockatrice, griffins, sphinx and wild boar – carved in bold relief. There's access up into the belfry of the castellated tower for an even better bird's-eye view of the city.

Further into Englishtown, next to Thomond Bridge, is **King John's Castle** (summer daily 9am–5.30pm, last admission 4.30pm; at other times check on ☎061/411201, bookings ☎061/361511). Built in the early thirteenth century, it retains much of its medieval structure. It was originally a five-sided fortress with four stout round towers; but these were shortened at a much later stage to accommodate artillery positions – though one was actually replaced as a bastion in 1611. Today, the flight of entrance steps from the main road runs up to large, pointed-arch gates set between two, more slender, towers. The steps replace the draw-bridge that would once have crossed a moat fed by the Shannon. In fact, the castle is probably more impressive from the outside, staring up at the cliff-like immensity of its walls, than it is from the inside, which is very bare. Recent **renovations** revealed archaeological remains dating back to the Viking raiders of the seventh century: the excavated area is now on display, complete with a visual interpretation auditorium.

The **treaty stone** stands on the far side of Thomond Bridge, on Clancy Strand on the west bank of the Shannon. In recent years it has been moved – only about twenty yards – and sandblasted clean. This, if you want to read symbolic significance into it, can be seen as an attempt to loosen a burden that was preventing the city from developing.

Irishtown

Back across Matthew Bridge you're in **Irishtown**, much of it now given over to grey council housing. Perhaps the brightest spark here is the **Custom House**, an eighteenth-century structure of harmonious Classical balance. Opposite, the **Town Hall** (Mon–Fri 9am–5pm) houses a small art gallery with portraits of local eighteenth- and nineteenth-century bigwigs and their prize animals. The city **museum** (Tues–Sat 10am–1pm and 2.15–5pm; free; ☎061/47826), housed in a fine Georgian end-house in St John's Square, close to St John's Cathedral, is also worth a look. Well-stocked in the most traditional of ways, it displays currency going as far back as the Viking period, guild regalia, historic maps showing the old walled towns of Englishtown and Irishtown, memorabilia of the various Fenian uprisings (notably a Pádraig Pearse letter from the 1916 insurrection) and various Stone, Iron and especially Bronze Age implements. Many of the mesolithic items (c.7000–4000 BC) were brought up from the Lough Gur area, and it's worth looking at the excavation photographs of this site before you visit it.

St. John's Cathedral, a nineteenth-century Gothic-revival monstrosity which boasts the tallest spire in the country (at 280 feet), is the seat of the Catholic diocese. Its two chief treasures are a fifteenth-century mitre and carved crozier, made by bishop Cornelius O'Dea. Inside, there's a sombre atmosphere appropriate to this most Catholic of cities; outside is a memorial to Patrick Sarsfield, unsuccessful Jacobite defender of the city. A short way north of the cathedral, on Lelia Street, you can see the best surviving section of the fifteenth-century **city walls**, built to guard the approaches from the North Munster territory of the O'Briens, with its Gaelic traditions, language and culture.

The Hunt Museum

The most interesting museum in Limerick, the **Hunt Museum** (May–Sept daily 9.30am–5.30pm; £1, students 60p; ☎061/333644), is housed in the National Institute of Higher Education (NIHE) some way from the centre. To get there, head out on the Dublin Road following signs to the NIHE. After a few miles take a left turn immediately after a *Maxol* petrol station for Plessay, follow the road round for another third of a mile, then turn left through the white gated entrance, to the reception at the three flag poles, and ask for the museum. This is one of the best conceived museums around, with art objects (mainly Irish antiquities but also European) of consistently high interest, beautifully presented and extensively documented. The museum owes much to the originator of the collection, John Hunt, who was also the enlightened creator of the Craggaunowen habitation project in County Clare (see p.287). Many of the objects here date from the Bronze Age; highlights include the **Antrim Cross**, one of Ireland's most important examples of ninth-century Early Christian metalwork, and thought to be a precursor of the high cross designs at Monasterboice and Kells. There's also a late Bronze Age shield, cauldron and bucket, wholly intact, and a thirteenth-century Limoges enamelled chasse.

Food and entertainment

For its size, Limerick is not particularly well-stocked with good, cheap places to **eat**. Nonetheless, it is a fair sized city, and you're in no danger of going hungry. The list below will give you some useful starting points. **Bars** there are in abundance, and in recent years Limerick has revived its reputation as a **musical** centre – particularly for contemporary and rock music. Local bands like *Tocandance* and *The Cranberries* are good examples, worth looking out for. Again, a selection of bars and places to see music can be found below. To find out what's going on in the music scene, and the arts generally, pick up a free copy of *Night Times*, which covers the whole mid-west region – from the tourist office, or at arts places listed below – or tune in to *Arts Facts* on Radio Limerick, 95FM. The *Belltable* and the *City Gallery*, listed below, are good places to make contact with the Irish arts scene, and are well worth visiting if you've more than half a day in the city.

Cafés and restaurants

Fat Freddie's Pizza, Theatre Lane, down an alley off Glentworth Street near the *Belltable Arts Centre*. Relaxing and affordable place with good food – not only pizza.

Cunningham's, Ellen Street. Another friendly place, though slightly more expensive (£10–15) – good vegetarian dishes.

The Vintage Club, Ellen Street. Pub/restaurant good for quick meals and sandwiches; decent wine selection too.

O'Donoghies, 6 Broad Street (☎061/410370). Café breakfasts and dinners a stone's throw from the *Limerick Holiday Hostel*.

Elana, O'Connell Street near Daniel O'Connell monument. Greek restaurant with good lunch menu.

Treaty Café, Nicholas Street (also known as *Dirty Dick's*). Friendly all-night café serving fish and chips and other basics; interesting photos of the war of Independence on the walls.

Belltable Arts Centre, 69 O'Connell Street (☎061/319866). Good café downstairs with home-cooked lunches and snacks. Daytime only.

George Bistro Restaurant, *Royal George Hotel*, O'Connell Street (☎061/44566). Restaurant with vegetarian choices.

The Groove, Cecil Street. Health food shop that does tasty takeaways.

Bars and music places

Arthur's Warehouse, 7 Robert Street (☎061/417616). Excellent new music venue: traditional on Mônday nights, live music with disco after Thurs–Sun. Also food.

Nancy Blake's, Upper Denmark Street (☎061/416443). Pub with traditional music Mon, Tues, Wed & Sun.

Tait's Tavern, 54 Parnell Street (☎061/418133). Traditional music Thurs & Sat, Jazz on Mon from 10pm.

The Vintage Club, Ellen Street (see above). Traditional music Wed & Fri.

James Gleeson, *The White House Bar*, 52 O'Connell Street. Ancient ale house, full of character (and characters); packed, but warm and friendly.

Tom Collins, Cecil Street. Quieter bar, popular with local arty types.

Grand Mariner, Catherine Street. Big on sport, with televised games always drawing a crowd. Near People's Park and next to *Lane Antiques*, which is also worth a look.

Barrington's Hospital Bar, Broad Street. Interesting, run-down old place displaying relics from the old hospital nearby (which is now the *Limerick Holiday Hostel*). Best at lunchtimes.

Boddies Bar, in alley off Foxes Bow, off William Street. Rock-and-roll shrine; loud music, dark and crowded.

Arts Centres and Galleries

Belltable Arts Centre, 69 O'Connell Street (☎061/319866); red doors under the granite arch. Interesting mix, usually including a summer season of Irish plays in July & Aug, with films on Sundays. Also some gallery space, exhibiting community and national artists (10am–8pm).

City Gallery of Art, Perry Square (☎061/310633; Mon–Wed & Fri 10am–1pm & 2–6pm, Thurs 2–7pm, Sat 10am–1pm; free). Situated in the People's Park, emphasises international contemporary art, with a lesser focus on Irish stuff; also has poetry readings.

All + 10 Sorts, 28–31 Windmill Street (☎061/413098). Lively, offbeat art scene.

Near Limerick: the Clare Glens

The **Clare Glens** on the Limerick/Tipperary border is a beautiful area of flowing falls, parts of which you can swim in: it makes a great day's excursion for cyclists. Head for MOROE (sometimes spelt Murroe), east of the city; Clare Glens is two miles north of this. A circular ride of some twenty miles could take this in, along with Glenstal Abbey and the village of **CASTLECONNELL**, a well known Irish music and Irish language centre in a scenic setting on the banks of the Shannon some seven miles from Limerick. **Currahchase Forest Park**, sixteen miles west of the city, is also a good ride, with a well-equipped campground (*Currahchase Caravan and Camping*; ☎061/396349; £3.50, plus £1.50 per person), picnic site, arboretum and the ruins of the home of poet Aubrey de Vere. To the south, it's not much further to Lough Gur (see below) and Adare (p.218).

South: The Road to Cork

Leaving Limerick city in the direction of Cork the main route is the N20, a fast and efficient but rather dull route south. If you have time to stop along the way a smaller road, the R512, has considerably more to offer – above all Lough Gur, site of a wealth of neolithic finds and one of County Limerick's chief attractions.

Lough Gur

Seventeen miles south of Limerick city, **Lough Gur** looks as though its waters have been accidentally spilt onto the Limerick soil. It's the county's only significant lake, and comes as a rare treat in the midst of an otherwise lustreless terrain. The area around the lake has been an extremely rich source of archaeological finds – though what exists now is often an extremely frugal sketch of what took place 5000 years ago. The lake is C-shaped, with a marshy area to the east that would complete the full circle.

In the middle of this circle is a small rise known as **Knockadoon**. Knockadoon's slopes are studded with faint remains of earthworks showing ring forts and hut foundations dating from 3500 to 1000 BC. The length of its less secure marshy side is naturally forested and guarded at either end by two medieval tower houses, Bouchier's Castle and Black Castle. Mary Carbery's nineteenth-century book, *The Farm by Lough Gur* (Mercier Press), gives a vivid contemporary account of life by the lough – the farm still stands up the road from the Neolithic huts known as the Spectacles.

Lough Gur must have been the perfect setting for a **Neolithic civilisation**. The lake provided fish, and the gentle hillsides produced berries, nuts and trappings for animal hunting, as well as protection from the elements – and detection. When the lake was partly drained in the middle of the nineteenth century, and its level dropped by three yards, prehistoric artefacts were found in such quantities that stories tell of whole cartloads being hauled away. This may not be such an exaggeration; visit museums across the world today, and you'll discover some find from Lough Gur on display. The most famous discovery was a bronze shield from 700 BC, perfect in its concentric rings of bosses, but for a hacking in two places by the reedcutter who discovered it. The finds here pair well with the Neolithic discoveries made in Meath; this was once a Neolithic living commune, where the *Brú Na Boinne* site is concerned with ritual and burial. Today there's abundant **birdlife** on the lake and, along with the grazing cattle, antlered goats, and lack of modern buildings, you get a strong intimation of the life of five thousand years ago.

Approaches: the Interpretive Centre and stone circle

The simplest approach to Lough Gur is to come off the R512 at Holycross. Follow the road to the northernmost section of the lake, keeping an eye out for a wedge-shaped **gallery grave**. The grave, typically, shows a long gallery space where the bodies of eight adults and four children from around 2000 BC were found. The gallery has parallel double walls of stone slabs filled in with rubble and what's called a septal slab at its back. The road then circles on round the marsh to an **Interpretive Centre** (May–Sept daily 10am–1pm & 2–6pm; £1.50; ☎061/85186). Housed in replica Neolithic huts, this attempts to give some idea of what life was like for the early inhabitants. From here the chief attractions on **Knockadoon** are easily accessible on foot.

A quarter of a mile north of the Holycross turn-off, the first thing you'll have seen is a gargantuan **stone circle** close to the main road, the most substantial of the area's prehistoric remains. Possibly the grandest example in the country, it has a ring of standing stones (*orthostats*) marking out an almost perfect circle. A posthole was found at the centre which must have held a stake, from which, with a length of cord attached, the circle could be struck. Some of the stones are massive, and are bolstered within their earth sockets by smaller boulders, which were then covered. Flints, arrowheads, blades and bowls were found within the enclosure, but little has been learned about the site's exact function. A circle of this size clearly demanded a good deal of social organisation and a strong sense of purpose; the obvious conclusion is that this was a great centre for religious rituals, and frustratingly little else can be said.

The castles and Knockadoon

If you're walking, an alternative approach to Knockadoon is across the stone causeway that leads from near the gallery grave to **Black Castle**. Possibly thirteenth-century, the castle is now weighed down by a swarthy camouflage of nettles, brambles and trees. It was once quite extensive, with a high curtain wall and square towers, and acted as a principal seat for the Earls of Desmond. The pathway north to Bouchier's Castle has three **Neolithic hut** site remains at various degrees up the hill slope. If you're intent on seeing them, you'll have to forage around among the wooded thickets. A 1681 map shows the Knockadoon peninsula as an island with a drawbridge sticking out of **Bouchier's Castle**. It's a typical fifteenth-century Desmond tower house of five storeys; but it's still privately owned and can't yet be visited (in any case, there's a better example at Castle Matrix, p.218).

Turning westwards from the Black Castle towards the lakeshore in the heart of the C, you'll see various ring forts and hut traces on the bare grassy slopes. It's not much, but even this scant evidence is enough to conjure up a thriving Stone Age community on **Knockadoon**. Rather than continue round along the bank of the lake, it's best to take this opportunity to cross back along the hilltop centre, where from a point known as **M** you can get penetrating views into Kerry and Cork, with Limerick spreading towards them in a swathe of low hills. **Crock** and **Bolin islands** in the lake are both *crannogs* which the mainland has now caught up with. They were built by laying down a ring of boulders, then the inner space was filled with earth and brushwood. **Garret Island** is a natural island with some stone remains of another Desmond castle.

Kilmallock

Eight miles further down the main road from Lough Gur, **KILMALLOCK** has some good Norman remains; a tower castle, a town gate, a Dominican friary and a medieval stone mansion on the main street. **St John's Tower Castle** stands in the middle of the street and was the town citadel (you can get the key at the bungalow across the road, but there's little to see here). Turn instead down the lane opposite and you'll find a tiny **museum** (Sat & Sun 2–5pm; otherwise see C Murphy, 8 Orr Street) which won't take a minute to get through, unless you lend an ear to the home-made audiovisual history of the town. One interesting fact that crops up, and which goes a long way to explain the prestigious-looking fortifications and friary bases, is that at the end of the sixteenth century Kilmallock had a population of 2000, compared to Dublin's 5000. Kilmallock's importance was swift to decline – its population today is only 1500.

Bruree

Three miles west of Kilmallock, **BRUREE** was the childhood home of **Éamon De Valera**, familiarly known as the "big man" or "Dev" to a population for whom he's been the most influential political instigator since the birth of the Free State in 1922. He founded the *Fianna Fáil* (Soldiers of Destiny) party in 1926, acted as premier of Ireland in 1932–48, 1951–54 and 1957–59, and assumed the honorary role of President from 1959 to 1973. This makes up a sizeable chunk of the Republic's history, and his grip on the nation has left an ambivalent understanding of his worth and integrity.

De Valera was the only leader of the 1916 Easter uprising to survive. His initial death-sentence was commuted to imprisonment because of his American dual nationality – he was born in New York, and at this time the British were sensitive to American neutrality in World War I. He escaped from prison in England and was unconstitutionally elected the first President of the Irish Republic in 1919; his almost miraculous survival had marked him out as the man to lead Ireland out of seven hundred years of British domination. The Republic immediately declared war on Britain, and when two years of struggle forced the British to negotiate, De Valera's was the leading rebel voice against the signing of the Anglo-Irish Treaty in 1921. He wanted to hold out for an all-Ireland Free State, rather than accept only 26 counties out of 32, as was laid down in the Treaty. This stance divided the Irish and provoked the Civil War of 1921–23. The one war he succeeded in keeping the Irish out of was World War II – at the end of which he had the gall to send official commiserations to the Reichstag on Hitler's death, so engrained was the bitterness of his battle with the British.

De Valera was brought up just outside Bruree in a small **cottage**, which has now been turned into a modest memorial of the family's household possessions, including a bulky trunk that was used for their return from exile in New York. The cottage is signposted nearly a mile down the road to the right at the eastern end of Bruree village (key from next house on the right, 150 yards further down the road). At the western end of Bruree village itself is the old schoolhouse, which has been turned into a **museum** (Thurs & Sun, key from house next door; 50p) stocked with memorabilia of the ex-premier and president, plus a few rural items of general interest.

Southwest: the Road to Killarney

The road to Killarney is by the far the most interesting route out of Limerick, catching the prim English beauty of thatched cottages in Adare and, much more importantly, taking in Castle Matrix, a Desmond tower house which has been brilliantly restored and gives a unique insight into life as it might have been lived in these castles.

Adare

Famously picturesque **ADARE** has cultivated nearly as many antique shops as pubs. In peak season, it will more than likely be infested with tourists snapping the wayside cottages that sit in a neat row, their purposefully quaint deep-brown thatch hanging in low fringes. The cottages represent the nineteenth-century ideal of romanticised rusticity, as realised by the third Earl of Dunraven (1812–71), landlord and master of Adare Manor and an eternal improver of circumstances for his tenants. Given that Adare is now probably regarded as the prettiest (and, it must be added, prissiest) village in Ireland, it's hard to believe that before the Earl's improvements it was one of the grottiest. The cottages today feature a **tourist information office** (July & Aug Mon–Sat 9am–7pm, Sun 9am–1pm; June Mon–Sat 9am–1pm & 2–6pm, Sun 9am–1pm; May Mon–Sat 9am–1pm & 2–6pm; April Mon–Sat 9am–1pm & 2–5pm; Sept & Oct Mon–Sat 9am–1pm & 2–5pm, Sun 9am–1pm; ☎061/396255), an antique shop and a **restaurant**, *The Mustard Seed*, whose fancy menu is matched by steep prices.

Adare Manor House, to the north of the village, is a huge, near fanatical assembly of castellations and turrets in limestone, built by the Earl to Gothic revival designs in 1832. This castle has only recently gone into private hands as a grand hotel (*Adare Manor*; ☎061/396566; £90!), cultivating the visits of very rich Americans – it costs even to walk into the grounds. The River Maigue flows by the estate a little further up, at the head of the village, and although an exciting looking triumvirate of **medieval buildings** beckons, a golf course steers its course next to all of them, inhibiting any snooping around you might want to do. You're meant to clear your intentions at the clubhouse (entrance a little further up the road) but you could probably slip from ruin to ruin without being noticed. It may not be worth the effort anyhow, for the **Desmond Castle** – interesting to explore as it looks – is completely bricked up and deemed unsafe. The fifteenth-century **Friary** appears far better preserved, but it was extensively restored as late as the mid-nineteenth century. All of these are perhaps easiest viewed from the bridge.

Back in the village there are ecclesiastical sites too, starting with an **Augustinian Priory** just by the bridge. Beautifully conserved, this still serves as the local Church of Ireland, its interior as close as any to the old medieval model. The **Trinitarian Abbey**, halfway down the main street, was founded in 1230 for the Trinitarian Canons of the Order of the Redemption of Captives, and is the only house of this order in Ireland. Today, it's Adare's Catholic church, with one of its turrets at the back a deserted columbarium. If you're thinking of staying over in Adare – there are a couple of **B&Bs** in the village and plenty more in the immediate surrounds – the *Old Courthouse* on the corner of the main street next the public toilet has **traditional sessions** most evenings during the summer.

Rathkeale and Castle Matrix

About eight miles on from Adare, **RATHKEALE** was once an important Geraldine town, and the main source of interest here is their one-time stronghold, **Castle Matrix** (May 15–Sept 15 Sat–Tues 1–5pm, other times by arrangement; ☎069/64284; £2, children £1). To get there, turn right at the south end of the exceptionally long main street, just after the bridge: the castle lies half a mile down the road, on the right. Castle Matrix is a fifteenth-century tower house built by the seventh Earl of Desmond, and would inevitably have met with the same ruinous fate as virtually all the other 427 tower houses that once existed in Limerick, or the 2700 that once stood throughout the country – but for the brilliant restoration work of current owner Seán O'Driscoll, an Irish-American military enthusiast. With his army expertise, he understood the design of the fortifications, and realised that measurements needed to be within an inch for the battlements on the parapets to be effective (in contrast, the ornamental battlements at somewhere like Bunratty in County Clare wouldn't have lasted long in a fifteenth-century siege).

Tower houses flourished between the fifteenth and seventeenth centuries, especially in these southern counties. They provided a robust enough mini-fortress for the shift in the times; Anglo-Norman confidence was increasing, resulting in an expansion of settlements. The big Irish estates were being broken up due to the fall of the old Gaelic chiefs, and more towns were cropping up, with land being cultivated in hitherto uninhabited areas. Tower houses took on a uniform plan, usually of four or five floors, the top floor being the living quarters, the bottom windowless and usually used for storage. Castle Matrix has a tiny chapel recreated on its top floor and a medieval bedroom on another floor. It's stocked with exciting *objets d'art*, including a jewel-encrusted nineteenth-century Gaelic harp made by Fall of Belfast; an ebony writing bureau imported by the Southwells from China and finally donated back to Matrix some years ago, now sitting in the Oriental Room; documents referring to the Wild Geese (Irish officers who fled to the continent at the beginning of the seventeenth century); and the most remarkable item of all to return home – the original deed of the Southwells (the Earls of Desmond), which Seán O'Driscoll came across accidentally in London's Portobello Road.

The castle derived its name from the *matres*, a Celtic sanctuary, on which it stands. The scattering of destroyed cashels and raths in the surrounding area give substance to the idea of an ancient sanctuary here. An annexe of the castle offers luxury **B&B** (including jacuzzi; ☎069/64284; £45), and gourmet banquets are also held at the request of groups. Alternatively, *Rathkeale House Hotel* offers food and accommodation for those living slightly less high on the hog (☎069/64322; £15).

Newcastle West

Between Rathkeale and Newcastle West a signpost points to **Ardagh**, the ring fort where the wonderful Ardagh Chalice was found in 1868 (it's now in the Dublin Museum). The site here is unimpressive, however, and it's not worth dragging yourself off the main road.

NEWCASTLE WEST should make the last, if very brief, stop on your way out of Limerick, to look at the almost perfectly preserved **Desmond Banqueting Hall**. The hall is on the main square and very little fuss is made of it; but it's part of a scattered and hidden complex of ruined buildings – a keep, a peel tower, a bastion and curtain wall. Even though this was once the principal seat of the Fitzgeralds, the town hasn't harnessed its history to its advantage. The hall is in a near perfect state of preservation, and ready for an inspired restoration. At present, apart from a marriage fireplace said to have been imported from Egypt, it's all bare. You can get the key from Mrs Maureen Nash at what used to be the old gatehouse, down the drive at the immediate right of the hall grounds. Again, there are several small **B&Bs** – try, for example, Mrs Kennedy on Bishop Street (☎069/62050; £12) – and you can also get food and rooms at the *River Room Hotel* (☎069/62244; £18).

There's another excellently preserved but entirely deserted tower house, **Glenquin Castle**, signposted left several miles off the Newcastle–Abbeyfeale road by a petrol station (head for Killeady). It has very good views of the countryside, but the effort to get here is really only worthwhile if you have a car.

West: the Road to Tralee

The **road to Tralee**, the N69, is the least interesting of the three major routes across Limerick. It runs parallel to the Shannon estuary, but mostly through flat alluvial land, without the compensation of having the waters alongside except for the last few miles into Glin.

The first sign of interest you'll spot is **Carrigogunnell Castle** – no more than a well-worn ruin, overgrown with shrubs and trees, but with striking views across the estuary's waist. It's probably not worth leaving the main road; catch sight of it as the road passes CLARINA, from where the ruin cuts a dramatic appearance atop its rocky outcrop.

The road passes a few more tower houses on the right and the **Currahchase Forest Park** (see p.214) on the left before reaching **ASKEATON**. Here, there's an Anglo-Norman **Friary** next to the River Deel, just off the main road at its second entry to Askeaton from the east. The friary was founded by the fourth Earl of Desmond, Gerald the Poet, in 1389. It now seems particularly hidden away, and has one of the loveliest cloisters you'll come across and some excellent window tracery. From the dormitory above, you can pick out the towering remains of the **Castle**, penned in towards the centre of the town. This is worth no more than a quick scout around (keys from Billy Casey at the house by the entrance gate); there's a large banqueting hall, very similar to the better example in Newcastle West, its vaulted ground-floor chambers remaining just within the walls. A very dodgy looking end tower (fifteenth-century) stands upon a rock in the centre of what was once an island in the River Deel. The castle's present decay does little to suggest its one-time Anglo-Norman prominence, when it flourished in the hands of the Earls of Desmond, until their fall to the Earl of Essex during the sixteenth century.

FOYNES is a moderately busy seaport, presently occupied with plans to host a museum that will celebrate the town's past as an aviation centre of flying boats. In the late 1930s and early 1940s, Foynes, as Limerick's only seaport, was the terminus for a transatlantic flying-boat service. Moving on, the afforested hillslopes that now appear mark a pleasant route along the estuary as far as GLIN on the Limerick–Kerry border.

travel details

Trains

From Waterford to Dublin (4 daily; 2hr 30min); Limerick (1 daily; 2hr 30min).

From Limerick two trains daily to Tipperary (1hr 30min); Cahir (1hr 50min); Clonmel (2hr 10min); Carrick-on Suir (2hr 30min).

From Limerick Junction to Dublin (4 daily; 1hr 50min).

Bus Éireann

From Waterford to Dublin (2 daily; 3hr 30min).

From Limerick to Dublin (10 daily; 6hr); Tipperary (6 daily; 50min).

Private buses

Pierce Kavanagh Coaches (☎01/734344) leave **from Dublin**, Liberty Hall on Fridays at 5.30pm for Cashel (8pm), Cahir (8.15pm) and Mitchelstown (9pm), continuing on to Cork and Bantry. A return service **from Bantry** leaves on Sundays at 3.30pm for Cork (5.15pm), Mitchelstown (6.10pm), Cahir (6.30pm), Cashel (6.45pm) and Dublin. Another service runs **from Thurles**, Liberty Square (Mon–Sat 8.45am) for Dublin, and **from Dublin**, Burger King, O'Connell St (Mon–Sat 6pm) to Thurles.

Funtrek (☎01/730852) runs daily services **from Limerick**, Roscrea and Nenagh to Dublin, and **from Waterford** to Dublin.

Waterford Travel Club (☎051/77177) runs daily services **from Waterford**, Hanover Street, to Dublin.

Rapid Express Club Travel, 32 Michael Street, Waterford (☎051/72149 and ☎01/6791549) has at least three buses daily from Waterford to Tramore (leaving Manahan's shop, Tramore approximately thirty minutes before leaving Waterford). Mon–Sat depart Waterford (Apple Market morning buses, afternoon buses from Bank of Ireland, Parnell Street) 8.30am, 1.45pm, 5.30pm; Sun 9.30am. For the return journey depart Dublin (Custom House Quay) 9am, 1.30pm, 6pm; Sun 6pm. Prices from as little as £5 return.

CHAPTER SEVEN

CORK

Cork, Ireland's largest county, is the perfect place to ease yourself gently into the exhilarations of Ireland's west coast. **Cork city** is the south's self-proclaimed cultural capital, and manages to be at one and the same time both a relaxed and a spirited place. There are no spectacular sights, but Cork has to be one of Ireland's most pleasurable and accessible cities. Always a port, and with an island at its core, Cork nestles well inland on the estuary of the River Lee, which sustains the city with that same clear, soothing atmosphere that characterises most of the county, and in particular its coast and rivers. In the east of the county maritime history is still more richly distilled, in the small ports of **Cobh**, **Youghal** and – most of all – **Kinsale**, all suggestive of a prosperity that Ireland could have had were it not for the systematic strangulation of its overseas trade by Britain. On the other side of this coin are the Anglo-Irish treasures: the Neoclassical perfection of **Fota House** near Cobh, and the outrageously sumptuous art treasures of **Bantry House** in the west. Both rank among the finest stately homes in Ireland.

Every county of Ireland's wild west coast has its devotees, and Cork is certainly no exception. The place elicits strong reaction from locals and visitors alike, and its rivalry with neighbouring Kerry is legendary. Critics like to call it tame or mild – even genteel – since it can only occasionally match the sheer wild physicality of coasts further north. But this quality probably has as much to do with the people, and the relative mildness of the weather, as with landscape. And west Cork is quite different.

In the main the charms of the Cork countryside are those of a gently rural backwater, but as you head west along a fabulously indented coastline of hidden bays and coves to the wild peninsulas of the extreme southwest, or through the ravine of Gougane Barra high above **Glengarriff** and **Bantry Bay**, the soft contours of a comfortable and easy prettiness slip away to reveal beauty of a more elemental kind. There's not as much of this as you might find in, say, Kerry, but in the **Cahir Mountains** careering up from Bantry Bay, the scintillating cliff scenery of **Mizen Head**, or the island-strewn **Roaring Water Bay**, teeming with birdlife, Cork has landscapes as exciting and dramatic as you'll find anywhere.

Cork City

Old **CORK CITY** – the second city of the Republic – is built on an island, the two channels of the River Lee embracing it either side, while nineteenth-century suburbs sprawl up the surrounding hills. The river gives the city centre a compactness and sharp definition which creates exciting tensions. It's a place of great charm, with a history of vigorous intellectual independence, and approached from rural Ireland, has a surprisingly cosmopolitan feel to it.

Evidence of Cork's history as a great mercantile centre is everywhere, with grey stone quaysides, old warehouses, and elegant and quirky bridges spanning the river. Many of the city's streets were at one time waterways: St Patrick's Street had quays for sailing ships, and on the pavement in Grand Parade are bollards where merchant vessels were moored up until the eighteenth century. Important port though Cork may be, however, it doesn't feel overridingly commercial, and the Lee is certainly not the river of an industrial town. The all-pervading presence of its waters reflects and seems to double any light, so that even on the cloudiest of days there is a balmy, translucent quality to the atmosphere which effects a calm on the visitor. Cork is a welcoming, friendly place. While it has the vibrancy to enliven and excite, the pace is always Irish, and somehow the island breathes enough space for all temperaments.

Some History

Cork (*Corcaigh*, meaning "marshy place") had its origins in the seventh century when **Saint Finbarr** founded an abbey and school on the site where the impressive nineteenth-century Gothic St Finbarr's Cathedral stands today. A settlement grew up around the monastic foundation, overlooking a marshy swamp where the city centre now stands. In 820 the **Vikings** arrived, bringing their usual violence and destruction, and wrecked both abbey and town. They built a new settlement on one of the islands in the marshes, and eventually integrated with the native Celts. The twelfth century saw the **Norman** invasion and Cork, like other ports, was taken in 1172. The new acquisition was fortified with massive stone walls, which survived Cromwell but were destroyed by Williamite forces at the **Siege of Cork** in 1690.

From this time on the city began to take on the shape recognisable today. **Expansion** saw the reclamation of marshes and the development of canals within the city, and waterborne **trade** brought increasing prosperity. Evidence of this wealth survives in the form of fine eighteenth-century bow-fronted houses, and the ostentatious nineteenth-century church architecture that decorates the city – sharp, grey and Gothic, much of it by the Pain brothers. Traces of the great dairy trade of that period can still be seen in the Shandon area.

More recently, Cork saw much violence and suffered greatly during the Anglo-Irish and Civil wars: the city's part in **Republican** history is well-documented in the local museum. The Black and Tans reigned here with particular terror, destroying much of the town by fire, and were responsible for the murder of Thomas MacCurtain, the mayor of Cork, in 1920. Cork's next mayor, Terence MacSwiney, was gaoled as a Republican and died in Brixton prison after a hunger strike of 74 days. A popular hero, his hunger strike remains one of the longest achieved in the history of the IRA. One of his colleagues in Cork prison, Joseph Murphy, achieved the longest fast on record, going 76 days without food.

As part of the Republic, Cork has continued to develop – as a port, a university town and a cultural centre – and to assert its independence of Dublin.

Arrival and Accommodation

One of the joys of Cork is the fact that its scale is human: most of what it has to offer can be explored on foot. **Buses** to the suburbs and outlying towns and villages all go from the **Bus Éireann station** at Parnell Place alongside Merchant's Quay (enquiries ☎021/508188), and most of these also pick up from the more central St Patrick's Street. There is a standard fare of around 60p within the city. The *Bus Éireann* station also operates an extensive nationwide coach

service, while the **train station** (enquiries ☎021/506766) is less than a mile out of the city centre on the Lower Glanmire Road. **Private buses** (see "Listings" and "Travel Details") operate from various central points, mostly along St Patrick's Street and from the junction of Western Road with Mardyke Parade. If you arrive by **ferry** you'll be at RINGASKIDDY, some ten miles out, from where you can catch a connecting bus into the centre. Coming in by **plane** you can easily pick up a bus for the fifteen-minute journey into town: a shuttle service from the airport operates every 45 minutes (until 6.30pm low season, till 11.15pm April–Sept). If you're **driving** remember that, as in all the major cities, a disc parking system is in operation: discs can be bought from newsagents or the tourist office.

The **tourist office** is on Grand Parade (☎021/273251; June–Aug Mon–Sat 9am–7pm; Sept–May Mon–Sat 9.15am–5.30pm), with the usual wide variety of information. They will book rooms for £1 for a local phone call, £2 long distance, and there's plenty of choice. There are two main concentrations of **B&Bs** – along Western Road, near the University, and at the opposite end of town on Lower Glanmire Road, near the railway station – and Cork also has plenty of **hostels** as well as a couple of **campgrounds**. Cork is a great city for **festivals**, the biggest of which are the **film festival** at the beginning of October and the **jazz festival** over the last weekend in October. If you are planning your stay to coincide with one of them, advance booking is essential. Without it you are liable to find yourself overcharged in an inaccessible and inconvenient private home.

Bed and Breakfast

Mrs Cross, *Antoine House*, Western Road (☎021/273494; £15).

Mrs Betty Coleman, *Westbourne House*, 2 Westbourne Villas, Western Road (☎021/276153; £15).

Mrs Donegan, *The Blarney Stone*, 1 Carriglee Terrace, Western Road (☎021/270083; £13.50).

Mrs Murray, *Oakland*, 51 Lower Glanmire Road (☎021/500578; £11).

Mrs Burke, *Kent House*, 47 Lower Glanmire Road (☎021/504260; £13).

Mrs Sheridan, *Tara House*, 52 Lower Glanmire Road (☎021/500294; £11).

Clare D'Arcy, 7 Sydney Place, Wellington Road (☎021/504658; £19). Worth paying a little more to stay in this beautiful Georgian town house.

Hostels

Isaac's, 48 MacCurtain Street (☎021/500011; dorms £5.50; dorms plus breakfast £7.50; B&B £13.50; bike hire £5 per day; credit cards). Certainly the plushest in town, but if you are intending on cooking your own food, the kitchen facilities become pretty cramped during high season.

Sheila's Cork Tourist Hostel, Belgrave Place, Wellington Road, up behind MacCurtain Street (☎021/505562; £5.50 for sharing in a 4- or 6-bedded room; £6.50 each in a twin room; £8 single; breakfast £1)). A good central alternative, friendly, well-run, with better cooking facilities and a garden to the rear.

Campus Hostel, 3 Woodland View, Western Road (☎021 343531; all year; £5). Tiny, friendly, but a good ten to fifteen minute walk from the centre of town along Western Road

An Óige Hostel, 1–2 Redclyffe, Western Road (☎021/543289; June–Sept £5.90, Oct–May £4.50; bike hire). Just before the *Campus Hostel*, predictably a bit more formal.

Kinlay House budget hostel, Shandon (☎021/508966; all year; £7 bed and breakfast; laundry facilities).

Cork City Independent Hostel, 100 Lower Glanmire Road (☎021/509089; £4.50–5). Handily situated about 100 yards from the train station.

Campsites

Cork City Caravan and Camping Park (☎021/961866; Easter to end Sept, plus jazz weekend; £3–3.50, plus £1 per car, £1 per person). The nearest to the centre of town, with a **launderette** on the site. Pick up a #14 bus from St Patrick Street or South Main Street (every 20 min) and the driver will put you down outside the site; last bus out of town runs at 11.15pm. To walk or cycle, climb Barrack Street beside Sullivans Quay, follow it for about half a mile, then take Lough Road on the left.

Bienvenue Caravan and Camping Park (☎021/312711; Easter to Oct 31; £3.50 per unit, 25p per person). Near the airport – the Airport/Kinsale bus stops 600 yards from the site, or follow the signposts to Kinsale and airport, and then the signs from the airport gates. Both campsites may increase charges at festival times.

The City

Cork has no really spectacular sights, but it's a fine place to wander: around the quays, through the narrow lanes, into the markets, up to Shandon. The ambience and sense of place are enjoyable in themselves, and for those with a taste for it there's plenty of nineteenth-century Gothic church architecture punctuating the river banks, and evocative remnants of a great mercantile past. Exploration on foot is rewarding – the city's medieval core is embedded in its central narrow lanes, and the meshing of its history can be felt embodied in its buildings, reflected in the constant flow of the Lee. But don't go expecting to be astounded. Enjoying Cork city is to do with tuning in to the pace and life of the place.

The island

The **city centre** is essentially the island, with its quaysides, pretty bridges, alleyways and lanes, plus that segment to the north of the River Lee that has MacCurtain Street as its central thoroughfare, and the lanes leading up to Shandon. The graceful wishbone arc of **St Patrick's Street**, with **Grand Parade**, forms the modern commercial heart, with a healthy smattering of the modish amenities generally associated with much larger European cities. Not that you are ever engulfed by commercialism; aggressive multinationals have not been allowed to dominate, and expensive fashion houses exist alongside modest traditional businesses. It is in such immediate contrasts that the charms of the city lie. A hundred yards from the elegant shop-fronts of St Patrick's Street you'll find **Coal Quay market** in Cornmarket Street – a flea market worthy of the name, well worth investigating if you are fascinated by the shabby side of a damp, rural life in its unchanged nineteenth-century setting. A minute's walk from Coal Quay Market down Paul Street brings still more variety in the bijou environs of French Church Street and Emmet Place. **Paul Street** itself is experiencing a resurgence of commercial and artistic activity with new restaurants, artists' studios, specialist bookshops and period clothes shops.

The eastern, downstream, end of the island is the more clearly defined: many of its quays are still in use, and it's here that you best get a sense of the old port city. Trips out into **Cork harbour** are available during the summer months – ask at the tourist office. In the west the island peters out in a predominantly residential area. Heading in this direction though, you can follow the signs off Western Road for **Fitzgerald Park**, home of the **Cork Public Museum** (Mon–Fri 11am–1pm & 2.15–6pm, Sun 3–5pm; free, Sun 20p), about a mile out of the city centre. Primarily a museum of Republican history, it has an excellent commentary on the part played by nationally significant local characters and events in the Republican

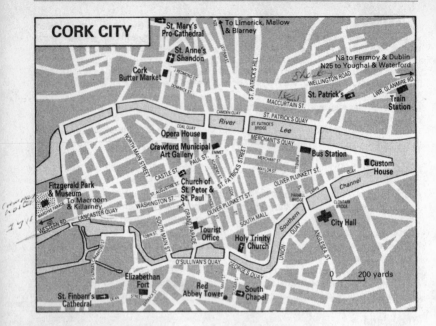

movement. There are exhibits of local archaeological and geological finds too, and a section on the history of the dairy trade. While in the park it's worth trying the **tearooms** – a cosy atmosphere with delicious homemade cake and soups, and a useful source of information for what's on in the arts, both in the city centre and at the University.

Shandon

North of the River Lee is the area known as **Shandon**, a sadly neglected reminder of Cork's eighteenth-century status as the most important port in Europe for dairy products. To get there head up John Redmond Street, or simply aim for the giant fish atop the church tower. The most striking survival is the **Cork Butter Exchange**, stout nineteenth-century Classical buildings recently given over to select craft workshops – expensive and very much geared to the US tourist market. The old **butter market** itself sits like a generously proportioned butter tub in a cobbled square: recently (rather disappointingly) renovated to house the *Irish National Ballet*, its future is now uncertain. Despite the air of derelelction, this part of town is worth a visit for the pleasant Georgian church of **St Anne's Shandon** (1750), easily distinguishable from all over Cork city by its weather vane – an eleven foot salmon. For £1 you can view the not particularly remarkable interior of St Anne's, and the old books, or for a much more worthwhile £1.50 you can climb the **tower** (Mon–Sat 10am–4.30pm), two of its sides finished in red sandstone, two in white limestone, for excellent views, and ring the famous bells – a good stock of sheet tunes is provided.

The stark precision of nineteenth-century Gothic which is repeated time and again in the city's churches may not be to everyone's taste, but here undeniably gives the city a rhythmic architectural cohesion. Both Pugin and Pain are very much in evidence, Pugin in the brilliant Revivalist essay of the Church of St Peter and St Paul on Friar Mathew Quay, with its handsome lantern spire, and in St Patrick's Church on Lower Glanmire Road. Best of all is William Burges' St Finbarr's Cathedral (built 1867–79); obsessively detailed, its impressive French Gothic spire provides a grand silhouette on the southwesterly shoulder of the city.

Food, drink and entertainment

As the second most populous city in the Republic and the nation's (self-proclaimed) cultural capital, Cork is a strangely unpretentious place, with plenty of good pub sessions and MOR discos, along with a smattering of more highbrow cultural events. The *Cork Examiner* is the local paper with mainstream what's on information. Other places to pick up on what's happening are *The Quay Co-op*, *The Other Place*, *The Triskel Arts Centre*, *The Phoenix* and the *School of Music* – all detailed below. There's also an excellent range of eating places.

Food

Bully's, 40 Paul Street (Mon–Sat noon–11.30pm, Sun 5–11pm). Wine bar serving pizzas, fresh pasta and fish (from around £5); popular with families and an older, discerning crowd.

Ciao Italy, Caroline Street, off Oliver Plunkett Street. Cheery atmosphere, cheap pizzas.

The Crawford Municipal Art Gallery, Emmet Place. An affordable off-shoot of the famous Ballymaloe restaurant near Cloyne.

Fitzgerald Park Café, next to the museum (Summer Mon–Sat 10am–5pm). Handy for the budget hostel, a cosy and convivial place much patronised by students, with reasonably priced, homemade soups and cakes. Another good place for what's on information.

Halpins, 14–15 Cook Street (Mon–Sat 9am–midnight; Sun 11am–11pm). Self-service delicatessen restaurant, serving delicious salads, seafoods, quiches and cakes; from £4 during the day; evening menu of steaks, curries etc £6–15.

Harlequin Café, 26 Paul Street (10am–6pm). Cheap and fairly wholesome café, though not all as homemade as its appearance might suggest. A nice spot to sit and watch the world drift past, and a good place to find out about drama and arts events.

Huguenot's, French Church Street (☎021/273357; Mon–Sat noon–10.30pm). Possibly the classiest place to eat well and cheaply in the city. Bistro-style restaurant serving salads, pastas, pancakes etc (£5–7). Despite swanky appearances, nobody minds if you just have a glass of wine, a coffee or a starter.

Luciano's, 8 MacCurtain Street. Swarthy café; great pizzas.

Café Mexicana, Carey's Lane. Enchilladas, tacos, tortillas etc from £5.50.

The Other Place, St Augustine Street (daily 10am–6.30pm). Off-shoot of the *Quay Co-op*; cheap, vegetarian café and second-hand and alternative bookshop.

Paddy Garibaldi's, Carey's Lane (Mon–Sat 12am–12pm, Sun 5pm–midnight). Friendly café-restaurant for burgers, steaks and pizzas; from around £6.

Pizza Pomodoro, Cook Street. Cheap pizzas in quiet, candlelit restaurant.

The Quay Co-op, 24 Sullivan's Quay (Mon–Sat 10.30am–6pm and 6.30pm–10.30pm). Delicious, large vegetarian and vegan meals, soups, puddings and teas, all in surroundings of wonderfully faded elegance. Meals from £2.50; dearer in the evenings.

The Raging Red Hag, Pembroke Street. Huge sandwiches to feed the ravenous poor.

The Triskel Arts Centre, Tobin Street, off South Main Street (open Mon–Sat 10.30am–5pm). Home-made bread, soups and salads; hot vegetarian and non-vegetarian dishes from £3; tasty and good value.

Thyme Out, French Church Street. Cheap vegetarian café.

Westimer, O'Sullivan's Quay (next to the *Quay Co-op*). Lively wild west theme diner; fun, young and squeaky clean. Burgers.

MORE EXPENSIVE

Arbutus Lodge Hotel, Montenotte (☎021/501237). Very pricey, but dazzling quality.

Le Chateau, 93 St Patrick's Street, next to the *Cork Examiner* (☎021/270370). Bar with good, French-inspired menu.

The Oyster Tavern, 4 Market Lane, off St Patrick's Street (☎021/272716). Old-fashioned atmosphere – all brass and polished wood.

Pubs

There are plenty of good watering holes in the city, and if all you want is a drink, you won't need a guide to find somewhere – though a couple of the city's older bars listed below are worth seeking for their atmosphere. Many bars have music, traditional or otherwise, and the following list should give some good pointers on where to find the best of this. As with any large city, though, venues and session nights change, so it's worth asking around for the best of the current action. Wherever you end up, this is not a difficult town to enjoy yourself in.

An Bodhrán, Oliver Plunkett Street. Traditional music (Mon, Tues & Wed).

An Spailpín Fánach, South Main Street. Traditional Irish music nightly; bluegrass Thursdays upstairs; bar food daily.

The Chambers, upstairs at 2 Anglesea Street. Boisterous bar playing house, disco and assorted dance music for a young crowd.

The Donkey's Ears, Union Quay. Lively bar with regular live blues/bluegrass (Sun & Tues); folk and rock (Mon), traditional Irish, folk and ballads (Wed), DJ playing house and hip hop (Thurs), reggae (Fri).

Georgia Browne, Washington Street. Lively bar playing rock, acid house; nightclub upstairs open till 2am; free admission if you are in before 11pm.

Isaac Bells, St Patrick's Quay (behind the *Metropole Hotel*). Very popular, lively bar playing reggae (Thurs & Mon evening), traditional Irish or folk (Wed & Sat evening), and jazz on Sunday, 5–8pm.

Loafers, 26 Douglas Street. Friendly bar with pleasant beer garden, attracts a bohemian clientele; probably the most relaxed place for gays to drink in the city.

The Lobby, Union Quay. A good spot to catch live music: traditional Irish sessions (Mon, Tues & Fri); upstairs bar, for which there is a cover charge, has just about any kind of music – rock, folk, pop, traditional – throughout the week.

The Long Valley, Winthrop Street. A must purely for the eccentricities of the owner and the clientele, the place also does good substantial sandwiches.

The Metropole Hotel, MacCurtain Street. Hotel bar: local jazz and old-style cabaret venue (Fri evenings all year and winter Sun lunchtime); traditional Irish and ballads (Wed & Thurs).

The Mutton Lane Inn, Mutton Lane, off Patrick Street. Convivial, old, traditional city centre bar.

The Phoenix, Union Quay. Traditional, blues and folk (Sun, Mon & Thurs); the bar upstairs attracts a younger crowd and offers videos, chart music, heavy metal and, on Friday nights, live rock bands.

The Vineyard, Market Lane, off Patrick Street. Quaint old bar given over to a young crowd; spacious enough to think as you drink.

Clubs

There are plenty of disco-type **clubs** around the city centre, easy enough to stumble upon late at night. Below are some of the (slightly) more interesting, again often with live entertainment.

De Lacy House, 74 Oliver Plunkett Street. Busy central club; MOR disco, bands, karaoke; big-name traditional Irish bands play here occasionally.

Mojo's, George's Quay. Bikers' pub/club with live blues (and occasional rock) Saturday nights and Sunday mornings; this is also a good spot for what's on info.

Sir Henry's, South Main Street (£3, concessions for unemployed). Nightclub lately invaded by very young acid-house devotees; Friday night is popular for its alternative dance music.

Elroy's, behind *Westimer*, Sullivan's Quay. Live bands till 1am at weekends.

Art, theatre, film and festivals

The latest hub of artistic activity in Cork is the **Triskel Arts Centre**, found down the narrow and dingy Tobin Street, off South Main Street (☎021/272022; concessions on tickets for students and unemployed). It has changing exhibitions of contemporary art, a film theatre, a continual programme of performance art, poetry reading, contemporary music, and a very good wholefood café. It is also an excellent source of information about what's on – Triskel will know about any theatre or music performances in the city.

Other **art galleries** include the *Crawford Municipal Gallery* in Emmet Place (Mon–Sat 10am–5pm), with a permanent collection of Irish and European painting and usually an interesting temporary exhibition. Nearby on Lavitt's Quay, the *Cork Arts Society* (Tues–Sat 10.30am–2pm & 3–5.30pm) is a good commercial gallery, with exhibitions of contemporary works changing every two weeks.

The **Cork Opera House** (☎021/276357), in Emmet Place, offers a full programme of drama, concerts both classical and popular, ballet, opera, review and variety; though very rarely anything at all out of the mainstream. For a more varied drama programme try **The Everyman Palace**, MacCurtain Street (☎021/501673), and for local small-scale productions try **Cork Arts Theatre (C.A.T.s)**, in Knapps Square, off Camden Quay. For classical concerts, look in at **Triskel**, the **School of Music**, on Union Quay, or the **City Hall**, Anglesea Street – ask at the tourist office or consult the *Cork Examiner* for details.

Cork has an extremely popular **international jazz festival** the last weekend in October. With music bursting out of every doorway, you don't need to go and see the big names to enjoy yourself if you are short of cash. It's a great time to be in the city, but advance booking for accommodation is strongly advised. There is generally a special Festival Accommodation Office to cope with the extra crowds – its location varies, so ask locally, or at one of the big venues or at the tourist office. There's also an important **film festival** at the beginning of October, with films screened at Triskel and the Opera House. The *International Choral Festival* is held the first weekend in May, and there is a folk festival during September: ask at the tourist office for exact dates.

Listings

Airlines *Aer Lingus*, 30 Patrick Street (☎021/274331); *Ryanair* (☎021/274444).

Airport Cork airport is 5 miles along the Kinsale road; ☎021/313131 for flight information.

Banks Branches of the *Allied Irish* in Patrick Street, North Main Street, Bridge Street and Western Road.

Bike Hire *Kilgrews Ltd*, 30 North Main Street (☎021/273458); *The Cycle Repair Centre*, 6 Kyle Street (☎021/276255), or from the campsite.

Bookshops *Waterstones*, Patrick Street; *Liam Russell*, Oliver Plunkett Street; *The Other Place* (second-hand and alternative books), St Augustine Street; *Collins*, Carey's Lane; *Mercier Bookshop*, 4 Bridge Street; *Eason's*, Patrick Street.

Bureau de Change At the tourist office.

Buses The *Bus Éireann* station (☎021/508188 for information) is in Parnell Place, alongside Merchant's Quay; local and intercity buses operate from here. *Bus Éireann* services cover the entire country, the main towns daily, smaller places less frequently. Check the detailed timetables for your intended route at the bus station if you're relying on getting somewhere. Several private bus companies also operate from Cork: see "Travel Details" at the end of this chapter.

Camping equipment *The Tent Shop*, Rutland Street, off South Terrace, offers camping gear for sale or hire; *Matthews*, Academy Street, for equipment and Gaz.

Car Hire *Great Island Car Rentals*, 47 MacCurtain Street (☎021/503536, 811609).

Chemists *Falvey's Pharmacy*, Bridge Street; *Denis O'Leary*, 8 Grand Parade (☎021/274563). For information on out-of-hours service, phone ☎021/965588.

Dental Emergencies Regional Hospital ☎021/545100.

Family Planning Clinic Tuckey Street, off Grand Parade (☎021/277544); *Cura*, Paul Street, offer free pregnancy testing (☎021/501444).

Ferries to France operate from Ringaskiddy, about ten miles from Cork. *Brittany Ferries*, 42 Grand Parade (☎021/277801) sail to Roscoff once a week; *Irish Ferries*, 9 Bridge Street (☎021/504333) operate services to Cherbourg and Le Havre. *Swansea–Cork Ferries*, 55 Grand Parade (☎021/271166). *Sealink*, for Rosslare–Fishguard, are based at the tourist office (☎021/272965).

Gay Info ☎021/271087 Wed 7–9pm.

Hospital Cork South Infirmary, Victoria Hospital, Old Blackrock Road (☎021/964333).

Hurley and Football Every Sun afternoon from Sept to June in GA Stadium, Blackrock.

Launderette MacCurtain Street, next door to the *Everyman Palace* theatre, Mon–Sat 9am – last wash 8pm.

Lesbian Line Thurs 8–10pm, ☎021/271087.

The Other Place, St Augustine Street. Second-hand bookshop and political campaigning centre; educational and social focus for gay and women's issues etc.

Public Baths Douglas Swimming Pool, Douglas Road (☎021/293073), in Churchfield on the north side of the city.

Rape Crisis Centre 27a MacCurtain Street (☎021/968086), or write to PO Box 42, Brian Boru Street.

Taxis *Arrow Cabs* ☎021/311311; *Cara Cabs* ☎021/505722; *Express Hackney Service* ☎021/507766.

Tourist office Grand Parade (☎021/273251; Oct–May Mon–Sat 9.15am–5.30pm; June–Sept Mon–Sat 9am–6pm, and until 7pm during July & Aug).

Trains The station (enquiries ☎021/506766) is on Lower Glanmire Road, about a mile from the centre; *Irish Rail*'s travel centre is right in the centre at 65 Patrick Street (☎021/504888 for all information).

Travel agents *USIT* have two offices in Cork: at 10–11 Market Parade (☎021/270900; Mon–Fri 9.30am–5.30pm, Sat 11am–4pm) and *UCC Student Travel*, near The Boole Library, University College (Mon–Fri 9.30am–5.30pm, Sat 10am–1pm).

Around Cork City

There are several good short trips that will get you out of Cork for the day, but back in time to take advantage of the city's nightlife. **Blarney** offers history and the scenic Lee valley; **Fota** has wild animals and eighteenth-century Classicism; and **Cobh**, water sports. It is also possible to visit **Kinsale** for the day from Cork, but allowing more time makes sense: once there you'll be reluctant to return, and probably find yourself lured further west around the coast.

Blarney

BLARNEY is an easy six miles from Cork city; buses leave the bus station every half hour. If you can manage to divorce the **castle** (Mon–Sat: May–Aug 9am–7pm; Sept 9am–6.30pm; Oct–April 9am–sundown. Sun: summer 9.30am–5.30pm, winter 9.30am–sundown) from the whole "Blarney phenomenon" it actually is a fine stronghold, built in 1446 by Dermot McCarthy, King of Munster. The **Blarney Stone** has been kissed by visitors for over a hundred years, the legend being that to do so gives you the gift of eloquent and persuasive speech. The most famous story of how the legend came about tells of one McCarthy – King of Munster and Lord of Blarney – who, supposedly loyal to the colonising Queen Elizabeth I, never actually got around to fulfilling any of the agreements between them, always sidetracking her emissaries with drinking, dancing and sweet talk. He was said to be able to talk "the noose off his head". In her frustration the queen is said to have eventually cried out "Blarney, Blarney, what he says he does not mean. It is the usual Blarney". And so the word entered the English language.

The stone itself is a four foot by one foot limestone block set in the battlements 83 feet above the ground, so kissing it requires a head for heights. If you want to do so, you'll have to join the queue in the castle keep from which you can watch everyone else (one at a time) being dangled backwards by the shins over the battlements aided by two strong men. This also gives you time to consider whether or not you really want to join in. According to a less challenging legend, the stone is half of the Stone of Scone, given to Cormac McCarthy by Robert the Bruce in gratitude for the support of 4000 men at the Battle of Bannockburn (the rest is in London, at Westminster Abbey). The views from the top of the castle are superb.

In the castle grounds, **Rock Close** is a nineteenth-century folly, a rock garden supposedly built around druidic remains. Authentic or not, it is a pity that myths are such big business around here, because without the commercials these ancient yews and oaks could create a potent atmosphere. **Blarney House** (June to mid-Sept Mon–Sat noon–5.30pm), nearby, is a nineteenth-century Scottish baronial-style mansion. Inside, it's oppressively lush and Victorian, despite some fine eighteenth- and nineteenth-century satinwood furnishings and Waterford chandeliers. (Admission to Blarney Castle £2.50, students £1.50; to Blarney House and Gardens £2, students £1.50; admission to both £4, students £2.50.)

The town

The **town of Blarney** functions chiefly as a tourist service centre geared to the American market – it is perhaps the only place in Ireland where you see not *Mná* and *Fir*, not Ladies and Gents, but "Rest Room". Naturally there are plenty of places to eat here – expensive but not impossible – and the majority of the pubs do bar food, which is generally the better option. One surprise is the **Blarney Woollen Mills**, one of Blarney's original industries, now doing very nicely out of the castle's visitors. It has a couple of shops here, and the smaller of the two is one of the best places in Ireland for woolly bargains. Alongside is a **tourist office** (daily June–Sept 9am–7pm), and you can **hire a bike** from *McGrath Cycles* (Stoneview; ☎021/385658) for some easy and scenic cycling from Blarney up the Lee valley.

Fota and Cobh

A visit to Fota House and Wildlife Park and the pretty harbour town of Cobh can be managed in a day on a return train ticket from Cork. Going by train really is the best option, taking you across the mudflats of an estuary teeming with bird-life. Both are situated on islands in the mouth of Cork harbour. **Fota Wildlife Park** (April 6–Sept 5 Mon–Sat 10am–5.15pm, Sun 11am–5.15pm; winter week-days until end Oct only; £2.70, students £2) is a small, pleasant park with apes, cheetahs, giraffes, red pandas and zebras among others all wandering about the landscaped eighteenth-century estate of Fota House.

The **house** itself may no longer be open (it's under threat of being sold to a private company and developed as an exclusive leisure complex), so check with the tourist office or ring first (☎021/812555): in the past hours have been April–Sept Mon–Sat 11am–6pm, Sun 2–6pm; Oct–March Sun & Bank Holidays 2–6pm (£2, students & unemployed £1). Originally an eighteenth-century hunting lodge, it was much enlarged in 1820. The building is one of Classical unity: Doric columns and plastered stonework outside are in complete harmony with the perfect Neoclassical interiors. Further Greek columns, high decorated ceilings and fine furnishings confirm the refined elegance of the lives led here. Fota is the perfect setting for the major collection of eighteenth- and nineteenth-century landscape paintings it houses, conveying as they do a pastoral idyll of a perfectly ordered world. In the estate is one of the most important **arboretums** in Europe, with a great variety of rare and exotic flowering shrubs and trees.

Cobh

Rejoining the train from Fota takes you out to the extremely pretty little town of **COBH**. Cobh (pronounced "Cove") is held in a quaint cup of land with steep, narrow streets climbing the hill to the Pugin Cathedral. One of the most enjoya-ble of these neo-Gothic monsters, it dominates the town, giving marvellous views out across the great curve of the bay to Spike Island. Thanks to its fine natural harbour, Cobh has long been an important port: it served as an assembly point for ships during the Napoleonic wars, and was a major departure point for steam-ers carrying emigrants to America. The first ever transatlantic steamer sailed from here in 1838, and the *Titanic* called in on her ill-fated voyage, too; a monu-ment to the victims of the *Lusitania* disaster stands in Casement Square. The port is still used by a substantial fishing fleet. From September to February, when it is awash with fishermen, the town's character changes completely.

First and foremost, though, Cobh is a holiday resort, itself an historic function. Ireland's first yacht club was established here in 1720, and from 1830 on the town was a popular health resort, imitative of English Regency resorts like Brighton, a style reflected in its architecture. The main square is flanked by brightly-painted Victorian townhouses, and the place has a robust cheerfulness, with all the amen-ities of a family resort: pitch and putt, tennis, swimming, and a stony beach. At the **International Sailing Centre** on East Beach (☎021/811237) you can hire sailing dinghies (£8 per hour, £40 per day), canoes (£4; £20) and windsurfing boards (£6; £15) – the centre also has accommodation available for long-term use. Further attractions are the **Cobh International Folk Dance Festival**, starting the second Sunday in July, and a **regatta** weekend in mid-August. You can also go **pony trekking** (*McCarthy's*, Tay Road; ☎021/811908) or on a **trip round the harbour** (*Marine Transport Services*, Atlantic Quay; ☎021/811485; £3). Cobh

tourist office, *Carrig Lodge*, Spy Hill (☎021/813301; Easter to Sept), which if you arrive from Fota by road you pass as you descend into the town, has maps and local information, and will give up-to-date information on *The Queenstown Project*, a **heritage centre** telling the history of the town from the American War of Independence until the present day. It's scheduled to open June 1992, and during June, July and August will be connected to Cork city and Fota by steam train (entrance charges will be £3.50).

If you want to stay, **B&B**s include *Westbourne House* (☎021/811391; £10), *Atlantic* (☎021/811489; £10–14.50) and *Ardeen* (3 Harbour Hill, ☎021/811803; £10). There's a **launderette** at 4 Park View(☎021/812146), behind the Clifton Bar on Midleton Street.

East of Cork

Beaches to the east of Cork city are unspectacular, and have nothing like the charm of the West. **BALLYCOTTON** has a little quayside, fine cliff walks for miles to the west, and a beach half a mile away. It overlooks Ballycotton Bay and the holiday villages of SHANAGARRY and GARRYVOE. **Garryvoe beach** is very long and sandy, but beset by caravans advancing upon the shore and very busy during high season. The east of the bay is flat and of interest only to bird watchers, its reed-infested estuary now a protected bird sanctuary. Here a river sidles its way, smooth and khaki, through the mudflats to the sea.

Inland, MIDLETON is a cheery market town, and four miles to the south is the sleepy, historic village of **CLOYNE**. There's not much to see here, but it's worth a look if you're passing through this part of the country. Its interest lies in its history; what was, rather than what is. One of Ireland's earliest Christian foundations, the monastery of Saint Colman, was established here in the sixth century. In medieval times the village continued to be of religious importance with the establishment of the See of Cloyne, a diocese which extended well into County Limerick. Reminders of this era, though, are few. There's a fine tenth-century **round tower**, from whose top, 100 feet up, there are superb views (key from Cathedral house, 50p) and you can also visit **St Colman's Cathedral**, a large building of warm, mottled stone originally built in 1250 but disappointingly restored in the nineteenth century. Inside, the grand and grim seventeenth-century Fitzgerald of Imokelly tomb and the alabaster tomb of George Berkley, the famous philosopher who was bishop here from 1734 to 1753, are worth a look. An Egyptian *tau* cross and the St Anthony's cross on the cathedral doorway are faint traces of earlier influences from the Mediterranean.

Off the Cloyne–Ballycotton road, *Ballymaloe House* (☎021/652531) is an exceptional **restaurant**, one of the most famous in Ireland; a meal here will cost you from around £25.

Youghal

YOUGHAL (pronounced "Yawl") is an ancient port at the mouth of the River Blackwater, where the counties of Cork and Waterford meet. In a small way it combines the richness of the Blackwater towns with the prettiness of Kinsale and Cobh. A picturesque holiday town, Youghal has real character, with a colourful history and some fine architecture to remember it by.

Youghal's walls were first built by the Norman settlers who established the town, but those which stand today were erected by Edward I in 1275. From medieval times the town prospered as one of Ireland's leading ports, trading with the continent, particularly France, and with England. Political disturbances and trade restrictions imposed on Irish ports by the English government, however, meant the town's growth began to slow in the mid-sixteenth century. It fell into the hands of the Earl of Desmond, and in 1579 the "Rebel" Earl (rebelling against Elizabeth I) sacked and burned the place. After Desmond's death, Youghal was part of the 40,000 acres granted to Walter Raleigh during the Munster Plantations, with which Elizabeth hoped to control Ireland. Raleigh, though, had little interest in Ireland, and spent most of his time composing poetry in an attempt to curry favour with the queen. In this he was abetted by Edmund Spenser, another local colonist, author of *The Faerie Queen*. Spenser proved to be capable of both great poetry and of barbarism in his dealings with the Irish: they eventually repaid him by burning down his castle Kilcolman, near Buttevant. Raleigh himself spent little time in Youghal, selling his land to Richard Boyle, the "Great" Earl of Cork (and father of the scientist), who then greatly developed the town as he did all his newly acquired land.

When Cromwell reached New Ross in 1649, the English garrison at Youghal went over to the Parliamentarian side, and so the town escaped destruction. Nonetheless the importance of the port continued to diminish through the seventeenth century. Still, the decline was only relative to its former stature, and there is enough fine eighteenth-century architecture to make it clear that a small but affluent class of merchants still prospered. Today Youghal is a quiet seaside resort, and the history preserved in its buildings continues to suggest prosperity earned through centuries of vigorous commerce, and offers an insight into the privileged lives of the early colonists.

The Town

Youghal's most famous landmark is the **clocktower** which bridges the long, curvy main street: a superbly proportioned Georgian structure of warm, plum-coloured stone. A century ago it was used as a prison, more recently it served as a museum, but it's now closed indefinitely. Steps leading off the tower climb the steep hill through little lanes to the top of the town, where the walls and turrets of the old defences still define the shape of the compact harbour.

The most charming buildings lie, in the main, on the landward side of North Main Street and in the lanes that run behind it. On Main Street itself the **Red House** is a fine example of domestic architecture: built in 1710, it clearly shows the Dutch influence of the original merchant owner. Here, too, are seventeenth-century almshouses, built by Richard Boyle to house Protestant widows. Lanes off to the west of this end of Main Street lead to the Elizabethan **Myrtle Grove**, known as "Raleigh's House" though there's no real evidence that he ever lived there; it remains a family home but is open to the public and worth seeing as one of the oldest unfortified houses in Ireland (May–Sept Tues, Thurs & Sat; £2; ☎024/92274).

Alongside you'll find the **Collegiate Church of St Mary's**, a large, simple, thirteenth-century building, one of the few of such age still in use in Ireland. The building has been greatly altered over the centuries, but still has interesting medieval tombs and effigies. Particularly notable are the thirteenth-century monuments in the south transept (key from Church Lodge, 2–5pm). Wrecked when the town was sacked by Desmond's men in 1579, they were later restored by Boyle, with the addition of effigies in seventeenth-century costume. Heading out of town towards Waterford, you pass the ruins of North Abbey, a thirteenth-century Dominican Priory of which little remains.

On the east side of North Main street is **Tyntes Castle**, a fifteenth-century tower house that is now sadly dilapidated (and, by the look of it, rapidly deteriorating). Edmund Spenser's widow married Robert Tynte, who lived here. Lanes off this side of the street lead to the **quayside**. Here it's all very quaint, almost too much so: warehouse buildings warm with the patina of age surround the harbour; yucca palms decorate the walkways, and the cultivated fields of Waterford across the water look very near.

Practicalities and Entertainment

The **tourist office** (open June–Sept ☎024/92390) is in Market Square, just behind the harbour, and there's plenty of **accommodation** nearby. The cheapest option is Mrs Helena James's *Hillside*, 6 Strand Street (☎024/92468; bed without breakfast £5). If you want **B&B** or mid-priced hotels there are plenty along the main streets and around the quayside – try Mrs P. Brooke's *Avonmore House*, South Abbey (☎024/92617; £12.50) or Mrs P. Foley's *Roseville*, Dolphin Square (024/92571; £12). The *Summerfield Caravan and Camping Park* (☎024/93537; June to early Sept; hikers'/cyclists' tents £2.25 plus 50p per person) is to the west of town, down by the beach: follow the Cork road and the site's signposted about a mile out of town off to the left. To the west of town, sandy (European Blue Flag) **beaches** stretch for miles. There's a **launderette** on North Main Street.

Every town selects which portion of its history it wishes to celebrate, and in Youghal the Raleigh connection takes first place. Thus the town celebrates music and potatoes in its **Walter Raleigh Potato Festival**, the last week in June and the first week in July. A close second is the use of the town as a location for the film of *Moby Dick;* memorablia and photographs from the making of the film are found in the bar by the quays.

During the summer months several of the bars in Youghal have regular **music** sessions – they cater for a family holiday crowd, but there's some interesting variety nonetheless. *The Nook* on Main Street has a traditional Irish night on Wednesday, and some kind of live band, free, every night from mid-July to mid-September; Saturday and Sunday only the rest of the year. The proprietor of this bar claims Youghal is the cheapest seaside town for drink: make of this what you will – he also claims Walter Raleigh used to drink in his bar. Similarly committed to giving visitors a good time is *The U-Tree* on Tallow Street (Youghal translates as yew-wood), further along the same stretch heading towards Waterford. There is some form of entertainment here – Irish music, country and western, discos or *céilís* – on weekends all year, more often during July and August, with a cover charge of around £1.50. *The Blackwater Inn* (Power's) and *The Anchor Bar* also have sessions, but Youghal has plenty of great, traditional **bars** too, such as **Buttimers**, by Market Dock.

There's no shortage of **places to eat**, but if you're feeling wealthy you should definitely check out *Aherne's*, North Main Street (☎024/92424) one of the finest seafood restaurants in Ireland, serving a wide range of shellfish. Their lunchtime menu is reasonably priced.

WEST CORK

West Cork is a place apart, its pace and character quite different to the rest of the county. The difference lies in both the land and its history, ensuring an undeniably separate identity. What it shares with the rest of Cork are the little fields that curl over and around gentle hills, and the all-permeating balmy atmosphere; but as you get sucked west, lulled by a hospitable familiarity, you gradually forget what you have left behind, happily succumbing to change. West Cork has none of the broad river valleys that serve the rest of the county, watering its pastures and nurturing towns at their crossing points. Nor does it have such fine harbours as Youghal, Cobh or Cork itself, whose flourishing overseas trade so enriched the main body of the county. Its allure is one of atmosphere, not history.

Blessed by the continual influence of the Gulf Stream, from spring onwards it's warm and appealing, with a colourful clothing of vegetation to distract from the underlying poverty of the soil. Of course it rains, but in late summer hedges are stuffed with bright crimsom fuchsia, and golden gorse thrives in otherwise barren places. Heading west the land becomes rockier, the life more difficult. Warm currents may take away the raw sting of ice, but winters here are hard, lashed by storms, and the landscape offers little comfort. Here poor land and the lack of safe anchorage have contributed to an historic poverty: conditions at Skibbereen during the famine years were among the most horrific recorded. Communities today are still small, and it's in this minor scale and remoteness that the charms of West Cork lie. What once meant poverty, disease and emigration now leaves an undeveloped rural backwater for anyone lucky enough to have the time and the resources to enjoy it. West Cork has retained a slow pace that, coupled with the warm appeal of the landscape and the gentleness of the people, seems far removed from the twentieth century.

Two styles of landscape are on offer: the **mountains** that share a border with Kerry in the North, wild, yet relatively accessible; and the heavily indented **coastline** riddled with hidden sandy bays and coves, empty of people. In the southwest the country breaks up into little islands and fragments of land seemingly spat out into the ocean. Immediately north of here, three ragged peninsulas finger their way out into the Atlantic: Mizen Head, Sheep's Head, and the Beara Peninsula.

Blow-ins and artists

The potential of this beautiful, unspoilt and remote countryside was first widely perceived over twenty years ago, when the area was subject to a significant social upheaval with the immigration of large numbers of Northern Europeans. "**Blow-ins**", as they're referred to, are people who have come to the area and have somehow managed to create for themselves an alternative lifestyle. Most of them are German, Belgian or Dutch and came here for a number of reasons: to escape political systems they abhorred at home; to distance themselves from nuclear issues; to escape pollution, overcrowding, stress; and to key into the perceived creative energies, and the romantic mysticism, generated by the West Coast.

This influx of outsiders began in the Sixties at a time when there was plenty of money to be earned in the major cities of Western Europe, and since then there has been a process of natural selection. Those who don't make a total commitment to the lifestyle no longer find it so easy to nip back to developed Europe, to earn swift cash with which to subsidise their romantic idyll. Consequently those who are still here are either survivors, or rich at home too. Missing the irony, many visitors consider them an intrusion, making the experience somehow less "Irish", less authentic. In fact the presence of "blow-ins" is positively beneficial to the budget traveller. While they may have originally settled with a vision of living off organic farming, craftwork and home-grown entertainment, the harsh realities of subsistence have borne a real resourcefulness, the most useful sign of which is the recent mushrooming of **independent hostels**. Many of these are tucked away in delightfully secret places the owner has discovered and now chooses to share with visitors, and they're often worth visiting purely for the setting or the very special personal atmosphere that's been created. Another spin-off from the "blow-in" phenomenon is the high incidence of **wholefood** shops in tiny towns; welcome indeed in an area where traditional grocery shops are poor at providing anything that doesn't come in a tin. Finally, West Cork has attracted a large number of people who have come here to be artists, some of whom have succeeded. A local **arts centre** may be nothing more than a shed, but it can hold surprises, so look out for them. Some of the work is folksy and boring, but you may also stumble across exciting stuff of refreshing originality. What adds to these centres' appeal is the deeper understanding of the land they can offer: the best work has been inspired by, and so reflects, the colours and textures of the landscape.

Travel in the west

The only way to get to know West Cork is slowly. It is possible to drive (or hitch) around the main N71 road quickly to see the beautiful views unfurl, to see one seascape replaced by another and then another by one of wild mountains, and for sheer scenery this *is* worth doing; but there is much more on offer if you have the time. Slow down, change gear, and follow whatever happens to come up. Whatever your planned route, if you relax into the place, you are bound to be sidetracked into going somewhere you've never heard of, and doing things you couldn't dream of. Time can lose all meaning, and you suddenly find your holiday expand beyond recognition.

The best way to do this is either by **bike**, which can take you off the main route to discover wonderful little sandy coves cupped around a view of mossy rock stumbling into the ocean, or by leisurely **hitching** – the kind where you don't decide too specifically where you intend to end up, and where you plan to enjoy walking much of the way. There is something about the meandering lanes, the occasional small communities and the coaxing, balmy atmosphere of the air that lures you away from any plans you might have thought you had, and it's very easy to see how so many "blow-ins" never quite got it together to return home.

Bus Éireann serves all areas of West Cork except the Beara Peninsula and the north side of Mizen Head; there's a service along Sheep's Head once a week. Major towns are connected daily; small towns and villages off the main roads are served less frequently, so if you are relying on public transport it's worth taking details of times and days of services you are likely to want while in a major bus station. Ask about return fares – often they are as cheap as single tickets if used on certain days. On certain routes private buses provide the only transport: see "Travel Details" at the end of this chapter for details.

If you have a tent, you can **camp** almost anywhere if you ask permission first, though the Beara Peninsula and the Caha Mountains are very rocky. The few official campsites are listed in the text. You'll find **hostels** at Kinsale, Timoleague, Dunmanway, Ballingeary, Clear Island, Sherkin Island, Bantry, Glengarriff, Adrigole, Castletownbere and Allihies.

The Inland option

Probably the most popular way to explore West Cork is to aim for the nearest bit of coast, usually Kinsale, and head west, enjoying the gradual change from pretty countryside to the barren island-spattered peninsulas as you go. But a more direct route inland does have its merits, and can also be used as a short-cut to the mountains of Kerry. Unless you yearn for the sea, it's just as beautiful. The secondary roads west of Cork city run up the Lee Valley, through beautiful countryside and a number of small villages. Chief of these is **MACROOM**, a focus for tourists and music enthusiasts heading for KILLARNEY. It's on a main road, and a relatively easy hitch through the mountains. The **Boggeragh Mountains** to the north of the Lee Valley appear as high, rolling moorland, unspectacular compared with other ranges in Cork and Kerry but particularly rich in archaeological remains: stone circles, standing stones, wedge tombs and ring forts. A leaflet, *Antiquities of the Boggeragh Mountains*, is available from the tourist office in Cork city – of great value in locating these sites. The Bantry road from Macroom is far quieter, leading into the mountains and the county's last remaining *Gaeltacht* region. There's a small, friendly **hostel** – *Tig Barra* – about a mile and a half west of the tiny village of BALLINGEARY (☎026/47016; open March 14–Oct 14; £4.50, camping £2.50); beyond here the road passes through the dramatic glacial valley of GOUGANE BARRA and down to Bantry Bay (see p.250).

Alternatively, taking the road south of Cork city to BANDON and then west to **DUNMANWAY**, brings you to very promising country of empty hills and lakes. Dunmanway is a plain country town, but *Shiplake House Mountain Hostel* here (☎023/45750; £4.50; double/family room £6 per person; camping £3; open March 15–Oct 31; at other times by arrangement for groups of four or more) is in a beautiful setting; to find it take the Castle road next to the *Market Diner* out of town, follow it for two and a half miles in the direction of Coolkelure (the road to Kealkill) and turn right at the hostel sign. It's a farmhouse hostel with bunks, a gypsy caravan for couples or families, laundry facilities, home-made bread and pizzas are available, as well as free **bikes** for exploring the surrounding hills and lakes. *Bus Éireann* run at least one bus from Cork to Dunmanway daily, and a bus from Dunmanway to Bantry and Glengarriff. A **private bus** runs a Dunmanway–Cork return trip at weekends; phone the hostel for details of times.

The coast: Kinsale

KINSALE has retained much of the flavour of its rich maritime history, and in many ways has more in common with the formerly affluent ports of Youghal, Cork and Cobh than with the impoverished and remote west, but it's an excellent place from which to begin your journey. The 18-mile road from Cork city travels through gentle rolling farmland and along the Bandon estuary. This easy, meandering coast is a favourite for fishing and bird watching; so alive with birdlife that it's rewarding even for the uninitiated. At Kinsale the harbour is broad, and cormorants and shags skim across its gentle waters. A tongue of land curls from the west into the centre of the harbour, protecting the town from harsh winds, and on this promontory are the ivy-clad ruins of Jamesfort, a ruddy castle built by the English James I.

Seeing the town: some history

Originally a fishing town and historically a sheltered harbour of strategic importance, Kinsale now does a healthy tourist trade. Its proximity to Cork and its picturesque and historic setting have enabled it to develop along tasteful, conservative
lines: there are plenty of valuable amenities, but tourism isn't allowed to run out of
control. Thanks to the visitors, local **history** is cherished and made accessible,
and maps of the "Kinsale Trail" are available free from the tourist office. The town
received its first royal charter from Edward III in 1333, but it was of little importance up until the **Battle of Kinsale** in 1601, a disastrous defeat for the Irish which
signalled the end of the Gaelic aristocracy as a power for the English to reckon
with. A Spanish fleet stood in the bay ready to support the Irish cause against
Elizabethan forces, but was unable to make useful contact with O'Neill and
O'Donnell attacking from the north. So the battle was lost, and although resistance
to English rule continued, six years later came "the flight of the Earls" – when the
Irish nobility fled to Europe, giving up the fight for their own lands.

It was also at Kinsale that, in 1689, James II landed with French support in an
attempt to regain his throne, and it was later the port of his final departure from
Ireland after the Battle of the Boyne. The town was an important naval base for the
English Crown in the seventeenth and eighteenth centuries, and the sixteenth-
century tower house in Cork Street – **Desmond Castle** – became known as *The
French Prison* when it was used to hold as many as 600 French prisoners during
the Napoleonic war. Nearby **St Multose Church** has traces of a medieval structure, and in the church porch are the town stocks from the eighteenth century.

This history is recorded in the **museum** (9am–5pm; 20p; ☎021/772044), bang
in the centre of town above the old market (1600) with its Dutch-style facade
(1704). More recent events are remembered even more closely: within the
museum is the musty old courthouse which had remained much the same from
the eighteenth century up until 1915, when the inquest into the sinking of the
Lusitania was held here and Kinsale suddenly became the focus for the world's
press. The *Lusitania* was a liner travelling from New York to Liverpool when it
was torpedoed by a German submarine off the Old Head of Kinsale, killing 1198
people. It remains a controversial incident: Germany claimed there was ammunition on board, the US said it contained only innocent civilians. Whatever the
truth, it has been seen as a catalyst for America's decision to enter World War I.
After the inquest it was decided that the courtroom should be left as a memorial.
The rest of the museum is a friendly and intriguing jumble of stuff: memorabilia
from the disaster; sixteenth-century royal charters and maps; local craftwork;
personal effects of the eighteenth-century giant of Kinsale; and a variety of
bizarre local inventions that never got any further than the local museum.

Beyond the town's centre, **James' Fort** (1601) is fun to clamber over, but if your
time is limited head instead for **Charles Fort** (1677), two miles out of town at
Summercove (mid-April to mid-June Tues–Sat 9am–5pm, Sun 2pm–5pm; mid-June
to mid-Sept daily 9am–6.30pm; £1, students 40p, heritage card; ☎021/772263). The
outer walls of this fort, barely touched by weather or gunfire, seem pretty innocuous, but they conceal a formidable war machine. Within is an awesome system of
barracks, ramparts and bastions, impressive testimony to the complexity and
precision of seventeenth-century military science. The barracks were occupied
until 1922, when the British left and handed the fort over to the Irish government.
Today they remain largely intact, with only the barracks' missing roofs to give the
place an eerily deserted feel. There are free guided tours every hour on the hour.

Practicalities

The **tourist office** (Mon–Sat 9am–7pm, Sun 9am–noon; ☎021/772234) is in the centre of town, next to the bus depot and cinema; when it's closed tourist information is readily available at *Barry's* shop (open until 8pm), opposite *The Spaniards* pub in Scilly, on the eastern coast road out of town. Kinsale **An Óige hostel** (☎021/772309, open all year, booking essential in July & Aug; Oct–May £3.80, June–Sept £5.50) is in a beautiful spot at SUMMERCOVE, two miles out of town beyond *Barry's*, and can be reached by following a pathway that follows the curve of the harbour. Alternatively *Dempsey's Hostel*, Eastern Road (☎021/772124; £4, private room £5; open all year)is a short walk from the town centre, just up the road to Cork. As always, the tourist office can help you out with **B&B** and hotel information, or try Mrs McCarthy's *Hilltop*, Sleaveen Heights (☎021/772612; £12), just off the Cork road, or Mr & Mrs R. Coppard at *Ashling*, Bandon Road (☎021/774127; £12.50). You can **camp** at Ballinspittle (below).

Kinsale is a well-known gourmet centre – it even has a **gourmet festival** the first week in October, crowded with the affluent well-fed – and has numerous expensive **restaurants**: one of the best is *The Blue Haven* in Pearse Street (☎021/772209), where there's a good value lunchtime menu. For more everyday food and drink, Kinsale is also famous for its quantity of **pubs**, many of which serve delicious seafood at the bar – oysters are the local speciality.

Ballinspittle

Seven miles southwest of Kinsale is the tiny village of **BALLINSPITTLE**, which has found fame in recent years for popular sightings of its miraculous moving statues. The peninsula to the south, the Old Head of Kinsale, guarantees superb cliff walks, and at the neck of this peninsula are the remains of a fifteenth-century De Courcy castle. The *Garrettstown House Holiday Park* **campsite** (☎021/778156, 775286; mid-May to early Sept; overnight hikers/cyclists £2; gas cylinders on sale and facilities for washing clothes) is clearly signposted from the centre of the village.

The Seven Heads Peninsula

The stretch of coast from Timoleague to Clonakilty is known as the **Seven Heads Peninsula**. It's a pretty, indented shoreline, good for walking and bird watching. The spruce village of **TIMOLEAGUE** sits inland on the muddy estuary of the Ardigeen River, dominated by the extensive remains of a **Fransciscan abbey** which was sacked in 1649. The much advertised **Castle Gardens** include a beautiful walled garden, but the ruins of Timoleague Castle itself are negligible, and not worth the entrance fee. Timoleague is only a small place, but it can boast *Pad Joes*, a good bar promising entertainment and **pub food**, and an excellent **independent hostel and restaurant**, *Lettercollum House* (daily; ☎023/46251; £5; private rooms £8; March 15–Nov 15). This is a friendly place, worth visiting for the food alone: seafood, lamb and vegetarian dishes, locally produced and lovingly prepared. Meals for hostellers start from £7.50; those not staying at the hostel are advised to phone and book for the restaurant in advance. You can **hire bikes** at the hostel, which makes it a perfect point from which to explore the Seven Heads Peninsula. There's also good **camping** at *Sexton's Camping* (☎023/46251), half a mile out of town.

At the broad mouth of the estuary, the village of **COURTMACSHERRY** is currently being developed as a safe, quiet family resort. It's certainly tranquil – when asked what happens here one local reckoned "the tide comes in and the tide goes out again". That's slightly exaggerated – if you're feeling rich you can go deep-sea angling or shark fishing (*Courtmacsherry Sea Angling Centre*; ☎023/46427), horse riding can be arranged through the *Courtmacsherry Hotel* (☎023/46198), and in the evenings you may find a singsong round the piano at the *Lifeboat Inn* or *Anchor Bar*. If you want to stay you can **camp** by the *Courtmacsherry Hotel* or at a site about two miles out of Timoleague on the Clonakilty road. Elsewhere around the Seven Heads Peninsula *Deasy's Bar* at RING, just east of Clonakilty, does **pub food**, while *Dunworley Cottage Restaurant* (☎023/40314), though pricey, is noted for its organic food.

Clonakilty

The busy little village of **CLONAKILTY**, birthplace of Michael Collins, has a growing reputation as a **traditional music** centre, thanks to the enthusiasm of local people; it's also home to the much respected, innovative **street theatre** group *Craic Na Coillte*, so any of the town's festivals are worth taking in. The **music/arts festival** provisionally scheduled for the last weekend in August should be just as popular as the busking festival it is going to replace, so expect accommodation to be tight. The traditional **Clonakilty Festival** (late June/early July) includes pub talent and debating contests.

The local **pub scene** is also exceptionally lively, attracting a lot of young people. There are plenty of excellent old bars: for music *De Barra's* on Pearse Street is probably the most popular place, with traditional or rock music more or less every night all year round. *Shanley's* in Connolly Street has MOR pop and Sixties sessions (7 nights a week in summer, 5 in winter); *Fiddler's Green*, Clarke Street, always popular with a younger crowd, has traditional, folk or Sixties pop bands on alternate Thursdays; and *O'Donovan's Hotel* (☎023/33250) has music nightly during July and August. *O'Donovan's* is also a good place to pick up what's-on information, and ask too if you can pop upstairs to have a look at their mini-museum of local history. **Pub food** is readily available – try *O'Donovans Hotel*, which serves till 10pm daily. *Fionnuala's*, 30 Ashe Street, is a cheap and cosy Italian restaurant, and there are a couple of more expensive places to eat that also do tourist menus: *The Sandlighter*, 4 Strand Road (☎023/33247), serves light meals from £5 and *An Súgán* (☎023/33719, 33498) offers a lunch menu at a similar price.

Pubs and festivals aside, Clonakilty makes a good base from which to explore the crazily indented coastline roundabout, especially enjoyable by bike. The best **beach** nearby is at INCHYDONEY, 4.5 kilometres to the south: formerly an island, it's now linked to the mainland by a causeway. Inland the recently excavated Lisnagun Early Christian **ring fort** can be found signposted off the road to Timoleague. Just over a mile north of town are the remains of the Templebryan **stone circle** – four of the original nine stones still stand, along with a central white quartzite pillar; to find it head out of town up MacCurtain Hill.

There's a **tourist office** in Rossa Street (☎023/33226; Mon–Sat July & Aug, closed between 1 & 2pm); **bike hire** from *Healy's Bikes*, Rossa Street (also repairs), *MTM Cycles*, Ashe Street (☎023/33584) or *Tom Sheehy*, Aston Square (☎023/33362); and plenty of **B&Bs**. Mrs Kathleen O'Sullivan's *Long House*, 15 Wolfe Tone Street (also known as Strand Road; ☎023/33011; £11), and Mrs

K.O'Neill's *Ashville*, Clarke Street (☎023/33125; £11), are both central, or you could try Mrs A. O'Driscoll's *Aisling*, Clogheen Road (☎023/33491; around £11). **Camping** is available at Dorothy Jennings' *Desert House* (head east out of the village and turn right at the *Jet* station; May–Sept; £3), near the shore and a mere 500 yards stagger from the pubs.

West to Skibbereen

You can pick almost any spot west of Clonakilty and be sure of satisfaction – it's a beautiful coastline with a frenzy of little bays and creeks, sandy coves and tidal loughs. There are tiny lagoons here and there, isolated along the shore from the main body of the sea, providing placid contrast to the furling white ocean spray. Each place has its own special charms – Rosscarbery, Glandore, Leap, Union Hall and Castletownshend – and at every turn there is some new delightful composition; a slither of trees, a bay, a tiny beach. If you take the main N71 you're never far from these places, with easy access by a couple of miles' walk or a short hitch.

Leap and Castletownshend

Of all these quiet little villages, **LEAP** holds the biggest surprise: *Connolly's* bar (☎028/33215), with arguably the best **live music** in West Cork and a great range of bands all year round: rock, traditional, bluegrass – just about anything that's on in the county will be on here. If you want to stay in the village there are a couple of **B&Bs**: Mrs Noreen Calnan, *Highfield* (☎028/33273; £11), and Mrs Eleanor Calnan, *Riverside* (☎028/33577; £10), or there's a **campsite** a couple of miles away at Glandore (☎028/33280; £3). There's a site too at Rosscarbery, just over five miles away, but an easier hitch along the main road: *O'Riordan's Caravan Park* (☎023/48216, 541825; £3–5 for two).

As you journey in this direction, there are scattered historic remains to punctuate your trip. The **Drombeg stone circle**, on the R597 minor road between Rosscarbery and Glandore, is one of the finest examples of a Recumbent Stone Circle in Ireland, its single recumbent stone marking the position of the midwinter sunset; it probably dates from the Early Bronze Age. Nearby is a **Fulacht Fiadh** of the same era: a stone trough used for cooking that would be filled with spring water and heated by throwing in hot stones from a fire. On a ridge overlooking Castletownshend is the **Knockdrum stone ring fort**, outside of which is a large rock with megalithic cup and ring marks. Pretty **CASTLETOWNSHEND** itself was the home of Edith Somerville of Somerville and Ross fame, authors of the "Irish RM" stories. The graves of the two are to be found in St Barrahane's churchyard.

Skibbereen

SKIBBEREEN, a cheerful place, smartly painted and set on the River Illen in a landscape of low wooded hills and pasture, is the main service and administrative centre for the south of West Cork. This traditional role is still remarkably alive: on Wednesday the cattle market still operates, drawing crowds from the surrounding country, and every Friday afternoon there's the regular country market. For travellers, it's a good place to stock up or to stop over – there are plenty of supermarkets and off-licences, a smattering of health food shops and delis, and of course plenty of pubs.

If you're after a **meal**, there's *Don Pasquale's* pizzeria, 31 Bridge Street (☎028/22429; open Mon–Thurs till 10pm, later at weekends; from £4.50); decent pub dinners are available at *MacCarthy's* at 68 Bridge Street, *Eldon's Hotel*, also on Bridge Street (☎028/21300), and *The Windmill Tavern* on North Street, which specialises in seafood. *The Kitchen Garden*, North Street, a wholefood and organic vegetable shop, has a cheap café attached, and *O'Donovan's* cafe, Bridge Street, serves particularly good homemade soups. The *West Cork Hotel* is more expensive (around £13 a meal), but eating here can be an engaging experience.

Though not particularly renowned for its **pub** scene, Skibbereen has plenty of intriguing old bars. In Bridge Street *McCarthy's* is a popular tourist spot that boasts weekend music sessions, and *Baby Hannah's* is a lively young place where you might stumble across a session if you are lucky. There's also a good traditional music shop – Jane and Kevin O'Farrell's *Jigs and Reels* on North Street (☎028/22420), where you can buy tapes, CDs, sheet music and instruments, and get the lowdown on any traditional music in the area.

The **West Cork Arts Centre** on North Street (☎028/22090; winter Mon–Sat 12.30–5pm, summer Mon–Sat 11am–6pm) is also worth checking out. It hosts monthly exhibitions which can be first-rate, stages occasional music and dance performances, and has a reference and slide library through which you can locate local artists. The **tourist office** (mid-June to mid-Sept Mon–Sat 9am–7pm, Oct–May Mon–Fri 9.15am–1pm & 2.15–5.30pm; ☎028/21766), is also along North Street and will put you on to **B&Bs**: a couple to try are *Illenside*, 18 Bridge Street (☎028/21605; £11.50), and Mrs McDonald's *Glen Ilen*, Mill Road (☎028/21269; around £10). You can get **Bus Éireann information** from *O'Cahalales* in Bridge Street, and hire **bikes** from *N.W. Roycroft and Son* in Ilen Street (☎028/21235; £7.50 per day, £30 per week).

Heading out of Skibbereen, Roaring Water Bay, Baltimore and Clear Island are all easily accessible to the southwest. A slight detour will take you by way of **Lough Hyne** (pronounced "ine"), a land-locked salt lake directly south of Skibbereen, linked to the ocean only by a very slender channel down which the receding tide returns to the sea. The lough, surrounded by hillsides dripping with lush, moist greenery, is a unique phenomenon, of great interest to marine biologists. From the head of the lake steep slopes, easily climbed, rise to panoramic views: eastwards along the coast to Kinsale; west across the length of the Mizen peninsula; and out across Roaring Water Bay.

Roaring Water Bay

The approach to Baltimore takes you through a landscape that is disarmingly low-key. Instead of some dramatic climax at this, the most southerly point of all Ireland, the land seems simply to be fading away: rocky terrain and scrawny vegetation accompany the windy, listless estuary, untidy with lumps of land that seem to have been tossed at random towards the sea. The whole ragged effect is as if the country is running out of substance; the landmass, already moth-bitten, is now fraying too. But as Roaring Water Bay – named after the roar from the waterfalls at Ballydehob – and Carbery's "Hundred Islands" come into full view this tailing off is put into spectacular context: the whole weight of Ireland is behind you, while ahead are dots, wracks and scraps of islands, petering out across the great open expanse of water to Sherkin and Cape Clear.

ISLAND FERRIES

Baltimore–Sherkin Island (£3 return) June–Sept depart Baltimore 9am, 10.30am, noon, 2pm, 4pm, 5.30pm, 7pm & 8.30pm; returning from Sherkin roughly quarter of an hour after these times. Winter 1–3 a day: ask at *Bushe's* bar or telephone ☎028/20125, eves 30566.

Baltimore–Clear Island (£7 return). July & Aug depart Baltimore 10.30am, 2.15pm & 7pm; returning at 9am, noon & 6pm: June & Sept depart Baltimore 2.15pm & 7pm; returning 9am & 6pm:

Oct–May depart Baltimore 10.30am & 5.30pm, returning 9am & 4pm. Times may change on Sun. If you stay at the youth hostel on the island, you get a £1 refund on your ferry ticket, so ask the warden to stamp it.

Clear Island–Schull (£6 return, £3 single) June and first week Sept depart Schull daily 2.30pm, return from Cape Clear 5.30pm; July & Aug depart Schull 10am, 2.30pm & 4.30pm; return from Cape Clear 11am, 3.30pm & 5.30pm (☎028/28138).

BALTIMORE, a delightful harbour village overlooked by a sixteenth-century O'Driscoll stronghold, is the last significant mainland settlement. Combining traditional fishing activities with tourism, it's also the departure point for ferries to Sherkin and Clear islands (see box): for most people this is the chief reason to come. During the last two weeks of July and the first weekend in August the yachting crowd descend en masse for the **regatta**: there are a few pricey restaurants to cater for them. At any time of year, though, you can get great seafood and steaks all day at *Casey's Cabin* (music on Sunday nights), about a mile towards Skibbereen. *Declan McCarthy's* bar by the harbour also serves seafood and has traditional, folk, ballads and jazz sessions (seven nights a week in summer, at least three during the winter), as well as cashing cheques and **changing money**. If you're staying, *Rolf's* **independent hostel** is cheerful and friendly (☎028/20289; £5; open all year but book ahead in July & Aug; organic produce on sale, light meals available; **bike hire** £6) or there is **bed and breakfast** accommodation at Ann Nolan's *Fastnet House* (£11) and at *Bushe's* bar, down by the quays (☎028/20119), where they also have **showers** for people camping or sailing. As well as the scheduled *Bus Éireann*, there is a private service that operates from the harbour to Skibbereen around 10–10.30am – check the exact schedule locally.

Sherkin Island

Tiny **SHERKIN ISLAND** is a delightfully pretty place: the considerable remains of a fifteenth-century Franciscan friary nestle down by the quayside, and little fuchsia-spattered lanes lead across the island to fine sandy beaches in the west. There are the remains of an O'Driscoll stronghold too, and the annual O'Driscoll clan gathering in June is a hectic five day event spread between Sherkin, Clear Island and Baltimore. For a community of only some ninety people, the island has an astounding **pub scene**, with sessions at *The Jolly Roger* attracting crowds from the mainland: if there's a band booked and you are staying in Baltimore, there's usually a late-night ferry laid on to take everybody home.

The place can get busy with daytrippers at bank holidays and in July and August; if you want to stay there are a few places that do **B&B** – Maureen O'Neill, the Post Office (☎028/20181; £10), *Cuina* (☎028/20384; £12) and *Island House* (☎028/20314). *Sherkin Island Hostel* is also open during the summer (☎028/20302) and if you want to **camp**, ask locally. If these are all full, it's worth asking at the pub for alternatives – a very helpful source of local information. Both *Garrison House* and *The Jolly Roger* do **bar food** during the summer: at other times you can buy supplies at the post office.

Clear Island

CLEAR ISLAND (*Oileán Chléire*) offers rather more to do, but it would be worth visiting for the ferry trip alone. There's an important ornithology station here, and on the 45-minute ride across Roaring Water Bay it's obvious that the place is paradise for wildlife enthusiasts. The bay is alive with seabirds – guillemots, cormorants, auks and storm petrels – and with luck you may see seals and, in warm weather, basking sharks. With even more luck you might find your boat raced by a playful dolphin or two, dodging around the bows and leaping out of the ocean to crash back down right alongside the ferry.

The hilly, rocky island seems to have been pinched in the middle where two inlets, North Harbour and South Harbour, almost meet. In the south, steep and inaccessible cliffs rise from the water; the North Harbour is perfectly sheltered. Roads climb up from here through hills covered in the coarse grass that seems to spread over everything; old walls, and houses long derelict. Sea pinks cling to rocky outcrops and honeysuckle clambers wherever it can. The island's high points give spectacular views back across the archipelago of Roaring Water Bay to the mainland.

The **bird observatory** at North Harbour has been here since 1959 and has complete records going back to that time. When it was set up, by an amateur group, this station was a pioneer of the constant observation of seabirds, and its work has done much for the knowledge of migratory patterns. Clear Island is one of the most important places for seabirds in Ireland, including some genuine rarities – especially plentiful are storm petrels, shearwaters, black guillemots and choughs. There is **hostel**-style accommodation available for ornithologists too, likely to be full in late spring and in September and October. If you are new to bird-watching, but fancy learning more, call in and see what's happening, though be warned that midsummer is not the best season.

Clear Island is also an isolated remnant of the *Gaeltacht*, where Gaelic is still spoken by about 160 islanders. During the summer Irish youth are sent here to practice the language. The island has a **festival** of drama, music, art and dance, *Féile Shamhna Chléire*, usually the bank holiday weekend of the last Monday in October. The **Heritage Centre** (June–Aug 3.30–5.30pm, and by arrangement – call at the house opposite; £1, students 50p), a steep, well-signposted walk from North Harbour, is a tiny museum of the domestic, fishing and seafaring history of the island. The island prides itself on being the birthplace of Saint Kieran, who supposedly preceded Saint Patrick by thirty years, but the holy well and stone that are attributed to him stand in a sadly unromantic spot by the road at North Harbour. The best of Clear Island's historic ruins is **Dún an Óir** ("Fort of Gold"), an O'Driscoll fort, impressive on a high, narrow splinter of rock which is now an island at high tide – a short walk west around the coast from the bird observatory. If you want to clamber over it, ask locally about the tides and the weather. Alternatively, great views of the castle can be had from the 200-foot cliffs to the south.

The **An Óige hostel** is at South Harbour (☎028/39144, open all year, very busy Sept & Oct; Oct–May £3.80, June–Sept £5.50); you can hire rowing boats from the warden. **Camping** is available on the way to Lough Errul to the west

(£2.50), and there are a number of **B&Bs**: try Mary Uí Drisceóil, *Cluain Mara*, North Harbour (☎028/39153) or Eleanor Uí Drisceóil, *Fáilte*, Glen East, up by the lighthouse (☎028/39135). Decent **pub meals** are available during the summer at *Cotters Bar*, North Harbour. You can often find fresh local bread, milk, eggs and goats' cheese on the island, and there's a good shop down by the harbour.

Mizen Head

The Mizen Head peninsula is a beautiful, remote finger of land poking its way west, to the north of the islands. It offers great sandy beaches and superb cliff scenery, getting wilder the further west you go. It's also an area rich in **archaeological sites**, from Bronze Age wedge graves contemporary with the first copper mining of Mount Gabriel, through Iron Age and early Christian ring forts, down to medieval castles. A leaflet, *Antiquities of the Mizen Peninsula*, available from the tourist office in Cork city, is worth getting if you want to locate these sites. Great care should be taken at the Mizen cliffs, as the land ends abruptly and without warning.

The most spectacular of the coastal scenery is at **Mizen Head** itself – sheer, vertiginous cliffs, with an offshore lighthouse linked by a little suspension bridge. Standing at this exhilarating spot it takes little effort to imagine the great number of ships that have been wrecked in Dunlough Bay to the north. A walk round to **Three Castles Head** brings in sight the curtain wall and two turrets of an O'Mahoney stronghold, one of twelve that were built along this peninsula in the fifteenth century. The setting makes this one truly spectacular. The whole of the peninsula's wild and empty northern coast, in fact, is one of sheer cliffs and stupendous views – an impossible route for hitching, but great for those with transport.

The south coast of the peninsula is more travelled, with small towns at Ballydehob, Schull and Crookhaven, and lovely sandy **beaches**. The best of these is the long and sandy strand at BARLEYCOVE, whose rolling breakers make it a favourite with windsurfers. Nearby is the busy little holiday resort of CROOKHAVEN, with a large **caravan and camping park** on the Goleen–Crookhaven road (May 14–Sept 10, £2.50); unless you want the facilities, though, there is no real need to use this – there are plenty of remote spots where you can pitch a tent for free. The only public transport along the peninsula is run by *Bus Éireann* as far as Crookhaven.

Schull

SCHULL, as well as being the place to catch the **ferry** for Clear Island (see box), is perhaps the most obvious place to stay on the peninsula: there's a **watersports centre** that requires neither advanced booking nor a massive bank balance, and plenty of cheery amenities aimed at holidaying families and an unpretentious yachting fraternity. An attractive, seaside market town, its sheltered, bulb-shaped harbour looks out over Carbery's Hundred Islands, while to the north Mount Gabriel rises to 1339 feet, offering wonderful views. To make this walk from Schull (nine miles there and back) head up Gap Road past the convent and you'll find a clear track all the way. From the top you can continue around the north side of the mountain, to return through Rathcool and Glaun. The domes at the summit of Mount Gabriel are aircraft tracking stations. As you walk, beware of unguarded mine shafts: this rough and rocky land was heavily mined for copper in the nineteenth century, and is still dotted with Cornish-style mining chimneys.

Schull is at its liveliest during its **festival and sailing events**. The local festival is usually held the first two weeks in July, very much geared for families with all sorts of sports activities, including terrier racing in the streets. Schull's international sailing festival for children is usually held the second week in July, when the town is awash with nautical teenagers; the yachting set proper swamp the town for the regatta held in Calves week (first week in August). As everywhere, festival time means **accommodation** can be difficult, and phoning ahead is advisable. If you want B&B try Louis O'Regan's *The Variety*, Main Street (☎028/28334; £11). If you fancy a spot of sailing yourself *Schull Watersports Centre*, The Pier (☎028/28554, 28351), organises sea-angling trips, dinghy hire (£20 a half-day), windsurfing (£6 per hour, £10 per half day) and diving, the last for the experienced only. If you want to go **horse riding**, try the *Schull Riding Centre* (☎028/28185), on Colla Road one mile southwest of Schull. **Bike hire** is available from Alan Murphy at *The Black Sheep* (☎028/28203).

As for **eating**, *Adele's Coffee Shop* in Main Street does excellent home-made cakes, soups, salads and fresh pasta; the delicatessen in the centre of town sells bread fresh from its brick-built steam oven, and there's plenty of good **bar food**: try *The Old Courtyard* or the *Bunratty Inn*. Schull is not a great place for music – most of what you'll find is pretty middle of the road – but if you want to track it down *An Tigin*, *The Old Courtyard* and *The Black Sheep* are the places to look. There's a bank and post office in town, and a very good **bookshop**, *Mizen Books*, in Main Street (☎028/28414), handy for rainy afternoons.

Ballydehob

BALLYDEHOB, a town of gaily coloured streets at the neck of the peninsula, was once known as the hippy capital of the West because it was said to have more "blow-ins" than locals. Heavily colonised in the Sixties, it still has traces of their influence – healthfood and artists for instance – and remains a liberal place compared to others of its size. For all this it's a sleepy town. Probably the liveliest place these days is *Coughlan's* on the Schull road, which serves up country and ballad sessions (Wed & Fri), local pop bands (Sat) and country music and dancing (Sun) to a fairly middle–aged crowd. There are a handful of places to **eat**: *Annie's Restaurant* (☎028/37292) serves home-made lunches (Tues–Sat noon–2.30pm) and good seafood from around £4.25 and evening meals, for which you should book in advance, from around £18. *The Forge Restaurant* (☎028/37312) serves midday meals, including decent vegetarian food, from around £4, evening meals from £14. *Duggans* restaurant on Main Street (June–Sept 9am–10pm, takeaway open until 12.30am; ☎028/37149) serves traditional meals at £3–8. There's a wholefood shop in Main Street, above which you'll find Kitty Kingston's **B&B**; the *Ballydehob Inn* (☎028/37139; £10) is similarly friendly. There's a **campsite** just a couple of hundred yards down the Durrus road (£2–2.50, including hot water and showers).

Ballydehob's nearest **beach** is three miles away at Audley Cove – a pebbly cove, secluded and personal, with lovely views of the islands. Two and a half miles out of Ballydehob towards Schull is the **Bookshop in the Bog** at Derryconnell (☎028/37317), full of antiquarian and military tomes, extremely difficult to find.

Sheep's Head

The peninsula north of Mizen, **Sheep's Head**, has a very ancient feel to it; barren land almost entirely devoid of people. There are only a couple of tiny villages here, and traffic is sparse – the sole weekly bus runs on Saturday – so don't try to hitch if you're going to need to return in a hurry. Nevertheless, if you have the time and the means, a tour down this sliver of old Ireland affords fabulous panoramic views over County Cork, the Beara Peninsula, and County Kerry from the top of Seefin, Sheep's Head's highest hill (1136 feet). The north coast looks down on the magnificent Bantry Bay, backed by the wild Caha Mountains.

Bantry

The beauty of **BANTRY** is its setting at the head of ever-turbulent Bantry Bay, which stretches thirty miles from the town to the ocean. The deep, churning blue waters of the bay, backed by the dramatic heights of the Beara's Caha Mountains and cowering, usually, under a notoriously changeable sky, form as dramatic a backdrop as any in Ireland. The town itself sits around a long square focussed at the head of the bay, with a slaty Regency Gothic church and a statue of Saint Brendan staring out to sea. In the immediate surrounds are lush wooded slopes with delightful walks and waterfalls; a safe haven, indulged between the ravages of the sea and the wilds of the rocky mountains. It's also a place of history and character – a commercial harbour, fishing port and market town, where the traditional market is still held on the first Friday of every month.

For centuries **Bantry Bay** attracted attempts from abroad to overthrow English rule. Once inside its shelter ships were protected from attack by the rugged mountains of the peninsulas on either side. In 1689 a French fleet sailed up the bay to assist James II, but was forced to return after an indecisive battle with Williamite forces. A century later, in 1796, Wolfe Tone arrived with another French fleet, and this time with revolutionary ideals, to try and overthrow the Protestant Anglo-Irish. Channel storms, however, had already reduced the fleet from 43 ships to 16 by the time it arrived, and the remaining vessels spent six days in the bay unable to land, even though, as Tone said, "we were close enough to toss a biscuit on shore". After this failure they were forced to turn back. Richard White, a local landowner, was rewarded for his loyalty to the English Crown at the time of the invasion by being made Baron Bantry.

Bantry House, Bantry Museum and other local sights

The Baron's home, **Bantry House** (daily 9am–6pm, till 8pm most summer evenings; ☎027/50047), nowadays provides an elegant vision of the rarefied life led by the Anglo-Irish aristocracy. Sumptuously decorated and packed with art treasures, it is well worth taking some time over. Much of the furniture is French Napoleonic, and there are Gobelin tapestries and Aubusson carpets, but what makes this house such a gem is the sheer variety of stuff that has been collected – much of it during the second earl's European wanderings in the nineteenth century. The setting is superb: ordered landscaped gardens look down over the bay, calmly asserting the harmony of the aristocratic order, unruffled by the ruggedness of the surroundings. **The Bantry 1796 French Armada Exhibition Centre** (daily 10am–6pm; £2.50, students £1.50; ☎027/51309) housed in one of the courtyards of the great house should open during 1992. It tells the story of Wolfe Tone's failed mission, and displays artefacts recovered from the wreck of the frigate *La Surveillante,* scuttled on Whiddy Island in 1797 and excavated in 1982.

Another side of the past is remembered with relish by the ladies who run the **Bantry Museum**, situated behind the fire station on Wolfe Tone Square (Tues and Thurs 10.30am–1pm, Wed and Fri 3–5.30pm; ☎027/50087, 50475). The museum is the collection of the local history society – domestic paraphernalia, old newspapers and everyday trivia of every sort – which the curators willingly demonstrate with an entertaining blend of history and gossip. The modern **library**, at the top of Bridge Street, is also worth a look. Built in 1974, it looks at first glance like some sort of spaceship, though the design was in fact inspired by a prehistoric dolmen: as adventurous a piece of modern architecture as you'll find in the west of Ireland, it's let down by a white facade that already seems thoroughly tacky.

One final thing worth going out of your way to see, just out of town, is the fine, early-Christian **Kilnaruane Pillar Stone**. Its worn carvings depict four men rowing, an apostle and the cross. To find it follow the main road south out of town and take the first turning on the left past the *Westlodge Hotel*: the stone is in a field 500 yards further on the right.

Practicalities

Finding **somewhere to stay** in Bantry should present few problems. **B&Bs** can be found on the square and along the Glengarriff Road. Ones to try include Mrs Evans, *Bay View House* (The Square; ☎027/50403; £10), Mrs O'Regan, *Sunville* (☎027/50175; £10.50), and Mrs Kramer, *The Mill* (Newtown; ☎027/50278; £11). If you feel like splashing out on a night or two of real luxury you can also enjoy bed and breakfast at **Bantry House** (☎027/50047), where for £45 you can sleep like an earl. The new *Bantry Hostel*, Bishop Lucey Place (☎027/51050; mid-March to Oct; £5, private room £6) is in a handy central location. The nearest official **camping** is four miles from Bantry at BALLYLICKEY along the Glengarriff road at *Eagle Point Caravan and Camping Park* (☎027/50630; May–Sept; £2.50), but there are plenty of farms nearer town where you can ask to pitch your tent in a field.

There are a handful of places to **eat**: the best of them has to be *O'Connor's* famous seafood restaurant, which for many people is a reason in itself to visit Bantry (☎027/50221) – they serve lunches from around £3.50, as well as dearer evening meals. *Ó Síocháin*, in Bridge Street, is a cheery café serving hearty lunches and seafood platters during the summer months (9am–6pm, till 10pm during summer); *The 5A* in Barrack Street is more of a hippy hang-out and similarly popular, the original vegetarian greasy spoon, serving soups, vege-burgers and delicious homemade cakes (Mon–Sat till 5pm or 6pm). *Peter's Grill* offers fried fish, steaks and grills (£3.50–£9), open throughout the day till late in the evening, and *Vickery's Inn Hotel Bar* in New Street does standard pub meals (10am–10pm).

Regular **pubs** are plentiful as ever: the *Anchor Bar* is a convivial place to start, with a good, friendly mix of locals and visitors. For traditional **entertainment** try *JJ Crowley's* for a mix of *ceilidhs*, ballads and country and western, or at weekends *The Bantry Bay* for local MOR pop and country rock bands and discos. *The Westlodge Hotel*, a couple of miles south along the main road, hosts the local Sunday night disco; the hotel also has a **swimming pool** open to non-residents.

Bus Éireann **buses**, connecting with Cork, Skibbereen, Glengarriff, Killarney and the Mizen peninsula, leave from outside *Crowley's Bar* (information inside), towards the harbour from the tourist office. For details of private bus services see the "Travel Details". **Bike hire** is available along the Glengarriff road, to the right just before the turning for the industrial estate (☎027/50278; £5 per day). The **tourist office** (☎027/50229; June –Sept) is on Wolfe Tone Square.

Local sporting opportunities include **sea angling**, **sailing** and **windsurfing** (for all of which contact John Crowley, ☎027/50030); **horse riding** at *O'Donoghue's Riding Stables*, Ardnatrush (☎027/63069); and **swimming**, **squash** and **pitch and putt** at the *Westlodge Hotel* (☎027/50360, 50557). There's also a **regatta** in August, and a **mussel festival** over the second weekend in May promising music, late bars and plenty of seafood. One local sport worth looking out for is **bowling**, a West Cork game played around Bantry on Sundays. A 28lb iron ball is thrown along country roads, and the winner of the game is the man (it's generally only men who play) who moves the ball over a prescribed distance with the fewest throws. If you come across handfuls of grass that have been dropped along a lane at intervals, it generally means a game has been or is being played along that route – clumps of grass are used as markers.

Glengarriff and the Mountains

Heading on from Bantry you're spoilt for choice: whichever way you travel, the scenery is magnificent. Heading **east** the road to Dunmanway and its fine independent hostel takes you through fabulous empty mountains, while the Pass of Keimaneigh further north leads through a steep, rocky ravine up to the Ballingeary hostel (see p.240), **Gougane Barra** and a corrie lake, the source of the River Lee. An island on this lake was the site of Saint Finbarr's hermitage before he founded his monastery at Cork city downstream. The remains on the island are, however, eighteenth-century. It's an area famous for its beauty, popular for daytrips, and there's a bar that does teas and sandwiches besides the lake. Gougane Barra has a forest park with nature trails, but up here you can walk wherever you please.

Glengarriff

Cradled between the Caha Mountains and Bantry Bay, **GLENGARRIFF** is an oasis of greenery. South-facing and sheltered by rugged mountains, it has a peculiarly gentle climate; oak and holly woodlands hug the shoreline while occasional palms flourish in hotel gardens. This picturesque juxtaposition has been exploited since the nineteenth century, when sensitive Victorians became alerted to the beneficial effects of the uniquely mild atmosphere in this pocket of lushness. Unfortunately, recent exploitation has resulted in a barrage of billboarding; ads for gift shops and boat trips have destroyed virtually all of the village's former character. When a coach tour meets Glengarriff nowadays, it's difficult to say which is the victim.

Despite the commercialism, Glengarriff is a great place to stay if you want to explore some of Cork and Kerry's most wildly beautiful countryside. There's an independent **hostel**, *O'Mahoney's*, three minutes walk from the centre of the village on the Bantry road (☎027/63097; £5, £4 camping), or you can get informa tion on local **B&B** accommodation from the **tourist office** in the main street (July and August; ☎027/63084). Better still you can stay outside town (and away from its excesses) at *Tooreen House* **independent hostel** (☎027/63075; March–Oct; £5, private rooms £6, camping £3; mountain bike hire £5 a day), a two-mile walk or easy hitch up the main Kenmare road. It lies on the right-hand side of the road and you should make sure that you're at the right place (look for the *Independent Hostel Association* logo, a bird flying across countryside, at the entrance) as there is another hostel on the opposite side of the road, a good mile before *Tooreen House*. At the real *Tooreen House* you'll be able to hear a gushing mountain river plunging over rocks. Superb for walkers with maps and compasses, it's a wonderful, wild place; huge areas of barren rock show odd patches of scrawny, rough vegetation, and then the occasional seam of brilliant deciduous woods. There is a real exhilaration up here as you watch the constantly changing patterns of weather over the mountains and the bay, with squalls of rain and pools of sunlight playing games of tag across the landscape.

Garinish Island

Walking down the street in Glengarriff you'll inevitably be hassled sooner or later by a stage-Irish boatman trying to sell you a ticket for **Garinish Island**. Sooner or later, you might as well give in; expensive as it is, the island trip is quite something. In 1910 the owner of Garinish conceived a plan to turn his island – then bare rock – into a floating oasis of exotic plantlife. All the topsoil had to be imported, and the resultant growth delicately nurtured for years. The end product is undeniably impressive: flowers and shrubs from all over the world flourish here, and through much of the year the place is ablaze with colour, in stark contrast to the desolate mountains of the Beara a stone's throw across the water. If you decide to visit the island you can cut the cost somewhat by getting a group together to share a boat; if you're staying at the independent hostel, ask there as they sometimes have trips arranged. Be warned, however, that whatever price you fix with the boatmen for the ten-minute trip out there past basking seals, you will be charged again the minute you step onto the jetty for the privilege of actually seeing the island (March & Oct Mon–Sat 10am–4pm (last landing), Sun 1–4.30pm; April–June & Sept Mon–Sat 10am–5.30pm, Sun 1pm–6pm; July & Aug Mon–Sat 9.30am–5.30pm, Sun 11am–6pm; £1.50, students 60p, heritage card; ☎027/63040).

The Beara Peninsula

The **Beara Peninsula**, barren and remote, seems to have an energy all of its own, bounding in great ribs of rock thirty miles out into the ocean. It is a fine place for tough cycling and energetic hiking, though you need to be prepared: the weather is notoriously changeable, and careful planning of routes, particularly the descent, is vital. Everywhere along the peninsula you are accompanied by fine views of the mountains and the sea, and there are occasional sandy beaches on either side. Take local advice before swimming, however, as currents can be treacherous.

In practical terms, there are enough good **hostels** to make lengthy exploration a viable proposition, but it's worth bearing in mind that a sparse population means there's little traffic of any sort – don't rely on being able to hitch back if you're in a hurry. If you're planning to **camp**, be aware that though there is no shortage of open land, a lot of it is very rocky. **Private buses** – the only public transport – connect the Beara communities with Glengarriff and Bantry four days a week, and there's also a service linking Castletownbere directly with Cork five days a week. Information on the former is available in Castletownbere at *O'Donohue's Corner House* (☎027/70007), for the Cork service contact *Super-van* (☎027/74003).

Adrigole

The first settlement along the coast, about fifteen miles west of Glengarriff, is **ADRIGOLE**, a string of houses stretching over a couple of miles with no real centre. *Adrigole Hostel* (☎027/60132; £5, camping £2.50; washing and drying facilities), a small wooden chalet with rocky mountains to the rear and Bantry Bay below, enjoys a wonderful setting on the R572 about 150 yards west past the junction for the Healy Pass. A shop and pub are nearby, and it's a perfect spot from which to do some walking. **Hungry Hill** rises to 2251 feet, a good climb rewarded by fabulous views, hidden lakes and waterfalls, while the steep road through the **Healy Pass** leads north to LAURAGH, County Kerry, where there is an *An Óige* hostel at Glanmore Lake (☎064/83181; April & May £3.50; June–Sept £4.50; closed winter).

Castletownbere

Beara communities have always relied heavily on fishing, and **CASTLETOWNBERE**, the peninsula's main town, is no exception. Set on Ireland's second largest natural harbour, it's periodically awash with French or Portuguese sailors. To serve them there's a handful of cafés, well-stocked shops, a chip shop and some pleasant pubs: *MacCarthy's* grocery shop is a bar as well, so provisions are available all hours; *Lynch's* bar has music at weekends, and Jackie Lynch also makes sensational seafood sandwiches. Should you feel the need, there is an occasional disco at *The Wheel Inn*, one mile out of town towards Adrigole; locals will tell you if there's anything on.

The town serves as a useful base from which to walk or cycle, or to catch a ferry for **Bere Island** which shelters the harbour; three ferries a day during July and August (and by arrangement at other times; ☎027/75009). Nearby coastal walks take you to the ruins of **Dunboy Castle** and **Puxley's Castle**. The former was where an Irish and Spanish force was besieged and overcome by the English in 1602, the latter the eerie, dilapidated shell of a Victorian Gothic mansion. This was the home of the Puxley family who made their money out of copper-mining; their story, and that of the mines, was used by Daphne du Maurier in her novel *Hungry Hill*. The castle itself was burnt down by the IRA in the 1920s, but its setting is idyllic: a placid inlet behind Castletownbere harbour fringed by rich woodlands, with stunning views of the wild mountains.

You can **camp** in the grounds of Puxley Castle for around £2–3. The *Beara Hostel* (☎027/70184), about two miles west of town on the road towards Allihies, should reopen in 1992 after improvements, though it's still likely to be pretty basic. The hostel is on an organic farm, and there is always produce available, as well as space to camp. **Bike hire** is available from D. Murphy (Bridge House; ☎027/70020) or at the *Super Valu* supermarket (£7 plus £10 deposit). There is a **launderette** at West End, Castletownbere.

On to Dursey Island

Moving on from Castletownbere you can head down to the remote, tiny villages at the end of the peninsula; a few houses, a shop and a pub being the typical set-up. This extreme of the peninsula saw some development in the nineteenth century when copper was mined, but little remains beyond the unguarded shafts; beware of these if you're walking. Six miles south of Castletownbere, off the road to the left, is the remote *Garranes Farmhouse Hostel* (☎027/73147, 73032; £5, private room £8; all year), clinging to a beautiful, ravaged coastline. The **hostel** is attached to the Buddhist *Dzogchen Beara Retreat Centre* and particularly welcomes people interested in joining their meditation classes; phoning ahead is strongly advised, however, as the hostel can be full of people on retreat at any time of the year. Note, also, that the nearest pubs and shops are six miles away. Tiny ALLIHIES, formerly a major mining centre, nowadays has simply a couple of pubs, a shop, a sandy beach, a new **independent hostel** right in the centre (*Bonnie Braes*; £4.50–£5; very small, and may be full in summer) and an **An Óige hostel** (☎027/73014; April & May £3.50, June–Sept £4.50) about a mile from the village. There is also a **campsite** down by the beach, and Veronica O'Callaghan's *Atlantic Seafood Restaurant*, which serves delicious food, is great value, and will make you feel you're being well looked after.

Perhaps the quietest of the islands to be visited off West Cork is **Dursey Island**, situated at the very tip of the peninsula, and fringed by high cliffs. Dursey's attractions include fabulous views, solitude, and the thrill of taking a very dodgy-looking cable car across the narrow and treacherous sound. You can walk up its hills for endless views westward over the ocean, with three great lumps of rock in the foreground: the Cow, the Calf and the Bull. For a day trip you need to get to the very end of the R572 in the morning. The cable car has no regular schedule, but generally it's difficult getting to the island between 11am and 4pm. If you want to stop over you'll need to pitch a tent, as the island has just a few houses – which claim to be the most westerly habitation in Europe.

travel details

Trains

From Cork: to Limerick Junction (8 daily; 1hr 10min); Dublin (7 daily; 2hr 30min–3hr); Killarney & Tralee (2–4 daily; 1hr 30min/2hr 15min).

Bus Éireann

From Cork: to Cork Airport April–Sept from 6.35am hourly, after 8.25am every 45min till 10.40pm; winter from 7.40am every 45min till 6.10pm; Dublin (3–4 daily; 4hr 45min); Limerick (5 daily; 2hr).

Private buses

Bantry–Dublin *Pierce Kavanagh Coaches* (☎01/734344, ☎056/31213). Departs Bantry (Courthouse) 3.30pm Sun, calling at Dunmanway, Cork (*Chateau Bar*, Patrick Street) 5.15pm, Cahir, Cashel, Dublin (Eden Quay) 9.30pm. Departs Dublin (Liberty Hall) 5.30pm Fri, calling at Cashel, Cahir, Cork (*Roches Stores*, Patrick Street) 10pm, Dunmanway, Bantry 11.30pm.

Bantry–Glengarriff–Castletownbere
O'Donohue's (☎027/70007). Mon: Castletownbere 7am & 4.30pm, calling at Glengarriff 7.45am and 5.20pm, arrives Bantry 8.15am & 5.50pm. Return from Bantry 11.25am & 8.20pm, Glengarriff 11.55am & 8.50pm, arrives Castletownbere 1pm & 9.45pm. Tues, Fri & Sat: Castletownbere 10.30am, calling at Glengarriff 11.20am, arrives Bantry 11.50am. Return from Bantry 3.45pm, Glengarriff 4.15pm, arrives Castletownbere 5pm.

Castletownbere–Cork *O'Donohue's* (☎027/70007). Depart Castletownbere 7.30am, Glengarriff 8.15am, Bantry 8.45am, arrive Cork 10.30am. Return from Cork (*Ivy Leaf Bar*, Parnell Place) 6pm, Bantry 7.45pm, Glengarriff 8.25pm, arrive Castletownbere 9.15pm. *Harrington's Buses* (☎027/74003) Depart Castletownbere Mon, Tues, Wed, Fri (& Sat in summer) at 8am to arrive at **Cork** 9.45am; Sun at 5pm to arrive at Cork 7.30pm. Services depart **from Cork** (*Ivy Leaf Bar*, Parnell Place) at 6pm on the same days, to arrive in Castletownbere at 8.30pm; Sun departure at 8pm.

CHAPTER EIGHT

KERRY

I f you've come to Ireland for the scenery, mountains, sea, and the remoteness, you'll find them all in **County Kerry**: miles and miles of mountain-moorland where the heather and the bracken are broken only by the occasional lake; smooth hills whose fragrant, tussocky grass is covered with sea pinks, speed-wells, thrift and red campion, and that fragment into jagged rocks as they reach the sea. The ocean looks enormous, and you can stand in the sunshine and watch a storm coming in for miles before you have to run for cover. The only catch is that a good part of the county is very much on the tourist trail.

The plus side of Kerry's long tradition of welcoming tourists is that it's very easy country to travel in, with plenty of accommodation and food in all price brackets. And, during the summer at least, transport is pretty good – though with some notable exceptions.

Broadly speaking, Kerry divides into four areas: the Dingle peninsula; the Iveragh peninsula, encircled by the Ring of Kerry, with Killarney in its hinterland; the Kenmare river, bordered to the north and south by the Iveragh and Beara peninsulas; and northern Kerry, from Tralee to the Shannon. Each section is quite distinct, and has its partisans. By far the most visited area – indeed the most visited in the whole of Ireland – is **Killarney and the Ring of Kerry**. Deservedly famous for the beauty of the adjacent lakes and mountains, this region is, predictably, geared up for tourism, and the principal roads and sights are often overburdened with visitors. Luckily, however, the real wilds are never far away, and whether you head for the mountains or the sea you can soon lose yourself and feel remote from modern civilisation. The **Dingle peninsula** is on a smaller scale than Iveragh, but equally magical: peppered with monastic remains, it has a contemplative atmosphere that makes you understand why people talk about the mystic quality of the west. Around **Kenmare** things are different again, with a tamed feeling about the scenery; one half of the Beara Peninsula actually belongs to more cultivated, genteel County Cork. To the **north**, flat, fertile farming land makes for less exciting scenery, but in contrast to the rest of the county there are many signs of a long-established Anglo-Norman presence.

KILLARNEY AND THE SOUTH

Killarney and the Ring of Kerry (the road running right around the **Iveragh peninsula**) attract huge numbers of visitors, particularly in high summer; be wary if you're looking for solitude. Fortunately, avoiding the hordes is fairly easy since mass tourism fixes only upon the most obvious attractions: Killarney, its lakes, the Gap of Dunloe, and the wholly insane notion of driving round the magnificent Ring of Kerry in a day. Strike away from these, and you'll escape the worst.

Killarney

Although **KILLARNEY** has been commercialised to saturation point and has little in the way of architectural interest, its location amidst some of the best lakeland, mountain and woodland scenery in Ireland offers some compensation. The town is essentially one main street and a couple of side roads, full of souvenir shops, cafés, pubs, restaurants and B&Bs. Pony traps and jaunting cars line up against walls while their weather-beaten owners talk visitors into extortionate trips through the surrounding country. It's all done with bags of charm, true to Killarney's long tradition of profitably hosting the visiting masses ever since its discovery as a resort in the mid-eighteenth century.

The town's Gaelic name (*Cill Áirne*, Church of the Sloe) doesn't imply a settlement of any great antiquity, and the Cromwellian Survey of 1654 found no town or village of that name. By 1756, however, a burgeoning **tourist trade**, soon fed by the growing Romantic attraction to lakes and mountains, had created Killarney: "A new street with a large commodious inn was designed to be built here, for the curiosities of the neighbouring lake have of late drawn great numbers of curious travellers to visit it", said a contemporary survey. The local landowner, Lord Kenmare, quickly spotted commercial opportunities and granted free leases for new inns and houses, building four major roads to connect his creation with the outside world.

That said, the town doesn't look particularly planned, and the only building of any distinction is the high Gothic revival style **cathedral**, built by Augustus Pugin in 1855. A particularly florid Victorian interpretation of medieval architecture, the cathedral inspires respect or derision, but is worth seeing either way. During the Famine, when building work ceased for five years, the covered area served as a hospital for victims of starvation and disease.

Practicalities: arrival and a room

The train and bus **station** is pretty central, off East Avenue Road; it's obvious where to go. Although there's plentiful accommodation of all sorts, Killarney is very crowded in high season and it's worth calling the helpful **tourist office**, on the main street by the town hall to make advance bookings (☎064/31633; July & Aug Mon–Sat 9am–8pm, Sun 10am–6pm; June & Sept Mon–Sat 9am–7pm; Oct–May Mon–Fri 9.15am–5.30pm, Sat 9.15am–1pm).

On thing the tourist office can't do is make specific recommendations of **B&Bs** – a shame since price and quality seem to vary a lot here. Nonetheless there are dozens to choose from. A couple of reasonable central options are *Aisling House* on Countess Road (☎064/31112; £13), and *Slieve Bloom Manor* (☎064/34237; £12.50), about half a mile out on the Muckross road.

The best of Killarney's **hostels** is the *Súgán Kitchen Hostel* (☎064/33104; £5, bike rental £4; often full, so worth phoning ahead), on Lewis Road, a few minutes' walk from the station. Cosy and relaxed, it has a wholefood bistro serving great food (three courses for around £6 for residents; more expensive for visitors), a laundry, and traditional music. The same family also runs the *Bunrower House Hostel* (☎064/33914; £5; formerly *Loch Lein Hostel*), near Ross Castle; bookings and free bus from the *Súgán*. If you stay at *Bunrower House* you can row and swim free in the hostel's own swimming area. The *An Óige* hostel (☎064/31240; June–Sept £5.90, Oct–May £4.50; booking essential in high season; free van service to and from the bus and rail stations, and bike rental at £4 a day) is three miles out along the Killorglin road, at Aghadoe. The *Four Winds Hostel* at 43 New Street (turn left outside the tourist office, left at the crossroads, and it's a few minutes' walk down on your right; ☎064/33094; accommodation for couples; £5.50, £5 with *ISIC* card; bike rental including mountain bikes from £4 a day) is extroverted and noisy; their minibus sometimes touts for business at the railway station. The *Park Hostel* (☎064/32119; £5, £4 with *ISIC*) is up the hill off Cork Road, opposite the petrol station.

There are a couple of other hostels too, and you can **camp** at the *Fossa Caravan Park* (☎064/31497; £5–6, 50p per adult) just past the Aghadoe youth hostel west of the town.

Staying further out

Finding somewhere to stay outside Killarney is perhaps a more attractive option, especially if you have transport. **B&Bs** outside town tend to be better value than the central ones – try the O'Connors at *Glebe Farmhouse* (☎064/32179; £11), some four miles north off the Tralee Road, or the Joys at *Forest Haven*, Long Guitane Road, Muckross (☎064/33757; £12). Among the best alternative **hostels** are *Donash Lodge* in Firies, on the main Farenfore to Dingle L103 road (☎066/64554; May–Sept; two family/double rooms; £4–6; camping possible); or *Woods Hostel* in the square at Milltown (see p.272). There's also an *An Óige* hostel at Loo Bridge, ten miles south of town and reachable on the Killarney–Kenmare bus (☎064/53002; £5.50; March–Sept).

Food, drink and entertainment

Places to **eat and drink** are so thick on the ground in Killarney that it seems pointless to list them. Nevertheless, cheap dinners are available at *Sceilig*, in the High Street; *Brian Mac's*, on the same road, is good for lunch, as is *A Taste of Ireland* on College Street. Evening **entertainment** is everywhere as you walk along the streets: the widely publicised "traditional" Irish music can seem pretty spurious when you are surrounded by busloads of other tourists, but it sounds great in places like *Jimmy O'Brien's* (near the Priory), the *Súgán Kitchen* (part of the hostel, also serves good food), or *The Laurels* (for Ireland's other folk tradition, country and western). *Tattler Jack's* is an ordinary pub with lively conversation.

In May, July and October there's **racing** at Killarney's racecourse on Ross Road, which, like any Irish race meeting, is well worth a detour. The tourist office can give details of **Gaelic football** matches; Killarney is a top team and feelings run high. If you're heading for Killarney in the spring, check out the **Pan-Celtic Week**, a gathering of artists and film-makers from Ireland, Scotland, Wales, Cornwall and Brittany; details from the tourist office.

Cycling and other practicalities

Even if you're not planning to bike round the Ring of Kerry, **cycling** is a great way of seeing Killarney's immediate surroundings (see below), and makes good sense because local transport is almost non-existent. *O'Callaghan Brothers* (College Street; ☎064/31465, 31175) are the local participants in the *Raleigh* scheme; bikes can also be hired from *O'Neill's* in Plunkett Street (☎064/31970). **Banks** and the **post office** can be found on New Street. Killarney's public **launderette** (Mon–Sat 9am–8pm) is in the little shopping mall off the High Street.

Around Killarney

The real reason for coming to Killarney is without doubt the surrounding landscape. Its three spectacular **lakes**, Lough Leane (the Lower Lake), Muckross Lake (the Middle Lake) and the Upper Lake, are only the appetiser. Behind them loom **MacGillycuddy's Reeks**, which have a grandeur out of all proportion to their height: rarely exceeding 3000 feet, they're still the highest mountains in Ireland. Much of this is contained within the huge **Killarney National Park**.

It was the Ice Age that formed the Killarney **landscape**. Glaciation has left its mark on the contorted limestone valleys of the Lower and Middle Lakes, and the nearby Devil's Punch Bowl and Horses' Glen show other signs: huge rocks smoothed to sucked-sweet shapes, and improbably teetering boulders. The lower slopes of the mountains are covered with what is often virgin **forest**, a joy to see in a country that has cut down almost all its trees. Almost everything seems to thrive in the local combination of high rainfall and humidity, and in the woods you'll find a rich mix of trees, dominated by oak but with bilberry, woodrush and woodsorrel, plus mosses, liverworts and lichens, sensitive organisms whose continued survival testifies to the clean air here.

As elsewhere in the west of Ireland, the Killarney area's **vegetation** includes a number of plants generally found only in quite different parts of Europe. The famous arbutus, or strawberry tree – so called from its bright red (and non-edible) fruit – for example, generally grows only in Mediterranean countries and Brittany. Some saxifrages, and the greater butterwort, with its fleshy purple flowers and sickly green leaf rosettes, are otherwise found only in northwest Spain and Portugal (see p.296 for more on the west's strange flora).

Knockreer Estate and Lough Leane

Oddly enough, given its origins as a tourist town, Killarney turns its back on the grand scenery to the west and south, hunching itself inwards so that you'd hardly guess at the delights that await you. But the gates of the old Kenmare Estate – now known as the **Knockreer Estate** – are just over the road from the cathedral, and a short walk through the grounds takes you to the banks of Lough Leane. The Browne family, earls of Kenmare, were unusual among the Irish peerage in that they never renounced their Catholic faith. Given lands confiscated from the O'Donoghues in the seventeenth century, they were subject in the eighteenth century to the penal laws which decreed that every Catholic landowner had to divide his property among his male heirs. The Brownes' estate remained intact quite simply because there was only one son in each generation.

At **Lough Leane**, the scenery is magnificent: tall wooded hills plunge into the water, with the mountain peaks rising behind to the highest, **Carrintuohill** (3414 feet). Ireland's last wild wolf was killed here in 1700, and when the weather's bad (as it often is) there's a satisfying similarity to early Romantic engravings. The main path through the Kenmare estate leads to the restored fourteenth-century tower of **Ross Castle**, the last place in Munster to succumb to Cromwell's forces in 1652. The story is that General Ludlow, having learned of a tradition that Ross Castle would never be taken from land, brought pre-fabricated ships from Kenmare and sailed them up from Castlemaine, whereupon the defenders – whom nothing else had budged – immediately surrendered. Near the water you can make out copper workings, last used during the Napoleonic Wars, and thought to date back 4000 years.

From Ross Castle you can **tour the lake** in large glassed-over boats like the *bateaux-mouches* that ply the Seine in Paris; but these don't make stops, and an alternative is to get a fisherman to take you out in a little craft with an outboard motor, or hire one yourself. This way, you can land on and explore the island of Inisfallen. (If you're navigating yourself, look for a limestone outcrop in the water. Inisfallen is the island to the left, about a mile out.)

Inisfallen

Of the thirty-odd small islands that dot Lough Leane, **Inisfallen** is the biggest and the most enchanting, particularly if there's no one else on it (which can easily happen as you watch the *bateaux mouches* grind by). The monastery founded here in the seventh century was an important scholastic centre for a thousand years. Brian Boru, the eleventh-century High King and victor over the Vikings at Clontarf in 1014, was allegedly educated here, and the twelfth-century *Annals of Inisfallen*, now in Oxford's Bodleian Library, are an important source document for early Irish history. Wandering round the island is a delight: heavily wooded, it's also scattered with monastic buildings – nothing from the original seventh-century foundation, but there's a small Romanesque church and an extremely ruined twelfth-century Augustinian priory. Eighteenth-century tourists were clearly awake to Inisfallen's charms: Lord Kenmare used to give parties for his influential friends here, and the gap in the wall of the Romanesque church is where he installed a bay window when the building was converted into a banqueting house. The picturesque ruin you see now is the result of further tinkering, around 1840.

Muckross and the upper lakes

The road from Killarney to the **Muckross estate** passes through unlovely territory dominated by huge modern hotels, and though jaunting cars from the centre will take you out to Muckross (cars are prohibited on the Muckross estate), it's more fun to hire a bike. Take the earliest turning right into the park that's available, to escape the busy main road. The first place to head for is **Muckross Abbey**, not only for the ruin itself – one of the best-preserved in Ireland, part Norman, part Gothic, though sadly despoiled by Cromwell's troops – but also for its calm, contemplative location, and the fact that it, like Ross Castle, hints at something predating Killarney's tourist history. Founded as a Franciscan institution by Macarthy Mor in the mid-fifteenth century, it was suppressed by Henry VIII; the friars returned again, but were finally driven out by Cromwell's army in 1652.

Back at the main road, signposts direct you to **Muckross House**, a solid, nineteenth-century neo-Elizabethan mansion designed by the Scottish architect William Burn. The **museum** (July–Aug daily 9am–7pm; March–June & Sept–Oct daily 9am–6pm; Nov–Feb Tues–Sun 11am–5pm; £2, students £1.50), while no great shakes, has a section on Kerry folk life where craftspeople (blacksmiths, weavers, potters) demonstrate their trades – but only at peak times. The excellent **tea shop** provides a good refuge from the rain, but the **gardens** – well known for their rhododendrons and azaleas – are the place to be when the weather is fine.

Middle Lake and the Meeting of the Waters

The estate gives access to well-trodden paths along the shores of the **Middle Lake**, and it's here that you can see one of Killarney's celebrated beauty spots, the **Meeting of the Waters**. Actually a parting, but highly picturesque nonetheless, it has a profusion of indigenous and flowering subtropical plants – eucalyptus, magnolia, bamboo, and an arbutus, or strawberry tree, on the left of the Old Weir Bridge. Close by is the massive shoulder of Torc Mountain, shrugging off the spectacular 60ft **Torc Waterfall**. There's a not terribly informative **visitor centre** by the car park for the waterfall; but the climb up the side of the mountain is worth doing, if only for the view across to Macgillycuddy's Reeks. On a good day, the Slievemish mountains on the far side of Dingle Bay are visible.

The Upper Lake

The **Upper Lake** is beautiful too, but still firmly on the tourist trail, with the main road running along one side up to **Ladies' View**, where the egg sandwich brigades queue up with their thermoses to admire the view – which is, in fact, truly amazing, including the Gap of Dunloe and the secretive Black Valley behind the lake.

The Gap of Dunloe

Although the **Gap of Dunloe** – a narrow defile formed by glacial overflow that cuts the mountains in two – is one of Killarney's prime tourist attractions, it's possible to find a modicum of solitude if you're willing to use your legs. **Jaunting cars** continually run here from Killarney's centre, a fact which, as the jarveys tout loudly for business, you're not likely to miss. One version of the trip, combining jaunting cars with a bus ride, sets off from the tourist office at 10.30am, transferring you to a pony and trap for the Gap itself, before returning to town at 5.15pm. Apart from being very overpriced, this entails being stuck in the traffic jam of bored ponies pulling traps up the Gap. The other option is to **walk**, ignoring the offers of rides that will assail you for the first half mile or so. If you peg out before the four miles are up, it's possible to haggle for a lift – the whole trip generally costs about £15 a car.

Kate Kearney's Cottage, at the foot of the road leading up to the Gap – a confusion of shops and sweating horses – is the last place for food and water before Lord Brandon's Cottage, way over the other side of the Black Valley. The best time to walk is late afternoon, when the jaunting cars have gone home and the light is at its most magical. The road – closed to motor traffic – winds its way up the desolate valley between high rock cliffs and waterfalls (Macgillycuddy's Reeks to your right, and the Purple Mountain, so called because in late summer it's covered in purple heather), past a chain of icy loughs and tarns, up to the top, when you find yourself in what feels like one of the remotest places in the world: the **Black Valley**.

Named after its entire population perished during the potato famine, and now inhabited by a mere handful of families, the Black Valley makes you begin to feel that you've left mass tourism behind. The fact that it was the very last valley in Ireland to get electricity is some measure of its isolation, and there are no pubs or shops here. Moving on, you can either carry on down to the Upper Lake (Lord Brandon's Cottage, food, boat hire and the quick way back to Killarney); or pick up the Kerry Way.

Walking the Kerry Way

The **Kerry Way** is part of a long-distance footpath that's intended to go right around the Iveragh Peninsula through Cahirciveen, Waterville, Caherdaniel, Kenmare and Kilgarvan – a sort of walkers' Ring of Kerry. At the moment it stops short around Sneem, on the peninsula's south coast. More than most of Ireland's long-distance footpaths, it's resonant of the culture, as well as the nature, of the area, consisting largely of green roads, many of them old drove roads, "butter roads" (along which butter was transported), and routes between Kerry's ancient Christian settlements. It's also one of the best ways of starting to explore the spectacular uplands of MacGillycuddy's Reeks.

The Kerry Way **starts** inauspiciously in Killarney, threads down through the Muckross estate and alongside the Upper Lake – road walking, most of it – before heading up to meet the Black Valley (see above). From the Black Valley, it heads on towards **Cloghernoosh** via a stony path that becomes a green road. After the footbridge over the stream running out of Curraghmore Lake, there's a stretch of bridleway, and from here on you're among the peaks, with exhilarating views of Carrintuohil to the north.

Next, the footpath follows the Lack Road, zigzagging up to a saddle point at the top, then skirting the side of **Lough Acoose** before reaching the **Glencar valley** (and the first tourist accommodation since the Black Valley). No longer traversing really high ground, the rest of the way into Glenbeigh is less exciting, although the stretch on **Seefin Mountain** above Caragh Lake is still spectacular.

Practicalities

All the usual **precautions** need to be taken seriously in a region where gales blowing in off the Atlantic can make the weather change rapidly. Bring waterproofs, walking boots, food, and a good map: the one-inch Map of Killarney District, covering most of the walk, is useful, while the half-inch Dingle Bay Ordnance Survey Map details most of the first leg, up to the Black Valley.

You should really fix up **accommodation** beforehand. The *An Óige* hostel in the **Black Valley** (☎064/34712; £5.50; open all year; ponies and boats for hire) sells supplies at strictly limited times, and an independent hostel, *The Mountain Lodge* (☎066/60173; £10; open Easter–Sept), a little further on in the **Bridia Valley**, does meals and sleeps just eight. To have dinner you need to arrive by seven (three courses £6.50, or soup for £2), the stream substitutes for showers, and you can also camp. It's roughly eight hours' walk from Killarney; hitching isn't recommended, since the nearest road seeing any traffic is eight miles from the start of the valley. Next stop is the *Climbers' Inn*, hidden among woodlands at **Glencar** (☎066/60101, £3–4); meals are available in the bar, decorated with a church pulpit, and there's a shop, bunkhouse accommodation and excellent advice on local walks and climbs. In **Glenbeigh** there are hotels and B&Bs (try the *Glenbeigh Hotel*, ☎066/68333, £20; or *Village House*, ☎066/68128, £13) as well as a hostel, *Hillside House* (☎066/68228; £4; March–Oct), which has private rooms, showers (50p) and a shop.

For more information on **mountaineering** in Kerry, contact the Killarney Mountaineering Club (☎066/61127); the Kerry Mountain Rescue Team is based at Killarney police station (☎064/31222, or ☎999 in emergency).

The Ring of Kerry

The 110-mile **Ring of Kerry**, which encircles the Iveragh Peninsula, can be driven around in a day, and most tourists view its spectacular scenery without ever leaving their coach or car. Consequently, anyone straying from the road or waiting until the buses knock off in the afternoon will be left to experience the long, slow twilights of the Atlantic seaboard in perfect seclusion. Part of the excitement of travelling round the Kerry coast comes from the clarity with which its physical outline stands against the vast grey expanse of the Atlantic. Every gully, bay, channel and island is as distinct as it is on the map, giving a powerful sense of place amidst the isolation.

If you really are limited to a **day's exploration** of the wild coastal scenery, it could be worth heading for Dingle, the next peninsula north, instead: its intimacy of scale means you can see a lot more without having to rely upon coaches or cars. **Cycling** the Ring itself takes three days (not counting any diversions), and a bike will let you get on to the largely deserted mountain roads; just be sure your machine has lots of gears, and you have plenty of energy – the combination of gradients and strong winds can be gruelling. You can pick up a useful **map** showing quiet cycling roads at the tourist office in Killarney for 50p. Public transport doesn't serve the entire circuit – the **buses** from Killarney only go as far as Cahirciveen (twice daily in July and August, once daily otherwise) – but during summer, flotillas of **coaches** ply the Ring. Most of them leave from opposite the tourist office, where you can get details, and for an extra charge will drop you off somewhere along the way, and pick you up the next day. Hitching is unreliable; while you're likely to get a lift from anyone who passes, traffic simply may not exist away from the main roads.

Killorglin to Cahirciveen

By travelling the Ring of Kerry **anticlockwise**, you get a gradual introduction to the wild grandeur of the coastline scenery, with the Dingle peninsula and the dim shapes of the Blasket Islands visible in the distance.

The first stop on the way out from Killarney is the pleasantly unexceptional hillside town of **KILLORGLIN**, whose main claim to fame is the **Puck Fair**, held over three days in mid-August, a bacchanalian affair with a wild goat captured and enthroned, plenty of dancing and drinking, plus a cattle, sheep and horse fair. These pagan-seeming rituals are in fact of much more recent origin, honouring the wild goats which, stampeding through the town, warned residents of the approach of Cromwell's army.

Next comes **GLENBEIGH**, where almost everything is given over to tourism; despite plenty of B&Bs and the *Hillside House Hostel* (see Kerry Way practicalities), the town illustrates the disadvantages of sticking rigidly to the Ring. However, there are wonderful views all along the coastline and across to Dingle, and by taking the road up past **Lough Caragh**, you'll find some of Kerry's best mountain scenery, full of deep silences and the magical slanting light of the west. If you're on a relaxed budget and are looking for comparative luxury, you could try *Glendalough House*, a mid-nineteenth-century country house on the shores of Lough Caragh (☎066/69156; £28–30). Alternatively, you could climb up to the three small lakes of **Coomnacronia**, **Coomasglaslaw** and **Coomsaharn** (good trout fishing, but you'll need a licence).

The lack of trees that contributes to the feeling of austerity in this area was not an original feature of the landscape; Sir William Petty, Cromwell's surveyor general, had an iron mine at Blackstones, and felled the forests to fuel a smelter.

Cahirciveen

At **Kells Bay** the road veers inland for Cahirciveen, giving you an opportunity to take a detour. Any of the turnings right will lead eventually to the sea, past bright fuchsia hedges, with little or no traffic. "One wonders, in this place, why anyone is left in Dublin, or London, or Paris, when it would be better one would think, to live in a tent, or a hut, with this magnificent sea and sky, and to breathe this wonderful air, which is like wine in one's teeth", wrote J. M. Synge of the Kerry landscape; and here for the first time you begin to understand how the Ring inspires such hyperbole.

CAHIRCIVEEN (*Cathair Saidhbhín*; pronounced "Caher-shivveen", stress on the last syllable) is a long, narrow street of a town and the main shopping centre for the western part of the peninsula, giving itself over cheerfully to the tourist trade in summer. A laid-back, unremarkable place, it has more relaxed attitudes to shopping hours than anywhere else on the peninsula, lending it an odd southern flavour; and there are plenty of friendly bars. For **B&B** try Mrs O'Donoghue at *Ocean View Farmhouse* (☎0667/2261; £12.50), half a mile out of town, or Mrs Quill at *Ard na Greine*, Valentia Road (☎0667/2281; £11); or there's an independent **hostel**, *Sive Hostel*, 15 East End (☎0667/2717; £5; open all year).

Beyond Cahirciveen, the main road takes the bulk of the traffic inland again towards Waterville, giving you an opportunity to explore the quiet lanes that lead out to Valentia Island and the peninsula's end. The *An Óige* **hostel** at Ballinskelligs (see below) makes a good base for exploring the area, as do the **holiday cottages** which abound here. These tend to get booked up ahead, so if you want to be sure of a place you'll need to book early in the year – they're administered by the Irish Tourist Board (see *Basics* for details) – but you can check availability on the spot with the Killarney tourist office. Staying here, the slow life works its spell; and you can buy fish direct from the boats at Reenard Point, where the ferry for Valentia Island departs.

Valentia Island

VALENTIA, an island now linked to the mainland by bridge, is Europe's most westerly harbour, and standing at Bray Head on the island's tip, there's nothing but ocean between you and Newfoundland, 1900 miles away. Valentia's significance is out of all proportion to its size: the first ever transatlantic telegraph cable was laid from here in 1857 – though permanent contact wasn't established until 1866 – and for years it had better communications with New York than with Dublin.

In contrast to the endless vistas west, the island itself is small, and consequently every scrap of land has been cultivated, forming a rolling patchwork of fields stitched with dry slate walls. Valentia's position in the Gulf Stream gives it a mild, balmy climate, and the abundance of fuchsias grown by the inhabitants in local hedgerows enhances its domesticated atmosphere. It's a homely, tame place to stay, though from July onwards the peace is disturbed by tourists.

Arrival and a room

Access is by **ferry** from Reenard to Knightstown (£1, ask at Cahirciveen post office for details: it runs only when the weather permits), or via the Maurice O'Neill Bridge, at the south end of the island, thirteen miles from the main coast road, and a difficult hitch. Once on the island there's no public transport at all. Accommodation is at a premium during the summer season, when most **B&Bs** in Knightstown and Portmagee raise their prices to around £16; a couple to try are Mrs Lyne's in Knightstown (☎0667/6171; £12) and Mrs Lynch's *Harbour Grove Farmhouse*, Portmagee (☎0667/7116; £12). The *An Óige* **hostel** has space for forty at cottages 1, 4 & 5 of the Coastguard Station in Knightstown, but for members only, and services are spartan (☎0667/6154; £5.50; open April–Sept). The independent hostel on the harbour front, the *Royal and Pier Hostel* (☎0667/

6144; £5; open all year) is never short of space, but damp and unfriendly. Midway between the bridge and Knightstown at Chapeltown, there's another independent, *Ring Lyne Hostel* (☎0667/6103; £5). Perhaps the best accommodation on the island, however, is at the *Valentia Heights* guesthouse (☎0667/6138; £20; meals available), overlooking the cliffs a couple of miles west of Knightstown.

Around the island
KNIGHTSTOWN is the focal village on the island and, facing Cahirciveen across the Portmagee Channel, affords fine panoramic views of the Kerry Mountains. A pretty harbour front with sprucely painted fishermen's cottages is dominated by the Victorian *Royal and Pier Hotel*; now damply dilapidated and something of a white elephant, it's currently being run as an independent hostel (see above). Tolerating rather than encouraging tourists, Knightstown is deeply old-fashioned, and if there are more than three in your group, you could feel something of an intrusion. About a thousand houses cluster around a slate church hidden within a dark rookery. The main street has a few well-stocked shops, a post office offering a good selection of Irish literature and free maps of the island; and a couple of **bars**. Uninspiring by day, these come to life after 10pm several nights a week, when locals playing accordions and pipes accompany rigorous Gaelic dancing, the faces of the participants (average age sixty-plus) showing serious concentration in this wild pastime.

From Knightstown, take the Kilmore road down towards the lighthouse, where there's a fine view of Valentia's empty harbour, the Beginis islands and tiny **Church Island**. This mere rock supports the ruins of an eighth-century cell, once inhabited by a solitary monk, a soulmate of the brotherhood on the nearby Skellig islands, whose only company was the sea birds. On a clear day you can also make out the sheer cliffs of the Blasket Islands beyond the Dingle Peninsula to the north.

Continuing west, the foreshore is an imposing clutter of megalithic slabs hurled together by the waves, with deep, limpid pools left by the winter storms. A couple of miles further on, a wonderful swimming cove combines intimacy with the grandiose, sheltered by lush, deciduous woods, with the whole of Kerry as its scenic backdrop. This appears to be part of the grounds of **Glanleam House**, former seat of the local magnate, the Knight of Kerry, attached to which are incongruously exotic gardens, but it's actually a public beach.

The fervour with which locals urge you to visit the **Grotto** is misplaced. A gaping slate cavern, it boasts a crude, municipal-baths blue statue of the Virgin (erected 1954) perched 200 feet up, amidst monotonously dripping icy water. Nevertheless, this is the highest point on the island, and a good walk for a clear day. But more exciting by far is the cliff scenery to the northwest, some of the most spectacular of the Kerry coast. The *Valentia Heights* guesthouse is nearby.

The Skellig Islands

From Valentia you get a tantalising view across a broad strip of sea to the **Skellig Islands** (*Na Sceilig*), apparently no more than two massive rocks. Little Skellig is a bird sanctuary, home to 40,000 gannets, and landing isn't permitted, but you can visit Great Skellig, or Skellig Michael as it's also called, and climb up to the ancient monastic site at the summit.

To get there, enquire at local shops in Reenard, Knightstown and Portmagee about **boat trips**, or call ☎0667/6124; the trips are dear at around £15 but, if the weather's good, make a fascinating and dramatic voyage. The boats run between Easter and September, when the weather gets too rough: September 1991 saw a party of civil servants stranded on Skellig Michael for three days. Once at sea, boats are followed by wheeling seagulls and, if you're lucky, puffins too. Oddly staid little birds that look like miniature flying businessmen, they come from the nature reserve of Puffin Island, further north. You'll also pass the huge, jagged arch of rock that forms **Little Skellig**, where gannets with six-foot wingspans career overhead, or make headlong dives into the sea for fish.

Skellig Michael looms sheer from the ocean, a gargantuan slaty mass with no visible route to the summit. From the tiny landing stage, however, you can see steps cut into the cliff face, formerly a treacherous monks' path. Nowadays there's also a road leading to Christ's Saddle, the only patch of green on this inhospitable island. From here, a path leads on to the arched stone remains of **St Finian's Abbey** (560 AD). Amongst the ruins are six complete beehive cells – drystone huts that have survived centuries of foul weather. The island is dedicated to Saint Michael, guardian against the powers of darkness, and patron of high places. Contrasted with Valentia, it's a wild, cruel place; an awesome sanctuary of devotion, even if the monks didn't remain here all year round to feel the violence of the elements. An amenity you may wish to avoid is the **Skellig Experience** (£3, or £15 including cruise round, but not landing on, the islands) – a "major, weather-independent tourist attraction" at Portmagee. On a wet day the interpretive centre, with information about Celtic monastic life, lighthouses and lighthouse-keeping, seabirds and aquatic life could be a pleasant refuge (and a "comprehensively stocked retail area" offers an opportunity for shopping therapy), but it's all too easy to see this as another example of theme-park Ireland.

On to Waterville

The stretch of coast between Valentia and Waterville is wild and almost deserted, apart from a scattering of farms and fishing villages. Sweet-smelling, tussocky grass dotted with wild flowers is raked by Atlantic winds, ending in abrupt cliffs or sandy beaches – a beguiling landscape where you can wander for days. The *An Óige* hostel (☎0667/9229; £5.50; open all year) in **BALLINSKELLIGS** (*Baile an Sceilg*) makes a good base and sells supplies. Monks from the Skellig islands retreated to Ballinskelligs Abbey in the thirteenth century, while the town itself, largely Gaelic-speaking, is the focus of the Kerry *Gaeltacht*, and in the summer it's busy with schoolchildren and students learning Gaelic.

WATERVILLE may be touristy, but it does it with a lot of grace. Popular as a Victorian and Edwardian resort and angling centre, it still has an air of consequence that sits oddly with the wild Atlantic views. Its few bars and hotels aside, the town is chiefly notable as the best base on the Ring for exploring the coast and the mountainous country inland. The hostel at *Waterville Leisure Centre* makes an excellent base (☎0667/4400; £5; open all year) and can supply information about surfing, mountaineering and riding in the vicinity. The *Butler Arms* (☎0667/4144; £40) offers a more comfortable option, redolent of bourgeois family holidays; cheaper **B&Bs** include Mrs Murphy's *Ashling House*, Main Street (☎0667/4247; £12.50), and Mrs McAuliffe's *Lake Rise*, Lake Road (☎0667/4278; £12.50).

From Waterville it's a long haul by bike or on foot up to the **Coomakista Pass**, but the effort is well worth it for the breathtaking views over the mouth of the Kenmare river, all greys and blues, the three rocks called the Bull, the Cow and the Calf, and beyond them the Beara Peninsula – most spectacular when the weather's good; when it rains you can see the squalls being driven in across the ocean. However, you can't hope to avoid lots of other tourists here.

WATERVILLE IN LEGEND: NOAH'S CHILDREN IN IRELAND

Waterville and Ballinskelligs Bay form the setting for one of the more wayward Irish legends. When the Biblical Flood was imminent, so the story goes, Noah's son **Bith** and his daughter **Cessair** found that there was no room for them in the Ark. So they and their retinue set sail for Ireland which, Cessair was advised, was uninhabited, free of monsters, reptiles and sin, and would therefore escape the flood. However, although 49 women survived to land along with Cessair in 2958 BC, only two men besides Bith made it. The three men divided the women between them, but when Bith and Ladra, the pilot, died, Fintan, the last man, was overwhelmed, and, to his eternal shame, ran away; upon which Cessair, who loved him, died of sorrow.

Derrynane to Kenmare

Tucked away on a little promontory of its own between the Ring of Kerry and the sea is **DERRYNANE** (pronounced "Derrynaan"), home of the family of **Daniel O'Connell**, the Catholic lawyer and politician who negotiated limited Catholic emancipation in 1829. You can visit his house, and Derrynane itself is a pleasant place, with wide, flat sand beaches, two miles of dunes, good swimming, and rocks glistening black with delicious mussels. Although fun in the daytime, like everywhere along this western seaboard it's most atmospheric at sunset, when the long twilight lingers; the Gaels believed that sunset and sunrise were points of transition (like stiles and gates) where it was possible to slip from the real world into the faerie one, and here you can see their point.

The **O'Connell House** (May–Sept Mon–Sat 9am–6pm, Sun 11am–7pm; Oct–April Tues–Sun 1–5pm; £1.50, students 50p) remodelled by Daniel O'Connell himself, is absolutely simple – a square slate tower and roughly elegant rooms with the slanting sea-light a constant presence. The O'Connells were an old Gaelic family who'd made their money trading and smuggling – the west of Ireland had a long tradition of trade with Europe in wine, spices and silks. Daniel O'Connell's uncle bequeathed him a fortune, giving him the financial independence necessary to devote himself to politics. Discrimination against Catholics was widespread, and closely experienced by Daniel: another uncle was shot dead because he would not give up his fine horse, as the law demanded of Catholics.

The immediate area has plenty of ancient forts and standing stones. On the way to CASTLECOVE, there's a sign on the left for **Staigue Fort**, two-and-a-half miles up a rough lane, a very well-preserved ring fort, possibly created as early as 1000 BC. The nearest **hostel** (with another fort 300 yards away) is *Carrigbeg* at **CAHIRDANIEL** (Cathair Dónall), just outside Derrynane Park on a bend in the road overlooking the sea; their breakfast of muesli and brown bread is a welcome relief from the ubiquitous bacon and eggs (☎0667/5229; £4.50; accepts only cyclists and hitch-hikers). Local **B&B** options include the *Scarriff Inn* (☎0667/5132; £14) and Mrs Sullivan's (☎0667/5124; £14). As the road winds onwards towards Sneem, there's good swimming, particularly at White Strand, past hedge-rows blossoming with both fuchsia and hydrangea.

Sneem

SNEEM (*An tSnaidhm*; pronounced "Shneem") is spectacularly set against the mountains, dominated by the 2245-foot Knockmoyle; but the village has lost something by selling out to tourism. Sneem's houses are washed in different colours – reputedly so that drunken residents can find their way home – and their picture-book prettiness juxtaposed against tourist shops and cafés has a touch of the surreal. Good local fishing is advertised by the salmon-shaped weathercock on the Protestant church. You'll probably want to push on to more interesting Kenmare, but if you do decide to stay here, try Mrs Sullivan at *Woodvale House* (☎064/45181; £13) or Mrs Drummond's *Rockville House* (☎064/45135; £12).

The approach to Kenmare along the estuary is unexciting, seemingly more in character with the Beara Peninsula opposite than with wild Iveragh, and you'll have a more scenic journey back to Killarney if you take the mountain road direct from Sneem. The two routes join up again at the spectacular **Moll's Gap**, north of Kenmare.

Kenmare and the Beara Peninsula

With its unlikely shops – delicatessens, designer boutiques and arty second-hand clothes shops – **KENMARE** feels like a foreign enclave, and you're more likely to hear English or German tones here than Irish. Neatly organised on an X-plan (laid out by the first Marquess of Lansdowne in 1775), the town is pleasantly cosmopolitan: besides the resident foreigners, it's the natural crossing-over point for everyone travelling up from Cork.

Kenmare was founded by **Sir William Petty**, Cromwell's surveyor general, to serve his mining works beside the River Finnihy. Petty was extremely active in (and benefited greatly from) the dealings in confiscated properties that went on after the Cromwellian wars. Many soldiers were paid by the impecunious govern-ment in land, but not all of them wanted to settle in Ireland, and so sold to dealers – such as Petty. His acquisition of land all over Ireland, including roughly a quar-ter of Kerry, was surely helped by his commission to survey the country on behalf of the government, when he investigated two thirds of the Irish counties in the amazingly short period of fifteen months. Petty's other achievements were no less remarkable: a professor of medicine at Oxford at 27, he was also a professor of music and founder member of the Royal Society in London; an early statisti-cian, economist and demographer; and politically astute enough to get yet more land and a knighthood out of Charles II, even though he had earlier served Cromwell faithfully. In Kerry he laid the foundations of the mining and smelting industries, encouraged fishing, and founded the enormous Lansdowne estate, which once surrounded the town; many buildings still remain today.

Evidence of much more ancient settlement is the fifteen-stone **stone circle** just outside the centre of town on the banks of the river; go up by the right of the market house that faces the park, past some Lansdowne estate houses. Walk up the lane at the cul-de-sac sign, and a few yards after it meets another lane coming in from the left you'll find the circle, behind a high ditch.

Kenmare practicalities

Kenmare has two independent **hostels**: the rather offputtingly clinical *Fáilte* in Henry Street (☎064/41083; £5, private rooms £6), and the ramshackle, disorganised *Kenmare Private Hostel* (☎064/41260; £5). There are also plenty of **B&Bs**, both in and just outside town; check vacancies at the **tourist office** on Main Street (☎064/41233; June–Sept). Mrs Hayes' *Ceann Mara* (☎064/41260; £14), on the outskirts of town, serves organically grown food. As for other **meals**, *The Pantry*, at 30 Henry Street, has a stock of wholefoods and healthfoods, plus organic vegetables and a wonderful range of unpasteurised cheeses; the *Dunboy Café*, at no. 16 opposite, lets you taste them in more comfort. *Án Leáth Phingin*, 35 Main Street (☎064/41559), in an old house with stone walls, wooden tables and a turf fire (burning even in June), is an excellent – though not cheap – Italian-Irish restaurant, with good seafood, and plenty of choice for vegetarians. *The Ivy Leaf*, also in Main Street (☎064/41589) specialises in fish and vegetable dishes. Kenmare's famous *Park Hotel* (☎064/41200; £84–120, just so you know) at the top of the main street, is also worth investigating, if only for a drink, despite the intimidating number of BMWs and Mercedes parked in the driveway.

The Beara Peninsula

Cross the river from Kenmare and you're on the **Beara Peninsula**, which Kerry shares with Cork. Beara has its followers, but after the wildness of the rest of Kerry, it can at first seem over-lush and polite, with more of the flavour of Cork. Even along the Kenmare river, though, the scenery is attractive enough and curiously, once you actually cross into County Cork, the Beara becomes far wilder (see p.253).

Turn right after the bridge, and the road runs through heavily wooded country alongside the Kenmare estuary, with a signpost to the left for **Inchiquin Lake** a few miles later. Following this, you soon quit the luxuriant vegetation as the bumpy road ascends rapidly to the lake, giving exhilarating views of the countryside left behind. A waterfall tumbles down from a second lake, and on the far side of Inchiquin Lake is **Uragh Wood**, one of the last surviving remnants of the ancient sessile oakwoods that once covered most of Ireland. The entire valley is packed with **plants**: large-flowered butterwort covers the meadows in spring, and you can find Irish spurge, saxifrage, arbutus and other flora specific to the southwest. At the lake itself, the surrounding hills seem to act as some kind of intensifier focussed on a tiny stone circle by the side of the water – bringing to mind the theory that these prehistoric monuments indicate earth forces. There's salmon, sea trout and brown trout fishing in both lakes, but, as always, check the licence position before you start.

Lauragh

Following the main road for **LAURAGH**, you're still in the enormous estate once owned by Petty. The gardens at **Derreen House**, for a long time one of the Irish residences of Petty's descendant the Marquess of Lansdowne, are open to the public, and stocked with plants that clearly luxuriate in the mild sea climate, including such exotica as tree ferns and bamboo, plus rhododendrons and camellias. Yet despite its magnificence, it doesn't compare with the wild and windswept grassy uplands. Head westwards from Lauragh, and you're soon over the border into Cork; south, the road climbs spectacularly above Glanmore Lough to Healy Pass – again, the county border – giving amazing views in both directions. There's an *An Óige* **hostel** up here (☎064/83181; June–Sept £4.50; April and May £3.50; closed winter).

DINGLE AND THE NORTH

In common with the rest of the far west, particularly the Gaelic-speaking areas, the **Dingle Peninsula** has almost fallen victim to its own romance. It's as if it has been telling stories about itself for so long that it has come to believe them: the remoteness and beauty, the hard life and poverty and, above all in the *Gaeltacht* areas, the language have all lent fuel to easy romanticising, creating the modern chocolate-box, almost mythologised picture of the west. In Dingle's case, the myth is strengthened by its location on the extreme western seaboard of Europe, its numerous early Christian remains, the wealth of Gaelic literature created on the now uninhabited Blasket Islands – and the fact that *Ryan's Daughter* and, in 1991, parts of "Far and Away", a new film starring Tom Cruise, were filmed here. Concern about the peninsula's reputation for fey other-worldliness is such that the local paper has found it necessary to assure Irish visitors that there are actually real night spots here.

All the same, a great nightlife is not the reason to visit this region. True, there are plenty of pubs in **Dingle town** – a small place reputed to have 52 of them – and lots of traditional music, perhaps even a *ceilí*. The town has been fortunate in only realising its tourist potential in the past few years; while Killarney is stuck with its tacky souvenir shops and pubs, Dingle has done an altogether more elegant job, mixing traditional places and new seafood restaurants.

But Dingle really scores with its **landscape** and antiquities. The former is spectacular, dominated by the 2627-foot **Stradbally Mountain**, while west of Dingle town lies a Gaelic-speaking region, strongly resonant of its history. Dingle also has probably the greatest concentration of Celtic monastic, and older, **ruins** outside the Aran Islands. On a fine day it can be exhilarating, with views out as far as the monastic settlement on Great Skellig, off the Iveragh peninsula; but it's more exciting still in the **rain**, when the cloud shifts down over the land and you find yourself in a white mist through which the dim shapes of oratories and beehive huts loom mysteriously.

Heading for Dingle: Milltown and Inch

Though most of the peninsula's delights are to the west of Dingle town, there are a few notable stopping points on the way, especially if you're cycling from Killarney. There's a magnificent ride taking the right fork at Aghadoe (where the youth hostel is); for the entire stretch up to Milltown, the very minor road offers wonderful views of the almost unreal looking MacGillycuddy's Reeks, to your left. At **MILLTOWN**, if you're exhausted already, there's an independent **hostel** in the Square (*Woods Hostel*; ☎066/67301; Easter–Oct; £5; camping). Otherwise, push on past Castlemaine Harbour and set out along the straight road beside the peninsula's edge, a seemingly endless ride if you're cycling against the wind.

THE DINGLE PENINSULA

To Killarny

Tralee

Ardfert

Barna Strand

Tralee Bay

Castlegregory

Slieve Mish Mountains

Castlemaine

Milltown

Killorglin

Castlemaine Harbour

Inch

Inch

Dingle Bay

Beenoskee 825 m

Anascaul

Brandon

Connor Pass

Lispole

Brandon Mountain 951 m

+ Gallarus Oratory

Dingle

Ballydavid

Milltown

Ventry

Smerwick

Ballyferriter

Dunquin

Dunmore Head

Slea Head

Inishtooskert

Blasket Islands

Great Blasket Island

Inishnabro

Inishvickillane

10 km

0

At **INCH** there's a break in the shoreline where a long, narrow sand-bar pushes out into Dingle Bay. Good bucket-and-spade territory when the weather's fine, its shifting dunes seem once to have been a place of Iron Age settlement. Inch also provides somewhere to **stay** before Dingle: high above the bay at Inch Heights, *Lios Dana*, the *Natural Living and Healing Centre* (☎066/58189; phone ahead), also has a B&B, and serves macrobiotic, vegan and vegetarian food. Anne Hyland, who also owns the restaurant in Anascaul, below, runs classes in relaxation, yoga, art and shiatsu. There are a couple of regular B&Bs, too, if all you're after is a bed for the night.

Soon the road turns inland for **ANASCAUL** (*Abhainn an Scáil*) where *Anne's Kitchen*'s good vegetarian and vegan food is worth stopping for. The village itself is a single street of brightly painted houses, pleasant enough but with a curiously safe, inland feel considering the proximity of the wild Atlantic coast. There are two B&Bs: Mrs O'Connor's *Four Winds* (☎066/57168; £11) and Mrs Flahive's *Lake View*, Ballintarmon (☎066/57122; £12) If you're not in a hurry to press on to Dingle, head northwards to **Anascaul Lake**. A string of increasingly rough tracks will bring you to the lake, overshadowed by the scree slopes of Stradbally Mountain: a secret-seeming place, despite the "Scenic Car Park" sign, with plenty of wilder country beyond.

Dingle Town

Getting to **DINGLE** (*An Daingean*) is easy. The **bus** leaves from outside Killarney's railway station at 10.35am every day, and there's a more frequent service from Tralee. Once you're here, there's not a huge amount to see; but the town is a peculiarly pleasant place to stay, devoted to fishing and tourism, and certainly makes the best base for exploring the peninsula. Though crammed with pubs, little restaurants and B&Bs, Dingle somehow never feels too crowded, and even if you don't like the way the place has geared itself up for tourism, you'll be glad when the weather's bad – which it often is – that there are plenty of places to hole up.

Essentially just a few streets by the side of Dingle Bay, Dingle has a hugely impressive natural **harbour** where the boats come in and **Fungi the dolphin** likes to play. Half-tame, Fungi is one of Dingle's main tourist attractions. It may sound silly, but there are people who talk of their meetings with this solitary, 300kg, maritime mammal in the terms of a religious conversion, and others travel hundreds of miles just to meet him (enquire at the tourist office about boats).

The solidity of the town's colour-washed houses suggests this was a place of some consequence, and Dingle was indeed Kerry's leading port in the fourteenth and fifteenth centuries. It later became a centre for smuggling, and at one stage during the eighteenth century (when the revenue from smuggling was at its height) even minted its own coinage. Contemporary reports describe the stone houses with balconies and oval windows, imparting a Spanish feel to the town. In the nineteenth century, Dingle was the focus of a uniquely successful attempt to woo the Kerry Catholics from their faith, when in 1831 the Protestant curate T. Goodman began preaching in Irish, establishing schools on the peninsula, and building houses as inducements for converts; these still stand at the edge of town.

Rooms and food

There's no shortage of **accommodation**, although a lot of Dingle's B&Bs are fairly pricey; the **tourist office** in Main Street (☎066/51188; July–Aug Mon–Sat 10am–7pm; June & Sept 10am–6pm) has an accommodation service. The handiest place to look for a central B&B is Dykegate Street, where there are several (try Mrs O'Connor's, for example: ☎066/51598; £13); *Doyle's* excellent restaurant (see below) also takes guests (☎066/51222 or 51476; £28). For standard old-fashioned hotel comfort, try *Benners Hotel* on Main Street (☎066/51638: £32–36). The *Westlodge/Westgate Hostel* (☎066/51476; £4.50, camping £2), just out of town on the Ventry road (turn right at the fish factory), is very basic, but has a common room with a coal stove and a big round table built for conversation. *Lovett's Hostel* (£4.50), opposite Moran's Garage on the other side of town, is more central but smaller – and since it has no phone you can't be sure of finding space. If both these independent hostels are full, you could try the *Seacrest Hostel* in Lispole, a few miles east, overlooking cliffs and beach (☎066/51390; £4, family rooms £5, camping £3; free pick-up from Dingle; mountain bike rental £3.50 a day; shop).

All of Dingle's **restaurants**, from the cheapest to decidedly expense-account places, serve excellent fresh seafood, landed just a few hundred yards away. The best way to find them is just to wander around and look; but *Greaney's*, on the corner of Dykegate and Strand Street, does good cheap lunches and dinners. *Éirí na Gréine* (the *Rising Sun*) in Lower Main Street is a useful place to get a packed lunch if you're going to spend the day cycling or walking, and also has sandwiches and tasty vegetarian meals. Moving upmarket, *Doyle's Seafood* (☎066/51174) in John Street is the best-known restaurant locally, and pioneered haute cuisine in Dingle. The often miraculous dishes are expensive, but worth it, in the evenings; there's cheaper bar food at lunch time.

For daytime, and for getting away from the weather if it rains, there's no better place than Dingle's truly excellent bookshop-café, *An Cafe Liteartha*, off Main Street. You can browse through the shelves (politics and local interest sections are especially good), tuck into home baking and soups, read the papers, and listen to the mingled sounds of rain and conversation in Gaelic and English. A more recent imitator is *The Island Man* bookstore and café, on Main Street (open until 10 at night; lunches at around £3, dinners more expensive).

Entertainment and bicycles

Life in the evenings is centred on Dingle's **pubs**, which between them offer **traditional music sessions** on just about any night you choose. *O'Flaherty's* in Bridge Street is a good place to start, with music most nights, or advice on where to find it somewhere else. *Mrs Nelligan's Pub* on Lower Main Street also has traditional music, in a slightly more staid setting, or try *Murphys* or the *Star Inn*, in Strand Street, for Friday or Saturday night revels with **dancing**.

Bikes are available for hire from *Moriarty's* in Main Street (☎066/51316), which participates in the *Raleigh* Rent-a-Bike scheme and has mountain bikes: useful on the punishing Conor Pass. *Paddy's* in Dykegate Street and *O'Sullivan's* in Strand Street also hire out bikes. **Special events** in Dingle include the mid-July cultural festival, *Dúchas An Daingin*; the Dingle Races in early August (well worth seeing); and the Dingle Regatta later in the month. See the tourist office for details.

West of Dingle

Unlike some *Gaeltacht* areas, the Gaelic-speaking area west of Dingle doesn't blow its own trumpet, and it's probably best not to expect too much of a linguistic experience. You may never hear a word of Gaelic spoken, and any written Gaelic is more likely to come from the stalwart Sixties relics who've established potteries and tea shops in the remotest parts of the peninsula than from native Gaelic speakers. But all around you, written into the wild landscape, are the relics of the **ancient Gaelic culture**. Ring forts, beehive huts, oratories and stone crosses are more prevalent here than almost anywhere else in Ireland; and the vigour of the Christian culture that set out from here to evangelise and educate the rest of Europe is almost palpable*.

Cycling around Dingle, you can put your bike in a ditch and take off up the mountainside to explore local beehive huts (a useful map of the local antiquities can be had from the tourist office for 50p); arm yourself with proper rain gear, and bad weather ceases to be a problem. **Buses** for Dunquin and Slea Head leave Dingle at 12.30pm every day, with additional services at 9am and 1pm on Mondays and Thursdays.

Towards Slea Head

The next town after Dingle is **VENTRY** (*Ceann Trá*), once the main port of the peninsula, and another fine natural harbour: a wide curve of sandy beach supporting a few houses, shops and a pub. Beyond it looms the enormous, gnarled shoulder of **Mount Eagle**, dropping almost sheer to the sea with only a precarious ledge for the road. It's in these inhospitable surroundings on the stretch out to Slea Head that the main concentration of **ancient monuments** can be found. What follows here can only be an introduction to the major sites; the minor ones alone could take weeks to explore. A good local **map**, such as the one available at the tourist office, is essential, while several excellent guides to the peninsula exist for real enthusiasts (available at bookshops in Dingle town).

First off there's the spectacular **Dún Beag**, a scramble down from the road towards the ocean about four miles out from Ventry (entry 75p). A promontory fort, its defences include four earthen rings, with an underground escape route, or souterrain, by the main entrance. It's a magical location, overlooking the open sea and the Iveragh Peninsula, its dramatic suitability to the setting only increased by the fact that some of the building has fallen off into the sea.

Between Dún Beag and Slea Head the hillside above the road is studded with stone beehive huts, cave dwellings, souterrains, forts, churches, standing

---

*This culture is vividly brought to life in Penguin's *A Celtic Miscellany*, a collection of epigrams, nature poems, satires and love poems translated into virile Gaelic idiom rather than the traditionally romantic Celtic twilight mode. "Pleasant to me is the glittering of the sun today upon these margins, because it flickers so", some ninth-century scribe noted in the margin of an illuminated manuscript; "Whether morning, whether evening, whether by land or by sea, though I know I shall die, alas, I know not when", runs a more sombre epigram, also of the ninth century; and a tiny example of the nature poetry of the same time goes, "Winter has come with scarcity, lakes have flooded their sides, frost crumbles the leaves, the merry wave begins to mutter". *An Cafe Liteartha* has copies.

stones and crosses – over 500 of them in all. The beehive huts can be deceptive – they were still being built and used for storing farm tools and produce until the late nineteenth century, so not all of them are as old as they look. But once you're standing among genuinely ancient buildings like the **Fahan group** (signposted, with a 50p admission charge) and looking south over a landscape that's remained essentially unchanged for centuries, the Iveragh Peninsula and (if they're not hidden by clouds) the two Skellig islands in the distance, you get a strong sense of past lives, with their unimaginable hopes and aspirations.

The Blasket Islands

At Slea Head the view opens up to include the desolate, splintered masses of the **Blasket Islands** (*Na Blascaodai*), uninhabited since 1953. The weather in Blasket Sound can be treacherous – two of the Armada's ships were shattered to matchwood when they came bowling round the head in September 1588 – but inhospitable as they seem, the islands were once the home of thriving communities. The astonishing body of **Gaelic literature** that emerged from these tiny islands (Maurice O'Sullivan's *Twenty Years A-Growing*, Peig Sayers's *Peig*, and Tomas O'Crohan's *Island Cross-Talk*) gives a vivid picture of the life of the islanders which, although remote, was anything but unsophisticated. Ironically, these literary works describe life among people who could neither read nor write; but their oral tradition emerges as far from primitive.

In the summer boats bound for **Great Blasket** (*An Blascaod Mór*) leave the pier just south of Dunquin every hour between 11am and 5pm (May–Sept in good weather; ☎066/56146, 56280; around £7 return). Whether or not you choose to stay over, Great Blasket's delights are simple ones: sitting on the beaches and staring out to sea, tramping the many footpaths that criss-cross the island, or trying to spot a seal. If you're staying, the island offers an amazing view of the sun sinking into the ocean; echoing the words of the Pogues' emigration song, *Thousands Are Sailing*: "This island that is silent now, but the ghosts still haunt the waves".

The comfortable **hostel** (☎066/56146; £9), in the house where Peig Sayers once lived, only sleeps ten, so it's best to telephone in advance. Bed and breakfast accommodation and free camping are also available, but there's no shop on the island, so you need to bring supplies. At the **café** (noon–5pm), overnighters can order good, cheap vegetarian dinners for around £5.

If the Blasket hostel is full, there's an *An Óige* one on the mainland a little further on at **DUNQUIN** (*Dún Chaoin*), with plenty of beds (☎066/56145; £5.90, under 18 £3.50; open all year); or **B&B** in the local *Kruger's* pub (☎066/56127; £13), where you may also come across some live music. The best place for daytime eating is the *Dunquin Pottery Café* (10am–8pm), with a spectacular view out across the Blaskets and, behind, a mass of mountain laced with a network of stone dykes.

Ballyferriter and Ballydavid

A couple of miles further round the headland, largely Irish-speaking **BALLYFERRITER** (*Baile an Fheirtearaigh*) can be bleak out of season, but in summer there are several cafés, plus a **heritage centre** (10.30am–6pm; £1, students 50p). The little northward lanes will lead you to impressive 500-foot hilltop walling at Sybil Head and the Three Sisters rock (with the Norman ruins of

Castle Sybil, built within an older promontory fort); or to Smerwick Harbour and **Dún an Óir**. In September 1580 at Dún an Óir (the Golden Fort), a band of Italian, Spanish, English and Irish supporters of the rebellion in Munster, backed by papal funds in support of Catholic Ireland against Protestant England, were defeated by the English. The rebels were massacred – men, women and children – as a warning to others; the poet Edmund Spenser participated in the indiscriminate slaughter.

At the other end of Smerwick Harbour lies **BALLYDAVID**, backed by the mass of Brandon Mountain and within easy reach of the cliffs at Ballydavid Head. **Brandon Creek**, just east of Ballydavid Head, is one of a number of contenders for Saint Brendan's sixth-century departure point, when he sailed off to discover the Islands of Paradise in the Western Ocean and, arguably, America.

Just outside Ballyferriter towards Ballydavid, on the strand at Muirioch, is a comfortable independent **hostel**, *Tigh an Phoist* (☎066/55109; £5, private rooms £6). In Ballyferriter itself the *Granville Hotel*, misleadingly marked *Ostan*, offers **rooms** of greater comfort (☎066/56116; £19.95–26.95, but enquire about special rates for longer stays): there are also several B&Bs, including *An Cat Dubh* (The Black Cat; ☎0667/56286; £9), just up the road from Smerwick Harbour, a café (9am–9pm) and supermarket that also does B&B; and near Ballydavid Mary uí Chíobain's *Ard na Carraige* (☎066/55295; £12.50) and the O'Gormain's *Caife na Mara*, Glaise Bheag (☎066/55162; £12).

Riasc, the Gallarus Oratory and Kilmakedar

A short way out of Ballyferriter – keep left on the main road, turn right over the bridge by a petrol pump, then right again – is the monastic site of **Riasc**. Recent excavation has revealed walls and foundations a few feet high, and the ruins evoke the early Christian monastery, dating from the tenth century.

The single most impressive early Christian monument on the Dingle peninsula, however, is the **Gallarus oratory**, a little further east. The most perfectly preserved of around twenty such oratories in Ireland, it looks almost too good to be true, though apparently it hasn't undergone any great restoration programmes. Though the oratory can't be dated with any great certainty, it's thought to have been built between the ninth and twelfth centuries (Christian architectural activity dates from the late sixth or early seventh century, but it wasn't until the ninth century that churches began to be built of stone rather than wood), and to represent a transition between the round beehive huts elsewhere on the peninsula and the later rectangular churches. The problem with this construction (and the reason why so many similar buildings have fallen down) is that the long sides tend to cave in – if you look carefully at the Gallarus oratory, you can see it's beginning to happen here too.

The next architectural stage can be seen a mile to the north in the rectangular church at **Kilmakedar**. Its nave dates from the mid-twelfth century, and the corbelled stone roof was a direct improvement on the structure at Gallarus. The site marks the beginning of the Saint's Road, dedicated to **Saint Brendan**, patron saint of Kerry, which leads to the top of Brandon Mountain – the route taken by pilgrims to Saint Brendan's shrine. If you want to follow this tough but historically resonant route up the mountainside, it's marked on the half-inch ordnance survey map. Alternatively, there's a marked route from the west beginning between Cloghane and Brandon.

Dingle's Interior

The interior of the Dingle Peninsula is dominated by two **mountains**, Brandon Mountain and Stradbally Mountain, separated by the steep **Conor Pass**. This mountainous terrain is excellent walking country: not only are there countless relics of the Celtic church and earlier to explore, but the area is dotted by a series of lakes that give the tussocky landscape some focus. There's an independent hostel at the foot of the pass on the northern side, the *Conor Pass Hostel* in Stradbally (☎066/39179; £5; open all year), from where it's also an easy journey to the good sandy beaches and swimming at Stradbally and Castlegregory.

Tralee

The main reason for being in **TRALEE** (*Trá Lí*) is that the train brings you here on your way to the rest of Kerry. It's a tatty, flyblown commercial town with nothing much to recommend it except the ways out: four buses a day go down the Dingle Peninsula every day except Sunday (when there's one).

Tralee is a point of orientation rather than somewhere to stay, and the helpful **tourist office** (☎066/21288; July–Aug Mon–Sat 9am–8pm, Sun 11am–3pm; May, June & Sept Mon–Sat 9am–6pm; Oct–April Mon, Tues, Thurs, Fri 9.30am–1pm & 2–5.30pm, Wed & Sat 9.30am–1pm) is in the Ashe Memorial Hall. If you do find yourself having to stay over, there are two **hostels** (as well as innumerable B&Bs): *Pitlochry* (☎066/23174; £5), a mile out of town at 31 Lisdara, just around the corner from a sports complex where you can swim, play tennis and so on, and *Drumtacker* (☎066/25209; £5), off the Listowel Road, another mile further out.

You can hire **bikes** in Tralee (though if you're headed for Dingle, it's a tough ride over the Conor Pass) from *J. Caball Himself* at Staughtons Row (☎066/ 21654), *Tralee Gas Supplies* in Strand Street (who also do mountain bikes, which may be useful; ☎066/22018); or Vincent O'Gorman in Ballydavid (☎066/55162). All these are part of the *Raleigh* Rent-A-Bike scheme.

Finding a cheap place to **eat** in Tralee isn't a problem – the town is full of them, though mostly pretty depressing. *Ruth's Wholefood Restaurant* is a daytime-only operation, with fresh spring-water from the owner's farm well supplied free. Another vegetarian restaurant, also daytime only, is *Bratts* in The Square. There are plenty of **pubs**, too; try *Kirby's Broque Inn* in Rock Street for jazz and traditional music, or *Crosty's*, in Castle Street. The **Folk Theatre of Ireland** has its home at the *Siamsa Tíre Theatre* in Godfrey Place, though their excellent performances don't draw the same crowds as the **Rose of Tralee International Festival**. Held in the last week of August, with much accompanying merriment, this is a beauty contest in which women, including foreigners who can demonstrate some credible Irish connection, compete for the dubious honour of Rose of Tralee. For those who are interested, details are available from the Festival Office in Lower Castle Street (☎066/21322).

Sights around Tralee

More worthy of your time than anything in Tralee itself is the ruined thirteenth-century cathedral at **ARDFERT**, five miles to the northwest. In a landscape littered with ruined ring forts, castles and churches, Ardfert was the site of a monastery founded by Saint Brendan in the seventh century, and later became the centre of the Anglo-Norman church in Kerry. There's also a Franciscan friary and two smaller, fifteenth-century churches.

It's also worth taking the road out to **Banna Strand** for the spectacular view over Tralee Bay, and its association with Sir Roger Casement, to whom there's a monument. In April 1916, on the eve of the Easter Uprising, Casement was captured by local police as he attempted to land at Banna Strand from a German submarine (see p.456 for more details). Tried and executed for high treason in 1916, his body was returned from England to Ireland in 1965 to be reinterred with full military honours. If you're driving, you can carry on round the cliffs of Kerry Head for more great vistas – south over Tralee Bay, north across the mouth of the Shannon.

North Kerry

This coastal road aside, **North Kerry** is unexciting – undulating farmland rolling up to the Shannon. The main road from Tralee heads up through **LISTOWEL**, a workaday Irish town that does, however, have a degree of literary distinction. In June it hosts a week-long **festival** of writers' workshops and meetings: Brian MacMahon, a local schoolteacher, is a strong proponent of the rigorous Irish short story tradition (for examples, try *The Sound of Hooves*, a recent volume of Kerry stories available locally). The time when Listowel – and surrounding places as far away as Tarbert and Ballybunnion – really come to life, however, is for the annual **Listowel races**, in the third week of September, when farming people from far and wide, their harvest in, take time off to eat, drink and lose money on the horses. There's plenty of accommodation here, ranging from the comfort of the *Listowel Arms* (☎068/21500; £21) to simpler B&Bs such as *The North Country House*, 67 Church Street (☎068/21238; £14), or Mrs Walsh's *Fairhill*, Cahirdown on the Tarbert road (☎068/21561; £13.50). Further advice from the **tourist office** (☎068/22590; June–Sept Mon–Sat 10am–6pm, Sun 11am–3pm).

From Listowel the main road continues to **TARBERT** on the Shannon estuary, and from there trails the river inland (through County Limerick) towards Limerick and Shannon Airport. Immediately north of Tarbert, the **car ferry** across the estuary provides a useful short cut into County Clare: there's no other river crossing west of Limerick (April–Sept Mon–Sat 7am–9.30pm, Sun 9am–9.30pm; Oct–March Mon–Sat 7am–7.30pm, Sun 10am–7.30pm; sailings every hour on the half-hour, return from Killimer on the hour; £6 single car, £8.50 return, £2 cycles; ☎065/51060).

Ballybunion and the Shannon Estuary

Turning aside at Listowel, **BALLYBUNION** lies about ten miles away on the coast at the mouth of the Shannon. It does have a kind of charm – it's the sort of sleepy resort that most people remember with a mixture of affection and horror from childhood holidays, and there are good sandy beaches – but unless you're beguiled by nostalgia you're unlikely to want to stay long. In addition to the complement of cheerful tat, pubs, and amusement arcades, two golf courses and the caves under the cliffs, provide something to occupy you if you do. A very faded notice on the wall of the *Atlantic Hotel* advertises roller disco. **B&Bs** in this holiday resort tend to be expensive (and full) in summer. A couple worth trying are *Invergordon*, Cliff Road (☎068/27246; £13) and *Doon House*, Doon Road (☎068/27411; £14), but you'll save a long walk around the *No Vacancy* signs by checking out possibilities first at the **tourist office** which operates in season out of a mobile caravan; check at the local post office for details of its whereabouts. They also have tourist information here.

If you've time to spare on your onward journey, you can allow yourself to be beguiled by the flatlands of the **Shannon estuary**, whose quiet plains are bathed in the oblique light of the west and dotted with monasteries and castles. The ruined fifteenth-century **Carrgafoyle Castle** rises miraculously from the water, joined to the land by a causeway; close by, a road separates two sheets of water, the land it's built on long since submerged.

Straight to Limerick: Castleisland

If getting to Limerick in a hurry is your main preoccupation, the faster route runs inland via Newcastle West. On this road **CASTLEISLAND** offers shops, and places to stop for a drink or a bite to eat. Nearby **Crag Cave** (July–Aug 10am–7pm, Mar–June & Sept–Nov 10am–6pm; £2.75, students £1.50; ☎066/41244) is an impressive limestone cave system extending a couple of miles undergound. If you're passing, the half-hour guided tour is enjoyable, with plenty of weirdly sculpted stalactites and stalagmites to keep you amused.

travel details

Trains

From Killarney to Tralee (4 daily; 35min); Cork (2; 1hr 45min); Dublin (2; 3hr).

Bus Éireann

From Killarney to Shannon Airport (summer only 1 daily; 3hr 10min); Tralee (2; 35min).
From Tralee to Limerick (3 daily; 2hr 20min); Cork (1; 2hr 30min).

Private buses

Funtrek (☎01/730852) runs one bus daily, two on Friday and Sunday, from Tralee, outside the *Brandon Hotel*, to Adare, Newcastlewest, Listowel, Killarney and Dublin.

CHAPTER NINE

CLARE

Physically, **County Clare** is clearly defined, with Galway Bay and the Shannon estuary to the north and south, massive Lough Derg forming its eastern boundary, and the Atlantic to the west. Strangely, although plenty of people visit, the county is sometimes glossed over by travellers as simply land between the magnificent scenery of Kerry and Galway. It's true that it doesn't have the scenic splendour of either of these and, for many, the north of the county is too bleak to be attractive. Nonetheless, Clare has a subtle flavour that, once tasted, can be addictive.

Clare is known as the "banner county", for its courageous political history, particularly in the fight for Catholic Emancipation; and the "singing county" for its strong musical traditions, which are still very much alive, and constitute a major reason for coming here. Both titles – the strong and the gentle – suggest something of the character of the place, and are echoed in the contrasts of the landscape.

The **Burren** heights in the north are startlingly stark and barren, while **Ennis**, the county's capital, is surrounded by low, rolling farmland. Fabulous cliff scenery stretches for miles round Clare's southern extreme at **Loop Head**, and is spectacularly sheer at the **Cliffs of Moher**, further north. In between are sandy

---

SHANNON AIRPORT

Arriving at **Shannon International Airport** – where Irish coffee was invented to placate stranded passengers – you're most likely to want to head for **Limerick**, barely fifteen miles away, for bus and train connections to just about anywhere in the country. **Ennis**, a similar distance, is also easily accessible, and a pleasant place to stop over if you're exhausted, plan to head north, or want to spend some time in County Clare.

Bus Éireann buses run to both towns: around 16 daily to Limerick (half-hourly in the morning, hourly in the afternoon, irregularly after 6pm; 45min; £4); slightly less frequently to Ennis. A taxi to either place will cost about £15.

The airport **tourist information office** (☎061/61664, 61565; May–Sept 6am–5.30pm daily; Oct–April Mon–Fri 6.30am–5.30pm, Sat & Sun 6.30am–4pm) is extremely helpful, and has full information on bus and train timetables and connections; they will also book accommodation for you for the usual small charge. There's also an **airport information desk**, right next to the tourist office, open to serve all flights: if there's no one there, pick up the phone and dial 0. The airport **bureau de change** is open every day from 7am until 5pm – though it sometimes closes early.

If all you want to do is find a bed for the night, the nearest **B&Bs** are a little over two miles away at Shannon Town: try Mrs Sheridan, 24 Dún an Óir, Tullyglass (☎061/362282; £12), Mrs Lohan, 35 Tullyglass Crescent (☎061/364268; £13); or marginally further away Mrs Moloney, 21 Coill Mhara (☎061/364185; £12) or Mrs Curran, *The Willow*, 18 Coill Mhara (☎061/364580; £11).

beaches and small seaside towns and villages. In the east, **Lough Derg** offers panoramic views across to the mountains of Tipperary from the slopes of the Slieve Bernagh and Slieve Aughtie mountains, and the opportunity for watersports.

This varied countryside holds plenty of specialist interest. The Burren is a major attraction for geology and botany enthusiasts, and is also rich in ring forts, dolmens and cairns in the north. The legacy of later communities is found throughout the county, in the thickly sprinkled medieval monastic remains, and tower houses of the O'Brien and MacNamara clans.

Ennis

The River Fergus, small and fast flowing, seems thoroughly in keeping as it runs through **ENNIS**, a bustling market town and the commercial capital of County Clare. You could easily see Ennis in a single afternoon – there are no towns of any size in the county – but it's worth staying longer if only for the plentiful traditional music.

The finest monument, **Ennis Friary**, lies right in the town's historic centre (guide/information service early June to mid-Sept 9.30am–6.30pm daily; at other times phone ☎065/29100; 80p, students 30p; heritage card). The Franciscan friary was founded by the O'Briens, Kings of Thomond, in 1242, but most of the existing building dates from the fourteenth century. At that time the Friary had 350 monks and over 600 pupils and was considered the finest educational institution in Ireland for the clergy and upper classes. In parts it remains striking: graceful lancet windows fill the east end of the chancel, while adjacent conventual buildings include cloister ruins and a stoutly barrel-vaulted sacristy or chapterhouse. There is much good sculpture too: look out for the small square carving on the jamb of the arch between the nave and transept, showing a half-length figure of Christ with his hands bound; the relief of St Francis with cross-staff and stigmata at the east end of the nave; and the carved corbels beneath the south tower showing the Virgin and child and an archbishop. The real sculptural highlight, however, is the fifteenth-century **MacMahon tomb** (now incorporated in the Creagh Tomb) which has fine alabaster carvings of the Passion.

Despite the beauty of the friary, Ennis today seems more proud of its later history, as capital of the unyielding "banner county" and a bastion of nationalism. A monument to **Daniel O'Connell** solidly dominates the old narrow streets that meet in **O'Connell Square**. In 1828 County Clare returned O'Connell to Westminster by such a huge majority that he had to be allowed to take his seat, despite the fact that he was a Catholic, which should have barred him at the time. He went on to force through parliament the Catholic Emancipation Act. It was in Ennis, too, that **Parnell** made his famous speech advocating the boycott in the land agitations of the late nineteenth century. **De Valera** was TD for the county from 1917 to 1959 (and *Taoiseach* for much of that time) and is remembered in a memorial outside the classical courthouse, and in the **De Valera Library Museum** on Harmony Row (Mon, Wed & Thurs 11am–5.30pm; Tues & Fri 11am–8pm; free), a small, local museum covering a history of national importance. Exhibits include an interesting collection of letters and telegraphs: from Daniel O'Connell seeking support in the forthcoming election; from De Valera while in prison expecting to be executed; from the Black and Tans threatening retribution for the kidnapping of two constables, and so on. The museum also houses a collection of weapons used by the Royal Irish Constabulary and the IRA and hosts changing exhibitions of modern Irish artists.

As for other things to search out, the town's status as a city demands that it has a **cathedral**, and a nineteenth-century building with a sharp spire stands icy and grey at the far end of O'Connell Street, at odds with this friendly town. More interesting is to wander the narrow, ancient lanes that run from O'Connell Street to the **old market place**, where a Saturday vegetable and livestock market is held.

Music

There's **music** throughout Ennis. Perhaps the best place to start is *Cois na hAbhann*, less than half a mile out on the Gort road (☎065/34158), a centre for local traditional music enthusiasts. Throughout the summer they have *Oíche Chéilí* and *Seisiún* evenings – both evenings of song and dance, though the latter is a more structured entertainment (July & Aug, Tues–Thurs; June & Sept, Thurs only; 9pm; around £3). These sessions also move around the county, so it's worth watching out elsewhere – tourist offices in the county have "What's On" information.

Ennis itself, for such a small town, has a surprising number of **bars** with traditional, cajun and rock sessions. For traditional Irish music try *Farrell's*, O'Connell Square (Mon & Thurs); *Brogan's*, O'Connell Street (Tues & Thurs); *The Old Ground Hotel*, O'Connell Street (Wed); or *P.J. Kelly's* in Carmody Street (Sat & Sun). *The Banner Arms* in Market Square is a lively place with rock, folk and cajun (Thurs–Sat) and *Patrick's Bar* in Market Street has traditional folk music and a fair amount of country and western. For the big name Irish bands and traditional music check out *Kearney's Bar* on Newbridge Road; for **pop** bands try *The West County Inn*, Clare Road, *Dilingers* in Market Street (Wed–Fri) and, one mile out on the Tulla Road, *Auburn Inn* (Wed–Fri). Obviously the crowd depends on the band, and it's really a matter of luck, but Ennis is so small you are unlikely to be hunting for long. For **discos** try *Queens Hotel*, Abbey Street (Thurs–Sun). There's also a **cinema** in Station Road.

Practicalities

There are direct bus connections between Ennis and **Shannon Airport** (same day arrival and departure enquiries, office hours, ☎061/61666; bookings ☎061/45556) thirteen miles away in the south of the county and the major airport on the west coast, with flights to Dublin, UK, Europe and the USA. If you're travelling by **train**, the nearest station is Limerick – there's a regular Ennis–Limerick bus service (1hr; 6 buses a day). **Bus Éireann** also run a service direct to Dublin on weekdays only, as well as a regular service to Galway (6 buses a day); see "Travel Details" for information.

There are plenty of **B&Bs** in the town centre, or you can book them through the **tourist office** which is just under a mile out on the Clare Road (☎065/28366; May–Sept daily 9am–6pm; winter Tues–Sat 9.30am–1pm & 2–5.30pm). Good possibilities include *Derrynane House*, O'Connell Square (☎065/28464; £14), *Woodquay House*, Woodquay, off Parnell Street (☎065/28320; £12) and *Ardlea House*, Clare Road (☎065/20256; £12.50); the *Old Ground Hotel*, O'Connell Street (☎065/28127; £40) is a friendly upmarket alternative. The cheapest place to stay in Ennis is the *Abbey Tourist Hostel* (☎065/22620; £4.95, doubles same price), beautifully run and situated just across the bridge from the Friary. *Walnut House* hostel (☎065/28956; B&B £8; double rooms from £5; bikes for hire; laundry facilities) is a much more basic alternative, found just over the traffic lights at the cathedral end of O'Connell Street. You can also **hire bikes** from *Michael Tierney*, 17 Abbey Street (☎065/29433; £7 a day, £30 a week). There's a **launderette** in Lower Market Street (Mon–Sat 9am–6pm). Alternative tourist information, including **what's on** around town, can be found more centrally at *Upstairs, Downstairs* (9am–9pm, daily), a gift shop on O'Connell Square.

For budget daytime **meals**, plenty of pubs serve decent food, but if lunchtime pubbing puts too much strain on your wallet, you have the choice of a couple of snack and salad bars in Parnell Street: try *Maison Neuve* (Mon–Sat 8am–6pm) or *Bewley's Coffee Shop*, in Bank Place, off O'Connell Square, which serves cheap light lunches and excellent coffee. The best hearty breakfast or lunch in Ennis is to be found in *The Sherwood Inn* in the new shopping centre (follow the lane beside *The Queen's Hotel* and look out for *Quinnsworth* – it's in there; open till 6pm, till 9pm Thurs & Fri). In the evening your choices are limited: the *O'Connell Bar Restaurant* serves meals from £3–6 (Mon–Sat lunchtime & 6pm–9pm). Other reliable late servers are *The Silver House* Chinese takeaway and restaurant in O'Connell St, from £5, and a chip shop in Lower Market Street, open until midnight. *Prince Dragon*, Lower Market Street, is a little dearer but worth it.

If you intend to visit a number of the region's **museums and castles**, it may be worth getting a *Shannon Heritage Trail Ticket* (£5.50, students £3, available from tourist offices), which gives free entrance to Bunratty Castle and Folk Park; O'Brien's Tower, Cliffs of Moher; Dunguaire Castle, Kinvarra; The Hunt Museum, University College Limerick; The Craggaunowen Project; Knappogue Castle; and Lough Gur Stone Age Centre.

Around Ennis

Ennis sits in a low-lying strip of land that runs from a deep inlet of the Shannon River right up to South Galway. To the east of the town are lush fields edged by white-grey walls and clumps of wild flowers: pinks, purples and yellows of willow herb and ragwort, the strong white horns of bindweed, and even the occasional orchid. Further out, the land breaks into little lakes and rivers before becoming gently hilly to meet the Slieve Bernagh mountains. This gentle farmland makes for easy cycling, and your trip can be punctuated by village pubs, and plenty of church ruins and castles.

East: Quin, Knappogue and Craggaunowen

One of the most pleasant rides eastward is to **Quin Abbey**, the area's best-preserved Franciscan friary, founded in 1433. The main church building is graceful, its slender tower rising clear over the high, open archway between chancel and nave, and making a distinct outline against the green of the surrounding pastures. Climb up a floor to the first storey, and you can look down on the Abbey's complete cloister that has not only the usual arches, but also slim buttresses. For all the uplifting beauty of the tower, the Abbey seems to be built on a human scale, to function as a place in which to live and worship rather than to impress and dominate.

On the other hand, the massy walls of **Knappogue Castle** emanate an awesome sense of power. Leave Quin and continue two miles south on the L31 to reach this huge sixteenth-century tower house (May–Oct daily 9.30am–5.30pm; £2.40, students £1.20; ☎061/71103). It was originally built by the Macnamaras, but they lost it to Cromwell, who then used it as his HQ – thereby, no doubt, saving it from the major damage he inflicted elsewhere. At the Restoration the Macnamaras managed to regain ownership of the castle, and hung on to it until 1800. It's been beautifully restored, and inside are boldly carved sixteenth-century oak fireplaces and stout oak furniture. At odds with the overall flavour of Knappogue, the nineteenth-century domestic additions are furnished as if eighteenth-century rooms, beautifully appointed with Irish Chippendale furniture and Waterford crystal. The main body of the castle is used for medieval banquets.

The Craggaunowen Project

The second left turning, two miles south of Knappogue, brings you to the **Craggaunowen Project**, tucked on the edge of a reedy lake under a wooded hillside (May–Oct daily 10am–last admission 5pm; £2.40, students £1.50). This is based around another fortified tower house, the ground floor of which houses a collection of sixteenth-century European wood carvings. The project itself aims to recreate a sense of Ireland's ancient history, with reconstructions of earlier forms of homes and farmsteads; a ring fort and a *crannóg*, for example. Young workers experiment with old craft techniques, using replicas of wooden lathes, kilns and other traditional methods, and double up as guides if asked.

The most adventurous and certainly the most famous of the working replicas here is Tim Severin's **Brendan**, a leather-hulled boat in which he and four crew successfully sailed across the Atlantic in 1976, to prove that the legend of Saint Brendan could be true. Saint Brendan's story – he was supposedly the first man to discover America – is recorded in a ninth-century manuscript, and the design of the *Brendan* is based on its descriptions, along with the features of curraghs still used off Ireland's west coast. The result is a remarkable vessel of oak-tanned oxhides stretched over an ash-wood frame. Craggaunowen is also the site of an actual **Iron Age road**, excavated at Corlea Bog, County Longford and moved to the site. Made of large oak planks placed across runners of birch or alder, it must have formed part of an important route across difficult bog. For refreshment, there's also a nice **tea shop** here, which serves delicious homemade cakes.

Eight miles beyond Craggaunowen, the village of **CRATLOE** is renowned for its oak-wooded hills overlooking the Shannon and Fergus estuaries, and is a particularly lovely spot for walking.

Bunratty

BUNRATTY lies right on the N18 Limerick–Ennis road – very handy for tour buses and inevitably very touristy. **Bunratty Castle** (daily 9.30am–last admission 4.15pm; Folk Park open until 7pm during July & Aug; adults £3.50, students £1.70; ☎061/361511) stands on what was once an island on the north bank of the Shannon. The Vikings of Limerick recognised the site's strategic importance for protecting trade, and so they fortified it – you can still see the moat. The first actual castle on the site was built by Normans, but they lost control and, in 1460, the Macnamaras built the castle that stands today. The exceptionally fine rectangular keep has been perfectly restored and now houses a large collection of furniture, tapestries, paintings and ornate carvings from all over Europe, spanning the fourteenth to the seventeenth century. In the castle grounds, **Bunratty Folk Park** is a complete reconstruction of a nineteenth-century village. In rural Ireland this hardly seems necessary, though you can watch people engaged in traditional crafts. The nearby *Durty Nellies* is a favourite tourist bar, regularly overrun by coach parties.

North: Dysert O'Dea and Corofin

Alternative routes from Ennis can take you north through low-lying country fretted with rush-bordered lakes. Seven miles north is **Dysert O'Dea**: take the Ennistymon road out of Ennis, after two miles take the right fork for Corofin, and it's up a road to the left. Dysert O'Dea is the site of the ancient monastic foundation of Saint Tola (d. 737), and was the scene of an important battle in 1318 when the O'Briens defeated the de Clares of Bunratty, thus preventing the Anglo-Norman takeover of Clare. There are remains of a Romanesque church (twelfth–thirteenth-century) with a richly carved south doorway and grotesque carvings of animal heads and human faces. Nearby is the base of a round tower and the twelfth-century *White Cross of Tola*, with carvings of Christ and a bishop in high relief, Daniel in the lion's den, and other intricate patterning. The **O'Dea Castle** nearby is a museum and archaeology centre (May–Sept daily 10am–7pm; £1.50).

COROFIN lies at the heart of the abundance of little lakes that wriggle their way north of here, their banks dotted with ruined O'Brien strongholds. The area offers good fishing and tranquil cycling, disturbed only by the wind scything its way through squeaky bullrushes, reeds and yellow water irises. The new *Corofin Village Hostel* (☎065/27683; dorms £5, private rooms £6, family rooms £20; camping £2.50; bike hire £5; rowing boat on Inchiquin lake £7 daily; laundry facilities) is a friendly, family-run place, very clean, dry and warm, and an excellent stop en route for the Burren. There is little to the village beyond a handful of houses, but there is a *Teach Cheoil* (music house) in the main street where traditional music is dished up with tea and brown bread in a pleasantly relaxed atmosphere (Thurs, July & Aug; £2; ☎065/27955). The village also boasts the **Clare Heritage Centre** (March–Oct daily 10am–6pm, other times by appointment) which portrays the traumatic period of Irish history between 1800 and 1860, and fills in the horrors that the Bunratty Folk Park omits: famine, disease, emigration and the issue of land tenure.

TRACING YOUR ROOTS

The Clare Heritage Centre has a genealogy service for those with origins in the county, holding details of around 2500 famililies – McMahon, Macnamara, Moloney and O'Brien being the most common names. If you want to research your roots in detail write to the centre a few months *before* your trip (they get especially busy here in July and August) and find out as much as possible before you visit (names, dates, marriages, deaths, location, occupation, parish etc). The more prepared you are, the more detailed the research the centre can do. An initial search costs £40, a full one £100. Alternatively the new library here is freely available: a morning spent poring over records will probably convince you just why it's worth paying a trained genealogist to do it for you!

Lough Derg

The west bank of **Lough Derg** is a seam of beautiful countryside set between bald, boggy mountains and the great expanse of the lake. It forms the county's eastern boundary and, isolated by the empty heights of the Slieve Bernagh and the Slieve Aughtie mountains, has a different character from the rest of Clare. The waterway's wealth of fish and bird life, and the quaint villages on either shore, have long made Lough Derg popular with a wealthy Lough-cruising set, whose exclusive brand of tourism means villages are fairly conservative and well-kept. The hunting, shooting and fishing crowd are well catered for, and tend to dominate the character of local pubs; but there are also pockets renowned for their traditional music sessions, attracting predominantly local crowds.

The main road north varies the scene, at times clinging to the lakeshore, at others gaining higher ground and panoramic views over the lough, its islands, and the mountains of Tipperary. It connects Portumna, County Galway, at the head of the Lough, with Killaloe at its southerly tip (both historic, picturesque towns), and laces together a handful of choice little villages.

How to go and where to stay

Access to the area is via Limerick or Portumna. *Bus Éireann* run at least one **bus** daily from Limerick to Killaloe, Tuamgraney, Scarriff and into the hills to Feakle. For timetable information phone Limerick ☎061/42433. Journeys along the shore north of Scarriff involve **hitching** or **cycling**, though this isn't such a good idea in the Slieve Bernagh and Slieve Aughtie mountains to the west. Here roads are empty, making hitching impossible, and deceptively steep and unsheltered, making cycling tough. You can **hire bikes** from *Guerins* (Mountshannon) for £3 a day, £18 a week.

The area has been opened up to the budget traveller by the *Lakeside Watersport Hostel and Caravan and Camping Park*, Mountshannon (☎065/27225): take the road north out of Mountshannon and it's the first turning off to the right. The **hostel** is open all year: accommodation is in caravans and chalets beside the lake, costs £4–5 and family rooms are available. Camping costs £4 per tent plus 50p per person; camping gaz is sold. The hostel is a great place for **watersports**; there is no need to book, and it's all very reasonably priced, with canoe hire £3, windsurf hire £5 per hour, rowing boat £4 a day, sailing boat £11 per day, motor boat £12 per day, and waterskiing £20 per hour.

Killaloe

At **KILLALOE** the Shannon narrows again after the Lough for the final stretch of this great river's journey to the sea. An old stone bridge still spans the waters at this traditional crossing point. The old part of Killaloe focuses around **St Flannan's Cathedral**, and the narrow lanes that run up the steep slopes to the west suggest the town's ancient origins. The Cathedral itself is a plain thirteenth-century building, impressive in its solid simplicity, with a low square tower, and straight, strong buttresses. Just inside the entrance is a heavily decorated Romanesque doorway from an earlier church, and alongside it the huge **Thorgrim Stone**, unique in its *ogham* and runic inscriptions (*ogham* is a form of the Latin alphabet associated with early Christianity, the runic forms are Scandinavian in origin), which is probably the memorial of a Viking convert. In the churchyard the stout, solid Romanesque **St Flannan's Oratory** dates from the twelfth century, and is complete with barrel-vaulted roof. Just over a mile north of town on the western shore of Lough Derg, **Beal Boru** is an earthen fort and possibly the site of Brian Boru's palace "Kincora", which was either here or in Killaloe itself.

Despite being a great spot for watersports, and popular with Lough cruisers and day-trippers from Limerick, Killaloe can offer only a handful of places to **eat**. *Morgan's Lounge*, in the eastern half of town, does pub grub at any time during the summer months, and *Patsy's* takeaway, on the same side of the bridge, is open till late daily throughout the year. The *Lakeside Hotel* serves snacks and sandwiches at any time – if you can't afford their restaurant it's uninspiring, but a haven of warmth and convenience. Nearby, upmarket *Peter's Restaurant* specialises in seafood. Across the bridge, up the hill opposite the Cathedral, *Morrissey's Piano Bar* serves food from noon, Monday to Saturday. If you want to **stay**, several B&Bs offer an alternative to the luxury of the *Lakeside Hotel* (☎061/376122; £25–30) – try Mrs Keogh's *Lakeside House* (☎061/376292; £12). For others, and help with booking, check at the **tourist information office** (Lock House, The Bridge; ☎061/376866; June to mid-Sept daily 10am–6pm).

Killaloe is not the best spot for **music**, but you can be lucky: *Sean Achaoi* in Bridge Street (west of the bridge) sometimes has traditional sessions and ballads at weekends; *The Anchor Inn* has a mixture of music – pop, traditional, ballads – on Saturday and Sunday, and an Irish Night on Wednesday with set dancing. Over the bridge in County Tipperary, *Morgan's Lounge* works hard to cater for the Limerick crowd with a mixture of folk and rock on Saturday and Sunday, and usually something on a couple of nights during the week in summer. Finally, the *Lakeside Hotel* has ballad and folk sessions on Saturday.

The West Bank

The villages along the scenic road north are all very small. Wealthy tourists into hunting, shooting and fishing tend to stay in fancy hotels, and amenities for other visitors are sparse – even campsites here cost above the average rate.

The best spot to stay, Killaloe and Portumna aside, is **MOUNTSHANNON**. It's amongst the prettiest of the villages and has a couple of cosy pubs-cum-grocery shops with music in the summer, a restaurant, and a hostel (see "How to go and where to stay" above), as well as the upmarket *Mountshannon Hotel* (☎0619/27162; £25) and a couple of tiny B&Bs. You can **hire bikes** and buy camping Gaz at *Guerins* grocery shop (daily until 7pm), and there's a safe swimming area at the lakeshore. From Mountshannon, too, you can take a boat to **Holy Island**, where there are ruins of a monastic settlement dating from the seventh to the thirteenth centuries.

North of Mountshannon, the beauty of the scenery fades as the main road leaves the lakeshore, and the mountains to the west become less dramatic. **WHITEGATE** is tiny, and dominated by a handful of bars. *Kate and Paddy's* is a friendly place catering for the hurling and hunting crowd, and offering traditional food – Irish stew, bacon and cabbage – at any time in the summer, plus occasional country and western and traditional sessions.

South of Mountshannon, **SCARRIFF** is a little farming town set high in rough, open country overlooking the lough. It's a handy place to pick up provisions, and the *Clare Lakelands Hotel* serves very good seafood and hot lunches daily from

£4. The hotel bar has music three or four nights a week from Easter to September, a mixture of country and western and traditional, plus discos on Saturday and Sunday. *O'Beirne's Cafe* also does good seafood and salads. *The Merriman Inn* serves midday pub lunches, and has traditional music in the summer. There's a *Bank of Ireland* here, open until 5pm on Mondays, and the *Allied Irish Bank* opens at *Melody's Pub* on Monday and Thursday (10am–12.30pm & 1.30–3pm). There's a **drycleaners and laundry** at *Hogan's*, Feakle Street. In nearby TUAMGRANEY, little more than a hamlet, *Hassett's Lounge* regularly has a variety of entertainers.

Clare's South Coast

The south coast of the county has glorious sandy beaches, stunning cliff scenery and a couple of popular family holiday resorts. Inland doesn't look so promising. Southwest from Ennis the country flattens out and becomes scrubby and barren: bog, marsh, the odd bit of cotton grass here, the occasional lump of thistles there, with only sporadic pockets of cultivated land. The bald flank of Slievecallan is to the north, and the outline of the Kerry hills to the south across the Shannon.

Kilrush and Scattery Island

At present, the best reason to stop in Kilrush is for a trip across the broad Shannon estuary to **SCATTERY ISLAND** – before it gets spruced up for mass consumption. Scattery was last inhabited in the late 1970s, and as you land the quay before you is dotted with overgrown, derelict cottages. Walking up the lanes, spongy with moss and bracken, you disturb the burrows the island is now riddled with, and rabbits pop out madly all over the place. Saint Senan founded a **monastery** here in the sixth century, and at one time there were seven monastic settlements. The community suffered greatly from Viking raids, but there are still the remains of several churches dating from between the ninth and the fifteenth century.

Wherever you wander on Scattery, you get the feeling of stepping back into a timeless past, a mythical world protected by its isolation in the Shannon estuary. But Scattery's most impressive feature has to be the **round tower**, perfect in form, the stone made a warm mustardy yellow by the lichen that covers it. Unusually for a round tower, the doorway here is at ground level (they were usually high up, reached by a ladder that could be withdrawn to make the tower impregnable). **Access** to the island is by small boat: in summer call down by the marina; if there is no one there either ask the tourist office to arrange a trip for you, phone Martin Brennan (☎065/52031) or make enquiries on ☎065/52133; the return trip costs around £2.50.

At the moment **KILRUSH** itself boasts traditional **Horse Fairs** in March, June, October and November, but the character of the place is changing rapidly. What was a muddy, tidal harbour is now a fine marina, the main thrust of the town's bid for the upmarket tourist trade, and in the **market square**, a statue of the Maid of Éireann (see box) looks resolutely down the broad main street to the quayside where it's all going to happen. Off to the right in Toler Street, the spacious **Saint Senan's Catholic church** is worth looking in for the Harry Clarke stained glass windows.

THE MANCHESTER MARTYRS

Statues of the Maid of Éireann, commemorating the **Manchester Martyrs**, are scattered around Ireland. In Manchester in 1867 a band of Fenians blew open the back of a Black Maria in an attempt to rescue some of their leaders, who had been arrested after an armed uprising. A police sergeant was killed in the explosion, and three Fenians were hanged as a result. The executions provoked demonstrations throughout England and Ireland, since many considered the sergeant's death to have been an accident and the trials rigged: these monuments are testimony to the strength of those feelings.

Practicalities

Local businesses, hotels, B&Bs and pubs are preparing for big changes, and behind the traditional facades, rooms are being assiduously upgraded. All this means that you can currently get high quality accommodation and **food** at reasonable prices. Particularly good seafood is available daily during summer at *Kelly's Bar*, Henry Street, from around £5, and in the evenings there's an *à la carte* restaurant upstairs. *The Haven Arms* in Henry Street also has good bar snacks. *Ryan's Deli*, Henry Street, does homemade pizzas, burgers and tacos, Monday to Saturday, 10am to 6pm.

The **tourist office** in the town hall in the main square (June–Aug Mon–Wed & Fri 10am–1pm & 2–5.30pm, Thurs 10am–1pm, Sat 10am–1pm & 2–5pm; ☎065/51577) will book **accommodation**: Mrs M. O'Mahony's *Ferry Lodge*, Cappa Road (☎065/51291; cross the river at the bottom of the main street), is friendly and palatial at around £12. Similarly hospitable is Mrs M. Daly's *St Martins*, Shannon Heights, Kilkee Road (☎065/51198; £11). For **camping**, *Aylevarroo Caravan and Camping Park* (☎065/51102, May 14–Sept 4; £4–5) is less than two miles from Kilrush on the N67 Killimer Road. As for **banks**, *Allied Irish Bank* and *Bank of Ireland* are both in Frances Street. *Bus Éireann* information for **buses** to Ennis and around the coast throughout the year, and to Galway and Cork during the summer, is available from *Crotty's* in the square. **Bike hire** is available at *Gleesons*, Henry Street (☎065/51127; £7–£8 daily), where they also stock camping gaz.

Onwards: the ferry to Kerry

If you're **cycling or driving on to Kerry**, you can cut out many miles and the mental congestion of Limerick city by heading for KILLIMER, five miles from Kilrush, and taking the **car ferry** to TARBERT (April–Sept Mon–Sat 7am–9.30pm, Sun 9am–9.30pm; Oct–March Mon–Sat 7am–7.30pm, Sun 10am–7.30pm; sailings every hour on the hour, return from Tarbert on the half-hour; £6 single car, £8.50 return, £2 cycles; ☎065/51060).

Kilkee

KILKEE, over on the Atlantic coast, is a small, busy seaside holiday town with all the amenities you'd expect: cheap cafés, restaurants, amusements and nightlife. Popular with the bucket-and-spade brigade, the town comes as a healthy piece of normality if the off-beat romanticism of the west coast has become too much.

There's a magnificent beach, a crescent of golden sand set in dramatic cliff scenery. The beach's westerly tip meets an apron of laminated rock strata known as the Duggerna Rocks, which protects it from the ravages of the Atlantic. Here, when the tide is out, deep, clear pollock holes form, filled with colourful marine life.

The area is a favourite for scuba diving and snorkelling, but even without equipment, exploration is rewarding. There are exhilarating walks for miles along the cliffs both to the north and, more spectacularly, to the south round **Loop Head**, where you can walk for sixteen miles along the cliff's edge past stack rocks, puffing holes (where the sea spouts up through crevices in the rock), and the natural Bridges of Ross. The other good way to see this peninsula is by **bike**; you can hire them at *Williams Pharmacy*, Circular Road (☎065/56041).

In the little church at **MONEEN**, near KILBAHA at the tip of the peninsula, is the nineteenth-century curiosity known as **The Little Arc**. In Penal times Catholics were forced to be both ingenious and secret in the practising of their faith. Here they were not allowed to worship on land, and so built a little hut on wheels which was kept on the beach and wheeled down below the high-water mark between tides, beyond the legal grasp of the local Protestant land vner. The priest would then say mass in it while the congregation stood around on the beach.

Practicalities

There is no shortage of **guesthouses and B&Bs** in Kilkee, though it's worth remembering that this is a popular resort and can be booked out in August. Addresses are available from the **tourist office** in The Square (☎065/56112; June–Aug daily 10am–1pm & 2–6pm). Near here in O'Connell Street both *Kincora* (☎065/56107; £13) and Mrs M. Hickie's *Bay View* (☎065/56058; £12) are good bets for B&B. The west end of Kilkee has accommodation, too, at Mrs Enright's, *Aran House* (☎065/56170) and at Mrs Haugh's, *Dunearn House* (☎065/56152), both around £12. The cheapest decent accommodation is at *Kilkee Hostel*, O'Curry Street (☎065/56209; £5), a friendly, family-run place right in the centre of town. Pitching tents is discouraged on the open land towards Loop Head, and would be very exposed to gales, but there are two **campsites** in town: *Cunninghams Caravan and Camping Park* (☎065/56430; open Easter weekend and May 14 to Sept 17; £4 per tent plus £1 per person; £2.50 per person for cyclists and hikers) is reached as you approach town from Kilrush by taking the first left after the Texaco station; the other site, far less attractive, is just up the Kilrush road from the main square. **Bus Éireann services**, departing from outside *Kett's* pub just along the Lahinch road, link Kilkee with Ennis and with towns along the coast.

There are plenty of bars and cafés to **eat** at during the summer. If you want to spend over £18 on a meal anywhere in the county you have two good options in Kilkee: *Manuel's Seafood Restaurant*, Corballwy, Kilkee (☎065/56211), one mile north of town is extremely popular both for the food and atmosphere; the same is true of *Krazy Krauts* (☎ 065/56240) rather more central, down on the seafront – booking is advisable for either. For **banks**, the *Bank of Ireland* and the *A.I.B.* are in O'Curry Street. As for **sport**, the choice is either pitch and putt or golf at the west end. **Strand races**, exciting informal horse races, are held on the beach, usually on the last weekend in August.

Heading North

The coastline north of Kilkee is one of fine cliffs and sandy beaches, though not all of them are accessible. **MILTOWN MALBAY**, eighteen miles north of Kilkee, is a Victorian resort, strangely situated some way inland. The place comes alive for the *Willie Clancy Summer School* held here (usually the first or second week in July), when it's packed with traditional music enthusiasts from all over the world. Two and a half miles away is **SPANISH POINT**, so called because it was here that survivors from wrecked Armada ships swam ashore, only to be executed by the High Sheriff of Clare. It's a holiday spot for nuns, and appropriately enough there's a very quiet **campsite**, *Lahiff's Caravan and Camping Park* (☎065/84006; April–Sept; £4.50), and *The People's Hostel* (☎065/84107; £5; laundry £2.50), in a bracing location overlooking the cliffs and an excellent, sandy swimming beach.

To the east of Spanish Point, **Slieve Callan** rises beside the main road to Ennis. Taking this road you pass KNOCKNALASSA, where there's an impressive wedge-shaped gallery grave, known as *Diarmuid and Gráinne's Bed* (after the Gaelic version of the Tristan and Isolde story). It's quite tricky to find: five miles along the road from Miltown Malbay you will pass a house with a newly thatched little barn alongside; the grave is about half a mile further east from here, tucked out of sight behind a hummocky rise to the left of the road. Follow the cows – it's worth seeing.

Back on the coast, **LAHINCH** is a busy family holiday resort with a fabulous broad sandy beach, ideal for surfing. Not far along the coast are two natural waterspouts. The town pitches itself at a conservative market, its two golf courses hosting major golf competitions in July and August (Lahinch Golf Club, ☎065/81003). While there's good **music**, both country and traditional, to be had in the bars, there's not a great deal to attract you to Lahinch; a characterless and very much a seasonal town that shuts down in winter. If you do stay, the new *Lahinch Hostel*, next door to the church, is very clean and pleasant (☎065/81040; dorms £5, family rooms £22 for four people; laundry facilities); you can **camp** at *Lahinch Camping and Caravan Park* (☎065/81424; May–Sept), which has a **launderette** for service washes and **bike hire** (£6 a day), and there are plenty of B&Bs – ask at the **tourist office** in the centre of the main street (June–Aug daily 10am–1pm & 2–6pm).

Towards the Burren

If you've come this far north, you're probably on your way to, or coming from, the Burren region: if so, the best stopover spots are at Ennistymon, inland, or Liscannor, on the coast. **LISCANNOR** has a couple of nice bars, a campsite (about three-quarters of a mile from the pubs as you head towards the cliffs), supermarket, post office and two **hostels**. *The Village Hostel*, Liscannor (☎065/81385; year round; £5) is right next to the bars. Spartan and musty, *The Old Hostel*, Dereen (☎065/81179; open all year; £4), is around two miles further west up the L54. The Cliffs of Moher **tourist office** can give further advice (☎065/71149; May–Aug daily 9.30am–6pm, March–April & Sept–Oct 10am–6pm). The sandy stretches towards Lahinch from Liscannor, towards the mouth of the river, are unsafe due to quicksand.

Ennistymon

ENNISTYMON, just over two miles inland from Lahinch, is an old market town (Tuesday is market day) with low shop-fronts, a pretty nineteenth-century Gothic church and some great old bars tucked away in the most unlikely of places. The town has a life, albeit a leisurely one, regardless of tourism, and its people enjoy **traditional music** and ballads in the **bars** year round: try *Phil's Bar*, *Daly's Bar*, *Nagles* or *Cooley's House*, all in Main Street and at weekends *The Falls Hotel*. The church at the end of the main street has been converted into a *teach cheoil* (ceili house) where you can catch evenings of traditional music: it's run by local enthusiasts so expect standards to be high (entrance around £3). Two traditional music festivals promise to be good in June 1992: the unaccompanied singing festival scheduled for the first weekend in the month (which should become an annual event), and the county *fleadh*, which will take place over the last weekend (and moves from town to town every year).

Ennistymon's setting is surprisingly green; nip down behind the *Archway Bar* and the **Cascades Walk** takes you alongside the River Cullenagh as it rushes over slabs of rock through the heart of the little town, with its slate-grey houses and wooded banks. Lodged at the side of these falls is a rudimentary hydroelectric power station housed in a shed providing electricity for the *Falls Hotel* – a resourceful piece of alternative technology. Ennistymon's eighteenth-century church stands on a hill above the town, from where you can see the blue river snaking its way out of the woods and beyond to the sea at Liscannor.

For **accommodation**, *The White House Hostel* (£4) is on the Main Street, up behind *Phil's Bar* – collect the key from Burke's Bar or from the chip shop down towards the church. There are several B&Bs too, including Mrs K. Cahill's, *Station House* (☎065/71149; £12), Mrs McMahon's *San Antone*, Church Street (☎065/71078; £12), and *McMahon's Bar* in Main Street, all reasonably central. Further accommodation and **tourist information** is available at *Kam Knitwear* (March–Nov 9am–6pm; ☎065/71387). *Bus Éireann* buses depart from the square for Ennis, Limerick and Dublin.

The Burren

The Burren (*Boireann* or rocky land) is a huge plateau of limestone and shale that covers over a hundred square miles of northwest Clare, a highland shaped by a series of cliffs, terraces, and expanses of limestone pavement, with little to punctuate the view. Bleak and grey, the Burren can come as a shock to anyone associating Ireland with all things green. It's an extraordinary landscape of stark rock, fading lower green fields, and above all the sky and the ocean. Its cliffs and terraces lurch toward the sea like huge steps of wind-pocked pumice. Bone white in sunshine, in the rain it becomes darkened and metallic, the cliffs and canyons blurred by mists. A harsh place, barely capable of sustaining human habitation, it was well summed up in the words of Cromwell's surveyor Ludlow: "savage land, yielding neither water enough to drown a man, nor a tree to hang him, nor soil enough to bury". There are no sweet rolling fields here, but stick with it and its fascination begins to emerge – cruel and barren as it is, there's a raw beauty about the place, and an exceptional combination of light, rock and water.

In recent centuries the Burren has supported a sparse population, living, like most of the west of Ireland, in harsh poverty. It was to this land, west of the

Shannon, that Cromwell drove the dispossessed Irish Catholics after his campaign of terror. Few could survive for long in such country. The area's lack of appeal to centuries of speculators and colonisers greedy to cream the fat off Ireland's lusher pastures has meant that evidence of many of the Burren's earlier inhabitants has remained. The place buzzes with the **prehistoric and historic past**, having over sixty Stone Age (3000–2000 BC) burial monuments, the most common types being wedge-shaped tombs, cairns and dolmens; over 400 Iron Age ring forts (500 BC–500 AD), which were defensive dwellings; and numerous Christian churches, monasteries, round towers and high crosses.

Geology and flora

The Burren has an austerity of almost mythical dimensions, suggesting ancient privations. The pavementing that stretches before you is a floor of grey rock, split by long parallel grooves known as *grykes*. Throughout the Burren, rainwater seeps through the highly porous rock and gouges away at the many underground potholes, caves and tunnels. The only visible **river** is the Caher at Fanore, but there are a multitude of underground waterways, and there are **lakes**, known as *turloughs*, that are peculiar to this landscape; they appear only after heavy rainfall, when the underground systems fill up, and vanish once again after a few dry days.

The panorama is bleak, but close up, **wild flowers** burst from the grooves in specks and splashes of brilliant colour. A botanist's delight and enigma, the Burren supports an astounding variety of **flora**, with arctic, alpine and Mediterranean plants growing alongside each other. The best time to see the flowers is late spring, when the strong blue, five-petalled spring gentians flourish. Here too are mountain avens, various saxifrages and maidenhair fern. Later in summer the magenta bloody cranesbill and a fantastic variety of elsewhere-rare orchids bloom: bee orchids, fly orchids and the lesser butterfly. More common flowers look stunning by sheer force of quantity: bright yellow birdsfoot trefoil and hoary rockrose, and milkwort. Obviously flowers must not be picked.

Nobody knows exactly how these plants came to be here, nor why they remain. It has been suggested that some of the Mediterranean flowers have been here since Ireland had a far hotter climate, but how they survived is a source of speculation: it may be the peculiar conditions of moist warm air coming in from the sea, the Gulf Stream ensuring a mild, frostless climate, and very effective drainage through the porous limestone. It's also thought that the bare rock absorbs heat all summer and stores it, so that the Burren land is appreciably warmer in wintertime than areas of a different geology. There's more on the Burren's geology in the **Burren Display Centre** in Kilfenora: proposals to open a new interpretive centre in the heart of the Burren are currently causing great controversy, with conservationists around the world joining the protests against it.

How to go and where to stay

The best way to get to know the Burren is slowly. The presence of some very good independent and budget hostels coupled with plenty of warm pubs in which to soak up the atmosphere of the "singing county" makes this a feasible and attractive proposition. There are **hostels** at Kinvarra, Fanore, Doolin, Lisdoonvarna, Lahinch, Spanish Point, Ennistymon, Liscannor, Corofin, and 7 km from Kilfenora in the heart of the Burren: details are given in the text, as are **campsites**, since, on all this rock, it can be difficult finding ground on which to camp. **B&Bs** can be found at all of the above, with the exception of Kinvarra.

You can get to the area by taking a *Bus Éireann* connection from stations at Galway or Limerick. There's a direct **bus** service from Limerick and Galway to Doolin and in summer at least one bus a day from Cork, Limerick and Galway passes through Ennistymon and Lisdoonvarna. **Bike hire** is available at *Byrne & Sons*, Ennis Rd, Miltown Malbay (☎065/84079); through John at the *Doolin Café* in Doolin (☎065/74429); at *Burke's* in Lisdoonvarna (☎065/74022); and at *Monks* pub down by the harbour in Ballyvaughan (☎065/77059). The following hostels also do bike hire: *Doolin Hostel*, Doolin; *The Bridge Hostel*, Fanore; *Doorus An Óige Hostel*, Doorus; and *Johnston's Hostel*, Kinvarra.

Seeing the Burren

To see the Burren's archaeological and ecclesiastical sites, go by car or bike; to get to know its landscape and flowers, go on foot. For either of these, the excellent Tim Robinson **map** *The Burren* (£3.50, available in tourist offices, good bookshops, or directly from him at Roundstone, County Galway; postage 75p) is usefully detailed and will make finding sites easy. There are two north–south routes across the Burren that are of particular **archaeological interest**; these run from Bell Harbour to Killinaboy and from Ballyvaughan to Leamaneh. If you're doing a lot of **walking**, a compass is a good idea as there's a shortage of easy landmarks. You're allowed to walk more or less where you want: a good start might be to follow the *Burren Way*, signposted from besides the entrance to *Ballynalacken Castle* (just north of Doolin) to Ballyvaughan. The big disadvantage if you have a car or bike is that this isn't a circular walk. Guided *Burren Bike Tours* are available for groups of four or more – ask for John at the *Doolin Café* (☎065/74429).

Kilfenora Caving and Outdoor Centre (☎065/71422), at KILSHANNY, near Kilfenora, is the place for **outdoor pursuits**: caving, gorge-walking and mountaineering cost £10 a trip, ponytrekking £6 per hour, and *The Bridge Hostel*, Fanore does caving trips during July and August.

Round the coast: the Cliffs of Moher

Circling round the Burren by the coastal route from the south, you arrive almost immediately at Clare's most famous tourist spot, the **Cliffs of Moher**. At their highest they tower 660ft above the Atlantic, and standing on the headlands that jut over the sheer, ravaged cliffs with their great bands of shale and sandstone, you can feel the huge destructive power of the waves. At points the battering of the water has left jagged stack rocks standing, continually lashed by white spume. Erosion is constant: during a storm nine years ago a section of the cliff fell, taking its picnic table with it. The cliffs have to be seen – ideally on a summer evening, when the setting sun is full on them – but be prepared for the oppressively commercial **visitors centre**, where readily-changed money and travellers' cheques are quickly spent on expensive food and souvenirs. Be prepared too for the professional Irish "characters", ready to sell you any baloney you're willing to buy, and the swarms of tourists newly armed with piercing tin whistles. Do see the cliffs, though – you can soon walk away from the crowds in either direction. The cliffs actually stretch for five miles, from Hag's Head, just west of Liscannor, to a point beyond **O'Brien's Tower** – a superfluous viewing point with telescope – some four miles south of Doolin.

Doolin

The village of **DOOLIN** itself, marked as *Fisherstreet* on some maps, has become *the* music mecca of the "singing county", and in fact of Ireland's West. By the time you get here, you'll no doubt already have met a good few traditional music enthusiasts on their way from across Northern Europe, and there are buses laid on from all over the place to bring them here. Without the music, Doolin would be a forlorn and desolate place, lodged beside a treacherous sandy beach at the tail end of the coast that climaxes with the Cliffs of Moher. Bold shelves of lime-stone pavement step into the sea by the pier, from which a **ferry** now runs to **Inisheer**, Inishmore, and very occasionally Inishmaan (June–Aug 10 trips daily 9am–8pm; April & Sept daily but less frequent; in winter by arrangement, weather permitting; ☎065/74189; £10 return).

Music may be its *raison-d'être*, but the village is now ruthlessly geared to providing **accommodation** for as many visitors as it's possible to squeeze into the place's three pubs, with over 100 hostel beds and a campsite as well as B&Bs. Despite their number, the **hostels** do get packed in August, so ringing ahead is a good idea (if they're full, try the ones in Liscannor and Ennistymon, a handy five and eight miles away respectively): in Doolin, choose from *The Rainbow Hostel* (☎065/74415; year round; £4.50; camping £2.50), *Aille River Hostel* (☎065/74260; March 15 to Nov 5; £4.50) and *Doolin Hostel*, (☎065/74006; £5–5.50; laundry and drying room, bureau de change, bike hire £5 to hostellers, £7 to non–hostellers). The **campsite** is by the pier (☎065/74127; open Easter & May–Sept; £1 plus £1 per person). For **B&B**, try Mrs Moloney's *The Horseshoe* (☎065/74006; £12.50) or *St Anthony's* (☎065/74357; £12), a couple of hundred yards either side of the world-famous *O'Connor's* pub.

Doolin's two other **bars** are around half a mile inland from *O'Connor's* – *McGann's* and *McDermott's*, both just as lively. Whatever day of the week you arrive in the summer, traditional music will be playing in all of them – though while the music will be fine, the "pub experience" might pall, as you can find yourself sitting amidst an audience rapt in reverential silence, awed at just being there.

Fanore and Ballyvaughan

North of Doolin, the coast remains spectacular, but bleak and empty. The first place to stop is **FANORE**, where the cosy independent *Bridge Hostel* (☎065/76134, March–Oct; £4.50) offers **bike hire** (£3) and **caving trips** (July and Aug, £5), but only has eighteen beds, so in July and August it's best to ring ahead.

Beyond, the scenic coast road to Black Head and Ballyvaughan is well worth taking. All along this North Clare coast, where the Burren borders Galway Bay, short stretches of well-tended farmland reach from the foot of the hills to the shoreline, and water glints through gaps in the high stone walls. To the south, the Burren slopes off and dissolves in subtle half tones, while way over Galway Bay the muted cobalt mountains of Connemara are hazy in the distance. There's a wealth of **birdlife** along these shores: cormorants, guillemots, terns, herons, grebes, fulmars, mallards, teals and swans, as well as sea-otters and seals.

BALLYVAUGHAN is an attractive village with a quay of neat grey blocks, beautifully poised between Galway Bay and the Burren. Its significance as a trad-ing centre has dwindled into tourism, but it makes a calm haven from which to explore the Burren hills. There's a cluster of shops, an expensive restaurant, and a Rent-an-Irish-cottage scheme (book, well in advance, through *Bord Fáilte*).

Free camping is possible down by the shore just beyond *Monk's* bar, which does good seafood and has **music** on Fridays and Saturdays throughout the year, and on other nights during the summer. The *Ballyvaughan Inn* offers standard home-cooked dinners from £5, plus music; and the *GAA* (Gaelic Athletic Association club) also occasionally has good sessions. The excellent *An Féar Gorta* tea rooms down by the quays serve great soups, cakes and salmon sandwiches (☎065/ 77023; June–Sept daily 11am–5.30pm). **Bike hire** is available down by the harbour (☎065/77059; June–Sept, £5 a day, £25 for 7 days). *Clare Coast Charter*, who operate expensive **sea angling trips**, are also based here (June–Sept ☎065/ 77014; off-season ☎065/21131).

From Ballyvaughan, interesting routes strike south through the heart of the Burren (see below). Sticking to the coast, you pass through BELL HARBOUR (*BEULACLUGGA*), at the southern tip of Muckinish Bay (where the road towards Killinaboy sets off, soon passing Corcomroe Abbey; again, see below), before approaching the border of County Galway.

South Galway Bay

Approaching the Burren from Galway you come straight to some of the best spots: tiny villages on the northerly edge, little settlements between glinting inlets and the eerie white Burren hills. These offer magical views across the wide expanse of Galway Bay, where changes in the broad sky are reflected in the bay's surface, and the shimmering silver and turquoise light bounces off the white-grey Burren rock. Kinvarra and Doorus are actually in Galway, but they're dealt with here since they're inextricably linked to the Burren.

Kinvarra

Set in the southeasterly inlet of Galway Bay, **KINVARRA** is a fishing village with a stone quayside that's almost too pretty; water laps the shore while swans drift to the side of Dunguaire Castle. This quaintness has been recognised, and for such a small place there are disproportionate amenities: a smattering of coffee shops, an expensive restaurant, a supermarket and some good bars. None of these set the little village off-balance, though, and the only environmental aberration is a bizarre development of modern thatched two-storey houses with Victorian gas lamps, worth noting as a lesson in bad proportion and absurd detail. **Accommodation** is provided by the cheerful, independent *Johnston's Hostel* (☎091/37164, May–Sept; £3.50, camping £2.50, bike hire £3) and there's enough variety in the area to warrant a reasonable stay between the rigours of Burren-walking and Galway city-life. An enjoyable **festival**, *Crumniú na mBád*, is held here on the last weekend in August, with the racing of Galway's traditional fishing vessels (Galway Hookers), singing and dancing. The **Hookers** come in four sizes – Bád Mór (Big Boat) and Leath Bhád (Half Boat), at around 40ft and 30ft, then the Gleoiteog (28ft) and the tiny Púcán.

The informative *Kinvarra: A Ramblers Map and Guide*, by Anne Korff and Jeff O'Connell, is worth getting if you intend to explore the immediate countryside: available in local shops and at Dunguaire Castle.

Dunguaire Castle (mid-April to Sept daily 9.30am–5pm; £1.70, students 95p; ☎091/37108), on the edge of the village, was built in 1520, and is a well-restored tower house, one of several used by Shannon Development for medieval banquets. These "castles" were in fact fortified houses, very much a fashion for wealthy landowners from 1450 to 1650, and found in their greatest concentration in East Clare, East Limerick and South Galway. If you've not yet been in one, this is a particularly good example, as the guide has a vigorous grasp of both local history and the political sense of the old building.

Doorus

In addition to all its other attractions, this part of South Galway is closely associated with the poetry of the **literary revival group** of Yeats, Lady Gregory, AE and Douglas Hyde; it was in what is now the *An Óige* hostel in **DOORUS** (out on the peninsula northwest of Kinvarra) that the idea of a national theatre was first discussed – later to become the Abbey Theatre in Dublin. The hostel was then the home of Count Florimond de Basterot, who entertained and encouraged the group (and also the likes of Guy de Maupassant and Paul Bourget). Given the political implications of the Irish literary revival, it's perhaps ironic that Count Florimond's cash came from French estates which his fleeing aristocratic ancestors had somehow hung on to, despite the Revolution.

Doorus itself is a small peninsula which was an island until the eighteenth century. The **village** has only a pub and a shop, but there are **sessions** in *The Travellers Inn* most Sunday nights, you can stay at the **hostel** (☎091/37173; bike hire £3; open all year – August is very busy, so ring ahead) and you can **camp** down by the beach. The gentle waters to the south are pleasant, tidal backwaters that contrast sharply with the wide sweep of beach to the north, which is stony but safe for swimming and surfing – there's a lifeguard on duty in summer. The beach at PARKMORE, to the northeast, however, is dangerous. Along this coast mussels are free for the picking – ask a local for the good spots. You can walk the wriggling coastline from Doorus down to Aughinish or back to Kinvarra, or cycle out to the Martello tower at Finavarra and around the inlet of Muckinish Bay towards Bell Harbour.

Inland: Kilfenora and the heart of the Burren

On the southern edge of the Burren, the tiny village of **KILFENORA** is home to the much publicised **Burren Display Centre** (mid-March to Oct daily 10am–5pm, June & Sept until 6pm; July & Aug 9.30am–7pm; £1.70, students £1.30; ☎065/88030). The centre clearly explains the basic geography and geology of the Burren (in English, French and German) with the aid of a landscape model and a film. Most people find the presentation helpful, though some consider it no more than an expensive geography lesson. At any rate, the centre has a very good **tearoom**.

Next door is **Kilfenora Cathedral**, certainly worth a visit for its High Crosses. The finest of these is the twelfth-century *Doorty Cross*, showing three bishops and what is probably Christ's entry into Jerusalem, with beautiful Celtic patterning. Nearby in the churchyard are remains of two other twelfth-century High Crosses, one near the northwest corner, one opposite the church door. Wander through the gateway behind the church to see a fourth cross, with a decorated crucifixion, in the field to the west. The Cathedral itself was built in 1190 and altered in the fifteenth century: it has a roofless chancel with a finely carved triple-light east window and two effigies of bishops, possibly fourteenth-century.

The Cottage Hostel (open all year; £5, camping £2.50) offers the best basic **accommodation** locally, right in the heart of the Burren, around seven kilometres from Kilfenora: take the Lisdoonvarna road and then the first road to the right (signposted "Ailwee Caves"). Follow this road straight ahead, north through NOUGHAVAL (with Gothic church to your right), past a phone box after about 1km, and then take a right turning about two kilometres after that. If you have the Tim Robinson map of the Burren it's marked as LISSYLISHEEN.

Lisdoonvarna

"LISDOONVARNA – for the crack and the women". The radio ad sets the tone for what the spa town of Lisdoonvarna's famous month-long **matchmaking festival** has become. Traditionally September is the time when, the harvest over, farmers come down from the hills to spend their hard-earned cash and look for a wife in a festival of singing, dancing and drinking. Today tradition wears a sad and sleazy face: it's a hugely promoted festival and the bars – in particular *The Hydro*, *The Matchmakers Arms* of *The Imperial Hotel*, and *The King Thomond* – heave with middle-aged money-spinners and the bewildered and lonely nervously cracking dirty jokes, drinking, singing and leering at any women brave enough to venture in. Between the crooning balladeers and the fortune-tellers' caravans the place bubbles with decades of repression and disappointment – a sad, archaic curiosity, fascinating in its own way. If you are here in September and want to drink amongst a younger crowd try *The Roadside Tavern* or *The Royal Spa*.

For the other eleven months of the year Lisdoonvarna remains a popular **spa** town: the spring waters here contain magnesia, iodine and iron, and reputably have restorative qualities. The town's principal sulphur spring is in the *Spa Wells Health Centre* (daily 10am–6pm; ☎065/74023), where you can take the waters in the pumphouse, or have a sulphur bath (£6), a sauna (£2), a shower (£1.50) or a massage (£6). Generally full of arthritic, elderly holiday-makers, the centre offers an invigorating afternoon for weary cyclists and walkers. The whirlwind tour of *The Lisdoonvarna Smoke House* (daily June–Oct, rest of year Mon–Fri; ☎065/ 74432, 74084), right in the centre of town, will fill you in on all there is to know about traditional methods of smoking fish: frankly, there's not much to it, but it's worth taking for the banter and the sliver of smoked salmon thrown in to tempt you to buy more.

If you want to eat, plenty of pubs serve **food**, and the *Royal Spa Coffee Shop* does filling meals – and particularly good home-made burgers – up until 9pm (daily, Easter–Sept). For anyone planning to stay there are plenty of **B&Bs** (though in August getting a bed for the night an be difficult) – *Sunny Bank*, Kincora Road (☎065/74185, £11–12) is extremely friendly, and the **tourist office** (June–Sept; ☎065/74062) can supply you with alternatives. There's a **hostel** too, *The Burren Holiday Hostel* (Kincora House; ☎065/74300; £4.50), right in the centre, and during the festival there's usually a field given over to campers.

Killinaboy and routes north

Heading east from Kilfenora you pass **Leamaneh Castle**, a fifteenth-century O'Brien stronghold, adjoining which is a four-storey building with mullioned and transomed windows (circa 1640). If you turn off north here, the R480 towards Ballyvaughan runs through an area littered with ancient remains. The most impressive of these are around **Caher Connell**, a well-preserved ring fort. Barely half a mile beyond this is Poulabrone **Megalithic tomb**, the most famous of the Burren's portal dolmens, dating from 2500 BC, and two miles further is Gleninsheen, a wedge-shaped tomb of similar vintage a short walk from the road.

A couple of miles further, now approaching Ballyvaughan, **The Aillwee Caves** (mid-March to Oct daily 10am–last admission 5.30pm; July & Aug 10am–last admission 6.30pm; £2.85; ☎065/77036) are two million years old, and the tour takes you through caverns of stalagmites and stalactites. It's very well lit, the tunnels are extensive and there are spectacular rock formations. However, these caves are privately owned, massively promoted, and the tour is very fast: the experience does not induce the wonder it should.

Continuing east from Leamaneh Castle you reach **KILLINABOY**, where a ruined eleventh- to fourteenth-century church has a striking *Sheila na gig* over the doorway: a carving of a naked woman with grotesquely exaggerated genitalia (*sheila* is the Gaelic equivalent of Julia, *gig* means breast) which was probably some kind of fertility idol. They're more usually found above castle doorways, and it may be that its siting here was intended as a warning against the sins of the flesh. From Killinaboy the road continues to Corofin (p.288).

Another road heads north from **Killinaboy to Bell Harbour**. There are many gallery graves around the early part of this road, climbing towards CARRON, and you also pass through a limestone valley with several ring forts, the most impressive of which is **Caher Commaun**, a ninth-century triple cliff fort to the east of the road. Further north, beyond TURLOUGH (like Carron, a tiny place), you'll see the mile-long road to the placid **Corcomroe Abbey** signposted on your right just as you approach Bell Harbour. A twelfth-century Cistercian foundation, its considerable remains are beautifully set in a secluded valley.

travel details

Bus Éireann
From Ennis: to **Limerick** (6 daily; 45min); Cork (3; 3hr); **Shannon Airport** (13; 45min); to **Dublin** 3–4 daily; 4–4.5 hours).

Getting to Doolin
June–Oct buses from Galway (2 a day; 3 hours), from Limerick (2 dailly; 3 hours); from Dublin (2 daily, via either Limerick or Galway; 6.5 hours).

Special package deals are available through *Bus Éireann* combining transport from Dublin, one night's stay (or more) in *The Doolin Hostel* plus a bus journey to anywhere else in the country all for £17; a similar deal from Galway or Limerick costs £14.

CHAPTER TEN

GALWAY, MAYO AND ROSCOMMON

G alway, Mayo and Roscommon mark a distinct change in the west of Ireland scene. Coming from the south, **County Galway** may at first seem a continuation of what has gone before in Clare and Kerry. And Galway city is in some ways the west coast town par excellence – an exceptionally enjoyable, free-spirited sort of place, and a gathering point for young travellers. But once you get beyond the city things start to change. The landscape is dramatically harsher and far less populous, and there are fewer visitors too.

Lough Corrib, which splits Galway in two, delineates another dramatic split in the landscape of the county, this time between east and west, inland and coast. To the east of the lake lies tame, fertile land which people have farmed for centuries, while to the west lies **Connemara**, a magnificently wild terrain of wind and rock and water. The **Aran Islands**, in the mouth of Galway Bay, resemble Connemara both in their elemental beauty and in their culture; the Galway *Gaeltacht* comprises the islands, Iar-Chonnacht, and some scattered communities in north Connemara and Joyce Country. Again, **Galway City** straddles the divide. A bridging point both physically and culturally, it's a fishing port, an historic city, and now the focus of an energetic social and artistic scene.

If you carry on up the coast you'll enter **Mayo**, where the landscape softens somewhat but is still relatively free of tourists. The pilgrimage centre of **Knock** and the attractions of historic towns like **Westport** aside, it's the coast which is once again the main draw. Physically it's as exciting and rugged as any in the Republic, and far less exploited, though the downside of this is that facilities for travellers are relatively thin on the ground. An exception is **Achill**, the largest Irish offshore island, which provides both some of the most spectacular cliffs and some practical necessities for travellers, as it's a moderately popular holiday resort. **Roscommon** is entirely landlocked, and less visited still. In a sense this is understandable, since there are few real excitements, and the land is for the most part flat and low-lying. Nevertheless the fine detail of this landscape, scattered with small lakes and large houses, has a slow charm. There are places that merit a look as you pass through, and in the extreme north, around **Lough Key**, there's some very attractive scenery indeed.

Galway City

The city of **GALWAY**, folk capital of the west, has a vibrancy and surly hedonism that make it unique. People come here with energies primed for enjoyment – the drink, the music, the "crack" – and it can be a difficult place to leave. University

College Galway guarantees a high proportion of young people in term time, maintained in summer by the attractions of the city's festivals. This youthful **energy** is an important part of Galway's identity, quite distinctive in a country plagued by emigration. Galway has become a playground for disaffected Dubliners, and folksy young Europeans return each year with an almost religious devotion. The city commands a vigorous loyalty: try doing the place down, and you're liable to find yourself in a fight.

Again in contrast to other Irish cities, Galway is experiencing a surge of economic **growth**, and is currently Europe's fastest growing city. Constant renovation is in progress in the small and crowded city centre, and during the summer it has the energy of a boom town, with an expanding number of shops and restaurants to cater for the increase in fashionable visitors and students.

Prosperity allows a vigorous independence from Dublin, reflected in the artistic dynamism of the city. It's a focus for the traditional **music** of Galway and Clare – Galway's status as an old fishing town on the mythical West Coast adding a certain potency – while the *Druid Theatre* has stimulated a new interest in drama here. At no time is the energy of Galway more evident than during its **festivals**, especially the *Galway Arts Festival* (the last two weeks in July), when practitioners of theatre, music, poetry and the visual arts create a rich cultural jamboree. It's a great time to be in the city, but be prepared for a squeeze on accommodation. The last weekend in July sees the place buzzing with the *International Busking Festival*, swiftly followed by the **Galway Races** (the first week in August), when accommodation is again at a premium. At the end of September, the *Galway Oyster Festival* completes the annual round.

Physically, the city is based around the **River Corrib** and its many millraces, sluices and massive old mills. Still dominating the centre, these are reminders of where the city's first boom came from.

History: the Claddagh

Galway originated as a crossing point on the River Corrib, giving an access to Connemara denied further north by the Lough. It was seized by the **Norman** family of De Burgos in the thirteenth century, and developed as a strong Anglo-Norman colony, ruled by an oligarchy of fourteen families. They maintained control despite continual attacks by the bellicose Connacht clans, the most ferocious of whom were the O'Flaherties. To the O'Flaherty motto "Fortuna Favet Fortibus" (Fortune Favours the Strong), the citizens of Galway responded with a plea inscribed over the long-vanished city gates: "from the fury of the O'Flaherties, good Lord deliver us".

Galway was granted a charter and **city status** in 1484 by Richard III, and was proudly loyal to the English crown for the next two hundred years. During this time the city prospered, developing a flourishing trade with the continent, especially Spain. However, its loyalty to the monarch ensured that when Cromwellian forces arrived in 1652 the place was besieged without mercy for ninety days. It was Cromwell who coined the originally derisory term "the fourteen tribes of Galway"; this didn't worry the Irish, who returned the disdain by proudly adopting the name as a title. The city went into a decline from the mid-seventeenth century onwards, and only recently started to revive.

The history of the **CLADDAGH**, a fishing village that existed long before Galway was founded alongside it, is quite distinct from that of the city proper. An Irish-speaking village of thatched cottages, the Claddagh was fiercely independent, having its own laws, customs and chief, and it has always remained a proud, close-knit community. Boat-building skills are still passed down through generations, though of course this work is on the decline, and the old vessels known as Galway Hookers are now used more by boating enthusiasts and for transporting turf to the Aran Islands than for fishing. It is from here that the famous **Claddagh ring** originates, worn by Irish people all over the world. It shows two hands clasping a heart surmounted by a crown and represents love, friendship and respect. It's worn with the heart pointing towards the fingertip when betrothed, the other way when married.

Arriving and Accommodation

You're almost bound to arrive in Galway at **Eyre Square**, also known as the J.F. Kennedy Memorial Park. The **Bus Éireann** and **railway stations** are off the south side of the square, while the **tourist information office** (July–Aug daily 9am–7pm; May–June & Sept Mon–Sat 9am–5.45pm; Oct–April Mon–Fri 9am–5.45pm, Sat 9am–12.45pm; ☎091/63081) is just off the southern corner at the junction of Victoria Place and Merchant's Road. Eyre Square is also the departure point for the cheap private buses. If you arrive by plane you can catch a bus from **Carnmore Airport** into the city centre at 11.30am and 12.55pm (Mon–Sat); a bus from Galway bus station to the airport departs at 11.15am and 12.40pm (Mon–Sat). The journey costs around £2 each way; hang on to your ticket if you arrive and are making the return journey midweek. A taxi to the airport costs around £6. There's an airport tourist office open for all arriving flights (May–Sept; ☎091/55252).

Accommodation

There are plenty of **hostels** in and around Galway, but they get very full during festival time and throughout August – ring ahead or arrive early. In the city centre are *Arch View Hostel*, Dominick Street (☎091/66661; £5–6.50; open all year); *Corrib Villa*, 4 Waterside (☎091/62892; £5.90; all year); *Eyre Hostel*, 35 Eyre Street (£5.50; summer only), a bit cramped though friendly; and *Woodquay Hostel*, St Anne's House, 23/24 Woodquay (☎091/62618; low season £5, high season £6.50; all year). The *Mary Ryan Hostel*, 4 Beechmount Avenue, Highfield Park (☎091/23303; all year), a twenty-minute walk from the centre, includes breakfast and a shower for £5.50 and has private rooms: walk via Taylors Hill Road, or take a #2 bus from Eyre Square to Taylors Hill Convent, from where there's a footpath to Highfield Park. As well as all these, there are plans to open a temporary *An Óige* hostel during the summer months – check with the tourist office.

There are a couple of hostels out at **Salthill** too: *Galway Tourist Hostel*, Gentian Hill, Knocknacarra, Salthill (☎091/25176; £5; all year) and *Stella Maris Hostel*, 151 Upper Salthill (☎091/21950, 26974; £5–6). Take a Salthill bus from Eyre Square to get there.

B&Bs are also plentiful in the city centre, with several in Prospect Hill at around £12: Seamus O'Flaherty's is at no. 34 (☎091/66302); Joan O'Sullivan's at 46 (☎091/66324); and Brigid Quilter's at 58 (☎091/61073). The R864 Salthill Road also has lots, though it's a little further out, as does College Road, heading east out of town. The tourist office will book for you, and at peak times this is worthwhile, as they should know where to look. If you want to pay more for a city centre **hotel**, there are some on Eyre Square itself, including the *Skeffington Arms* (☎091/63173; £28) and *Currans* (☎091/62445; £16), or try the *Atlanta* in Dominick Street (☎091/62241; £20).

You can **camp** in the centre for free on the grass down by the Spanish Arch, otherwise there are campsites at *Ballyloughane Caravan Park* on Dublin Road (April–Sept; £6 per unit; ☎091/55338), and several in Salthill, the pleasantest being *Hunter's Silver Strand Caravan and Camping Park*, about four miles west on the coast road (April–end Sept; £4–5 per unit, 20p per person; ☎091/92452, 92040).

The City

Eyre Square is an almost inevitable starting point. This small park, set in the middle of a traffic interchange, is one of the places to which everyone seems to gravitate, the other being the Shop and Quay Street area. It's used as a performance space during festivals, and outdoor sessions can start up here at any time, the relaxed atmosphere lending itself to improvisation. Visually, though, the place is a mess. A sentimental statue of the writer Pádraic Ó Conaire, a seventeenth-century doorway, a couple of cannons from the Crimean war and a clutter of disused flagpoles all detract from what should form the focus of the square: Eamonn O'Donnell's splendid sculpture, whose arcs of rusted metal and gushing white fountains evoke the sails of the Galway Hookers, and recall the city's maritime history. It is worth calling into the **Eyre Square Centre**, however: building of this shopping mall in the late 1980s revealed impressive sections of medieval city walls, and these are now preserved within the new complex.

Galway's centre is defined by the **River Corrib**. Issuing from the Lough, it thunders under Salmon Weir Bridge and wraps itself round the full body of the city, meeting the lively **Shop and Quay Street** areas at Wolfe Tone Bridge, where it flows into the bay. Such is the social pull of Shop and Quay streets that many visitors never make it beyond the bridge, and see the river as the city's boundary. This is a big mistake, as over the bridge is the Claddagh, and about a mile and a half west of that is **Salthill**, Galway's commercial seaside town. The **Claddagh** now appears as a small area of 1930s corporation housing, but it's worth getting to know for some of its excellent bars and cheap eats. From any of the bridges you can wander beside the pleasant walkways of river and canals, checking out the industrial archaeology, watching salmon make their way upstream, anglers fly-fishing in the centre of the city and cormorants diving for eels, while gawky herons splash through watery suburban back gardens. At the harbour, a walk out around the stone pier places the city in its impressive setting, with a level coastline stretching to the west and the eerie Burren hills washed and etched in half tones across the bay.

Architecture in the centre

The prosperity of maritime Galway and its sense of civic dignity were expressed in the distinctive **town houses** of the merchant class, remnants of which are littered around the city in the form of finely carved doorways, windows and stone slabs bearing armorial carving. The **Browne doorway** in Eyre Square is one such monument, a bay window and doorway with the coats of arms of the Browne and Lynch families, dated 1627. Just about the finest medieval town house in Ireland is **Lynch's Castle** in Shop Street, now housing the *Allied Irish Bank*. The Lynches were Galway's most prominent family for three hundred years. A local story relates that in 1493 James Lynch Fitzstephen, mayor of the

GALWAY CITY/309

town, found his own son guilty of the jealous murder of a Spanish visitor, and that such was the popularity of the lad that no one in the town would take on the job as hangman – so the boy's father did it himself. The house, dating from the fifteenth century, has a smooth stone facade decorated with carved panels, medieval gargoyles and a lion devouring another animal. Step inside for a detailed history of the building and its heraldry, and to view two pieces of Galway silver: the seventeenth-century sword and eighteenth-century mace. In Market Street, outside Saint Nicholas's Collegiate Church, is the similarly styled **Lynch's Window**. In Bowling Green, a lane just off Market Street, is a gift shop which was formerly the home of **Nora Barnacle**, wife of James Joyce (Mon–Sat, £1).

Down by the harbour stands the **Spanish Arch**; more evocative in name than in reality, it's a sixteenth-century structure that was used to protect galleons unloading wine and rum. Behind it is a fine piece of medieval wall, and next door is the uninspiring **Galway Museum** (May–Sept Mon–Fri 10.30am–5pm), where the only things of real interest are old photographs of the Claddagh and a few examples of sixteenth- and seventeenth-century stone carving from around the city.

Churches and University

Two of Galway's churches are of particular, if radically different, interest. The **Collegiate Church of Saint Nicholas** is the largest medieval church in Ireland, having been built in 1320 and enlarged in the next two centuries. Dedicated to Saint Nicholas of Myra, patron saint of sailors, it's decorated with finely chiselled carvings and gargoyles, akin to the style of Lynch's Castle. The **Cathedral of Our Lady Assumed into Heaven and Saint Nicholas**, in hideous contrast, was commissioned about twenty-five years ago by the then Bishop of Galway, Michael (pronounced Mee-hawl) Brown – hence its nickname, *The Taj Michael*. It sits on the banks of the river like a huge toad, its copper dome seeping green slime down the formica-bright limestone walls. Inside the horrors continue in a senseless jumble of stone, mahogany and Connemara marble. It's so remarkably awful that it demands attention, and viewed from a long distance its sheer bulk does achieve a grandeur of sorts.

On the road behind the cathedral is the more restrained **University College Galway**, a mock-Tudor imitation of an Oxbridge college, which was opened in 1849 at a time when the majority of people in Connacht were starving. The university has the dubious distinction of having conferred an honorary degree on Ronald Reagan. More importantly, it is now UNESCO's base for an archive of spoken material in all Celtic languages, and summer courses for foreign students are held annually in July and August.

Escape to the river

If a restful trip on the water appeals, at nearby **Woodquay** you can either hire a rowing boat (May–Sept) or take the Lough Corrib river cruise (1pm, 3pm & 4.30pm; £5), which goes five miles up the river through flat countryside punctuated by derelict castles, out into the open expanse of the lough. Both are very pleasant options.

Salthill and the beaches

Beyond the Claddagh lies **SALTHILL**, Galway's seaside resort, complete with amusement arcades, discos, seasonal cafés and a fairground – as well as scores more hotels and B&Bs. Salthill **tourist office** is on the front (generally open June, July & Aug daily 9am–6pm; ☎091/63081). The huge **Leisureland** amusement complex is used as a venue for big concerts, and also has a swimming pool (summer daily 10am–9.30pm). **Lower Salthill** has a long promenade with a series of unspectacular but safe and sandy beaches. Even on a hot summer's day it's never so busy as to be oppressive, and its great asset is the view over a glittering expanse of water to the Burren. West of here, **Upper Salthill** is a mess of a suburb that sits around its golf course, despoiled by huge billboards and caravan parks.

Probably the nicest of the sandy beaches immediately west of Galway City is the small one at **White Strand**, nestling beneath a grassy headland about three miles out of the centre. Here, in a small inlet backed by a copse, is also the area's pleasantest **campsite**, the *Silver Strand Caravan Park*. The nearest pub to this site is *The Twelve Bens*, just over a mile west. Galway's other special beach is **Ballyloughrun**, east of the city; this too has a campsite alongside, and can be reached by taking the public footpath along by the railway line, or by either the Renmore or the Merlyn Park bus from the station.

Food and entertainment

If the "crack" has eluded you so far on your travels, Galway is where you're going to find it. The **bars** are the social lungs of this town, and even the most abstemious travellers are going to find themselves sucked in. You are guaranteed to find **music** somewhere – probably in a bar – and similarly there's absolutely no problem finding places to eat.

Eating

Finding tasty, filling **food** at any time of day is easy in Galway, and relatively cheap. Any of the places below should serve you well.

McDonagh's Seafood Bar, 22 Quay Street (☎091/65001). A must for seafood; nip in for a thick and creamy seafood chowder, or stay for a full meal – nobody minds what you order, you just get the feeling that someone actually wants to feed you. Open throughout the day and evenings.

Food For Thought, Lower Abbeygate Street, and also in the back of the tourist office. Cheap wholefood and vegetarian snacks and light meals.

The Hungry Grass, Cross Street. Good, wholesome sandwiches.

The Country Basket, 3 Cross Street. Café serving good value wholefood lunches, including at least one decent vegetarian option.

The Round Table, 6 High Street. Dishes up huge traditional lunches around midday – roasts, pies and gavy etc in a wholly unpretentious setting. £3.50–4.50.

Naughton's (*Tigh Neachtain*; ☎091/66172), 17 Cross Street, corner of Quay Street. Pub with restaurant upstairs.

MacSwiggens, Eyre Street. Good lunchtime pub grub.

The Cellar Bar, Eglinton Street. Another pub where you can get lunch.

L'Hermine, Upper Abbey Street (☎091/68539). Crêperie run by French staff, serves delicious crêpes, tartes and coffee.

Quay Street Wine Bar and Restaurant, Quay Street(☎091/65942). Slightly pricier than similarly convivial eateries round about – but then wine in Ireland is expensive.

Sev'nth Heaven, Courthouse Lane, Quay Street (☎091/63838; daily noon–midnight). Popular restaurant/wine bar serving pizzas, quiches and vegetarian food at lunchtime and pasta in the evening.

Nora Crúb, 8 Quay Street (☎091/68376; Mon–Sat 9am–9pm). Vegetarian dishes, seafood and steaks.

The Brasserie, Middle Street (☎091/61610; Mon–Sat noon–10pm). Pizza, tacos and ribs.

Fat Freddy's, Quay Street. Great atmosphere, great pizzas; one of the cheapest places to get an evening meal.

Blue Raincoat Restaurant, The Long Walk, Spanish Arch (☎091/64642). Imaginative fish menu; expect to spend over £12.

Conlon & Sons, Eglinton Street. Traditional fish and chips with class; up to 25 fish dishes, and a wine licence. Eat in or takeaway at only slightly higher than normal prices.

The Kebab House, 4 Dominick Street (daily noon–3am). Takeaway offering delicious, sizeable helpings.

Sharma, Flood Street. Indian restaurant and takeaway.

Moran's. A real hedonistic splurge; situated on the estuary south of Clarinbridge, three miles out of Galway (see below). *The* place (in season) to enjoy a plate of native oysters, sitting out on the riverbank while the sun sets.

Bars and music places

To experience Galway city you have to frequent one of the lively **bars** with which the place teems. **Traditional music** is performed in many of them; some of it will be depressingly over-amplified, but you can hit a great session on any day of the week and at almost any time of the day during the summer months. The bars of Shop and Quay Streets are especially good, as are those over the bridge around Dominick Street. You can't really go far wrong; those listed below are popular in the main with a young crowd, but there are plenty more well worth exploring. Look out for *The Word*, Galway's free listings magazine.

Naughtons, 17 Cross Street. Popular with locals and visitors alike.

The Quays Bar, Shop Street. Opposite *Naughtons*, similarly popular and with a room at the rear for occasional traditional Irish and bluegrass bands, cabaret etc.

Monroe's, Dominick Street. Another lively spot and one of the best places to catch traditional Irish, cajun or blues.

Mick Taylors, Dominick Street. A relaxed place where you might catch a session anytime.

The Crane Bar, 2 Sea Road. Renowned for its traditional sessions.

MacSwiggens, Eyre Street. Another lively, popular young spot.

An Púcán, Forster Street. Music on a regular basis; popular with boozy, tub–thumping tourists. Can be fun.

Sally Long's, 33 Upper Abbeygate Street (☎091/65756). Good for live rock bands.

The Cellar Bar, Eglinton Street (☎091/63966). Sunday morning jazz sessions.

The King's Head, Shop Street. Sunday morning jazz sessions and diddle and stomping, traditional Irish in the evenings.

Síamsa, 45 Dominick Street (☎091/55479). Irish traditional music and folk theatre run and frequented by Gaelic enthusiasts. Admission is usually free, though during the summer it has special programmes costing £3.

The Castle, Salthill (☎091/25583). Music venue only, but often good.

C.J.'s, Salthill. Another Salthill music place.

The Hangar at the *Hilltop Hotel*, Dalysfort Road, Salthill (☎091/21349). Particularly good for **country blues** gigs.

O'Connell's, Salthill. Boisterous bar with a name for traditional music and singalongs.

Discos

Galway has its fair share of **discos**, though most of those right in the centre of town are pretty run of the mill

Bentley's, Prospect Hill. Pub until midnight, disco afterwards; if you're in before 11pm you won't pay an admission charge.

Zachs, Prospect Hill. Close to Bentley's – the same comments apply.

Central Park, Upper Abbeygate Street. Something of a cattlemarket.

Bransky's, Westside Tavern, in the Westside Shopping Centre by the ring road to Salthill (☎091/24648, around £3). Decent disco, probably a better bet than those in town.

Warwick Hotel, Salthill. Something of a student hang-out: can be fun.

The Arts

Galway is experiencing a real growth in artistic activity. It's the home of the versatile **Druid Theatre Company** (☎091/68617; tickets £6, students £5), in Chapel Lane, off Shop Street; a relatively young company, it produces six new plays a year – many of them new Irish works – and undertakes extensive tours. If you're lucky enough to be in Galway City when they're on, book a ticket in advance, as they play to packed audiences.

Look out too for the **Punchbag Theatre Company**, a small, new company based in the city down by the quays (☎091/65422), committed to performing new Irish plays along with the classics. Galway's **Irish-language theatre** is *An Taibhdhearc* in Middle Street (☎091/62024, 63600). The **Galway Arts Centre**, Nun's Island (☎091/65886), is used as a performance space for dance, theatre and music, as well as having a lively programme of visual arts exhibitions. It's also a good place to find out what is going on in the arts locally.

Inside the old quad of the university campus is a **gallery** which has occasional art and photographic exhibitions. The city's **cinemas** are the *Town Hall Cinema*, Courthouse Square, and the *Claddagh Palace*, Lower Salthill.

Listings

Airport Carnmore Airport flight enquiries, ☎091/55569; *Aer Árann* at Minna (☎091/93034). Airport tourist office, open May–Sept for all arriving flights (☎091/55252).

Bike Hire Ball Alley Lane, off Eyre Square/Williamsgate Street (June–Sept daily 9am–6pm; £5 daily, £25 weekly; ☎091/66219). *Round-the-Corner Bike Hire*, Queen Street, behind the tourist office (£5–7 daily, £25–30 weekly, also available at Seapoint, Salthill; ☎091/66606, 21559, 52360). *Station Rent-a-Bike*, opposite the station (£5 daily, £25 weekly; repairs undertaken). *Europa Bicycles*, Earls Island (☎091/63355).

Bookshops *The Pedlar Bookshop*, Quay Street, has a secondhand and new Irish section, also maps. *Hawkins House* bookshop, Churchyard Lane, includes comprehensive feminist and Irish-language sections. *The Salmon Bookshop and Writers' Centre*, The Bridge Mills (☎091/62587), specialises in poetry and drama.

Buses *Bus Éireann* (enquiries ☎091/63555) run four **buses** to Dublin daily, with a range of special fares worth checking out. *North Galway Club* (enquiries and bookings ☎093/55492) run a similarly priced coach between the two cities; booking a day in advance is advisable especially for Friday travel.

Camping equipment *Great Outdoors*, Eglinton Street (☎091/62869).

Health *University College Hospital*, Newcastle (☎091/24222); Family Planning Clinic(☎091/62992).

Horse riding *Clonboo Riding School*, Clonboo Cross, Corrundulla (near Annaghdown; ☎091/91362).

Launderettes *The Launderette*, Sea Road (Mon–Sat 9am–6pm); *Laundrex*, Old Malte Arcade, High Street (Mon–Sat 8.30am–6pm); *Launderette*, 153 Upper Saithill.

Left luggage Ball Alley Lane bike hire (see above), or at the station for 80p.

Lesbian and Gay information *Lesbian Line* (Wed 8–10pm; ☎091/24810).

Lib ry Galway County Library, Hynes Building, St Augustine Street.

Music *Mulligan*, 1 Cross Street (☎091/64961). Traditional, country, folk and blues – cassettes, vinyl and CDs.

Police Mill Street (☎091/63161).

Sailing *Galway Sailing Club*, Rinville, Oranmore, five miles from the city (☎091/94527).

Trains *Irish Rail* (enquiries ☎091/61444) have four direct trains from Dublin Heuston Station on weekdays and two on Sundays: others connect via Athlone.

Travel Agents *USIT*, at the New Science Building on the university campus (Mon–Fri 10am–5pm; ☎091/24601), is the best agent for youth and student travel. *Corrib Travel*, in the centre of town in Cathedral Building, Lower Abbeygate Street (☎091/63879, 68318), deals with *Slattery's*, *Supabus*, *Eurotrain*, student flights and youth fares.

Windsurfing At Rusheen Bay (☎091/57486, 25295).

Galway Bay and the south

The countryside of the southwest of the county, around the southern shores of Galway Bay and on towards Clare, is some of the prettiest in Galway, and was greatly loved by Yeats, Lady Gregory and others associated with the Gaelic League. The main N18 road round Galway Bay from Galway is a busy one, passing through the villages of Galway's **"Oyster country"** – ORANMORE, CLARINBRIDGE and KILCOLGAN (where the main road leaves the water to head south towards Ennis) – and bringing plenty of visitors, particularly during the **Oyster Festival** over the first weekend in September. The most famous of the Oyster pubs are *Paddy Burke's Oyster Tavern* at Clarinbridge and *Moran's of the Weir*, in a beautiful waterside setting at Kilcolgan. Two miles south of Kilcolgan, off the KINVARRA, road stands **Drumacoo Church**, a fine stone building of about 1200, with a Regency Gothic chapel of iron alongside, rusting and derelict.

The villages of DOORUS, AUGHINISH and KINVARRA, on the south shore of Galway Bay, are covered in the section on "The Burren" in County Clare (p.295) as you're more likely to be visiting them from that direction.

Sticking with the Ennis road, you'll find **Coole Park**, the old demesne of the house of Lady Gregory, much visited by Yeats, and the subject of some of his most famous poetry, two miles to the north of GORT. All that remains of the house itself are some crumbling walls and a stable yard, but the grounds and the lake are now a particularly beautiful forest park. Its **autograph tree**, bearing the graffiti of George Bernard Shaw, Sean O'Casey, Augustus John and others, has been incarcerated in railings and barbed wire to stop the less famous getting in on the act. A mile-and-a-half northeast of Coole, **Thoor Ballylee** is signposted off the N18. This is a sixteenth-century tower house which Yeats bought in 1917, renovated, and made his home for the next ten years. It's now open to the public (April–Sept daily 10am–6pm; £2), and has rare and first editions of his works on display.

Four miles southwest of Gort, just off the Corofin road, are the remains of **Kilmacduagh**, a monastic settlement founded by Saint Colman Mac Duagh around 632. The sheer quantity of buildings – dating from the eleventh to the thirteenth centuries – is more impressive than any particular architectural detail: a cathedral, four churches, the *Glebe House*, and a round tower 115 feet high, all on one site. And the setting, against the shimmering, distant Burren slopes, lends something magical to the ancient, grey stone.

THE ARAN ISLANDS

The **Aran Islands** – **Inishmore**, **Inishmaan** and **Inisheer** – lying thirty miles out across the mouth of Galway Bay, have exerted a fascination over visitors for decades. Their geology creates one of the most distinctive landscapes in Ireland, the limestone pavement giving the islands a stark character akin to the Burren of County Clare. This spectacular setting contains a wealth of pre-Christian and early Christian remains, and some of the finest archaeological sites in Europe. And it's not only works in stone that have survived out here: the islands are Gaelic-speaking, and up until the early part of this century a primitive way of life persisted, a result of the isolation enforced by the Atlantic.

History

The Aran Islands abound with evidence of their **early inhabitants**: the earliest ring forts possibly date from the Iron Age, the majority from the Early Historic period. The next group of people to figure are the **Christians**, who came here to study at the foundation of Saint Enda in the fifth century and went on to found Iona, Clonmacnoise and Kilmacduagh. However, the earliest surviving ecclesiastical remains date from the eighth century.

As Galway's trade grew, so the strategic importance of the islands increased, and in **medieval** times control of them was disputed between the O'Flaherties of Connaught and the O'Briens of Munster, the latter generally maintaining the upper hand. In 1565 Queen Elizabeth resolved the dispute by granting the islands to an Englishman on condition he kept soldiers there to guarantee the Crown's interests. In the mid-seventeenth century the islands lost their political usefulness; the Cromwellian soldiers garrisoned there simply transferred to the new regime after the Restoration and became absorbed into the islands' traditional way of life.

After the decline of English interest and influence, the islands fell into poverty, aggravated in the nineteenth century by rack-renting. That rents should be levied on this barren rock suggests a cruel avarice, and not surprisingly, Aranmen were active in the **Land League** agitations: acts of defiance included walking the landlord's cattle blindfolded over the Dún Aengus cliff edge. Despite this link with the general political movement on the mainland and the islands' use as a refuge for Nationalists during the War of Independence, it is their isolation that has allowed the continuation of a unique, ancient culture. Ironically, this very isolation has been a source of interest for outsiders in the twentieth century.

The Gaelic Revival

With the burgeoning fascination for all things Gaelic from the 1890s onwards, the Aran Islands, along with the Blaskets, became the subject of great sociological and linguistic enquiry, the most famous of their literary visitors being J.M. Synge. His writings brought the islands to the attention of other intellectuals involved in the **Gaelic Revival**, and the notion of a surviving community of pure Gaels provided fuel for the Nationalist movement. In fact this notion was misconceived. The distinct physical type found on Aran – the dark skin, large brow and Roman nose – is, some argue, the legacy of the Cromwellian soldiers who were left on the islands.

In 1934 Robert Flaherty made his classic documentary *Man of Aran*, which recorded the ancient and disappearing culture he found here. (The film can be seen during the summer in Halla Rónáin, Kilronan, at 3pm, 5.30pm & 8pm; £2.) While the **folklore and traditions** recorded in the film are obviously on the decline, much remains: some of the women of Inishmaan still wear the bright red patterned shawls; the men occasionally wear the traditional grey-blue tweed sleeveless suits. *Currachs* – light wood-framed boats covered formerly with hide, now with tar-coated canvas – are still used for fishing, and for getting ashore on the smaller islands when the ferry can't pull in. I even witnessed, as in the film, a man fishing with a simple line off the edge of a 200-foot cliff. Fishing is still very much a way of life on Inishmaan, while tourism is the major earner on Inishmore and Inisheer. This means that, though their purpose will change, knowledge of these customs will not vanish, and tourism may even help ensure the language survives, as Gaelic provides the islanders with a curtain of privacy against the visitors.

TRANSPORT TO THE ISLANDS

Several **ferry companies** operate between Galway and the Aran Islands, but they are rivals and won't let you mix your journeys between services on one ticket. A return to any of the islands costs in the region of £12, and it's usually possible to buy tickets on the boat. With any of these ferry services it's a good idea to check on the times of return journeys with the skipper, since weather conditions can mean alterations.

Island Ferries (or *Aran Island Ferries*; ☎091/61767, 72273), Victoria Place, Eyre Square, Galway, behind the *Allied Irish Bank*. The only company to serve all three islands all year round. In summer (June–Sept) boats leave Rossaveal (with a connecting bus from Galway) five times a day for Inishmore and at least once a day to the two smaller islands; during winter there are two daily to Inishmore and one a day to Inishmaan and Inisheer. A return fare to any of the islands costs £12, students and hostellers staying at *Mainistir House Hostel* on Inishmore £10. This is the company to use if you want to visit more than one of the islands and return to Galway – round trips are negotiable for £18–20. If you do plan on travelling between the islands check the schedule closely as doing so can be more complicated and time consuming than you might at first imagine. For example boats from Inishmore to Inishmaan depart only on Monday and Thursday at 8am.

Inter Island Boat Services (☎091/93336, ☎088/551663) leave SPIDDAL (11 miles west of Galway, 7.5 miles east of Inverin Hostel) for all three islands at 10am daily from Easter to the end of September; phone for schedule at other times. The booking office is at the pier at Spiddal, though advance booking is not usually necessary (£12 return, students £10).

Aran Ferries (☎091/68903, evenings ☎091/92447) are based at the Galway tourist office. Their service direct from Galway City (late May to early Oct, £15–18 return) takes just 90 minutes. Departures from Rossaveal for Inishmore are at 10.30am, 1.30pm and 6.30pm (operates April–Oct, £12–15 return); a connecting bus to Rossaveal leaves the tourist office an hour and a half before the boat departs (bus journey costs £3 each way). Reductions of £2 are available for students, interailers and hostellers staying at *Aran Islands Hostel* or *Dún Aengus Hostel* on Inishmore). Bicycles are carried free. **Package deals** from Galway are available and well worth considering: return ferry and B&B £22; return ferry and hostel £15. If you want to plan your trip well in advance this company also does deals with *Irish Rail*, offering a return fare from **Dublin** plus two nights B&B on Inishmore for £49. With any of these deals, it is adviseable to check *which* B&B or hostel you will be staying in, and whereabouts it is on the island, before you buy your ticket – some are miles from the pubs.

Doolin Ferries (☎065/74455) sail from Doolin (County Clare) to Inisheer (mid-April–end-Sept; 1–8 daily); and to Inishmore mid-May to end August (once daily).

Aer Árann (☎091/93034) are based at a new airstrip at Minna, west beyond Rossaveal. From spring 1992 they will offer **flights** to all three of the islands: three flights daily throughout the year (less on Sundays), and during the summer months a non-stop shuttle service seven days a week. A connecting bus from Galway City meets all flights. The return fare is £25, bookable at the *Aer Árann* desk in the tourist office, where it is also worth asking about **fly/sail** deals. There are no student reductions on flights and it is not possible to take a bicycle on the plane. Island airport numbers are: Inishmore ☎099/61109, 61131; Inishmaan ☎099/73007, 73002; Inisheer ☎099/75014.

Getting there

There are no problems sailing to **Inishmore** at any time of the year; flights, however can be delayed in bad weather. On **Inisheer** and **Inishmaan** you're at the mercy of the weather and you can occasionally get cut off from the mainland during winter if the weather breaks.

It is possible to do a **day trip** from Galway to any of the islands, and from Doolin (Co Clare) to Inisheer and Inishmaan, but you really need two full days to see the main sites of Inishmore alone. Staying over on Inishmaan is the only way to experience its bewitching silence, and though Inisheer is so small that a day trip from Doolin is feasible, an overnight stay gives a priceless dimension to a visit – a taste of the islands' elemental forces. Though they are always considered as a group, each of the islands has its own distinct flavour and pleasures.

Provisions on the islands are slightly more expensive than on the mainland, and you can only buy *Gaz* bottles on Inishmore if you are thinking of camping.

The most detailed **map** of the islands is produced by Tim Robinson of Roundstone, available on Inishmore and at bookshops and tourist offices in the Galway and Clare area. In fact the Aran Islands are quite easy to explore and the map isn't essential for finding the major sites. It is, however, of great value to those interested in the detailed archaeology and in Gaelic place names.

Inishmore (Inis Mór)

Although there's some truth behind the attitude that does down **Inishmore** as the most tourist-orientated and least "authentic" of the Aran Islands, its wealth of dramatic ancient sites overrides such considerations. And though there does tend to be a sudden rush of camera-wielding visitors with the arrival of the morning ferry, Inishmore is big enough to absorb them quickly.

It's a long strip of an island, a great tilted plateau of limestone, with a scattering of **villages** along the sheltered northerly coast. The land slants up to the southern edge, where tremendous **cliffs** rip along the entire length of the island. Walking anywhere on this high southern side, you can see the geological affinity with the Burren of County Clare, and visualise the time when these islands were part of a barrier enclosing what is now Galway Bay. As far as the eye can see is a tremendous patterning of stone, some of it the bare formation of the land (the pavementing of grey rock split in bold parallel grooves), some the form of dry-stone walls that might be contemporary, or might be pre-Christian. The textures blur so that it's impossible to make sense of planes and distances, the only certainties being the stark outline of the cliffs' edge and the constant pounding of the waves below. Across the water in contrast are the Connemara mountains, coloured pink and golden and slatey blue in the evening sun. Up the bay is Galway, now an insignificant speck, and around to the southeast, appearing as just a silvery ridge, are the Cliffs of Moher.

Practicalities: transport and accommodation

The best way to **get about** Inishmore is by a combination of cycling and walking. *Aran* **bicycle hire** is beside the pier in Kilronan, where the ferry docks (£4–5 per day, £20 a week); *Costello's Bike Hire* (☎099/61241, May–Oct; £4 per day) is opposite the *American Bar* further up the lane. Bear in mind that in high season all bikes are likely to go with the arrival of the ferry at 11.30am. **Pony buggies** will take you on a round tour for about £20 for a group of four, or there's a **minibus** tour of the island that leaves Kilronan around 12.30pm (£4). If you have limited time you can take the public minibus up the island through the villages that stretch over seven miles to the west – MAINISTIR, EOCHAILL, KILMURVEY, EOGHANACHT and BUN GABHLA – and walk back from any point. The bus leaves Kilronan grocery shop, up behind the hostel, every two hours between 9am and 5pm (£2 one-way). The village of KILLEANY, a mile and a half to the south of Kilronan, has to be either walked or cycled to.

If you're looking for **places to stay** there are three **hostels** on Inishmore. *Aran Islands Hostel*, Kilronan (April–Sept; £5; ☎099/61255) is very near the pier, handy if you want to spend the night in the pub below, noisy if you don't. *Dún Aengus Hostel* (£5) is out at Kilmurvey – both of these can *only* be used if you have travelled on an *Aran Ferries* boat (bookable through the tourist office in Galway). *Mainistir House Hostel* at Mainistir (☎099/61169) has deals with *Island Ferries* (see box), but will accommodate you however you have arrived. It's open all year and the charge of £6.50 includes bed linen and an "alternative" continental breakfast (double rooms £8.50; laundry facilities). The sitting and dining areas are a cut above average hostel standards, it's all non-smoking, and there is good food available, "vaguely vegetarian" – subject to the temperament of the proprietor. Check the time of the evening meal if you want to be sure to eat here.

B&Bs can be booked through the **tourist office** (June to mid-Sept Tues–Sun 10am–6pm, July–Aug daily), a couple of minutes' walk from the pier in Kilronan. Mrs Gill, *Ard Éinne*, Killeany (☎099/61126), and Olwyn Gill, *The Cliff House*, Kilronan (☎099/61286), are open all year, both charging around £10–12, and in the summer there are others. There is a basic **campsite** (no showers; £1) an easy walk from Kilronan: take the lane heading west out of the village and turn right in front of *Joe Watty's* pub. Alternatively it's just about possible to pitch a tent down by the idyllic beach at Kilmurvey, a lovely sweep of white sand looking out over to the Connemara mountain range; anywhere else is either bare rock or a treasured piece of cultivatable land. Should you stumble across a likely spot, finding the owner and asking permission is essential.

The island's main **grocery shop** is in the lane behind *Aran Islands Hostel*, and there's a second by *Joe Watty's* bar. Kilronan has a **post office**, with a public phone (and cardphone) outside, and the *Bank of Ireland* opens here Wednesday only (10.15am–12.30pm & 1.30–3pm). You can also **change money** at the tourist office, the Post Office and *Carraig Donn*, a craft shop selling hand-knitted Aran sweaters by the pier at Kilronan, open seven days a week from April to October – this last will also advance cash on credit cards.

The island

Inishmore's villages are strung along the main road that runs the length of the northern shore, the hub of activity being **KILRONAN**, where the ferry lands. There are some some great sandy **beaches**: the one at **KILMURVEY** (four miles west of Kilronan) is safe and sheltered, with fabulous views of the Connemara mountains, or you could take the main road to its eastern extreme and then walk north to get to the safe beaches from Carraig na gCailleach, through Carra na Loinge, down to Poll an Ghabhna. Tucked closer to **KILLEANY**, three quarters of a mile to the south, is Tra Mor (Cockle Strand), safe for swimming; little over a mile further on, near the airstrip, is Tra na Ladies, which looks nice, but where you can get caught by tides or sinking sand. You can **walk** just about anywhere so long as it doesn't look like someone's garden, but be careful when walking anywhere on the south of the island in poor visibility, as the cliffs are sheer and sudden.

Dún Aengus and the forts

The most spectacular of Aran's prehistoric sites is Inishmore's fort of **Dún Aengus** (signposted from Kilmurvey, three-quarters of a mile), a massive semi-circular ring fort of three concentric enclosures lodged on the edge of cliffs that plunge 300 feet into the Atlantic. The inner citadel is a twenty-foot-high, eighteen-foot-wide solid construction of precise blocks of grey stone, their symmetry echoing the almost geometric regularity of the land's limestone pavementing and the bands of rock that form the cliffs. Standing on the ramparts you can see clearly the *chevaux-de-frise* outside the middle wall, a field bristling with lurching rocks like jagged teeth, designed to slow down any attack.

The place is tremendously evocative, and it's easy to understand how superstitions have survived on the islands long after their disappearance on the mainland. Visible west of the cliffs of Inishmore under certain meteorological conditions is the outline of what looks like a mountainous island. This is a mirage, a mythical island called *Hy Brasil* that features in ancient Aran stories as the island of the blessed, visited by saints and heroes. Until the sixteenth century *Hy Brasil* was actually marked on maps.

Dún Eoghanachta is a huge drum of a fort, a perfect circle of stone settled in a lonely field with the Connemara mountains a scenic backdrop. Its walls are sixteen feet thick, and inner steps give access to the parapets. Inside are the foundations of the ancient drystone huts known as *clocháns*. The stronghold is accessible by tiny lanes from Dún Aengus if you've a detailed map, otherwise retrace your steps to Kilmurvey and follow the road west for just over a mile, where it's (poorly) signposted off to the left.

Dún Dúcathair (the Black Fort) is especially worth visiting for its dramatic location. It's a promontory fort, and what remains is a massive stone wall straddling an ever-shrinking headland precariously placed between cliffs. The eastern gateway fell into the sea early in the last century, leaving the entrance a perilous twelve inches from the sheer drop. Inside are the curved remains of four *clocháns*. It's about a two-mile walk from Kilronan – head south out of the village for three-quarters of a mile, take a turning to the right (signposted to "Cliff House") and follow the lane to the cliffs. Once at the cliff edge you can see the fort on the second promontory to your left.

The **dating** of these forts is tricky: Dún Aengus and Dún Dúcathair are probably from the first century BC, whereas Dún Eoghanachta and **Dún Eochla** (just south of Eochaill) could have been constructed at any time between the first and seventh centuries AD, or possibly earlier. The massive buttresses of Dún Eochla are nineteenth-century additions, but the forts have generally been kept in exceptional condition.

Church sites and clocháns

From the fifth century onwards the Aran Islands became a centre of monastic learning, the most important of the eremitical settlements being that of Saint

Enda (Eanna). At the **seven churches**, just east of **EOGHANACHT**, there are ancient slabs commemorating seven Romans who died here, testifying to the far-reaching influence of Aran's monastic teaching. The site is in fact that of two churches and several domestic buildings, dating from the eighth to the thirteenth centuries. Here **Saint Brendan's grave** is adorned by an early cross with interlaced patterns and, on the west side, part of a Crucifixion carving. There are also parts of three high crosses, possibly eleventh-century, and in the southeast corner of the graveyard, alongside the slabs of the Romans, lie several ninth-century slabs incised with crosses and inscriptions.

The most interesting of the ecclesiastical sites on Inishmore, however, is **Teampall Chiaráin**. Take the low road from **MAINISTIR** (opposite *Joe Watty's* pub), follow the lane parallel to the shoreline, and you'll come to it, a simple twelfth-century church on an old monastic site. Alongside is **Saint Kieran's Well**, a long U-shaped spring backed by huge blocks of plant-covered stone. It's very pagan-looking – such wells often held sacred significance in pre-Christian times, and were sanctified in name with the arrival of Christianity. Similarly, some of the tall stones that stand around the site look pre-Christian even though they have crosses inscribed on them. The one by the east gable has a hole in it that may have held part of a sundial, and nowadays people sometimes pass handkerchiefs through it for luck.

Teampall Bheanáin, on the hill behind KILLEANY, is a pre-Romanesque oratory of around the sixth or seventh century, dedicated to Saint Benen. It's distinguished by its very steep gable ends, and by its unique north–south orientation. In all probability it used to form part of the great early monastic site that existed at Killeany.

The finest of Aran's *clocháns* is **Clochán na Carraige**, just north of Kilmurvey. This nineteen-foot-long drystone hut has a corbelled roof whose arrangement is probably an Early Christian design. There are fifty lesser examples of such huts on Inishmore.

Food, drink and entertainment

Not surprisingly, **seafood** is the great speciality on the island. *Dún Aonghasa* in Kilronan (☎099/61104; June–Sept daily 10am–10pm; Oct–June daily noon–9pm), has probably the most varied menu, and is good value for anything from light snacks up to full meals. *Dormer House*, behind the hostel in Kilronan, is a friendly B&B that also feeds non-residents; it's all home cooking and a full meal will cost around £10. *An tSeanchéibh* is a self-service place in Kilronan (April–Sept; ☎099/61228; midday meals from £6, evenings from £7) that also specialises in seafood. Kilronan also has a chip shop, open daily in summer until 10pm, and later if there is a *céilí* on.

You can punctuate your cycling or walking with lunch, tea or snacks at *Man of Aran Cottages* in Kilmurvey, used as a set in the film (June–Sept 11.30am–4.30pm daily; they plan to serve evening meals too; ask at the tourist office if you are going to be staying near this part of the island).

The **pub** beneath the hostel in Kilronan is convivial enough, but it's still a good idea to wander away from here to sample some of the island's other bars: *The American Bar*, *Joe Watty's* further west, *John Dirrane's* at the top of the road as it slopes down to the beach at Kilmurvey, or *Tigh Fitz* bar in Killeany. In addition to this there are **céilís** in Kilronan parish hall (June–Sept Fri, Sat & Sun; winter Sat; £2), and a **disco** in Kilronan parish hall on Thursday nights.

Inishmaan (Inis Meáin)

Coming from Inishmore you are immediately struck by how much greener **Inishmaan** is. Brambles and ferns shoot from walls, and bindweed clings to the limestone terraces. Here the stone walls are a warm brown and seem to almost glow with yellow moss. They're remarkably high – up to six feet – and form a stone maze that chequers off tiny fields of lush grass and clover. Yet despite this verdancy, the island still feels dour and desolate. Farming here is at subsistence level; farm buildings and cottages are grubby and dull, and soggy thatches sag over low doorways. The only sudden splashes of colour are from tiny cultivated gardens – the bright reds, pinks and oranges of geraniums, gladioli and carnations.

The island is shaped something like an oyster shell. It rises in clear levels from the soft dunes of the north, through stages of flat naked rock, up to minuscule green pastures, then again up a craggy band of limestone (along which sit the main villages of the island), eventually levelling out on higher ground to meet the crinkled blowhole-pitted southerly edge. Inishmaan is the least visited, least touched by tourism of the three islands, though it has had visitors since the turn of the century. J.M. Synge stayed here for four summers from 1898, recording the life and language of the people. His play *Riders to the Sea* – which influenced Lorca's *Blood Wedding* – is set here, and his book *The Aran Islands* provides a fascinating insight into the way of life he found. **Synge's Chair**, a sheltered place on the westerly cliffs overlooking St Gregory's Sound, was his favourite contemplative spot. Traces of the ethnic **culture** he discovered remain. Some of the women still wear traditional brightly coloured shawls; Gaelic is the main language, though English is understood; and the islanders get on with what they've always done: farming and fishing. There's no hostility to visitors, but tourism isn't the islanders' concern. If you want to be impressed or entertained, you'll have to look elsewhere.

Forts and churches

One of the most impressive of the Aran forts is Inishmaan's **Dún Conchúir**, loosely dated between the first and seventh centuries AD. Its massive oval wall is almost intact, and commands great views of the island, being built on the side of a limestone valley. (In myth, Conchúir was the brother of Aengus of the Firbolg.) To the east, the smaller **Dún Fearbhaí** stands above the village of BAILE AN MHOTHAIR and looks out over the little eighth-century **Cill Cheannannach** by the shore. In this context the interior of the island's modern church, just below Dún Conchuir, comes as a shock: garish, stylised windows of virulent turquoise and purple from the workshop of Harry Clarke. Stepping outside, the old magic reasserts itself, with the island's ancient graves and wells.

Eating, sleeping and other practicalities

Inishmaan's indifference to tourism means that amenities for visitors are minimal. The **shop** in the main street of the central village has limited provisions: tinned foods, bread and milk. *Pádraig Ó Conghaile's* **pub** is a haven of luxury in such a setting: warm and friendly, and excellent **snacks** are available at any time, with **music** sessions at weekends. There are few other going commercial concerns on the island: a seasonal café below Dún Conchuir and an expensive Aran knitwear shop, which also houses the **Inishmaan Museum**, a fascinating photographic archive of island history, all documented in Gaelic. **B&Bs** are cheaper than on the mainland (around £10), though if you have an evening meal it may nearly double the price. If you want to book ahead, the only one you can phone is Mrs A. Faherty (☎099/73012); if you arrive on spec, ask at the pub. Most farmers will let you **camp**, but remember to ask them – all land belongs to somebody here. There is no chemist or doctor on the island, and **emergencies** are dealt with by a nurse who serves all three islands (☎099/75006). A **public phone** is located outside the post office, and the *Bank of Ireland* operates on the first and third Tuesday of every month.

Inisheer (Inis Oírr)

Inisheer, at just under two miles across, is the smallest of the Aran Islands. Tourism has a key role here; Inisheer doesn't have the archaeological wealth of Inishmore, or the wild solitude of Inishmaan, but the introduction of regular day-trip ferry services from Doolin promises a constant, if small, flow of visitors. This new service also now makes for a handy route from County Clare to Connemara. Of course tourism threatens the very stuff of its attraction – the purity of ethnic traditions and a romantic isolation – but for the moment Inisheer retains its old character, and for some it's a favourite place.

A great plug of rock dominates the island, its rough, pale grey stone dripping with greenery. At the top the fifteenth-century **O'Brien's castle** stands inside an ancient ring fort. Set around it are low fields, a small community of pubs and houses, and windswept sand dunes. Half buried in sand just to the south of the beach is the ancient **church of Saint Kevin**; still in use in the last century, it is now used only to commemorate him as the patron saint of the island every June 14.

Practicalities

The **tourist information office** (June–Aug daily 11am–7pm), in a hut by the pier, will give you a map and a list of **B&Bs**, all of which cost around £8–10. The *Co-op* (☎099/75008) will also do this for you, and will deal with phone reservations for advance booking in high season – the first weekend in August and Whit weekend are usually booked up well ahead. The *Bru* **hostel** (☎099/75008; £5.50; open all year) is new and comfortable, with meals available. The only **camping** is on the official site (☎099/75008; £2 per tent, 50p per person, showers 50p).

The island's main **festival** is its *currach* racing and sports day, normally held on the second Sunday in August. There are a handful of places to get a cooked **meal** on Inisheer: *Radharc na Mara* (June–Sept, until 9pm) does breakfasts and lunches (£3–4) and evening meals (£7–8) and the *Óstán Inis Oírr* (*Hotel Inisheer*, June to mid-Sept; ☎099/75020) does bar food and meals for non-residents, from 9am to 9pm, with evening meals from £6.50. Both the hotel bar and *Tigh Ruairí* bar have **music** any time of the week during the summer. There is no bank on the island, but you can change currency (though not travellers' cheques) in the shop.

CONNEMARA

Dominated by two mountain ranges, **Connemara** is exceptionally beautiful. The **Twelve Bens** and **Maam Turks** glower over vast open areas of bog wilderness, while to the southwest the land breaks up into myriad tiny islands linked by causeways, slipping out into the ocean. The whole area has superb beaches, huge sweeps of opalescent white sand washed by clear blue water. Chance upon good weather here and you feel you've hit paradise; even on the hottest of days the beaches are never crowded.

This is country you visit for its scenery rather than its history. There is little evidence of medieval power in west Galway, either ecclesiastical or secular, beyond a few castles along the shore of Lough Corrib, and the occasional one further west. The great exception is the profusion of **monastic remains** dotted over the little islands off the west coast. Mainland settlements up until the nineteenth century were widely scattered, and the area has always been sparsely populated, due to the poverty of the land. There's never been much to attract marauders or colonisers, and any incursions have involved a battle against the terrain as much as against the people. It's easy to see how such a land would remain under the control of clans like the O'Flaherties for centuries, while gentler landscapes bowed to the pressure of foreign rule. In the famine years the area suffered some of the worst of the misery, and a thinly peopled land was depopulated further as people chose to escape starvation by emigration, despite its dangers and uncertainties.

Continued economic deprivation and isolation have meant that an ancient rural way of life has continued for far longer here, so Connemara is still Irish-speaking, the largest of the *Gaeltacht* areas. A *Gaeltacht* summer school is held in **Spiddal**, and **Casla** (Costelloe) is the home of the new *Raidió na Gaeltachta* radio station. English is spoken too, however, and the only difficulty for the visitor is that the signs on the roads, and on some buses, are often in Gaelic only.

For all its beauty, the dramatic mountain landscape of west Galway is surprisingly undeveloped in terms of tourism, owing in part to the infamous Irish weather and in part to the fact that walking has not been the popular recreation in Ireland that it is in other, more urbanised European countries. If you're in search of solitude, you won't have to go far to find it.

Transport, accommodation and other practicalities

Bus Éireann services link all villages on major routes between Galway, Oughterard, Roundstone, Clifden and Cong. They are reliable, although infrequent, often with only one service daily. Timetables can be picked up in Galway bus station. Connections from Clifden to Westport only operate on Thursday.

Hostels and **B&Bs** are both in reasonably good supply throughout Connemara, and you can **camp** more or less anywhere, bearing in mind that a lot of the area is bog and therefore very wet. Away from towns and villages, you may have trouble getting hold of water; very irritating when in the middle of a bog! *Gaz* bottles or canisters are available in Galway city, at *Keogh's* in Oughterard, *Michael Ferron's* in Roundstone, *Peter Veldon's* in Letterfrack, and in Clifden at *The Twelve Bens*, *Stanleys* and *Millers*. *Bord Fáilte* approved **campsites** are listed in the text.

If you intend to go **walking** bear in mind that the mountains here are potentially **dangerous**. There is no organised mountain rescue service such as you get in European countries that are more developed for mountain sports. The Ordnance Survey 1:126,720 maps are based on surveying done in 1837 and are inaccurate, especially above 1000ft. If you are doing any serious walking it is worth getting either the *Connemara Map and Guide Booklet* (£6.50), or *The Mountains of Connemara* (£5.50), a map and guide to eighteen walks, including The Western Way. Both are produced by *Folding Landscapes* of Roundstone, Connemara, County Galway, and can be obtained in tourist offices in the west of Ireland, or by post (add 75p p&p). **Bike hire** is available at Clifden, Galway, Roundstone, at several hostels (mentioned in the text) and from Gerard Coyne in Tullycross (☎095/43499).

Most of Connemara's more beautiful **beaches** are safe for swimming, including Clifden, Lettergesh, Dog's Bay, Gurteen Bay, Renvyle, Ardmore, Mannin Bay, Aillebrack, Omey, Letterfrack, and Spiddal. It is, however, a very varied coast, so if in doubt, ask about safety locally.

Finally, being the *Gaeltacht*, **signposts** are often in Gaelic, as are names on buses (even Galway is sometimes *Gaillimh*); where common these are added in parenthesis in the course of the guide. Variations in the Gaelic spellings are common – sometimes the "An" is omitted.

Iar-Chonnacht

Draw a large triangle between Maam Cross, Rossaveal and Galway and you've defined the area known as **Iar-Chonnacht**, an open and bleak moorland of bog. Occasional white-splotched boulders lie naked on the peat that stretches to the skyline; any grass that survives is coarse and wind-bitten, and, but for small pockets of forestation, the bog has no trees. It's difficult, wet walking country, but numerous lanes and *boreens* lead to tiny loughs set in the granite hollows of the hills – good for fishing for brown trout, sea trout or salmon. The moorland reaches its highest point near Lough Lettercraffoe on the **Rossaveal to Oughterard road**, giving fine views down onto **Lough Corrib**, whose green and wooded shores are a vivid foil to the barren west.

Galway to Oughterard

If you're heading for the dramatic **walking country** of the mountains and plan to base yourself at Clifden, the road to take from Galway is the N59 through Oughterard. It makes the easiest hitch and most pleasant cycle ride from Galway, avoiding the boring strip development down to Spiddal, and taking you instead along the shore of island-flecked **Lough Corrib**, past crumbling ruins. These include the main sixteenth-century O'Flaherty fortress of **Aughnanure Castle**. A six-storey tower house standing on a rock island surrounded by a fast-flowing stream, Aughnanure was one of the strongest fortresses in the country at the time of Cromwell's blockade of Galway (1652–54). It has now been restored and is open to the public (mid-June to mid-Sept 9.30am–6.30pm, otherwise key with caretaker; 80p, students 30p, heritage card; ☎091/82214; guided tours on request).

OUGHTERARD itself is a small town serving fishing-based tourism, from where you can hire boats out onto the lough. Approached from the east, Oughterard can beguile you into thinking that Connemara is going to be a populated, thriving, developed place, but arriving from the west it seems a lush, green oasis, the beech trees that line the banks of the river sumptuous and luxuriant after the barren wilds of the bog. If you want to stop over there are plenty of **B&Bs**: Mrs O'Meara's (☎091/82635; £12) is a friendly place to stay. Alternatively there is the *Lough Corrib Hostel* in Camp Street (☎091/82634; all year; £5, camping £3).

The main N59 road then takes you through the hamlets of **MAAM CROSS** (*Crois Mám*), where there's a craft shop, petrol station and a pub which serves rather uninspiring food all day, and RECESS, where all you will find is *Joyce's* bar and shop. Five miles further west, close in under the rugged peaks of the Twelve Bens, is *Ben Lettery An Óige* hostel (*Binn Leitrí*; ☎095/34636; June–Sept £5.50, Oct–May £3.80).The nearby castle of **Ballynahinch** was once the home of the land-owning Martin family, now a hotel with a bar open to non-residents (☎095/31006; £50). On Ballynahinch lake are the remains of an old O'Flaherty castle, known as *Martin's Prison* after the use it was put to by Ballynahinch's most famous son, Dick Martin – aka **Humanity Dick** (1754–1834). The story behind the name is that Richard Martin, originally dubbed "Hairtrigger Dick" because of his duelling prowess, spent his adult life campaigning for animal rights, and any tenant he caught causing suffering to animals was thrown into jail in the castle. Dick was known to have fought duels on behalf of threatened animals, and when asked why he did so replied: "Sir, an ox cannot hold a pistol". More constructively, he pushed various acts through parliament protecting farm animals from maltreatment, and was instrumental in founding the *RSPCA*.

West around the coast

The **coast road** is the alternative route west from Galway, passing through the *Gaeltacht* villages of BARNA (*Bearna*) and **SPIDDAL** (*An Spidéal*). The *Spiddal Craft Centre* is a collection of workshops showing high-quality sculpture, ceramics, weaving and jewellery, open all year. Spiddal itself, which has a small beach and boats to the Aran Islands, can be surprisingly lively for such a tiny, drive-through town; it's part of the *Gaeltacht* and you can catch good sessions in the pubs here. *Spiddal Village Hostel* (☎091/83555; £4–5) is the cheapest place to spend the night; if you want **B&B** there's plenty of choice – try Mrs Concannon's *Dún Lios*, Park West (☎091/83165; £11). Five and a half miles west of Spiddal there are also **hostels** at INVERIN (*Indreabhán*): an *An Óige* one (☎091/93154; Oct–May £4.50, June–Sept £5.90), and the *Connemara Tourist Hostel*, Aille (☎091/93104; all year; £5).

Beyond **ROSSAVEAL** (another departure point for the Aran Islands) the land breaks up into little chains of low-lying islands, linked to one another by natural causeways. These islets, more gentle than the main body of Connemara, make a perfect place to get lost: meandering around the inlets and gullies you experience a happy disorientation.

The beach at **CARRAROE** (*An Cheathrú Rua*) is a strand made up of tiny fragments of coralline seaweed, and the *Réalt na Maidine* bar (☎091/95193) here offers both bar food and B&B. Near ROSMUCK, a speck of a hamlet, is the cottage of the republican and poet **Pádraig Pearse**, who was executed after signing the 1916 proclamation. The cottage where he wrote plays in both English and Irish is open to the public (mid-June–mid-Sept daily 9.30am–1.30pm & 2.30–6.30pm; 80p, students 30p, heritage card; ☎091/74292). At CARNA you can wander out onto Mweenish Island and look out to Saint Mac Dara's Island, where the remains of a monastery still stand. Such was the former reverence for the saint that fishermen would dip their sails three times when passing the island. A three-day festival, *Féile Mhic Dara*, is still held in July in Carna. There is a budget **hostel** here too, *Carna Hostel* (☎095/32240; £4.50).

Roundstone

The only settlement of any size in the area is **ROUNDSTONE**, a fishing village at the foot of the Errisbeg mountain. Curving its back to the Atlantic, the quaint stone harbour looks across its sheltered waters to the magnificent Twelve Bens of Connemara. Fishing is the main source of income, along with an unobtrusive tourism that makes the most of the unique prettiness of the setting and the glorious beach at Gurteen Bay. A huge sweep of white sand with lucid blue water, this is really very seductive. There's a **campsite**, the *Gurteen Caravan Site* (☎095/35882; March–Sept £3.50–4.50), a mile and a half west of Roundstone; it also has a launderette. An Industrial Development Authority complex is discreetly tucked away to the west of the village, where you can wander around the various studios and see traditional instruments being made (flutes, goatskin *bodhráns*, whistles and harps), visit pottery workshops and call in on *Folding Landscapes* – the people who produce the maps.

It's an easy couple of hours' walk from Roundstone up to the top of **Errisbeg** – follow the fuchsia-flooded lane up the side of *O'Dowd's* bar and then the track ahead. The views are panoramic: the frilly coast of isthmuses and islets runs out to the south, while the plain of bog to the north is vast and open, punctuated only by the irregular glinting surfaces of dozens of little lakes, like sinister jellied eyes on the stark face of the landscape. It's through this wilderness that the **bog road** runs, the source of such superstition that some local people will not travel along it at night. Around the turn of the century, two old women, who lived in the road's only dwelling, robbed and murdered a traveller who'd taken refuge with them, and the road is considered to be haunted. From Errisbeg the view across the bog to the Connemara mountain ranges is tremendous. To the west, extensive beaches of white sand scoop their way north – Gurteen, Dog's Bay, Ballyconneely, Bunowen and the coral strand of Mannin Bay – each one echoing the beauty of the last.

As far as **food and drink** go, Roundstone has a couple of expensive restaurants, some tea shops, and a handful of nice bars with music at weekends. There's particularly good pub grub at *O'Dowd's Bar*, and also in their *Seafood Restaurant* (Easter–Sept noon–10pm; ☎095/35809). Other popular bars are *Connolly's*, *Keanes Hilltop Bar* and *Vaughan's Lounge* in the *Roundstone House Hotel*. You can **hire bikes** from *Michael Ferron's* shop (£5 a day, £25 a week). To go **pony trekking** contact James de Courcey, Errisbeg, Roundstone (☎095/35803), who takes treks on beaches or in the mountains for around £10 per hour. There are several places for **B&B** – try Pádraic and Carmel Faherty, *Connolly's Bar* (☎095/35863; £12), Patricia Keane, *Heather Glen* (☎095/35837; £11), or Mrs C. Lowry, *St Josephs* (☎095/35865; £11).

Clifden

Because of the dramatic grandeur of the Connemara mountains and the romantic pull of Galway, you expect **CLIFDEN** (*Clochán*) – known as the capital of Connemara – to be something special. In fact it's a very small place with only two significant streets. Its great asset is its position, perched high above the deep sides of the boulder-strewn estuary of the Owenglin River. The circling jumble of the Twelve Bens provides a magnificent scenic backdrop, and the broad streets seem consciously to open out, to take in the fresh air of the mountains and the Atlantic. Gimlet spires of matching nineteenth-century churches pierce the sky, giving Clifden a sharp, distinctive skyline.

Clifden seems to be trying hard to cultivate the cosmopolitan atmosphere of Galway. Lots of European tourists come here, but, aiming to serve all tastes, the town somehow misses the mark. Bars have loud disco music blaring out onto the streets – exactly the kind of thing most Gaelophile Europeans have come to get away from. It attracts a fair number of young Dubliners too, revving up the life of this otherwise quiet, rural town. The place is at its most interesting when it's busy being Irish: during the annual **Connemara Pony Show**, for example, on the third Thursday in August (entrance around £2). This is for the sale and judging of Connemara ponies: tough, hardy animals, well suited to a harsh bog and mountain existence, yet renowned for their docile temperament. Clifden also has a community festival in the last week of September.

Practicalities

Clifden is an obvious base if you're hostelling or camping, despite its limitations, and even despite the fact that although the Connemara mountains *look* magnificent from here, they are not at all accessible without transport of one kind or another. *Bus Éireann* **buses** leave from Market Street, with three buses to Galway daily in the summer, and one a day for the rest of the year. The **tourist office** is in Market Street (mid-May to mid-Sept Mon–Sat 10am–6pm, July–Aug also Sun noon–4pm; ☎095/21163).

There's plenty of hotel and B&B **accommodation** in the centre of Clifden, though everything can be very busy in July and August. *Corrib House* on Main Street (☎095/21346; £9) is the cheapest in town, and very friendly. Others, all around £10, are: *The White Heather Guest House,* The Square (☎095/21085); Mrs M. King, *Kingstown House*, Bridge Street (☎095/21470); Mrs K. Morris, *Ben View House*, Bridge Street (☎095/21256); and John and Barbara Lydon, *Benbawn House*, Westport Road (☎095/21462). A couple of central pubs offer rather more upmarket rooms: *Barry's* on Main Street (☎095/21287; £20) or *Alcock & Brown* (☎095/21086; £22). At the other end of the scale there are two **hostels** next door to each other on Beach Road right in the centre of town: *Leo's* (☎095/41132; all year, £5, private rooms £7.50, camping £3), a friendly place with cosy turf fires, and the *Clifden Hostel* (£4.50, private rooms £5, bike hire £4–5).

There are plenty of places for **bike hire**: the B&B next door to the tourist office rents them out during the summer at £5 a day, £25 a week, as do *John Mannion*, Bridge Street (☎095/21160) and *Joyce's Garage*, Market Street. Clifden's **launderette** is in Main Square. **Pony trekking** is organised at *Errislannan Manor* (☎095/21134; closed Sun; £10 per hour), about a mile beyond the Alcock and Brown Memorial, south of Clifden on the L102. **Windsurfing** is available at the boat club, Coast Road. *The Island House*, Market Street (☎095/21379) organises **guided walks** focussing on the archaeology and natural history of Connemara, an excellent way to explore the countryside, especially if you are travelling on your own or if you don't have a car or bike (tours last four to five hours and cost around £11).

As for **food and drink**, there's no problem getting provisions in Clifden, and the town's two main streets harbour plenty of places to eat. On Market Street *Mannion's* bar is plain, but one of the nicest for drink, music and food; *The Old Skillet* serves fresh crabmeat, smoked salmon and soups at very reasonable prices; *The Coffee Shop* does delicious coffee and cakes and *Linda's Crafts and Coffee Shop* serves soups and healthy breakfasts. For **evening meals** at £12 and upwards try *O'Grady's Seafood Restaurant* or *Doris's Restaurant*. Round the corner on Main Street *The Marconi Bar* serves light meals from £4–6 and *Corrib House Restaurant* offers a seafood menu from £8. Just off Main Square *Kelly's Coffee House* does cappucinos, sandwiches and home-made ice-cream.

There's little traditional **music** on offer, but it's worth looking in *King's* bar on the square during the summer, or taking in a Traditional Irish Night at the town hall (July & Aug, Tuesdays, 9pm; £2.50).

Around Clifden

Clifden offers easy access to some beautiful scenery. To get to the **Twelve Bens** you will need to cycle, hitch or skilfully manipulate the bus service. For more spontaneous walking, take the westward **coast road** out of Clifden (past the hostels) to a fine, sandy beach and a path that follows the shore of Clifden Bay. The shell of a nineteenth-century Gothic castellated mansion that you pass on the way was the home of John D'Arcy, who founded the town. Running north from beside the hostels, the **sky road** takes you to more desolate countryside and the long thin inlet of Streamstown Bay. Stick to the road and you'll eventually come down to the little village of CLADDAGHADUFF, where at low tide you can walk across to **Omey Island**. There are excellent beaches here. In the bay three miles north is the little village of CLEGGAN, where you'll find a comfy **hostel**, *The Master's House* (☎095/44746; all year; £5, private rooms £6), and the ferry for the island of **Inishbofin** (see below).

To the immediate south of Clifden there's equally pleasant country. A fourteen-foot aeroplane wing carved in limestone sticks out of the bog four miles from Clifden on the **Ballyconneely road**, as a melodramatic memorial to the landing of **Alcock and Brown** at the end of their pioneering non-stop transatlantic flight in June 1919. Beyond this is the coral strand of Mannin Bay, excellent for swimming, as is that at Doonlonghan.

Inishbofin

The island of **INISHBOFIN** is a mellow, balmy place, quite different from the mainland. It's more fertile, its sandy beaches are sheltered, and there's a general softness to its contours. The only jagged features are the cliffs to the west (the *stags*), a fine vantage point for viewing seals basking on the shore. Even the high, heathery moorland soon gently descends to the placid **Lough Boffin**, rimmed with rustling water iris and bullrushes. The lough is the scene of the island's most durable **myth**, a story that explains how it got its name. Several versions of the tale exist, but the basic elements are constant. For eons the island lay shrouded in mist under the spell of an enchantment, but one day two lost fishermen came upon it and lit a fire by the shore, thus breaking the spell. As the mist cleared they saw an old woman driving a white cow along the strand. She hit it with a stick, and was instantly turned to rock. Taking her for a witch, the men hit her and they too immediately turned to rock (*Inis Bó Finne* means "Island of the White Cow"). The only white cow you'll see on the island today (and on postcards) was born on the morning of a local girl's wedding, and given to her as a marriage gift by her father, so perpetuating the romantic association.

The known **history** of the island starts in the seventh century, when Saint Colman arrived here from Iona after a quarrel with Rome over the method of calculating the date of Easter. No remains exist of the monastery he founded, but ruins of a thirteenth-century church stand on the original site in a sheltered vale beside the lake in the east. Later the island was taken over by the O'Flaherties, and then Grace O'Malley is supposed to have fortified the place for her fleet. Coming into the island's long protected harbour you'll see the remains of a sixteenth-century castle, low on the hummocky terrain. It was taken and strengthened yet further by Cromwell, who used Inishbofin – and other west coast islands – as a kind of concentration camp for clerics. The most chilling reminder of his barbarity is the rock visible in the harbour at low tide. Known as **bishop's rock**, it was here that Cromwell chained one unfortunate ecclesiastic, then let his troops watch the tide come slowly in and drown him.

Getting there, eating and sleeping

You can visit Inishbofin on a day trip from Clifden, even without a car. Take the 8am bus to **CLEGGAN** (summer Tues & Fri), which returns at around 7.30pm – but check with the driver. **Ferry** tickets are available from *Coynes* in Cleggan, *The Island House*, Clifden, or on board the *Dún Aengus* or *The Queen* (sailings depart Cleggan 11am and return from Inishbofin at 5pm daily, and there is at least one extra sailing a day during the summer months; return fare £10, further information ☎095/45806 or 44750).

There are two **hotels** on the island, both of which have **restaurants** open to non-residents. A midday meal in *Day's Hotel* (☎095/45827; £16) will cost you around £5, evenings £12 or more; the *Doonmore Hotel* (☎095/45806; £17) is marginally more expensive all round. If you're on a slim budget then take advantage of *Day's* excellent bar food, available all day. *Miko's* **pub** is very friendly and has **music sessions** any time of the week during the summer season, and at weekends in winter. If you want to book **B&B** (around £14) in advance, write to Lena Schofield, Horseshoe Bay, Inishbofin, County Galway; to rent a cottage contact Frances Concannon, Post Office, Inishbofin. The *Inishbofin Island Hostel* (☎095/45855; April–Sept; £5) is an extremely friendly place. There's an island shop, with the usual limitations on supplies – in particular, no Gaz – and *Miko's* pub will change travellers' cheques.

You can **camp** on any of the open common land. A particularly good spot is at the east end of the island at Rusheen beach, from where you're treated to the glorious sight of the Connemara mountains lurching into the sea. The only places that are dangerous for swimming are at Tra Geall, just beneath Doonmore, opposite the island of Inishark in the west.

The Connemara National Park

The **Connemara National Park** typifies the scenic splendour of west Galway. Its chief functions are to promote the area's natural beauty while conserving this area of bog, heath and granite mountains. The park includes part of the famous **Twelve Bens** range – Benbaun, Bencullagh, Benbrack and Muckanaght – all of which are for experienced walkers only. Less threatening are the spectacular Polldark River gorge and Glanmore valley, and the multi-faceted granite Diamond Hill – though problems of soil erosion here have led to the Park discouraging a walk to the top: ask at the visitors centre for the current state of play.

The park's **visitors' centre** (May–Sept daily 10am–6.30pm; ☎095/41054; admission £1, student 40p, heritage card), near Letterfrack, is a good source of information on the fauna, flora and geology of the area. It's also the focus for the bogland conservation work that's going on roundabout, and the herbarium here is worth looking at if you're interested in botany. The staff can suggest safe hiking routes of varying length and difficulty, and you can leave details of your own route and intended time of return – an invaluable service in this potentially hazardous landscape. The centre has kitchen facilities available for walkers, an indoor "picnic" area, and a new tearoom. In July and August a botanist leads a guided walk of about two-and-a-half hours, currently leaving at 10.30am on Monday, Wednesday and Friday, though it's wise to ring and check this schedule. As well as offering facilities to outsiders, the centre is doing much to raise local awareness of the value of the area as a tourist amenity – particularly important in view of the current threat of goldmining in the area.

Letterfrack and Tullycross

LETTERFRACK itself is an orderly nineteenth-century Quaker village in a rugged setting. The village is tiny, but there's good food, and occasionally music, at *Veldon's* and *The Bard's Den*. There's also a post office, phone, shop and bureau de change and a new independent hostel *The Old Monastery* (☎095/41132; all year; £5, private rooms £7.50, camping £3; bike hire), a perfect base for walking in the National Park. Two miles east of here, the towers of **Kylemore Abbey** sit in a rhododendron-filled hollow against lush deciduous slopes. Its white castellated outline, perfectly reflected in the reed-punctured lake, has made it the subject of many a postcard, but Kylemore is in fact a phoney Tudor building created by a nineteenth-century Liverpool shipping magnate. A girls' boarding school now occupies the house; visitors are welcome to its restaurant and pottery showrooms, but otherwise the interior is private. You can, however, walk through the woods to see the medieval-style Victorian church, with its interior of Connemara marble.

Alternatively, a detour round the Renvyle Peninsula off the N59, northwest of Letterfrack, takes you through **TULLYCROSS**. A Rent-an-Irish-Cottage scheme operates in the village, the cottages fully incorporated into the main street with a view to helping visitors mix in with the local social life. The effect is pretty suburban – rather like a set for a Gaelic series of *Neighbours*. Nearby **Renvyle House** is of immense interest in Irish literary and political history. At one time it was visited by the great Edwardian comic twosome Somerville and Ross, authors of *Stories of an Irish R.M.*, but the house's most famous owner was Oliver St John Gogarty, the distinguished surgeon, writer and wit. An associate of the Gaelic League, he attended the literary evenings of Yeats, Moore and AE (George

Russell), and is immortalised as "stately plump Buck Mulligan" in Joyce's *Ulysses*. Renvyle House is now a hotel (☎095/43511, 43444; £35), also offering facilities such as horse riding, windsurfing and a swimming pool to non-residents. About a mile west of the hotel is a ruined O'Flaherty **castle**, superbly overlooking the sea. The coast road to the east offers magnificent scenery, a great route for the **hostel** at Killary Harbour if you are cycling, and some lovely sandy beaches.

Killary Harbour and around

Inland, the N59 route to **KILLARY HARBOUR** is faster and similarly beautiful. The lightly wooded shore around Ballinakill Harbour provides a brief luxuriant interlude before the landscape of wild bog and granite reasserts itself with ever increasing austerity. The *An Óige* **hostel** at Killary (☎095/43417; June–Sept £5.50, March–May & Oct £3.80), where Wittgenstein finished writing his *Philosophical Investigations* in 1948, has a deeply ponderous setting at the mouth of Ireland's only fjord, a cold dark tongue of water which cuts eight miles into the barren mountains. The hostel is five miles of extremely difficult hitching off the N59, so be prepared to walk. There's a shop at the hostel open evenings, otherwise you have to go to LETTERGESH shop and post office. From the hostel walk south, past the adventure centre (see below); take the right turn before the crest of the hill, and keep on for about one and a quarter miles; the shop is the first big house on the left, with a phonebox outside. A *Bank of Ireland* van operates from here at 1pm on Thursdays. There are good sandy beaches in the vicinity.

The *Little Killary Adventure Centre*, Salruck, Renvyle (☎095/43411), runs courses in mountain walking, climbing, sailing, canoeing, sailboarding, archery and orienteering. Courses start from £65 for a weekend, £225 a week, and are generally booked well in advance, though it is often possible to join a course for part of a week or weekend. Further north, **LEENANE** has plenty of **B&Bs** from which to enjoy this dramatic landscape, most recently used as a location for the film "The Field": Mrs Hamilton's *Bayview House* (☎095/42240; £12); Mrs Hoult's *Hillcrest House*, Clifden Road (☎095/42244; £11) and Mrs Wallace's *Avondale House* (☎095/42262; £11) are all reasonable options. If you're heading towards Cong, in County Mayo (p.342), the desolate, empty road takes you through MAUM and on past *Cornamona Hostel* on the shores of Lough Corrib (☎092/48002; April–Sept; £4.50), just nine miles from Cong.

MAYO

Often seen as simply a passage between scenic Galway and literary Yeats country, **Mayo** is little visited – though it's hard to see why. Like Galway to the south and Sligo to the north, it has a landscape of high cliffs, lonely mountains and bright fuchsia hedges; in the wild, boggy area to the northwest are the vestiges of a *Gaeltacht*; and on Lough Conn there's some of the best fishing in Ireland. Yet, with the exception of the Georgian town of **Westport** and **Achill Island**, the biggest of the Irish offshore islands and a traditional Irish holiday resort, Mayo is off the west of Ireland tourist trail. This is all the more incomprehensible since the railway will take you right out to Westport, on the coast, and the opening of the new international airport at Knock has made the northwest more accessible. Mayo is bound eventually to become busier, but for the moment it remains wonderfully empty.

The Barony of Murrisk – and Clare Island

Unless you're flying into Knock (see p.341), you'll probably enter Mayo by road from Galway, via the spectacular scenery of **Killary Harbour**, part of the lobe of land between the Galway border and Westport that's known as the **Barony of Murrisk**. This is country as rugged and remote as anything you'll find in the west, and two ranges of hills, the Mweelrea Mountains and the Sheefry Hills, provide terrain for energetic walking, mountaineering, riding, fishing and canoeing.

Delphi and Louisburgh

The road due north from Killary threads along a narrow valley which opens up, briefly, for a famous salmon and sea-trout lough-fishery with the unlikely name of **DELPHI** (in the local pronunciation, "Delph-eye"). The story behind the name involves the first Marquess of Sligo, whose seat, misleadingly, was at Westport. The flamboyant Marquess, a friend of Lord Byron, was caught in the sway of romantic Hellenism, and in 1811 set sail for Greece to search for antiquities. He swam with Byron off Piraeus, and rode with him overland to Corinth; but when he got to Delphi, he suffered a bout of homesickness, finding that it reminded him of nothing so much as his fishery at home in County Mayo. After numerous adventures, and some pillaging of ancient sites, the Marquess returned home to reminisce. Nowadays, there's an **adventure centre** (☎095/42208) at Delphi, offering supervised instruction in windsurfing, mountaineering, canoeing and so on. **Pony trekking** is based at the *Drumindoo Stud* (☎098/66195). Luxurious **accommodation**, plus a taste of the area's history, can be had at *Delphi Lodge* (☎095/42213; £30–35, minimum stay 2 nights), an 1830s sporting lodge by the lake, built for the Marquess of Sligo in a surprisingly austere style.

North of Delphi, the road runs alongside sombre **Doo Lough**, also known as the Black Lake, and over desolate moorland before reaching **LOUISBURGH**. Pronounced "Lewis-burg", this is one of the few instances where a town this side of the Atlantic has been named after one on the other: it was renamed after Henry Browne, uncle of the first Marquess of Sligo, had taken part in the capture of Louisburgh, Nova Scotia, in 1758. Louisburgh is essentially little more than a crossroads, but its planned buildings give it an incongruous air of importance, and it's a pleasant enough place to stay. The *Granuaile Interpretive Centre* (☎098/66195) provides useful information about the historical resonances of the scenery and on local flora and fauna, with a thirty-minute video: there's also a coffee shop and craft shops.

Louisburgh makes a good base for exploring the sandy **beaches** that run along the north coast as far as Murrisk Abbey, as it has some good **self-catering accommodation** (details on ☎098/66260) and a number of **hotels** including the reasonably priced *Durkan's*, in Chapel Street (☎098/66140; £15). Just outside Louisburgh, at Old Head (on the Westport Road), there's a **campsite** with showers and launderette (☎098/66021; £4.50 plus 50p per person; June–Aug). Another good beach is the **Silver Strand**, claimed grandiosely in the local tourist leaflets to be second only to Florida's Key West. You can reach it by turning southwest at the crossroads just outside Louisburgh on the Killary road; it has a couple of **B&Bs** – *Silver Strand House* (☎098/66021; £12) is homely and comfortable. The *Céilí House Café* (☎098/68656; booking advised), not far away at Killadoon, is worth going out of your way for: run by a young German couple it offers snacks all day and special five-course "sunset dinners" of unusual seafood dishes: if it's clear, the sunset is worth the price of the meal in itself.

Clare Island

Follow the road from Louisburgh west along the strand to the land's tip, and you reach **Roonagh Quay**, where a boat leaves twice a day for **CLARE ISLAND**. (The bus from Westport runs at least twice a day and will drop you two miles away in Louisburgh.) The crossing takes 25 minutes; boats leave morning and evening – check times with the tourist office in Westport (☎098/25711) or with the *Bay View Hotel* on the island (☎098/26307). Fares are £6 return, £4 for students. Although it's tiny – only fifteen or so square miles – Clare Island rises to a height of 1522 feet in a massive shoulder of land that dominates everything around. There's not much here besides the hills, some ruins, and some unfrequented sandy beaches, but there's plenty of walking, and you can go pony trekking, or water-ski, sailboard or fish.

The island is famed above all as the stronghold of **Grace O'Malley**, or Gráinne Ní Mháille (c.1530–1600; often corrupted to **Granuaile**), the fearless and none too scrupulous pirate. The daughter of Owen O'Malley, chief of the western islands, she made herself queen of the Clew Bay area when he died, and earned her place in Irish legend by being one of the few Irish chiefs to stand up to Elizabeth I, insisting on being treated as her regal equal when they met in London in 1575. Continually mentioned in sixteenth-century dispatches, her exploits included dissolving her marriage to her second husband, Sir Richard Burke of Mayo, by slamming the castle door in his face and stealing all his castles. Her own castle is at the eastern end of the island and she – or a close relative – is buried in a tomb on the north side of the ruined thirteenth-century Cistercian abbey halfway along the south coast of the island.

You can **stay** overnight on Clare Island, at the *Bay View Hotel*, which isn't outrageously expensive (around £18) and also organises local watersports.

Croagh Patrick and Murrisk Abbey

The land between Louisburgh and Westport is dominated by the strange, perfectly conical silhouette of **Croagh** (pronounced *croak*) **Patrick**, which at 2513 feet is by far the highest mountain in the immediate area. The sandy beaches of the shore peter out at Bertra Strand, just short of MURRISK and the ruins of **Murrisk Abbey**, a house of Augustinian friars set up on the shore of Clew Bay by the O'Malley family in 1457.

Looking out over the hummocky islets of the bay, the abbey is the best starting point if you want to climb the mountain. On the landward side, a little saint's head carved in the wall peers glumly up the slope – it's a very tough **climb**. Still, there's a surprise when you get to the top; the summit isn't conical, as it looks from the bottom, but forms a flat plateau, with a little chapel and a breathtaking view: on a good day you can see right from the Twelve Bens in the south to the mountains of Achill Island in the north, the Nephin Beg east of the island, and on to the Slieve League in Donegal.

In 441 **Saint Patrick** spent the forty days of Lent on the mountain in prayer and fasting, and it's from here that he is supposed to have sent the reptiles of

Ireland crawling to their doom. Just to the south of the summit is the **precipice of Lugnanarrib**, where he stood, ringing his bell, then repeatedly hurling it over the edge, each time taking with it a stream of toads, snakes and other creepy-crawlies. Luckily he didn't have to go down to the bottom to get his bell back – helpful spirits did the job for him. There's a pilgrimage to the top of Croagh Patrick, which is carried out by some 60,000 people, some of them in bare feet, every year on the last Sunday of July.

A fine place to stop for **refreshments** after a climb, barefoot or not, up the mountain, is *Glosh House*, a restaurant overlooking the sea and specialising in seafood and vegetarian dishes. It also does Irish breakfasts and sustaining afternoon teas.

Westport

Set in a picturesque eighteenth-century landscape on the shores of Clew Bay, **WESTPORT** is a comfortable, relaxed town, still recognisably Georgian, with a leafy mall, octagonal square, a canalised river and one of Ireland's great stately homes, Westport House. In the summer it's tremendously lively, with Irish, British and French visitors returning annually to re-sample its charms, and a couple of excellent festivals.

The town was planned by the architects Richard Castle and James Wyatt, and its formal layout comes as quite a surprise in the midst of the west. In its heyday Westport was very prosperous, fattened by the trade in linen and cotton cloth and yarn. In 1817 the monthly sales of linen were worth £3000, and of yarn £1000, figures that were quite staggering at the time. However, like many places throughout Ireland, Westport was hit hard by the Act of Union of 1801. Though local landowners like the first Marquess of Sligo (the one who swam with Byron) supported the Act in the belief that it would be of economic benefit, the reverse was in fact true: Irish hand looms were no competition for the new spinning jennies in Britain's industrial towns, the national linen and cotton industries declined, and Westport's economy was ruined. Mass unemployment forced a choice between reverting to subsistence farming, or starting a new life in America.

Its quiet Georgian beauties and its loud modern streetlife apart, the reason Westport is on the tourist trail nowadays is **Westport House** (Mon–Sat 10.30am–6.30pm, Sun 2–6pm; admission to house £3.50, zoo £2.50, both £4.50), a mile or so out of town towards Clew Bay. Beautifully designed in 1730 by the ubiquitous Richard Castle, with later additions by Thomas Ivory and James Wyatt, this was one of the first Irish houses opened to the public – and it's had a go at any and every way of making money. There's a zoo park in the grounds and horse-drawn caravans for hire, while the dungeons (which belong to an earlier house) have everything from a trace-your-ancestor service to a machine that claims to tell you whether or not you're sexy. On the plus side, though, the dungeons also contain a fairly useful secondhand bookshop; and the house and location are wonderful if you can ignore the commerce. Inside the house there's a *Holy Family* by Rubens, a violin which used to belong to J. M. Synge, and, on the first floor, a room with lovely Chinese wallpapers dating from 1780. A lot of the mahogany in the house was brought back from Jamaica by the first Marquess, who was instrumental in freeing slaves during his time as governor there.

On the walls of the staircase, a series of paintings of local views by James Arthur O'Connor, commissioned by the second Marquess in 1818 and 1819, show an idyllic nineteenth-century landscape; bustling activity as sailing boats are unloaded at Westport Quay, an overweeningly romantic version of the dramatic scenery at Delphi. This was wishful thinking – Westport in the 1810s was already overshadowed by the changes in the relationship with England, and by 1825 was finished as an industrial centre.

Practicalities: rooms and food

For cheap accommodation you've a choice of three independent and one *An Óige* **hostels**. The newest and most central, the *Old Mill Hostel* (☎098/27045; £5.50), converted from part of an eighteenth-century complex of mills and warehouses, is on James Street, up from the Octagon. Alternatively there's the roughly stone-built *Granary*, past *Ryan's Hotel* on Quay Road, just before the road forks (☎098/25903; £4.50), and *Summerville* (☎098/25948; 4.50, private room £5.50; mid-March to mid-Oct), a sort of svelte Georgian bungalow, full of sagging sofas and pretty, faded chintzes – once part of an Anglo-Irish estate – a mile and a half out of town on the Louisburgh road overlooking Clew Bay. The large *An Óige Club Atlantic* (☎098/26644; £5.90) is also new, clean and comfortable: it's opposite the train station on Altamont Road, and very close to Fair Green, where buses stop. If you want to pitch a **tent**, *Parklands Caravan and Camping Park* (☎098/25141; £4–5; May–Aug) is on the Westport estate; there's more camping further out at Old Head.

The **tourist office**, in the Mall (June–Sept Mon–Fri 9am–6pm, Sat 10am–6pm; Oct–May Mon–Fri 9am–5.15pm; ☎098/25711) can help with other accommodation. There are dozens of **B&Bs**: try Mrs Sheridan at *Altamont House*, Ballinrobe Road (☎098/25266; £12.50), Mrs Reidy's *Clooneen House*, Castlebar Street (☎098/25361; £13) or Mrs Kelly's *Dún na Mara*, Castlebar Street (☎098/25205; £12). Moving upmarket, you may be put off by the olde-worlde pretensions of the *Olde Railway Hotel* (☎098/25166; £35, cheaper weekend rates), but its location, facing the canalised river on the leafy Mall, could hardly be better: they'll also fix up canoeing, hill climbing, pony trekking and golf.

There are plenty of places to **eat**. The *Continental Café and Healthfood Shop*, High Street (☎098/26679), serves hearty soups and home-made bread and is also an excellent information centre (open only until 6pm). Two budget options, with sustaining salads and soups, are *McCormack's* (open only until 6pm) and *The Crockery Pot* (open until 9pm), both in Bridge Street. Other good places are *Anthony Hoban's* pub on James Street (☎098/25020), with value-for-money home-cooked meals in the evening; the more expensive *Carvery and Seafood Bar* in the *Olde Railway Hotel* (12.30–3pm & 6.30–10pm); or at the other end of the scale try the burgers at *Nevada* on Mill Street (open till late). Out at The Quay (see below), *Quay Cottage* (☎098/26412), at the entrance to Westport House, serves enormous salmon salads and plenty of vegetarian food, but is rather pricey; nearby *Moorings Restaurant* (☎098/25874; booking essential) is also excellent, and probably better value.

Festivals, nightlife and entertainment

If you want to see Westport at its liveliest, try to make it for the **Westport Street Festival**, in the second week of July, with free street concerts and general carousal. The season stretches from then until the **Arts Festival** at the end of September. Even if you don't coincide with a festival, you'll find plenty to do. There are two main centres of activity, the town centre, and the fast-developing complex of shops, pubs and restaurants around The Quay by the entrance to Westport House. In the centre, the best **music pubs** are on Bridge Street, where *The West* is hugely popular (arrive early and stay put) and *Matt Molloy's Bar*, owned by the eponymous member of *The Chieftains*, features occasional musical celebrities. The best **dancing** takes place on Fridays and Saturdays at the *Castlecourt Hotel*, Castlebar Street (until 1.30am; £4 admission includes bar meal).

Out at **The Quay**, the waterside complex of refurbished buildings is guaranteed to be humming until late on any summer evening. *The Towers*, overlooking Clew Bay, is a waterside musical pub with excellent seafood. The *Asgard* bar/restaurant (☎098/25319) is also worth a look, while up the drive to Westport House you'll find the *Wagon Wheel Bar*, always crowded and featuring Brendan Shine every Tuesday in season.

For a rather quieter evening of Irish culture, look out for theatrical events at the **Wyatt Theatre**, in the Town Hall on the Octagon, where there are good amateur productions of Irish drama.

Daytime activities, sightseeing apart, are plentiful. If you're lucky with the weather the best **beaches** are at Bertra, six miles out on the Louisburgh road, and Mulrany, 18 miles away on the Achill road. **Cycling** from Westport is rewarding, if strenuous – there are hills in almost all directions except towards Newport: bike hire is from *J.P. Breheny & Sons*, Castlebar Street (☎098/25020). **Horse riding**, which will let you get right off the road, is available half a mile out of town on the Castlebar road at the *Drummindoo Equitation Centre* (☎098/25616) and also at Westport House. The **sea angling** in Clew Bay is magnificent, and there are also good opportunites for salmon and trout in nearby lakes and rivers – details from the *Sea Angling Centre* in town. **Sailing** in sheltered waters can be arranged through the Mayo Sailing Club in Rosmoney – good facilities and teaching for newcomers.

North to Newport

The road north out of Westport, bordered by bright fuchsia hedges, follows the shore of Clew Bay to **NEWPORT**. A neat, trim little town unashamedly devoted to tourism, Newport's main boast is that one of Grace Kelly's ancestors once lived here. It's also a centre for sea angling; if you go into the swanky *Newport House Hotel* (around £48 a night; ☎098/41222) in the evenings you'll see massive sea trout – caught by guests earlier in the day – laid out for less energetic guests to admire.

You may well be tempted to hurry on to Achill or the wild Erris Peninsula, but Newport is a serviceable base for both the sea and the Nephin Beg mountains. If you do **stay**, the *Skerdagh Outdoor Centre*, three miles out of Newport on the L137, functions as a hostel and also arranges bicycle hire, rock climbing, orienteering, hill walking and canoeing (June–Aug, but group bookings taken at other times; ☎098/41500). There's **self-catering accommodation** at Loch Morchan at Kilbride, just outside Newport (☎098/41221), or if you want to drink in the comfortably urban atmosphere of Newport itself, try the *Black Oak Inn* on Medlicott Street (☎098/41249; £12). For **horse riding** and pony trekking the contact is ☎098/36126; permits for **fishing** are available from the *Newport House Hotel*. Tourist **information** can be had from the stand at *Darac Crafts* in the Main Street (☎098/41116).

Achill Island

More than with most places in the west, you need good weather for **ACHILL ISLAND**. Although it's the part of County Mayo most developed for tourism, this means no more than a few hotels, B&Bs and hostels, and if it rains there's simply nothing to do but pack up and head for Westport or Sligo. Given good weather, though, Achill can be magical, especially for campers, who can live at the water's edge. Achill's sandy beaches never seem overcrowded, although they attract plenty of (mostly Irish) tourists in high summer. Inland, the bogland and mountains are dotted with ancient relics – standing stones, stone circles and dolmens. The largest of the Irish offshore islands (although it's connected to the mainland by a road bridge), Achill was Irish-speaking until very recently. Tourism here seems to have had an almost entirely beneficial effect: before its arrival, islanders subsisted to a very great extent on money sent home by emigrant relatives.

The bridge that crosses to the island will bring you first to **Achill Sound**, where there's a small **tourist office** (☎098/45384; July & Aug Mon–Sat 10am–6pm) and a number of souvenir shops. These can be discouraging, but it's best to ignore them – they're in no way typical of what's to come. More useful are a post office and **bike hire**, at the *Achill Sound Hotel* (☎098/45245; £6 per day). Achill Sound is not the best base for exploring the island, but if you decide to go no further a new independent **hostel**, the *Wild Haven* (☎098/45392; £5) does offer the comforts of warm duvets and an open fire.

Seeing the island

A combination of walking and cycling is the most pleasurable way to get to know Achill, although the island can be fairly strenuous going (hitching is a viable alternative, especially in season when the island is full of visitors). **Slievemore**, Achill's highest mountain at 2205 feet, is a massive pile of quartzite and mica. This is the first place to make for if you're driving, with fabulous views. At its foot, on the seaward side, are the **Seal Caves**, burrowing way back under the mountain; you can visit them by boat from Dugort (see below). On Slievemore's southern slopes stands a **dolmen** with a stone circle at each end, and a booley village of huts formerly used during summer pasturing – a reminder of a much newer, but equally outdated, transhumant way of life. Close to Dugort, some ruined buildings and scattered gravestones are all that's left of a village known simply as **The Settlement**. It was founded in 1834 by a Protestant vicar, the Reverend E. Nangle, who bought up sixty percent of the island and built schools and a printing press in an ultimately unsuccessful effort to evangelise the islanders.

Continuing anticlockwise you come to **Croghaun**, a whisker lower than Slievemore at 2195 feet, whose seaward side boasts spectacularly high cliffs. On the eastern side is **Corrymore Lodge**, where the notorious land agent Captain Boycott once lived (see p.343). The best approach to the summit is via **Lough Acorrymore**, above Corrymore Lodge: from the top you're treated to another magnificent view of the Belmullet Peninsula and the scattered islands, while mountains rise spectacularly in the southeast.

Keel and Dugort

The best bases for exploring Achill are Dugort or **KEEL**, nine miles from Achill Sound on the south side of the island. There's a wonderful two-mile sandy **beach** here, at the east end of which are the fantastic Cathedral Rocks, eroded into a series of caves and pillars by the wind and water. They are backed by the **Minaun**, at 1532 feet another mountain worth climbing for the view. Close to the southern tip of the island is Kildownet Castle, a stronghold used by the pirate queen Grace O'Malley.

The *Wayfarer Hostel* is right on the strand at Keel (☎098/43266; £5; March–Oct); the **campsite**, right by the beach, charges £3–4 for tents (☎098/43211; open June–Sept); other than these, there's not much in the way of cheaper accommodation, certainly fewer B&Bs than in Dugort – you could try *Island House*, Dookinelly (☎098/43180; £12), or for rather more luxury the Achill Head Hotel (☎098/43131; £18). There's also a post office and shops. *The Beehive* is a new handicrafts and coffee shop in a replica beehive hut; you can rent **bikes** at *O'Malley's Island Sports* (☎098/43125). For **music**, try the *Village Inn* or the *Annexe Inn*.

Two miles west of **DUGORT**, the *Valley House Hostel* (☎098/47204; £4.50; April–Nov) was once home to the woman whose story is told in J.M. Synge's *The Playboy of the Western World* – her rejected suitor burned down a barn and tossed her onto the flames. The house now has four-bed rooms, and the luxury of a bar. *Atoka House*, at Valley Crossroads, is a comfortable **B&B** (☎098/47229; £10), with a good, cheap restaurant attached. *McDowell's Hotel* in the village itself also does good B&B (April–Sept; ☎098/472051; £14) with excellent food, including vegetarian, and runs frequent traditional music sessions. Dugort's two **campsites** are the *Seal Caves Caravan and Camping Park* (☎098/43262; £4–4.50; April–Sept) and *Lavele's Golden Strand Caravan and Camping Park* (☎098/47232; £4; April–Sept).

The Belmullet Peninsula and Bangor Erris

The **Belmullet Peninsula**, a flat slab of land that seems tacked onto the mainland almost as an afterthought, is the one part of Mayo where some Gaelic is still spoken. It's sparsely populated, but its houses tend to be scattered evenly rather than grouped into villages, in the way that's characteristic of the west of Ireland,

THE FRENCH INVASION

On August 22, 1798, three warships flying British colours anchored at Kilcummin, near Killala. The Protestant Bishop Stock, relieved that they were apparently English and not the rumoured French invasion fleet, sent his two sons and the port surveyor to pay their respects. They were immediately taken prisoner; the **invasion** had begun. After a brief resistance, Killala succumbed to the French, and at sunset that evening a French soldier climbed to the top of the Bishop's Palace and replaced the British flag with a green flag with a harp in the centre, bearing the words *Erin go Bragh* (Ireland for Ever).

Wolfe Tone, the inspirational leader of the United Irishmen, had been working since his exile from Ireland in 1794 to secure foreign aid for his planned insurrection against the British. However, by the time the first French expedition (of 1100 men under General Humbert) reached Killala, rebellion had already been all but crushed. Not only was there a military mismatch between the French professional soldiers and the few poorly armed Irish novices who joined them, but there were ideological clashes, too. The French had expected that liberation from British rule would appeal to Catholics and Protestants alike, and were further confused to find and you're hardly ever out of sight of habitation. The seaward side of the peninsula is raked by Atlantic winds to the extent that almost no vegetation can survive. The landward side, overlooking Blacksod Bay, is much more sheltered and has some **beaches**, notably at Elly Bay. To the east and north the land rises, though the cliffs are not hugely spectacular. There's an impressive castle at **Doonamo Point**, its wall cutting off the neck of the peninsula and enclosing three clocháns and a circular fort.

BELMULLET itself is a functional little village, its streets perpetually mired with mud from the bogs. The surrounding district of **Bangor Erris** as a whole is bleak; there are people who fall in love with its uncompromising lack of comforts, but it can also make you understand why a lot of Irish people have mixed feelings about conservationist enthusiasm for the black bog – you can't grow anything on it, it's dirty, and it's horrible to live in. Inland, the moors of the Barony of Erris, in contrast to the Belmullet Peninsula, really are deserted.

For **accommodation** on the peninsula, there's *Kilcommon Lodge* at PULLATHOMAS (☎097/84621; £4), an independent hostel that also does bed and breakfast and meals; or head for Belmullet itself, where the *Western Sands Hotel* (☎097/81096; £11) has basic rooms and there are numerous B&Bs. BANGOR ERRIS has another hostel, *Owenmore Riverlodge* (☎097/83497; £4; May–Sept), and there's an *An Óige* one at POLLATOMISH (☎097/87842; £4.50; April–Sept).

Heading east, the coastline is wonderfully dramatic, with some terrific walking country. **Benwee Head** is a massive cliff of almost 820 feet, with great views of the Donegal cliffs to the northeast and the **Stags of Broadhaven**, a series of seven 300-foot rocks which stand a mile and a half off the coast. Further east, near PORTURLIN, the waves have carved the rocks into weird, contorted shapes, including the Arches, a thirty-foot opening in the cliff which the brave – or foolhardy – attempt to row through in good weather at low tide. At BELDERRIG an excavation of a Stone Age settlement is in progress, but there's little to see as yet. East again, a detached rock with a fort on it at **Downpatrick Head** has some puffing holes which send up tall plumes of water in rough weather.

---

the Irish volunteers greeting them in the name of the Blessed Virgin and apparently having no idea of the significance of the French Revolution.

The rest of the story is sadly predictable. With some heroic fighting, the Franco-Irish army took Killala, Ballina and Castlebar, but on September 8, near the village of Ballinamuck in County Longford, seriously depleted in both numbers and weapons, it was defeated by the united armies of Lord Cornwallis and General Lake. The French were taken prisoner and returned to France; the Irish rebels were hanged.

A month later, sailing with another French force from Brest, Wolfe Tone was himself captured – along with the French fleet – off the coast of Donegal. He was subsequently courtmartialled and condemned to death. Despite his insistence that he should be treated with military honour, and therefore shot, he was sentenced to hang. Before that could be carried out, he cut his throat with a pocketknife, and died after seven days of agony. He came to personify the tradition of revolutionary violence in the cause of an independent Ireland.

The events of 1798 led directly to the Act of Union with Britain three years later, while the land agitation that spread throughout the country laid the foundations for land reform, Catholic emancipation and, eventually, the long process that led to Irish independence

Killala

KILLALA, overlooking Killala Bay as the coast curves back round towards Ballina, is a must, both for the magnificent local scenery and for its historical connections. Scene of one of the most significant events in Irish history – the unsuccessful French invasion organised by Wolfe Tone in 1798 (see box) – it's a pleasantly run-down seaside town, so small it's difficult to believe it's a bishopric, with lovely wild sea coasts and some good roads for cycling. As far as sights go, the highlights are an attractive quayside and a fine round tower, but it's the historic atmosphere that's the real attraction here.

If you want to stay there's an *An Óige* **hostel** in an old, stone house near the centre of town (☎096/32172; £5.50) and just a couple of **B&Bs** – try Mrs Carey's *Rathoma House* (☎096/32035; £12.50), four miles out of town, or Mrs Caplice's *Avondale*, Pier Road (☎096/32229; £12). Most local newsagents sell Bishop Stock's *Narrative* of the events of 1798 – a surprisingly sympathetic account of the uprising.

Inland: Lough Conn and Castlebar

The road from Killala to Ballina quickly leaves the drama of the northern coast and runs through flat farm country. It's remarkable only for two abbeys on the Moy estuary, **Moyne** and **Rosserk**, both of them founded in the fifteenth century. Rosserk, with a tower at the water's edge, is the bigger and more poetic of the two, but both have good cloisters.

There's nothing very much to recommend the busy town of **BALLINA**, except as a place to stock up on provisions and information. There's a **tourist office** open in the summer (☎096/70848; June–Aug Mon–Sat 10am–6pm), *Keehane's* in Arran Street is a reasonable bookshop, and the West of Ireland **cycling club** is based at *American House* on Station Road (☎096/21350) – it also has **accommodation** (£16), and you may find they're more interested in getting you to stay than in giving information. There are plenty of other B&Bs and small hotels around, and food in the bars or at *American House*.

Lough Conn

The main attraction of **Lough Conn** is for fishermen: the lake itself is rich in trout, and the River Moy is a delight for salmon anglers. If this is your thing then the place to stay would be the marvellously eccentric *Mount Falcon Castle* (☎096/21172; £40), run by the indomitable Constance Aldridge a few miles out of Ballina, which has its own fishing. If you're staying elsewhere you'll need to check the position on licences locally. Other **accommodation** is in plentiful bed and breakfasts around the lake, or at one of two independent hostels – *Cooltra Lodge* (☎094/56640; £4.50; June–Sept) in PONTOON, between Lough Conn and Lough Cullen, or *Gannons Hostel* in the pretty town of FOXFORD, three miles away. There are B&Bs in Foxford too, or try *Healy's Hotel* (☎094/56443; £25) in Pontoon, where the restaurant specialises in home-cooked Irish food using local produce.

Relaxed, raffish **CROSSMOLINA**, at the top of Lough Conn, has more places, including the comfortably run-down *Dolphin Hotel* (☎096/31270; £12), or on the lakeshore not far south, *Enniscoe House* (☎096/31112; £40) is a Georgian mansion run as farmhouse accommodation. It isn't cheap, but the owner, Susan Kellett, is putting together a heritage centre and is happy to show visitors round the house, as long as they ring first. Enniscoe is a good example of easygoing Georgian attitudes to architecture: originally built in the mid-eighteenth century as a three-storey house, it was extended in the 1790s (and damaged in 1798 when the French army marched down the back avenue) to include a grand facade overlooking Lough Conn. The result inside is two completely different structures whose floor levels and room sizes don't correspond at all.

East of the lough the country is flat and generally unexciting: if you want to explore further head west, where the **Nephin Beg** range of mountains has impressive walking country.

Castlebar and around

CASTLEBAR, although it's the county town of Mayo, is another place that offers little reason to hang around. The tree-bordered green is attractive, and the main street has all the facilities you might need conveniently gathered together, but since the demise of the annual rock festival there seems to be little going on. Historically, it's notable for a Franco-Irish victory in 1798, known as the Castlebar Races, at which General Humbert's army routed a stronger force commanded by General Lake. Should you need to stay, there's plenty to choose from – the *Imperial Hotel* (☎094/21961; £21) is ideally situated on the green, B&Bs concentrated mainly on the Westport road, where you could try *Nephin House* (☎094/23840; £11) or *Devard* (☎094/23462; £12).

Seven miles south of Castlebar on the Ballinrobe road is **Ballintubber Abbey**. Founded in 1216 by Cathal O'Connor, King of Connacht, it's an important site and ought to be atmospheric. Sadly that's not the case. It's been grossly over-restored, and around the church the Stations of the Cross form a kind of ghastly theme park in stone, including representations of an empty tomb, an inexplicable dolmen, and some human figures whose overall impression is obscurely pornographic.

Between Castlebar and Foxford, at **STRADE**, is the **Michael Davitt Museum**, which preserves a number of mementoes, and documents the activities of the Land League in which Davitt played a major part.

Knock

Ever since an apparition of the Virgin Mary, accompanied by Saint Joseph and Saint John, was seen on the gable of the parish church of **KNOCK** in 1879, it has been a place of pilgrimage. As a passer-by in Ireland, it's surprisingly easy to forget the all-pervasive influence of the Catholic church, but at Knock you're brought slap up against it. Whatever you may believe about the possible veracity of the apparitions, Knock rates for Catholics, along with Lourdes in France and Fatima in Portugal, as one of the leading modern miraculous confirmations of their faith. A massive and ugly church with a capacity of twenty thousand was opened in 1976, the pope visited the shrine in 1979, and in 1986 a new international **airport** was opened at nearby CHARLESTOWN.

When Monsignor Horan, a local priest, first hatched the plan for the new airport it seemed a crazy and profligate idea, and there were years of bitter controversy over this apparent waste of public funds. In fact it has proved remarkably successful, and as well as bringing in pilgrims to see the shrine, the airport has had the effect of opening up the northwest of Ireland for travellers – to the extent that Mayo is in reach of London for weekend breaks, and house prices in the county are booming as wealthy inhabitants of southeast England buy their second homes. The Lourdes to Knock run is also used by fishermen from the southwest of France to reach the lake fisheries of the west of Ireland.

The **airport** (situated three miles from Charlestown at the junction of the N17 and N5) is open from 9am to 6pm daily, serving many UK airports including Luton, Stansted and Coventry. An *Aer Lingus* shuttle service to Dublin connects with major international flights. There's a **tourist information office** in the airport, open to greet arriving flights (☎094/67247; closed Tues & Thurs in winter), and another in Knock itself (☎094/88193; May–Sept daily 10am–6pm); ask them for details of transport – most of the time you seem to have to rely on taxis to Charlestown (a major crossroads where you can pick up buses and there are a number of B&Bs) or Knock.

As a **town**, Knock is nothing much to look at. The scene of the apparitions has been glassed in to form a **chapel**, and pilgrims can be seen there praying at all hours. Other than that, and the religious tat shops, it's not a place to hang around, unless you've just flown in and need a **place to stay**. If this is the case, there's no problem finding somewhere. There are a couple of hotels, such as the *Belmont* (☎094/88122; £20), and numerous B&Bs: try Mrs Carney's *Burren*, Kiltimagh Road (☎094/88362; £12), or *Mervue*, overlooking the shrine (☎094/88127; £12).

Cong and around

CONG lies between Lough Mask and Lough Corrib at the point where the dramatically mountainous country of Connemara to the west gives way to the flat and fertile farmland that makes up the east of County Mayo. A picture-book pretty village that caters for plenty of tourists, it's also the site of the ruined **Cong Abbey**, which was founded in 1128 for the Augustinians by Turlough O'Connor, King of Ireland (though it's probably built on a seventh-century monastic site). The doorways represent the transition between the quite different styles of Romanesque and Gothic. The cloisters look just a little bit too good to be true: they were partially rebuilt in 1860. At its height, Cong Abbey had a population of some 3000, and the practicalities of feeding such multitudes can be glimpsed in the remains of the refectory and kitchen by the river, where a fishing house over the water contains a fish trap beneath the floor. The **Cross of Cong**, a twelfth-century ornamented Celtic cross originally made in County Roscommon for the abbey, gives an indication of the wealth and status of the foundation – it's now on show at the National Museum in Dublin. From the abbey there's a pleasant wander through woods down to the river.

It's also worth taking a look at the **canal**. In the 1840s attempts were made, as a famine relief project, to dig a canal between Lough Corrib and Lough Mask. The river that links the two, though you can get to it at various points, including the Pigeon Hole, a mile or so north of Cong, runs underground through porous limestone for most of its length. This might have been an indication of what would happen to the canal: the porosity of the rock meant that the water just drained away, and Cong is left with a dry canal, complete with locks.

Cong's big house is **Ashford Castle**, at the point where the river meets Lough Corrib, now converted into a luxury hotel (☎092/46003; £50–90). Although its history goes back to the thirteenth century, what you see is essentially a Victorian castellated reconstruction.

More realistic prices are on offer at the *An Óige* **hostel** (☎092/46089; £5.50), signposted from the centre of the village, and the *Quiet Man* independent hostel (☎092/46511; £5), on Abbey Street; the latter is named after the John Wayne film shot locally, which is shown here every night. There are also numerous reasonable **B&Bs**: try Mrs Bourke at *Woodlands*, Caherduff, The Neale (☎092/46067; £13), half a mile out of town, or Mrs Coakley, also a short way out at *Hazel Grove*, Drumshiel (☎092/46060; £12). The *Rising of the Waters Inn* (☎092/46316; £12) has simple rooms and good bar food.

Around Cong: Ballinrobe

Loughmask House (not open to the public), on the shores of Lough Mask a couple of miles due north of Cong, was the home of the notorious **Charles Boycott**, a retired captain of the British army and land agent to Lord Erne. His behaviour toward the tenant farmers during the Land League unrest of the 1880s made him one of the victims of Parnell's "moral Coventry" policy, subsequently known as "boycotting". As Parnell himself put it in a meeting in Ennis in 1880:

> *You must show what you think of him on the roadside when you meet him, you must show him in the streets of the town, you must show him at the shop counter . . . even in the house of worship, by leaving him severely alone, by putting him into a sort of moral Coventry, by isolating him from the rest of his kind as if he were a leper of old, you must show him your detestation of the crime he has committed.*

Taking the Ballinrobe road, you pass one of the mysterious monuments that abound in Ireland. On the right-hand side of the road stands a massive stone-stepped **pyramid**, with an inscription, almost indecipherable, including the name George Browne and some worn Roman numerals, dating it somewhere in the eighteenth century. The Brownes are the family who occupy Westport House; but the reason for the pyramid remains obscure. **BALLINROBE** itself is probably worth visiting only if you're here in the third week of July, for the **Ballinrobe Races**. This is Irish racing as you've imagined it, with a great atmosphere at a picturesque and compact course; there's excellent viewing and it's all very relaxed and amateur.

EAST GALWAY

East Galway cannot rival the spectacular landscapes of west Galway or County Clare, nor their romantic isolation. Nonetheless, to hurry through east Galway without seeing what the place does have to offer would be a mistake. A lot of the land here is low-lying and easily cultivatable, which made it attractive to earlier settlers. They've left not only a network of roads and villages, but also a wealth of historic remains, particularly medieval monastic sites. The east of the county has nothing like the strong ethnic culture of the west, but towards the south the musical traditions of County Clare wash over the county boundaries and form an important part of the region's culture. And while the landscape is never exciting, some of it is very pleasant, notably the lakesides of **Lough Derg** at **Portumna**, and the delightful southern shore of **Galway Bay**, which becomes particularly special where the heights of the Burren of County Clare become a part of the scene.

Transport and accommodation

In contrast to Connemara, transport in east Galway is easy. Galway to Dublin **trains** call at Athenry and Ballinasloe (for train information phone Athenry ☎091/44020 or Ballinasloe ☎0905/42105), and there are *Bus Éireann* services to surrounding towns. *North Galway Club* runs a Dublin to Galway **coach** that picks up in Tuam, Athlone and Ballinasloe. **Hitching** is relatively easy too, since the area is well served by busy main roads. **Bike hire** is available from *P. Clarke & Sons*, Dunlo Street, Ballinasloe (☎0905/42417) and Tony Cunningham, Dominick Street, Portumna (☎0905/41070).

There are independent **hostels** at Aughrim, near Ballinasloe, and at Kinvarra, and an *An Óige* hostel at Doorus, as well as plenty of **B&Bs** around Tuam, Athenry, and Ballinasloe. **Tourist offices** at Tuam (in the Mill Museum; July–Aug Mon–Sat 10am–6pm; ☎093/24463) and Ballinasloe (July–Aug Mon–Sat 10am–6pm; ☎0905/42131) can give more information on accommodation around the region, and make bookings.

East of Lough Corrib

The east shore of Lough Corrib provides a gentle route between County Mayo and Galway City, less dramatic than the Connemara roads. The lake shore and the many rivers are popular with fishermen (for trout and salmon in summer, pike in winter), and visitors with no taste for field sports have a number of medieval ruins to admire.

Beside the lough

Two miles north of HEADFORD, virtually on the border of County Mayo, is **Ross Errilly** (or "Ross Abbey"), the biggest and best-preserved Franciscan abbey in Ireland. It was originally founded in the mid-fourteenth century, but the bulk of the buildings belong to the fifteenth – the Franciscan Order's greatest period of expansion. The church buildings themselves are impressive, with a battlemented slender tower (typical of Franciscan abbeys) and well-preserved windows, and there's a wonderful tiny cloister, but it's the adjacent domestic buildings and the picture they give of the everyday life of the Order that are perhaps the most interesting. Stand in the cloister with your back to the church and ahead to the right is the refectory, with the reader's window-side desk up in the far northeast corner. Straight ahead is a second cloister (this one without arcading), and behind that the bakehouse. To the northwest of this second courtyard lies the kitchen, where you can see a water-tank used for holding fish, and an oven which reaches into the little mill-room to the rear.

Five miles south of Headford, a detour off the main road leads you right down to the Lough shore and the ruined Franciscan friary of **Annaghdown** – far less impressive than Ross Errilly – and a nearby Norman castle. It was at this friary, after all his voyaging and preaching, that Saint Brendan finally died, nursed by his sister, who was head of Annaghdown nunnery. The road loops back to rejoin the main Galway road. **Traditional music** enthusiasts might want to sample the B&B at the seventeenth-century *Cregg Castle*, Corandulla (☎091/91434; £15), which has evenings of music and storytelling (Fri, £5) and set dancing (Wed, £1.50) and a range of music classes throughout the week.

Tuam and around

Northeast County Galway is served chiefly by the small market town of **TUAM**. There's little here to detain you, but should you wish to sniff out the scant remnants of the town's former importance, have a look inside the Church of Ireland Cathedral on Galway Road. It's primarily a nineteenth-century building, but a magnificent Romanesque arch, showing strong signs of Scandinavian influence, and the accompanying east window, have survived from a twelfth-century chancel. The shaft of an ornamented high cross is set in the wall near the west door. It's a great shame that so little remains of medieval Tuam. A monastery was founded here in the sixth century by Saint Iarlath, a disciple of Saint Enda of Inishmore, and in the medieval period Tuam became not only an archdiocesal see, but also the power centre of the O'Conors of Connaught. The high cross in the town square dates from the twelfth century: it's highly decorated but actually a bit of a patchwork, as the head and the shaft don't really belong together. Should you need to stop over in Tuam, there's no shortage of **B&Bs**: try Mrs Clarke, *Chessington House*, Ballygaddy Road (☎093/24584; £11), or Mrs O'Connor's *Kilmore House*, Kilmore, Galway Road (☎093/28118; £11), half a mile out of town. In the central Square, the *Imperial Hotel* (☎093/24188; £21) offers rooms and food. Tuam is also the home of the *Saw Doctors* – the band some see as the eventual successors to U2 – though this doesn't seem to be reflected in any great wealth of entertainment or music locally.

Dunmore and Knockmoy abbeys

Yet more medieval ruins are dotted roundabout: if you're heading through Dunmore in the northeast of the county, there's **Dunmore Abbey**, an Augustinian priory of 1425, and just to the west of the town a Norman castle built by the de Berminghams. Alternatively, seven miles south of Tuam off the N63 Galway–Roscommon road, **Knockmoy Abbey** is a Cistercian foundation of 1190 – though the central tower is probably a fifteenth-century addition. The most remarkable feature of the abbey is on the north wall of the chancel, where you'll see one of Ireland's few medieval frescoes. Extremely faint (only the black outlines are original colours) it depicts the legend of the Three Dead Kings and the Three Live Kings. Under the dead kings an inscription reads "We have been as you are, you shall be as we are"; the live kings are out hawking. Underneath this is a picture of Christ holding his hand up in blessing, and a barely visible angel with scales.

East to Ballinasloe: Athenry

Chances are you'll see **ATHENRY**, if at all, from a train. The place is more renowned for the song *The Fields of Athenry* – which you're unlikely to have got this far without hearing – than as a tourist centre. Still, if you've time to kill between connections, it's worth nipping out of the station to take a look at its remains of Anglo-Norman power – so much a feature of east Galway and so conspicuously absent in the west of the county. The town was founded by the de Berminghams, and large portions of its Norman town walls have survived, along with a tower-gate, five flanking towers, and a market cross. On the edge of town stands a bold thirteenth-century **castle**, again built by the de Berminghams, its stout, three-storey keep still impressively intact (Mon–Fri 8am–5pm). If you're looking for **B&B** try Miss Gardener's, Old Church Street (☎091/44464) or Mrs O'Connor's, Swan Gate (☎0915/44681), both £10–11.

Loughrea

LOUGHREA, on the main road to Ballinasloe, is like Portumna (see below) in that it's a lakeside market town. But it's much smaller, and tiny Lough Rea can't compare with the beauty of Lough Derg for a setting. In the thirteenth century Richard de Burgo founded a **Carmelite Monastery** here, which still stands in an excellent state of preservation next to the abbey. The town also has a late-nineteenth-century **Cathedral**, the interior of which demonstrates the development of the modern Dublin School of Stained Glass – an acquired taste. Much earlier religious art is on display next door in the **Loughrea Museum** (Mon–Fri 9.30am–4.30pm, Sun 3–5pm; at other times ask at the church for the key). This small museum includes episcopal vestments and carved Crucifixes from the seventeenth century; beautifully simple silver and gold chalices from as early as 1500; penal crosses; and a few rare wood carvings from the twelfth and thirteenth centuries. The Kilcorban *Virgin and Child* is the earliest of only three such carvings that have been found in Ireland.

In a field two miles to the north of Loughrea, near BULLAUN, stands the **Turoe Stone**. A superb, rounded pillar-stone, this is decorated with the bold swirls of Celtic La Tène art, a style found more typically in Brittany. The finest of its kind in Ireland, it dates from the third or second century BC and was probably a phallic fertility stone, used in pagan rituals.

Aughrim and Kilconnell Friary

Tiny **AUGHRIM**, on the road just short of Ballinasloe, makes a good base from which to explore some of the ecclesiastical remains of the area. *Hynes* **hostel** (☎0905/73734; open all year; £4.50; camping £3) is attached to the local pub, which has music at weekends during the summer. The hostel has only twelve beds, so it's worth ringing ahead in July and August; during the horse fair it's booked up way in advance. In 1691 Aughrim was the scene of a key battle of the Williamite War, in which the Irish and French forces were defeated; a small **museum** in the local primary school has finds connected with the battle.

Four miles to the northwest are the very beautiful remains of **Kilconnell Friary**, a Franciscan foundation built near the site of the sixth-century church of Saint Conall, which gives the place its name. The friary held out successfully against Cromwellian attack in 1651. The ruins are extensive, with additions to the early-fourteenth-century building showing that there was increased monastic activity here in the later Middle Ages. There's a very pretty arcaded cloister, and in the north wall of the nave are two splendid canopied wall-tombs.

Ballinasloe

Galway's eastern boundary is one of water: Lough Derg, the Shannon, and the River Suck. The tourist-geared villages are again catering mainly for the fishing fraternity, but there is enough of historic interest to warrant leisurely exploration. **BALLINASLOE** is the main town in east Galway. Important as a crossing point of the River Suck since 1124 when Turlough O'Conor, King of Connaught, built a castle here, the remains that can be seen today date mainly from the fourteenth century. You're only really likely to be here if you've come for the famous **horse fair**, which starts on the first weekend in October and lasts for eight days. The largest of the ancient fairs left in the country, drawing horse dealers from all over Ireland and England, it gives a fascinating glimpse of a slowly dying way of life. The bartering is very much a game, though a serious one. Generally, both parties know the value of the beast in question, but enjoy the bartering ritual anyway, with its possibilities of outdoing an opponent. The logic seems to be that if you're not up to the bartering, you don't deserve the right price for the animal. This system of exchange is threatened by EC regulations which insist that animals be sold by weight, a sorry demise for an ancient tradition.

If you intend to visit the fair, you'll have to book accommodation well in advance. The main **hotel** in town is *Hayden's* in Dunlo Street (☎0905/42347; £23): for **B&B** in the town itself try Mrs Molloy, *Ashling*, Old Mount Pleasant Avenue (☎0905/42457; £10), or there's Mrs N. Mulqueen's *Adare* (☎0905/43282; £10), and Mrs Burton's *Woodlands* (☎0905/43123; £10), both on Dublin Road half a mile out.

Clontuskert Abbey and Clonfert Cathedral

The countryside to the south of Ballinasloe makes a dull setting for two fine pieces of ecclesiastical architecture, well worth taking in if you're staying in the area, or heading south towards Portumna and Lough Derg. The first is **Clontuskert Abbey**, five miles south of the town. From the road it looks impressive in this open countryside, like some iron-grey battleship adrift on the flat and muddy approaches to the Suck. The church is the only sizeable remnant of the abbey complex, with a Perpendicular west door of 1471, carved with figures of the saints.

Nine miles further south is **Clonfert Cathedral**, on the site where a Benedictine monastery was founded around 560 by Saint Brendan. In subsequent centuries the monastery was pillaged, but towards the end of the twelfth century the church was rebuilt, and dedicated to Saint Brendan. There's a superb Romanesque doorway made up of six arches, each a perfect semicircle, and richly carved with heavily stylised plants and animals. The capitals are Romanesque cubes carved with crazy, bold animal heads. The Bishop's Palace beyond the cathedral – now derelict as a result of an accidental fire – was the home of Sir Oswald Mosley after his release from prison in 1949.

Portumna

PORTUMNA, on the north shore of Lough Derg, is a traditional market town and Shannon crossing point, happy to be cashing in on the exclusive tourism that drifts its way on the Lough cruisers, yet still retaining a friendly and unpretentious character. Close to the shore is **Portumna Priory**, for the most part a fifteenth-century Dominican building, though its delicately arched cloisters are built around the remains of a much earlier Cistercian foundation. Nearby **Portumna Castle,** a fine early seventeenth-century mansion with Jacobean gables (something of a rarity in Ireland), is currently undergoing renovation, though completion is clearly a long way away. Nobody minds if you take a look via the fields to the rear. The castle's estate is a wildlife sanctuary with a large herd of fallow deer and Japanese sika.

Portumna really has more in common with the other little towns on the luscious scenic strip that lines Lough Derg, catering for the more conservative tourism of the Lough cruisers. There's a **tourist office** here during the summer months and several good **B&Bs** in the centre. It's easy **camping** country too – just ask a farmer – and in the summer there are **public showers** down by the lough jetty (July and August only). Swimming is relatively safe on the lake but not on the river. There are two very friendly places to **eat**, both in the main street: *Peter's Restaurant*, a fast-food place that will rustle up whatever you fancy, and *Clonwyn House*, which does traditional cooked meals any day any time.

Although small, Portumna has an astounding 21 **pubs**, and there's no shortage of ballad sessions, but no traditional music, unless you catch one of *Clonwyn House*'s Sunday night *céilís*, when the old folk come in to do their set dancing. Thursday nights they have ballad sessions here and Saturdays the place generally has a local pop band. The *Bank of Ireland* is in Clonfert Avenue, open until 5pm on a Wednesday, and the post office is in Abbey Street. There's also a **launderette** – *Frank's* in Brendan Street.

ROSCOMMON

Roscommon has the unjust reputation of being the most boring county in Ireland. A long sliver of land running from south to north, it's the only county in Connacht without any sea coast, though it is bounded for almost its entire western border by the upper reaches of the Shannon. Although most of the county is either bog or good grassland pasture, on the Sligo and Leitrim border the Curlew mountains rise high and wild. Chances are you'll be approaching the county from the south, which is not its best aspect: the most worthwhile places are Boyle, in the far north, and Strokestown in the east, approached from Longford.

Roscommon and Castlerea

There's nothing much to **ROSCOMMON** Town, pretty much in the centre of the county, but it's an oddly pleasant place to spend time and soak up the atmosphere. Its solid tone is set by heavy stone buildings such as the Bank of Ireland, once the courthouse, and the **county jail**, which now houses a collection of shops and has a toothed top that gives the town a characteristic silhouette identifiable for miles around. The jail was the scene of all public hangings in the county, and used to have a woman hangman called Lady Betty, whose own sentence for murder had been revoked on condition that she did her gruesome job for free.

Roscommon boasts two impressive ruins: on the Boyle road out of town, the enormous and well-preserved **Roscommon Castle** was built by the Normans in 1269, burnt down by the Irish four years later, and rebuilt in 1280. Remodelling clearly continued for some time – there are some incongruously refined windows among the massive walls. The other ruin, in the lower part of the town, is the **priory**. Roscommon takes its name from a Celtic saint, Saint Coman, who was the first bishop here, and under whom the see became well known as a seat of learning, having close ties with the more famous abbey at Clonmacnoise in County Offaly. The priory ruin, however, is Dominican, dating from 1253. Amazingly enough, despite the religious persecution that followed the Reformation and the

Plantations, the Dominicans managed to hang on well into the nineteenth century, the last two incumbents, parish priests of Fuerty and Athleague, dying in 1830 and 1872 respectively.

Accommodation around Roscommon is not exactly plentiful. The *Royal Hotel* (☎0903/26317; £25), on Castle Street right in the centre, is one of those fine, upstanding inns that still exist in rural Irish towns: good fun, plenty of locals in the bar, comfortable, but not especially cheap. Otherwise, you've a sprinkling of B&Bs to choose between. These include Mrs O'Grady's *The Villa* (☎0903/26048; £12) and Mrs Campbell's *Westway* (☎0903/26927; £10) on the Galway road or, a mile out on the Sligo road, Mrs Dolan's *Munsboro House* (☎0903/26375; £14). There's a **tourist office** open in the summer (mid-June to Aug Mon–Sat 10am– 6pm; ☎0903/26342).

Castlerea

CASTLEREA in the west, Roscommon's third most important town after Roscommon and Boyle, is an unprepossessing place, and the only real reason for going there is to visit **Clonalis House** (June to mid-Sept; £1.75), just outside the town to the west. Clonalis is the ancestral home of the clan O'Conor, which claims to be Europe's oldest family, dating back to one Feredach the Just in 75 AD. The house is a Victorian pile, stuffed with mementoes and archival material, including the harp of the blind musician Turlough O'Carolan (1670–1738).

Strokestown

In the east of the county, on the N5 from Longford, **STROKESTOWN** is a gem of a planned town whose reason for existence is **Strokestown House**, once the centre of the second biggest estate in Roscommon after Rockingham. The enormously wide main street – reputedly the result of an ambition on the part of an early owner to have the widest street in Europe – ends abruptly in a castellated wall with three Gothic arches, behind which lies Strokestown House.

It's a graceful Georgian residence designed by Richard Castle on a plan – a central block with two side wings linked by curved arms – whose adaptability as a sort of glorified farmhouse ensures that it turns up again and again throughout Ireland. Sold by the family of the original owners to the local garage in 1979, the house has never gone through an auction and therefore retains everything from furniture to early papers. A lot of restoration work has already been done, and there are ambitious plans for a museum on the Famine, plus a restaurant and the conversion of one of the yards into a kind of time-share arrangement, with gyms and tennis courts to finance it all.

The house is already open to the public (May–Sept Wed–Sun noon–5pm; £2, students £1; ☎078/33013) and makes a good place to get to grips with the Anglo-Irish tradition. Its story is a fairly typical one. Originally a massive 27,000 acres, the estate was granted to one Nicholas Mahon in reward for his support of the house of Stuart during the English Civil War. The original house, finished around 1696, was fortified but not particularly grand; only one room of it survives, the stillroom in the cellar, which has just been restored by the Irish Georgian Society. As the family became richer and more secure, it made more grandiose additions, and the current house dates essentially from the 1730s, with some early-nineteenth-century alterations. One of its really extraordinary features is a gallery that runs the length of the kitchen, allowing the lady of the house to watch what was happening there without having to venture in; on Monday mornings she would drop the week's menu down from the gallery.

Strokestown's owners included one particularly nasty piece of work, Major Denis Mahon, who is believed to have been one of the first landowners to charter less-than-seaworthy vessels (the notorious **coffin ships**) to take evicted tenants to America during the Famine. Whether or not the ships he hired actually arrived at their destination isn't known, but his activities were reported and censured in contemporary newspapers both in Ireland and abroad. In 1847 he was shot dead on his own estate.

Meanwhile, one of the house's charms is that it's not stuck in a Georgian time warp like many of the grand houses you can visit, but is clearly a home that's been well lived in for hundreds of years. To give a measure of the interconnectedness of Anglo-Irish society even in comparatively recent times, the lady who sold the house to the garage, the redoubtable Mrs Olive Hales Pakenham Mahon, married the heir to the Rockingham estate in 1914, thus uniting the two biggest estates in Roscommon, though the land empire set up by this dynastic marriage crumbled very soon afterwards. Also in the house, in one of the upstairs bedrooms, is a painting of horses and stooks of corn by Woodbrook's Phoebe Kirkwood (see below).

For **accommodation**, the *Strokestown Arms* (☎078/33302; £16) has a prime position just outside the house's gates. If it's full try B&B with Percy French (☎078/33300; £15) or Mrs Cox, two miles out of town at *Church View House* (☎078/33047; £13).

Boyle

It's disparagingly said that County Roscommon doesn't have any towns. It does, and **BOYLE** is one of them. Although it's not a place marked out by particular charm or beauty, there's enough here to keep you entertained for at least a one-night stopover. Boyle grew up around the greatest estate in County Roscommon, **Rockingham**, and although the estate was disbanded long ago and the house – in what is now the Lough Key park – was burned down in 1957, the town is still marked by their ghostly presence. The main street, for instance, was planned as an avenue to lead up to the house.

In Boyle itself the most charismatic building is the Cistercian monastery, **Boyle Abbey** (mid-June to mid-Sept daily 9.30am–1.30pm & 2.30–6.30pm; 80p, heritage card; ☎091/74292) consecrated in 1220 and one of the early results of the arrival of foreign monastic orders in Ireland during the medieval pan-European upsurge in spiritual life. In 1142 a group of monks sent to Ireland by the founder of the Cistercians, Saint Bernard of Clairvaux, at the instigation of Saint Malachy, established the great abbey of Mellifont in County Louth. Clonmacnoise, the important Celtic monastery on the banks of the Shannon in County Offaly, was quickly abandoned, and within twenty years monks from Mellifont had settled at a site beside the River Boyle here at *Mainistir na Buaille*.

The abbey is small and compact, in very pale stone, well enough preserved to let you see how the monks must have lived. You still go in through the gatehouse (a sixteenth- or seventeenth-century addition), and there's a wonderful church – basically twelfth century – with Gothic arches down one side of the nave,

Romanesque down the other. Keys are obtainable from *Abbey House*, next to the monastery. This is also a guesthouse and, wedged between the rushing river and the abbey, is one of the best places to **stay** in Boyle (☎079/62385; £13; Feb–Nov); there are plenty of other B&Bs and a couple of hotels – the 250-year-old *Royal* (☎079/62016; £25) is a solid country inn where the river rushes by your bedroom window.

Lough Key Forest Park and Woodbrook

The road out of Boyle towards the **Lough Key Forest Park**, part of the old Rockingham estate, leads through the gate of the grounds, itself a Gothic fancy, and past a castellated lodge. The park has been thoroughly and relentlessly amenitised, with a terrible wood-and-glass restaurant at the side of the lake, and masses of tarmacked car-parking on the former site of the great house. Yet the stable block, church, icehouse and temple – the graces of an eighteenth-century estate – give an impression of what it must have been like: and, with boats for hire and plenty of ring forts to explore, it's a pleasant enough place to spend a sunny day.

A little further out of Boyle on the Carrick-on-Shannon road, **Woodbrook** is another old Anglo-Irish house. It's not open to the public, and the reason for mentioning it is that it's the subject of a remarkable book, *Woodbrook*, written by an Englishman, David Thompson, who worked there for most of the 1930s as tutor to the Kirkwood family's two young daughters. Sometimes naive, sometimes sentimental, it's strong in its documentation of the passing of Anglo-Irish culture.

travel details

Trains

From Galway: to Athenry (4 daily; 15min); Athlone (4; 1hr); Portarlington (3; 2hr); Dublin (4; 2hr 30min).

From Westport: three daily to Castlebar (14min); Castlerea (1hr 10min); Roscommon (1hr 30min) and Dublin (3hr 30min).

Bus Éireann

From Galway: to Dublin (4 daily, 3hr 45mins); Limerick (5; 2hr); Cork (4; 4hr); Clifden (3; 3hr); Doolin (2; 1hr 30min).

Private buses

Funtrek (☎01/730852) run one bus a day, two on Friday **from Galway**, Imperial Hotel, to Athlone, Ballinasloe, Loughrea and Dublin.
North Galway Club (☎093/55492) departs **from Galway**, Kiltartan House, Forster Street daily for Dublin (Mon–Sat 8am). Departs **from Tuam** Cathedral daily for Dublin (same hours as above). Departs **from Dublin**, Ormond Quay, for Galway (Mon–Sat 6pm) and Tuam. There are summer connections to Dublin Airport.

Feda O'Donnell Coaches (☎075/48114) depart **from Galway** Cathedral (except Sun evening departures, which leave from Eyre Square) daily for Letterkenny, Co Donegal, serving many towns along the way including Knock, Sligo, and Donegal town, and continuing on to Gweedore (dept Galway Mon–Thurs 4pm, Fri 5.30pm, Sat 10am, Sun 8pm. Depart **from Letterkenny** Mon–Thurs 9am, Fri 10.30am and 4.30pm and Sun 3.30pm).

Nestor's (☎091/97170) from Galway *Imperial Hotel* to Dublin airport and city (8am daily). Dublin–Galway departs Tara Street Station 6pm daily.

CHAPTER ELEVEN

SLIGO AND LEITRIM

C ounties Sligo and Leitrim pair up well, offering a distinctively luscious and
gentle scenery that contrasts with the wilder streaks of Donegal and
Mayo, yet is equally far removed from the dullness of Longford and
Cavan to the east. **Leitrim,** one of the most neglected counties in the
country, is an area of lakelets and low mounds, and presents a singularly withdrawn face to the outside world. **Sligo,** phenomenally underrated, is the more
enticing of the two, having the beautiful mountains of **Benbulben** and
Knocknarea, and the enchanting **Gill** and **Glencar** loughs. Much of the terrain
is gently undulating farming land, allowing long cross-country views to the higher
outcrops in the county's far corners: the **Ox Mountains** range to the west, the
Bricklieve to the south and the **Dartry** to the north. And at **Streedagh** and
Mullaghmore you'll find some of the country's finest beaches.

Sligo is rich in historical terms too. Especially interesting are the extensive
Neolithic cemetery at **Carrowmore,** to the west of Sligo town, and the large
prehistoric village at **Carrowkeel,** on top of the Bricklieve Mountains. The wealth
and variety of legends covering its terrain has no rival, and its modern literary
associations are no less strong, as this landscape and its culture inspired the
greatest of Irish poets, **W. B. Yeats.** His poetry is saturated with the atmosphere
of Sligo, and his presence still makes itself felt above all at places such as the
island of **Innisfree** on Lough Gill and **Lissadell House.**

Sligo Town

SLIGO, with a population of about eighteen thousand, is, after Derry, the biggest
town in the northwest of Ireland and a real focal point for the surrounding area.
The first recorded mention of Sligo dates from 807 AD, when the town was
sacked by the Vikings, and by the thirteenth century it had become the gateway
between Connacht and Ulster, with a castle (since destroyed) on what is now
Castle Street. The Middle Ages was a period of sporadic violence, most notably
between the Anglo-Norman Maurice Fitzgerald and the O'Connells. Thanks to its
strong defences, Sligo was the last of the western garrisons to surrender to
Williamite forces after the Battle of the Boyne.

The town suffered during the **Famine,** when its population fell by a third
through death and emigration, but by the end of the last century things had
picked up to the extent that it was described in guidebooks as "a progressive and
busy centre". The upswing has continued to the present day, and in summer the
streets are always crowded with visitors – but if you have a chance to look at the
photos of old Sligo hanging in the County Museum on Stephen Street, you'll
appreciate how remarkably constant the look of the town has been. The tightly
packed and narrow **back streets** make it feel a little like Latin Quarter Paris, with

grocery stores and bars on the street corners open late into the evening. Apart from the Dominican Abbey there's not much left in the way of sites that recall the town's long history, but the old-fashioned market town atmosphere and the equally atmospheric old pubs make it an ideal base for exploring the surrounding countryside and sights.

The Town

The thirteenth-century **Dominican Abbey** has had a chequered history, having been destroyed a couple of times by both accident and design since its foundation. Its life as a religious foundation came to an end in 1641, when the whole town was sacked during the Ulster rebellion. These days the abbey makes a good place to have a picnic as its walls still stand and the chancel and high altar, with fine carvings, are in a good state of preservation. If the abbey is locked you can get the key from the caretaker, Mr A. McGuinn at 6 Charlotte Street, although you won't be missing much if you just take a look through the gates.

The **Municipal Art Gallery** (July–Aug 10.30am–12.30pm & 2.30–4.30pm; rest of year Tues & Fri 10.30am–12.30pm; free), housed in the County Library on Stephen Street, possesses many paintings and pencil drawings by Jack Yeats, brother of the poet. His work has a strong local flavour, and his later efforts like *The Graveyard Wall* and *The Sea and the Lighthouse* are especially potent evocations of the life and atmosphere of the area. If you're going to be heading north into Donegal, look out for *Early Morning in Donegal Lough* by Paul Henry, which will give you a taste of things to come. Also worth more than a passing glance are the paintings by George Russell, better known as AE, the mystical poet and contemporary of W. B. Yeats.

In the same compound as the library but situated just by the entrance gate are the **Sligo County Museum** and **Yeats Memorial Museum** (Mon–Fri 10am–5pm, Sat 10am–1pm), which basically comprise two rooms. Along with the interesting old photos of Sligo, the more unusual items in the local history section include a sequence of excellent nineteenth-century sketches of the monastic ruins on Inishmurray, and a double-weight hundred-year-old firkin of bog butter. Memorabilia in the Yeats museum include photographs and commentary of his funeral, lots of letters and photos of the man himself, and the Nobel Prize medal awarded him in 1923. Before you rush out, read a bit of the long article on Michael Coleman, one of Ireland's most famous fiddle players; Fritz Kreisler, the greatest of classical violin players, wrote at the beginning of the century that even he could not attempt the kind of music Michael Coleman played, even if he practised for a thousand years.

Just down the road, at Douglas Hyde Bridge, the **Yeats Memorial Building** (☎071/42693) is the headquarters of the *Yeats Society* and venue for the *Yeats International Summer School*. Inaugurated about thirty years back, the gathering has become something of an academic institution, attracting scholars from all over the world.

By far the most interesting historical set piece in Sligo is **Hargadon's Pub** on O'Connell Street. An exclusively male establishment until ten years ago, it's a fine old talking pub, with dark recesses and shut-off rooms, and shelves of nineteenth-century earthenware stout jugs. Note the little swivel windows at the far end of the serving bar, where the whiskey could be slipped through with little fuss by either drinker or landlord.

Another place of great interest is an old butcher's shop turned sculpture studio, **Michael Quirke's** on Wine Street. A butcher for twenty-seven years, Michael Quirke began in the 1980s to sculpt the figures of Irish mythology in windfallen wood. Every feature of these small carvings bears the mark of his encyclopaedic knowledge of every legend or myth that was ever dreamed up about Ireland – if you get a chance to listen to him, it will be one of the most inspiring moments of your stay. So far his work isn't too expensive (£30 upwards), but it's getting increasingly popular. For souvenirs of a more traditional kind, *Dooney's* in O'Connell Street sells excellent Irish tweed and knitwear at well below Dublin prices – which is still far from cheap.

Practicalities

Buses and **trains** both arrive at the station, handily placed on the western edge of town in easy walking distance of almost everything. Sligo's **tourist office**, on Temple Street (July & Aug Mon–Sat 9am–8pm, Sun 10am–2pm; rest of year Mon–Fri 9am–5pm; ☎071/61201), is the headquarters for Sligo, Donegal, Leitrim, Monaghan and Cavan – a wide brief which means it often has little hard information to give out. They do, however, offer car hire, money exhange and an **accommodation** booking service.

Rooms and transport

If you're staying in Sligo town itself **B&B** is probably the best option. Nearest the station is a place at 34 Wolfe Tone Street (£11); or try *Sheelin* on Union Street (£12); *Renaté House*, 9 Upper John Street (☎071/62014; £13); or *An Crúiscín Lán* (The Full Jug), Connolly Street (☎071/62869; £12.50), a friendly place with a bar and cheap pub meals. There are also dozens on Strandhill Road, heading away from town from the station. Moving upmarket, try the *Bonne Chere*, 44 High Street (☎071/42014; £25), again with a bar and meals.

There are also **hostels**, all charging £5 a night. The *County Hostel*, on Lord Edward Street, is very handy for the railway station but has nothing else to recommend it. The more popular independent *White House Hostel* (☎071/45160), on Markiewicz Road, is much more pleasant, and includes breakfast in the price, but gets very crowded in the summer. The official *An Óige* place is *Eden Hill* on Pearse Road (☎071/43204).

For **bike hire** try *Raleigh Rent-a-Bike* (☎071/67560), at the back of the *Silver Swan Hotel*, or *Conway Brothers*, 6 High Street (☎071/61370). For **minibus tours** around Lough Gill and other north Sligo areas contact John Houze (☎071/42747); the tours depart from the tourist information office at 9.30am and 1.30pm from June to September (£4–5); there are also **walking tours** from the tourist office in summer. For **boats** on the river and around Lough Gill – one of the best ways to spend time here – contact Peter Henry at *The Blue Lagoon*, Riverside.

Eating

Every pub in Sligo seems to serve a **bar lunch**, and with so much competition the food is excellent value – a decent meal for around £2. Away from the pubs, *Fortes Café* on Markiewicz Road does main courses from about £1.90 and three-course meals from £2.75, and the *Ritz Restaurant*, 35 O'Connell Street, does a four-course lunch for £4. The *Cottage Coffee Shop*, upstairs at 4 Castle Street, has a cheap and varied hot and cold menu with vegetarian specials; *Lyons Café* at the top of O'Connell Street is another good café serving meals or drinks throughout the day.

Up a price category, *Gullivers* on Grattan Street serves good American-style food (burgers, pizzas, chicken, fish, from £4.50) in a busy atmosphere, open till midnight. *Beezies Dining Salon* at 45 O'Connell Street has a similar saloon theme and is also open till late, with a bar, occasional entertainment and five-course meals from £10 – as well as smaller meals. Excellent lunches are served at *The Cellars*, 30 O'Connell Street.

Cosgrove's, a **delicatessen** on Market Square, is something of a tourist attraction in itself, with a nineteenth-century interior and a craft shop attached. You can get picnic supplies here or from *Kate's Kitchen* on Market Street .

Pubs and entertainment

When it comes to **pubs**, Sligo does well. To find out what's happening in the way of entertainment get hold of a copy of *The Sligo Champion*, which lists music in pubs and other entertainment.

Hargadon's (see above) is one of the most enjoyable places to drink and talk, with several snugs and no distractions. For **traditional music**, the two best regular spots are *T.D.s* on Adelaide Street, and the *Leitrim Bar*, across the river on

The Mall: both have something happening most nights throughout the year. *MacLynn's* on Old Market Street is cosy and usually crowded, there's an open fire in the bar, and folk/traditional music almost nightly in summer, less often the rest of the year. *Hennigan's Pub* on Wine Street is fairly seedy, but has pop/rock once a week, usually Thursday, and mainly traditional stuff on Sunday. *Comhaltas* have sessions on Wednesdays in the *Silver Swan Hotel*, Hyde Bridge, a venue for other types of music most other nights and an excellent Sunday lunchtime jazz session. The *Clarence Hotel* on Wine Street has a live band every Friday and Saturday, with a dance floor. The *Trades Club*, on Castle Street has good traditional sessions from 9.45pm every Tuesday, sometimes with a brilliant young violinist and, from time to time, Lord Templemore on spoons – arrive early to ensure getting in (the entrance is an ordinary house door and is easy to miss).

The big new **nightclub** in town is *Toff's* at the *Embassy Lounge*, Riverside; *Zanadus* on Teeling Street also has **discos** (Wed & Fri–Sun 11pm–1.30am; £4 including food). *The Blue Lagoon*, Riverside, has traditional music on Monday and Tuesday and discos on Thursday and Saturday.

The *Hawk's Well Theatre* on Temple Street (below the tourist office) often has a reasonable programme of **plays**, and the *Gaiety Cinema* on Wine Street has four screens showing a variety of **films**.

Around Lough Gill

The 24-mile circuit of **Lough Gill**, a broad lake with luscious woodland covering the small hills that rise off its indented banks, makes a great day trip by bike from Sligo. There are also plenty of shorter walks, and this is one of the most enjoyable ways to spend time around Sligo. To **walk** to the lake – little over an hour away – set off from Bridge Street along Riverside on the south bank of the Garavogue, until you come after about a mile to Doorly Park. Follow the path through the park, hugging the river, until it rejoins the road, which leads eventually to a lakeside jetty. Here the entire length of Lough Gill is spread out before you.

If you have transport, the northern shore is much the more interesting, and is reached from town by taking The Mall past the hospital, turning onto the L16 at the garage, and then following signposts for the **Hazelwood** estate on the right. A left turn off the road leading into the estate grounds will bring you after half a mile to **Half Moon Bay**, where there's a picnic site and a nice lakeside walk. Wooden sculptures by various artists are ranged in the woods around – the most stunning is a set piece of chariot and horses, set in its own artificial dell.

THE LEGENDS OF LOUGH GILL

A place of such natural beauty inevitably features in **legend**: Lough Gill's story tells of a warrior called Romra who had a daughter named Gille ("beauty" in Irish). One day Gille was seen bathing by Omra, a friend of Romra. Omra was captivated by the girl, and she wasn't altogether indifferent to him; but when Romra got to hear about it, a fight ensued in which Omra was killed and Romra received wounds from which he later died. Grief-stricken, Gille drowned herself, and from the tears of her doubly grief-stricken nursemaid Lough Gill(e) was formed. According to another tale, the silver bell from the Dominican Abbey in Sligo lies at the bottom of the lake. Only those free from sin can hear its pealing.

Back on the L16, there's nothing to stop for until you near the Leitrim end of the lake, when the road begins to skirt the shore on its approach to **Parke's Castle** (June–Sept 10am–6pm; £1), a romantic-looking seventeenth-century fortress positioned only yards from the water. Look out for the narrow passage that runs under the wall to carry *curraghs* onto the lake, and for the small sweathouse (a kind of turkish bath), whose therapeutic steam was intended to be followed by a freezing dip in the lake.

Rounding the eastern side of the lake, into County Leitrim, provides the most enjoyable contact with the lake until a steep road runs up to the left towards Manorhamilton (see below), with the main road veering away from the lake and on to the village of DROMAHAIR. At the entrance to the village a signpost points out a path to **Creevylea Abbey**, a Franciscan friary founded in 1508. Now mostly ruined, it still has some fine sculptures in the cloister arcade: look out for Saint Francis with the stigmata, and another of him preaching to the birds from a pulpit. Until a few years ago the place was used for burials, and some of the tombstones date from as recently as the 1970s.

Innisfree Island and back to town

The return journey to Sligo is frustratingly remote from the lake, and the sole diversion – to **Innisfree** – is really only for the avid enthusiasts of Yeats' poetry.

> *And I shall have some peace there, for peace comes dropping slow,*
> *Dropping from the veils of the morning to where the cricket sings;*
> *There midnight's all a glimmer, and noon a purple glow,*
> *And evening full of the linnet's wings.*

The Lake Isle of Innisfree

The shore opposite the island is a good three miles from the main road; if you want to go over, a small boat is available in summer. The south road back into Sligo passes **Cairns Hill Forest Park**. From the car park a path leads to a cairn on top of Cairns Hill, with a view across to a second cairn on the peak of Belvoir Hill. These are reckoned to be the tombs of Romra and Omra, though another legend makes them out to be the breasts of a monstrous hag, with Lough Gill as her navel.

North of Sligo Town

Leaving Sligo along the coast to the north, almost immediately there's the possibility of a short detour to **ROSSES POINT** (bus #286 from Sligo), via the promontory that forms the north side of Sligo Bay. This (or Strandhill, p.363) is the place to go for a day's outing to the beach, a perfect picture-postcard scene, with the streaks of Coney and Oyster islands guarding the entrance to the bay, and the distinctive beauty of Knocknarea standing behind. A sea marker called the *Metal Man* marks the deepest part of the channel for Sligo-bound boats; placed there in 1822, it was called by Yeats the "Rosses Point man who never told a lie". The tip of the headland, **Deadman's Point** (now an upper-crust recreation centre), took its name from a sailor who was buried at sea here with a loaf of bread thoughtfully provided by his comrades – they weren't sure whether he was really dead but wanted to despatch him quickly so they could make port before the tide turned. For seafood, head for *The Moorings Restaurant*, in the village at Rosses Point. There are a couple of small hotels and lots of B&Bs out here too.

Drumcliff, Benbulben and Glencar Lough

Sticking to the main N15 road out of Sligo you'll bypass this small peninsula, to reach water again at **DRUMCLIFF** (bus #290 or #291), an early monastic site probably better known as the last resting place of **W. B. Yeats**. His grave is in the grounds of an austere nineteenth-century Protestant church, within sight of the nearby Benbulben, as the poet wished. You could easily miss the simple gravestone bearing the epitaph from Yeats's last poem:

> *Cast a cold eye*
> *On life, on death.*
> *Horseman, pass by!*

In 575 Saint Columba founded a **monastery** here, and you can still see the remants of a round tower to the left of the road and a tenth-century High Cross – the only one in the county – on the right. The east face of the cross has carvings of Adam and Eve, Cain killing Abel, and Daniel in the lion's den; the west face shows scenes from the New Testament, including the Presentation in the Temple and the Crucifixion. Local excavations have turned up a wealth of Iron and Bronze Age remains too.

At 1730 feet, **Benbulben** is one of the most dramatic mountains in the country, and its profile changes constantly as you round it. According to the Fionn Mac Cumhaill legend it was here that Diarmuid was killed by the wild boar, its bristles puncturing his heel – his one vulnerable point. Access to the slopes is easy, but you need to take care as there are a lot of dangerous clefts into which the unsuspecting walker can all too easily plunge – especially as it's invariably shrouded in mist. There are **hostel** facilities at the *Yeats Tavern* (☎071/63117; £4.50) in Drumcliff, about a hundred yards past the church. It's part of the roadside pub, and although handy for drinks and basic eating, you won't want to spend more than one night there. There's also **B&B** at *Castletown House* (☎071/63204; £11) and numerous others roundabout.

Just to the east of Drumcliff, but best reached from the T17 road to Manorhamilton, is **Glencar Lough** (bus #125 or #283 from Sligo), set into the back of Benbulben. Follow the road round the northern edge of the lake passing the recently reopened mine sheds on the left (barium is mined here), until you see the "Waterfall" signpost. From the nearby car park a path leads up to the waterfall itself, which at nearly fifty feet high is worth going out of your way for, particularly after heavy rain. There are more waterfalls, visible from the road, in the upper reaches of the valley, although none is quite as romantic as this one. For an even better mountain walk continue along the road to the eastern end of the lake, where a track rises steeply northwards to the **Swiss valley**, a deep rift in the mountain crowned with silver fir.

Cooldrumman and Lissadell House

Beyond Drumcliff the first left turn off the main road (signposted "Lissadell") runs to CARNEY village, to the north of which is an area known as **Cooldrumman**, where the **Battle of the Book** took place. This battle followed the refusal of Saint Columba to hand over a psalm book copied from the original owned by Saint Finian of Moville, in defiance of the High King, who ruled that just as a calf belongs to its cow so every copy belongs to the owner of the book from which it is made. Columba won the battle at a cost of 3000 lives; repenting the bloodshed he had caused, he then went into exile on the island of Iona.

In Carney a signpost to the left indicates the way to **Lissadell House** (June to mid-Sept Mon–Sat 10.30am–noon & 2–4.30pm; £2; bus #290 or #291 from Sligo; ☎071/63150), a nineteenth-century stately home whose popularity is mainly due to its Yeats associations. This was the home of the Gore-Booth family, who produced several generations of artists, travellers and fighters for Irish freedom. During the Famine Sir Robert Gore-Booth mortgaged the place to feed the local people and doled out rations from the hall. His grand-daughters Eva Gore-Booth and Constance Markiewicz were friends of Yeats (his *In Memory of Eva Gore-Booth and Con Markiewicz* is displayed at the gate) and took part in the 1916 rising. Constance was condemned to death by the British for her participation, but was pardoned and went on to become the first British female MP and then Minister of Labour in the Dáil's first cabinet. The house is full of relics of the colourful lives of its inhabitants, with odd touches like the dining room's full-length mural portraits of family members and retainers, painted by Count Casimir Markiewicz (Constance's husband).

Walks around Lissadell: Ellen's Pub

The area around Lissadell has some lovely **walks** and reputedly the warmest patch of sea on the Sligo coast. Also worth seeking out is *Ellen's Pub*, whose cottage-home atmosphere draws people from miles around. Céilís are sometimes held in the back room, and on Friday, Saturday and Sunday from June through to September musicians gather here to belt out tunes on fiddles, accordions and banjoes. There's a relaxed attitude to the licensing laws, so relaxed in fact that the pub was closed down for a while in 1986. To find it, follow the road past the turning for the Lissadell estate, bear right away from Maugherow church, turn left at the pub/grocery store at the crossroads and then take the second right – it's another mile straight on. Hitching is possible, because everyone knows where you're trying to get to if you're anywhere in the area.

Raghly Point to Mullaghmore

To the west of Lissadell is RAGHLY, a small harbour with a forlorn pier and raised beach from where there are good views of the bay and surrounding mountains. On the way there you'll pass **Ardtermon Castle** (closed to the public), the seventeenth-century fortified manor house once occupied by Francis Gore-Booth, an ancestor of the Lissadell House Gore-Booths. Ten years ago the place was more or less a ruin, but since then it has been well restored by its German industrialist owner.

The next stop along the coast is sandy **Streedagh Strand** (7 buses daily from Sligo), most easily accessible by taking the main road to Grange (see below) and following the signposts from there, as roads on the Raghly peninsula are hard to disentangle. The substantially German-inhabited colony of this whole area has earned it the nickname of "Little Bavaria", and the prices of some of the chalets at Streedagh Strand itself (up to £50,000) have provoked a degree of antipathy from the locals. The beach itself is a fantastic stretch of sand, superb for long walks or horse riding by the waves (there are several stables in the district), and when the tide is at its lowest you can walk round to the caves at the southern end to do some fossil collecting. At the very north end of the beach is *Carraig na*

Spáinneach (Spaniards' Rock), where three ships of the Spanish Armada foundered. There are numerous anonymous burial stones nearby, said to mark the mass graves of some 1100 sailors who either drowned or were butchered by the British and the locals.

Grange, Moneygold and Cliffony

At GRANGE itself there's not much of worth apart from a old boys' bar off to the right, over the bridge. However, if you venture inland (past the pub) you'll get a changing perspective of Benbulben as you approach the **Gleniff Horseshoe**, a scenic road that runs along a glen on the flank of the Dartry range, and gives easy access to the top of Benbulben.

MONEYGOLD, a short way beyond Grange, offers excellent **accommodation** at the *Moneygold Riding and Language Centre* (☎071/63337; hostel accommodation £5, B&B £8), where you can also try organically produced cheeses and sample local fish and shellfish. The hostel organises very cheap **bike hire** and **horse riding** on Streedagh Strand; and you can help work on the small farm for a week or more and earn yourself free food and accommodation. CLIFFONY, a couple of miles on again towards Bundoran, is remarkable for the **Creevykeel Court Tomb** (just past the village by the roadside), one of the most extensive Neolithic sites in the country, comprising two roofless tombs within a stone court.

The Mullaghmore peninsula

Mullaghmore headland is the most attractive of all the promontories north of Sligo Town. A left turn at the Cliffony crossroads takes you onto it, past **Classiebawn Castle** (closed to the public), a Disneyland-looking construction built by Lord Palmerston; it became the home of Lord Mountbatten shortly before he was killed by the IRA in 1979, when his boat was blown up in the bay.

MULLAGHMORE itself is a dainty place with a peaceful skiff-filled harbour and a very good beach. If you're spending some time here, there's good walking to be had along the rocky shelves of Mullaghmore Head, at the end of the village, where the ocean waves crash constantly within feet of you. Alternatively, you could explore the area on horseback: mounts can be hired from the stables on the crest of the hill. If you're wondering what all the nuns are doing in Mullaghmore, it's because the village has a convent holiday home at which they can relax after the rigours of their parishes. Non-ecclesiastical travellers can **camp** in the sand dunes as long as they're inconspicuous, and the *Beach Hotel* (☎071/66103; £28) offers **B&B** and good food; *Pier Head House* (☎071/66171; £22) also has rooms, a bar and food. *Lomax Boats* hires out fishing boats (£80 a day; maximum 6 persons; rods £4 per day), and can arrange trips to Inishmurray in summer (see below). For a quiet pint try *Annie's Bar*.

Inishmurray Island

The island of **INISHMURRAY**, about four miles offshore, has been deserted since the 1950s, but the trip out to it is more than worthwhile for its ruined sixth-century monastery, its church and its early Christian gravestones, some of the best-preserved in the country. In addition to *Lomax Boats*, trips are run by Mr Christy Herrity, *Carns*, Moneygold (☎071/63365; £75 for maximum group of 10), and Mr Mulligan, *Dún Ard*, Mullaghmore (☎071/67126). The crossing takes 75 minutes, and you can spend several hours on the island.

West of Sligo Town

Taking the route directly west out of Sligo Town – the Strandhill Road – you'll be heading in the direction of Knocknarea mountain. A right turn off this road runs down to Sligo Bay, where concrete markers delineate a low-tide crossing to Coney Island. More excitingly, a left turn eventually takes you into a fieldscape studded with over sixty megalithic tombs, the **Carrowmore Megalithic Cemetery** (mid-June to mid-Sept daily 9.30am–6.30pm; 80p, students 30p, heritage card; ☎071/61534). Over sixty tombs have been located here – the oldest predating Newgrange by some 700 years – and though half the stones have disappeared, this is still the second-largest such site in Europe after Carnac in Brittany. It's an intoxicating meander alongside the dolmens, stone circles and cairns, under the eye of the big mother cairn of them all – *Medb's Cairn*, on top of **Knocknarea**. The easiest ascent of the mountain is along the path that meets the road skirting its southern flank (the western slopes are too difficult). The 60-foot cairn on the summit is said to be the tomb of Queen Medb of Connaught, but as she was killed elsewhere it's unlikely that she's buried here; experts reckon that the 40,000 tons of rock were put here by Neolithic farmers – but it has yet to be excavated to find out why.

Towards the end of the headland, at **STRANDHILL** (bus #285 from Sligo), there's a large, wild beach along which the sea sweeps massive boulders in winter. Sligo airport is close by, and it's a thrilling sight to see the small *Aer Lingus* planes coming in over the top of *Medb's Cairn*. At the end of the airstrip stands the tenth-century **Killaspugbone Church** (access across the beach), where Saint Patrick allegedly tripped on the threshold and lost his tooth. A beautiful casket in which the sacred tooth was enshrined – the *Fiacal Pádraig* – is now in the National Museum in Dublin, but the whereabouts of the tooth is a mystery. The old Strandhill village was sited here until the drifting sand forced the villagers to move a few centuries ago. In modern Strandhill village look out for *Dolly's Cottage*: sessions take place some evenings, and during the day it's a kind of folk museum (July & Aug daily 3–5pm).

Ballysadare to Enniscrone

The main road south and then westward from Sligo, flanked by the northern foothills of the Ox Mountains and the innocuous coastline of western Sligo county, is scarcely an enthralling route, yet a few things crop up on the way to Mayo that are worth a mention. If you're cycling, take the road running parallel to and nearer the coast. **BALLYSADARE**, situated at the head of a beautiful bay with striking views back to Knocknarea and Benbulben, has the remnants of a seventh-century monastery and a pre-Romanesque church, neither really worth stopping for. *The Thatch Pub*, at the very southern end of town, is an old-fashioned pub where you should be able to hear a traditional tune or two (Thurs all year; plus open sessions Tues in summer).

Easky and the Ox Mountains
Just after SKREEN comes the turn-off for the **Ladies Brae Scenic Route**, one of only two trails across the vast **Ox Mountains** (*Sliabh Ghamh*, stony mountain) into south Sligo. Following the course of a tumbling stream between forests of fir, the road ends not far from COOLANY. Much of the Ox range consists of

unexciting heathery slopes and flat boggy upland, but the second route across the mountains – starting with a left turning off the road just before Easky (see below) – takes you up through the gorgeous setting of **Easky Lough** and then down a dramatic descent of the southwestern face of the range into the area surrounding Tobercurry (see below).

Originally a monastic settlement, **EASKY** was a vital link in the anti-Napoleon coastal defensive chain, as two nearby Martello towers attest. These days the place is acquiring a bit of a reputation as a surfers' paradise, which means increasing numbers of tourists. At the mouth of the salmon-rich Easky River are the ruins of the fifteenth-century **Rosalee Castle**, which many of the locals are convinced is cursed (key from Mrs Mary Morrissey, above *Clerk's* shop). A few years back it was all set to be renovated with government money, and a committee was set up to steer the village into a new tourist-fed prosperity. Suddenly the chairman of the committee dropped dead, then the secretary drowned, and finally, before the project was hastily disbanded, the treasurer choked on a steakbone and was rushed to hospital. Maybe this is why the village signs read *GOD BLESS YOU* as you leave. The only **pub** of any singularity is *Sheila Sullivan's*, a talking pub for the old fellas.

Enniscrone

ENNISCRONE, on the east side of Killala Bay and the western boundary of County Sligo, is a popular seaside resort for the Irish, with caravan sites hidden away in the sand dunes, plus the traditional golfing amenities. There's a sweeping three-mile crescent of sandy beach, with ten Victorian bath-houses, built to exploit the health-giving properties of seaweed and hot sea-water.

One other thing you can't fail to notice in Enniscrone is a powerful metal sculpture of a black pig in someone's front garden on the main street (the mythical Black Pig was chased across Donegal Bay and came ashore at Enniscrone). It was supposedly commissioned by the council, then appropriated by the house's owner when the unprepossessing final result was rejected. The local **tourist office** is on Main Street (☎096/36202). There are numerous **B&Bs**: try *Central House* on Main Street (☎096/36234; £13) or the *Castle Arms Hotel* (☎096/36156), where you can also get a drink and a bite to eat.

South of Sligo

The single stop-off sight in the village of **COLLOONEY**, five miles south of Sligo where the N4 and N17 separate (bus #247, #267, #275 or #285 from Sligo), is the **Teeling Monument** at the northern entrance to the village, built to commemorate Bartholomew Teeling, hero of the Battle of Carricknagat. The battle, which was fought nearby, occurred during the rebellion of 1798, when a combined Franco-Irish force – on its way to Ballinamuck in County Longford – was held up by a single strategically placed English gun. Teeling charged up the hill and shot the gunner dead, turning the tide of the engagement. After their defeat at Ballinamuck the French were treated as prisoners of war, but 500 Irish troops were massacred. Irish-born Teeling, who was an officer in the French army, was later hanged in Dublin. The monument links Teeling and his fallen comrades with subsequent generations of Irish freedom fighters.

Towards Lough Arrow

The more appealing route south from here, to Lough Arrow, involves a turn off the N4 at DRUMFIN, along the road that goes through the geriatric village of RIVERSTOWN. Several miles on, standing by the roadside behind a modern bungalow, is **Heapstown Cairn**, a Neolithic passage tomb as large as *Medb's Cairn* and traditionally the last resting place of Ailil, brother of King Niall of Tara. A lot of the cairn stones have been plundered for building material, but even in its diminished state the cairn remains impressive, best appreciated by climbing it and taking in the view from the top. What's most fascinating about the view is the perfect central position the cairn takes in relation to the surrounding circle of hills, some with cairns on their peaks.

One option from here is to go down the eastern shore of **Lough Arrow**, whose blue waters are set with ringlets of isles. When the sun is shining there are few spots to beat it, especially if you can take a rowing boat onto the tranquil lake – keep your eye out for boats lying by the banks and then ask at a nearby house. The road round the southern edge of the lake goes through BALLINAFAD, at the back door of the Bricklieve Mountains. The road into Ballinafad from the Curlew Mountains of Roscommon gives the most stupendous view in the whole of Sligo, right up to Benbulben – it's worth backtracking up the hill to get it. **Ballinafad Castle** (left off the road at the top of the village) is a sixteenth-century building remarkable only because its huge circular towers and squat walls are of thirteenth-century design.

Carrowkeel and Keshcorran

The other and more interesting route southwards from the Heapstown cairn takes you along the top of Lough Allen to meet the N4. Cross at CASTLEBALDWIN and climb the road leading up behind *McDermot's Pub* for the Bronze Age **Carrowkeel Cemetery** – be warned that it's a long and fairly arduous walk, but the panorama on the way is marvellous. Comprising fourteen cairns, a few dolmens and some fifty-odd pieces of stone foundations, the site is the most important cairn colony west of Sliabh Na Caillighe in northwest Meath. Several cruciform passage graves set in the cairns are still roofed, the smaller ones with great lintel stones, the larger with corbelled vaults. To get to the cemetery follow the ascending road for a few kilometres, turn left as signposted, follow the track round the hill's flank, through the gateway, next left round the side of the opposite slope and the cairns will be signposted forty yards up through the heather.

Also of interest in the area are the caves on the hill of **Keshcorran**, which you can get to by rejoining the main road across the mountains, then turning left down the hill, taking every descending turning until you reach a major road where the pub *The Traveller's Rest* stands. Take a right here towards KESH, and after the *Foxes Pub* and grocery store a fingerpost points right – after a couple of hundred yards you'll spot the line of caves cut into the forehead of the mountain. The caves have no depth at all, but the feeling of isolation is immense at this spot. It was here that the baby Cormac Mac Airt, later to be the greatest of all the High Kings who ruled at Tara, was reared by wolves. On the last Sunday in July, in a reflection of ancient pagan rituals, locals still gather by the caves for sessions of prayer.

Ballymote and Tobercurry

If, instead of taking the Lough Arrow route from Collooney, you follow the N17 southwest, you could make a diversion along the L11 to the small market town of **BALLYMOTE**. Its fourteenth-century castle, built by Richard de Burgo (the "Red Earl of Ulster"), was once the strongest in Connacht, but has associations with major defeats – it was O'Donnell's before he lost at the Battle of Kinsale, and it was James II's possession before he lost at the Boyne. The village sports a couple of nice old bars: *Sally's*, towards the east end of town, which has a dark wooden interior for serious drinking (music Sat & Sun); and *Hayden's* on the main southern street (occasional open sessions). For **accommodation** enquire from John Perry at *The Corran Restaurant*. He will arrange B&B (£8–9) or just a bed at the standard hostel price (☎071/83372); the restaurant is the best place to eat, and the proprietor acts as local information service. The *Castle Hotel* (☎071/83342; £12) also offers beds and meals.

The most stylish **B&B** in the vicinity, however, is at *Temple House* (☎071/83329; B&B £25, dinner £18; April–Nov), three miles from here on the shores of the lake. Founded by the Knights Templar and expanded in 1560, this is one of the grandest and oldest Anglo-Irish houses ever built in Ireland, on a 950-acre estate, with 97 rooms, five of which are for B&B guests. To get there take the left fork off the Collooney end of town; it's near the N17 to Tobercurry.

Tobercurry

The district around **TOBERCURRY** – and south Sligo in general – has a reputation for **traditional music**: Michael Coleman, the greatest of Irish fiddle players, came from here, and it's also where the *Chieftains* had their roots. Today the town and the surrounding area is economically very depressed, with boarded-up houses a common sight, and scenically it's not too exciting either. Tobercurry town is a busy little market centre, usually devoid of tourists. The **tourist information** is based in *Killoran's Traditional Restaurant*, where you can eat well and cheaply – don't miss out on the famous fresh salmon from the River Moy. The restaurant also has a dance floor at the back, where it holds boisterous Irish evenings (June–Sept Thurs 9.30am–12.30pm). In the second week of July the town has a **music week**, featuring short courses in music and Irish dancing. For **accommodation**, Anne Killoran can arrange free camping or a bed at the standard hostel rate; there are also several standard B&Bs such as Mrs Jackson's *April House* on the Ballymote road (☎071/85141; £13). *Carricks* sport and fishing tackle shop, a few doors down from *Killoran's*, hires out rods, and in the *Lough Talt Inn*, a few miles up the Ballina road, boats can be hired for trout fishing on the lake.

Gurteen and the far south

The L133 runs down to **GURTEEN**, once another thriving centre for traditional music, now a place with something of the scent of a ghost town. Yet some of the finest musicians in the country still live up in the hills, and from time to time they might come down to strike up a tune. *Teach Murray* has a session on Mondays, and the *Róisín Dubh* has spontaneous music making.

Lough Gara, tucked away in the southernmost pocket of the county, is not as appealing as the map suggests it might be, having a very undramatic surrounding shoreline. **Moygara Castle**, signposted near the lake, is similarly anticlimactic, with just one of its original four towers left intact.

County Leitrim

The **Leitrim** scenery is more distinctive than it's normally given credit for, but the county has no places of historical interest, and is not an area that will detain you for long unless you're a boating or canal enthusiast. It stretches fifty miles from County Longford to its slim two-mile coastline at **Tullaghan**, and is neatly split into a north and south section by the vast interruption of **Lough Allen**, the first lake on the River Shannon. The southern half is the more interesting, owing mainly to the presence of the **Shannon**, though the lake-peppered terrain to the east of the river also merits exploration. The northern section, around **Manorhamilton**, is a contrastingly mountainous territory; its most beautiful features – **Glencar** and **Lough Gill** – are shared with Sligo, and are best approached from there.

Carrick-on-Shannon

The small county town of **CARRICK-ON-SHANNON**, beautifully positioned on a wide stretch of the Shannon just below Lough Key, is a major **boating** centre, and its marina is full of pleasure boats and Shannon cruisers. It also makes a good base from which to cycle round the southern loop of Leitrim or to investigate Lough Key and Lough Boderg in Roscommon, and there's good coarse fishing to be had.

The single piece of historical interest the town has to offer is the minuscule **Costello Chapel**, at the top end of Bridge Street. Billed as the second smallest chapel in the world, it was built in 1877 by the fanatically devout businessman Edward Costello as a memorial to his wife, who died young that year. The couple's lead coffins, protected by thick slabs of glass, lie in two sunken spaces on each side of the tiny, beautifully tiled aisle. Also worth a call is **Cyril Cullen's** pebbledashed Georgian house and factory shop, *Summerhill* (on the road to St Patrick's Hospital), where he sells porcelain figures and his own distinctive knitwear designs – he breeds his own Jacob sheep for their wool. You may be lucky enough to get a chance to hear his 150-year-old harp made by J. Fall of Belfast, the first craftsman to take up harp-making after O'Carolan's death.There are only two such instruments in Ireland, the other being in Pádraig Pearse's memorial house in Dublin. You might also be shown his marvellous collection of Bridget Gore-Booth paintings.

Practicalities

Carrick boasts a number of small hotels and one of the best **hostels** in the country, the *Town Clock Hostel* (☎078/20068; £4; July–Sept only), which is situated at the junction of Main and Bridge Streets. **Camping** is allowed on the river bank by the bridge, just in front of *Michael Lynch's* boat hire, and you can use the washing facilities at the Clancy's supermarket nearby. More upmarket accommodation is on offer at numerous **B&Bs**, especially on Station Road and out on the Dublin road – try *Sunnybank*, Station Road (☎078/20988; £11) or *Attyrory Lodge* on the Dublin road (☎078/20955; £12) – or **hotels** such as the simple *Mariners Reach* on Bridge Street (☎078/20068; £13).

There are plenty of **pubs** in town. *Seán's Plaice* (sic) has a very jovial atmosphere with noisy sing-alongs on a Sunday morning, and is good for food too. *Burkes Bar*, just a few doors up from *Seán's*, has traditional music on Thursday nights. If you're looking for a place where silence is golden, then try *Armstrongs*, next door to the Costello Chapel. The *County Hotel* has traditional music sessions every Friday during July and August, with a small cover charge. *The Anchorage Bar*, near the bottom of Bridge Street, is the place where the youngsters hang out (music Oct–March on Sun, and on Wed during the rest of the year).

For **food** try *Cryan's*, at the bottom of Bridge Street, where you can get a three-course meal at a reasonable price. The *Coffee Shop*, also in Bridge Street, has very nice home bakes and is the best place for a snack lunch. For picnic provisions, *Doherty's Bakery* on Main Street is the place to go. *The Bookshop*, over the road from *Doherty's*, has a good selection of Irish literature and general contemporary stuff.

Carrick's **tourist office** (☎078/20170; May–Sept) is on the quay on the Roscommon side of the river. *Michael Lynch*, on the same side, but before the tourist office, has **boats** for hire (£15 per day with outboard; maximum 5 people), and there are numerous companies which hire out **Shannon cruisers** (2- to 10-berth) by the week. By 1993 it is hoped that the Ballyconnell–Ballinamore canal will be open again, linking Lough Erne with the Shannon and providing an unbroken 150-mile navigable stretch. For shorter **excursions**, *White Dolphin Boats* organise trips up the river leaving from the bridge on the hour (10am–5pm; £3.50 per person). Hire of **bikes** and fishing tackle is available at *Geraghty's* on Main Street.

South of Carrick

As with most of Leitrim, there's little of dramatic interest in the area south of Carrick, but if you're passing through there are a couple of places where you could at least slow down a bit. The village of **JAMESTOWN**, on the main Longford road, is a regal plantation town – the main road passes through a gate in the old estate walls. The Georgian mansions and the wooded river banks create the aristocratic feel of a bygone age. Excavations in the summer of 1989 at nearby **DRUMSNA**, another riverside village, unearthed huge stretches of a Stone Age wall, one of the oldest artificial structures in the world. It's been estimated that it would take a labour force of 30,000 men ten years to build its full length. *Taylor's Lounge*, right by the bridge, does bed and breakfast. A plaque on the wall records that Anthony Trollope began his novel *The MacDermots of Ballycloran* here in 1848; the MacDermots were great Catholic landowners during the eighteenth century, then were ruined by the Penal Laws.

DROMOD is the home village of one of the most extraordinary characters in Leitrim, a Kerryman called **James McCarran**, whose chaotic antique shop is almost as intriguing as the stories he tells. If he tries to sell you a saddle from the Battle of Hastings, think twice before shelling out. **ROOSKY**, on the Shannon a mile or so down the road, has just one attraction – *The Crow's Inn*, which has sessions on Thursday nights, with uilleann pipes and dancing; and even that is on the Roscommon side of the river.

Mohill

To the east of these villages is **MOHILL**, reached by turning off the main road at Drumsna or Dromod. A sculpture on the main street commemorates its most famous son – **Turlough O'Carolan** (1670–1738), the blind harpist and composer (he wrote "The Star Spangled Banner", among others). The last of the court bards, he lived by travelling round the chieftains' households playing his new compositions. He was also reputed to have been as great with the whiskey bottle as he was on the harp; it's said that on his deathbed he asked for a cup of the stuff, and finding that he hadn't the strength to drink it, touched the cup with his lip, saying that two old mates shouldn't part without a kiss. The **Lough Rinn Estate** near Mohill, recently opened to the public, is a large expanse of woodland with a carefully nurtured conglomeration of unusual plants, shrubs and trees. The mansion house is open for guided tours (11am, 11.30am, noon, 2pm, 3.30pm, 4pm and 4.30pm), but there isn't much to see really. *Fitzpatrick's* pub is more entertaining, with sessions on a Tuesday night.

North of Carrick

A couple of miles north of Carrick (#277 bus) is the county's namesake, **LEITRIM** village. It's a tiny one-street place with a lovely canalside setting – best appreciated from the pub on the bank. Though its name translates as "the back of the old cow's arse", **DRUMSHANBO** (four miles north from Leitrim) would make a decent alternative base from which to see south Leitrim. It sits at the southern tip of Lough Allen, noted as having the best pike fishing in Europe. Every June the village holds a festival of music and dance – details from the **tourist office,** based at Mrs Mooney's **B&B** on the corner of the High Street and the Carrick road (☎078/41013; £11). You can **camp** for free in a field a little way down the Carrick road, near the heated swimming pool complex (Irish dancing in the *Teach Cheoil* Mon night in summer; music on other summer evenings). The holiday cottages on the opposite side of the lake from the pool have a good restaurant that's a touch less pricey than the high-quality *Highbank House* on the High Street. For cheaper eating there's a cafe out the Manorhamilton end of town. The pea-green thatched *McManus* bar on the High Street has a music session every Thursday evening, but a much more interesting bar to drink in is *Conway's*, at the head of the Manorhamilton road. There are a couple of **buses** a day in the direction of Dublin, usually at 8am and 6pm (☎078/31174). **Bike hire** is available from the garage on Convent Street, going out in the Dowra direction, or from *McGrath's Cycle Shop*, opposite the tourist office. Rowing **boats** can be hired from Mrs McGuire, who lives in the large house to the side of the holiday homes.

Neither bank of Lough Allen is particularly attractive, but the eastern route along the bottom of **Slieve Anierin** is the better bet, taking you up to the county border at DOWRA. Just before the village there's a rewarding climb up into the Iron Mountains (take right turn off by *John Ryan's* pub/grocery store on side of the road); a very rugged track for much of the way, it twists and turns to follow the run of the river that cuts between the rock faces.

To Ballinamore

The best move from Drumshanbo is to take the Ballinamore road into the array of lakes that attracts most of Leitrim's tourism. This route makes a pleasant trip on a bike, as many of the lanes skirt the shores as they wind between the hills. Two of these hills have legendary names – **Sheemore** and **Sheebeag** (the hill of big fairies and the hill of the little fairies; there's a well-known Irish set-dance by the same name). As with all such enchanted hills, this pair are supposed to open up on *Samhain* (Hallowe'en), when their gods and goddesses roam the land.

Sheemore lies a couple of miles before KESHCARRIGAN on the south side of Lough Scur; unfortunately it's not signposted, so you might have to question a few of the locals for directions. Topped by a cairn and a St Patrick's Cross, the hill commands the best view across Leitrim; the cairn is believed locally to be Fionn Mac Cumhaill's grave. On your way again along the south of Lough Scur you'll pass a dolmen by the roadside before reaching **Sheebeag**, which has a gorse-covered cairn but is less exciting than its bigger brother. To get there follow the road straight on rather than turning left into Keshcarrigan, and take a sharp right up the hill and continue for a mile or so.

There's nothing much doing in Keshcarrigan apart from some traditional music every Friday night in *McKeown's* bar. FENAGH has a few more bars, and the ruins of a monastery and two churches founded in the seventh century by Saint Caillain. The key for the ruins are kept at the *Kealadaville B&B* (☎078/44179; £11), a hundred yards up the Mohill road.

It's not far from here to **BALLINAMORE**, which has a heritage and folk museum in the library building halfway down its main street. Highlight of the dull collection seems to be the "authentic detachable shirt collar worn by executed 1916 patriot Seán MacDiarmada" – and if you don't believe it there's a photograph of the man to prove it. For drinking and listening to a bit of music, try *Reynolds* on a Thursday night. *Caroline's Restaurant*, at the bottom of the main street, is a nice place to eat. There are plenty of places to stay, including *McAllister's Hotel* (☎078/44068; £15) and Mrs Gormley's B&B (☎078/44082; £10), both on the High Street.

North Leitrim

Focal point of the mountainous area north of Lough Allen is **MANORHAMILTON**, lying in the saddle of five valleys. Manorhamilton was founded on top of a strategic plateau by Sir Frederick Hamilton, a Scots colonist, during the seventeenth century; his castle was destroyed in the 1650s, but the ruins can still be visited. Today it's a handsome crossroads town, but with little happening to drag you all the way up there.

The road over to **KILTYCLOGHER** makes an exhilarating scenic drive, but although the village is trim and pretty there's nothing that should detain you after you've seen the **Seán MacDiarmada** statue. He was born here, and was executed in Dublin in 1916 for his part in the uprising. The route on up from here to Kinlough runs along the eight-mile western shore of **Lough Melvin**, whose only remotely picturesque spot is the paltry ruin of **McClancy's Castle**, standing on an islet a few yards from the northern end of the lake. It was here that the eight survivors from the three Spanish galleons wrecked off Streedagh Point finally found refuge.

KINLOUGH, near the tip of the lake, is a wholly undisturbed village, and has a surprisingly interesting little folk museum at the Manorhamilton end. Part of the museum is the old *McCurran's Bar* (key from the grocery store across the road), where a half-bottle of Guinness stands fermenting on the wooden bar counter, and a poteen shaped like a diving bell stands by the wall. There's another more conventional room to the museum, with folk and historical knick-knacks crammed into every available space; a newspaper cutting shows De Valera on his way to the Dáil for the first session of the new Irish Free State. There are a couple of small B&Bs, including *Bluerock*, on the Dartry road (☎072/41610; £12).

TULLAGHAN, a few miles away, is a dreary resort on a dreary strip of coast.

travel details

Trains
From Sligo: three trains daily run to Collooney (10min); Ballymote (20min); Boyle (40min); Carrick-on-Shannon (50min); Dublin (3hr 20min).

Bus Éireann
From Sligo: to Belfast (1 daily; 6hr); Galway (3 daily; 3–5hr).

Private Buses
Funtrek (☎01-730852) operates daily services **from Sligo** Wine St car park to Carrick-on-Shannon and Dublin.

CHAPTER TWELVE

MONAGHAN AND CAVAN

Fishermen apart, nobody comes to **Monaghan** or **Cavan** for a holiday. That's not to say there isn't some very enjoyable countryside – there's plenty – but it just doesn't compete with the grandeur of Sligo and Donegal, nor the expansive beauty of Fermanagh. These counties sit side by side as if one is a physical imprint of the other – Monaghan all small hills, Cavan all small lakes. County Monaghan is renowned for being drumlin country – rashes of rounded hills that diminish as you head west into Cavan where the land breaks up into a crazy pattern of tiny lakes. Both landscapes have their charms, both their practical difficulties. If you're walking or cycling in either county, a compass can be very useful – the terrain isn't inaccessible or dangerous, but there's such a network of winding, crisscrossed roads that you can very easily get lost. In Monaghan the drumlins all look similar, while the myriad lakes of Cavan enforce constant twists and turns. Cyclists should be aware that a lot of the minor roads are riddled with potholes, and dodging them slows you down considerably.

With County Donegal, Monaghan and Cavan share the peculiar identity of being historically part of **Ulster*** yet nowadays included in the Republic. Donegal's coastline links it with the West; but Monaghan and Cavan are far more involved with and affected by the North. As **border** counties they inevitably shelter a lot of Republican activity for purely geographical reasons, but there's also a strong affinity between Cavan and Monaghan people (Protestant and Catholic) and their Ulster neighbours – until Partition, they shared a culture and a history. Cavan and Monaghan communities are intermittantly touched by the North's violence, and appreciate that they don't have to live it every day. Republicanism just south of the border can appear stronger than in the North; the aims here are clear, and people are not worn down by daily facing the realities of the conflict. It's no more appropriate to assert your opinions on Irish politics here than in the North – at the very least people find it intrusive. It's also advisable to steer clear of the border itself, which can be quite tricky; it twists and turns, and signposting is rarely better than minimal.

Although the border has sharpened political and social definitions, there is a sense in which it also shelters both of these counties. You'll probably be struck by the old-fashioned feel of the countryside: while slow, rural ways are as prevalent in other Irish counties, the sharp contrast with the industrialisation and British development over the border makes them more striking here. Uncertainty about the future and the possibility of violence has slowed development, leaving an unhurried rural ordinariness that constitutes much of these counties' appeal. They are not gaily painted for tourists, nor visibly quaint, and

---

*Confusingly, the name Ulster has come to be used to describe Northern Ireland. In fact, the ancient province of Ulster consisted of nine counties: at Partition, Monaghan, Cavan and Donegal were severed from the six counties which now form the North.

there's a dour Scottish severity in many of the villages, particularly in Monaghan – clear evidence of the Ulster planters. But as you explore you'll find both counties have real charm, understated and quiet.

COUNTY CAVAN

There's little of historical interest left in **County Cavan**, and what there is often lies in the landscape itself. In former times the region was even more water-riddled, boggy and forested than it is today. This complex of lake and bog was extremely difficult for foreign invaders to penetrate and control, and also made the land less desirable. Only the most durable relics have survived. There are plenty of **court cairn tombs** in the region, evidence of Neolithic peoples from as early as six thousand years ago, but they're hard to find unless you know what you're looking for. Similarly invisible are the lakes' *crannógs* – man-made islands built as early as the Stone Age, but more typically developed as secure settlements from the first century AD, and now melted back in to the general landscape, indistinguishable from natural islands. **The Celts** had their principal pagan shrine at **Magh Sleacht** near present-day Ballyconnell. Several Celtic stone idols bearing bold representations of the human head have been found in the lake areas of Cavan and Fermanagh, particularly potent pagan symbols. Some of them were found in circumstances suggesting that they were deliberately hidden in recent times to deny them their power, a sign of their continuing folkloric importance. Sadly, though, none of these idols can be seen in their original setting, and most now form part of the collections of the National Museum in Dublin or the Fermanagh County Museum at Enniskillen.

When **Saint Patrick** established his seat at Armagh, he also set up a monastery at Kilnavert. Rather than crudely asserting a new dogma, the proselytising Christians allowed pagan and folkloric traditions to continue, mingling them with the new creed. The filtering through of the new faith was fairly rapid; but more brutal invaders found the area far harder to penetrate. The network of lakes and waterways proved difficult to negotiate, and foreign invaders arrived with neither knowledge of the terrain, nor the physical means needed for conquest. The **O'Reilly** family, who dominated Cavan from the beginning of recorded history to the seventeenth century, continually blocked Anglo-Norman attempts to take control, and this explains the lack of Norman developments in the region.

Despite Elizabeth I's attempts to divide and rule by creating the **County of Cavan** (more a piece of propaganda than a sign of real political strength) and playing one Irish barony off against another, it was only after the failure of the Irish cause at the Battle of Kinsale that Cavan received the stamp of foreign invaders. Ancient Gaelic ways were crushed by the Jacobite plantation and the county was divided up between English and Scottish settlers. Every parish was to have a Protestant church, and the new town of Virginia was built in memory of Elizabeth. As usual, the best land was given to the English and Scottish newcomers, leaving the Irish population to face poverty and the loss of religious freedom.

The rebellion of 1641 was a direct result, and **Owen Roe O'Neill**, the Ulster Confederate leader based at Cavan, played an important part, defeating the British General Munro at Benburb to the north of the county in 1646. However, O'Neill failed to follow his victory through, and the Irish Confederates were eventually defeated. After O'Neill's death in 1649, Cromwell quickly took control of

Cavan and the resulting confiscation of land and property from the Irish guaranteed the Protestant domination of the county.

Until Partition, Cavan's subsequent history was much in line with the rest of Ulster. In the eighteenth and nineteenth centuries the linen and woollen industries ensured a measure of economic growth – though Cavan was always one of the poorer parts of the province because of the difficulties of the land; and the Famine of 1847 brought large-scale emigration. At **Partition**, Cavan was included in the Republic, thus retaining its Irishness; but it shared the fate of Monaghan and Donegal in being torn from its historic and cultural Ulster identity.

Getting around Cavan: where to stay

Cavan town is very much the transport centre of the county, and it's here you're likely to arrive. *Bus Éireann* (☎049/31353 for information) connects Cavan town with all major towns in the Republic and the North, and **private buses** run to Dublin. As for accommodation, the only **independent hostel** in the county is in Ballyconnell (see below) but there are plenty of B&Bs in Cavan Town, Bailieborough, Belturbet, Cootehill, Killeshandra, Kingscourt, Lough Gowna and Virginia. As everywhere, people will usually let you **camp** in their fields if you ask, but if you want the amenities of a campsite try *Lakelands Caravan and Camping Park* at SHERCOCK (☎042/69206; open Easter & June to mid-Sept; laundry facilities; £3) in the east of the county, and *Lough Ramor Caravan Park* at VIRGINIA in the south (☎049/47447; mid-April to Sept; £2 per unit, 25p per person).

Lough Oughter and Cavan Town

The focus of scenic interest in County Cavan is the complex of tiny lakes which riddle the north of the county. They're known collectively as **Lough Oughter**, and form part of Upper Lough Erne. The land here is so fretted with water that its very fabric seems to be disintegrating. Contours are provided by very low, unassuming hills while the waters are edged with reeds, spindly silver birch and alder. Everything is on a small scale, but the landscape has a subtle attraction nonetheless, and the roads making their way through the labyrinthine network of lakes are quiet and empty. It makes little sense to head for a particular point in Lough Oughter – it's hard to tell when you've got there anyway – and the best plan is probably just to enjoy the gentle confusion.

The county is renowned for its **fishing**, and a conservative tourism is growing which neither scars the land nor disturbs the peace. Forest parks have been developed, not to encourage families to bring the kids, but to give fishermen access into the heart of the lake complex. Everywhere the stillness is profound. The nicest of the little towns serving fishing visitors are Belturbet, Virginia, and Cavan Town itself. BELTURBET sits prettily on a hill besides the River Erne, an angling and boating resort, while VIRGINIA is picturesquely situated beside Lough Ramar, and adds golf to these amenities. Both are straight-laced, well-kept towns. Five miles west of Belturbet in **BALLYCONNELL**, the county's one **independent hostel**, the friendly *Sandville House Hostel* (☎049/26297; March–Nov; £4; camping and bike hire available), is well-placed just off the main R200 road to West Cavan and Sligo. Housed in a converted barn alongside a large Georgian house, the hostel is not heavily used because of its remoteness, but if you do find your way here you're liable to stay longer than planned. A good stop on your way west, it also offers a retreat *from* the West if the West Coast experience gets too much. The *Slieve Russell Hotel* (☎049/26444; £30), atop a hill outside town, makes a considerable contrast, and seems designed to announce that its owner has made it big locally: inside it's less brash, and the dining room is the best place to eat round here, albeit expensive. There are a couple of regular B&Bs too. To the southeast, there's also the pretty village of BUTLERSBRIDGE, with a notoriously enjoyable bar, the *Derra Garra Inn*; touristy, but it serves good food throughout the day (10.30am–10.30pm).

Cavan Town
CAVAN Town grew up around an abbey, but nothing remains of this beyond its memory and an eighteenth-century tower beside the burial place of Owen Roe O'Neill. Today it's a pretty subdued place. It has two main streets: Main Street is the principal artery of shops and bars, while Farnham Street has an older character with some very nice stone Georgian houses, a Classical courthouse of warm sandstone and a huge Catholic cathedral, built in the Forties, that surprisingly succeeds in confirming status and a sense of place without being overbearing.

For **bed and breakfast**, try Mrs McMahon's *New County*, 38 Farnham Road (☎049/31694; £12); or, ten minutes' walk out of town, Mrs P. Adams' *Shandra*, Golflinks Road, Lisdaran (☎049/31183; £11). For rather more luxury the *Farnham Arms* on Main Street (☎049/32577; £24) has rooms as well as a pleasant bar and pub meals. Other useful facilities include a **launderette** (*The Laundry Basket*, on Dublin Road), a **travel agent** (*McGinnity Ltd*; 2 Coleman Road; ☎049/31811) and a **tourist office** at Farnham Street (June–Aug Mon–Sat 9am–6pm, Sept–May Mon–Fri 9am–5pm; ☎049/31942). You can **hire bikes** from *Bicycle Tours* on Farnham Street (☎049/31932). *Bus Éireann* buses also leave from Farnham Street.

Around the county

Some three miles west of Cavan, on the R198 to CROSSDONEY, stands the modern Protestant Cathedral of **Kilmore**. The modern structure is of little interest, but set in the wall is an impressive Romanesque doorway, removed here from a monastery that stood on Trinity Island, three miles to the west in Lough Oughter. Its deep, chunky carving is superbly intricate, and repays detailed attention. Follow the narrow road that runs north from here to the hamlet of GARTHROTTEN, and you can enter **Killykeen Forest Park**. Here **Clough Oughter** is a thirteenth-century circular tower built on a *crannóg*, the best of its kind in Ireland.

Alternatively from Crossdoney, you can follow the road round the west side of Lough Oughter, through KILLESHANDRA and MILLTOWN. In contrast to the dearth of viewable history in the county as a whole, Mrs Faris's *Pighouse Collection*, a **folk museum** at Corr House, CORNAFEAN (open anytime, but ring ahead to check she's in; ☎049/37248; adults £1.50, kids 50p), is a massive accumulation of miscellaneous remnants of the past. To get there, take the Killeshandra road from Crossdoney, bear left at the Arva signpost, then first right – it's difficult to reach without transport. Three huge barns are full of dusty junk, only a small part of which, the section on domestic utensils and furniture, has so far been catalogued and labelled – the rest you rummage through and interpret for yourself. There's a vast and fascinating range of stuff which includes (for example) a fine collection of embroidered eighteenth-century waistcoats, Victorian and Edwardian evening gowns, samples of old lace and a huge collection of porcelain cheese dishes.

Further on, just south of Milltown, you'll find **Drumlane Church** and **Round Tower**. A monastery was founded here by Saint M'Aodhog in the sixth century, and Augustinians from Kells took the place over in medieval times. The church itself is plain and roofless, but its setting beside a lake, and its size in such an intimate landscape, are impressive. The earliest parts of the building are thirteenth-century, but it was substantially altered in the fifteenth century, from when the carved heads outside the doorways and windows date. The round tower is eleventh-century, and of good, clean stonework.

West Cavan

To the northwest of Milltown and Killeshandra, **West Cavan** sticks out like a handle, tracing the line of the border. It's quite different from the rest of the county; wilder and higher, with peat-covered hills, granite boulders, and mountain streams. In this bleak inhospitability it has more in common with the wilds of Donegal than the more intimate Cavan lakeland. The **Cavan Way** is a signposted walk of seventeen miles that takes you through rugged terrain from Dowra to Blacklion, where it meets the southwestern end of the **Ulster Way**. Small maps of the route can be picked up in tourist offices. From the heights above Blacklion there are spectacular views over Lough MacNean and the Fermanagh lakeland, to the Sligo and Leitrim mountains in the west, and on a clear day to the heights of south Donegal. Along the route **Shannonpot** is the source of Ireland's mightiest river – the Shannon – and figures heavily in Irish myth, though it's little visited.

DOWRA and BLACKLION themselves are tiny and remote; the former high on the young Shannon before it fills Lough Allen, the first of many lakes, the latter a border crossing point. Both have **B&Bs** which are almost certain to have space, though it's still safer to phone ahead and check – they all charge around £10. In Blacklion try Christina McManus's *Benbrack House* (☎072/53025) or *Loughmacneann House* (☎072/53022), both in Main Street; in Dowra ask at the *Hi Way Inn* (☎078/43025).

COUNTY MONAGHAN

Monaghan's countryside is first and foremost *drumlin* country. **Drumlins** are softly rounded mounds of land left by retreating glaciers at the end of the Ice Age, and the exceptional number of these small hills packed together in County Monaghan serves as a very good example of what text books call "basket of eggs" topography – a reference to the land's appearance from on high. The result at ground level is that the soil is poor, and the land is broken up into small units which are difficult and uneconomic to farm. The drumlins are grass-covered, and light hedgerows stitch their way across them, marking out the fields. Initially it's a charming scene, but it soon becomes repetitive: the pathways between drumlins are pretty enough, but once you're round or over one small hill the next is much the same. Little lakes provide occasional relief, and are excellent for fishing, but they're nothing like as numerous as in Cavan.

The feel of this landscape has been captured in the poetry and prose of **Patrick Kavanagh**, rated by many as Ireland's finest poet after Yeats. He was born in Inishkeen in the south of the county, and his writing evokes the poor quality of peasant life – and something too of the monotony of the rural landscape.

Particularly in the north of the county, the terrain has led to an insane criss-crossing of lanes: a compass is a good idea, as is an awareness that all available maps are unreliable. It makes for delightful walking if you're not in too much of a hurry: in these hilly areas you can wander undisturbed for miles along the labyrinth of ancient tracks and lanes – though it is advisable to try and avoid the border. If you know what to look for you can seek out the sites of court tombs, forts and cairns from the Bronze Age. Many of them, thanks to the underdevelopment of the land, have remained virtually untouched. The best megalithic sites in the region are the Lisnadarragh wedge tomb, **Dún Dubh**, at TIRAVERA; and the **Tullyrain triple ring fort** near SHANTONAGH.

But most of Monaghan's towns and villages have very clear origins in the seventeenth and eighteenth centuries. The influence of Scottish **planters** and English colonists is obvious in the number of Planters Gothic and Presbyterian churches; in the planned towns, and the landscaped estates developed around conveniently picturesque lakes. Stark, stern architecture reflects the character of the hard-working and hard-driving settlers who came here determined to extract prosperity from farming, and from the linen industries which they introduced. Probably the most extreme examples of such discipline are the dour, austere stone cottages of GLASLOUGH, cold and orderly in the north of the county. Like Cavan, Monaghan's cultural identity is deep-rooted in her Ulster history.

Practically speaking, while you'll have no problems finding **B&Bs** in towns like Monaghan, Carrickmacross and Castleblayney, decent **places to eat** are surprisingly hard to come by, especially in the evening, and you may find yourself resorting to takeaways more often than you'd like.

Monaghan Town

You're most likely to find yourself in **MONAGHAN Town** while on your way to somewhere else, but the actual fabric of the place is quite interesting as you pass through. Monaghan Town epitomises what makes this county very definitely Ulster, and yet quite distinct from Cavan. The planning of seventeenth-century settlers, the prosperity of the eighteenth-century linen industry (largely the achievement of Scots Presbyterians), and the subsequent wealth and status of the town in the following century are all very much in evidence.

Three central squares are linked by a chain of lanes, a layout not, in fact, altogether typical of Plantation towns. At the centre is the **Diamond** – the name given to all these Ulster "squares" – in the middle of which stands a grandiose Victorian drinking fountain, the kind of memorial strongly reminiscent of any nineteenth-century industrial British city, yet strangely out of place in rural Ireland. When it was placed here, the earlier seventeenth-century Scottish settlers' cross, with its multifaceted sundial, was shifted to Old Cross Square, where it still stands. Alongside the Diamond is **Church Square**. Here a Classical courthouse, a solid Victorian bank and hotel, and a very pretty Regency Gothic church, large and spacious, stand together, conferring a strong sense of civic dignity. The town's former importance as a British garrison town is quite clear, and a large obelisk commemorates a colonel killed in the Crimean War. Everything about the place suggests a conscious attempt at permanency, buildings placed with a view to posterity; even the rounded corners of the most mundane buildings and their boldly arched entries – both features unique to Monaghan – suggest strength and pride.

Beyond Church Square, at the top of Market Street, is a pretty, arched **Market House** built in 1792. A solid, graceful building of well-cut limestone, with finely detailed decoration of carved oak leaves and oak apples, this houses the **tourist office** (June–Aug Mon–Sat 9am–6pm, Sept–May Mon–Fri 9am–1pm & 2–5pm; ☎047/81122). In the opposite direction, Dublin Street leads down to **Old Cross Square**. At number ten stands the birthplace of Monaghan's most famous son, **Charles Gavan Duffy** – a nationalist who was instrumental in the founding of the Irish Tenant League. He was also the co-founder, along with Thomas Davis, of *The Nation*, a paper which was to disseminate politically sensitive ideas. Beyond, high on a hill out of town, **St Macartan's Catholic Cathedral** commands views over the whole town and surrounding countryside. It's a Gothic Revival building of hard grey sandstone, completed in 1892; the spire is very tall, and the interior, complete with an impressive hammer-beam roof, is spacious. As you stand on the steps looking out over the surrounding land you get a real feeling of its era – it's a most successful nineteenth-century statement of religious liberation and pride.

As well as being a busy commercial and administrative centre, Monaghan looks after the county's vigorous and sometimes violent history at the award-winning **Monaghan County Museum** (Hill Street; June–Sept Tues–Sat 11am–5pm, Oct–May Tues–Sat 11am–1pm & 2–5pm; free). This has a permanent collection of archaeological material, prehistoric antiquities, examples of traditional local crafts, domestic utensils, and paintings, prints and watercolours from the late eighteenth century to the present day. Recent acquisitions include textiles and banners, but the museum is most proud of the **Cross of Clogher**, a processional cross dating from around 1400. Contemporary art exhibitions are also held here. The **Heritage Centre** (Broad Road; Mon, Tues, Thurs & Fri 10am–noon and 2–4pm; Sat & Sun 2–4pm; £1, students 50p; ☎047/82529) tells the story of the religious order of Saint Louis, with an intelligent display meticulously put together by one of the sisters; you're guided through it with a cassette recording.

Practicalities

Bus Éireann (☎047/82377) link Monagahan with all major towns in the Republic and with Armagh, Belfast, Derry, Omagh and Strabane in the North. **Private buses** connect with Dublin (P.J. McConnon; ☎047/82020; see "Travel Details"). For longer distance transport, *O'Hanrahan Travel* (59 Dublin Street, ☎047/81832, 81133) is local agent for *Transalpino*, *Eurotrain*, *Slatterys* and *Supabus*.

Decent **B&Bs** include *Ashleigh House*, 37 Dublin Street (☎047/81227; £12) and *The Cedars*, Clones Road (☎047/82783; closed Dec; £10), and there's the usual clutch of small **hotels**, including the *Westenra Arms* on The Diamond (☎047/82298; £25). There's no **campsite**, but you should be able to find somewhere to pitch a tent if you ask at a farm out of town. None of the **places to eat** are particularly inspiring: the *Courthouse Bar* in Church Square serves bar lunches daily (from £2.50); the *Coffee Shop Restaurant* offers chicken, burgers and chips (Mon–Sat 9am–8.15pm, Sun 5–7.30pm) while the fast food at *Tommies Restaurant* (7 Glaslough Street; noon–3.30pm) includes steaks, roasts, grills, pizza and curry, to eat in or take away. *Genoa Restaurant and Ice-Cream Parlour* (61 Dublin St; daily noon–7.30pm, takeaway till around midnight) serves home-made pizzas, burgers and fried chicken as well as excellent ice cream.

As far as **entertainment** goes, there's little beyond occasional music in **bars**. In Dublin Street *McKenna's* has occasional rock and blues bands, and *The Shamrock Bar* has less frequent, similar music. There are a couple of local **theatre** groups who are very active: if your visit happens to coincide with a local production it's well worth going to see them. The local **jazz festival** takes place over the first weekend in September.

The rest of the county

Unless you're heading for the North, there are two main routes out of Monaghan: west to Clones, or south to Carrickmacross, the county's second town. On the latter route you'll pass first through **CASTLEBLANEY**, whose two proud broad streets hinge upon a fine Georgian courthouse at what was once the market square. Castleblaney was built by English colonists to serve the needs of a large estate, beautifully situated beside Monaghan's largest lake, **Lough Muckno**, and this is still the town's finest asset. When the English picked their spot they knew what they were about: it's a particularly attractive demesne of mixed woodlands and gentle slopes beside placid waters. The estate is now a forest park, with clearly signposted walks around beautiful grounds. *Hope Castle Caravan and Camping Park* is a thoughtfully concealed **campsite** amidst the trees (June–Aug; £2.50–3.50; ☎042/45031) that attracts families and fishermen in search of peace and quiet. **B&Bs** include Mrs Fleming's *Lochbeg* (Corracloughan, just outside town; ☎042/40664; £12) and Mrs Coogan's *Hazelwood House* (Annahale, Dundalk Road; ☎042/46009; £12). For **food** there's *Joan's Pantry* (Mon–Sat), a delicatessen and café serving light, wholesome lunches, or a Chinese restaurant a few doors down (evenings only).

Carrickmacross

CARRICKMACROSS is the county's second most important town, boosted in the nineteenth century by a prosperous lace-making industry. The town has one broad main street; a Planters Gothic church stands at one end, a large Georgian house at the other. In between lies a bustling array of pubs, shops and Georgian houses. Just outside town, landscaped parkland of sumptuous oaks and beeches surround **Lough Fea**. Further out, some three miles down the Kingscourt Road, is the **Dún a Rí Forest Park** with more good wooded walks. The massive *Nuremore Hotel* is very expensive (☎042/61438; £60), but there are plenty of **B&Bs** near the centre of Carrickmacross, up the Derry Road past the Texaco filling station: try Mrs Hanratty's *Cloughvalley House* (☎042/61246; £10); Mrs Martin's *Nocdale*, 9 Ard Rois Avenue, Cloughvalley (☎042/61608; £11); or the *Shirley Arms* on Main Street (☎042/61209; £15). *M&S* **launderette** is on Main Street (9am–6pm, closed Sun & Wed).

Inishkeen

INISHKEEN, to the east of Carrickmacross, is the birthplace of **Patrick Kavanagh**, which is not, in itself, any very good reason to visit. There's a small plaque bearing some of his verse in the village and the house he lived in is well signposted – but you can't go in and it's an entirely uninteresting building. In a more distant past Inishkeen was the site of a sixth-century monastic centre: scant remains of the abbey and a round tower survive. The **Folk Museum** (by arrangement only ☎042/78102) deals with local history, folklife and the old Great Northern Railway. For **entertainment**, Daniel McNello's *Kavanagh Hide Out* has country music sessions every weekend.

Clones

In quite the other direction from Monaghan, in the west of the county, **CLONES** (pronounced Clo-nez) is a busy, friendly market town barely half a mile from the border. Situated on top of a hill, its streets give a good perspective over the surrounding countryside. The town as it appears today dates from 1601 when the English took it over and started to develop it. It's very obviously an Ulster town, with large Presbyterian and Methodist churches to rival the usual Catholic and Church of Ireland offerings. The solemn and impressive **St Tiernach's church** (Church of Ireland) gives out onto the fine Diamond, and there is some evidence of eighteenth-century prosperity in the town's handful of Georgian houses. There are also traces of Clones' earlier identity, the most impressive being the weathered, deeply-carved **High Cross** which stands in the Diamond. Depicted on it are Adam and Eve, Abraham's sacrifice of Isaac, Daniel in the lion's den and, on the north side, the Adoration of the Magi, the miracle at Cana, and the miracle of the loaves and fishes. Though worn, there's still a strong impression of the richness of the carving. In the sixth century Saint Tiernach founded a monastery at Clones. It became an Augustinian **abbey** in the twelfth century, and the tumbled-down traces of this can be seen in Abbey Street, along with those of a Round Tower. Just on the edge of town is an ancient rath (an enclosure used as a dwelling) of three concentric earthworks.

Nowadays, of course, the town's chief claim to fame is as the home of **Barry McGuigan**, the former world-champion boxer. His supporters club is the *Diamond Hotel*, which also happens to be one of the best places for **bar food** in the county (Mon–Sat 10am–6pm). There's excellent food too at the *Lennard Arms Hotel* (daily, anytime; it's also on the Diamond; ☎047/51075) which offers **B&B** from around £14; *Creighton's* in Fermanagh Street is the other option if you're looking for somewhere to stay (☎047/51284; £15).

Just east of Clones is the remarkable Tyrone Guthrie Foundation at Annamakering, Newbliss. Commemorating the famous Shakespearian director, the centre offers a retreat and workspace to writers, artists and composers from all over the world. So if you're carrying that unfinished novel in your backpack contact the director, Brendan Loughlin (☎047/54003) – but be warned that the place is very oversubscribed.

travel details

Bus Éireann

From Cavan: to Belfast (2 daily; 3hr–4hr 40min); Dublin (6daily; 3hr).

From Monaghan: to Belfast (7 daily; 2hr); Dublin (7 daily; 2hr 15min).

Private buses

Wharton's Bus (☎049/37114) runs a daily service **from Cavan**, outside the *Lakeland Hotel* (Mon–Sat 8am, Sun 7pm) for Dublin. Departs **from Dublin**, opposite the gates of the Rotunda

Maternity Hospital, Parnell Square (Mon–Sat 5.45pm) and on Sun (8.30pm) from outside *Wynn's Hotel*, Abbey Street.

P.J. McConnon's (☎047/82020) buses **from Monaghan** to Dublin depart Church Square twice daily (Mon–Fri 8.05am & 8.30am, Sat noon & 3pm, Sun 5.45pm & 6.30pm), returning from Parnell Square (Mon–Thurs 5.15 & 6.15pm, Fri 3pm, 4pm, 5pm, 5.45pm & 6.15pm, Sat 11.30am, 4.30pm, 5.30pm & 6.15pm, Sun 8.15pm).

CHAPTER THIRTEEN

DONEGAL

Not many people would disagree with the assertion that **County Donegal** has the richest scenery in the whole country. Second only in size to Cork, it has a spectacular two-hundred-mile coastline, an intoxicating run of headlands, promontories and peninsulas that rises at **Slieve League** to the highest cliffs in Europe. Inland is a terrain of glens, rivers and bogland hills, of which the best-known parts are the **Glencolumbcille** Peninsula and around **Ardara** and **Glenties** in the southern part of the county. Well served with a string of hostels, the Glencolumbcille area attracts more visitors than any other, yet the landscape of northern Donegal is, if anything, even more satisfying, especially the **Rosguill** and **Inishowen** peninsulas, and the interior region sometimes called the **Donegal Highlands** – around **Errigal** mountain, **Lough Beagh** and **Lough Gartan**. Other noteworthy areas are the **Rosses** and **Bloody Foreland**, which are reminiscent of the more barren stretches of Connemara and make up the strongest *Gaeltacht* districts in the county. The only piece of Donegal not worth spending some time in is the eastern half of the county which shares more low-lying fertile ground with counties Derry and Tyrone.

The county's original name was *Tír Chonaill*, which translates as "the land of Conal", one of the twelve sons of Niall of the Nine Hostages. Subsequent to the **Flight of the Earls** in the early seventeenth century the English changed the name to that of their main garrison *Dún na nGall*, "the fort of the foreigner", which has a certain irony, because Donegal always eluded the grip of English power, mainly due to its wild and untillable terrain. In 1923, at the time of Partition, the Protestant leader **Carson** let it remain with the Republic, reasoning that its Catholic population would probably have voted the county and the whole of the North back into the Republic at a later stage. Hence the peculiarity of its being the most northerly piece of the island, yet belonging to the South, to which it's attached by just a thread of land.

Bundoran and the road to Donegal Town

BUNDORAN (*bun dobhráin*, mouth of the Doran River) is one of Ireland's liveliest seaside resorts – with three miles of blue flag beaches – busy day and night with mainly Northern Irish holidaymakers and courting couples strolling around the amusement arcades, souvenir shops and pubs. The town centre is concentrated into a mile of main street with the tiny river and bridge separating the western part of town (known as the West End) from the Catholic East End with its tackier atmosphere, pubs, B&Bs, eating places and golf course. As an introduction to the county of Donegal it's entirely misrepresentative, and unless you really want to seek out the boisterous holiday atmosphere, Bundoran is probably best viewed from the window of a bus.

If you do stop, the chief attraction is a lovely, golden-sand beach known as **Tullan Strand**, a bracing stroll along the coastal promenade away from the northern end of the town beach. The walk takes in rock formations known as the **Fairy Bridge** and the **Puffing Hole** with the Atlantic thundering below and appetising views across to the much more rewarding Glencolumbcille Peninsula. Along with the beach at Rossnowlagh, Tullan Strand is reckoned among the most exciting surfing spots in the world, which also makes them some of the most dangerous for swimming.

A more recent attraction for the tourists is **Waterworld** (☎072/41230; £3, £2 children), a complex of heated pools with wave machine and waterslides.

Bundoran practicalities

There's a tourist office (☎072/41350; June to mid-Sept) on the bridge, with details of accommodation and a booking service. The cheapest **place to stay** in Bundoran is the basic *Homefield Holiday Hostel* (☎072/41288; £4; large kitchen, sitting room and washing machine): to get there take a right turning at the church just before the bridge in the West End. Its main function is as an activity centre, so it's often full of hearty young groups. **B&Bs** are plentiful along and just off the main street – try for example *Kieran House* (East End; ☎072/41345; £11; April–Sept) – getting better as you cross the bridge into West End, where many have wondrous views of Donegal Bay: *Atlantic View*, West End (☎072/41403; £11.50); *Glena*, almost next door (☎072/41245; £10); *Conway House*, 4 Bayview Terrace (☎072/41220; £11; April–Sept); and *Bayview House*, Main Street (☎072/41296; £14). There are also lots of resort **hotels**, chief of them the big old *Great Northern* (☎072/41204; £35), dominating the golf course right on the headland.

For **eating** there are plenty of simple cafés like the *Kitchen Bake*, in a converted chapel on the main street, for excellent cakes, coffee and snacks; an ideal stop between buses. The *Angler's Restaurant* offers a good three-course meal for less than £5. More upmarket but still not overly expensive is the *Fitzgerald Hotel* (just over the bridge in the West End) with a tourist menu at £7.50. The newly opened *Whistling Oyster*, on the main street, offers varied seafood dinners from £10 in a bar-room setting.

Most **pubs** in Bundoran are pretty ordinary, and permanently crowded with northern holidaymakers in season. Two to try in the West End are the *Seashells Tavern* (also does bar snacks and accommodation) and the new *Bradog Bar*, where an intimate session involves fifteen musicians every Monday. Opposite the latter, the *Imperial Hotel* serves amazing value bar lunches from £2.

Cycles can be hired at *Michael Goodwin's* shop in the West End. If you want to go **horse-riding**, check out the *Stracomer Riding School* (☎072/41685), just out of town off the Ballyshannon road, which offers fabulous pony-trekking over sand-hills and beaches.

Ballyshannon

BALLYSHANNON, four miles on at the mouth of the River Erne, more genu-inely marks the beginning of county Donegal, though it too is quickly passed through by most tourists who are eager for the scenic splendour further north. In fact it deserves a quick look, and at the time of the **Music Festival** (first week-end in August, a bank holiday) you shouldn't miss it on any account. This is one of the most popular festivals of traditional music in Ireland, with a mix of the biggest names and unknown talents: if you want a room you'll need to book in advance, although if you turn up unannounced a floor will always be found for yourself and your sleeping bag.

The town stands a few hundred yards upstream from a ford, at the point where the river's fresh water begins to mix with that of the ocean. All the interest lies up the steep, northern slope, and is easily combined in a single, straightforward stroll. The main arteries here form a wishbone, and halfway up the left-hand branch, just left off the road and past an overbearing Masonic Lodge, is the grave-yard where the poet **William Allingham** (1824–89) lies: his grave is a plain white marble slab by the left side of St Anne's church. Allingham was born in Ballyshannon and, like T. S. Eliot, began work in a bank (the *Allied Irish* has a bust of the poet and preserves the words scratched by him on a windowpane). He later become a poet of national significance – his verse, although usually very light in tenor, is uniquely sonorous in its descriptive lilts and rhythms:

> *Up the airy mountain*
> *Down the rushy glen,*
> *We dare not go a'hunting*
> *For fear of little men*
> *Wee folk, good folk,*
> *Trooping all together,*
> *Green jacket, red cap,*
> *And white owl's feather*
>
> *By the craggy hillside,*
> *Through the mosses bare,*
> *They have planted thorn trees*
> *For the pleasure here and there;*
> *Is any man so daring*
> *To dig one up in spite,*
> *He shall find the thornies set*
> *In his bed at night.*

From the graveyard there's a marvellous panoramic view looking down over the town and out to the surrounding hills north and south. Down at the pier you can see the backs of the tall, old warehouses lined along the river bank, their basement walls dripping with seaweed, and also the ancient isle of **Inis Saimer** just out in the river. There's only a wooden summerhouse on the island now, but it claims to have sheltered the first colonisation in Ireland, around 3500 BC, offering safety from the ferocious beasts that would have roamed the forests on the mainland. The water here seems to teem with fish and you'll find anglers still trying to catch them well into the night, with only the smell of the bakery behind them as company. Looking further out, to the mouth of the estuary, the view also takes in the white dunes of FINNER, nowadays the site of a large Irish Army camp.

Abbey Assaroe and beyond

Back on the road, a left turn by the thatched pub at the top of the hill takes you out along the Rossnowlagh road, where a second left turn (marked by a finger-post sign, "Fishing") takes you down to the scant remains of **Abbey Assaroe**. Founded by the Cistercians in 1184 it's pretty barren now, and Allingham's hundred-year-old description remains apt:

> Grey, grey is Abbey Asseroe.
> The carven stones lie scattered in
> briar and nettlebed
> The only feet are those that come
> at burial of the dead.

Following the road down past the abbey and round to the left, you'll come to a restored **mill** beside a lively little stream. This makes a pretty picture of mill-race and rotating cog wheels and there's an **interpretive centre**, *The Watermills* (☎072/51580), with coffee and craft shop, display centre and working water wheels. There's a less obvious natural beauty to be found if you pass through the log gate next to the old bridge and go on up along the stream's left bank. Within a few minutes you'll come across two man-made **caves**. One is a small grotto known as the Catsby; the other (now around 30 yards deep) is said to have once reached all the way under the Abbey and run for two miles towards Rossnowlagh. The grotto was once a site for Penal Masses, services that had to be held secretively during the enforcement of the Penal Laws during the eighteenth century – and you'll find in the Rossnowlagh museum the carved stone known as the Monk's Head that once sat above the entrance.

Back in the mill area, head back up the hill for a few yards and watch out to the left for a little track, beginning with a stone stile beside a bungalow, that runs down to the shore of the **bay**. Saint Patrick is said to have once stepped ashore here, and today there are several rusted metal crosses perched on small stony outcrops and a tree covered in tattered ribbon mementos. It goes without saying that there's a natural well that sprang up at the spot where the saint's foot touched the shore; you'll find it down by the furthest cross. Bless yourself with its water three times and your prayer for a cure will be answered.

Ballyshannon practicalities

There are plenty of **B&Bs** around Ballyshannon, but few that are very convenient unless you have transport to get to them. In town try *Hillcrest* or Mrs Donagher's, next to each other at the top of Castle Street by the *Abbey Cinema*, and each charging about £10, or a place opposite *The Thatch Pub* on Bishop Street. Others are mostly out on the Donegal and Rossnowlagh roads. *Duffy's Hostel* is some way out on the Donegal road at the corner with Cluainbarron Road (☎072/51535; £4.50; March–Oct; some bikes for hire). **Hotel** accommodation includes the *Imperial* (☎072/51147; £24), up the main street on the way to the churchyard, and the *Royal Millstone*, pretty much opposite.

Restaurants lie mainly on the right-hand road: there are several reasonably priced options including *Cúchulainn's* on Castle Street (fast food, healthy portions), the popular *Grime's Kitchen Bake*, handy for buses just up from the bridge, whose upstairs coffee rooms have marvellous fresh cakes and pastries, and the *Shamrock* Chinese restaurant, back over the bridge and straight ahead fifty yards – everyone heads here after the pubs, and it's much better than most Irish Chinese restaurants. For a bit more style try *Danby House*, a few hundred yards out the Rossnowlagh road. The best **pub** in town is *Seán Óg's* (pronounced *Oags*), with **traditional music** every Wednesday night and rock on Saturday; others worth a try are *The Thatch Pub* on Bishop Street, with thatched roof and cottage-kitchen interior and the *Green Lady* on the bridge opposite the bus station, the current youth mecca, with frequent live music.

As well as its August music **festival**, Ballyshannon has a number of other festivities worth looking out for. There's a **drama festival** of mainly Irish plays in the week of March 17th (St Patrick's Day); the **Allingham Festival for Writers** over a weekend at the beginning of October; and traditional **harvest fair** celebrations around the middle of September, a rural affair with crowds from the surrounding countryside. The rest of the time you can fill your evenings at the *Abbey* **cinema**, at the north end of town by the Donegal road (following restoration, this will have several screens, a theatre and restaurant); there are Monday night Irish **dance classes** in the Market yard if you want to learn a few steps; and Gaelic football every other Sunday. At BALLINTRA, four miles along the Donegal road, there's **horse racing** in the open fields on the first Monday in August.

The **bus** depot is down at the bridge: six departures a day to Bundoran, three to Derry, four to Donegal, one or more to Rossnowlagh, and a couple a day to Sligo and Dublin.

Rossnowlagh

ROSSNOWLAGH, on the coast away from the main Donegal road, is a short diversion well worth making, for a magnificent long stretch of beach raked by Atlantic surf and, to the south, good cliffs for walks. Appropriately named ("The Heavenly Cove"), it has a waterskiing, surfing and canoeing club beside the *Sand House Hotel* which unfortunately is private: however, one of the many surfing buffs will probably be able to help you out with equipment or at least advise where else to get your hands on it.

The **Franciscan Friary** nearby has a captivating one-room museum (daily 10am–6pm) crammed with Stone Age flints, Bronze Age dagger blades, penal crosses, pistols and other local miscellany. This includes a lovely set of uilleann pipes with green felt bag and very handsome regulators, a fiddle that belonged to the great piper Turlough MacSuibhne, and a seventeenth-century Flemish painting on glass (*The Christ of Pity*) used as a devotion plate. A mile north of Rossnowlagh towards BALLINTRA (itself an unappealing place) lies **Glasbolie Fort**, a huge earthen rampart twenty feet high and nearly 900 feet round. It's said to have been the burial place of a sixth-century High King of Ireland.

Donegal Town

DONEGAL TOWN is not the most exciting of places, but it is making an effort. It's not even the county capital (which is Letterkenny) and the lasting impression is one of traffic jammed around the busy (triangular) **Diamond** at the centre, the old market place. Just about the only thing to see in town is the well-preserved shell of **Donegal Castle**, on Tirchonaill Street by the Diamond, overlooking the River Eske (mid-June–Sept daily 9.30am–6.30pm; 80p, students 30p, heritage card; ☎073/22405). A fine example of Jacobean architecture, it dates originally from the fifteenth century, but was substantially rebuilt by Sir Basil Brooke in the early seventeenth century, and combines strong defence with domestic grace – note the mullions, arches, gables and no fewer than fourteen fireplaces, over the grandest of which are carved the escutcheons of Brooke and his wife's family, the

Leicesters. The castle tower on the right as you enter (topped by Brooke with a Barbizon turret) was originally a stronghold of the O'Donnells, who ruled Donegal between the thirteenth and sixteenth centuries before fleeing to Spain around 1600. It was then transformed by Brooke (also responsible for the design of the town) who added the mansion to the left where the kitchens and bakery would have been found on the ground floor, with living quarters on the floor above.

In the Diamond stands an obelisk commemorating the compilers of the famed **Annals of the Four Masters**. The *Annals* were put together in Donegal Abbey, on the coast close to Bundoran, and show years of research which collected all known Irish documents into a history of the land beginning in 2958 BC and ending at the time of writing, 1616 AD. The first entry dates back forty years before the Flood, and relates to a visit of Noah's granddaughter to Ireland. There's good shopping around the Diamond, especially the *Four Masters* book-shop and *Magee's* department store.

Down at the **quay** a French anchor is displayed, probably dating from the time when French troops were being ferried across to the aid of Wolfe Tone's rebellion in 1798. On the left bank of the River Eske not far from here stand the few ruined remains of a **Franciscan Friary**, while on the opposite bank a woodland path known as the **Lovers Walk** runs out alongside the bay with a nice view onto its many sandy islets and stony shoreline. The only real reason to stay long in Donegal town, though, is to explore the surrounding countryside, especially in the direction of the **Blue Stack Mountains** which rise at the northern end of **Lough Eske** (see below).

Arrival and a room

Buses stop outside the *Foodmarket* on the Diamond, with the timetables displayed in the office behind the newsagents, where luggage can also be left. One advantage of staying in Donegal is that you've plenty of choice. There are literally dozens of **B&Bs** scattered around the town, but many of them are very small, so to avoid a lot of walking it's simplest to call at the **tourist office** on the Quay (May–Sept Mon–Sat 10am–1pm & 2–6pm; ☎073/21148; also has bureau de change; currently being expanded). All have standardised their prices at £11.50–12: a couple of the larger ones to try if you arrive out of hours are *Arranmore House* (Coast Road; ☎073/21242) and *Windermere* (Quay Street; ☎073/21323), and there are others on Quay Street, which is a good place to be based. At the other end of the scale, the *Abbey Hotel* on the Diamond (☎073/21014; £30) is central and comfortable.

There are also two **hostels**, the independent *Peter Feely's* (Bridge End; ☎073/22030; £5; cramped and often crowded, but jovial atmosphere) and the *An Óige Ball Hill Hostel*, about three miles out in a former coastguard station on the north side of Donegal Bay (☎073/21174; £5.50; open all year). Again this tends to be busy, but it's right on the shore (swimming is safer at a second beach twenty minutes' walk away), you can **camp**, and you can rent **horses** nearby (contact Anne Carney, on the Ball Hill road; £6 an hour; pony trekking for beginners).

Food, drink and entertainment

Eating places are plentiful, though as ever the pubs seem to offer most choice. Alternatives include fast food at *Southern Dixie* opposite the tourist office

(11.30am–1.30pm, until 3am on Fri & Sat); *Talk of the Town* (on the Derry road opposite the cathedral), with very good value lunch specials; and the *Atlantic Café* (town end of Derry road), good for a substantial cheap meal. The tea room in *Magee's* store on the Diamond serves good light lunches, or the *Abbey Hotel* will feed you rather more substantially. *Foodland Supermarket* (by where the buses congregate on the Diamond) has a great selection of cheeses, meat and fruit – the last such stock you're likely find in the county.

As for **pubs**, they're as ubiquitous as ever. The *Old Castle Bar*, next to the castle, has an excellent new restaurant plus high quality music and dancing till 2am most nights. *Tír Chonaill*, opposite the *Ulster Bank* on the Diamond, is good for a quiet pint: one room caught in time. The *Abbey Hotel* on the Diamond has a **disco** and dance on Sunday night (10.30pm–2am; £4; sometimes on Friday too in the summer), and **Irish nights** (not for the purist) from Monday to Wednesday in July and August. Others are mainly out on the Derry road, Main Street: the *Star Bar* is a lively place with sing-songs and live acts, the *National Hotel* has more traditional music in the lounge at weekends, and best of all is *The Schooner*, just past the cathedral, with a nautical interior, original nineteenth-century bar, and music almost every night. In LAGHY, three miles south on the Sligo road, *Carlin's* pub has old-time dancing on Tuesday, and Irish nights in summer.

Other practicalities

The *Apollo* **launderette** (Mon–Sat 9am–6pm) is on Upper Main Street just past the cathedral. **Bikes** and **fishing tackle** can be hired from *O'Doherty's* (☎073/ 21119; Main Street), which is also a useful stop for supplementary information about the region. The owner is very knowledgeable and has photocopied local maps for sale (10p) marking out all the interesting sights in the surrounding countryside and also the best fishing spots in the south Donegal area; **fishing permits** are also issued here. There's a **cinema** on the Derry road opposite the *National Hotel*.

If you're after souvenirs, or simply a way to fill a wet afternoon, then it might be worth heading out to the **Craft Village**, three-quarters of a mile from town on the Sligo road. The workshops are leased to professional craftworkers who you can see in action if you visit: some of their work is worth a look.

Inland from Donegal: Lough Derg

Southeast of Donegal Town, the corner of the county tucked into a fold in the border is replete with little lakes well stocked for fishing. The largest of these, **Lough Derg** (the Red Lake), is the most often visited. In the middle of the lake is a rocky islet known as **Station Island**, which has long served as a retreat for Catholics who feel in the need of rigour and solitude to recharge their faith. Today it still thrives as a strong centre for pilgrimage (especially June–Aug) and the island cannot be visited for any other reason – though some casual travellers and non-believers do get some sort of stimulation out of passing through this ancient ceremony, lasting a minimum three days. Participants go without sleep or food (bar black tea and toast) and walk barefoot over rocks, praying at selected points. It seems particularly popular with Irish students studying for exams – or waiting for the results. In the Northern Irish poet Seamus Heaney's book, *Station*

Island, a number of poems deal with the mystique surrounding this ritual. To get there you have to approach by the L84 from PETTIGO or a #115/289 bus from Ballyshannon should drop you nearby.

Lough Eske

Lough Eske (whose name means the Lake of the Fish) lies less than five miles upriver from Donegal, with the Blue Stack Mountains rising behind. It's no longer a particularly great fishing spot, though it is known as a place to catch char, a tasty nine-inch-long species of the salmon family. They lurk in the depths at the centre of the lake, moving out to the shallower edges around late October where they can easily be fished using worms. The sandy banks of the River Eske are also known for freshwater oysters – some of which are reputed to contain pearls – but they're a protected species so you mustn't take them. Two or three miles along the Ballybofey road, by the lake's edge, is a complex of chalets owned by a Swiss millionaire, Harvey's Point (☎073/22208): this includes the region's best **restaurant**, with an à la carte menu from about £15, and a range of seafood from £20.

The most enjoyable way to get to this area of soft beauty, especially if you're cycling, is to take the minor road which runs north of the river (from Donegal Town, turn off Killybegs road a little way above the hostel), though you can also take the main Derry road (the N15) and turn off by the *Naomh Aengus* B&B. Either route will bring you to a forgotten and afforested estate at the southern end of the lake with the ruins of one of the Brooke family's old fortified houses (1751) at its centre. This estate is now owned by the Forestry Commission but is relaxed about visits from the public. Circling the lake clockwise from here, you'll pass the western gate of the estate and then a farmyard: a hundred yards or so further on look out for a gap in the hedge on the left where you'll find hidden a massive cauldron nearly six feet high and six feet round. This is a **Famine Pot**, manufactured in Britain and shipped over to Ireland by English landlords. It would be filled with Indian meal (a substitute porridge) and placed in a field where local people would come during the Famine and fill their own smaller pots to take home.

The Blue Stack Mountains

Carrying on up the western shore you'll reach the point where the river flows in at the lough's northern tip. Nearby, a dirt road runs off to the left to take you into the **Blue Stack Mountains**. At the top of the pathway that leads on from the track, there's a very fine waterfall from where, if you want to continue, the **Ulster Way** leads by Lough Belshade (*Bél Seád*, the lake with the jewel mouth). If you're intending to tramp around the mountain range it's best to keep to the skirts of the hills, for there are many marshy patches on lower ground; be prepared for misty patches to descend during bad weather. If you're only making a day trek of it then the photocopied maps from *O'Dohertys* are good enough for bringing you back safely if you lose your sense of direction; there's hardly any danger in the area apart from that of being caught by the descending mist. For longer and more intense trekking enquire at *O'Clery's Bookshop* in town about Ordnance Survey maps of the area.

Towards Glencolumbcille

The most appealing route on from Donegal Town is the one which follows the north shore of the bay all the way out to Glencolumbcille, near the point. The first turning off this road will lead you down to **Holmes beach** and *Ball Hill* hostel. **MOUNTCHARLES**, the first place of any size on the main road, has little to offer beyond the atmospheric *Cellar Club* in the basement of the *Seamount Hotel*. There's good jazz and sometimes folk here every Thursday (£2.50, which includes food) – well worth a night out. **FROSSES**, a mile or so inland off the road between Mountcharles and Inver, is a pleasant, tiny village that has traditional music every second Saturday of the month in *Frosses Hall* (open session begins 9pm; listen out for the singer Rita Gallagher). The cemetery here has the graves of two of Ireland's famous literary figures: the novelist Seamus MacManus and his wife, the very underrated poetess Eithne Carberry.

The hamlet of **INVER** and its small strand, just a few hundred yards off the road, is worthwhile scenically and also to have a drink (or hear traditional music on Wed, Fri & Sun) in the *Rising Sun* pub. Inside, this has a ceiling in the shape of the hull of a boat, and stone shelves for the spirit bottles – it is also the birthplace of Thomas Nesbitt, inventor of the harpoon gun.

Dunkineely and Bruckless

At **DUNKINEELY** another deviation from the main road takes you down a long, narrow promontory to **St John's Point**, where a crumbling castle stands at the tip. As you head out, there are great views over Donegal Bay, especially back towards the narrow entry of Killybegs bay, with **Rotton Island** at its mouth. There's a B&B in the village, *Seaview* on the main road. A little further on, approaching **BRUCKLESS**, you'll spot a magical little lagoon staked out with poles for rearing mussels. Look out for a "handknit" sign at the top of a track that will lead you down to a dwelling where you can buy oysters (about £4 a dozen) and mussels (£1 a kilo). On the other side of the lagoon you can see an eighteenth-century Georgian house, which now offers stylish and not too expensive **B&B** (*Bruckless House*; ☎073/37071; £20). There's also a **hostel** here, *Gallahers Farm Hostel*, Darney, Bruckless (☎073/37057; £5).

Killybegs

Shortly beyond Bruckless the road runs away from the bay, and there's a right turn which cuts off the peninsula, heading directly for Ardara. If you stick to the coast road, however, you'll round Killybegs Bay and arrive in the most successful fishing port in the country, **KILLYBEGS**, where tons of top-quality fish are hauled onto the quaysides daily. This marks the halfway point to Glencolumbcille, and also the point where the scenic interest changes dramatically for the better. The mile-long approach road around the bay is idyllic and the town itself is perched on a slope, its gleaming whitewashed buildings huddled around cramped narrow streets.

In summer the place is abuzz with traffic, mostly heading down to the quay, where you can purchase the fish after watching the fleet come in in the early evening. A huge **sea angling festival** takes place here in the second half of July; and you can go sea angling any time with one of six boats that go out daily. A small **town festival** takes place in early August. Picturesque though Killybegs is, it isn't exactly overflowing with interest, and most of the pubs are aimed squarely at working fishermen: there's **entertainment** in a ballad session on Friday and Saturday in the *Lone Star* pub; sessions Thursday to Sunday 10pm to 1am at *Hughies*, both on the road out to Kilcar; and music at the *Harbour Bar* and in the new *Cope House Hotel*, again on the Kilcar road.

If you're staying, it's worth calling at the church at the top of the hill for a glimpse of the **McSweeney tombstone**, covered in Celtic carving. The cross standing on the hillock nearby is an ugly specimen that stands to remind one of ugly times, the penal days.

Practicalities

There's a new **tourist office** just before the post office on the road into Killybegs. As for **accommodation**, B&Bs are plentiful at around £12, there are rooms at the *Lone Star* (☎073/31518; £18) and the *Cope House Hotel* (☎073/31834; £20), or you could try the excellent *Hollybush Hostel*, one mile before Killybegs on the main road (☎073/31118; £4.50, camping £2). The adjoining pub – favoured by local farmers and fishermen – has open sessions every Sunday and sometimes Friday and Saturday during the summer. The hostel owner also hires out bicycles and fishing tackle, and can arrange boat hire for sea-fishing (£80 per day, all tackle supplied; up to 10 people per boat). There's **self-catering** accommodation at *Glenlee Holiday Homes* (☎073/31183; sleep 4–9, from £200 a week in high season), opposite the *Spar* shop on the Kilcar road, with local bungalows over-looking the bay.

Places to **eat** include *Melly's Café* by the harbour, with the usual cheap snack food, and the *Sail Inn* and the *Lone Star*, both on the Kilcar road, with competitive seafood-based menus. The *Cope House Hotel* has a good restaurant with daily specials for under £10 and an innovative wine list. *McGeehan's* **buses** leave from outside the *Pier Bar* for Ardara and Dublin: enquire at *Hegarty's* grocer shop by the bus stop.

Kilcar to Slieve League

The road on to **KILCAR** divides just after the *Blue Haven Restaurant* (old-time Irish evening on Thurs), a few miles out of Killybegs, and once again it's best to follow the coast, with fine views all the way. In Kilcar itself look out for *Piper's Restaurant Pub* which has a *comhaltas* every Wednesday and occasionally other cultural entertainments. *McGeehan's* **buses** leave from outside *John Joe's* bar at 7.50am for Dublin via Killybegs and Ardara, and for Glencolumbcille at 10.50pm.

Between Kilcar and **CARRICK**, a little over a mile away, you'll come upon one of the jolliest independent hostels in the country – *Derrylahan Hostel* (☎073/38079; £3.50; camping available). This is an ideal base for exploring the elementally beautiful countryside around Carrick, especially Teelin Bay and the awesome **Slieve League cliffs** to the west. In Carrick itself the *Slieve League* **pub** is a must, its shelves piled with the largest variety of whiskies you'll ever come across – Middleton, Redbreast, Chinese, Hewitt's triple-distilled single Scottish lowland malt, Glenfiddich, etc – served by a loquacious Pioneer (the name given to a religious abstainer from drink), Paddy Carr. The **traditional music festival** that the pub organises over the last weekend in October is one of the more popular and successful in the region.

The road to **TEELIN** (*tigh linn*, house of the flowing tide) follows the west bank of the River Owenee, whose rapids and pools are good for fishing. The village is Gaelic-speaking and rich in folklore, which has been recorded over the last half-century by Seán Ó' hEochaidh, Donegal's great folklorist. The best pub in town is the *Rusty Mackerel*, at the entrance to the trail of village buildings – it's easily noticed by its garish colour and mural painting of one of its old fisherman regulars.

Slieve League

There are two routes up to the ridge of **Slieve League** (*sliabh leic*, mountain of flagstones) – a less-used back route (follow the homemade fingerpost pointing to *Baile Mór* just before you come into Teelin) and the road route that follows the signs out of the village to BUNGLASS (*bunglas*, the end of the green) which turns out to be exactly what it says, the end of the grass way above a sheer drop. These claim to be the highest sea cliffs in Europe, and standing here that seems all too likely. The sea moves so far below it seems like a film that has lost its soundtrack, and the near two-thousand-foot high face of Slieve League glows with mineral deposits in tones of amber, white and red. They say that on a good day it is possible to see one third of the whole of Ireland from the summit.

Both routes up are walkable and very enjoyable (though it's a great deal easier to drive): the former looking up continually at the ridge known as the *One Man's Path*, on which walkers seem the size of pins, and the frontal approach swinging you up and round in the most spectacular way to one of the most thrilling cliff scenes in the world, the **Amharc Mór** (great view).

If you want to make a full day of it, you can follow *One Man's Path* onto *Old Man's Path* (simply because it's a few inches wider) over the crest of the mountain and then bound down the heather-tufted western slope and make your way across towards the verdant headland of **MALINBEG**, where there's a paradisical crescent shaped golden strand enclosed by a tight rocky inlet. The path is accurately named. In places it's only a few feet wide, and in wet or windy weather it can be extremely hazardous. On a fine day, though, it's a spectacular – if terrifying – traverse. Malinbeg itself is a village of white bungalows, with the land around ordered into long narrow strips. Three miles offshore lies **Rathlin O'Birne island**, a place with many folklore associations: there are occasional boats across, but nothing to see beyond some early Christian stone relics and a ruined coastguard station.

Beyond Malinbeg it's relatively easy to extend your walk through MALINMORE (the large *Glenbay* hotel serves teas) onto Glencolumbcille. The whole distance from Teelin can be comfortably completed in six hours.

Glencolumbcille

Approaching **GLENCOLUMBCILLE** (the Glen of St Columbcille) by road you cross a landscape of desolate upland moor, its oily-black turf banks stitched into patches of heather and grass, where not even sheep seem able to survive. After this, the rich, verdant beauty of the Glen (as it's invariably known) comes as a welcome shock. Less than forty years ago this area was on its last legs, a typical example of rural depopulation: its new lease of life is owed to the former parish priest, Father James MacDyer, who introduced a series of collective enterprises – in knitting, agriculture and tourism – that are sending goods out of the valley and bringing people (visitors and new residents) in.

Development has done nothing to diminish the natural beauty of the place however. Its central buildings are painted up in radiant colours – the village church in lavender, a whitewashed semi-detached estate for the newly married, one old pub in submarine yellow and another in a Mediterranean sky-blue.

Glencolumbcille village is widely known as a place of pilgrimage, a status it's held since the seventh century AD, in consequence of the time **Saint Columba** spent in the valley. Every June 9 at midnight the locals commence a barefoot circuit of the cross-inscribed slabs that stud the valley basin, finishing up with mass at 3am in the small church.

The **Folk Village**, next to the beach, usually has tourists tripping over one another on the strictly guided tours (Easter–Sept Mon–Sat 10am–6pm, Sun noon–6pm; £1.50). There's free access to the **National School** replica, which has a display of informative photographs and research projects, and a section on the American painter Rockwell Kent, who painted marvellous treatments of the area's landscapes. Also open at no charge is the **Sheebeen** house, where you can try a taster of seaweed wine and other concoctions such as honey, fuchsia, elderberry (most much better than they sound) and then buy a bottle – you can also pick up some whiskey marmalade while you're there.

From behind the hostel (see below), **cliff walks** steer off around the south side of the bay above a series of jagged drops. Rising from the opposite side of the valley mouth, the promontory of **Glen Head** is surmounted by a Martello tower. On the way out you pass the ruins of **St Columbcille's Church**, with its "resting slab" where Saint Columba would have lain down exhausted from prayer. (To clear up the confusion, Columba and Columbcille/Colmcille are the same person – the latter is the name by which he was known after his conversion, and means "the dove of the church".) North across this headland you can climb and descend again to the forgotten little cove of PORT a few miles away. Absolutely nothing happens here, though Dylan Thomas once stayed at Glenlough, the next, almost inaccessible, valley, renting a cottage for several weeks and then disappearing early one morning without paying.

Practicalities

The tea house at the Folk Village does cheapish **food**, and sells watercolours as a side line. Another place to eat in the village is the *Lace House Restaurant* on the main street above the **tourist office** (☎073/30116), with freshly baked bread and evening meals. In summer, one of the nearby pastiche holiday cottages does B&B; others are available for weekly rental. You can also stay at the beautifully positioned *Dooey Hostel* above the fine shingle strand at the mouth of the valley (☎073/30130; £5, £3 camping). To walk there, keep on the village road as far as the Folk Village (see below) and then take a path up to the left: in wet weather the longer route, by road, may be easier. **Buses** for Donegal Town leave from *Biddy's Bar* at 7.30am (*McGeehan's*) and 8.25am (*Bus Éireann*), with additional *McGeehan's* services 2.50pm on Friday and 3pm Sunday.

Courses in Gaelic, painting, archaeology, hill-walking and set dancing are run from the *Oideas Gael School* (☎073/30051) in the village; accommodation is also available there. Ring ahead for information and bookings.

Maghera and Ardara

Leaving Glencolumbcille you can either retrace your steps along the coast or take the road through the heart of the peninsula towards Ardara. This takes in the dramatic **Glengesh Pass** (*gleann géis*, the glen of the swans), winding down through wild but fertile valley land. Just before reaching Ardara a road to the left runs along the northern edge of the peninsula for five and a half miles to **MAGHERA**, with narrow **Loughross Beg Bay** on one side and steep mountains rising from the road on the other. A mile before Maghera you'll pass the transfixing **Essaranka Waterfall**, and Maghera itself (tea house in the village) is an entrancingly remote place, backed by an exceedingly beautiful glen and fronted by a strand that runs along to an intriguing series of caves. One of the larger caves is said to have concealed a hundred people taking refuge from Cromwell's troops; their light was spotted from across the strand and all bar one (who hid on a high shelf) were massacred. Some of the caves are only accessible at low tide and you'll need a torch; if you do visit, take great care and stay out of the water, as there are extremely strong currents – tourists have been drowned. Behind the village a tiny road runs up into the glen, a former hideout of poteen smugglers.

Ardara

ARDARA is a pretty big town by Donegal standards, and also one of the best places to buy **Aran sweaters**, sometimes at half the price you'll find further south. *Molloy's Tweed Factory*, a mile or so out of the southern end of town, is the biggest outlet, but *Kennedy's*, at the top of the hill, is handier (its owner is also a mine of local tourist information), and all the stores are well stocked with hand-loomed knitwear and tweeds. The town itself has been declared a heritage centre (one of thirty nominated by *Bord Fáilte*), which qualified it for a substantial EC grant: this is being put towards an **interpretive centre** in the old Law Courts by the bridge, which should be open by the time you read this.

Ardara is also a great place for **pubs**, dozens of which seem to be crammed into its L-shaped main street. For a quiet drink try the ancient *Pádraig MacGiola Dé*, to the south (guaranteed to be an experience – avoid the loos), or the *Corner House* bar at the corner of the L – old and poky, and very suitable for a morning bottie when buying the groceries. For a livelier time you shouldn't miss *Peter Oliver's* (music every night June–Sept; traditional dancing every Wed in hall at back; £1); the publican himself is a musician, and there are fiddles, button accordion, banjo, mandolin and *bodhrán* on the wall ready to play. *Nancy's*, by the bridge, a cosy 200-year-old pub run by the same family for seven generations, is also excellent, with something happening most nights during the summer (listen out for the fiddler John Gallagher).

Best place to **eat** is *Woodhill House*, a seventeenth-century house half a mile from the centre (follow the signposts off the Donegal road), which is worth a visit even if you're not hungry: there's a bar, often with music, and the restaurant offers an innovative menu, changed daily, in a lovely setting, well worth the £15 or so it will cost. Less fancy meals are available at the *Nesbitt Arms*, for good bar lunches and huge platters of Irish cooking in the evening; and the *Lobster Pot*, a distinctly superior chip shop by the bridge, open till 2am or later at weekends. **B&B** is available at *Laburnum House* (☎075/41146; £10) and *Homeward Bound* (☎075/41246; £12) both right in the centre, or for places with sea views a short way out on the Portnoo Road try *Greenhaven House* (☎075/41129; £12) or *Bayview House* (☎075/41145; £12). Both *Woodhill House* (☎075/41112; £22) and the *Nesbitt Arms* (☎075/41200; £20) have rooms of considerably more style. A *McGeehan's* bus leaves for Dublin from outside the post office daily at 8.30am.

From Dawros Head to Crohy Head

The **Dawros Head Peninsula**, immediately north of Ardara, is much tamer than Glencolumbcille, with many tiny lakes (great for fishing, get licence in Ardara) dotting a quilt of low hills. The terrain of purple heather, fields, streams and short glens makes a varied package for the enthusiastic walker. You don't get many outsiders here, but the caravan and camping sites of PORTNOO and NARIN are densely populated with Northern Irish tourists. As you approach Narin, just before the pastel-shaded Kilclooney church, look back to the right and you'll spot the **Kilclooney Dolmen**, probably the most elegant in the country. (The Narin end of the peninsula in general is rich in these remains.) The spearheaded two-and-a-half-mile-long **Narin Strand** is a wonderful beach, safe for bathing, and at low tide you can walk out to **Iniskeel Island** where there are the ruins of two twelfth-century churches with some cross-inscribed slabs.

The most worthwhile sight on the peninsula is **Doon Fort**, which occupies an entire oval-shaped islet in the middle of Lough Doon. To get there take a left out of Portnoo and then left again alongside a lake where you'll see a sign for boat hire: this leads to the farmhouse of Mr McHugh, who will row you out to the island for a small charge. The idyllic setting, rarely disturbed by visitors, makes the hassle worth it: although its walls are crumbling, the fort has been untouched for over two thousand years. The walls stand fifteen feet high and twelve feet thick – their inner passages were used in the Fifties for storing poteen. Two other lakes nearby, **Lough Birrog** and **Lough Kiltoorish**, also have ruined castles, both built by later Irish chieftains, the O'Boyles. Their stones, however, have mostly been carted away for house building, slid across the ice when the lakes froze over.

If you want to **stay** on the peninsula, *Carnaween House* in Narin offers good B&B (☎075/45122; £12), or you could hire a caravan at *Dunmore Caravan and Camping Park*, by the golf course in Narin (☎075/45121; £60–150 a week; camping £4.50 plus 30p per person), but there's little chance of a vacancy in midsummer. *Dawros Bay Hotel*, north of Rossbeg, offers very basic accommodation at hostel rates (☎075/45252; £4 per bed, £3.50 breakfast); it's well-placed for headland walks, but the nearest grocery store is by the harbour in Portnoo. The *Lake House Hotel* in Portnoo (☎075/45123; £16) offers a great deal more comfort

Inland to Glenties, Fintown and Doochery

GLENTIES is a village of Plantation grandeur (courthouse, old lodge and high-land hotel) set at the foot of two glens. It also sports the largest **disco** in the northwest, the *Limelight* (situated at the north end of town, its clientele seems exclusively under sixteen) and no less than thirteen bars on the only street. Another community attraction is a beautiful **church** designed by the contemporary Derry architect Liam McCormack, at the Ardara end of town; the vast sloping roof reaches down to six feet from the ground, and the rainwater drips off the thousand or so tiles into picturesque pools of water.

The **St Conall's Museum and Heritage Centre**, opposite the church in the Neoclassical courthouse (June–Sept Mon–Fri 11am–1pm and 2.30–5pm, Sat & Sun 2.30–6pm; £1; ☎075/51265), is well fitted out with items from all periods, including an interesting set of pleas submitted to the courts during the Famine; there's also an Edison phonograph that'll play "It's a Long Way to Tipperary". The town's most famous son was **Patrick MacGill** (*Children of the Dead, The Rat Pit*), a navvy turned author and the inspiration for a huge **summer school** – which draws hundreds of people to exhibitions, workshops and debates – and literary festival held in his honour each year in the last week of August.

Although there's little in the way of entertainment, there are plenty of places to **drink** – *Paddy's Bar*, *Wee Joe's Bar* and *McMonagle's Riverside Bar* are all good. If you want **traditional music** head for the *Glen Tavern*, three miles out on the Ballybofey Road, beautifully situated by the river at the foot of the Blue Stacks; the star turn is local fiddler Vincent Campbell, who may come down if a session strikes up – otherwise there are sessions on the last Saturday of the month at 9.30pm. **Eating** out is a problem – the only decent option is the *Highlands Hotel* (which is excellent, and very much the centre of town life – it also has weekend discos and a small art gallery), though there are a number of takeaways on the main street, including *Jim McGuiness's*, where the *McGeehans* buses for Letterkenny and Ballybofey stop.

Accommodation is limited too – there's **B&B** at *Kelvon House* at the north end of town (£12) or the *Claradon*, less than a mile out on Glen Road (☎075/51113; £12; Easter–Oct), or more expensive rooms at the family-run *Highlands Hotel* (☎075/51111; £16).

Fintown and Doochery

The trip inland to Doochery via Fintown and then down the Gweebarra valley to the coast at LETTERMACAWARD is a fine scenic loop. **FINTOWN**, nine miles northeast of Glenties, is a ramshackle roadside place set beside a lake at the foot of towering mountains. Once again, the setting has a mythical colouring – it was here that Fergoman was attacked by wild boars, and cried out so piteously that his sister was driven to distraction and dived into the lake, where she drowned. There's a bar and B&B – *Finian's Rainbow*.

DOOCHERY lies five miles northwest across a route that cuts against the grain of the hills. It's a desolate but delightful journey, through moorland streaked by turf banks, where bulbous knuckles of rock force the road to duck and lunge from side to side. The village itself has a few pubs and a grocery shop, as well as a new **hostel**, *The Lodge* (☎075/46151; £4; April–Sept): it makes a delightful base. Nine miles northeast, up the Gweebarra River, is the Glenveagh National Park (see below), while five miles downstream are the headlands at Lettermacaward.

The **Dooey Point headland** makes a scenically interesting little detour if you have time in hand. The northern shore, on Traweenagh Bay, is the more gratifying, with a fine stretch of beach backed by sand dunes. Classic thatched cottages and abandoned Volkswagens are two of the main characteristics. On the southern side is **Corr Strand**, fertile ground for mussels and clams, with a handy bar nearby.

The Crohy Head Peninsula

The southern approach to **Crohy Head** curls round the headland's central mountains, looking down onto a rocky shelf of coastline from which plumes of spray rise like geysers. As you come round the headland to the final approach up to the three-storey *An Óige* **hostel** (one of the best in the country; ☎075/21330; £5.50; April–Oct), the globular outline of **Aranmore Island** appears, close to the Rosses coast. The hillside below the road can be dangerous at points because of a remarkable landslip known as the *tholla brista* (broken earth), but this, and the great sea stack known as *an briste* (the breeches), make the headland an even more dramatic experience for the walker.

The one-pub fishing village of **MAGHERY** lies at the foot of the north side of the headland. Its most unusual feature is the tall wall that runs by the abandoned mansion house at the far side of the short strand: called the *Famine Wall*, this windbreak was built by the villagers for the landlord, who devised the task so that he could pay them a wage as famine relief. Mrs Wallace's *Bay View House* (☎075/21672; £11) offers a couple of rooms for **B&B**, and meals. **Minibuses** run daily from Maghery to Dunglow and back, usually at 10am.

The Rosses

The **Rosses**, a vast expanse of rock-strewn land and stony soil, is one of the last strong *Gaeltacht* areas. Dotted with over 120 tiny lakes, the crumply terrain stretches from Dunglow in the south to Crolly in the north. The coastal route between these two boundaries is infinitely more rewarding than the more direct inland route.

Upper Rosses: Dunglow

With its bustle of shoppers and its multitude of pubs, **DUNGLOW** is an easy place to settle into, but there's little other than ad hoc entertainment to make lingering worthwhile. It's at its liveliest for the midsummer *Mary of Dunglow* festival, a parochial variation on the *Miss World* idea that provides a good pretext for general festivities and late-night drinking. The town is also synonymous with the rejuvenating work of **Paddy the Cope** (1871–1966), who envisaged the salvation of these poor communities through co-operative ventures. He founded the *Templecrone Co-operative Agricultural Society* (the "Cope") in 1906, and today *Co-op* supermarkets throughout the Rosses – megastores in West Donegal terms – stand as a testament to him. Copies of his entertaining autobiography *My Story* are available in a local edition from the supermarket in Dunglow.

The *Tír Chonnaill* **bar** at the top end of the street is a genuine old-timers' bar with not a note of music interfering; the *Atlantic Bar* has rock music every Saturday and traditional on Fridays and Sundays. The *Central Bar*, in the middle of Main Street, has recently re-opened (summer only) after more than twenty years in which nothing seems to have been touched – a fascinating old place. For **eating**, *Doherty's Restaurant* is a good low-priced grill which also has a speciality of squid provençal for as little as £3.50. There are numerous **B&Bs** here – try Mrs McCole on Mill Road (☎075/21094; £12) – as well as a couple of small hotels: the *Midway* (☎075/21251; £15) on the main street also provides meals and a bar. *Doherty's* **private buses** run daily in July and August, through Fintown and Letterkenny to Derry.

Burtonport

Passing the smoking funnels of a kelp factory, the coastal route heads off in the direction of **BURTONPORT**, half a mile off the main road. A settlement of a handful of houses and pubs, it's the embarkation point for Aranmore Island or, if you can find someone to take you out, for the smaller islands hereabouts. With the establishment of government buildings on **Rutland Island** in the eighteenth century this area became the first English-speaking district in the whole of Donegal. The English connection endures. Until a few years ago a colony of post-hippies known as the *Screamers* ran an organic commune on another island; their departure coincided with the arrival of three eccentric ladies from England, who live in immaculate, formal Victorian style in the white mansion at the entrance to Burtonport. Known as the "Silver Sisters", Miss Tyrrell, Miss Lucinda and their young maid are an engaging sight, doing their shopping in the village dressed in bonnets and sober black garments edged with white lace. They welcome only visitors with a serious interest in their anachronistic way of life, and not the merely curious.

The village has little to say for itself, and its **pubs** now look somewhat lifeless. The *Skipper Tavern* is the only one where you might hear traditional music. For **eating**, *Kelly's Arran Bar* will probably be able to offer you a plate of mussels for a few quid, and even salmon and lobster when in season. Otherwise you'll have to make do with pies and fish and chips. Mrs McGinley, down by the pier, does **B&B** (☎075/42047; £12.50).

Aranmore Island

It's a twenty-five minute journey out to **Aranmore Island**, through the straits between the nearest cluster of islands (Rutland, Inishfree, Inishcoo and Eighter), and then across a free expanse of water to the island's main village, LEABGARROW (7 boats daily in summer; £2). There's an **An Óige** hostel here (no telephone; £4.50; May–Sept). The high centre ground of bogland and lakes reaches a greater altitude than anywhere else in the Rosses, and has great views back to Burtonport. A few roads crisscross the island, the villages being ranged in true Rosses style round the rim of the eastern and southern sides – the western and northern shores are uninhabited, and perfect for walking. Intriguingly, there's no *Garda* on Aranmore, so you see very few cars with tax discs, and might catch sight of a ten-year-old popping into the driver's seat and setting off. The **pubs** (of which there are only six or seven) also tend to keep open into the early hours – which is helpful, as there really is no other form of nightlife. The most dramatic of the several beaches is at the lighthouse end of the island, approached by a set of steps down the side of a perpetually crumbling cliff.

Lower Rosses

The road up through the Lower Rosses to Gweedore passes through a wild and crazed terrain of granite boulders and stunted vegetation. On the coast, the especially beautiful sections are along the lip of **Cruit Island Bay** (a couple of miles north of Burtonport) and the **Rannafast** headland, which rises between ANNAGARY and **CROLLY**. As you come down the hill into Crolly, look out for a sign pointing to **Leo's Tavern** – on most nights it has traditional music, and as Leo is the father of the family group *Clannad* and the singer Enya, you may well catch them on a home visit at family reunion times of year. The large *Teach Phaidí Óig* pub used to be one of the great traditional music-making places, but events are nowadays far less regular.

Lough Keel – tucked into the back of Crucknafarragh mountain to the southeast – allegedly contains Ireland's answer to the Loch Ness monster, glimpsed on numerous occasions over the past few years.

Inland: the Derryveagh Mountains

The central area of North Donegal rivals any of the best bits of the Donegal coastline, and if you're travelling northwards from the south of the county, makes a far better destination than the Bloody Foreland. The road to get onto is the one that goes through the hamlet of Gweedore (see below), along the northern shore of Lake Nacung, and into **DUNLEWY**, where an *An Óige* **hostel** (☎075/31180; £5.50; open all year) nestles by Lough Dunlewy (aka Lake Nacung) at the foot of **Errigal Mountain**. Quite often the area is shrouded in mist, but on a clear day the beauty of Errigal is insurpassable, its silvery slopes resembling Hokusai's images of Mount Fuji. Should you venture into the one and only **bar** in Dunlewy, be careful as you enter the lounge – the dartboard hangs a couple of inches to the side of the door.

Glenveagh National Park

For the **Poisoned Glen**, turn off just below the church at the eastern end of the lough – the route continues over the bridge, and then you should follow the bank of the river deep into the gorge, always heading for the col up at the shoulder of the Derryveagh Mountains. It's not an easy tramp, for a lot of the ground is marshy, but it's the beginning of one of the finest wild walks imaginable. From the col the view behind is as fantastic as that in front, where the Glenveagh River flows into Lough Beagh. You're now in the **Glenveagh National Park** and may well see deer hereabouts. Going straight down the hill, head for the road, which you should then follow for a short distance before bearing down the old disused vehicle track that will take you down the barrel of the glen. The Glenveagh River writhes its way to a tiny sandy shore at the head of the lake, where rhododendrons and tall spruces grow. Waterfalls plummet down the sheer cliff sides on the other side of the lake, and **Glenveagh Castle** (May–Oct Tues–Sun 10.30am–6.30pm) now appears above the tree tops on a small rocky knoll. The grandeur of this walk into the heart of the estate is far greater than that of the routine approach on the north side of the lake, beautiful as that is. The castle itself, a battlemented nineteenth-century creation swathed in flower gardens, looks best from below.

The most interesting way to get from Glenveagh Park to Lough Gartan, in the next valley east, is to follow the three-mile track across the mountain bog tops (possible to drive), which is the only track leading off the Glenveagh estate road. On weekdays between the beginning of September and the end of February you're forbidden to leave this road or any other recognised footpath – it's the deer-hunting season, and you may get shot.

Lough Gartan

The environs of **Lough Gartan** are one of the supreme beauties of Ireland. **Saint Columba** was born into a royal family here in 521 AD; his father was from the house of Niall of the Nine Hostages and his mother belonged to the House of Leinster. If you walk over from Glenveagh you'll pass his birthplace – take the first road right at the first house you see at the end of the mountain track, and you'll come to a colossal cross marking the spot. Close by is a slab locally known as the **Flagstone of Loneliness**, because the saint used to sleep on it, thereby giving the flagstone the miraculous power to cure the sorrows of those who lie upon it. During the height of the emigrations, people used to come here the night before departure in the hope of ridding themselves of homesickness. Archaeologically it's actually part of a Bronze Age gallery tomb, and has over fifty cup marks cut into its surface.

Going back to the track leading downhill will bring you to a main country road, where a left turn will take you towards the remains of a church known as the **Little Oratory of St Colmcille**. It's an enchanting ruin, no larger than a modern living room, with a floor of old stone slabs with grass growing up through the cracks. To one side is the *Natal Stone*, where the baby Columba first opened his eyes; to this day pregnant women visit the slab praying for a safe delivery.

Glebe House

Go back down the country lane in the direction you came from and follow on round to the left and you'll reach **Glebe House** (Easter week & late May to early Oct Tues–Sat 11am–6.30pm, Sun 1–6.30pm; £1). Set in beautiful gardens on the northwest shore of the lake, the house is a gorgeous Regency building richly decorated inside and out. The kitchen has various **paintings** by the Tory Island group of painters, most remarkably James Dixon's impression of Tory from the sea. A remarkable collection of paintings and sketches adorns other parts of the house, including international names like Kokoschka, Renoir, Braque, Picasso and Dégas. The study is decked out in original William Morris wallpaper and there are Chinese tapestries in the morning room. It's well worth buying the guidebook and taking the tour.

Heritage and outdoor pursuits

Moving on round the northeast of the lake, in the direction of Church Hill, a right turn immediately after crossing the bridge will take you down to the modern **St Colmcille Heritage Centre** (Mon–Sat 10.30am–6.30pm, Sun noon–7pm; £1.50; ☎074/21160), on the opposite shore from Glebe. The exhibition space is largely devoted to tracing Columba's life and the spread of the Celtic church throughout Europe. It's not as boring as it sounds, for there are a few intriguing items – very beautiful stained glass windows of Biblical scenes by Ciaran O'Conner and Ditty Kummer, and a step-by-step illustration of vellum illumination and calligraphy. The road to the heritage centre continues a little further on to the **Gartan Outdoor Pursuit Centre**, where it's possible to book a **hostel bed** for the night (☎074/37032) – a must if you're going to have any chance to enjoy the area to the full. Continuing east from here towards Letterkenny, you ascend from the northern shore to Church Hill, with superb cross-country views as far north as the peninsulas.

The Rock of Doon and Kilmacrennan

Lying a few miles northeast of Gartan, **The Rock of Doon** and **Doon Well** are reached by taking the last right turn off the L77 just before it reaches the N56, which runs into Kilmacrennan; this will bring you into a rural dead-end right next to the well. Just as you come into the area of the well, the road runs along the bottom of the large bushy outcrop that is the **Rock of Doon**. For centuries this was the spot where the O'Donnell kings were crowned before a great gathering of their followers. The inauguration stone on the summit is said to bear the imprint of the first Tír Chonaill king, a mark into which every successor had to place his foot as his final confirmation.

The **well** itself is marked out by a bush weighed down with offerings left behind by visitors – looking just as you'd imagine a school play representation of the burning bush that confronted Moses. You're meant to take off your shoes as you approach, and be well intentioned before taking the water. You'll probably pick up a story or two of dramatic conversion and miracles effected by the water, which is sent to Irish emigrés all over the world.

KILMACRENNAN is a sweet-looking inland village further downstream on the Leannan River, but there's no reason to hang around there. The *Village Tavern* has reasonably priced pub grub.

Letterkenny

Ever since Derry was partitioned into the North, **LETTERKENNY** has been Donegal's major commercial centre – there are loads of shops including some excellent craft outlets, and two new shopping centres are currently being built. It has an ebullient bustle about it which, in the context of its surrounding blanket of green fields, reminds one of a typical Cork town. Although it's just at the edge of Lough Swilly, there's no water in sight, and the main visual element is the file of advertising down the main street. The only notable sight is the huge nineteenth-century **cathedral**, with its intricate stone-roped ceiling and gaelicised Stations of the Cross. Frankly, the only real reason you're likely to be here is that so much transport passes through, and it's a handy place to catch up on shopping or the business of changing money and sending mail.

For comprehensive **tourist information** head for the Chamber of Commerce, Port Road (☎074/24866); in season they run **day trips** to Glenveagh National Park (depart 11am, £5). There are two **hostels**: *Rosemount Hostel* at 3 Rosemount Terrace, in a terraced house at the back of Upper Main Street (☎074/21181; £4; June–Nov); and *Letterkenny Tourist Hostel*, High Road (☎074/25238; £4; all year). **B&Bs**, of which there are plenty, include *Belvedere House*, Ballaghderg (☎074/23031; £11), Covehill House, Port Road (☎074/21038; £12.50) and *Ard na Greine*, Sentry Hill (☎074/22490; £12). *Gallagher's Hotel*, on Upper Main Street (☎074/22066; £19), is the pick of the more expensive places, very central.

The *O'Boyce Snack Bar* offers the cheapest, fastest and most basic **food** in town; it's handy to the bus station, down by the roundabout at the Derry side of town. In the big shopping centre directly behind the bus station, the *Oasis Bar* has a variety of reasonably priced lunches; there's also a delicatessen in the shopping centre. Closer to the heart of town, you'll find good pub lunches at the *Central Bar* on Main Street. *Bakersville*, on Church Street on the way up to the cathedral, is a good coffee shop, using all wholefood ingredients. In the evenings, more substantial meals are available at *Pat's Pizza*, 9 Market Square (☎074/21761), with a good three-course tourist menu for less than £5, or if you want to go the whole hog try *Carolina House* (☎074/22480), a mile-and-a-half out on the Ramelton road, with an à la carte menu from around £20, booking essential.

As ever there are plenty of **bars**, a few of which offer Irish music. *McGinley's* has music most nights and vegetarian food; *Downtown* also has music many nights and a disco on Wednesday; the *Cottage Bar* may also have music: all are close together on Lower Main Street. The *Three Ways Inn*, about a mile out the main Derry road, holds occasional *comhaltas* evenings. There are even three **nightclubs**, of which *Nero's*, on Port Road, is currently the most favoured and there's a three-screen **cinema** nearby.

An indication that you're approaching the North is that the *Sinn Féin* office occupies a Main Street shop at the southern end of town; it has literature from the prisons and the usual socialist and republican material. Finally, there's a **Bureau de Change** (11am–6pm) and **post office** on the main street, and a **launderette** just a couple minutes' walk down from Main Street to the ring road below.

The Gweedore and Cloghaneely districts

The southwest edge of **Gweedore** district, on the coast immediately north of the Rosses, is marked by the villages of Bunbeg, Middletown and Derrybeg, their cottages sprinkled across a blanket of gorse and mountain grasses. Some buildings are grey and decaying, some are roofless or grass-covered, others are at various stages of completion. It's a dispiriting kind of landscape, and it continues like this right up the coast and round the **Bloody Foreland** to Gortahork and Falcarragh in the Cloghaneely district.

BUNBEG, it must be said, has a gorgeous little harbour packed with smallish trawlers – it's half a mile from the village along an enchanting rollicky road. In summer it's possible to negotiate a boat trip from the pier to offshore islands such as Inishinny, Inishmaine, Inishirrer, Umfin, Inishfree, Owey and Gola, which was reluctantly abandoned but to which the fishermen often return. The **beach** further up the coast is approached from the road running north out of the village, by taking any track off to the left. The most popular bar in Bunbeg is *Teach Hiúdaí Beag*, once a great spot for traditional music but now quieter than it used to be. You can **eat** extremely well at *Mooney's Restaurant* (five-course dinner £12); *Micky Gallagher's* has cheap bar grub, while *Sergeant Pepper's* is a good place for kebabs and pizzas. The *Ostan Gweedore* holds **discos** (Wed, Fri & Sun; £2.50), and has country and western music on Wednesdays. **Rooms** here are expensive: the *Ostan Gweedore* (☎075/31177; £35) is at least luxurious; *Brookvale House* (☎075/31149; £20) is also pretty comfortable.

At GLASSACH, a few miles after Derrybeg, the road climbs abruptly to the **Bloody Foreland**, a grim, stony, almost barren zone, crisscrossed by stone walls. The road turns eastwards at KNOCKFOLA, hugging the side of the mountain, with the bogland and its hard-worked turfbanks stretching below towards the Atlantic. At **MINLARACH** (*Mín Lárach*, the gentle spot) you should be able to spot the distinctive shape of Tory Island far out to sea. A road runs down to the pier, from where you can pick up a boat to take you out to the island; Bunbeg and Dunfanaghy are other possible departure points. In the dead of winter a trip is virtually impossible, and at any time of the year you must be prepared to be stranded for anything up to a fortnight if the weather takes a sudden turn for the worse. Minlarach has a few pubs and grocery store, handy if you're waiting for a boat.

Tory Island

With its ruggedly indented shores pounded day and night by the ocean, **Tory Island**, though only eight miles from the mainland, is notorious for its inaccessibility. The island is completely treeless and, it's claimed, ratless too – thanks to the intervention of Saint Columba, who arrived here in 500 AD. There's no hotel or guesthouse on Tory – you simply bring a sleeping bag and enquire about a floor to sleep on. It has two villages – West Town and East Town; the former possesses the church, school and post office, and two of the island's three shops. There's no pub, but the community hall is pressed into service for drinking and music.

In winter nothing could equal the austerity and harshness of this place, and most of the island's hundred or so inhabitants decamp to the mainland for the worst months. An idiosyncratic brand of Gaelic is their first tongue, and it's indicative of their independence that they refer to the winter migration as "taking a visit over to Ireland". Fishing is still the staple trade, but some of the men supplement this a little through **painting**, a circumstance which originated in a chance encounter between the English painter Derek Hill and one of the fishermen, **James Dixon**, in 1968. Dixon (now dead) had never lifted a brush before the day he told Hill that he could do a better job of painting the Tory scenery, but he went on to become the most famous of the island's school of primitive painters. (Glebe House has a remarkable painting by him – see "Lough Gartan", above.)

It's no surprise to learn that potent legends are attached to the island. **Balor of the Evil Eye** (the Celtic god of darkness) supposedly had his residence on Tory, the remains of his castle standing on the eastern cliffs. There's also said to be a crater in the very heart of the island that none of the locals will approach after dark, for fear of incurring the god's wrath. Another superstition focuses on the **wishing stone** in the centre of the island, three circuits of which will lead to your wish being granted. It was utilised to defeat invaders by wrecking their ships – the British gunboat the *Wasp*, sent to collect taxes, was caught in a sudden storm that killed all but six of its crew. The islanders have never paid tax since.

Some monastic relics from Saint Columba's time remain on Tory, the most unusual of which – now the island's emblem – is the **Tau Cross**. Its T-cross shape is of Egyptian origin, and is one of only two such monuments in the whole of Ireland. It is now relocated and set in concrete on Camusmore Pier in West Town. There are other mutilated stone crosses and some carved stones lying around, several by the remains of the Round Tower.

Gortahork and Falcarragh

The first town you'll come across to the east of the Bloody Foreland is nondescript **GORTAHORK**. The *Teach Bhillie* is an old mens' drinking place, while the *Irish College* – up to the right after you pass *Whorskey's* on the left – has céilís every night throughout July and August. The bar in *MacFadden's* hotel (☎074/35267; £20) has snack lunches and a reasonably priced Sunday carvery lunch.

FALCARRAGH is more interesting, and has more to offer by way of pubs, shops and other amenities. The local tourist committee have recently made available **hostel rooms** down at **Ballyconnel House** – take the coast road at the village crossroads, and the gateposts of the estate are beside the main road where it bears left. Set in 500 acres of woodland, the house was built in the midseventeenth century, once belonged to one of the great landlords of the area, Sir John Olphert, and was taken over by the State in 1923. It's planned to open a heritage centre and museum here. There's more regular tourist **accommodation** at the *Shamrock Lodge* independent hostel (☎074/35859; £5) and at a few B&Bs in the countryside nearby. For **eating**, *John's Café*, at the Gortahork end of town, is the best place. The *Gweedore* has **music** of varying kinds most nights in July and August, and does lunches and evening meals.

Falcarragh **beach** is reached by following the coast road for a few miles – eventually the dunes will appear behind a car park. This is one of the more beautiful strands on this northwest coast, but a strong undercurrent makes it unsafe for bathing.

Leaving Falcarragh, the road to Dunfanaghy opens up a significantly milder landscape, with the green grass now beginning to outstrip the ruggedness, and the odd reed-fringed lake with swans by the roadway.

Horn Head and around

DUNFANAGHY, a resort town seven miles from Falcarragh, is the gateway to the Horn Head peninsula. It's an aristocratically self-conscious Plantation town, whose strongly Presbyterian atmosphere makes quite a contrast to anything west or south of it. The measure of the place is given by the fact that its one and only memorial was raised in honour of an agent for the estates of a nineteenth-century landlord. It hasn't a single fast-food outlet or café, but instead proffers several hotels and an art gallery (mostly soft Irish landscape impressions, supplemented by an assembly of heavily polished antique knick-knacks) just on the outskirts of the west end of town. *Dan Devine's* is the liveliest and cosiest **bar**, with friendly bar staff. For **eating**, *Danny Collin's* pub offers soups and pricey but delicious seafood; the **hotels**, *Arnold's* (☎074/36208; £26) and *Carrig Rua* (☎074/36133; £25), also offer food.

Horn Head is magnificent, a 600-foot rock face scored by ledges on which perch countless guillemots, puffins and gulls. The best view of the cliffs, seastacks and caves is from the water, but the cliff road is vertiginous enough in places to give you a good look down the sheer sides. To get there take the slip road at the Falcarragh end of Dunfanaghy village; it descends to skirt the side of a beautiful inlet before rising steeply to go round the east side of the head. A spectacular vista of headlands opens up to the east – Rossguill, Fanad and Inishowen – but none can match the drama of Horn Head's cliffs, their tops clad in a thin cover of purplish heather.

Moving east again, the road follows the side of **Sheephaven Bay**; signposted turn-offs run to the popular holiday spots PORTNABLAGH and MARBLE HILL STRAND, the latter possessing a vast sweep of silver sand.

The Creeslough area

The sleepy village of **CREESLOUGH** stands on a slope commanding gorgeous views across the head of Sheephaven Bay. Part-way down its main street is one of Liam McCormack's churches, its whitewashed whorl and backsloping table roof reflecting the thickly set **Muckish Mountain** nearby. You can see the mountain from within the church – it's usually enswirled in mist, or what is known locally as the Donegal *smir*. Creeslough and Falcarragh make the best launching pad for a climb up the mountain; from Creeslough follow the road out to Muckish Gap, down at the southern face, and from there the route ascends the grassy slopes to the flattened summit. There are pubs and grocery stores in the village, but it's otherwise fairly uninteresting, and not a place you would choose for an overnight stay.

The coastal road northwards onto tl.e Rossguill peninsula offers a couple of worthwhile diversions. **Doe Castle**, to the left just before Lackagh Bridge, has been superbly reconstructed. The tall central keep, standing within a bawn and rock-cut fosse, was the original fortress of **McSwyney Doe** whose graveslab is now fixed to its wall. The carving on the stone is faint, but its intricacy makes it historically important; the seven-speared fleur-de-lys at the top represents the close family connections with Scotland, and other carvings show a fox, cow, dolphin and eagle, as well as Celtic tracery. A walk around the battlements affords a view of the southernmost corner of Sheephaven Bay; when the tide is out the whole peaceful expanse looks like a desert, with only a slim channel of water gliding through the sandbanks. If the castle gate is padlocked, a key is kept in the cottage fifty yards back down the approach road.

Lackagh Bridge is an even better viewpoint, the curving silty shoreline lying downstream, and a ginger-brown picture of rushes and heather reaching deep into the hills. Immediately after the bridge there's a turn-off to **GLEN** (two miles), a roundabout way to Carrigart that's worth taking for the scenery and the opportunity to drop in at the *Old Glen Bar*. This is a low-ceilinged place, smoky and atmospheric, with music at weekends and most other nights as well. If solitude is what you want, this is a good area to explore: apart from Lough Glen, there are several other lakelets in the district, all enclosed in a silent, rocky landscape.

The Rosguill Peninsula

CARRIGART is the back-door entrance to the extremely beautiful and very manageable **Rosguill Peninsula**. It's a beguiling village, whose **bars** define the essence of the place: *P. Logue's,* at the west end of town, is a welcoming sort of hideaway. Also note *MacGettigan's* grocers, at the eastern end of the main street, with its old-style wooden counter and shelving, and a tempting array of bottles in the window.

The route onto the peninsula starts by the side of the church; follow this road for a little, then fork left, and you'll be going past the rabbit-infested dunes at the back of a fantastic and usually deserted beach. The three-mile strand runs in a scimitar's curve all the way back round to the bottom of Sheephaven Bay – it's a marvellous four-hour walk to Doe Castle, though when the tide comes in you could have to do a mile or so of the journey on the lanes. **DOWNINGS**, at the top of the strand, is a small and sprightly holiday centre, patronised mainly by Northern Irish tourists (especially from Belfast), with caravan sites hogging the rear end of the beach and holiday chalets creeping up the hillside behind the village.

The one **pub** you should be sure to head for is the *Harbour Bar*, at the far end of the village (traditional music Tues, Thurs & Sat), which usually attracts the *Gaeltacht* crowd during the summer months. The *Fleet's Inn*, at the centre of the village, runs discos during the summer, when there are also nightly folk sessions, often lasting until 3am, at the *Beach Hotel* opposite. If you want to stay, the *Beach Hotel* is one possibility (☎074/55303; £16) or there are a couple of B&Bs – try *Bay Mount* (☎074/55395; £12).

The main street runs on round the west side of the headland to become the panoramic **Atlantic Drive**, first passing by a slip-road that runs down to the pier. Just before the pier is the only nourishing eating place on the whole peninsula – the *Coffee Shop*, great for home-made everything (11am–8pm).

If, instead of taking the left fork to Downings, you go right, you're on your way to the **hostel** at Trá Na Rosann beach (see below). This route goes by the *Singing Pub* (traditional music Sat), sited on a turning up to the left. Opposite this turning and down to the right is **Mevagh Church** graveyard. It has an early Christian cross and an intriguing slab into which some cup-like cavities have been carved. And there's one gravestone that cannot but bring an appreciative smile: *Pat MacBride 1910–86, Shoemaker and Philosopher.*

The hostel – and some views

The peninsula's *An Óige* **hostel** (☎074/75142; £5.50; open all year) is perfectly placed at the northeastern corner of the headland, right next to the Trá Na Rosann beach. The management are very friendly, there's virtually no curfew, and the views from the dorms are great. Fish can be bought from the fisherman who lives in the bungalow behind the hostel, and a grocery van stops by every Monday around midday.

The hostel at first sight looks like an Alpine refuge out of *The Sound of Music*. One of the first things you should do on arrival is belt up the hillside immediately behind – at the summit the view is stupendous. You'll see long, narrow Mulroy Bay and a seemingly endless length of mountain ridges behind it. Further round there's the bombastic height of Horn Head, while closer in rises the central hump of the Rossguill Peninsula, and the **Trá Na Rosann** strand serene and untouched below. The remainder of the headland back towards **Mulroy Bay** stretches only as far as a caravan site and another beach at MELMORE (not safe for bathing); the coastal rocks on the way harbour the odd cove and cave.

Rossguill practicalities

For transport, *Patrick Gallagher's* private **bus** service leaves Letterkenny's Market Square for the peninsula at 6pm, and leaves Downings at 10.45am every morning. It's quite easy to **hitch** to the hostel, as everyone knows exactly where you're heading. For **cycle** hire try *Charlie Coyle Cycles* (☎074/55427), based on the Creeslough road just outside Carrigart, in the bungalow next to the clump of fir trees. The only **bank** in the area is in Carrigart (Mon–Wed & Fri 11am–2pm, Thurs 11am–1pm).

The Fanad Peninsula

The **western** route onto the **Fanad Peninsula** has marvellous patches of idyllic scenery close to the Mulroy Lough and near the northwest corner, where the low-lying headland resembles the Rosses. But on the whole it's not the most inspiring of routes.

MILFORD makes for a fairly drab beginning to the western route; **CARROWKEEL**, a bit further on, offers a bit more excitement, being a popular holiday place. The *Mulroy Ballroom*, one of the few remaining Sixties showband ballrooms, carries on the tradition with an Irish night (every Wed, June–Aug); it's on the Milford road out of town. Opposite is the *Rockhill Campsite Park* (tents £5, plus 30p per person; pony trekking available), providing the only basic **accommodation** in the place. The *Village Restaurant*, at the northern end of the village, has an expensive but wide-ranging menu.

The road north from Carrowkeel runs along the water's edge up to BALLYWHORISKEY, at the top of the peninsula, where the landscape becomes flatter, with dwellings spread out in the *Gaeltacht* manner. A left turn at the FANAD DRIVE signpost, just outside an old grey school building, will take you through hillocky and boulder-strewn terrain to a few small beaches and a pier; from here you can return to the main road to Fanad Head (see below). The large **Ballyhiernan Strand**, further along towards the head, has a few caravan sites behind its grassy dunes if you're seeking a place to kip down for the night.

The Eastern Route: Rathmelton

The road crawling up the **east** side of Fanad is a much more interesting route. It starts at **RATHMELTON**, a sedate and neat little village that attracts Dublin yuppies and which because of its many Georgian houses has been granted heritage status. The main part of town sits attractively on the eastern bank of the broad black flow of the Leannan River, famous for its salmon. There are some fine stone warehouses on the banks, parts of which have been converted into bars and bistros. The *House on the Brae* coffee shop sells home-baked **food** (entrance facing the river); more substantial but more upmarket is *McDaid's* restaurant and wine bar right on the junction of the quay road and the high road. *Chez Michel's*, turn left after the bridge, serves good couscous and seafood. For a smidgeon of entertainment, the *O'Donnell Arms* puts on traditional music on a Friday night and country and western on a Saturday. If you're only passing through, *Sweeney's Tavern* is the nicest refuge for a stopover drink.

Rathmullan

Next stop north, **RATHMULLAN**, looks pretty with its long row of seafront housing following the curve of the bay, but the beach itself is to be avoided, having two sewer pipes running down to the water's edge. In 1587 **Red Hugh O'Donnell** was lured into a British merchant ship here, on the pretext of a merry drink, and ended up in Dublin jail for six years; and in 1609 it was the departing point for the **Flight of the Earls**, the event that marked the end of the Gaelic nation.

The view across to Fahan on the Inishowen Peninsula is enticing (a small ferry-boat operates in summer), but otherwise the only thing to delay your passing through is **Rathmullan Friary**, one of the better-preserved historical ruins in

Donegal. The original part of it was built by Rory MacSweeney in 1508 and then presented to the Carmelites. George Bingham plundered it in 1595 and used it as a barracks, and in 1618 it was further adapted as a castle residence by Bishop Knox. Only the chancel area continued to serve as a church until its eventual abandonment in 1814. Today you can see traces of Gothic doorways and narrow window apertures.

On the way into Rathmullan there's very good **eating** to be had at the *Water's Edge Restaurant*, and the comfortably old-fashioned *Pier Hotel* (☎074/58115; £15) serves excellent fresh salmon for a fraction of what you'd pay at swanky *Rathmullan House*, nearby. Sea angling can be arranged locally.

Towards Portsallon
Four miles north of Rathmullan, on the Portsallon road, a signpost to the left indicates a little track that leads towards the tenth-century **Drumhallach Cross Slab**; only four and a half feet in height, it has delightful carvings of two figures sitting on the arms of the cross sucking away at their thumbs. This curiosity is linked by local folklore with Fionn Mac Cumhaill, who one day burned his thumb while tending to the salmon of knowledge, and immediately stuck it in his mouth – thereafter doing the same whenever he needed to be wise. The lower figures on this front face are harder to make out, but are meant to represent bishops.

Back on the main route, the road climbs to give great views across to Dunree Head and the Urris range of mountains, on the Inishowen Peninsula. Just approaching the summit of this climb, and above the patch where the oyster beds lie, is a tin-roofed cottage offering home baking – handy for little **Bunnaton Hostel** (☎074/51022; £4.50 plus £1 for bedding), an old coastguard station half a mile away. To get there follow the path off to the right down by the clump of fir trees. There's a small shop here, a couple of bikes for hire, and great walks nearby. The hostel overlooks a small cove with a rocky beach, and also has a nice view inland up the valley of **Glenvar**, which will take you across to Carrowkeel on the western side of the peninsula.

Continuing north, the road rises until you're running along the cliff-top approach to the most spectacular views on the peninsula at **Saldanha Head**. From here you're looking down onto the three-mile stretch of golden sand at Balinstocker Strand. The tiny village of **PORTSALLON**, on the other side of the strand, was once a great holidaying spot, but is now more of a ghost resort, with its grand crenellated hotel abandoned down on the front. Just in front of it, however, is *Rita's Bar*, still thriving in its Fifties decor, with wooden bar counter and shelves for sweets and bottled drinks.

Fanad Head
Though some stretches are forested, most of the five-mile route north from Portsallon to Fanad Head is through humpy and barren land, with clusters of granite pushing through marshy ground. By the roadside there's a **Holy Well**, decked out with a crazy collection of mementoes – beads, prayer books, plastic knife and fork, a golf tee, badges, mugs, bottles, medicine bottle and so on. Before reaching the Head, there is one other curiosity worth taking in – the rock formation known as **the Great Arch**. Follow the signpost on the right of the road, then take the path down to the new house, and finally cross the fields to the rocky strand. You'll see the arch to your left, a sort of natural *Arc de Triomphe* with the sea crashing all around it. Only half a mile off the same main road at this

point but to the left (signposted) is *Knock Donnely* **B&B**, just before Shannagh lake (☎074/31050; £11); they offer vegetarian **meals** throughout the day. The road straight on from the B&B will lead you away from Fanad Head and over towards the western tip of the peninsula.

If you return to the main road, you'll find that it leads straight on to **Fanad Head**, where you'll find a dramatically placed cliff-edge lighthouse and its namesake public house. The *Lighthouse Tavern* doesn't live up to its situation, serving hot toddies out of the microwave, but allegedly has wild country and western sessions (July & Aug Tues, Fri & Sun), and the views. The road from here runs on down to the low rocky coast, where the pebble beach emits a strong hiss as each wave gets sucked back down its slope.

The Inishowen Peninsula

Rarely sought out by tourists due to a combination of its northerly location and its proximity to the "troublesome" North, the **Inishowen Peninsula** is perhaps the great overlooked treasure of the Irish landscape. It's a diverse and visually exciting terrain, where the views usually encompass the waters of the loughs or the Atlantic waves. Every aspect of the land is superb – the beaches (especially **Fahan**, **Tullagh** and **Pollan**), the towering headland bluffs (**Malin**, **Inishowen**, **Dunaff** and **Dunree**) and the central mountain range, with **Slieve Snaght** (*sliabh sneachta*, the mountain of the snows) at the centre of it all. Its name derives from **Eoghán**, who was made First Lord of the island by his father Niall, the High King of Ireland. Phases of the peninsula's history before and after Eoghán have left a legacy of fine antiquities, from the **Greenan Fort** to a host of beautiful early Christian crosses (**Cloncha**, **Mura**, **Carrowmore** and **Cooley**).

Western Inishowen

The most stimulating of all the Inishowen sights, the ancient fort known as the Grianán of Aileach, is a short way off the western route into the peninsula from Derry city. The turning is past BRIDGE END, on the south side of the Letterkenny–Derry road, by the Liam McCormack-designed **Burt Church**, probably the most beautiful new church in all Ireland. The seating is set concentrically, under a whitewashed ceiling that sweeps up into a vortex to allow sunlight to beam down directly upon the altar; the allusions in every detail to Neolithic sepulchral architecture (especially Newgrange) are fascinating and very atmospheric.

The **Grianán of Aileach** (a mile up the hill from the church) was already 1700 years old when the Alexandrian geographer Ptolemy showed it on his map of Ireland in the second century, and most people today find it the most impressive of all the pagan antiquities left in the country. It was said in the years after Christ to have been the base of various northern Irish chieftains. Here Saint Patrick supposedly preached in 450 AD, and baptised Eoghán, the founder of the O'Neill clan. In the twelfth century it was sacked by Brian, the King of Thomond, in retribution for a raid on Clare, with the result that a large amount of its stone got carried away. What you see today owes a lot to the reconstruction by a Dr Bernard in the late nineteenth century. It's enclosed by three earthen banks, but its most stunning asset is the view across the primordial jumble of mountains and hills far away to the west and the loughs to each side of Inishowen immediately to the north.

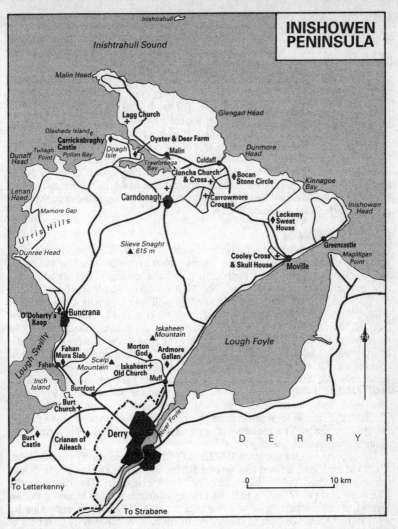

INISHOWEN PENINSULA

Inishtrahull

Inishtrahull Sound

Malin Head

Glengad Head

Lagg Church

Glashedy Island

Carrickabraghy Castle

Oyster & Deer Farm

Dunaff Head

Tullagh Point

Doagh Isle

Pollan Bay

Malin

Culdaff

Dunmore Head

Trawbreaga Bay

Cloncha Church & Cross

Bocan Stone Circle

Kinnagoe Bay

Lenan Head

Carndonagh

Carrowmore Crosses

Inishowen Head

Mamore Gap

Urris Hills

Slieve Snaght ▲ 615 m

Leckemy Sweat House

Dunree Head

Cooley Cross & Skull House

Moville

Greencastle

Magilligan Point

O'Doherty's Keep

Buncrana

Iskaheen Mountain

Lough Foyle

Lough Swilly

Fahan Mura Slab

Morton God

Ardmore Gallan

Scalp Mountain

Fahan

Iskaheen Old Church

Inch Island

Burnfoot

Muff

Burt Church

River Foyle

Burt Castle

Crianan of Aileach

Derry

D E R R Y

To Letterkenny

0   10 km

To Strabane

Fahan and Buncrana

To get back towards the western coast of the peninsula from here the safest bet is to return to Bridge End and turn onto the road to **FAHAN**. The beach at Fahan is delightful, as are its monastic ruins. The first abbot was Saint Mura (one of six saints in the one family), and what remains today from his time is the **St Mura Cross Slab**, a spellbinding example of early Christian stone decoration, though it's a shame that it hasn't yet been cleansed of its lichen. There's said to be a rare Greek inscription on its side, but it's hard to locate.

The high street at **BUNCRANA**, a few miles north, is one long carnival parade of shops, each with a name saluting one or other of the local clans –

Casey, McLoughlin, Hegarty, O'Doherty, Grant, McGonagle. The town is packed out during the summer, for this is the Derry people's unrivalled seaside resort. Amusement arcades are here by the dozen, as are **B&Bs** in the Victorian backstreets towards the shore – try, for example, Mrs Doherty's *St Brigid's* (☎077/61319; £11) or Mrs McConigly at *Kinvyra*, 14 St Oran's Road (☎077/61461; £10). For **eats** in the town check out the Italian cooking at *Cassidy's Coffee Shop* on the left-hand side just as you round the corner into the main street. *Dorrians* on the main street is also a good bet for a substantial lunch. The place is crammed full of **pubs**; if you're looking for a plain and unpretentious b r try *Roddens*, and for a more upbeat venue try *O'Flaherty's*, which often has music.

The left turn that runs down to the pier at the north end of the main street will take you onto the coastal path to **Stragill Strand**, a beautiful and isolated stretch of golden sand. There's a **campsite** here, from which you can go on to get to Dunree Head by following the track away from the beach up to the main road. The view across **Lough Swilly** at this point is extremely satisfying, with the closed-in feel of a large mountain lake.

Dunree to Doagh Isle

Perched on a headland overlooking the mouth of Lough Swilly, just past the tiny village from which it takes its name, **Dunree Fort** began life as a Martello tower and was then enlarged into a fortress. It now has a museum of predictable military memorabilia (June–Oct Tues–Sat 10.30am–6pm, Sun noon–6pm; £1). A steepish climb going north out of the village will take you past a scattering of weatherbeaten thatched cottages before you cross a small bridge close to the **Gap of Mamore** (*madhm mór*, the great mountain pass), looking like a bite taken out of the Urris Mountains. From here the road spirals steeply downwards, an ever wider and more spectacular view of the flat foreground to Dunaff Head opening up with every bend. The mile-long **Tullagh Strand**, to the east of Dunaff Head, is a safe bathing beach, with a camping and caravan site just behind it (☎077/76289, 76138); *Marky's Tavern*, by the roadside, has music at weekends. The road from here works its way inland between the mountains to CLONMANY, a village of predominantly cream-coloured terraced houses and a few grocery shops. The backdrop of mountains on all sides shields it from any thought of an outside world.

The popular holiday village of **BALLYLIFFEN** makes an earthy contrast, with a hotel at each end, a disco and several **B&Bs**. Try Mrs K. Grant, *Pollin House*, Carndonagh Road (☎077/76203; £11) or Mrs McLaughlin, *The Vartry*, at the Clonmany end (☎077/76370; £12). Its principal attraction is the beautiful **Pollan Strand**, at the northern tip of which stands the ruin of **Carrickabraghy Castle,** an O'Doherty defence built in the sixteenth century. Weathered by centuries of spray and seasalt, the stones of the tower show colours ranging from the darkest hues through oranges and reds to golden yellows. The strand itself has wonderfully wild breakers, which unfortunately make it dangerous to swim.

The castle sits on the western side of a promontory called **Doagh Isle**, which you can drive onto by a road to the east of Ballyliffen. You shouldn't miss a trip onto it, for **Trawbreaga Bay** (*trá bréige*, the treacherous strand), on the eastern side, is an exquisite piece of coastline. The mouth of the bay is bewitching – if you walk onto the beach here you'll find the sea has fashioned the rocks into myriad shapes and colours.

Carndonagh

Just before you turn into **CARNDONAGH**, coming from the Ballyliffen direction, there's a church on the corner of the turn-off. Against the church wall is the elegantly shaped and decorated seventh-century **Donagh Cross**, with two diminutive pillar stones to its right and left. The pillar stones show figures with rather large heads, while the cross depicts evil little characters jumping out of its Celtic interlacings – all of which harks back to the pagan Druidic religion. A few other decorated stones stand by the entrance. The buildings of Carndonagh town are stacked up the hillside, near the crown of which stands the all-surveying Catholic church. The town **museum**, in the basement of the Wesleyan church, near the base of the hill as you come from the Ballyliffen direction (July & Aug Mon–Sat 2–4pm) has many intriguing folk items. For **accommodation** try *Teirnaleague*, left off Church Street then on for a mile (☎077/74471). The *Sportsman's Inn*, on the Diamond, does stews and salads, and may have traditional music on a Saturday night. Carndonagh has a **folk festival** in the third week of July but it's not one of the more lively ones.

East of Carndonagh – the ancient sites

Not far to the east of Carndonagh are a neighbouring set of historical remains – the Carrowmore High Crosses, the Cloncha Cross, the Bocan Stone Circle, and the Temple of Deen. To get to the **Carrowmore High Crosses** take the Moville direction out of Carndonagh for four miles, then take a right forty yards after the signposted turning for Culdaff: the two plain crosses are eighty yards up the road, one on each side. These and a few meagre building stones are all that remains of the ancient monastery of Saint Chonas. For the **Cloncha Cross and Church** get back to the Culdaff turning and follow it for a couple of miles until you see a small bungalow with a garden hedge of small firs – the site is behind it. This was once the most important monastic foundation in Inishowen, a status borne out in the beautiful designs carved on the cross's stem. Inside the church are a few more carved stones, the outstanding piece being a tenth-century tombstone.

For the other two sites, take a right here towards Moville and then a left uphill for fifty yards – the **Bocan Stone Circle** is through the first field gate on the left. Only a handful of the stones still stand, among a scrapyard of fallen ones; they were all placed here at least three thousand years ago. There's a fine vista of the surrounding ring of hills, with which the stones seem deliberately aligned. On the other side of the main road from the circle is a gallery tomb known as the **Temple of Deen** (go a little further along towards Moville and take a right up as far as the wire barrier – you'll spot it from there). It's nothing extra special, but it's possible that what is exposed today is only the central chamber of an immense cairn. Unfortunately, no archaeological work has yet been done on either this or the stone circle. **CULDAFF** is the nearest base for all of these places, but apart from having a quaint little pier and ancient stone bridge there is little to entice you down there. For **accommodation** try *McGrory's Guest House, Bar & Restaurant* (☎077/79104; £13) or *Culdaff House* (☎077/79103; £12).

To Malin Head

Four miles north of Carndonagh is **MALIN** village, tucked picturesquely into the side of Trawbreaga Bay. A Planter settlement, with an overtly charming central green, it has only one pub, which must make it unique for its size (the *Malin*

Hotel also has rooms; ☎077/70606; £19). A little way north of Malin a signpost shows the way to **Five Fingers Strand**, across the bay from Doagh Isle – it's worth the diversion for the ferocity of the breakers on the beach and the long walks on its sands. The beach hit the headlines when a large IRA cache of arms was found buried here. Back on the main road, you'll quickly come to a left turn to take you straight on for Malin Head; a more devious route is to take a left that veers off this road and a left again at the next signpost, which brings you to the top of a hill overlooking Five Fingers Strand – one of the most captivating views of this part of the peninsula. Going downhill from here feels like a slightly less intoxicating version of the descent from the Gap of Mamore, and is decidedly more thrilling than the direct lowland road.

Malin Head, the northernmost extremity of Ireland, might not be as stupendously over-the-top as other Donegal headlands, but is nevertheless excellent for windy and winding coastal walks. Look out for a large chasm in the cliffs known as Hell's Hole and the now-deserted **Inishtrahull Island** that aptly translates as the *Island of Yonder Strand*.

Eastern Inishowen

The route from Derry to Inishowen Head along the Lough Foyle side of the peninsula is the nightclubbing circuit for the youth of Derry, and you'll see cars, buses and hitchers racing down here on Friday and Saturday nights. Favourite destinations are the mock-Tudor *Tiffanys/The Ture Inn*, a few miles on from **Muff**, *The Point Inn* at **Quigley's Point**, a few miles further on again, and *Scamps* at **Redcastle**, several miles on again. Scores of new bungalows hog the slopes to capture their slice of the panorama.

The first few miles of the road entering this part of Inishowen belongs to the British sector of the north of Ireland: you'll approach the army checkpoint a half-mile short of the border at CULMORE POINT.

Muff and around

The tiny village of **MUFF**, just a few minutes' drive north of the border, has the only **hostel** in the whole of the peninsula. The independent *Muff Hostel* is a very cosy and welcoming place (☎077/84188; £5); you get there by taking a left turn at the end of the village, just before the *Burmah* petrol station. *Mrs Reddin* on the main street offers a **B&B** alternative (☎077/84031; £11). The village itself is not quite as dead as it looks: *The Carman's Bar* has Irish music on a Wednesday and it's possible *The Squealin' Pig* will have some traditional music on a Friday and Sunday; the pub with the toreador and flamenco mosaic outside has country and western music and dancing from Friday to Sunday. For **eats** the town café has steaks and pies. *Lough Swilly* **buses** run six or more times a day from Derry.

The countryside immediately around Muff has several interesting megalithic remains. In the **Iskaheen** district (the hostel area) there are some standing stones not far from the sparse ruins of an old abbey that marks the spot where Eoghán, son of Niall of the Nine Hostages, died of grief for his brother Conal. To get to the more impressive of the stones from the abbey go past the nearby St Patrick's Church for a quarter of a mile, by the garden packed with elves, and then go up into the second field up behind the new-looking bungalow; from the stone you have the best view of the whole area.

Another nearby site worth seeking out is the **Ardmore Gallan** stone. Dating from the Bronze Age, it's a striking monumental stone standing all on its own in a farmer's field. It is heavily carved with symbolic forms, having forty small cup-dents and a large vertical valley down the middle of one face. To get to it, take a left off the Moville road about half a mile out of Muff, then up the lane at the side of the red-doored house; follow the road straight up and then take a right turn to the farmyard at the end – the stone is in the far side of the field in front of the yard.

Also to be recommended is the fourteen-mile trip across the mountains through **Gráinne's Gap** and on to Buncrana on the western side of the peninsula (see above). There are fantastic views back down onto the Foyle estuary from the gap, and the inland scenery is all trickling burns, heathery boggy slopes lined with turf banks, and rocky granite outcrops.

Moville and around

Set on a gentle hillock beside the Foyle, **MOVILLE** is a very agreeable seaside resort of the convalescent variety – one can imagine a grandfather clock ticking away in every household. It's handy for a rocky shoreline walk that you can pursue as far as Greencastle without too much difficulty (although at a few points you'll have to circumspectly walk across the bottom of a few private gardens). The village will rarely stir itself to offer anything more than even a tingle of excite-ment, but if you're on the lookout for somewhere to shrug off a rainy day, then try *The Prospect Bar* down by the gaudily painted Temperance Hall – which has folk and ballad singing (Thurs, Fri & Sat). *Rosatos*, on the Carndonagh road, is the best place for a snack and a cosy drink. For **accommodation** try Mrs McGroarty's, at the top end of Main Street (☎077/82091; £11) or the *Foyle Hotel* (☎077/82025; £16). You can hire bikes at *The Bike Shop*, halfway up the same street.

There are a few historical pieces in the district, most notably the **Cooley Cross** and **Skull House**, signposted off to the left of the main road a quarter of a mile before Moville. Follow the turn-off up the steep hill for about a mile, always bear-ing right, and it's there – an ancient Celtic wheel-cross, guarding the entrance to a walled graveyard. There are very few examples of this kind of cross with the pierced ringhole in its head – the hole was once a pagan device used to clinch serious treaties, the hands of the opposing parties being joined in amity through it. The Skull House, in the graveyard, is in the form of the type of tomb usually kept for saints, and in this case it's probably that of **Saint Finian** (the one who argued with Columba), whose monastery this was. If you peep through the front hole you'll see some bones.

Greencastle to Kinnego Bay

Though its harbour is surprisingly ugly, **GREENCASTLE** has a pleasant view across to the extensive golden sands of Magilligan Strand on the British side of Lough Foyle. At dusk you'll see the area across the water begin to sparkle with lights like a ship at sea – these are the lights of the prison camp, just hidden behind the dunes. By the road to Stroove (see below) are the ruins of a four-teenth-century **Richard de Burgo** castle, built on a rocky knoll to guard the narrowest part of the lough. De Burgo saw it as the greatest castle building enter-prise in Donegal, and hoped it would be just the job to quell the local Inishowen chieftains, the O'Donnells and the O'Dohertys. But the O'Dohertys in the end took control of the castle, until they finished up bickering among themselves and causing most of the damage seen today. It's in no great shape, with gaping breaches right round its circular enclosure making it look like a large mock-up of a stone circle, but viewed from the shore it's still an impressive sight. Next door is **Greencastle Fort**, a fortress built in the Napoleonic era; designed as a lookout post, it unsurprisingly affords good views across the estuary. Back in the village, *The Ferryboat* bar on the seafront offers meals and **B&B** as well as drink (☎077/81021).

At **STROOVE** (pronounced "shroove") the scenery jumps into a more exciting gear, with lovely clambering walks along its coastline to the lighthouse. There you'll have to return to the road to reach the small beach, from where doughtier walkers can resume the clamber as far as the cliffs of the awesome **Inishowen Head**. An easier way to the Head is to simply follow the road until it turns left, where you go straight on up the hill; a car can make it up the first couple of miles, but after that you run the risk of getting stuck in a rut. From the Head, it's a beautiful but tiring walk to **Kinnagoe Bay**. The alternative route entails going back to the main road and following it to the right turn by the thatched cottage in Stroove – this will take you over the headland through two beautiful glens, where fields set at impossible angles line the valley sides. Approached by a precipitous descent, Kinnagoe is one of the most secluded sandy beaches around, tucked between the rocky walls of headland against which the waves throw spray as delicate as lace embroidery. A plan on a roadside plaque shows where three of the Spanish Armada ships sank just off the coast; most of the ships' wreckage discovered over the last twenty years is now on view in Derry's Foyle College. The nearest **B&B** is back in Stroove, with Mrs Gillespie (☎077/81020; £11).

travel details

Bus Éireann
From Donegal: to Dublin (3 daily; 5hr).
From Letterkenny: to Dublin (3 daily; 5hr).

Private buses
Funtrek (☎01/730852) operates a daily service **from Letterkenny** to Dublin.

For connections to Galway, see that chapter's "Travel Details".

THE NORTH

I nfluenced by television reports and coverage in the less than clear-eyed press, a large portion of the British population regards Northern Ireland as a place in which sectarian violence is the dominant factor of everyday life. It's not. There *are* ravaged streets, security checkpoints, armoured patrols and fortified army and police headquarters, but you'll encounter them only in the major pressure-points: chiefly parts of **Belfast** and **Derry City**, and along

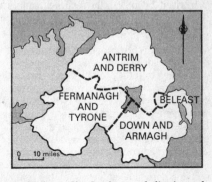

the border, where security is deliberately high profile. In the rural districts of counties **Antrim** and **Derry** you'll scarcely be aware of the "troubles", and even in **Down** and **Armagh** – whose towns feature regularly in the British media's litany of outrage – there is little risk of encountering antagonism towards British travellers.

Yet the caricature is more potent than the reality. Despite the fact that the North is generally as hospitable as the Republic, it's little frequented by tourists. Only a few areas see any at all – the coastline of **County Derry** (including the magnificent black basalt geometry of the **Giant's Causeway**); the green **Glens of Antrim**; and the **Mourne Mountains**, to the south of Belfast. These might be the most immediately appealing landscapes, but exploring the rest can be a rewarding experience. Away from the spectacular coastline, the country settles down into rolling farmland punctuated by the planned towns of the merchant companies that were entrusted with the resettlement of this region in the seventeenth century. The inland counties of **Tyrone** and **Fermanagh** are dotted with traces of their history – archaeological sites, castles, ruined churches, raths and dolmens. Fermanagh, centred on **Lough Erne**, is a good place to head towards for watersports and fishing; scenically, Tyrone is duller, though it rises both physically and in terms of interest towards the wild and desolate **Sperrins** in the north.

Perhaps the main characteristic is how like the south the North is – roads may be a little better, some towns a little wealthier, and you'll see the odd English-style phone box and post box, as well as more flags, murals and graffiti than you're used to – but the background remains one of stone houses and pubs amid lots of water and green fields.

Crossing the border: security

Although at times an inconvenience in terms of delay, **crossing the border** is easy enough. For the uninitiated, however, the experience can seem bizarre, and even unnerving. Irish formalities are almost non-existent, but approaching the British side the road is flanked by wide screens of corrugated iron and overlooked by a tower of the same, all festooned with barbed wire. A couple of speed ramps encourage you to slow down. At this stage a soldier carrying an automatic rifle is likely to approach your car window or board your bus; it is extremely rare to be asked for a passport, but drivers should have their licence handy – be prepared for a cursory search and questions about the purpose of your journey.

As far as everyday **travel** in the North is concerned, you're likely to be surprised by how little security matters affect you. As long as you use your common sense, and take care in certain areas of Belfast and Derry, you should have no trouble at all.

CHAPTER FOURTEEN

BELFAST

BELFAST, the capital of Northern Ireland, is not somewhere you can be indifferent to. A third of the population of the North live here, and they grab more than their share of world headlines. On the streets roam armoured vehicles and heavily armed patrols, and there are regular searches and checkpoints. On the other hand, the tourist authorities try to portray their city as some kind of Hibernian Rio – a farcical idea but also one to which the city's magnificent setting of mountains, pellucid skies and the great natural harbour of Belfast Lough does lend some credence.

If you've never been, it is almost certainly not what you expect. Belfast, though it no longer has any real relationship with its lough inlet or its major river, the Lagan, is a city by water. To look at, it is a wholly English creation of the Victorian period – a parody, almost, of the great industrial cities of the English Midlands and North, and once their great rival. It is a predominantly Protestant city but also one divided by religious factionalism, either fiercely (in West Belfast) or less openly (in the middle-class suburbs). The Troubles are all too apparent, yet it is not really a dangerous place to visit, and in the midst of all the signs of modern depression it remains a beautiful city, and a storehouse of Victoriana. No part of the city is more than a few miles from the foothills of the surrounding mountains, and in many parts the hills magically appear at the end of each street.

To visit Northern Ireland without seeing Belfast would be to avoid the issue. This is the voice of the North – pronounced in an accent which is the harshest and loudest in the land (to achieve authentic local pronunciation, try saying Northern Ireland as *Norn Iron*). In purely practical terms, visiting is dead easy. Normal life continues, albeit in a way that can come as a shock to a newcomer, the people are strikingly friendly, and, statistically at least, you're safer here than in virtually any other city of comparable size. Accommodation, food and transport are all well-organised, and if you feel the need to escape you can rapidly get to almost anywhere else in the North, or there's good transport on the main road and rail routes down towards Dublin.

As far as **what you should see** goes, it's experiencing the city itself that comes top of the list. This need not take more than a couple of days, though Belfast is also an easy base from which to visit virtually anywhere else in the North. In the city centre, concentrate on the glories that the Industrial Revolution brought; grandiose **Victorian buildings** as self-satisfied as any the British Empire created. And magnificent Victorian **pubs**. **West Belfast** offers a more contemporary vision – a depressed, working-class area where Northern Ireland's sectarian divisions are at their most starkly apparent. It may not sound like a tourist attraction, but it's certainly an eye-opener; and the ephemeral (but sometimes exceptionally talented) art of the mural painters who have claimed this part of the city for their own gives a fascinating insight to the current temper of the North.

The development of the city

Belfast began its life as a cluster of forts built to guard a ford across the River Farset, a river that nowadays runs underground, beneath the High Street. The Farset and Lagan rivers form a valley that marks a geological boundary between the basaltic plateau of Antrim and the slaty hills of Down: the softer red Triassic sandstones from which their courses were eroded are responsible for the bright red colour of the Belfast brick that pervades the city today.

In the early days, however, Belfast was very slow to develop, and indeed its history as a city doesn't really begin until the seventeenth century. A **Norman** castle was built here in 1177 but its influence was always limited, and within a hundred years or so control over the Lagan valley had reverted firmly to the Irish, under the **O'Neills** of Clandeboye who had their stronghold in the Castlereagh Hills. Theirs was the traditional Irish pastoral community, booleying their livestock and families between the hills and valley plain. Then, in 1604, **Sir**

Arthur Chichester, a Devonshire knight whose son was to be the first Earl of Donegall, was "planted" in the area by James I, and shortly afterwards the tiny settlement was granted a charter creating a corporate borough. By the restoration era of 1660 the town was still no more than 150 houses in five or six streets, and Carrickfergus at the mouth of the lough held the monopoly on trade.

The eighteenth century: the United Irishmen

By the end of the seventeenth century, things were looking up: French Huguenots fleeing persecution at home brought skills which rapidly improved the fortunes of the local linen industry, and by the turn of the century the population had reached about 2000. In 1708 the town was almost entirely destroyed by fire, but it was only a temporary setback: throughout the **eighteenth century** the cloth trade and shipbuilding expanded tremendously, and the population increased ten-fold in a hundred years. It was a city noted for its liberalism. In 1784 Protestants were overwhelming in their generosity to help build a church for the Catholic population. And in 1791, three Presbyterian Ulstermen formed the society of **United Irishmen**, a gathering embracing Catholics and Protestants on the basis of common Irish nationality. Belfast was the centre of this movement and thirty Presbyterian ministers in all were accused of taking part in the 1798 rebellion – six were hanged.

Despite the movement's Belfast origins, the rebellion in the North was in fact an almost complete failure, and the forces of reaction backed by the wealthy landlords quickly and ruthlessly stamped it down. Within two generations most Protestants had abandoned the nationalist cause and Belfast as a sectarian town was truly born. In the **nineteenth century** Presbyterian ministers like the Reverend Henry Cooke and Hugh (Roaring) Hanna began openly to attack the Catholic church, and the **sectarian divide** became wider, and increasingly violent. In 1835 several people were sabred to death in Sandy Row, and sporadic outbreaks of violence have continued from that day on. Meanwhile, the nineteenth century saw vigorous commercial and industrial expansion. In 1888 Queen Victoria granted Belfast city status; the city fathers' gratitude to her is stamped on buildings throughout the centre. By this time the population had risen to 208,000 and, with the continued improvement in both the linen and shipbuilding industries, the population exceeded even that of Dublin by the end of the century.

The twentieth century

This century has been less kind. Although **Partition** and the creation of Northern Ireland with Belfast as its capital inevitably boosted the city's status, decline has been fairly constant over recent years. Bombing in World War II destroyed much of the city, and in the past ten years great tracts of West Belfast have been pulled down in a belated attempt to improve living conditions. Outside the centre, this is a very modern-looking place. Nowadays the city is struggling very hard for **revitalisation** and billions of pounds are being poured in – from Britain and the European Community – in the hope that economic revival might bring with it some kind of more hopeful future. The linen industry, which had disappeared almost completely, is undergoing a modest revival in high-fashion clothing, and shipbuilding is also surfacing again after reaching rock bottom.

The phone code for Belfast is ☎0232

BELFAST

To Crumlin & Belfast
International Airport

To Larne, Belfast Castle,
Cave Hill & Zoo

(Greyhound &
Stock Car Racing)

Dunmo
Park

ARDOYNE

CRUMLIN ROAD

FLAX STREET

Brookfield
Mill

WOODVALE ROAD

CRUMLIN ROAD

York
Rail S

ANTRIM ROAD

Mater
Hospital

CLIFTON ST.

Crumlin Road
Gaol

SHANKILL

SHANKILL ROAD

SPRINGMARTIN

Li
Ferry

Belfast Cathedral

NORTH ST.

Conway
Mill

DIVIS ST.

Divis
Flats

Tourist
Information

CASTLE ST.

FALLS

SPRINGFIELD ROAD

FALLS ROAD

St. Peter's
Cathedral

ALBERT ST.

City Hall

SPRINGFIELD ROAD

Royal Victoria
Hospital

GROSVENOR ROAD

B.B.C.

BALLYMURPHY

FALLS ROAD

Bus Station &
International
Airport Terminal

GT. VICTORIA ST.

WESTLINK

DONEGALL ST.

WHITEROCK ROAD

City Cemetery

DONEGALL ROAD

DONEGALL ROAD

Arts Theat

TURF
LODGE

Falls Park

GLEN ROAD

Botan
Sta

Y.W.C.A.

UNIVERSITY ST.

Queen's

ANDERSONSTOWN ROAD

Milltown
Cemetery

MOTORWAY M1

Y.W.C.A.

Queen's U

Botanic
Gardens

EGLANTINE AVE.

Ulster
Museum

To Crumlin

To Lisburn

Lyric
Theatre

ANDERSONSTOWN

LISBURN ROAD

ADELAIDE PARK

MALONE ROAD

Queen's Elms
Residences

Gov
B

(Gaelic
Football!)

Casement
Park

Belfast
Boat Club

STRANMILLIS ROAD

To Derry & Dublin

King's Hall

MALONE

LISBURN ROAD

FINAGHY

Arrival

If you **fly** into Belfast you'll arrive either at **Belfast International Airport**, in Aldergrove, 19 miles from the city (airport coaches to Great Victoria Street Bus Station, Mon–Sat half-hourly 6.40am–10.20pm, Sun hourly 7.15am–10.15pm; ☎08494/22888 for airport information), or at **Belfast Harbour Airport**, four miles out (train from Sydenham Halt to Central Station or take a taxi; ☎457745).

Of the **ferries** to Northern Ireland, only the Isle of Man and Liverpool services actually come into Belfast Harbour: the rest dock at Larne, twenty miles to the north. **Donegall Quay**, where the Liverpool ferries dock, is only a short way north of the centre of town: it's easiest to take a taxi from here, or walk through to Great Georges Street where you can pick up city buses to the centre. At **Larne Harbour** *Ulsterbus* services connect with ferry arrivals, running to Great Victoria Street Bus Station, and there are also trains from the harbour to York Road Station.

Coming in by **rail** you'll be at the Central Railway Station (☎230310, 235282) on East Bridge Street, a little way east of the centre (the only exceptions are the trains from Larne Harbour to York Road). A special rail-link bus service runs between the two stations every ten minutes or so, passing through the city centre on the way.

Long-distance **buses** arrive either at Great Victoria Street Bus Station (actually in Glengall Street behind the *Europa Hotel*: services to the west – Armagh, Tyrone, Derry, Fermanagh and west Down – as well as to the Republic and for airport and ferry services) or Oxford Street (for the north and east – Antrim, Down and east Derry). Both of these are extremely central, and well served by city bus services. ☎320011 for *Ulsterbus* information, or there's a brilliant touch-screen computerised **information service** at the Victoria Street station which has full timetables, and information on places to visit and accommodation throughout the whole of northern Ireland.

Regular tourist information is available from the helpful **tourist office**, River House, 48 High Street (☎246609; Mon–Fri 9am–5.15pm, Sat 9am–2pm); they have lots of brochures and maps, and an accommodation booking service.

Accommodation

There's no shortage of **places to stay** in Belfast, ranging from the famous city-centre *Europa Hotel* (on Great Victoria Street by the bus station; from around £90 double; ☎327000) to the youth hostel, but the great majority in fairly ordinary B&Bs from around £10 up. At peak times it may be worth taking advantage of the tourist office's booking service, as they'll know where the vacancies are.

Hostels and student accommodation

Belfast International youth hostel, almost three miles south of the centre at 11 Saintfield Road (the A24 towards Newcastle, bus #38 or #84 from Donegall Square East; £7.50; ☎647865). Just about the cheapest, especially for lone travelers, but price is the only reason to stay: it's a long way out, strictly run, with an 11.15pm curfew, lock-out during the day, compulsory chores, and only two showers.

YMCA, 3–5 Malone Road (☎668347; £10 sharing, £11.50 single). Near the University, and a better bet if you're looking for this type of accommodation, with single rooms (some tiny) and breakfast. Takes men and women.

YWCA, Queen Mary's Hall, 70 Fitzwilliam Street (☎240439; £10 sharing, £11.50 single). A little further from the university, otherwise very similar to the YMCA.

Queen's University lets out student rooms out of term. If you have student ID these are exceptional value, though they are meant to be booked in advance: contact *Queen's Houses*, 14–16 Upper Crescent (☎245133 ext 3740) or *Queen's Elms*, 78 Malone Road (☎381608, 668535). Prices are as low as £6.50 (bed only) for students, though for adult non-students they can be close to B&B prices.

Bed and breakfast

A high proportion of the **B&Bs** are in the university area, south of the centre, especially on Botanic Avenue, Eglantine Avenue and Malone Road. There are dozens, all very similar. Unless otherwise stated, those listed below will charge £12–13:

Botanic Lodge Guest House, 87 Botanic Avenue (☎327682).

Liserin Guest House, 17 Eglantine Avenue (☎660769).

Eglantine Guest House, 21 Eglantine Avenue (☎667585).

East Sheen House, 81 Eglantine Avenue (☎667149). One of the best.

Pearl Court House, 11 Malone Road (☎666145).

Malone Guest House, 79 Malone Road (☎669565).

Beaumont Lodge, 237 Stranmillis Road (☎667965).

Camera House, 44 Wellington Park (☎660026; £22–27). A very luxurious B&B, much better than most Belfast hotels.

Ash-Rowan, 12 Windsor Avenue (☎661758; £25). Similarly superior B&B.

Camping

The nearest **campsites** to the city centre are:

Jordanstown Lough Shore Park, some six miles north in Newtownabbey (Shore Road, Newtownabbey; ☎868751, 863133). Basically a caravan site, but with some tent pitches.

Belvoir Forest, about four miles south. Much nicer, but you need a permit in advance to camp here (from the *Forest Service*, Department of Agriculture, Room 34, Dundonald House, Belfast; ☎650111 ext 456).

Getting about

Although you can walk easily enough around the centre, distances to the more outlying attractions can be considerable, and many of the places to stay are also some way out. Fortunately there's an excellent city bus service that covers almost anywhere you're likely to go, and abundant, relatively inexpensive taxis.

Buses

Almost all **buses** set off from Donegall Square, right at the city centre, or the streets immediately around, and the best way to start is to pick up the map which outlines the main services from the tourist office (you can also phone for bus information on ☎246485). The fare for city centre journeys is 60p, and there's a zone system which comes into operation as you head further out. You can pay on the bus, but you'll save time and a little money if you buy a **multi-journey** ticket in advance (£3.80 for eight journeys, from newsagents and other shops throughout the city). You push the ticket into a machine on the bus (or get the driver to do it) to cancel one journey each time you travel – two people can use the same ticket as long as the ticket is cancelled twice. For journeys across zones, you again have to cancel the ticket twice. *Ulsterbus* also serve the routes from the city centre to Lisburn, via either the Falls and Andersonstown roads, or Lisburn Road. These leave from either Glengall Street, or the Grosvenor Road (☎320011 for details.)

Taxis and driving

Black taxis, which run along set routes into West Belfast, picking up and dropping passengers anywhere along the way, can also be extremely handy, and at less than £1 a journey (for each passenger) they're also cheap. The ones which operate into the Catholic areas (all of these go up the Falls Road itself) set out from the Smithfield area of Castle Street, and some of them will be prepared to give you a tour round Catholic West Belfast for £6–7 an hour. Cabs servicing Protestant areas run from North Street, slightly further north, and charge much the same, though they may find the idea of a tour round Protestant West Belfast a slightly strange one. Some Belfast people are reluctant to use these cabs, believing that the money raised goes into the hands of sectarian racketeers on whichever side. **Regular taxis**, based at the rank in Donegall Square and others throughout the city, charge a minimum £1.50, which rapidly starts to increase on the meter if you're going any distance.

If you're **driving** you need to be careful about where you park your car: it's made abundantly clear that you're not allowed to leave it unattended in a few city centre **control zones** (clearly marked with black-and-yellow signs). There are, however, plenty of car parks, and many city streets have pay and display parking in operation.

The City Centre and the sights of Belfast

Donegall Square, in the centre of which stands the City Hall and from all around which buses and taxis set out for every part of the city, is very much the physical heart of Belfast. To the immediate north is the main shopping and commercial area, to the south entertainments and accommodation. Most of the grand old Victorian buildings so characteristic of the city are within walking distance, especially to the north and to the east, towards the river. Further out, **north Belfast** boasts Cave Hill, with its castle and zoo, and plenty to see on the way there. **South Belfast** has the "Golden Mile", with its pubs and entertainments, stretching out past the University, the Botanic Gardens and Ulster Museum. In the **east**, across the river beyond the great cranes of *Harland & Wolff*, lies suburbia, and very little of interest apart from Stormont Castle, the former Northern Irish parliament. Working-class **West Belfast**, by contrast, seems almost a separate city in its own right; divided from the rest by the lanes of the Westlink motorway.

Around the City Hall

The **City Hall** presides over Belfast city centre, a handy landmark for visitors and principal departure point for city buses. A self-satisfied looking building, quadrangular and squat, its once white Portland stone is now milky-grey and its architecture echoes all the styles the British Empire borrowed from – turrets, saucer domes, scrolls and pinnacle pots. In the eighty-odd years since it was built, any functional civic purpose the building has had has been secondary to its role in propagating the ethics of Presbyterian power. This is clear at the main entrance,

CENTRAL
BELFAST

Harland & Wolff
Shipyard

River Lagan

¼ mile

0

QUEEN'S QUAY

River Lagan

To Liverpool
Ferry Terminal

DONEGALL QUAY

Custom
House

ALBERT SQ.

QUEEN'S
SQUARE

CORPORATION ST.

EXCHANGE STREET

OXFORD STREET

MARLBOROUGH ST.

ANN STREET

LAGANBANK ROAD

Bus Station

Cattle
Market

Central
Train Station

EAST BRIDGE STREET

OXFORD STREET

Oxford St.
Bus Station

Royal Courts
of Justice

VICTORIA STREET

Prince Albert
Memorial
Clock Tower

VICTORIA STREET

Northern Ireland
Tourist Board

SKIPPER STREET

WARING STREET

HIGH STREET

BRIDGE STREET

DONEGALL STREET

NORTH STREET

Belfast
Cathedral

Art College

ROYAL AVENUE

Central
Library

NORTH STREET

WINE TAVERN ST.

Shankill Black
Cab Rank

PETER'S HILL

Smithfield
Market

SMITHFIELD

MILLFIELD

KING STREET

Falls Black
Cab Rank

DIVIS STREET

Lost Property
Office
(Police Station)

ANN STREET

CORNMARKET

Post
Office

CASTLE PLACE

British Rail
/Sealink

CALLENDER STREET

DONEGALL SQ. N.

DONEGALL PLACE

ARTHUR ST.

FOUNTAIN STREET

Bord Fáilte

CASTLE STREET

Aer Lingus

British
Airways

COLLEGE STREET

WELLINGTON PLACE

VICTORIA SQUARE

CHICHESTER STREET

Taxi Rank

Buses

DONEGALL SQ. E.

Linenhall
Library

City Hall

DONEGALL SQ. W.

DONEGALL SQ. S.

MAY STREET

JOY STREET

RUSSELL STREET

LINENHALL ST.

Arts Council
Gallery

Ulster Hall

BEDFORD STREET

Group Theater

WELLINGTON STREET

Crown
Liquor Saloon

To University,
Ulster Museum &
Botanic Gardens

COLLEGE SQUARE EAST

GREAT VICTORIA STREET

Movie Theater

Opera House

GROSVENOR ROAD

GLENGALL STREET

Europa
Hotel

Bus Station/
International
Airport
Terminal

QUEEN ELIZABETH BRIDGE

QUEEN'S BRIDGE

where stands Queen Victoria, portrayed as Empress, her maternal gaze unerringly cast across the rooftops towards the Protestant Shankill area. At her feet, sculpted in bronze, are proud figures representing the City Fathers' work ethic; a young scholar, his mother with spinning spool, and father with mallet and boat. More powerfully intransigent than the symbolic domineering of any of the building's statuary, however, is a banner high up among the colonnades, embracing the main drum, which proclaims the Unionist catchphrase, *Belfast Says No*, an expression of their opposition to the Anglo-Irish Agreement signed in 1985.

The City Hall does, however, offer the only real opportunity to be shown around one of Belfast's many classical buildings: there are 45-minute guided **tours** daily at 10.30am and 2.30pm (July–Sept only) and at 10.30am on Wednesday throughout the rest of the year; admission is free and access is through a security entrance at the rear (opposite Linenhall Street). Inside, the **main dome**, and an unreachable whispering gallery, are 173 feet above you – modelled on that of St Paul's in London, the dome has zodiac signs, both painted and in stained glass windows, around its rim. The marbled **entrance hall** itself is palatial, with staircase pillars and colonnades, and there are bronze and marble statues as well, two of which portray Frederick Robert Chichester, Earl of Belfast (1827–1853): the first, upright and stalwart-looking, stands on the principal landing, while the other, Frederick reclining on his deathbed, has been hauled out of the rain into the Octagon entrance porch.

Also on the principal landing is a **mural**, executed in 1951 by John Luke, celebrating Belfast's traditional industries, now mostly dead – ropemaking, shipbuilding, weaving and spinning. Oddly though, the central position in the picture is given to the Town Crier, perhaps a reference to Belfast having the oldest continuously running newspaper in the world (*The Newsletter*, since 1737). The tour also takes in the **robing room**, where the trick is to ask to try on one of the cloaks for a snapshot. The building's highlight is the **council chamber**, the walls wainscotted in hand-carved oak and its centre filled with councillors' pews and a visitors' gallery (open only on the first of the month), both also in oak. It's a very civilised scene (at least when the council is not in session – meetings are notoriously stormy), hung with portraits of British Royalty and aristocracy; the seating puts the majority Unionists on the far side, with the rest of the parties on the near side, while the everpresent press sit in between.

Linenhall Library

At the northwest corner of Donegall Square stands the **Linenhall Library** (Mon–Wed & Fri 9.30am–6pm, Thurs 9.30am–8.30pm, Sat 9.30am–4pm), Belfast's oldest library, established in 1788. Irish-language and reference books occupy the first floor, fiction is on the ground floor. The library contains probably the best collection of early Belfast printed books in the country. On the second floor, its "Political Collection" is a unique accumulation of over 40,000 publications dealing with every aspect of Northern Irish political life since 1968 – a range of literature that encompasses every election poster printed since then, as well as documents ranging from party political ephemera to doctoral theses sent in from all over the world. This radical approach is not a new departure for the Linenhall: one of the institution's librarians was Thomas Russell, executed in Downpatrick in 1803 for inciting rebellion in sympathy with Robert Emmett's 1798 uprising down south.

The library is an independent institution and you're free to examine its collection: it has a fancy computerised catalogue, on the first floor; free, but a donation is welcome. There are also excellent facilities for tracing family trees, if you're interested; as well as all the daily newspapers and a good tea room.

St Malachy's Church

Between the back of the City Hall and the BBC, on Alfred Street, look out for the turrets of the strange and wonderful **St Malachy's Church** (1844), reckoned to be the finest late Georgian building in Belfast. The interior resembles nothing so much as an inverted wedding cake, and the fan-vaulted ceiling is modelled on that of Henry VII's chapel in Westminster Abbey. The Department of Environment and city council have recently granted planning permission for an office block which would block the front view of the church, a decision which has caused much controversy, especially among Catholics (it's a Catholic church).

The commercial centre: Cornmarket

The streets leading north off Donegall Square North take you into the **city centre** proper, downtown Belfast. The grand old department stores here, in creams, pinks and browns, have only recently been transformed into a flood of up-tempo shops. Mercifully, though, it's only the ground floors that have been converted, leaving the lofty grandeur of the floors above undisturbed. New structures, too, go up swiftly, but they at least tend to reflect the rhythm and sheer hulk of their nineteenth-century forebears. Much of this zone is pedestrianised (though buses go through), and the whole area is cordoned off by security barriers at the major points of entry – and blocked off completely by green military railing at all other routes. That said, there's really little to discover in this area, apart from a few necessary amenities. There are also three recent shopping complexes, The High Park Centre (just off High Street), which has a wide range of shops, multi-storey car parking plus a good range of cheap places where you can eat during the day; the more upmarket Castle Court Centre, on Royal Avenue; and the York Centre in York Street (the continuation of Royal Avenue).

The pedestrianised **Cornmarket**, marked by a cap-hooded bandstand painted red, is where the various cults gather; skinheads, punks, Mods and drunks, though most prevalent are the religious chanteurs. This spot (near enough) is also where Henry Joy McCracken was hanged, after leading the Antrim rebels in the ill-fated (and in the north almost farcically unsuccessful) 1798 rebellion.

From the Entries to the docks

Nearby, along Ann Street, and off down any left or right turning, you're in among the narrow alleyways known as the **Entries**. There are some great old saloon **bars** down here, like *The Morning Star* in Pottinger's Entry, with its large frosted windows and Parisian café-like counter; *The Globe* in Joy's Entry; and *White's Tavern* in Winecellar Entry (off High Street), the oldest pub in the city. **Crown Entry** was where the "Society of United Irishmen" was born, led by the Protestant triumvirate of Wolfe Tone, McCracken and Samuel Nielson: Nielson printed his own newspaper in this area, the *Northern Star*, full of the French revolutionary ideals of liberty, equality and fraternity – inflammatory material which got him hounded out of town. Also in Crown Entry, Sheridan, the playwright (of *School for Scandal* fame) had his "pathetic" comic school.

Across the High Street, to the north, there used to be a similar set of Entries that ran through to Waring Street, but many of them were destroyed by bombing during World War II. Still, this end of the **High Street**, with the Farset River running underground (and invisible) below, is the oldest part of the city, its atmosphere in places redolent of the eighteenth century. At the docks end of the High Street is the **Prince Albert Memorial Clock Tower**, built in 1867–69 and wilting slightly off the perpendicular. It's a strange memorial, especially as Prince Albert never had anything to do with Belfast, but it's a handy landmark. And beyond here are more of the grand old classical-style buildings that stud Belfast (see below).

Across the river: East Belfast

The Prince Albert Memorial is a good position from which to view the world's second and third largest cranes, *Goliath* and *Samson*, across the river in the *Harland & Wolff* **shipyard** in East Belfast. They are the city's proudest international asset: among others, the ill-fated *Titanic* was built here and the shipyard is nowadays said to possess the largest dry dock in the world – over 600 yards long and 100 yards wide. Unfortunately, the area is very security conscious, as its workforce has always been predominantly Protestant, and access is impossible without making a formal application.

In fact there's virtually no reason to cross the river into **East Belfast** at all. **Van Morrison** fans might get a thrill from seeking out the many streets that feature in his songs, and there are a couple of pleasant **parks**, but few more concrete reasons to come. For transport buffs, the **Witham Street Gallery**, in Witham Street off Newtownards Road (Mon–Sat 10am–5pm; buses #16, #21, #22 or #24 or train to Bridge End station) is a collection of carriages, cars, trams, trains, bicycles and motorbikes that forms part of the Ulster Folk and Transport Museum (see "Down and Armagh"), and its exhibits are rotated with the ones there. The nucleus of the exhibition is the collection of Thomas Edens Osborne, a local bicycle dealer who was an associate of John Dunlop (of tyre fame): it runs from the earliest vehicles to Northern Ireland's most recent and disastrous association with the motor industry, De Lorean.

Stormont, the former home of the Northern Ireland assembly, is also east of the city, off the Newtownards road (#16 or #17 bus from Donegall Square). You can't visit the house itself – which is now occupied by civil servants – but it's an impressive sight, a great white Neoclassical mansion crowning a rise in the middle of a park at the end of a magnificent long, straight drive. You can wander freely in the **grounds**, a popular place for a walk; also here, though obviously not open to the public, is **Stormont Castle**, the office of the Northern Ireland Secretary.

From the Albert Memorial to the Cathedral

North of the Albert Memorial are a series of grand edifices which grew out of a similar civic vanity as that invested in the designing of the City Hall. The **Customs House**, a Corinthian-style building designed by Charles Lanyon between 1854 and 1857, is laid out just behind the memorial in the shape of a letter E. Unfortunately, it's not open to the public, leaving you unable to verify stories of fantastic art masterpieces stored in its basements – though it is known that Anthony Trollope, the nineteenth-century novelist (and not-so-well-known inventor of the pillar box), once worked here as a surveyor's clerk.

Another of Lanyon's designs, the **Belfast Banking Company** building (1845, now the Northern Bank), is at the Donegall Street end of Waring Street. Originally an eighteenth-century Assembly Rooms, it was transformed by Lanyon into a palazzo-style remodelling of Barry's *Reform Club* in London. On the same street, you'll also stumble upon the **Ulster Bank** (1860), an indulgent Italianate building of rich yellow sandstone, fronted by a spate of fluted pillars and, up on the parapet, with decorated Grecian urns at the sides of an allegorical representation of war maidens. There's a surround of intricately wrought iron railing and a few reassembled Victorian street lamps, too, stubby but quaint.

St Anne's Cathedral

The most monolithic of all these grand buildings, however, is the Protestant **Cathedral** of St Anne's, a neo-Romanesque basilica started in 1899. It's at the junction of Donegall Street and York Street, close to the beached buoys of the modern Art College. There's a glorious west door, but its over-riding significance is that the body of **Lord Edward Henry Carson** is entombed underneath the nave floor. Carson (1854–1935) is a name that Ulster has never forgotten: the bodily symbol of Partition, he's seen either as the hero who saved Ulster, or the villain who sabotaged the country's independence. A Dubliner of Scots-Presbyterian background, Carson took the decision in 1910 to accept the leadership of the opposition to Home Rule, which in effect inextricably allied him to the Ulster Unionist resistance movement – an association which is about the only thing for which he is remembered. Yet his personality and integrity went far deeper than this. He abhorred religious intolerance and, behind the exterior of a zealous crusade, he sincerely believed that Ireland couldn't prosper without Britain, and only wished that a federalist answer could have involved a united Ireland. Nonetheless, this was the same man who, as a brilliant orator at the bar, and in the role he loved the most, brought about the humiliating destruction of Oscar Wilde at his trial in 1895.

Clifton House

As it continues north Donegall Street becomes Clifton Street, which takes its name from **Clifton House** (1771–74). Better known as the "Poor House", or the "Charitable Institute for the Aged and Infirm", it's in handsome Georgian style, of pedimented brick with an octagonal-based stone spire at its rear and symmetrically projecting wings to its sides. This is one of the simpler but more effective buildings that Belfast has to offer, yet was designed by an amateur architect and local paper merchant, Robert Joy, uncle of the hapless Henry Joy McCracken. The Institute was built at a time of much poverty and unrest, brought about by the Donegalls' eviction of tenants when their leases started running out – the very same Donegalls whose name is tagged to so many of Belfast's streets.

South Belfast: the university area and the river

The university area occupies part of the stretch of **South Belfast** now known as "The Golden Mile", starting at the Opera House on Great Victoria Street and reaching past the University, up into the Malone, Lisburn and Stranmillis roads. It's an area in which you're likely to find yourself spending much of your time, since it's littered with eating places, pubs and bars, B&Bs and guesthouses. Dozens of restaurants have sprung up here in the last few years, the gourmet explosion said to have been triggered by the refurbishment of the grandiose, turn-of-the-century **Grand Opera House** in 1980. In December 1991 a bomb in the adjacent *Europa Hotel* cause extensive damage to the Opera House, which is likely to remain closed for some time.

The Golden Mile

Among the welter of attractions on the Golden Mile is one of the greatest of Victorian **gin palaces**, the *Crown Liquor Saloon*; now a National Trust property but still open for drinking. The saloon has a glittering tiled exterior – amber, carmine, rouge, yellow, green, blue and smoke-grey – resembling a Spa Baths more than a serious drinking institution. The rich, High Victorian stucco-work continues inside, too: the scrolled ceiling, patterned floor and the golden-yellow and rosy-red hues led John Betjeman to describe it as his "many coloured cavern". With your drinks, grab a snug and shut the door (best to avoid the busy lunchtime and mid-evening periods): it's like sitting in a railway-carriage compartment, with snatches of conversation creeping over from the neighbouring snugs. There's no let-up in decoration in here either, the mirrors painted, the oak panelling sporting flourishes of friezework (like the heraldic beasts guarding each snug entry) and the mounted gun-metal plates provided for striking matches. The push-button bell activates an indicator on a board above the bar, though it's just as much an experience to order at the bar from the white-aproned and black-bowtied staff – the bar counter a gorgeous S-curve of tile work, with exotically carved timber dividing screens.

The **Golden Mile** itself buzzes with activity in the evening, even on a weekday as long as it's in term time. As a rule, the cheaper restaurants are at the city end of Great Victoria Street, with the more expensive ones up the Stranmillis Road and in and around the skirts of the BBC in Bedford Street. There's a plethora of accommodation, too, in amongst the grid pattern of the broad, tree-lined streets surrounding the University campus, much of it in the old three-storey Victorian homes. The area also has two excellent antiquarian **bookshops** on Dublin Road, Roma Ryan's *Books and Prints* and *Prospect House Books*, both pretty good for Irish material, though the prices are not giveaways by anyone's standards; and also a few secondhand bookshops, the best being *Bookfinders* (Mon–Sat 10am–5.30pm, Thurs until 7pm) at 47 University Road.

Sandy Row

Before heading straight into the University quarter, sidestep off Great Victoria Street into **Sandy Row**, which runs parallel. A strong, working-class, Protestant quarter with the tribal pavement painting to prove it, it's one of the most glaring examples of Belfast's divided worlds, wildly different from the Golden Mile's cosmopolitan sophistication, yet only yards away. In Donegall Road, off to the west, are some of the murals which characterise these sectarian areas – see under "West Belfast", below. Sandy Row used to be the main road south and, although hard to credit today, it was once a picturesque, shoelace stretch of whitewashed cottages.

The University area

Back on the Golden Mile, and just past the southern end of Sandy Row, are three churches (Moravian, Crescent and Methodist) whose distinctive steeples frame the entrance into the **University quarter**. It's a highly characteristic area, many of the terraces leading up to the university buildings representing the final flowering of Georgian architecture in Belfast. The **Upper Crescent** is a magnificent curved Neoclassical terrace, built around 1845 but sadly neglected since, and now used mainly for office space. The **Lower Crescent**, perversely, is straight.

It's **Queen's University**, though, that's the architectural centrepiece of the area, flanked by the most satisfying example of a Georgian terrace in Belfast, University Square, where the red brickwork has mostly been kept intact, with the exception of a few bay-windows put in by the Victorians. The terrace now houses various faculty buildings. The **Union Theological College** on College Park, which was temporarily the site of the Northern Ireland assembly until Stormont was built in 1932, closes off the vista between the terrace and the university. Not surprisingly, given its Italianate lines, this is another Lanyon design, as is the University College itself, built in 1849 as a mock-Tudor remodelling of Magdalen College, Oxford. Across the road from here is the Students' Union, a white 1960s design.

Botanic Gardens and Ulster Museum

Just to the side of the University are the **Botanic Gardens**, first opened in 1827 and deservedly the most popular of Belfast's gardens – compact, with walks well sheltered from the noise of surrounding traffic. Within the gardens is the **Palm House** (Mon–Fri 10am–5pm, Sat & Sun 2–5pm; free), a hot-house predating the famous one at Kew Gardens in London, but very similar in style, with a white-painted framework of curvilinear ironwork and glass. It was the first of its kind in the world, another success for Lanyon who on this project worked in tandem with the Dublin iron-founder Richard Turner.

Also in the Botanic Gardens you'll find the **Ulster Museum** (Mon–Fri 10am–5pm, Sat 1–5pm, Sun 2–5pm; free; buses #69, #71, #72, #83 or #85), re-sited here in 1929 and expanded in 1972 with a concrete extension that matches the Portland stone surprisingly subtly. You'll need a fair bit of stamina to get round the museum, since it's a monster of a collection. Displays run from a dinosaur show, through reproductions of early Irish Christian jewellery, to the history of the post office in Ireland, waterwheels and steam engines, local archaeological finds, Irish wildlife, rocks, fossils and minerals – the list is exhaustive and exhausting. Still, everything is well-explained and well laid out, and if you're keen to know about crocodiles' digestive systems or see a 35-million-year-old mackerel, then you could happily spend a full day here. (Though if you have the time, the museum is much more enjoyable taken in several small doses.)

The various **art collections** are excellent: try the top floor for modern work by Francis Bacon or Henry Moore and, best of all (and the one thing you won't see elsewhere), the Irish artists represented – Louis le Brocquy, Paul Henry and Belfast's own most acclaimed painter, Sir John Lavery. The museum's **Girona exhibition**, treasures from the Spanish Armada ships which foundered off the Giant's Causeway, and the museum's showpiece, can't be viewed at present.

Further south: the river and Giant's Ring

To go beyond the University area is to head through the glades of middle-class suburbia – an area that is singularly uninteresting. However, a ten- to fifteen-minute walk out on Stranmillis Road (the name derived from *struthán milis*, "sweet stream") will take you to the **Lagan Towpath**: follow the signs to the Lagan Meadows. The newly tarred towpath can be tramped for about eight miles to Lisburn, passing old locks and lock-houses, rapids, woodland and marshes. The waterway opened in the late 1790s, ready to carry the newly discovered coal from Lough Neagh, but its utility declined with the advent of the railway in 1839. Today, it's been harnessed as part of the *Ulster Way*, for rambling and canoeing enthusiasts. Travelling south towards the affluent Malone Road area, you'll find the internationally-renowned **Mary Peters Track**, part of the Malone Playing Fields, which is just off the Upper Malone Road. Set in what amounts to a natural amphitheatre, with the Castlereagh Hills in the distance, the track, established by Olympic gold medallist Mary Peters, is on the European Grand Prix Athletics Circuit.

Less of a walk, but just as interesting, is to head a couple of miles up the river path to Shaw's Bridge, and from there up a country road, following signs to Edenderry, along Ballysillan Road; and lastly a right turn up Giant's Ring Road. Here, the **Giant's Ring** is a gargantuan, ceremonial burial ground or meeting place, its grassy interior the size of three football pitches, contained by a twenty-foot-high circular earthen rim. You wouldn't be far wrong to think that its inwardly sloping wall would make an excellent speed-track circuit, for in the eighteenth century it was used for horse racing – six circuits making a two-mile race, with the punters jostling for position on the rampart's top. Most captivating of all is the huge dolmen left at the central hub of this cartwheel structure. As a single megalithic remain it is immediately more impressive even than the great structures of the Irish High Kings at Tara, though here there's little information concerning its origins and usage. The ground chosen for the site, high above the surrounding lowlands (probably once marshy lake), is an impressive one: there's a powerful feeling that the great dramas and decision-making of the ancient northeast must have been played out here. If you want to do the walk in just one direction, *Ulsterbus* #22 passes below the site three times a day.

North Belfast: Cave Hill

North Belfast's attractions amount to no more than a castle and the city's **zoo**, out on the Antrim Road (daily 10am–5pm; buses #2, #3, #4, #5 or #6), both conveniently next door to one another on the slopes of Cave Hill. In truth, though, it's **Cave Hill** itself that should be your real target.

Several paths lead up from the castle estate to the hill's summit – a rocky outcrop known as "Napoleon's Nose" – where there's an unsurpassable strategic overview of the whole city and lough. From here you can't help but appreciate the accuracy of the poet Craig Raine's aerial description of the city in his *Flying to Belfast* – like "a radio set with its back ripped off". Cave Hill was once awash with Iron Age forts, for there was flint (for weapon-making) in the chalk under the basalt hill-coverings. In 1795, Wolfe Tone, Henry Joy McCracken and other leaders of the United Irishmen stood on the top of Cave Hill and pledged "never to desist in our efforts until we have subverted the authority of England over our country and asserted our Independence".

Belfast Castle (and its wooded estate) is open to the public, recently upholstered and restored but, sadly, virtually empty of period accoutrements – the one exception is the recently reopened basement kitchen. It stands on the former deer park of the third Marquis of Donegall, whose wish it was for the sandstone castle to be built here to the designs of Lanyon and his associates, in 1870. Consequently, the exterior is in the familiar Scottish Baronial style, inspired in part by the reconstruction of Balmoral Castle in Aberdeenshire in 1853: six-storey tower, a series of crow-stepped gables and conically peak-capped turrets. The most striking feature of all, however, is the serpentine Italianate stairway that leads down from the principal reception room to the garden-terrace below. There are two **restaurants**, one nouvelle-cuisine and expensive, the other much simpler.

West Belfast

West Belfast has always been the city's working-class area. Here, in the eighteenth century, the flax and linen mills were established which in turn produced the relentless, gridded street pattern, lined with housing for the workers and their families. The overcrowded conditions were deplorable, and the sectarian riots of 1886 – the worst of the nineteenth century – inspired the creation of two separate neighbourhoods, Catholic and Protestant. In 1968 and 1969 this division was pushed to its limit when sectarian mobs and gunmen evicted over 8000 families from their homes in the city, mainly in Catholic West Belfast.

Today, however, West Belfast is no Beirut. It's as safe an urban area as any for the stranger to stroll around, and although it's principally residential, several of its sectors are worth investigating. Of most interest are the partisan **mural paintings** seen in both Catholic and Protestant areas, an ephemeral art with new murals replacing old ones as the houses they're painted on are demolished. As you wander the back streets, you'll be captivated (sometimes captured) by the extraordinarily open friendliness of the people, an experience that's the high point of many people's stay in Belfast: you'll not come across this openness in any other part of the city, more remarkable here given the rigours of life in West Belfast.

The busy **Westlink motorway**, which effectively separates West Belfast from the rest of the city, linking Motorways 1 and 2, seems innocent enough as it sweeps across the city, but there are those who see it in a more sinister light, as part of the security process. Certainly it's handy for the police and army, restricting east–west access to a handful of the main arteries. These points, overhead bridges and roundabouts, are virtual border crossings, easily sealed and easily monitored. It looks menacing too: a footbridge over the motorway walled and roofed to keep missiles away from the cars passing below.

The Falls

Two routes lead into the heart of the **Falls** area (known as Andersonstown); one along Grosvenor Road, the other through Divis Street. The latter is the more infamous and is also the route that carries the main injection of black taxi-cab traffic into the area. The taxis assemble in ranks at the end of Castle Street, in the Smithfield area, their routes strictly into the Catholic enclaves; a printed sign in Gaelic (one of the few official-looking ones of its kind in Belfast) should be enough to emphasise the point for you. Rides are set at a fixed rate of around 50p and the cab leaves once it's full. The drivers, incidentally, are said to be Republican ex-prisoners.

Smithfield itself used to have a large, covered bazaar which has now been replaced by **Smithfield Retail Market** – actually a set of small shop units rather than a traditional open-air market. The area has recently undergone large-scale redevelopment by private developers (another shopping complex) and Belfast City Council also have plans to extend and improve the Smithfield market itself. There is a reminder of the old character of the area in Winetavern Street, with several bookshops and junky antique places.

The Divis Flats and Divis Street

Crossing the Westlink via Divis Street confronts you immediately with the single most devastating symbol of disillusionment in the area – the **Divis Flats**. The flats take their name from Divis Mountain, the highest in the surrounding bowl of hills, whose name translates – poignantly – as the "mountain of tears". The twin spires rising behind the flats belong to **St Peter's Catholic Cathedral**, a nineteenth-century Gothic design, modelled on the spires of Cologne cathedral. At the base of the flats, the moonscape wasteground is the only play area for the children. It's fringed with a necklace of kerbstones, placed there by the community to keep out joyriders, who used to trek here from all over the North.

The flats themselves are a structural disaster. Ugly, grey, punctured by coloured cardboard and window glass, the ceilings and beams are cracked, sewage outlets blocked (by infestation with rats), the detritus flooding from one home to another, the lifts broken, the stairways unlit, asbestos visible – while unemployment in the blocks exceeds eighty percent. To have begun building Divis (in the late 1960s) at a time when the rest of Europe already regarded such structures as failures was a decision of the blindest ignorance, and in 1983 the Divis community set up a "development committee", its main objective to bring about the demolition of the flats. A few blocks have already gone and total destruction is expected in around seven or eight years' time. Or maybe longer. The last block to be demolished will almost certainly be **Divis Tower**, capped by a military fort of corrugated iron sheeting. Along with its sister fort, further south next to the roundabout at Donegall Street, this is one of the few high-rise places round here that has no problem with the lift, as supplies and personnel are flown in by helicopter. If you're keen to have a closer look at the flats, no one will take offence: in fact, having been ignored for so long, your intrusion will probably be welcomed.

A little further up Divis Street, on the other side of the road, is a gable wall **mural**, striking because of its pacifist content; a Madonna and Child, serenely centred in a pale blue sky and surrounded by little white clouds. Predictably, though, even this traditional theme doesn't go untainted. Below the scene is a turbulent sea, its violent waves a bile-green, and the swaddling-clothes are finely streaked in the creases with blood-red.

The Falls Road

Moving on, you enter the **Falls Road** proper, which continues for a further two miles out past Milltown Cemetery (see below) and into Andersonstown. There's a life and activity along this route the like of which you'll find nowhere else in Belfast, with the possible exception of the Shankill Road – shared taxis being flagged down, the odd collection of loitering males, an armed foot patrol edging its way along, and kids and prams being pushed through the streets. Most of the interest is concentrated in the **Lower Falls** (which is the area you've now entered), the road's left-hand side flattened and rebuilt with redbrick terraced estates of two-up and two-downs. The right side of the road is more of a hotch potch, taking in the bright blue swimming baths (target of an IRA bomb in 198 that killed two Catholic civilians), the DHSS (known as "the Brew") cooped up in an awning of chicken wire, a weary-looking Victorian library, and a *Worshippers of Peace* Convent.

Over the road from here, a mural expresses solidarity with the African National Congress (ANC), Nelson Mandela's portrait enlarged in a semi-silhouette; though the ANC was swift in its rejection of any such support from the IRA. By now, too, you'll have noticed the blockade of iron sheeting which divides the streets. Called the **"Peace Line"**, it has the Protestant working class living directly on the other side. Down one of these streets, Conway Street (by the DHSS), stands the old Conway Mill, recently revitalised by a concerted community effort, spearheaded by community activist Father Des Wilson. Inside you can buy the wares of the few small businesses that operate out of here, or you can get a square meal and mug of tea for 50p in the small community canteen on the second floor.

Further on you'll pass the redbrick buildings of the **Royal Victoria Hospital**, on the left as you head towards Andersonstown. Since the Troubles began, the Royal, as it's known locally, has been internationally acclaimed for its ability to cope with the consequences. Just beyond the Royal in a disused church at 216 Falls Road is the **Cultúrlann MacAdam O' Fiaich**, a centre for Irish speakers. The Irish language is thriving in Catholic areas of Belfast and throughout the north: the first Irish-speaking primary school is now over twenty years old, and the first secondary school opened in 1991.

There's little to see beyond here, although a few hundred yards further down the Falls Road, on the left across a small rubble patch, is one of the more powerfully evocative of the Republican murals. It carries the words of Mairead Farrell: "I have always believed we had a legitimate right to take up arms and defend our country and ourselves against the British occupation". Farrell, a prominent member of the IRA, was gunned down by an SAS team in March 1988 (along with Sean Savage and Danny McCann), in the controversial and much-publicised Gibraltar murders.

Milltown Cemetery

Follow the road on for another mile and it'll lead to **Milltown Cemetery**, recognisable by the army encampment opposite the entrance. A peaceful place, it's significant as the main Republican burial ground in Belfast – and was also the site of grenade-throwing and shooting in 1988 at the funeral of Sean Savage, one of the IRA men killed by the SAS in Gibraltar. Enter through the stone arch and you're immediately surrounded by a numbing array of Celtic and classical crosses. If you're in search of the Republican plots, continue directly on from the entrance for about a hundred yards, then veer right, heading towards a corrugated warehouse shed just outside the perimeter of the cemetery. Along the way are two plots, marked off by a low green border fence. The nearer one holds a large memorial tablet listing the Republican casualties in the various uprisings from 1798 to the present day. The far plot contains a modern granite-block sculpture, and also the graves of Bobby Sands, Mairead Farrell, Sean Savage and others. Once you start to look, it's not difficult to spot the graves of many other victims of the Troubles, a devastatingly long list of (usually young) men and women. The M1 motorway lies below, at the bottom of the burial park: it was onto this stretch of road that Michael Stone, the Loyalist attacker, was pursued after he'd opened fire at the funeral of Sean Savage.

The Ballymurphy murals

There's one last set of **murals** worth taking in, up behind the Falls area in the **Ballymurphy Estate**. To get there, turn right off the Falls Road up Whiterock Road, passing alongside the City Cemetery wall and its slogans ("He is not your son but what if he was" and "The West has the best Vote Sinn Féin"). Once over the brow of the hill, take the next right into Ballymurphy Road, heading towards Springhill Avenue.

This whole area is in the process of being levelled to make room for new housing, but in the meantime the burnt-out hulks of masonry couldn't possibly look more depressing. The only relief is in the colour of the mural paintings. One carries the proclamation "Our day will come", showing three paramilitaries with guns raised in front of the tricolour; another nearby is an astonishing contrast, depicting a peaceful, nineteenth-century scene of reaping the hay on a sunny harvest day. Turn past this last mural up towards Springfield Road and, a hundred yards or so up on the left, you'll see two of the most highly regarded gable-wall murals in Belfast.

The first is an enlarged copy of a Jim Fitzpatrick mythological piece, dazzlingly well executed by a young Belfast man, **Gerry Kelly**. Mural painting has taken on such a standing in the community that a competition is held to elect an annual winner: Kelly has been responsible for many Republican murals and this particular one was elected the winner for 1988. It shows an over-muscular, helmeted warrior in athletic pose, brandishing a smoking blade in his right hand with sunrays colourfully torpedoing out in concentric circles from around him. It celebrates the arrival of the *Tuatha Dé Danann*, said to have been the fourth of the six legendary colonies which invaded Ireland, arriving in 1896 BC. Legend has it that they came from four cities in the northern Greek islands, from where they learned their druidry and magic. The character here, Lug – best-known king of the Tuatha – is portrayed as protector of the Catholics.

The other mural here couldn't offer a more strikingly realist alternative. Painted in memory of the eight IRA men ambushed and shot by the British security forces at Loughgall in May 1987, it lists the names of the dead men alongside representations of them in black caps and combat uniform: in the background are the green Armagh hills, a fiery sky and blue water, the usual symbolism of territorial claims. A little further up on the right are lesser murals; a portrait of Bob Marley; a small twelve-piece set showing the demise of the Union Jack, fragment by fragment, giving rise to the Starry Plough; a humorous cartoon mural on "low profile"; and a "Free Leonard Peltier" appeal. Peltier was a North American Indian said to have been framed by the FBI – another example of the community's need to feel solidarity with other oppressed groups around the world.

The Shankill and Crumlin Roads

The Protestant areas of West Belfast receive much less attention from visitors, yet they're no less interesting – and no less deprived in terms of unrest and economic misfortune. Suffering in West Belfast operates more on a class scale than a sectarian one. For the outsider, this area is particularly rich in murals and if you want to see them, the Protestants have their own taxi-ranks, with shared cabs departing from the top of North Street – fares again are around the 50p mark.

Shankill Road

Crossing the Westlink into the **Shankill Road** (its name comes from *sean chill*, the old church), the graffiti begins to tell a different story; one says "The British army is welcome in Ulster". A little way up on the left is a typical Ulster Volunteer Force mural, its centrepiece the outline of the six counties, without the rest of Ireland. At either side of the province stand two paramilitaries, one a 1912 Ulster Volunteer Defender in "home guard" attire, the other a contemporary Loyalist in all-black body and head gear. Accompanying them is the slogan "They fought then for the cause of Ulster. We will fight now".

An alleyway on the right here will lead you into the **Shankill estate**. Almost immediately you'll find yourself in the midst of the greatest concentration of wall paintings around (there are more in Percy Place, nearby). In conception and technique, Protestant mural painting is markedly different from the Catholic tradition. Here, instead of sophisticated artwork, the execution is simple, symmetrical and largely unsymbolic. One mural depicts a thin William of Orange on his white horse; others show flag waving, the emotive expression of loyalism as a creed. Slogans abound – "One faith, one Crown; Ulster Scotland, United we stand", and others which need no explanation, mostly executed in red, white and blue.

Further up the Shankill Road, on the wall of a Protestant social club on the right, another mural is a seventieth anniversary commemoration, comparing the volunteers of the Somme to the UVF prisoners of war in Long Kesh – a message to the British authorities to get their priorities in order. Eighty yards further, on the left, a monochrome drawing again commemorates the UVF of 1912. It has four volunteers, with rifles firing in the course of battle, positioned around their armoured vehicle – a statement that alludes to their fight being in defence of their property.

Crumlin Road

The **Crumlin Road**, too (you can easily make your way across from any point here), offers several gable walls for mural musing. Most are faded, but there's a prominent set at Queen's Land Street, with a particularly unusual one in which shamrocks and the harp (traditional emblems of the Free State) are depicted alongside the red hand of Ulster. Others on the street depict the Star of David, possibly a statement of solidarity with Israel against the PLO and hence the IRA – the PLO/IRA link is tacitly acknowledged by all.

Heading back towards the city you'll pass an army encampment, set back from the road, with a tentacled iron sheeting corridor and lookout post. Further down, you pass between the courthouse and the notorious Crumlin Road jail, with their underground connecting tunnel. Finally, at **Carlisle Circus**, the roundabout with the missing statue that was once of Ian Paisley's nineteenth-century counterpart, Roaring Hanna, there's a mostly unimpressive mural chronicling the death of William McCullagh, a leading UDA man who was shot dead on the Shankill Road by the INLA in 1981, in retaliation for a spate of sectarian murders carried out by Loyalists.

Donegall Road

Other Loyalist murals can be seen along the **Donegall Road**, west off Sandy Row. As you cross the railway bridge approaching the Westlink you'll catch sight of a very large wall painting on the gable end of Roden Street; it can be seen clearly from Donegall Road itself. It bears the mottos "Quis Separabit" and "In memory of John McMichael", with the abbreviated initials of four of the organisations under his command, the UFF, UDF, LPA and DSD. McMichael was killed in December 1987 by a bomb placed under his car. As well as being a leading member of the UDA he was responsible for forming its political wing, the Ulster Loyalist Democratic Party and for formulating the UDA document "Common Sense".

Not far from the roundabout on the Westlink is a photogenic mural of King William, this time on a very indignant white horse, rearing out of the waters of the Boyne. The Protestant Donegall Road ends at this intersection, and the same road continues on the other side as the Catholic Sraid Dun Na nGall – the only road in West Belfast that the communities can really be said to share.

Food, drink and entertainment

This is a big city, and it's rarely hard to find something to eat, or to keep yourself amused in the evenings, even if the latter more often than not means drinking in a pub. In the last resort, there are plenty of **takeaway** and **fast-food** places around the city centre, many of which will still be open when the pubs close. Many of the best places to eat and drink are just south of the city centre, along the Golden Mile.

Eating

Breakfast

If you're staying at a B&B, chances are you'll emerge in the morning full of enough fried food to keep you going all day, but if you do want **breakfast** you'll find plenty of cafés ready to dish up a good old-fashioned "Ulster Fry".

Bonne Bouche, Fountain Street in the centre. Here you'll be stuffed with bacon, eggs, sausage, tomato, potato bread, soda bread and pancake, all for around £1.

Isibeals, High Street. Another good bet for breakfast, though mainly a burger place.

Golden Mile

This is definitely the place to head for food. Down the **Golden Mile** you're spoilt for choice, and all you really have to do is wander down Great Victoria Street until you see something that takes your fancy. In the evening it's also much the liveliest part of town. A few to look out for include (from the top down):

Boyne Bridge Tavern, Sandy Row, across the road from the tobacco factory, very handy for the bus station. Limited, meaty menu but good value.

The Archana, Amelia Street, behind the *Crown Liquor Saloon*. Indian restaurant, very cheap for lunch Monday to Wednesday, eat-all-you-can buffet Sunday evening.

Moghul Restaurant, Great Victoria Street. Another Indian place nearby, again with lunchtime and Sunday night specials.

Ruby King, Great Victoria Street. Decent Chinese restaurant.

Harveys Pizzas, 95 Great Victoria Street (☎233433; noon–midnight). Popular pizza joint; four-course lunch for £4.25.

La Belle Epoque, 103 Great Victoria Street (☎323244). Fancy, expensive French restaurant – main courses around £10.

The Butler Delicatessen, Dublin Road (Mon–Fri 8.30am–7pm, Sat 9am–6pm, Sun noon–7pm). A good deli where you can also sit down and eat.

Chez Delbart, also known as *Frogities*, 10 Bradbury Place, off Great Victoria Street (☎238020). Good food at good prices, though you often have to queue. Serves wine or bring your own bottle (there's a shop across the road) for £1 corkage.

Speranza, 16 Shaftesbury Square (☎230213). Massively popular Italian. Three courses for under a tenner; expect to queue.

Roscoffs, 7 Lesley House, Shaftesbury Square (☎331532). Thought by some to be the best restaurant in Ireland. Modern. Expensive. Book.

Bookfinders, University Road just before the University. Second-hand bookshop serving healthy lunches in room at the rear.

Saints and Scholars, University Road, Cheap and cheerful student place, good for vegetarians.

Students' Union Cafeteria, second and third floors of the Union building, lunchtime only. Adequate and cheap.

Rajput, 461 Lisburn Road. Further out, beyond the Golden Mile, but handy for some B&Bs. A good Indian restaurant.

Friars' Bush, 159 Stranmillis Road (☎669824). Again much further out, does excellent four course meal including wine for under £15.

Centre

Despite the obvious attractions of the Golden Mile, there will be times when you won't be there: in the centre there are plenty of lunch places, especially in the pubs. Most serve food at lunchtime.

Kelly's Cellars, 30 Bank Street, down the side of the *Allied Irish Bank*. One of the best places for lunch.

Capstan Bar, 10 Ann Street. Good pub grub.

Bradan Bar, 83 May Street. More pub lunches.

Kitchen Bar, Victoria Square. Has astonishing Irish pizzas with a soda-bread base.

White's Tavern, Winecellar Entry. Claims to be the oldest pub in the city, but the food's fine.

The Deer's Head, round the corner from the tourist office. Recently refurbished pub, superior bar snacks.

Spice of Life, 62 Lower Donegall Street, opposite St Anne's Cathedral. Good vegetarian fare in what claims to be Belfast's only wholefood restaurant.

The Upper Crust, Lombard Street. Salad bar, guaranteed to be packed with shoppers and office workers at lunchtime.

West Belfast

In West Belfast there's not a great deal of choice, but there are two of the cheapest places to eat in the city.

Conway Mill, Conway Street, off Falls Road. Community centre where you'll get a basic but substantial main dish and a mug of tea for under £1.

Mill Diner, Crumlin Road, part of the Brookfield Mill complex (Mon–Fri 9am–3pm). Excellent value sandwiches and light meals.

Pubs

The situation with **pubs** is very much the same as with restaurants: the liveliest are on Great Victoria Street or down around the University, and if you start drinking at the *Crown* you can do a substantial pub crawl without moving more than about 100 yards from where you started.

Golden Mile

The Crown Liquor Saloon, Great Victoria Street opposite the *Europa Hotel*. The most famous and spectacular pub in Belfast (see p.434) with a clientele that likes to think itself intellectual (there's no music). Good repertory of Ulster food – champ, colcannon etc. – and also Strangford oysters in season, usually gone by early afternoon.

Robinsons, Great Victoria Street, next door. Slightly less glamorous version of the *Crown*; may be closed for refurbishment.

The Britannic Lounge, Amelia Street, above the *Crown's* side entrance. Sedate, cosy and faintly exclusive (and more expensive than usual), this place even has a uniformed foyer attendant. Has some interesting *Harland & Wolff* pictures and memorabilia, including items from the *Britannic* liner itself, the sister ship of the *Titanic*.

The Beaten Docket, Great Victoria Street, just below the *Crown*. Packed with fashion-conscious youngsters upstairs and down. Very loud music.

The Linenhall, Clarence Street, round the corner from the BBC. BBC accent control zone. A very self-congratulatory place, yuppy and arty, but a pleasant bar – food at lunchtimes, but best in the evenings when they sometimes have music in the (otherwise closed) back lounge.

Cratchets, Lisburn Road at the corner of Camden Street, near the University. Another trendy crowd.

Lavery's Gin Palace, Bradbury Place. Snazzy outside but a regular pub within, with a student and local crowd. Popular, though for no apparently special reason. Next door is Belfast's first *McDonalds*.

Students' Union, University Road. Basement bar and first-floor "speakeasy" with lots of heavy student drinking, but good-natured and cheap. You're really meant to be a student to drink here, but no one seems to mind.

The Eglantine Inn, Malone Road. Known to the students who pack it out as the "Egg". Very crowded, with a disco bar upstairs for the smart casual set.

The Botanic Inn, Malone Road opposite the "Egg". Perhaps inevitably, known as the "Bot". Again almost entirely students, and plenty of atmosphere.

The Empire, Botanic Avenue, just up from the station. Cellar bar in a former church with a boisterous beer-hall atmosphere. Good value food.

Centre and docks

Maddens, Smithfield. Great, unpretentious, atmospheric pub. Lots of locals drinking in two large rooms, one upstairs, one downstairs. Serves cheap stew and soup. Brilliant sessions.

Morning Star, Pottinger's Entry. Fine old-fashioned bar, busy in the day, quiet at night. Other good bars in the Entries include *The Globe* (Joy's Entry), *White's Tavern* (Winecellar Entry) and the *Kitchen Bar* (Victoria Square), which probably possesses the smallest urinal in the world.

Pat's Bar, Prince's Dock Road, in the north of the city by the docks, off York Road, easiest reached by taxi. Recently renovated in traditional style, with two bars (one large, one small) and open fires.

The Rotterdam, Pilot Street, also in the docks near *Pat's*. Great place with good music – see below.

The Liverpool, Donegall Quay, virtually opposite the Liverpool ferries. Small, two-roomed place with a pool table. Friendly and handy if you're waiting for the boat.

Music

As so often in Ireland, the best entertainment you'll find in Belfast is music in the pubs. Some of the main sessions and venues are listed below – often the same places already recommended for a simple drink – but you should look out for posters or check the listings in the *Belfast Telegraph* for up-to-date details. The tourist office also has details, updated regularly.

The Linenhall, Clarence Street. Jazz on Saturday afternoons.

Students' Union, University Road. Officially you must show a student pass or get a Queen's student to sign you in, though pleading may work. Folk evening in the upstairs bar on Thursday. Riotous atmosphere and great fun: plenty of mock *céilí* swinging goes on because none of them know how to do it properly.

The Elbow, Dublin Road. Intimate pub, part of a complex which includes one of Belfast's best nightclubs, *PIPS*.

Errigle Inn, 320 Ormeau Road. Traditional sessions on Monday nights.

Limelight, Ormeau Avenue, near the BBC. Basically a disco/nightclub, with cabaret on Tuesday, Friday and Saturday, and bands on other nights of the week (£2).

Kelly's Cellars, 30 Bank Street. Folk music on Saturday afternoons, Blues on Saturday nights.

Maddens, Smithfield. Excellent traditional sessions on Monday, Wednesday and Saturday from around 9pm: sometimes as many as twenty musicians with music going on upstairs and downstairs at the same time.

The Liverpool, Donegall Quay. Traditional sessions on Sunday evenings and some Saturdays.

Pat's Bar, Prince's Dock Road. Sessions irregular but great when they happen.

The Rotterdam, Pilot Street. Music most nights, ranging from jazz and blues to folk and traditional.

Film, theatre and other entertainment

When it comes to other forms of entertainment, Belfast reveals itself as little different from any British provincial city – there's not a lot going on. Again the *Belfast Telegraph* will have details of just about everything. As far as film goes there are plenty of mainstream **cinemas** showing the usual general release stuff – big downtown ones include the four-screen *Cannon* (Great Victoria Street; ☎222484) and three-screen *Curzon* (Ormeau Road; ☎681373) – but the only really enterprising place is *Queens Film Theatre* (University Square Mews off Botanic Avenue; ☎667687), with two screens showing slightly more esoteric stuff.

Theatre is concentrated south of the city centre. Sadly the *Opera House* on Great Victoria Street (☎241919), Belfast's most prestigious venue, is currently closed – but it's worth checking the status. The *Arts Theatre* on Botanic Avenue (☎224936) shows mostly comedy or very popular stuff: the *Lyric Theatre*, in a much more isolated position further out on Ridgeway Street (☎660081) takes on more serious drama, especially from the Irish heritage.

The **classical music** performed in the city rests mostly in the hands of the Ulster Orchestra at the *Ulster Hall* on Bedford Street (☎241917; it's also used for big rock and pop concerts); you may also catch concerts – professional and amateur – at the *Whitla Hall*, Queen's University (☎245133). The biggest pop and **rock gigs** are staged at *King's Hall*, Balmoral.

There are a few **art galleries** to browse round if you have the time on your hands. The *Arts Council Gallery* on Bedford Street exhibits mainly contemporary art (it also has a good coffee shop) as does the *Tom Caldwell Gallery*, a private basement gallery on Bradbury Place. The *Malone Gallery* (31 Malone Road) shows more experimental contemporary works and is probably the most interesting of the three.

Slightly more offbeat amusemements include **ten-pin bowling** and **Quasar** (indoor, hi-tech war games) at the *Belfast Superbowl*, 4 Clarence Street West (☎331466). For **festivals** see the listings section below.

Listings

Airlines *British Airways* (9 Fountain Centre, College Street; ☎240522); *Aer Lingus* (46 Castle Street; ☎245151); *British Midland* (Suite 2, Fountain Centre; ☎225151); *Dan Air* (☎0345/ 100200); *Loganair* (☎247979).

Airports Two airports serve the Belfast region. *Aldergrove International Airport* (☎08494/ 22888) is used by all international flights and most major British airlines (including the *British Midland* and *British Airways* shuttles). Buses run every half hour to Great Victoria Street Bus Station, but if you're heading straight to Derry, or any other train station on that route, you can save time and money by taking a taxi to Antrim train station. *Belfast Harbour Airport* (☎457745) has direct services with smaller operators from many British provincial airports. Catch a train to the city centre across the dual carriageway (Sydenham Halt station) or take a taxi (£4).

Banks Most of the major UK banks are allied to the following Northern Irish ones, all of which have city centre branches: *Ulster Bank Ltd* 47 Donegall Place (☎320222); *Allied Irish*, 2 Royal Avenue (☎246559); *Bank of Ireland*, 54 Donegall Place (☎244901); *Northern Bank*, Donegall Square West (☎245277); *Trustee Savings Bank* 4 Queens Square (☎325599). Remember that British cash cards will work in their machines.

Bike hire *Ernie Coates*, 108 Grand Parade (☎471912); *Bike-It*, 4 Belmont Road (☎471141).

Bookshops *Just Books* (7 Winetavern Street) is an alternative community bookshop stocked also with magazines and political postcards; *Roma Ryan's Books and Prints* and *Prospect House Books* on Dublin Road are good for antiquarian tomes; *Bookfinders* at 47 University Road, good second-hand bookshop; *University Bookshop* on University Road; *Waterstones* on Royal Avenue; *Dillons* on Fountain Street.

Buses ☎246485 for city bus information, or pick up a timetable from the kiosk on Donegall Square West. Most routes operate from points around Donegall Square. Services outside Belfast are operated by *Ulsterbus* from either the Great Victoria Street Bus Station (actually in Glengall Street, behind the *Europa Hotel*; services to the west and the Republic) or Oxford Street, near the main railway station (for the north and east). ☎320011 for *Ulsterbus* information, or use the computer at the bus station.

Car Hire *Avis*, 69 Great Victoria Street (☎241414; also at Aldergrove Airport, ☎08494/22333, and Belfast Harbour Airport, ☎240404); many other big names at the airports. *Bairds Rentals* on Boucher Road (☎247770) are usually cheaper.

Family Planning Clinics *UPAA* 338a Lisburn Road (☎667345); *LIFE* Bryson House, Bedford Street (☎229241); *CURA* (☎644963).

Ferries *Sealink* (Larne–Stranraer) are on Castle Lane (☎327525); *P&O European Ferries* (Larne–Cairnryan) are based at Larne harbour only (☎0574-74321); *Belfast Ferries* (Belfast–Liverpool) are at 47 Donegall Quay (☎326800); *Isle of Man Steam Packet Company* (Belfast–Isle of Man) is on Northern Road (☎351009).

Festivals *Belfast International Festival at Queens* (2–3 weeks in Nov) claims to be Europe's second biggest arts festival after Edinburgh; *Belfast Folk Festival* (3 days in Sept); *Royal Ulster Academy Annual Exhibition* (Ulster Museum, 3 weeks in Oct); *Orange Day* on July 12 (and marching season all around this date).

Hospitals Shaftesbury Square Hospital, near the University (☎329808); Belfast City Hospital, Lisburn Road (☎329241); Royal Victoria Hospital, Falls Road (☎240503). ☎999 for emergency service.

Left Luggage Due to the obvious security considerations, there is, unfortunately, no official place where you can leave your luggage.

Markets The *St George's Casual Retail Market* (also known as the *Variety Market*) in May Street (Tues & Fri mornings) is the liveliest: the Friday Food and Variety market is by far the more popular with about 200 traders taking part; on Tuesday it's more of a fleamarket type affair, selling new and secondhand clothes and a variety of junk. The *Smithfield Retail Market*, at the back of the new Castle Court development (West Street/Winetavern Street) is also pretty good; it operates from about 30 shop units and sells new and secondhand goods and clothes. For **antiques**, try the Saturday market at *Alexander The Grates* (Donegall Pass; open all day), which sells local bits and pieces at very reasonable prices.

Police ☎999 for emergency service. Main city centre police station is in North Queen Street.

Post Office General Post Office, Castle Place.

Tourist Information The Northern Ireland Tourist Board are in High Street (☎246609). *Bord Fáilte*, for the Republic, can be found at 53 Castle Street (☎327888).

Trains Nearly all trains operate from the Central Station on East Bridge Street (☎230310, 230671). Trains for Larne Harbour (and the ferries) use York Road Station (☎235282). The two are connected by a shuttle bus service. Botanic Station on Botanic Avenue is handy if you're heading north for Portstewart or Derry.

Travel Agents *USIT*, 31a Queen Street (☎242562); *American Express*, 9 North Road; *Thomas Cook*, 11 Donegall Place.

Welfare *Gay Counselling Service* and *Lesbian Line* (☎222023 Mon–Thurs 7.30–10pm); *Belfast Rape Crisis Centre* (☎249696).

Women's Centre 19 North Street Arcade (☎243363, 231674).

travel details

Trains

From Belfast: to Lisburn (approx 4 an hour; 15min); Portadown (approx 2 an hour; 30min); Dundalk (5; 1hr 20min); Dublin (6; 2hr); Larne Harbour (2 an hour; 45min); Derry (6 daily; 2hr 20min); Coleraine (8 daily; 1hr 35min).

Ulsterbuses

From Belfast: to Derry (2 daily; 1hr 30min; also 3 via Omagh, 3hr); Antrim (10; 35min); Ballymena (8; 50min); Portrush (2; 2hr); Newry (9; 1hr 10min); Monaghan (3; 2hr); Enniskillen (6; 2hr 15min); Sligo (1; 4hr); Portadown (2; 55min); Dublin, connecting with *Bus Éireann* service at Monaghan (3 daily, 4hr) or at Newry (5, 5 hr); Cork, connecting with *Bus Éireann* (1 daily, 11hr); change at Cahir for Waterford (11hr), at Roscrea for Limerick (9hr), or at Athlone for Mullingar (6hr 40min); Galway, connecting with *Bus Éireann* (2 daily, 6hr 30min) via Cavan (3hr).

CHAPTER FIFTEEN

ANTRIM AND DERRY

The northern coastline of counties **Antrim** and **Derry** is as spectacular as anything you'll find in Ireland: certainly it's the major reason to make your way north of Belfast. From most of the coastline, on good days, the Mull of Kintyre is clearly visible, and much of the population, predominantly Protestant, derives originally from Scotland. Unlike other parts of the North, the region attracts lots of tourists and perhaps because of this, it's one of the parts where you'll feel most comfortable travelling – the odd red, white and blue kerbstone and anti-Catholic graffiti apart, there's little evidence of the Troubles up here. The two main attractions are side by side. The nine **Glens of Antrim**, in the northeast corner, closest to Scotland – green fertile fingers probing inland from high cliffs – are immediately followed to the west by the weird geometry of the **Giant's Causeway**. And along the way are plenty of firm, white strands and rocky heights, relatively unfrequented except for a couple of boarding-house resorts.

Thanks to the Scottish connection, the main point of arrival for the area is the decidedly unlovely port of **Larne**, which marks the Irish end of the shortest crossing from Britain. From here, the main road follows the **coast** all the way round to the attractive resorts of **Portrush** and **Portstewart**, though if you don't have a car this doesn't make getting around as easy as you'd think – buses are few and far between. Hitchhiking, though, isn't difficult. The **train**, alternatively, cuts a less interesting **inland** route through dull farming country – though you can reach either end of the coastline from Belfast, with trains to both Larne and Portstewart. But the rest of the stops on the way to **Derry** are at some fairly grim inland towns: **Antrim**, **Ballymena** and **Coleraine**. The other inland route is the A6 road from Antrim to Derry, passing through and near some of the counties' **planters' towns**, the most impressive of which is **Moneymore**.

If transport can be a problem, then at least **accommodation** is easy, with a good sprinkling of *YHA* hostels, plenty of campsites, and unpretentious, reasonable B&Bs where you're generally assured of a friendly welcome. Indeed, the coastline represents the acceptable face of Northern Ireland, and the people are usually very keen to reassure you that life here is normal.

Larne

Arriving by sea is always impressive, but unfortunately, approaching **LARNE** this way – from Cairnryan or Stranraer – gives you no indication of what's to come. It's a plain, prim, boring town, whose graffitied walls proclaim untidily, in case you hadn't guessed already, that there's "No Popery Here".

Larne's **history** is tied up with its geographical convenience as a landing stage. Norse pirates used Larne Lough as a base in the tenth and eleventh centuries; Edward Bruce, brother of Robert, landed here in 1315 with a force of 6000 men in his attempt to urge the Irish to overthrow the English; and in 1914 the Ulster Volunteers, opposed to the Irish Home Rule Bill, landed German arms here.

History apart, though, Larne is not a place to hang around. The only real landmark is the **round tower**, at the entrance to the port, and even that's a reproduction. The other sight is the ruined, sixteenth-century **Olderfleet Castle**, which cowers among the industrial wasteland of the harbour. Frankly, unless you're waiting for a ferry, the best thing about Larne is the road out: you can either head up to the enticements of the Antrim coast, or straight in towards Belfast.

If you're stuck, then **tourist information** is available from the council's offices in Victorian Road (Mon–Fri 9am–4.45pm; ☎0574/72313); in summer, look out for the temporary tourist office in a caravan in the car park at **Murrayfield shopping centre** (Mon–Sat 10am–6pm; ☎0574/71313). Both will book B&B **accommodation** for you, which is plentiful. The nearest **hostel** is at BALLYGALLY (see below) five miles north up the A2. **Ferry information** is on ☎0574/74321; see *Basics* for more details of the crossings.

The route south to Belfast

Although all the real interest lies to the north of Larne, many people first take the opportunity to head **south to Belfast**, a quick enough option. Arriving in Larne by boat you'll see, on your left, the spit of land called **Islandmagee** – not, in fact, an island at all, but a peninsula seven miles long and two miles wide, attached to the mainland at its southern end. Tapering from high, black basalt cliffs on the east coast down to Larne Lough on the west, its history is sadly representative of these parts: in 1642 the population was massacred by the garrison at Carrickfergus, further south down the coast – some of the victims are said to have been hurled over the cliffs.

Ballycarry

Both road (the A2) and rail run down the coast from Larne towards Belfast, cutting across the neck of the peninsula. **BALLYCARRY**, just off the main road, has the remains of the first Presbyterian church to be built in Ireland. The tradition is an enduring one: kerbstones are painted red, white and blue, and a gable-end carries a colourful mural – the first of many you'll see in this region – showing a man on a prancing horse, with the caption, "Remember William, Prince of Orange 1690".

The **church**'s graveyard contains the tombs of some of the supporters of the 1798 uprising, including that of James Burns, whose cryptic gravestone requires the following key to decipher: the numbers 1, 2, 3 and 4 represent the vowels a, e, i and o, and 5 and 6 the letter w. There's also a grand Masonic memorial of 1831, which bears a patriotic poem about Ireland: "Erin, loved land! From age to age, Be thou more great, more famed and free" – not, at this stage, about Ulster or the union with Britain.

Carrickfergus

Once you've turned the corner at WHITEHEAD, you're into Belfast Lough and fast approaching the city's conurbation. About halfway from Larne to Belfast, **CARRICKFERGUS** is an unremarkable, halfhearted sort of seaside town. The one real point of interest is **Carrickfergus Castle**, one of the earliest and largest of Irish castles. Built around 1180 by the Anglo-Norman invaders (and in continuous use until 1928), it reflects the defensive history of this entire region. In 1315 it underwent a year's siege before falling to the combined forces of Robert and

Edward Bruce; after which it was retaken and held by the English for most of the next three centuries. In 1760 the castle was overwhelmed by a French force, and hurriedly recaptured; and in 1778 the American privateer, Paul Jones, fought a successful battle with the British vessel "HMS Drake", America's first naval victory. The story is that Belfast citizens – most of the Protestants were sympathetic to the American Revolution – rushed out to cheer the victors. If you want a military view of the province's history of armed struggle, then the castle contains a **Cavalry Regimental Museum** (Mon–Sat 10am–6pm; Sun 2–6pm, until 4pm Oct–March; 75p), full of weapons and armour.

Otherwise, Carrickfergus claims plenty of literary associations, though not all of them are tangible: the Restoration dramatist, William Congreve, lived in the castle – his father was a soldier – until he was eight; Jonathan Swift's first sinecure was at Kilroot, just outside Carrickfergus, and it was there, between 1694 and 1696, that he wrote *The Tale of a Tub*; and the poet Louis MacNeice spent his childhood in Carrickfergus. Still, none of these claims to fame are as tenuous as that of the connection with the American president, Andrew Jackson, whose parents emigrated from Carrickfergus in 1765. The **Andrew Jackson Centre** (daily 10am–5pm; June–Aug also 6–8pm) isn't even their home, but a reconstruction of an eighteenth-century thatched cottage, with a little museum.

One reason to give Carrickfergus a little more time might be the **annual fair**, *Lughnasa*, which is tackily medieval – with wrestlers, archers, minstrels and people dressed up as monks – but great fun nonetheless. It's held at the beginning of August; check the dates with the **tourist office** on Castle Green (June–Aug only), or at the Town Hall (☎09603/51604).

The Glens of Antrim

Northwest of Larne lie the nine **Glens of Antrim**, cutting back from the sea to wild country behind. It's a curious landscape, with enormous contrasts between the neat, seaside villages and the rough moorland above, and its well-defined topography gives first-time visitors the strange sensation that they know it well already.

Until the present coast road was blasted out of the cliffs in 1834, the Glens were extremely isolated, despite their proximity to the Scottish coast. They were also one of the last places in Northern Ireland where Irish was spoken: perhaps surprisingly, Gaelic remained widely spoken in the North far longer than in the south. **Transport** is still a problem here. The only service to run from one end of this coast to the other is the daily Belfast–Portrush express (sets off from Belfast early morning and returns late afternoon; £4.60 single, £8 return). The Larne–Cushendall **bus** runs six times daily (Mon–Sat; £3.75 single, £6.70 return), although some services stop at Carnlough, ten miles short of Cushendall. In July and August there's a once-daily service in each direction; check times with local tourist offices. **Hitching** is generally fine, though you'll often be told the tale of a German woman student who was murdered on a ride north from Larne in 1988. **Cycling** is heady but strenuous, and don't rely on being able to hire a bike: one of the few places that has some is *Coffee and Crafts* (☎02667/71800) outside Cushendall. One alternative means of getting about is **pony trekking**, which can be a delight in the Glens in good weather. The main centre is at Ballycastle, at the northern extremity of the glen-fractured coast; see p.456.

Larne to Glenarm

Taking the road northwards out of Larne, you leave the dull suburbs behind fairly quickly, the view broadening out to take in the open sea and, beyond it, the low outline of the Scottish coast. The first place you come to is **BALLYGALLY**, with a wide, wild bay and a sandy beach embraced by hills. There's something about the sobriety of the architecture that makes it look more like Scotland, an impression heightened by the crow-stepped gables of **Ballygally Castle**, built by seventeenth-century planters. You can call in here for a drink – it's now a hotel with, they tell you, a ghost in the dungeon bar – although it's more impressive from the outside. If you're heading on towards the Glens, there's nothing much to keep you in Ballygally, but there is a modern **youth hostel** (210 Coast Road; ☎0574/583355; closed Mon Oct–March).

The southernmost of the Glens, **Glenarm**, is headed by a village of the same name, which grew up around a hunting lodge built by Randal MacDonnell after Dunluce Castle, further up the coast, was abandoned. Glenarm became the major seat of the Earls of Antrim, something that might lead you to expect that **Glenarm Castle** would be worth seeing. But major rebuildings in the eighteenth and nineteenth centuries have left it a fairly horrendous compilation of styles, an unexciting amalgam of turrets and portcullises that deny each others' impact.

GLENARM village itself, though, is a delight, and very much a taste of what's to follow, with a broad main street of colour-washed buildings leading up to an imposing gateway, the old estate entrance, which now leads into the glen itself. The lower part of the glen is blighted with Forest Service conifers, but carry on and you reach National Trust land, and far better walking. There's nowhere much to **stay** in Glenarm, but should its charm beguile you, try *Margaret's Cafe* (☎0574/84307) on the main street, which does a very reasonable B&B for £10.

Carnlough and Waterfoot

CARNLOUGH stands at the opposite side of the next bay northwards, at the head of **Glencloy** – the "glen of hedges". The village's most striking feature is the sturdy, white limestone architecture: until the 1960s Carnlough's way of life was tied up with its limestone quarries. The centre of the village, all built in shining, white stone, was constructed by the Marquess and Marchioness of Londonderry in 1854. Over the main road there's a solid stone bridge that once carried the railway which brought the limestone down to the harbour; while the harbour itself, with an impressive breakwater, plus the clock tower and courthouse, are also of limestone.

Cheap **B&B accommodation** is thin on the ground in Carnlough, though you could try the *Bethany Christian Guesthouse* at 5 Bay Road (☎0574/85667; £12), full of religious paraphernalia, or cheaper rooms above NcCauley's Pub in Bridge Street (☎0574/85669; £10). Otherwise the **tourist office** (☎0574/85210), inside the Post Office on Harbour Road, can help. If you're **camping**, there are two small caravan sites, *Bay View Caravan Park* (☎0574/85685) and *Whitehill Caravan Park* (☎0574/85233), that allow tents. *Black's Pub*, also on Harbour Road, is the place to head for **music**, with sessions most nights. The solid *Londonderry Arms Hotel*, once owned by Winston Churchill, is worth a stop for a drink, too, if only to admire the bizarre collection of mementoes of the 1960s steeplechaser, Arkle.

From Carnlough the road skirts round a gaunt shoulder of land to **WATERFOOT**, a short strip of houses with a cheap **inn** that comes to life in the evenings. There's also a B&B at *Glen Vista*, 245 Garron Road (☎02677/71439; £9). Waterfoot is the scene of the *Feis na nGleann*, one of the great competitive Irish sporting and cultural festivals, held in July.

It's **Glenariff**, though, Waterfoot's glen, that is the real attraction. Wide, lush, and flat-bottomed, it's abruptly cut off by the sea, while a few miles up the glen is the *Glenariff Forest Park*, which – though it costs to enter – has a **campsite** (☎02667/37232; contact the head forester in advance) and a spectacular series of **waterfalls**. You could cheat, though, and see some of the waterfalls by taking the forest park road and turning left at the *Laragh Lodge* sign; stop at the restaurant.

Between Waterfoot and **Red Bay** pier, there's a series of **caves** with an odd history. The so-called "school cave" was where lessons were conducted for the children of Red Bay in the eighteenth century; a practice made necessary by the oppressive Penal Code that outlawed Catholic education. And the largest of the caves, "Nanny's Cave", forty feet long, was the home of the redoubtable distiller of illicit poteen whiskey, Ann Murray, who died, aged 100, in 1847.

Cushendall and around

CUSHENDALL lies at the head of three of the nine Glens of Antrim, on the shores of Red Bay, and may become a busy port, if a projected ferry service between Red Bay and Scotland materialises. For the moment, however, it remains delightfully understated, its charming colour-washed buildings grouped together on a spectacular shore. The red sandstone **tower** at the main crossroads was built in 1809 by one Francis Turnly, an official of the East India Company, as "a place of confinement for idlers and rioters"; there are plans to turn it into a tourist and heritage centre. Meanwhile, the **tourist office** (☎02667/71415) is housed in a portacabin off the Glenballyemon road, where you can check for details of **dancing and traditional music** in local pubs: *Joe McCullum's*, in Mill Street, is worth a try, sessions usually taking place on Thursday and Saturday throughout the summer.

Cushendall is probably the best base for exploring the Glens of Antrim, and accordingly it's well provided with **accommodation**. In addition to bed and breakfast places, there's a **youth hostel** on Layde Road (closed in Dec–Feb and on Tues Oct–Mar; ☎02667/71344; £6) – leave town by Shore Street, go left at the fork, and look out for the youth hostel sign on the wall; and a **campsite** on the hill to the north of the town (☎02667/71520; £2–3). You can **hire bikes** from Martin O'Lane, 54 Trana Road (☎02667/71800; £3 per day, £10 deposit).

Short walks from Cushendall
Beyond Cushendall, the land rises sharply and the main road swings away from the coast, which is good news for walkers. A clifftop path, running northwards from the beach, takes you to the calm ruins of the thirteenth-century **Layde Old Church**, chief burial place of the MacDonnells. It's nothing spectacular, although if you have family roots to trace in the Glens it may be worth checking out; the tourist office staff at Cushendall have been cataloguing the gravestones and can tell you more about the people buried there.

The other trip from Cushendall is to what's known as **Ossian's Grave**, on the main road to Cushendun (see below). There's a double fake involved here:

Ossian, the legendary son of Fionn Mac Cumhaill, was the supposed author of the Ossianic Cycle of poems, translated and popularised – and largely fabricated – by James Macpherson in the 1760s. This was to give impetus to the early Romantic movement, particularly in Germany and Scandinavia. However, the tomb doesn't actually have anything to do with Ossian as it's a Neolithic court grave. All the same, standing in a sloping field above the valley, with views to Glendun, Glenaan, and, in the distance, Scotland, it oozes spirit – as good a place as any to reflect on the shaky origins of the first Celtic literary revival.

Beyond the grave runs **Glenaan**, one of the smallest of the glens, soon petering out as little more than a dip of red reeds and black seams of peat between two hills of heather and cotton grass.

Cushendun to Fair Head

CUSHENDUN is an architectural oddity. On a windswept bay, it was once a fashionable resort, almost entirely designed, between 1912 and 1925, by the stylish architect of Portmeirion in Wales, Clough Williams-Ellis. However, it has nothing of the twee Italianate style that has made Portmeirion famous: built to a commission from Ronald McNeill, the first (and last) Lord Cushendun, and his Cornish wife, Maud, Cushendun's houses are of rugged, rough-cast whitewash with slate roofs – a Cornish style which clearly weathers the Atlantic storms as efficiently here as in Cornwall.

All of Cushendun is National Trust property, and it shows. It's a tiny and welltended place where tourists – and everyone else – seem peculiarly out of place; but there's a **hotel**, a couple of guesthouses and a (municipal) caravan park that also allows **camping** (☎026674/254). If you need information, the **tourist office** (☎026674/506) is in the main street.

North from Cushendun, there's not much point in taking the main road, which runs inland, unless you have to: it traverses some impressively rough moorland, but you'll be missing some of the best of the northern coastline. Edged with fuschia and honeysuckle, the coastal road switchbacks violently above the sea to **Torr Head**, the closest point on the Irish mainland to the Mull of Kintyre in Scotland, only thirteen miles away – it's said that Protestants from this coast used to row from here to church on the Scottish mainland. You can also pick up the signposted **Ulster Way** around here, although it swings inland immediately after Cushendun, joining the coast again at Murlough Bay: despite the spectacular views from the top of Carnanmore mountain, the coastal route is probably better.

That said, people will tell you that the **Ballypatrick Forest Park**, on the main road, is worth seeing. It's not, unless you're thrilled by the idea of a one-way driving route past things like fjords and even prehistoric cairns marked out like a fairground ghost train. **Camping** is allowed in the park, but check with the Forest Service in Belfast (☎0232/650111 ext 456) before turning up.

The coastal route: Murlough Bay

Murlough Bay is probably – perhaps because of the absence of a main road – the most spectacular of all the bays along the northern coast. From the rugged clifftops, the hillside curves down to the sea in a series of wildflower meadows that soften an otherwise harsh landscape. As much as anywhere else on the Irish coastline this is a place for just spending time and drinking it all in.

The **stone cross** by the second car park is a memorial to **Sir Roger Casement**, an extraordinary figure who was both a successful administrator for the British and a martyr for the Nationalist cause. Following a brilliant career in the Belgian Congo and Peru, he was given a knighthood in 1911. But, believing that Britain's involvement in World War I could give Ireland the opportunity for independence it needed, he negotiated with Germany for military aid and, at the height of the fighting, arranged for a German submarine to land a shipload of arms at Banna Strand on the Kerry coast. His plans were discovered, however, and he was arrested and hanged.

The last headland before Ballycastle is **Fair Head**, with massive cliffs rising over six hundred feet all the way round, and a really spectacular view across the North Channel to the Scottish islands – Islay, the Paps of Jura and, beyond them, the Mull of Kintyre. It's easy to believe that local Protestants could row across the channel to church on Sundays; and seeing the landscape makes even more sense of the confusion of land ownership between Ireland and Scotland. Rathlin Island (see below) was hotly contested right up to the seventeenth century, while the MacDonnells owned land both here and on Kintyre. (Kintyre, incidentally, was considered dangerous enough to English interests to be settled, or "planted" – with people from elsewhere in Scotland – in the seventeenth century, just as Ireland was.) **Lough na Cranagh**, one of three lakes in the hinterland behind the cliffs, has an oval island that is actually a lake dwelling, a *crannóg*, with an encircling man-made parapet wall.

Ballycastle

Situated at the mouth of the two northernmost Antrim glens, Glenshesk and Glentaise, the lively market town and port of **BALLYCASTLE** divides the glens from the Causeway coast, and is a base for touring in either direction. As such it has the air of a family resort, and is pleasant enough, particularly if you find yourself passing through at the time of the *Fleadh Amhrán agus Rince*, the three-day music and dance **festival** in June, or the **Ould Lammas Fair** in late August. This last event is more than just a tourist promotion: Ireland's oldest fair, it dates from 1606 when the MacDonnells first obtained a charter, and has sheep and pony sales as well as the obligatory stalls and shops. You may be able to find the edible seaweed, dulse, and the tooth-breaking yellow toffee (it's so hard you break it with a hammer) called "yellow man", delicacies that feature in a sentimental song that originates in Ballycastle:

> *Did you treat your Mary Ann*
> *To dulse and yellow man*
> *At the Ould Lammas Fair in Ballycastle-O?*

Ballycastle still has a solid, prosperous air about it that derives from the efforts of an enlightened mid-eighteenth-century landowner, Colonel Hugh Boyd, who developed the town as an industrial centre, providing coal and iron ore mines, a tannery, brewery, soap, bleach, salt and glass works. Ballycastle's prosperity, though, really depended on its coal mines; lignite was mined at Ballintoy, on the coast a few miles further west, but that enterprise came to an abrupt end in the eighteenth century when the entire deposit caught fire, continuing to burn for several years.

Ballycastle proper is a couple of miles inland, linked to a little resort on the coast, from where boats leave for Rathlin Island (see below). At the seafront there's a memorial to Guglielmo Marconi, the inventor of the wireless, who in 1898 made his first successful transmission between Ballycastle and Rathlin. If you're looking for a B&B, this is the place to stay, as there's a good sandy **beach** close by.

A little way out, on the main road to Cushendall, are the ruins of **Bonamargy Friary**, founded by the dominant MacQuillan family around 1500. A number of members of the rival MacDonnell family are also buried here, including the hero of Dunluce Castle, Sorley Boy MacDonnell, and his son Randal, first Earl of Antrim (see p.462). An indication of the strength of the Irish language in these parts is that the tomb of the second earl, who died in 1682, is inscribed in Gaelic as well as the usual English and Latin: the Irish inscription reads "Every seventh year a calamity befalls the Irish" and "Now that the Marquis has departed, it will occur every year". The **Margy River**, on which Bonamargy Friary stands, is associated with one of the great tragic stories of Irish legend, that of the Children of Lir (see p.150), whose jealous stepmother turned them into swans and forced them to spend three hundred years on the Sea of Moyle (the narrow channel between Ireland and the Scottish coast).

Practicalities

If you're going to **stay** in Ballycastle, as well you might, the **tourist office** in Sheskburn House on Mary Street (☎02657/62024) can point you in the right direction. The harbour end of Quay Road is packed with **B&Bs** – try Ardagh House at no. 50 (☎02657/63875; £10) – and the last house on the left incorporates the independent *Castle Hostel* (☎02657/62337; £5); there are also several **caravan sites** which take tents, the nearest being *Silver Cliffs Holiday Village* (☎02657/62550), where you can also rent self-catering chalets (around £50 per person per week) and ready-pitched tents – it has lots of facilities including a swimming pool. If your budget is more generous, the *Marine Hotel* (£34), at the bottom of Quay Road on the waterfront, is very comfortable.

The usual range of fast **food** and tea shops can be found in town and on the front: there are good bar lunches at *McCarroll's* on Anne Street and at the *Marine Hotel*. *Wysners*, 16 Anne Street, has a daring and inexpensive menu, and is next door to the famous butcher of the same name. If you're after nightlife, you'll find Ballycastle's **pubs** surprisingly lively – *McCarroll's* has music on Thursdays; the *House of McDonnell*, on the main street, is young and lively; even better is the bar at the *Antrim Arms*, next door, with a magnificent range of whiskeys and a host rich in Ulster wisdom; finally the *Angler's Arms*, down on the seafront, is a cosy bar in which to end the evening.

There's **pony trekking** on offer in Ballycastle, too, at the *Loughaveema Trekking Centre* (☎02657/62576), on the Ballyvennaght road. **Corrymeela**, the famous centre for cross-community reconciliation (☎02657/62626), is just a few miles out of town.

Rathlin Island

Ballycastle is the departure point for rugged **Rathlin Island**, six miles and a fifty-minute boat trip offshore, and just twelve miles from the Mull of Kintyre in Scotland. In summer, **boats** go every day (call *Rathlin Ferries*, ☎02657/71207; or *Rathlin Venture*, ☎02657/63917; fares are £5 return, children £2.50); in winter the boats go only on Monday, Wednesday and Friday. In winter, it can get too rough for the boat to make the trip; and note that the boat doesn't always come back the same day, so it's worth making sure in advance that you can stay on the island as accommodation is strictly limited.

Rathlin is an impressive, cliff-ridden island, its vegetation stunted by salt winds, its barrenness seemingly in keeping with its stormy history. It was the first place in Ireland to be raided by the Vikings, in 795 AD, and has been the scene of three bloody massacres, one by the Scots and two by the English. In 1595 the mainland MacDonnells sent their women, children and old people to Rathlin for safety from the English, but that didn't stop the English fleet, under the Earl of Essex (whose soldiers included Sir Francis Drake), from slaughtering the entire population; Rathlin was deserted for many years afterwards.

The island's cliffs are good bird watching country, particularly **Bull Point**, on the western tip. The foot of the cliff is riddled with caves, many of them accessible by boat only in the calmest of weather, and many also filled with detritus from wrecked ships, which storms have brought to the surface. **Bruce's Cave**, on the northeast point of the island, below the lighthouse, is a cavern in the black basalt where, in 1306, so the story goes, the despondent Robert the Bruce retreated after being defeated by the English at Perth. Seeing a spider determinedly trying to spin a web persuaded him not to give up – and he went back to Scotland to defeat the English at Bannockburn. You can hire a boat to see the cave, but only in calm weather.

There's not much in the way of **accommodation** on Rathlin: just a couple of guesthouses – *Rathlin Guest House* (☎02657/63917; £9) and the *Rathlin Dive/ Holiday Centre* (☎02657/63915; £10 B&B in dormitories with kitchens) – and a **campsite**. Life on the island is simple and uncomplicated, but not entirely basic, so you'll also find a restaurant, a pub and two shops. (All the electricity on the island, incidentally, comes from generators, and since there's only really one bit of serviceable road, Rathlin residents don't have to pay road tax.)

West to the Giant's Causeway

The Ulster Way joins the coast at Ballintoy, just west of Carrick-a-rede Island, but there are a couple of places between here and Ballycastle that are worth seeing. The first of these, **Kinbane Castle**, is a decaying sixteenth-century fortification on a long, white headland, built by Colla Dubh, brother of the redoubtable Sorley Boy MacDonnell. The pathway is slippery and badly eroded, but it's worth climbing up to the castle to inspect these Irish defences against the English.

As you draw level with **Carrick-a-rede Island**, you'll see the **rope bridge**, the second biggest tourist attraction in these parts. Strung eighty feet above the sea, between the mainland and the island, the bridge leads to a commercial salmon fishery on the southeast side of Carrick-a-rede – but its main function seems to be to scare tourists, something it does very successfully. Walking its sixty foot length, as the bridge leaps and bucks under you, is enough to induce giggles and screams from the hardiest of people. The bridge is taken down in September, when the salmon fishing season ends, and put back up in April.

BALLINTOY itself has a dramatic harbour with a dark, rock-strewn strand contrasting oddly with the neat, pale stone breakwater. In the summer it's lively with boats and visitors, but in winter it's bleak and exposed. The little white church that stands at the top of the cliff is a replacement of the one where local Protestants took refuge from Catholics in 1641, before being rescued by the Earl of Antrim. A landlord of Ballintoy in the eighteenth century was Downing Fullerton, who founded Downing College in Cambridge; the staircase and oak panelling were removed from the castle at Ballintoy when it was demolished and taken to Cambridge. In good weather you can hire boats for fishing and trips along the coast. **Sheep Island**, the bizarre rocky column standing just offshore, is home of a colony of cormorants. In the summer, **boat trips** run out from Ballintoy, past Sheep Island, to Carrick-a-rede (£1).

Continuing up the coast, **White Park Bay** is a delight, a mile-and-a-half sweep of white sand with a **youth hostel** that makes a good base for exploring (☎02657/31745; £5.50; bike rental available). A footpath from Ballintoy leads past here to **PORTBRADDAN**, a hamlet that's hardly more than a few houses. The interest lies in the brightly coloured bit of ecclesiastical architecture that is, supposedly, the smallest church in Ireland – twelve feet by six and a half. Needless to say, there are other contenders.

Dunseverick Castle

From here the coast path leads round a headland and through a spectacular hole in the rock and then, by degrees, up to the cliffs of **Benbane Head**, which is where the bizarre geometry of the Giant's Causeway really begins in earnest. The road almost meets the path at **Dunseverick Castle**, now no more than the ruins of a sixteenth-century gatehouse, but once capital of the old kingdom of Dalriada and the terminus of one of the five great roads that led from Tara. It was, naturally enough given its location, one of the main departure points for the great Irish colonisation of Scotland that took place from the fifth century onwards. Dunseverick also features in one of the great Irish love stories, the ninth-century *Longas mac n-Usnig*, or "The fate of the children of Uisneach". Deirdre, the betrothed of King Conor, falls in love with his bodyguard, Noisi. Together with Noisi's two brothers – the sons of Uisneach – they flee to Scotland. Fergus, one of Conor's soldiers, believes the king has forgiven them and persuades them to return home. Landing at Dunseverick (or, some say, Ballycastle), they take the high road to Conor's court at Armagh, but the king kills the brothers and seizes Deirdre, who dashes her head against a stone and dies. And Fergus, outraged, destroys Conor's palace (though not, apparently, the king himself).

The Giant's Causeway

Ever since 1693, when the Royal Geographical Society first publicised it as one of the great wonders of the natural world, the **Giant's Causeway** has been a major tourist attraction. The highly romanticised pictures of the polygonal basalt rock formations by the Dubliner, Susanna Drury, which circulated throughout Europe, did much to popularise the Causeway: two of them are on show in the Ulster Museum in Belfast, and copies are in the visitor centre at the site. Not everyone was impressed, though. William Thackeray ("I've travelled a hundred and fifty miles to see *that*?") especially disliked the tourist promotion of the Causeway, claiming in 1842 that "The traveller no sooner issues from the inn by a back door which he is informed will lead him straight to the causeway, than the guides pounce upon him." And although the Causeway is probably less overtly moneymaking now than at almost any time since the late seventeenth century, it still attracts plenty of people: there's a massive and over-appointed visitor centre (see below), and a minibus on the site rules out the necessity for any physical exertion whatsoever. But even in high season, it's easy enough to escape the crowds by taking to the cliffs.

For sheer strangeness, the Causeway can't be beaten. Made up of an estimated 37,000 black basalt columns, each a polygon – hexagons by far the most common, pentagons second, and sometimes figures with as many as ten sides – it's the result of a massive subterranean explosion some sixty million years ago, that stretched from the Causeway to Rathlin and beyond, to Islay, Staffa (where it was responsible for the formation of Fingal's Cave) and Mull in Scotland. A huge mass of molten basalt was spewed out onto the surface and, as it cooled, it solidified into what are, essentially, crystals. Simple as the process was, it's difficult, when confronted with the very regular geometry of the basalt columns, to believe that their origin is entirely natural. The Irish folk versions of their creation (see box) are certainly more appealing.

The best way to **approach** the Giant's Causeway is undoubtedly along the cliffs, preferably on a wet and blustery day when you're scared you'll lose your footing along the muddy way. The waymarked **North Antrim Cliff Path**, cut into the cliffside alongside the black geometric configurations, runs all along this stretch of coast. **Public transport** to and from the Causeway is well organised in summer: an open-topped **bus** (the "open topper") runs in July and August four times daily between Coleraine (where the stop is opposite the railway station) and Bushmills, stopping at Portstewart, Portrush, Portballintrae and the Causeway; you can flag it down anywhere along the way. If you're travelling by **train** from Belfast, the line ends at Portrush, from where you can either catch the open topper, or the #172; more details on ☎0265/43334.

FIONN MAC CUMHAILL: THE CAUSEWAY LEGENDS

Two versions of the **legend** of the creation of the causeway are current. The romantic version is the everyday story of a love affair between giants: the Ulster warrior, Fionn Mac Cumhaill (Finn McCool), became infatuated with a giantess who lived on the island of Staffa, off the Scottish coast (where the Causeway resurfaces), and built the great highway to bring his lady love to his side. This tale is recounted, alongside the scientific account, in the visitor centre's exhibition – along with some fanciful embellishments, such as an estimate of Fionn's height calculated on the basis of a large shoe-shaped stone that's known as his boot. A more robust tale has Fionn involved in a row with a Scottish giant. He built the causeway to go over to Scotland for a punch-up, but on seeing the size of the other giant lost his nerve and fled home. Safe in Ireland, he had his wife tuck him up in an outsize cot – when the Scots giant arrived in pursuit he saw the size of Fionn's "baby", and in turn took fright and fled, never to be heard of again.

Visiting the Causeway

The Causeway's **visitor centre** (summer daily 10am–7pm; winter 10am–4pm; ☎02657/31855) has a craft shop, coffee shop and audio-visual displays, but it's not a place to linger unless you're very cold or very wet – the real excitement is outside. There's a paying exhibition that doesn't tell you a great deal, its one interesting exhibit one of the **trams** from the tramway that used to run between the railway station in Portrush and the Causeway. Opened in 1883, it was the first electrically powered tramway in Europe, and ran on hydroelectric power generated from the River Bush. The tramway wasn't built simply for the tourists: it was thought that the area would be developed for iron mining, and the tram-owner, William Traill, planned to make his fortune. There was some concern over the possible dangers of using hydroelectricity, and Traill sought to allay fears by dropping his trousers and sitting on the live rail – it was only later that he admitted that he'd suffered a severe shock. The line was closed in 1949, although there are apparently plans to reopen it.

Taking the tarmacked **path** from the visitor centre (and dodging the minibus that's laid on) brings you to the **Grand Causeway**, where you'll find some of the most spectacular of the blocks, and where most of the crowd lingers. If you push on, though, you'll be rewarded with relative solitude and views of some of the more impressive formations, high in the cliffs. Many of them have names invented for them by the guides who so plagued Thackeray and his contemporaries – the Organ and the Harp, for example – but at least one, **Chimney Point**, has an appearance so bizarre that it persuaded a ship of the Spanish Armada to think it was Dunluce Castle, a couple of miles further west, where they might get help from the MacDonnells: instead, the Girona was wrecked.

Before you reach Chimney Point, **Port-na-Spania** is the place where the ship foundered in September 1588. The treasure she was carrying was recovered by divers in 1968, and some of the items are on show in the Ulster Museum in Belfast (though a planned big exhibition hasn't yet materialised). Carrying on, you climb up to **Benbane Head** on a wooden staircase and can then return to the visitor centre along the tops of the cliffs.

The **boats** that ply for trade at the Causeway will show you the caves that aren't accessible from the land: Portcoon Cave, 450 feet long and 40 feet high; Leckilroy Cave, which you can't go into; and Runkerry Cave, an amazing 700 feet long and 60 feet high.

Bushmills to Portrush

The next stop on the main road beyond the Causeway is **BUSHMILLS**, whose main attraction is the **Old Bushmills Distillery**, on the outskirts of town. Whiskey has been distilled here legally since 1608, making it the oldest licit distillery in the world and it's well worth making the free **tour** (Mon–Thurs 9am–noon & 1.30–3.30pm, Fri 9am–noon; ☎02657/31521). The great claim about Bushmills whiskey is that it's distilled three times, instead of the twice that's usual in Scotland; but perhaps the biggest surprise is just how unsubtle a business the industrial manufacture of alcohol is, despite all the lore that surrounds it. Basically, you're shown round a massive factory where an extraordinary range of (mostly unpleasant) smells assails your nostrils, making it difficult to imagine that the end product is something that will delight the taste buds. All the same, at the end of the tour you're offered a tot of the hard stuff: the best bet is the unblended malt, representative of what goes on in Bushmills itself, as the grain whiskey that goes into the blend is almost all distilled in Cork; alternatively ask for a tot of Coleraine whiskey, only a tiny amount of which is still produced. They also serve hot toddies, which may be more in order in winter. To find the distillery follow the signs from the cenotaph in the centre of town – it's barely a quarter of a mile.

Accommodation is mostly strung out along the Causeway road, where for example you'll find the *Carnside Guesthouse*, 23 Causeway Road (☎02657/31337; £12), two miles from the distillery with a Causeway view. Just about the only cheap place in Bushmills itself is *Ardevin* (£11), on the road out to the distillery. The best rooms in town are at the recently renovated *Bushmills Inn*, 25 Main Street (☎02657/32339; £29), a former coaching **inn** with cottage-style interior complete with secret room and peat fires. Also attached is the excellent *Barony Restaurant*, with an à la carte menu for around £15; at the least you should pop in for a drink in the gaslit bar while waiting for the bus (which stops outside). There's marginally less expensive luxury at the *Auberge de Seneirl* (☎02657/41536; £20), a converted nineteenth-century schoolhouse discreetly signposted off the Coleraine road. It's pricey by guesthouse standards but is well equipped – swimming pool, sauna, jacuzzi, solarium – and has a **restaurant** with excellent French food. The owners aren't keen to take guests who don't want to eat in the restaurant, but it can be an excellent place to hole up after the rigours of walking the cliffs.

Portballintrae

A detour of a couple of miles along the minor coast road from Bushmills will take you to **PORTBALLINTRAE**, a decorous little place with a friendly **hotel** if you fancy staying over – the *Bayview Hotel* (☎02657/31453; £25), on the front at 2 Bayview Road. There's good **fishing** from the tiny harbour. The bus between Bushmills and Coleraine stops here.

Dunluce Castle

A couple of miles further west, where the main road rejoins the coast, sits sixteenth-century **Dunluce Castle** (Tues–Sat 10am–7pm; closes at 4pm Oct–March), easily the most impressive ruin along this entire coastline. Sited on a fine headland, high above a cave, it looks as if it only needs a roof to be perfectly habitable once again. Its history is inextricably linked with that of its original owner, **Sorley Boy MacDonnell**, whose MacDonnell clan, the so-called "Lords of the Isles", ruled northeastern Ulster from Dunluce. English incursions into the area culminated in 1584 with Sir John Perrott laying siege to Dunluce, forcing Sorley Boy ("Yellow Charles" in Gaelic) to leave the castle. But as soon as Perrott departed, leaving a garrison in charge, Sorley Boy hauled his men up the cliff in baskets and recaptured the castle, later repairing the damage with the proceeds of the salvaged wreckage of the Girona. Having made his point, Sorley Boy made his peace with the English, and his son, Randal, was created Viscount Dunluce and Earl of Antrim by James I. In 1639 Dunluce Castle paid the penalty for its precarious, if impregnable, position when the kitchen, complete with cooks and dinner, fell off during a storm. Shortly afterwards the MacDonnells moved to more comfortable lodgings at Glenarm, and Dunluce was left empty.

However, it remains an extraordinary place. The MacDonnells' Scottish connections – Sorley Boy's son continued to own land in Kintyre – show in the gatehouse's turrets and crow-step gables; the seventeenth-century Great Hall, medieval in plan but Renaissance in style, has tapering chimneys of the Scottish style; and there's a strange touch of luxury in the *loggia* that faces – oddly – away from the sun.

You can see the **cave** below the castle without paying to go in. Piercing right through the promontory upon which Dunluce stands, with an opening directly under the gatehouse, it's a spectacular scramble, particularly in wild weather.

Portrush, Portstewart and Castlerock

The coastline west of Dunluce, to **Magilligan Point**, is a major holiday spot, the twin resorts of **Portrush** and **Portstewart** filled with tourists in July and August, mainly from the rest of the North. **Castlerock**, too, gets its fair share of beach-goers, but the Inishowen Peninsula, on the other side of Lough Foyle, is now well in sight, and the beaches on the Republic side are often more exciting and less crowded. From Magilligan Point, site of a high-security prison as well as a nature reserve, the coastline – overlooked by the dramatic crag of **Binevenagh** – is flat and undramatic, some of it consisting of land reclaimed from the sea to grow flax for the eighteenth-century linen trade.

Portrush

PORTRUSH, built on the Ramore Peninsula, has sandy beaches backed by dunes, running both east and west, and everything you'd expect from a seaside resort, including summer drama staged in the Town Hall and plenty of amuse-ment arcades. Thanks to students from the University of Ulster at Coleraine, many of whom choose to live here, it's a considerably livelier place than you might expect, even out of season. The **beach** is long and sandy: to the east, towards Dunluce, it ends in the **White Rocks**, where the weather has carved the soft, limestone cliffs into strange shapes, the most famous of which is the so-called "Cathedral Cave", 180 feet from end to end. On a rather different level, Portrush's newest attraction is **Waterworld**, by the harbour: "an all-weather holi-day paradise with water flumes, slides, sauna, jacuzzis, aquarium and restaurant".

Nightlife is quite a serious business here. It centres on the disco at *Kelly's Hotel* and *Tracks* nightclub, and there are loads of convivial pubs. The *Ramore Restaurant* (at least £15 a head; expensive wine) serves good food, or the excel-lent *Rowland's Restaurant*, 92–94 Lower Main Street (☎0265/822063) has a three-course set menu for under £10, while there are plenty of cheap Chinese restau-rants, fish and chip shops and the like. The *Singing Kettle* on Atlantic Avenue is a coffee shop that offers healthier alternatives. The *Harbour Inn* is probably the nicest bar in town; it also has a decent modern restaurant.

Accommodation ranges from the *Eglington Hotel*, by the station at 49 Eglington Street (☎0265/822371; £26), not bad value for what you get, to dozens of **B&Bs** most of them very friendly and welcoming. Try, for example, *Glenkeen Guest House*, 59 Coleraine Road (☎0265/822279; £12), which has won tourist board awards; *Malvern House*, 36 Mark Street (☎0265/823435; £9); or two on Bath Terrace, *Rest-a-While* at no.6 (☎0265/822827; £10) and the *Clarence* at no.7 (☎0265/823575; £10). There are also lots of **campsites** in the area – though most of them are actually fairly unattractive caravan parks that take tents. Closest are the *Golf Links Hotel Caravan Park*, 140 Dunluce Road (☎0265/823539) and the municipal *Carrick Dhu Caravan Park*, 12 Ballyreagh Road (☎0265/823712). The **tourist office** (☎0265/823333; April–Sept Mon–Fri 9am–5pm, also weekends mid-June to mid-Sept) will book a place for you: it's in the Town Hall, and has plenty of information and maps of the Causeway Coast too.

Portstewart

Like Portrush, **PORTSTEWART** (which is actually across the county border in Derry) is full of Victorian boarding houses. Of the two, Portstewart has always had more airs and graces: the railway station is said to have been built a mile out of town (holidaymakers had to make the rest of the journey by steam tram) to stop vulgar people from coming. Certainly it's much more sedate – basically a family resort. In terms of sheer location, though, Portstewart wins hands down. Just west of the town is **Portstewart Strand**, a long, sand beach firm enough to drive on – which the locals delight in doing – with some of the best surfing in the country. Again, a good place if you hit fine weather and feel like getting out your bucket and spade. The best way to take the sea air is the bracing **cliffside walk** which runs between the beach and the town, passing battlements and an imposing convent.

There's slightly less here in the way of **accommodation**, though there is an independent **hostel**, *Inverness*, at 4 Victoria Terrace (☎0265/833789; £5). **Guesthouses** are mostly along the main road by the bay – the Town Hall **tourist office** (☎0265/832286) can help with bookings if you have any problems – or there's the *Edgewater Hotel*, 88 Strand Road (☎0265/832224; £28.50), with a breathtaking view from the lounge bar. There's a municipal **caravan park**, *Juniper Hill*, at 70 Ballyreagh Road (☎0265/832023; camping £6). *Morelli's*, on the promenade, is justly famous for its **ice cream**, and also serves snacks and Italian **food**. In the evenings *Nero's* **nightclub** is the newest place in town, with a pleasant pub attached.

Castlerock and Mussenden Temple

Beyond Portstewart, the coastline rears up as great cliffs once more, before settling down into monotonous flatness beyond Magilligan Point for the run into Derry. There's a long sand beach at **CASTLEROCK** (and a heated swimming pool, too) and, at the A2 crossroads a mile south of Castlerock, **Hezlett House** – a long, low thatched building of wood-cruck construction. It's a building method that's common in England, but enough of a rarity here to warrant preservation by the National Trust.

Further west along the A2, a pair of huge, ornate Pompeiian gates on the left mark the entry to **Mussenden Temple**, a domed rotunda clinging precariously to the cliff-edge. This is almost all that is left of the great estate of Frederick Harvey (1730–1803), fourth Earl of Bristol and (Anglican) Bishop of Derry, the enthusiastic traveller after whom all the *Hotel Bristols* throughout Europe are named. The "Earl Bishop", as he was known, commissioned Michael Shanahan to build the temple in honour of his cousin Mrs Frideswide Mussenden, who died before it was finished. It was then used as his summer library and, with characteristic generosity and a fairly startling lack of prejudice, the Earl Bishop allowed Mass to be celebrated in the temple once a week as there was no local Catholic church. The inscription on the frieze translates, smugly, as "It is agreeable to watch, from land, someone else involved in a great struggle while winds whip up the waves out at sea".

Inland: Coleraine and Limavady

Given the attractions of the coast, it's almost impossible to see why anyone would want to visit the two towns immediately inland, though you'll pass through if you're heading for Derry City, and Donegal, by the most direct route. **COLERAINE**, designated a joint conurbation with Portrush and Portstewart, is entirely unprepossessing. There's a big, pedestrianised shopping centre, anonymous and depressing. The one thing Coleraine does have going for it is a major campus of the University of Ulster, a bone of contention with the people of Derry, many of whom believe that the only reason the University didn't go there was that the authorities wanted it to be in a predominantly Protestant location.

There's a new **tourist office** on Railway Road by the station (☎0265/44723), which is very helpful and will try hard to convince you of the attractions of the place. In summer a **cruise boat** operates from Coleraine Marina (☎0265/44744), and will take you up and down the River Bann or on short sea jaunts – prices from £3. Also in summer there are interesting environmental **walks** (under the title *Talks and Tours*, details from the tourist office), and there's a fine **theatre** here too, the *Riverside*. The Coleraine campus provides cheap **accommodation** in the summer holiday (☎0265/44141), and there are B&Bs if you really want to stay.

Just a mile south of Coleraine, on the eastern bank of the river, **Mountsandel** is a two-hundred-foot mound, apparently the earliest-known dwelling place in Ireland, though the recent discoveries in Boora Bog in County Offaly must run it fairly close. The post-holes and hearths of the wooden houses that once stood here have been dated at around 7000 BC.

Limavady

LIMAVADY is a great improvement on Coleraine, though not exactly a holiday attraction either, with a broad main street that's still recognisably Georgian. Number 51 was the home of Jane Ross, who noted down the famous *Londonderry Air* – better known as *Danny Boy* – from a travelling fiddler in 1851. The **Roe Valley Country Park**, a couple of miles south of Limavady, preserves Ulster's first hydroelectric domestic power station, opened in 1896, with much of the original equipment intact, and a small weaving museum. There's also a **campsite** (☎05047/62074) if the ones on the coast didn't appeal. Tourist information is available from the Council offices at 7 Connell Street (☎05047/22226)

Derry City

DERRY lies at the foot of Lough Foyle, immediately before the border: a major crossroads where the coast road meets the faster, duller route direct from Belfast, and from where roads head on west into Donegal and the Republic, south into Tyrone. Ireland's fourth largest city, and the second largest in the North, its size makes it Belfast's sister city, but it has a markedly different atmosphere, being two-thirds Catholic. Within Ireland, Derry is highly regarded both for its characteristically caustic humour – best caught in the busier bars and at the football matches at the Brandywell – and for its musical pedigree, having produced names as diverse as Dana, Phil Coulter, The Undertones and many less well known. This last claim to recognition is misleading, though – Derry may produce musicians, but its own music scene is largely inaccessible to outsiders.

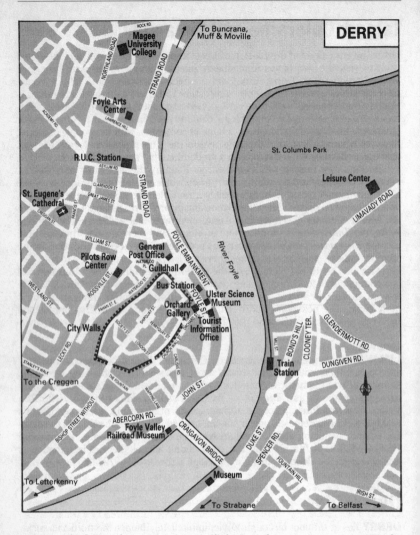

Approached from the east in winter twilight or under a strong summer sun, the city presents a beguiling picture, with the spread of the **River Foyle** and the rise of the city's two hillsides, terraced with pastel-shaded houses from which rise the hueless stone spires of the ever-present Church Orders. This scenic appeal apart – you'll get a similar overview from the city cemetery in the Creggan – Derry at first sight seems to have little to tempt you to stay overnight, for all the richness of its history. Yet there are things worth seeing, all of them enclosed within the seventeenth-century **walls**, themselves the most significant reminder of the city's past. And four miles or so out of the centre, across the border on the Letterkenny road, is an unmissable sight – the Grianán of Aileach, a stone fort that is the oldest habitation left standing in Ireland.

Outside of Ireland, the name of Derry brings to mind the troubles of recent years, difficulties with which the Bogside and the Creggan are inextricably associated. Don't be put off by this. Unlike Belfast, the cutting edge of violence has here receded considerably in the past few years, and a resurgence of optimism is being felt for the first time since the early Sixties. Moreover, the southern border is no more than a few miles away, making the city handy for a day excursion that anyone should jump at.

Historical background

Derry's original name was *Daire Calgaigh* meaning "the oakwood of Calgach", a warrior who led the Caledonians at the battle of the Grampians. This name remained in use until well after the coming of Saint Columba, who founded a monastery here in 546 AD; then, in the tenth century, the settlers renamed the spot *Doire Cholmcille*. As the annals of the city record, the settlement suffered frequent onslaughts, first from the Vikings, later from the Anglo-Norman barons de Courcy and Peyton. In 1566, Elizabeth I of England sent a small task force in a failed attempt to pacify such troublesome chieftains as Shane O'Neill, but at the end of the century the uprising of Hugh O'Neill, Earl of Tyrone, provoked another English invasion, this time successful. It paved the way for the first wide-scale "planting" of English and Scottish **settlers** in the reign of James I. *Doire* became anglicised to **Derry** and then, in 1613, "London" was bestowed as a prefix after land within the newly drawn borders of the county was awarded to the Twelve Companies of the Corporation of London. Today the entrance routes to the city bear the two different names – "Welcome to Londonderry, an historic city" and "Welcome to Derry, a nuclear free zone" – reflecting the changing sectarian majority on the city council.

The **seventeenth century** was the most dramatic phase of the city's evolution. The city walls withstood successive sieges, the last of which (in 1688–89) played a key part in the Williamite army's final victory over the Catholic King James II at the Battle of the Boyne – the Derrymens' obduracy crucially delaying the plans of James and his ally Louis XIV. Seven thousand of the city's thirty thousand inhabitants died during the fifteen-week **siege** (the longest in British history), the survivors being reduced to eating dogs, cats and rats. The suffering and heroism of those weeks still have the immediacy of recent history in the minds of Derry's citizens, who commemorate the siege through the skeleton on the city coat of arms, and the lyrical tag "maiden city", a reference to its unbreached walls.

After the siege many Derry people emigrated to America to avoid the harsh English laws, and some of their descendants – such as Daniel Boone and Davy Crockett – achieved fame there. George Farquhar (b. 1678), a Derryman who chose to stay, achieved fame as a playwright. Derry's heyday as a **seaport** came in the nineteenth century, a period in which industries such as linen production also flourished. It was a Derry weaver, William Scott, who established the world's first industrialised shirt manufacturers, cutting the shirts in Derry and sending them to the cottage women of Donegal for stitching. After **Partition**, the North–South dividing line lay right at Derry's back door, and the consequent tariffs cut off a lot of its traditional trade.

Civil Rights

Though Derry remained relatively peaceful, its politics were among the North's most blatantly discriminatory, with the substantial Catholic majority denied its civil rights by gerrymandering which ensured that the Protestant minority maintained control of all important local institutions. On October 5, 1968, a 2000-strong **civil rights march** – demanding equality of employment and housing, and other political rights, and led by a Protestant, Ivan Cooper, and a Catholic, John Hume – came up against the batons of the Protestant police force and the B Specials. It is an event which is seen by many as the catalyst of the present phase of the Troubles: faith in the impartiality of the RUC was destroyed once and for all, and the IRA was reborn a year or so later.

The Protestant Apprentice Boys' March, in August 1969, was a further step – the RUC attempted to storm the Bogside (from where stones were being thrown at the march), and for several days the area lay in a state of siege. The Irish prime minister, Jack Lynch, moved units of the army to the border and set up field hospitals for injured Bogsiders. In the mounting tension that ensued, British troops were for the first time widely deployed in the North, and many of the demands of the Civil Rights movement were forced on Stormont from Westminster. Then, on January 31, 1972, came **Bloody Sunday**. Thirteen people were shot dead when British paratroopers (who subsequently claimed that they had been shot at first) opened fire on another unarmed civil rights march.

These days the city is controlled by the SDLP, which attempts to be scrupulously non-sectarian. In this they seem to have been successful (at least in Northern Irish terms), and they also pursue an enlightened arts policy which has succeeded in making this a lively and unexpectedly entertaining place to visit.

Arriving and Accommodation

Northern Ireland Railways run about six **trains** a day from Belfast to Derry (information on ☎0504/42228), and there are also frequent **buses** to all parts of the North and the Republic: *Ulsterbus* (☎0504/262261) serves all the main Northern Ireland destinations and Dublin, at frequencies ranging between twice weekly to Dublin, and twelve weekly to Strabane; *Bus Éireann* operates a good network, connecting Derry to towns as far away as Galway and Dublin; and *Lough Swilly Bus Services* (☎0504/262017) have services across the border into north Donegal. Good roads enter the city from all directions, making it very straightforward to **hitch**. You can also **fly**: *Aer Lingus* operate from Dublin to Eglinton Airport (☎0504/810784), seven miles out on the A2 road, and there are also flights to Glasgow, Manchester and Gatwick.

The **tourist information** office is handily situated in the city centre, across from the bus station. Housed in a pagoda-like accretion, it contains both a *Bord Fáilte* office and a branch of the *Northern Ireland Tourist Board* (July–Sept Mon–Fri 9am–8pm, Sat 10am–5pm; Oct–June Mon–Fri 9am–1pm & 2–5.15pm; ☎0504/267284; *Bord Fáilte* ☎0504/369501). Grab a free pocket guidebook for up-to-date information.

Accommodation

There's a limited choice of **accommodation** in Derry, although the budget choices should be expanded considerably with new places opening to coincide with *Impact 92*.

B&Bs are fairly thin on the ground in the centre, but you could try the following, all charging around £10: *Clarence House*, 15 Northland Road (☎0504/265342); *Florence House*, 16 Northland Road (☎0504/268093); Joan Pine, 36 Great James Street (off Strand Road; ☎0504/269691); or *Quinn's*, 49 Clarendon Street (off Strand Road; ☎0504/264842). There's a **youth hostel** at 15–17 Lower Nassau Street and an independent hostel on Strand Road. Rooms are also seasonally available at the university; student rooms are let from approximately mid-June to mid-September, a week each side of Easter and a week each side of Christmas (£7 for students, £12 otherwise; Mon–Fri ☎0504/265621 ext 5218).

The City

The **walls** of Derry – some of the best preserved historical defences left standing in Europe – are the obvious starting point for a walkabout of the city, though iron sheeting and rolls of barbed wire laid down by the military make it impossible to walk right round. A mile in length and never higher than a two-storey house, the walls are reinforced by bulwarks and bastions, and a parapeted earth rampart as wide as any thoroughfare. Within their circuit, the original medieval street pattern has remained, with four **gateways** – Shipquay, Butcher, Bishop and Ferryquay – surviving from the first construction, in slightly revised form.

You're more than likely to make your approach from the Guildhall Square, once the old quay. Most of the city's cannons are lined up here, between Shipquay and Magazine gates, their noses peering out above the ramparts. A reconstruction of the medieval **O'Doherty Castle** was built here a few years back, and now houses local history exhibits and acts as an **interpretive centre** (☎0504/265238); the exterior blends well with the walls, but inside only a very roughshod estimation of sixteenth-century style has been attempted.

Turning left at Shipquay Gate into **Bank Place**, access to the walls' promenade is pretty immediate and opens up an unhampered stretch that runs nearly to the Ferryquay Gate. Several sculptures have been placed at strategic points on the walls by the English artist Antony Gormley, their gaping eye sockets looking out in diametrically opposite directions from a single body – a frank comment on the city's ideological split. Aesthetics aside, the figures provide welcome visual relief against the office buildings that swamp the immediate view.

Just off steeply sloping Shipquay Street as you penetrate towards the heart of the old city is **Derry Craft Village** (Mon–Sat 9.30am–5.30pm), an Inner City Trust project with shops and workplaces representing a range of traditional crafts in a purpose-built traditional stone village complex. This new venture is still expanding and well worth a visit – the elegant *Boston Tea Party* coffee shop is a good place to sit and take it all in.

Saint Columb's Cathedral and the Fountain area

The Protestant **Saint Columb's Cathedral**, built in 1633 in a style later called "Planter's Gothic", was the first cathedral to be constructed in the British Isles subsequent to the Reformation. On show in the entrance porch is a cannon shell fired during the siege by the besieging army, to which was attached their terms of surrender. The cathedral was used as a battery during the siege, its **tower** serving as a lookout post; today it provides the best view of the old city. The present spire dates from the late Georgian period, its lead-covered wooden predecessor having been stripped to fashion bullets and cannon shot. Inside, an open-

DERRY
CITY WALLS

timbered roof rests on sixteen stone corbels carved with portraits of past bishops; hanging above the nave, flags brought back from various military expeditions give the interior a strong sense of the British Empire. Other things to look out for are the finely sculpted reredos behind the altar, the eighteenth-century bishop's throne, and the window panels showing scenes as diverse as the relief of the city on August 12, 1689 and Saint Columba's mission to Britain. In the **chapter house** are more relics of the siege, plus the grand kidney-shaped desk of Bishop Berkeley and mementoes of Cecil Frances (1818–95), wife of Bishop Alexander and composer of the famous hymns: "Once in Royal David's City" and "There is a green hill far away".

Immediately outside the walls here is the **Fountain** area, to reach which you'll first need to pass by the **Courthouse**, built of white sandstone in crude Greek revival style, and then cut down through a passageway tucked into the left of the Bishop Gate arch. The Gate itself was remodelled for the first centenary of the siege, but today is defaced by a mangle of fences and scaffolding, underneath which skulks an army breezeblock hut. Before passing the glare of the RUC men, take a glance at the surrounding pieces of eighteenth-century architecture, evident even in boarded-up Dean Street. The Fountain area is a housing estate that sticks into the Catholic west bank like a sore thumb, with a single road entrance close to the Craigavon Bridge. It's of interest solely for its Union Jack kerb paintings and huge wall murals – one reads "LONDONDERRY/ WESTBANK LOYALISTS/STILL UNDER SIEGE/NO SURRENDER" in direct reply to the more famous Catholic "FREE DERRY" mural in the next valley.

The Bogside

If you want to avoid the Fountain, back-track down Bishop Street towards the Diamond, taking a left to the west section of the walls, or just follow the path round the outside. The Double Bastion on the west wall has now been taken over by the British army, its signal mast and cameras monitoring the activity in the valley below. The streets under surveillance are those of the **Bogside**, where, at the start of the Troubles, young Catholics were caught up in an advancing disarray of army and police, who replied to bricks and petrol bombs with tear gas, rubber bullets and careering Saracen armoured cars. The area at the foot of the escarpment has been redeveloped in the form of a dual carriageway, a new estate of tenement flats and empty concrete precincts. But clinging to the opposite hillside is a classic urban landscape, with turn-of-the-century terraces of stucco facades, blue tile roofs and red chimney stacks.

Most eye-catching in this panorama is an isolated wall bearing the slogan "YOU ARE NOW ENTERING FREE DERRY" – for the first two years of the Troubles the territory beyond was the notorious "No Go area", the undisputed preserve of the IRA. This autonomy lasted until 1972, when "Operation Motorman" was launched; the IRA men who had been in the area were warned, though, and got across the border before the invasion took place. Further across to the right of the wall stands the memorial pillar to the thirteen Catholic civilians killed on **Bloody Sunday** by British troops. The soldiers immediately claimed they were fired upon, a claim that was later disproved, though some witnesses have come forward to report seeing IRA men there with their guns. To the right of this area once stood the Rossville flats, by far the most famous part of the Bogside – Derry's Divis in fact. Further up the Westland Road, which runs up by the *Bogside Inn* – a former IRA stronghold, where the gunmen would set their revolvers on the bar while drinking – is a busy mural grouping the silhouetted faces of Bobby Sands, Che Guevara and Lenin; other murals are now faded, evidence of the greater stability of recent years.

Two museums

Finally, there are a couple of museums worth visiting. The new **Ulster Science Centre**, 32–38 Foyle Street (Mon–Sat 10am–5pm; £1.25; ☎0504/370239), opposite the tourist office, is thoroughly enjoyable (even if it is designed mainly for kids), with fascinating hands-on displays and regularly changing exhibitions. The **Foyle Valley Railway Centre**, on Foyle Road by Craigavon Bridge (☎0504/265234), is more interesting than it might sound. The highlight is a short ride up the Foyle Valley on a steam train, but there are also plenty of old engines and models, plus extensive displays on the history of railways in the area, a sad tale of decline enthusiastically explained.

Food, drink and entertainment

Although **eating** out in the city has improved dramatically over the last few years, you still won't be put out by a bewildering choice. Shipquay Street has the widest variety, including *Epicure* (Mon–Thurs & Sat 9am–5.30pm, Fri 9am–9pm), which does very tasty and reasonably priced pizzas and home-baked food. Even cheaper are *Anne's* on William Street, decorated with black-and-white photos of the Troubles in Derry, and the very sociable *Leprechaun* on the Strand. *Piemonte Pizzeria* on Clarendon Street is the best pizza place in town. The *India House*, 51–55 Carlisle Road, is an excellent Indian – main courses around £6. As ever, you can also get lunch in many of the pubs: the *Linenhall* in Linenhall Street and the *Monaco Lounge* beside the main post office, for example.

Bars and traditional music

What Derry lacks in restaurants, it makes up for, inevitably, in the **pubs**. For plain drinking and talk, the student set congregates at the *College*, *The Strand Tavern* and *Andy Cole's*, all grouped at the bottom of the Rock Road, and of course in the campus bar in Magee College grounds (where beer is 80p a pint). Other congenial and conversational places are *The Clarendon Bar*, 44 Strand Road; *Badgers Place*, 18 Orchard Street, with an older crowd; *The Metro* on Bank Place; and *The Forum* on Foyle Street behind the bus station – a big, friendly new bar with music at weekends.

Traditional music in the city is not as exciting as it once was: the venues that remain are all grouped in and around **Waterloo Street**, just outside the northern section of the walls, a mostly Catholic working-class area. The *Dungloe Bar* claims to be the most regular music-making place here, with traditional stuff on Monday and Wednesday evenings and a two-piece folk band on Thursdays and Fridays. Other sessions take place at the *Rocking Chair Pub* and the *Gweedore Bar*, which has a function room upstairs with good music and dancing, and often stays open until 1am. Elsewhere, the *Phoenix Bar*, on Park Avenue in the Rosemount area, has traditional music on a Tuesday evening, as does the *Pilot's Row Centre* (7.30–9.30pm), which also offers classes in Irish dancing, music and language. The *Bogside Inn* on Westland road has music on a Thursday evening.

For livelier **nightlife** head for Shipquay Street, where the *River Inn* and *Townsman* pubs and the cavernous *Squire's* nightclub all attract a young crowd.

Another popular thing to do on Friday and Saturday nights is cross the border, to nightclubs at Quigley's Point, Redcastle and the White Strand, Buncrana.

Arts and other entertainment

The Derry arts scene is a surprisingly active one, especially thanks to **Impact 92**, a year of arts and entertainments in the city which aims to raise the profile of Derry and attract both visitors and working artists of all sorts. There's been some local controversy about the "high art" nature of many of the events, but it certainly looks set to liven things up. Further information from the tourist office, or the *Impact 92* offices at 8 Bishop Street (☎0504/265686).

Classical music thrives in the city through the Londonderry Arts Association, with around a dozen concerts a year held in the Great Hall of Magee University College. Orchestral concerts by the Ulster Orchestra are held much less regularly in the Great Hall of the Guildhall. The vanguard of **theatre** in the city is *Field Day*, one of Ireland's most notable companies, principally directed by a set of Derrymen (Seamus Heaney, Seamus Deane and Brian Friel) and a few other artistic luminaries (Tom Paulin and Stephen Rea). Their repertoire comprises mainly new work by contemporary Irish playwrights dealing with historical-political themes, and they invariably premiere in Derry, normally in the Guildhall during September.

The **visual arts** are also attracting a lot of international attention, thanks largely to the highly innovative contemporary art programming of the *Orchard Gallery* in Orchard Street; a visit there is a must – and watch out for the exhibitions it sometimes arranges in the *Foyle Arts Centre*, off Lawrence Hill, or at other venues around the city. The *Heritage Library*, on Bishop Street, occasionally has local artists' work on display.

Several **arts festivals** take place at regular times throughout the year, the most interesting of them being the *Foyle Film Festival* (late October) and the *North West Arts Festival* (early November). In addition, **Halloween** is traditionally an excuse for riotous celebration, with fireworks, fancy dress, and partying in the streets. The tourist information office will have further details. There's a **cinema** at the city end of the Strand Road and another next to the *Orchard Gallery* on Orchard Street.

Listings

Banks Principally situated on Shipquay Street and Waterloo Place.

Bicycle repairs *Sackville Cycles*, 5 Sackville Street (☎0504/268330); *McClean Bros*, 108 Spencer Road (☎0504/43171).

Bookshop *Bookworm* on Bishop Street is one of the best bookshops in the country, comprehensive and with excellent coverage of contemporary and historical Irish works.

Car Hire *Hertz*, c/o *Desmond Motors*, 173 Strand Road (☎0504/360420).

Hospital Accident and emergency department, Altnagelvin Hospital on the Belfast Road (☎0504/45171); contact this number for **dental** emergencies after working hours or at weekends.

Launderette 147 Spencer Road.

Library The Central Library (Foyle Street) has a good selection on Irish studies and local history.

Market Bottom of Orchard Street every Saturday.

Newspapers The Catholic *Derry Journal* (Tues & Fri) is good for entertainment listings; the Protestant local paper is the *Londonderry Sentinel* (Wed).

Taxis Black cabs run from Foyle Street and most operate in a similar way to those in Belfast, functioning like minibuses to ferry the Catholic community to and from their housing estates. If you want a regular taxi, call: *Auto Cabs* (☎0504/45100); *Blue Star Taxis* (☎0504/264888); or *Quick Cabs* (☎0504/260515).

Police ☎0504/265161.

Women's Centre 7 London Street, for information and advice (Mon–Fri 9.30am–5pm; ☎0504/267672).

Southern Derry: Dungiven and the planned towns

South of the A6, the Derry to Antrim road, the landscape settles down into a pattern more familiar to the Republic: fertile farming land, rising to the **Sperrin Mountains**, punctuated by small, planned towns. The pattern is subtly different from the south, though, because the grants of land here were not made to individuals, but to various London Guilds or companies. Consequently, there isn't the strange, late-flowering feudalism that you see in the south, with its repeated archetype of big house and surrounding town, but rather entirely **planned towns**, often built on green-field sites selected by professionals, who specialised in doing just that.

Coming from the coast, **DUNGIVEN**, 18 miles east of Derry, provides a small shock, as it's the first place where there's an army control zone (no unattended vehicles) and (periodically) a heavy military presence. Originally an O'Cahan stronghold, Dungiven was given to the *Skinners' Company* to settle in the seventeenth century. The remains of the O'Cahan fortifications are incorporated into the ruined nineteenth-century **castle**, whose battlemented outline gives Dungiven a particular flavour when approached from the south. This was the scene of the 1971 attempt to set up an independent Northern Ireland parliament.

Dungiven Priory, signposted down a footpath a little way out of the town towards Antrim, gives a taste of the pioneering life of the early plantation settlers, and of the continuity of tradition. No more than a ruin, the Augustinian priory stands on an imposing, defensible site on a bluff above the river. Founded in 1100 by the O'Cahans, it belongs to the first wave of European monastic orders which arrived in Ireland to supplant the Celtic church. The church contains the tomb of Cooey na Gall O'Cahan, who died in 1385, rated as the finest medieval tomb in Northern Ireland: beneath the effigy are six bare-legged warriors in kilts, presumably denoting Scotsmen, who represent the O'Cahan chieftain's foreign mercenaries, from whom he derived his nickname, na Gall, or "of the foreigners". At some point, the O'Cahans added a defensive tower to the west end of the church and later – when Dungiven was granted to the *Skinners' Company*, in the person of Sir Edward Doddington – this was enlarged to become a two-and-a-half storeyed defensive manor house. There's an evocative artist's impression on the site of what that building looked like.

Although the church hasn't been used since 1711, Dungiven Priory remains a religious site of sorts. The tree knotted with rags – handkerchiefs, torn-off bits of summer dresses, socks – stands over a deeply hollowed stone, originally used by the monks for milling grain, and now an object of pilgrimage for people seeking cures for physical illness.

Draperstown, Moneymore, Magherafelt and Upperlands

South of Dungiven, well into the Sperrin Mountains, are more of the **plantation towns** of the London companies, most of them characteristically planned around a central diamond. **DRAPERSTOWN**, unsurprisingly founded by the *Drapers' Company*, is essentially a junction, with well-mannered houses facing each other in a very grand street plan. The real gem, though, is **MONEYMORE**, to the southeast, also built by the Drapers, and reconstructed by them in 1817 – graceful, pedimented buildings facing each other across a wide, main street topped by an Orange Hall (plenty of red, white and blue kerbstones here). It was the first town in Ulster to have piped water; amazingly, as early as 1615. Just outside Moneymore, **Springhill** (Easter week 2–6pm daily; May, June & Sept Sat & Sun 2–6pm; July & Aug Fri–Wed 2–6pm) is a typical example of the fortified manor houses built by the early planters. Dating from the late-seventeenth century, it's a lovely bit of sober, whitewashed architecture, housing a good costume collection.

MAGHERAFELT, granted to the *Salters' Company* by James I, has another wide, sloping main street with Union Jacks fluttering everywhere. Of more delaying interest, just north of MAGHERA, at **UPPERLANDS**, you can get some idea of the impact of the new eighteenth-century technology on the area. The **Middle House Museum** here is a private textile museum owned by the Clark family: in 1740, Jackson Clark dammed the river to provide power and installed linen finishing machinery here. If you want to look around, phone Wallace Clark (☎0648/ 42214, 42737) in advance to arrange a guided tour.

South Antrim: Ballymena to Belfast

South Antrim is unlikely travelling country, largely rolling (and unexciting) farmland, with places whose names are familiar because you've heard them so often on the news: Ballymena, Antrim and Lisburn. Still, you're likely to see something of most of these towns as the train from Belfast passes through them on the way to the northern coast.

Ballymena and Gracehill

BALLYMENA (pronounced, incidentally, "Ballamena", unless you're a BBC newsreader) is a fine, upstanding Protestant town that could have been transplanted straight from the Scottish lowlands. Indeed, most of its Plantation settlers came from the southwest of Scotland, and the Ballymena accent still retains traces of Scottish lowlands speech. Like many Northern Irish towns, its prosperity derived from the linen trade, while the alleged tightfistedness of its residents earned it the sobriquet the "Aberdeen of Ireland". A mile and a half west of Ballymena is **GRACEHILL**, a reminder of the curious mixture of religious oppression and tolerance that has characterised Northern Ireland's history: at the same time as Ireland's Catholics were suffering heavy penalties, the country was welcoming dissenting Protestant groups, among them the Moravians (the United Brethren), who built a model settlement at Gracehill. The elegant square survives, with separate buildings for men and women, whose main trade was making lace and clocks. Segregated in life, the sexes remained divided in death, and in the graveyard you can walk down the long path that separates the graves of the men from those of the women.

Antrim

ANTRIM, by way of contrast, is a tacky and depressing town, the sort of place that despite its recent growth – the population has trebled in the last fifteen years – isn't really given a chance by either the Troubles or the grim economics of Northern Ireland. If you've time to kill, there's a tenth-century **round tower** in Steeple Park, a mile out of town, indicating the site of an important monastery that flourished between the sixth and twelfth centuries; and a pretty, if unremarkable, eighteenth-century cottage, *Pogue's Entry*, off the main street (ask for the key at *Simpson's* newsagents at 32 Church Street). **Belfast International Airport** is just four miles south of Antrim, but luckily this doesn't mean that you have to stick around – the transport links to Belfast are much better than to Antrim.

Lisburn

LISBURN, practically a suburb of Belfast, and a grimy, uninteresting sprawl of cut-price shops, is also best ignored. Again, there are few clues to its past as an important linen town. After the revocation of the Edict of Nantes in 1685, which removed French and Dutch Huguenots' freedom of worship, large numbers of them were persuaded to come to Ulster, where they founded the linen trade. Bleach greens were set up along the banks of the Lagan River; the first of them started in 1626 at LAMBEG, a mile downstream from Lisburn. The place has given its name to the big drums which appear in the Orange marches, deriving from the military drums of Prince William's army. The **museum** (Tues–Sat 11am–1pm & 1.45–4.45pm; closed Sat in winter) in Lisburn's Market Square has a permanent exhibition on the development of the linen trade.

Long Kesh

The political prison of **Long Kesh,** or **the Maze,** which lies to the south of Lisburn and is clearly visible from the main M1 motorway, incorporates the notorious H-Blocks which were the focus of the 1981 **Hunger Strikes**, in which Republican inmates demanded the reinstatement of political status. The prison, erected on an old airfield soon after the Troubles began, housed hundreds of activists, Loyalist and Republican, interned without trial by the British government. Originally all inmates – convicted prisoners as well as internees – had special category status (a kind of POW status), in conjunction with the Emergency Powers legislation under which they had been convicted, but when the British Government phased out internment in late 1975, special status went with it. From March 1, 1976, the prison was in the peculiar position of housing the last of these special category prisoners as well as – in the H-blocks – those convicted after this cut-off date, who were now classified, and treated, as ordinary criminals.

The IRA campaign for the reinstatement of status began in 1976 when Kevin Nugent, in refusing to wear prison clothes, initiated what become known as the "blanket protest" (quite simply, draping a blanket around himself instead of wearing prison clothes). By 1978 this had escalated into the famous "dirty protest" in which Republican prisoners refused to undertake ordinary prison duties such as emptying chamber pots, resorting instead to smearing the cells with their own excrement in order to get rid of it. In 1981 a concerted hunger strike led to the deaths of ten men, including Bobby Sands, provisional commander of the IRA men inside the prison, who had, significantly, been elected MP for Fermanagh–

South Tyrone six weeks into his fast. None of this succeeded in budging the government who steadfastly refused to back down in the face of what they believed was nothing more than moral blackmail. The motivation for the hunger strikes was made manifestly clear in a piece of contemporary graffiti that appeared in Republican areas:

> *I'll wear no convict's uniform*
> *Nor meekly serve my time*
> *That England might brand Ireland's fight*
> *Eight hundred years of crime.*

travel details

Trains
From Derry to Dublin Connolly Stn (6; 2hr 20min); Belfast (6; 2hr 20min); Portrush (6; 1hr); Coleraine (6; 40min); Ballymena (6; 1hr 20min).

Ulsterbus
From Derry to Dublin (3; 4hr 40min); Sligo (1; 2hr 45min); Donegal (1; 1hr 10min); Monaghan (3; 2hr 5min).

Private buses
Funtrek (☎01/730852) runs a daily service **from Derry** bus depot to Dublin via Monaghan, Omagh and Strabane.

CHAPTER SIXTEEN

DOWN AND ARMAGH

D own and Armagh occupy the southwest corner of Northern Ireland, between Belfast and the border. It's territory where all too many of the names are familiar from the news, and certainly the border areas, especially South Armagh, have borne more than their share of the Troubles. But it's also very attractive country, especially around the coast, with a rich history which takes in **Saint Patrick** – who sailed into Strangford Lough to make his final Irish landfall in County Down, founded his first bishopric at Armagh, and is buried at either Downpatrick or Armagh, depending whose claim you choose – and the constant defence of Ulster from invasion.

Heading south from Belfast, the glowering **Mourne Mountains** dominate every view, and it's in this direction that most of the attractions lie. If you simply take the main roads in and out of Belfast – the A1 for Newry and the border or the M1 motorway west – you'll come across very little to stop for: it's in the rural areas, the mountains and coast that the charm of this region lies. Probably the best option is to head east from Belfast around the Down shore, through the **Ards Peninsula** or along the banks of **Strangford Lough**, towards **Newcastle**, the best base for excursions (on foot) into the Mourne Mountains. Along the way there are plenty of little beaches, early Christian sites and fine houses to stop for. Immediately outside Belfast in this direction – easy day trips from there – are the **Ulster Folk and Transport Museum**, one of the best in the North, and the overblown suburban resort of **Bangor**. Beyond the Mournes a fine coast road curves around to **Carlingford Lough** and the border.

Inland there's less of interest, certainly in County Down. **Armagh City**, though, is well worth some of your time for its ancient associations, cathedrals and fine Georgian streets. South Armagh has some startlingly attractive country, especially around **Slieve Gullion**, though its border position makes travelling here a less appealing proposition than it might otherwise appear.

COUNTY DOWN

In **County Down** it's the coast, and the Mourne Mountains at the southern extremity, that you're heading for. The big towns in the north, **Newtownards** and **Bangor**, are not at all attractive, but beyond them the A2 road clings to the coast all the way round to Newry, or lesser routes follow the shores of Strangford Lough towards **Downpatrick** and its associations with the arrival of Saint Patrick. There are numerous small resorts around the coast but **Newcastle** is the biggest, and in some ways the most enjoyable. It's also the ideal place to start your exploration of the mountains.

Transport is pretty good on the main roads, with frequent buses connecting anywhere of any size, but yet again if you want to explore the countryside in any depth you'll need your own transport: much of Down is ideal cycling country.

Routes east from Belfast

Heading east into County Down from Belfast, you've a choice of two routes: the A2, which heads up to Bangor and follows the coast right around the edge of the county, to wind up in Newry; or the A20 directly east to Newtownards, at the head of Strangford Lough. Following the **A20** you'll pass **Stormont** (p.432), four miles from the city centre.

Once you get on to the dual carriageway after DUNDONALD, the single interesting sight is **Scrabo Tower**, standing on a rocky, gorse-clad knoll of a hill – actually a long extinct volcano. Getting to the tower after you've spotted it is quite a circuitous business, but follow the signs to *Scrabo Country Park* and you'll arrive in the car park just below. Up close it looks quite monstrous, like some giant rocket in its launcher, hewn out of rough black volcanic rock. It was built in 1857 as a memorial to the third Marquess of Londonderry, General Charles William Stewart-Vane, in gratitude for his efforts on behalf of his tenants during the Great Famine. The spot was originally a Bronze Age burial cairn, probably the resting place of one of the grand chieftains of the area. It's now very popular with sightseers, who come mostly for the wonderful views across Strangford Lough and the healthy, blustery weather that often curls around the side of the hill. The woodland immediately behind is country park open to the public (information from the warden's office; ☎0247/811491); in contrast to the tamed, prosperous countryside roundabout, Scrabo is the only piece of ground for miles around to feel at all wild. **NEWTOWNARDS**, a place strong on manufacture but unexciting for the traveller, is evenly spread out below. What you see of it from Scrabo is probably as much as you'd ever want to: if you do visit there's a ruined Dominican Priory, an ancient market cross, and a Scrabo stone market house (1765), now the Town Hall/Arts Centre.

The Ulster Folk and Transport Museum

The **A2** towards Bangor is both more scenic and more interesting, and still within easy reach of a day trip from Belfast. There's a lovely fifteen-mile walk between HOLYWOOD (pronounced "Hollywood") and Helen's Bay, along a mildly indented estuary coast with some beautiful silvery sand beaches, especially the small crescent-shaped ones at Helen's Bay itself. The railway runs between the path and the road, with a couple of stations where you can pick up services on towards Bangor.

At CULTRA station you can alight for the **Ulster Folk and Transport Museum** (May–Sept Mon–Sat 11am–6pm, Sun 2–6pm, until 9pm Wed May & June; Oct–April Mon–Sat 11am–5pm, Sun 2–5pm; £2.20; ☎0232/428428; *Ulsterbus* #1 from the Oxford Street terminus will also stop here), one of the most fascinating in the North. The main site is an open-air museum, still being added to, where about twenty typical buildings from all over the North – and ranging back as far as the eighteenth century – have been gathered and rebuilt, as far as possible in authentic settings and with furnishings as they would have been. The idea is that you can walk from one part of Northern Ireland to another, amid scenes typical to each: to this end traditional farms have also been created, and assorted livestock roams between the buildings. You start with a gallery where there are exhibitions, permanent and temporary, on Ulster's social history, and an introduction to

BEL

Lough Neagh

Lisburn

Dungannon

The Argory

Moy
Charlemont

Lurgan

Craigavon

River Lagan

Hillsborough

Benburb

Ardress House
Portadown

Loughgall

Blackwaterdown

Richhill

River Bann

Dromore

D O W

Armagh

Tandragee

Banbridge

Hamiltonsbawn

Scarva

Legananny Dolmen

A R M A G H

Gosford
Forest Park

Markethill

Castlewella
Forest Pa

Monaghan

Keady

Rathfriland

Newtownhamilton

Bessbrook

Hilltown

Spelga Dam

Derrymore
House

Newry

Ballymacdermot
Cairn

Narrow
Water C.

Killevy Church

Slieve Gullion
573 m

Jonesborough

War on
Point

Rostrevor

Ulster Way

M o u r n e M

Fairy Glen

Crossmaglen

Forkill

Omeath

Greencas

Dundalk

Cooley Peninsula

To Liverpool

To Douglas
(Isle of Man)

Belfast Lough

Grey Helen's
Point Bay

Bangor

Crawfordsburn

Copeland Island

Holywood

Donaghadee

The Ulster Folk
Museum

Stormont
Parliament House

Millisle

Newtownards

Scrabo Hill

Comber

Mount
Stewart
Gardens

Greyabbey Ballywalter

Ards Peninsula

Mahee
Island

Strangford
Lough

Saintfield

Portavogie

Rowallane
Gardens

Ballynahinch

Killyleagh

Audley's
Castle

Portaferry Kearney Point

Castleward House

Strangford

Inch
Abbey

oughinisland

Saul

Kilclief

Ballyquintin Point

Downpatrick

Killard Point

Clough

Dundrum

Killough

Ardglass

Dundrum Bay

St. John's Point

Newcastle

Tollymore
Forest Park

Irish Sea

Annalong

0   15 miles

the buildings you'll see. From here you walk around the grounds, visiting the various buildings (not all of which are always open); they include a small village street with church and rectory, two schools, various typical farm dwellings, and a forge and other buildings used in light manufacture.

On the far side of the main road, across a bridge, are the **transport galleries** (an annexe of the Belfast transport museum), where the exhibits include every conceivable form of transport from horse-drawn carts to lifeboats and a vertical take-off plane, but especially veteran cars (and, of course, a De Lorean). Outside the galleries there's a miniature railway, which runs on summer Saturdays, and back in the main section there's a handy **restaurant**, located in the Education Centre.

Helen's Bay

If you're not walking, **HELEN'S BAY** is signposted a mile off the A2, or it's another stop on the Belfast–Bangor rail line. It's a rather smug but restful little place, with a red-painted baronial-style station and a big pitch and putt course. **Grey Point Fort** (open Easter–Oct daily 9am–5pm; winter Sun 2–5pm; ☎0247/85362), a little to the left of the bay and on the walking path, is positioned to command the mouth of Belfast Lough, along with its sister fort at Kilroot on the other side. The fort has what you'd expect by way of quarters, engine house and stores, as well as an impressive battery of gun emplacements, ready to challenge the shipping that entered the lough during the two world wars. In the event, the two six-inch breech-loading guns were never fired except in practice, but they still look pretty impressive. The Battery Observation Post and Fire Command Post are today manned by dressed-up mannequins, like stills taken from a war movie – though they're now staring straight into a growth of trees that have sprung up to obscure the view. There's also a selection of photos showing the original guns and their positions; but it's really as a viewpoint with an atmosphere of military history, rather than the other way round, that the fort is worth visiting nowadays.

The fort, and in fact the whole short stretch of coast from Helen's Bay, is actually part of the **Crawfordsburn Country Park**, an estate handed down from the Scottish Presbyterian Crawford family, then acquired by Lord Dufferin (whose mother Helen gave her name to the bay) and now in public hands. Its glens and dells are replete with beeches, cypresses, exotic conifers, cedars, the usual burst of rhododendrons and also a Californian Giant Redwood. Perhaps the best walk (well marked) is to follow the pathway back from Grey Point to the top of the bay's beaches, and turn inland by the stream (Crawford's Burn). This will take you up through the best of the woodland, under a fine nineteenth-century rail viaduct (still in use), and up to a waterfall at the head of the glen. The **Park Centre** has a restaurant (a bit pricey) and a video show on the area's chief attractions; you can also **camp** on the estate. **Helen's Tower**, which can be seen from a considerable distance, was built by Lord Dufferin in the nineteenth century to honour his mother, and as a famine relief project.

CRAWFORDSBURN village is on one of Ireland's most ancient highways, an ancient track that ran from Holywood to Bangor Abbey – now the B20 – and has a nice but twee (as with many things in this part of the world) early seventeenth-century **pub**, *The Old Inn*, which serves cheap lunch specials.

Strangford Lough and the Ards Peninsula

The three most scenic routes south through County Down are all to the east. The **Ards Peninsula** stretches out an arm to enclose the waters of **Strangford Lough**, with only the narrowest of openings to the sea in the south, and it's around the lough's waters that most of the area's interest is concentrated. Ancient annals say the lough was formed around 1654 BC by the sea sweeping in over the lands of Brena. This created a beautiful, calm inlet, the archipelago-like pieces of land along its inner arm fringed with brown and yellow bladderwrack and tangle weed, and tenanted by a rich gathering of bird life during the warmer months, and vast flocks of geese and waders in the winter. It makes a sporting haven for small boats and yachts, and several attractive stopping-off places for the land-bound make the road along the lough's western bank the most interesting of all routes leading south from Belfast.

Bangor and the outer arm

Surprisingly perhaps, the least interesting of the three possible routes is the coastal trip along the peninsula's outer arm from Bangor down to Portaferry. **BANGOR** has been a popular seaside resort for Belfast people since Victorian times, but today it's pretty dull – as much a suburb of Belfast as a holiday spot – and its attractions, apart from a vast new marina, rather tawdry. There are, however, plenty of facilities for visitors, and scores of **B&Bs**, concentrated especially in Queen's Parade, Princetown Road and Seacliff Road. What history the place has, as yet another ancient monastic settlement, has entirely disappeared, and Bangor's one claim to historical fame now lies in the Ambrosian Library in Milan. This is the *Antiphonarium Benchorense*, one of the oldest known ecclesiastical manuscripts, consisting of collects, anthems and some religious poems. It came originally from the great Bangor Abbey (one of the most powerful for nearly 800 years), though had it remained here it would surely have perished with the abbey's destruction.

Moving south along the Ards coast, you'll find many **camping sites** along the A2 – at DONAGHADEE, MILLISLE, BALLYHALBERT and CLOGHY, to name a few – but it's far from the most attractive coastline hereabouts. Just about the only minor piece of interest is the late eighteenth-century **Ballycopeland windmill** (April–Sept Tues–Sat 10am–7pm, Sun 2–7pm; Oct–March Sat 10am–4pm, Sun 2–4pm), a mile west of Millisle. This claims to be the only working windmill in Ireland. You'll find a great deal more to detain you if you follow one of the shores of the lough.

Along the western bank

Leaving Scrabo Tower on the A20, you'll pick up signs for COMBER (famous only for its potatoes) and then Downpatrick, with a turning to *Castle Espie Wildfowl and Wetland Centre* on your left (daily 10.30am–sunset; £1.80) – it has a variety of ducks, geese and swans, plus a coffee shop and art gallery. Immediately after the conservation centre you'll see the excellent *Old Schoolhouse Restaurant* by the roadside, unmistakable with a fire engine lodged in its front garden; there's a fair priced Sunday lunch (otherwise open Tues–Sat 7–11pm; ☎0238/541182). From here, you can wind along the very edge of the lough, on a series of minor roads.

Travelling this route is enjoyable in itself, but there are a couple of spots worth making for. First of them is **Mahee Island**, named for Saint Mochaoi, the first abbot of the island, who died tragically, burned in his cell. Heading past crumbling Mahee Castle (currently undergoing repairs) at the entrance to the island, and over the causeway, you come to the Celtic **Nendrum Monastic Site** a few hundred yards further on. It's a gorgeous spot, surrounded by drumlins and the lough's waterways. This was once a sizeable establishment, with church, round tower, school and living quarters all housed in a *cashel* of three concentric wards, which is itself probably even earlier. Today, the inner wall shelters the ruined church, and a reconstructed sundial uses some of the original remnants. There's an illuminating reconstruction map at the site and a helpful visitors' centre.

Back on the road along the lough, follow the signs to Ardmillan, Killinchy (*Balloo House* here is an excellent restaurant, with garden) and then Whiterock for **Sketrick Island** (which itself is not signposted). As with Mahee Island, there's a castle to guard the entrance, now no more than a shattered reminder. *Daft Eddy's Pub and Restaurant*, behind the castle, offers bar snacks as well as a more elaborate restaurant menu. An equally daft competition known as the **Hen Island race** takes place here in October, when craft constructed from oil drums and crates are ridden and paddled between Sketrick and the nearby Hen Island.

The tiny coves and inlets at the feet of little drumlins continue as far as Killyleagh, almost any of them worth exploring. The best way to do this would be to **hire a sailing boat** for a day or more, which you can do at RINGAHADDY, about halfway down the lough, from Alan McGarvey at *Strangford Lough Charters* (☎0238/541186; £15–35 per day, £150–200 per week, depending on season).

Killyleagh

Approaching **KILLYLEAGH**, what looks like a huge child's sandcastle comes into view, wholly out of character with the area. This began life as a John de Courcy castle in the late twelfth century, but went through a major overhaul by the Hamilton family in the nineteenth century to give it the Bavarian schloss appearance it has today. It's still a private house, and when viewed close up it's much more gaunt, with a squat mixture of high step crenellations, turrets and cones. The stone outside the castle gates commemorates the town's most famous son, Hans Sloane (1660–1753), physician to King George II and founder of both the British Museum and Kew Gardens – London's Sloane Square is named after him. Through rather more obscure connections, Prince Andrew was created Baron Killyleagh on his wedding day in 1986, the Duchess of York having some ancestors from here.

The lough's eastern shore

Over on the Ards Peninsula, the eastern edge of Strangford Lough is not as indented as its opposite shore, but betters it in having a major road (the continuation of the A20) that runs close to the water virtually all the way down. The scenery is delightful, and there are two places to stop off en route to Portaferry – the Mount Stewart Gardens and Grey Abbey.

Mount Stewart

The National Trust-owned **Mount Stewart House and Gardens** (June–Aug Tues–Sun noon–6pm; May & Sept Wed–Sun 2–6pm; April & Oct weekends 2–

6pm; ☎0247/74387) lie five miles southeast of Newtownards. The **gardens**, only part of an eighty-acre estate, are laid out on a grand scale. The trees and shrubs here are no more than sixty to seventy years old, but they've grown at such a remarkable rate that they look twice that. This is principally due to the microclimate, which is unusually warm and humid – the gardens get the east coast sun, causing a heavy overnight dew, and the Gulf Stream washes the shores only a stone's throw away; surprisingly for so far north, conditions here rival those of Cornwall and Devon. It was Lady Londonderry, wife of the seventh Marquess, who laid out these gardens from about 1920 on, and a thorough job she made of it; titles include the Mairi Garden (after her daughter), Italian Garden, Spanish Garden, Peace Garden, Sunk Garden, Shamrock Garden and many more; well worth visiting in the blooming season.

The **House** is also worth a visit. It was once the Irish seat of the Londonderrys, one of whom, Viscount Castlereagh, acted as Foreign Secretary under Pitt in the late eighteenth and early nineteenth centuries, and is best remembered for guiding the Act of Union into operation. Among the splendid (and occasionally eccentric) furniture inside, much of it once again the work of Lady Londonderry, is a set of 22 empire chairs used by the delegates to the Congress of Vienna in 1815, including the Duke of Wellington and the Prince de Talleyrand; the chairs were a gift to the Viscount's brother Lord Stewart, another high-ranking diplomat of the time. The European connection is flaunted further in bedrooms named after various major cities; Rome, St Petersburg, Madrid, Moscow and also Sebastopol (from the time of the Crimean war). One of the most notable and largest paintings in the house (and in Ireland for that matter) is *Hambletonian* (1799) by George Stubbs, showing the celebrated thoroughbred being rubbed down after a victory at Newmarket. A little to the east of the house, the **Temple of the Winds** is a remodelling of the Athenian *Tower of Andronicus Cyrrhestes* by James "Athenian" Stuart (1713–88), one of the pioneers of Neoclassical architecture. The Temple is set on a promontory overlooking Strangford Lough, making it a great place for bird watching.

Grey Abbey

A short diversion from Mount Stewart will take you to CARROWDORE, in the middle of the peninsula, and the grave of the Ulster poet, **Louis MacNeice** (1907–63). Continuing on the shore road, however, **Grey Abbey** (April–Sept Tues–Sat 10am–1pm & 2–6pm, Sun 2–6pm; Oct–March Tues–Sat 10am–1pm & 2–4pm, Sun 2–4pm) is only a couple of miles further on: approaching from the north, take a left turn in the village of GREY ABBEY. Typical of the Cistercian, or "white monks" order, of which Mellifont was the mother house, Grey Abbey sits in remote parkland beside the fresh running water of a rivulet, a perfect example of the kind of idyllic setting the Cistercians used to seek. Even today, that setting is barely disturbed, and reason in itself to visit, with a substantial set of ruins to complete the picture.

The abbey was founded in 1193 by Affreca, daughter of the King of Man and wife of John de Courcy, as a thanksgiving for having made a safe sea-crossing during a storm. Its plans conform pretty much to the same shape as all Cistercian abbeys, with a church at one end and the living and working quarters of the monks ranged around a cloister, and its structure was realised in a very plain manner, without distracting embellishments. Grey Abbey is unusual for Ireland, though, in showing early Gothic features at a time when late Romanesque work was still common here. Among the best-preserved remains are the **west door**, much of whose carved decoration can still be made out, and the church in general. Another unusual feature is that the church is a simple hall, with no aisles around which the monks could process.

Outside the church, the guide notes on display help you to imagine the covered alleys and walks of the elongated rectangular cloister that would have been overshadowed on three sides by buildings which are now no more than stumps. These would have included the Chapter House, dormitories and refectory. There's a **B&B** in the village (*Gordonall*, 93 Newtownards Road; ☎0247/74325; £12) if you want to stay in these parts: the village itself is known for its antique shops.

Portaferry

PORTAFERRY marks the bottom end of the peninsula and the only place of any real size beyond Newtownards. It's the home of the **Northern Ireland Aquarium** (☎02477/28062), but the main attraction is the marvellous **sunset** looking across the "Narrows" to Strangford. In July the **Galway Hookers Regatta** livens the place up – the traditional boats sail round from Galway to be welcomed by the *Portaferry Yacht Club*, and every pub has virtually 24-hour music sessions.

The pubs are good at just about any time of year, in fact, and if you're looking for somewhere to **stay**, there's B&B for around £10 with the Adairs (22 The Square; ☎02477/28412) or a little way out at *Millview Farm* (8 Abbacy Road, ☎02477/28030), or there's the *Portaferry Hotel* (10 The Strand; ☎02477/28231; £25), which also has a decent restaurant. **Ferries** leave regularly (every half hour or so; 50p on foot, £2.10 per car) for the five-minute ride across the lips of the lough to Strangford.

The Lecale Peninsula

Jutting around the bottom of Strangford Lough, the **Lecale Peninsula** is above all **Saint Patrick's country**. Ireland's patron saint was originally a Roman Briton, first carried off as a youth from somewhere near Carlisle in northern England by Irish raiders. He spent six years in slavery in Ireland before escaping home again and, at the age of thirty, decided to return to Ireland as a bishop, to spread Christianity. Christianity had actually reached Ireland a while before him, probably through traders and other slaves, and Saint Patrick was not in fact the first bishop of Ireland (then on the edge of the known world) – but he remains far and away the most famous. He arrived in Ireland this second time, according to his biographer Muirchú (also his erstwhile captor, converted), on the shores of the Lecale region, and his first Irish sermon was preached at Saul in 432 AD. Today the region commemorates the association with sites at Struell Wells and Saul, as well as at Downpatrick town itself.

Downpatrick

DOWNPATRICK, the county capital, is not somewhere you come for a vibrant nightlife. In modern times it seems depressed and rather lethargic, awaiting the invigorating kiss of economic revival. On the other hand its history is a rich and well-preserved one, with the major sites conveniently concentrated at one end of town, around the **Hill of Down** on which the Cathedral now stands. This was once a rise of great strategic worth, fought over long before the arrival of Saint Patrick made it famous. A Celtic fort of mammoth proportions was built here, and was called first *Arús Cealtchair*, then later *Dún Cealtchair* (Celtchar's fort). Celtchar was one of the Red Branch Knights (see "Armagh", below), a friend of the then King of Ulster, Conor MacNessa, and, according to the *Book of the Dun Cow*, "an angry terrific hideous man with a long nose, huge ears, apple eyes, and coarse dark-grey hair". The *Dún* part of the fort's name went on to become the name of the county, as well as the town.

By the time the Norman knight **John de Courcy** made his mark here in the late twelfth century, a settlement was well established. Pushing north out of Leinster, and defeating Rory MacDonlevy, King of Ulster, de Courcy dispossessed the Augustinian Canons who occupied the Hill of Down to establish his own Benedictine Abbey. He flaunted as much pomp as he could to mark the occasion, and one of his festive tricks was to import what were supposedly the disinterred bodies of Saint Brigid and Saint Columba to join Saint Patrick, who was (supposedly again) buried here. One of the earliest accounts of Patrick's life asserts that he's buried in a church near the sea; and since a later account admits that "where his bones are no man knows", Downpatrick's claim seems as good as any.

The site of the three graves is meant to be just to the left of the tower entrance and is marked today by a rough granite slab, put there around 1900 to cover the huge hole created by earlier pilgrims searching for the saints' bones. The cathedral built by de Courcy was destroyed in the fourteenth century, and a new abbey erected in the early sixteenth century was even more short-lived. Today's **Cathedral** (open to visitors 9am–5pm) dates basically from the early part of this century, though it incorporates many aspects of earlier incarnations. Its most unique feature is the private box-pews, characteristic of the Regency period and the only ones remaining in use in Ireland.

The centre of town

Leaving the cathedral and retracing your steps a little down English Street, crowded with Georgian houses, the eighteenth-century jail has undergone some renovation and now houses both the **Down Museum** and the **St Patrick Heritage Centre** (summer Mon–Fri 11am–5pm, Sat & Sun 2–5pm; winter closed Sun & Mon; ☎0396/5218). The heritage centre occupies the gatehouse, and has a video and display of illustrations telling the Saint Patrick story, principally through his own words from his autobiographical *Confessions* (the short video also provides a handy summary of what the rest of the peninsula has on offer by way of relics of the saint). The three-storey Georgian **Governor's House**, in the centre of the walled courtyard, includes a local history gallery with a fascinating set of photographs of Loughinisland (see below) and its people at the beginning of this century. The cell block at the back of the enclosure (still awaiting restoration) once held the United Irishman Thomas Russell, who had already survived the 1798 uprising but was found complicit in Robert Emmett's rebellion and was duly hanged in 1803 from a sill outside the main gate of the jail.

Turn downhill between the jail and the fenced-up courthouse, and you come to the **Mound of Down**, a smaller prominence half submerged in undergrowth. It's in fact sixty feet high and inside its outer ditch is a horseshoe central mound of rich grass. Once a *rath*, or round hillfort, it was considerably altered and enlarged to create a Norman motte-and-bailey style fortification, with a *bretasche* (a wooden archery tower) at the centre. Its view back onto the Hill of Down shows up clearly the attractions the Hill had for its earliest settlers.

Inch Abbey

Over to the other side of the Quoile Marsh lie the remains of **Inch Abbey**. Unfortunately, you can't get over to it from here, due to the river, and it's vexing to be only a handshake away – its setting and atmosphere are amongst the most exquisite of all these Cistercian sites. The only access is a mile out along the Belfast Road, taking the left turn down Inch Abbey Road just before the *Abbey Lodge* hotel. It's signposted from here down another left turning. The site (50p entrance) was once an island, and its early church was replaced by de Courcy with the Cistercian Abbey. The monks were shipped over from Furness Abbey in Lancashire with the intention of establishing a strong English centre of influence – no Irish monks were ever allowed to be part of it. Not unexpectedly, little of it is now left standing, having undergone its allotted burning in 1404, with monastic life completely finished off by the mid-sixteenth century. Still, it makes by far the most satisfying memory of the Downpatrick area, with a picturesque setting among small glacial drumlins and woodland, and strolling up the valley sides (now a nature reserve, created when a flood barrage downstream turned this part of the river from saltwater estuary to freshwater marshy lake) is a very pleasant way to pass time.

Downpatrick practicalities

The **tourist information**, not terribly useful, is based at the Leisure Centre out on the Clough Road (Mon–Fri 10am–10pm, Sat 10am–6pm, Sun 2–6.30pm); a new place is being built at the nearby **railway station**, which should be better stocked with information. The **bus station** is also on the Clough Road.

You won't find much exciting to **eat**, but you won't starve either. The *Abbey Lodge Hotel* does a three-course Sunday lunch for under £10, and bar food on weekdays. The *Gatsby Bar* on Clough Road does good pub lunches, as do the *Old Mart*, opposite the Downtown Shopping Centre, *Rea's Pub*, on the same street, with a big open fire, the *DeCourcy Arms* and *Dick's Cabin*, both on the Belfast Road; the last two are popular **music** venues. There may also be occasional performances in the excellent new **Down Arts Centre** (in the refurbished old town hall on Irish Street; ☎0396/615283); there's an art gallery, coffee bar and performance space here. Another good coffee shop in the centre is *Oakley Fayre*, with the usual home-baked pastries. Should you want to **stay** try the *Abbey Lodge Hotel* (☎0396/4511; £20) or B&B at Mrs McCormick's *Rivendell*, 69 Saul Road (☎0396/2695; £11), *Hillcrest*, 157 Strangford Road (☎0396/612583; £10) or *Havine Farm*, 51 Ballydonnell Road (☎0396/685242; £11).

On the trail of Saint Patrick

The nearest of the surrounding Saint Patrick sites, within a couple of miles of Downpatrick, is **Struell Wells**. To get there, head out on the Ardglass Road, then turn left just past the hospital, then right down a narrow track into a secluded rock-faced valley. The waters here were once a grand old centre for pilgrimage and their miraculous healing powers recorded as far back as medieval times. In 1744 Walter Harris described the scene at their height: "vast throngs of rich and poor resort on Midsummer Eve and the Friday before Lammas, some in the hopes of obtaining health, and others to perform penance." Mass is still said here on midsummer night, and people bring containers to carry the water home with them; but if you're not looking for health or penance, there's still the joy of spotting one of the tiny gems of Irish landscape beauty – a hideaway rocky dell with an abundance of yellow-flowering whin, its underground stream rechannelled to run through the wells' purpose-built bath houses.

The next Saint Patrick landmark is at **SAUL**, not much further from Downpatrick off the Strangford Road. Saint Patrick is said to have landed nearby, sailing up the tiny Slaney River, and it was here that he first preached, immediately converting Dichu, the lord of this territory. Dichu gave Patrick a barn as his first base (the town's name in Irish is *Sabhal*, meaning barn), and the saint frequently returned here to rest from his travelling missions. Today a memorial chapel and round tower in the Celtic Revival style, built of pristine silver-grey granite in 1933, commemorate the place as "the most ancient ecclesiastical site in the land, the cradle of Christianity". Two cross-carved stones from between the eighth and twelfth centuries still stand in the graveyard, though there's not a trace of the medieval monastery built here by Saint Malachy in the twelfth century.

Back on the Strangford Road, a few miles further on between Saul and Raholp, **St Patrick's Shrine** sits atop *Slieve Patrick*, a tract of hillside much like a slalom ski-slope, with the stations of the cross marking a pathway up. The summit (no more than a twenty-minute climb) offers a commanding view of the county, a vista of the endless little bumps of this drumlin-filled territory.

Loughinisland

Loughinisland lies in quite the other direction, inland from Downpatrick, but it's probably the most worthwhile of all the sites associated with Saint Patrick, and indeed one of the most idyllically tranquil spots in County Down. It comprises a reed-fringed lake contained by ten or so little drumlin hills, one of which forms an island in the lake. Here, across a short causeway, are the ruins of three small churches, set next door to each other. To get here from Downpatrick, take the Newcastle road out past the racecourse, then look for the right-hand turning to Loughinisland. The most interesting of the churches is the smallest one, **MacCartan's Chapel** (1636), which has an entrance door no taller than four or five feet. It was used by both Catholics and Protestants until they quarrelled on a wet Sunday around 1720 over which camp should remain outside during the service. The Protestants left and built their church at SEAFORDE instead.

Around the Lecale Coast: Strangford

If you're coming by ferry to Lecale from the tip of the Ards Peninsula, and following the A2 round the coast, you'll arrive at tiny **STRANGFORD** village, directly opposite Portaferry. Its small harbour makes a pleasant setting for watching the to and fro of the ferry boats, and the *Lobster Pot*, on the front, has a welcome pub garden and middle-of-the-range prices for evening meals. But there's little else, and nowhere to stay.

Immediately around Strangford are a few houses and castles worth visiting, the first of them on the road back towards Downpatrick. **Castleward House** (July & Aug Wed–Mon noon–8pm; May & June Wed–Sun noon–6pm; April, Sept & Oct Sat & Sun noon–6pm), the eighteenth-century residence of Lord and Lady Bangor, is now owned by the National Trust. It's a positively schizophrenic house, thanks to the opposed tastes of its creators (they later split up): one half (the Lord's) is in the Classical Palladian style, the other (the Lady's) neo-Gothic, a split carried through into the design and decor of the rooms within. Outside there are pleasant gardens and preserved farm buildings. There's also a sixteenth-century tower house (Old Castle Ward) inside the grounds, and another, **Audley's Castle** (fifteenth-century), just outside on the lough shore. It has a superb view across the lough, though there's a better example of a tower house just south of Strangford. On your way back to the main coast road, **Audleystown Cairn** is marked across the fields to the right – though access isn't easy as it's in a field which usually seems full of bulls.

The Ardglass road

A couple of miles south of Strangford, **Kilclief Castle** (Easter–Sept Mon–Fri 10am–7pm, Sat 10am–4pm, Sun 2–4pm) is another, slightly earlier fifteenth-century tower house, in much better condition than Audley's Castle. One of Ireland's earliest tower houses, this was originally the home of John Cely, Bishop of Down – until he was defrocked and thrown out for living with a married woman.

By now you're on the A2 heading down towards Ardglass, but there remain a couple of things worth stopping for. Half a mile or so before you reach Ardglass, the ruin of fifteenth-century **Ardtole Church** is well signposted just a few hundred yards off the road. It's set on the spur of a hill, which gives it a fine perspective out to sea and back across the undulating flat of Lecale. Once dedicated to Saint Nicholas, patron saint of sailors, this church was used by English fishermen until a quarrel broke out with the Irish around 1650. The story goes that the fishermen tied a sleeping Irish chief to the ground by his long hair so that he couldn't get up when he awoke. Tradition has it that Swift got the similar episode in *Gulliver's Travels* from this tale, and certainly the Ardtole region runs amok with tiny drumlins – very much like the description of the Lilliputian mountains.

Also signposted off the Ardglass Road (a mile's drive and a quarter of a mile's walk) is **St Patrick's Well**, set on a wonderful rocky shore. The well is easily spotted – it looks rather like a sheep dip, but with a crucifix at its head. Its holy water has turned into something closer to stagnant consommé than an ever-youthful source of new life.

Ardglass

ARDGLASS is set on the side of a lovely natural inlet. Its domestic buildings, rising steeply from the harbour (*ard glas* in Irish means the green height), are interspersed with seven fortified mansions, towers and turrets. These date from a vigorous English revival in the sixteenth century, when a trading company first arrived to found a colony here. The best preserved of the fortifications, and the only one open for visits, is **Jordan's Castle**, next door to the *Anchor* pub on the Low Road (Easter–Sept Mon–Fri 10am–7pm, Sat 10am–4pm, Sun 2–4pm). The most elegant and highly developed of all the Down tower houses, this now contains the local museum. The tall, crenellated building with white plaster trimming up on the hill was once **King's Castle**; its nineteenth-century renovation is obvious, as is modern work to turn it into a nursery. The lone ornamental-looking turret on the hilltop is **Isabella's Tower**, a nineteenth-century folly created by Aubrey de Vere Beauclerc as a gazebo for his invalid daughter.

In the nineteenth century, Ardglass was the most thriving **fishing** port in the North; and even today, as well as the prawns, herrings and whitefish brought in by the fishing fleet, there's very good rod fishing to be had off the end of the pier for codling, pollack and coalfish. Even the *Spar* supermarket on the quay is wonderfully stocked with a fantastic range of seafood (scallops, monkfish, oysters, salmon etc), enough in itself to entice a quick shopping visit. It's also sometimes possible to buy direct from fishing boats or from the cannery on the quay. You can get **food** and a **room** at the *Ardglass Arms* on Kildare Street (☎0396/841228; £18); alternatives are *Aldo's* popular Italian restaurant and Mary Donald's farmhouse B&B (☎0396/841466; £10), one mile out on the Downpatrick road.

From Killough to Clough

KILLOUGH, a few miles on, is an unworldly village stretching around a much larger harbour than Ardglass – now silted up. The A2 passes through Killough's main street: a fine avenue of sycamores with a string of picturesque cottage terraces at its southern end, this makes an unlikely major thoroughfare. It was the Wards of Castleward who built the harbour in the eighteenth century, and there's still a direct road running inland, virtually in a straight line, from Killough to Castleward.

From the southern end of Killough you can head out to **St John's Point** – much favoured by bird watchers – on which lie the ruins of one of the North's best examples of a pre-Romanesque church. It's an enjoyable two-and-a-half-mile walk. The tiny west door of the tenth-century church has the distinctive sloping sides, narrowing as the doorway rises, that were a common feature of these early churches. Also still apparent are the *antae*, enclosures created by the extension of the west and east walls to give extra support to the roof. Excavations in 1977 showed up graves that extended under these walls, indicating that an even earlier church existed from the early Christian period, probably made of wood. There's a black-and-gold striped lighthouse on the nail of the point.

From Killough, the A2 passes long, sandy beaches at MINERSTOWN and TYRELLA STRAND before reaching **CLOUGH**, a crossroads village between Downpatrick and Newcastle and the inland ending of the Lecale region. It has a Norman motte and bailey, as pristinely preserved as a carpet of mown grass, with a poor remnant of a thirteenth-century stone keep stuck in the middle. The site, just behind a petrol station at the Belfast end of the village, has surprisingly good views considering its low-lying position – across Dundrum Bay inlet towards the Mournes and back over to Slieve Croob in central Down. Presumably because of its position astride several main roads, Clough has a number of **B&Bs**, charging around £10: they include *Woodhill* (☎039/687240) and *Teach Chuillinn House* (☎039/687662), both on Moneycarragh Road, and *Timakeel*, 27 Claragh Road (☎039/6778751).

The road to Newcastle

Heading south along the coast from the Lecale region, **DUNDRUM** lies beside a hammer-headed tidal bay, only a few miles down the road from Clough. Above the town are the quite spectacular ruins of a large Norman **castle** (summer Tues–Sat 10am–7pm, Sun 2–7pm; winter Tues–Fri 10am–4pm, Sat 10am–4pm, Sun 2–4pm); to get to it, take the steep turning up the hill from Dundrum village, a fifteen-minute walk. The castle has a central circular *donjon* (with a fine stairway in its walls), a fortified gateway and drum towers, all set upon a motte and bailey. In its time it was described as the most impenetrable fortress in the land. Some say it was a de Courcy fortress, designed for the Knights Templar; but the circular keep, a rarity in Ireland, is not at all in keeping with the other fortresses de Courcy built to defend the stretch of coast from Carlingford right up to Carrickfergus. De Courcy's successor, de Lacy, is a more likely candidate – his Welsh connections tie in with the castle's similarity to the one at Pembroke, Wales. If you're lucky, your visit might coincide with the real McCoy soundtrack of live gunfire from the shooting range down by the Murlough Sand Dunes (a National Trust reserve beside the bay), which sharpens the atmosphere of the scene superbly.

There's a **B&B** in Dundrum (*Mourneview House*, 16 Main Street; ☎039/675457; £11), and both the *Dundrum Bay Inn* (169 Main Street; ☎039/675209), at the south end of the village, and the *Murlough Tavern* have simple rooms and serve good meals and snacks.

Newcastle and around

NEWCASTLE, with its lovely stretch of sandy beach, is the biggest seaside resort in Down – packed with trippers from Belfast on summer weekends – and also the best base for excursions into the Mourne Mountains. The mountains' highest peak, **Slieve Donard**, rises just behind the town; at 2796 feet it's also the highest peak in Ulster, yet it makes an easy and safe climb. The town itself isn't exactly exciting, but it's well equipped to send you pony trekking, or fishing on the river, and for the inevitable rainy day there are indoor alternatives at the Newcastle Centre and Tropicana Complex on the promenade (summer only; ☎03967/22222), with swimming pools, water slides and playgrounds.

Places to stay include the only official **youth hostel** in this region in a terraced house on the seafront (30 Downs Road, near the bus station; ☎03967/22133; £5.90), and lots of hotels and **B&Bs**. Cheaper central ones include Fountainville Guest House, 103 Central Promenade (☎03967/22317; £11) and *Carlton House*, 15 South Promenade (☎03967/22123; £10): for much the same price you can stay at the **YMCA** (*Rathmourne House*, 143 Central Promenade; ☎03967/24488; £10.50) or the **YWCA** (*Glenada Holiday Centre*, 29 South Promenade; ☎03967/22402; £10).

The best of the more upmarket **hotels** is the very obvious Victorian redbrick *Slieve Donard Hotel* (☎03967/23681; £30) on Downs Road near the youth hostel; the *Brook Cottage Hotel*, 58 Bryansford Road (☎03967/22204; £15) might be more fun at half the price. There are also two semi-detached National Trust properties *Murlough Cottages* on the shore of Dundrum Bay (sleep 4–6; longer periods only; contact Mrs Whatmough ☎03967/51311). Obviously, these get booked up well in advance, but you may be lucky out of season. There are also eleven **caravan/**

camping sites around the town. Newcastle's **tourist information office** is at 10–14 Central Promenade (☎03967/22222; summer Mon–Sat 9.30am–8pm, Sun 2–6.30pm; winter Mon–Sat 9.15am–5pm).

Mario's Italian Restaurant on the front is the best place for evening **meals** and Sunday lunches. The *Donard Hotel* on Main Street also does reasonable lunches. Otherwise there are plenty of cafés and chip shops scattered among the amusement arcades.

Walks nearby

There's little to see in Newcastle itself – though the hideous modern Catholic church is hard to miss – but in the immediate surrounds are several pleasant **parks** created from the estates of old houses. The nearest is **Donard Park** on the slopes of Slieve Donard. There's a good walk along the Glen River from the town centre to the park, and if you keep following this path uphill you'll emerge on the other side and eventually come to the Saddle, a col between the two mountains of Slieve Donard and Slieve Commedagh; from here, via Trassey Burn, you can go straight into the heart of the hills. **Tollymore Forest Park** is a little further away, two miles inland along the Bryansford Road, and considerably bigger and better equipped. It also creeps up the northern side of the Mournes, and its picturesque trails wind through woodland and beside the river. You enter the park by one of two ornate Gothic folly gates – there are more follies in BRYANSFORD nearby – and there's an information centre and café in an elaborate stone barn.

Castlewellan Forest Park is also inland, outside the elegant market town of CASTLEWELLAN. A wonderful **arboretum**, dating originally from 1740 but much expanded since, is its outstanding feature: the sheltered south-facing slopes of its hills, between the Mournes and the Slieve Croob range, allow exotic species to flourish. There's trout fishing in its main lake and coarse fishing in the smaller lakes; there's also a café in the 1720 Queen Anne style farmstead and courtyards, near the main entrance. The Baronial castle to which the grounds originally belonged is now the property of a Christian conference organisation, and it offers a very few cheap rooms (☎03967/78733). Inside the park, **Dolly's Brae** (one of the westernmost hills) is often remembered at Loyalist celebrations as the site of one of the greatest victories against Catholic uprisings.

The Mourne Mountains

The **Mournes** are a relatively youthful set of granite mountains, which explains why their comparatively unweathered peaks and flanks are so rugged, forming steep sides, moraines and occasional sheer cliffs. Closer up, these give sharp, jagged outlines; but from a distance they appear much more gentle, like a sleeping herd of buffalo. The wilder topography lies mostly in the east, below Newcastle, although the fine cliff of **Eagle Mountain**, to the southwest, is wonderful if you can afford the time and effort to get there, and the tamer land above Rostrevor has views down into Carlingford Lough that can rival any in Ireland.

Newcastle is by far the best base if you want to do any serious walking or climbing in the Mournes, and the route outlined above through Donard Park is the obvious starting point. A climb to the peak of **Slieve Donard** (a relatively easy ascent on a well-marked trail to a massive hermit cell on the summit) should be one of the first things you do, not least for its view across the whole mountain-scape, which can help you pick out your preferred route. In summer at least (winters can be surprisingly harsh) there are plenty of straightforward hikes in the Mournes that require no special equipment, with obvious tracks to many of the more scenic parts. For further information, and maps, go to the Newcastle tourist office or to the youth hostel there. There are also, of course, more serious climbs: **climbing courses** in the Mournes are run by the *Northern Ireland Mountain Centre* in Newcastle (☎03967/22158), but they must be booked at least two weeks in advance (contact *The Sports Council for Northern Ireland*, House of Sport, Upper Malone Road, Belfast; ☎0232/381222).

Among the highlights are the route that follows Trassey Burn beyond Donard Park up towards the **Hare's Gap**, where minerals have seeped through the rock to form precious and semi-precious stones – topaz, beryl, smoky quartz and emeralds – in the cavities of the **Diamond rocks** (hidden behind an obvious boulder stone on the mountainside). Around this point in spring, you might get the chance to hear the song of the Ring Ouzel bird, which migrates from Africa to breed in these upland areas.

Other heights worth chasing include **Slieve Bingian**, beyond the Hare's Gap, and reached through the Brandy Pad passes by the Blue Lough and Lough Bingian; **Slieve Commedagh**, with its Inca-looking pillars of granite; and **Slieve Bearnagh**, up to the right of the Hare's Gap. Also, try and cross the ridge from **Slieve Meelmore** to **Slieve Muck**, the "pig mountain", descending to the shores of Lough Shannagh, where there's a beach at either end – useful for a dip, though the water's freezing. In the panorama beyond the Hare's Gap, the places not to miss are the eastern slopes of the **Cove Mountain** and **Slieve Lamagan**. If you're sticking to the roads, all you can really do is circle the outside of the range, though there is one road through the middle, from Hilltown to Kilkeel.

The western slopes

The landward side of the Mourne Mountains are a patchwork of fields divided by stone walls; attractive, especially in the morning light, but with nothing of pressing interest. **HILLTOWN** has a main street extraordinarily well provided with pubs (supposedly because it was once a smugglers' hideaway, where the spoils would be divided), and it's still a crossroads where numerous roads meet. But most of the time its atmosphere is that of a ghost town. Little over a mile from Hilltown on the Newcastle road is the handsome **Goward dolmen**, known locally as "Pat Kearney's big stone". It's well signposted off the road, though the last quarter mile of track is severely potholed.

Drumena Cashel, back in the same direction off the A25, is one of the better preserved ring forts, or defended homesteads, in the area. It has a T-shaped underground chamber intended to give shelter from the Vikings – though this is only twelve yards long, and seems better suited to its peace-time function of providing cold storage for food. The stone foundations of a few circular beehive huts (known as *clocháns*) also remain. The puzzling aspect of the cashel is its position *below* the summit of the hill; possibly a compromise between the needs of defence and those of comfort, so there would be some shelter from the harsh winds that curl through the area.

The Mourne Coastline

The A2 south along the coast from Newcastle, trailing the shore around the edge of the mountains and then looping inland around Carlingford Lough, is a spectacularly beautiful drive – though villages become increasingly politicised as you approach the border. There's no shortage of **camping and caravan sites** along this coastal run – try *Annalong Marine Park* (☎03967/68736); *Ballymartin Caravan Park* (☎06937/62881); *Chestnut Caravan Park*, on the beach at Cranfield near Kilkeel (☎06937/62653); *Kilbroney Caravan Park*, Rostrevor (☎06937/38134); or *Moygannon Caravan Site* at Warrenpoint (06937/72346). **B&Bs** are also plentiful in Annalong, Rostrevor and Warrenpoint.

Annalong

The first place worth stopping at south of Newcastle is the small fishing harbour of **ANNALONG**. Its name in Irish is *Áth na Long*, or the ford of the ships, and the town's a pleasantly relaxed seaside attraction during the summer, with a stony beach and Slieve Binnion providing a grandiloquent backdrop. In the harbour pleasure craft are tied up alongside the fishing boats and small trawlers. There are a number of small **B&Bs** here – for example Mrs Gordon, 32 Majors Hill, (☎03967/68348); Mrs Stevenson, 237 Kilkeel Road (☎03967/68345); and Mrs Whyte, 57 Kilkeel Road (☎03967/68849) – and a **camping/caravan** site (*Marine Park*, summer only) that's landscaped in the shape of a shamrock. The only blot on the horizon is the powerful smell of herring wafting up from the harbour.

The campsite is just off the main road, and a path from it gives immediate access to an early nineteenth-century **cornmill**, still in working order and open for visits (June–Aug Mon–Sat 11am–6pm, Sun 2–6pm; Easter–May Sat 11am–6pm, Sun 2–6pm; 50p), down by the walled harbour and the beach. The village itself goes about its maritime work in its narrow streets much as it always has done, and it comes as a surprise in this out-of-the-way part of the North to find the grey harbour walls adorned with the familiar ritualised Protestant graffiti – Ulster 1690, UVF and a Union Jack flag. The only Republican effort (IRA) is sneaked in on the seaward side of the walls, lending an almost humorous touch to the imbalance of the sympathies in this particular spot. Right on the harbour, the *Harbour Inn* has inexpensive **food** at lunchtime. *The Fisherman*, on the Kilkeel Road, has an extensive fish menu.

Kilkeel

Continuing south, there's a good small beach just outside the hamlet of BALLYMARTIN. **KILKEEL** is a much grander version of Annalong, remarkable mainly for the even heftier stench of fish from the canneries on the harbour. The biggest excitements here are the fish auctions that take place on the quayside when the fishing boats come home, and the annual summer **harbour festival**. Both Kilkeel and Ballymartin have **places to stay**. In Kilkeel there are a couple of hotels – *Cranfield House*, 57 Cranfield Road (☎03967/62327) and *Kilmorey Arms*, Greencastle Street (☎03967/62220) – both of which also serve food, and numerous B&Bs (try *Mourne Abbey*, 16 Greencastle Road, ☎03967/62426; *Homesyde*, 7 Shandon Drive, ☎03967/62676; or Mrs McKibben, 181 Moyad Road, ☎03967/63444); Ballymartin has just small B&Bs such as Mrs McCormick's at 3 Ballymartin Village (☎03967/62077) or Mrs Bingham's, 6 Ballykeel Road (☎03967/62521).

Not far from Kilkeel, **Greencastle Fort** (April–Sept Tues–Sat 10am–1pm & 1.30–7pm), on a point of land at the mouth of Carlingford Lough, is worth a diversion off the main route. The fort is a comparatively well-preserved Anglo-Norman edifice, with a unique rock ditch, built in the same year (1261) as Carlingford Castle on the southern side of the lough. After succumbing to several attacks from the local Magennis clan, and falling to Edward Bruce in 1316, it collapsed into complete ruin after the Cromwellian invasion and today sits forlornly next to a working farmstead, for tourist use only. It's wide open to the blustery winds that sweep up the lough, and it takes great imaginative effort to summon up warmth from the great fireplaces, and fill the large window frames. But much of the structure is still here, to its full height (you can climb up the corner turrets and have full run of the top storey), plus there's a sandy beach below, and photographic views up the mouth of the lough.

Rostrevor and Warrenpoint

Beyond Kilkeel the road turns inland, to follow the lough shore round towards Newry. Four or five miles out of Kilkeel a signpost points to the **Kilfeaghan Dolmen**, a mile inland then a short walk through a couple of fields and kissing gates. This polygonal stone is enormous, and could only have got here during the retreat of the glacial drift.

Further up the lough, **ROSTREVOR** sits at the point where the waters dramatically begin to narrow towards Newry; and also where the population and political climate turns more in favour of the Catholic communities of County Armagh and those of the ever-nearing border. It's a picturesque town of Victorian terraces and friendly pubs, clambering up the slopes of **Slieve Martin**. A steep forest drive leads up the mountain from the back of the town, a long and winding ascent, really only of use to motorists, though rewarded at the top with wonderful views across to the Cooley mountains over the border. Again there are just a couple of tiny **B&Bs** in town, the best of them probably *Still Waters* at 14 Killowen Road (☎06937/38743; £10) and *Mandalay*, 31 Killowen Road (☎06937/38234; £10). **Camping** is available at two caravan parks, one each in Kilbroney Park and Rostrevor Forest Park. Big, inexpensive steaks are popular at the *Top o' the Town* (known as *Annie O's*) in Church Street. The **Fiddler's Green Festival** in August is a big, enjoyable event, attracting folk musicians from across Europe.

Warrenpoint

WARRENPOINT is equally picturesque, with a colourful esplanade of seafront housing and a spacious central square. It's much more of a traditional seaside resort than Rostrevor, with a **tourist information** kiosk occupying a pagoda-like hut on the seafront, and good places to spend a night. There are handy **boat trips** across to Omeath on the opposite side of Carlingford Lough, leaving from just in front of the *Marine Tavern* (July & Aug only Mon–Sat 1–5pm, Sun 1–7pm, tides permitting; 5min).

If you want to stay, **B&Bs** include the *Waterfront Guest House*, 6 Seaview (☎06937/73629; £10), *Glen Rosa*, 4 St George's Street South (☎06937/72589; £10), and *Fernhill House*, 90 Clonallon Road (☎06937/72677). There's cheap **eating** at the *Diamond Restaurant* on the main square, and cosy **drinking** at *Molly McCabes*, at the bottom of the road that runs uphill from the square, where the old boys gather to drink bottled stout only – it can accommodate twelve people at the most. Warrenpoint also has something of a tradition of singing pubs: there's regular **céilí** dancing in St Peter's Gaelic Hall and **traditional sessions** in the Forresters' Hall on the seafront (every Wednesday 9–11.30pm, with every third Wednesday being the big one). These days, though, there are even more **discos**, for which locals come from miles around: biggest are at the *Marine Tavern* (Wed, Fri & Sat 9.30pm–1.30am) and the *Carlingford Bay Hotel*, also on the seafront (Thurs, Sat & Sun). You can **hire bikes** at *Stewarts* (☎06937/73565).

Less than a mile from Warrenpoint along the Newry road is the ruined **Narrow Water Castle**, built in the sixteenth century to guard the entrance of the river that flows from Newry into the lough. In this serene setting, it's hard to imagine that sixteen British soldiers were blown up here by the IRA, on the same day that Lord Mountbatten was killed in Mulloughmore Bay in 1979. There are very slight remains of an earlier castle nearby, and on the other side of the road an avenue leads up to New Narrow Water Castle (a private residence) whose private **gallery** is worth checking out if you're interested in contemporary art (☎06937/73940).

Newry

Although **NEWRY**, astride the border of Down and Armagh, is this area's most important commercial centre, it's the least attractive proposition for a visit. The town here has always been a garrison, guarding the borders of Ulster at the narrow point between the mountains known as the Gap to the North, but there's no trace at all of the early fortresses that were fought over so often. Rather what you see dates mostly from the eighteenth and nineteenth centuries, when a canal (the first in the British Isles) brought ships right up from Carlingford Lough into town, and with them trade and considerable wealth. This business has gone, however, and these days Newry is probably best known from the news: the town and its immediate surrounds were repeatedly bombed by the IRA in the 1970s, and even now it's frequently a hive of army and police activity. Given its central position you're highly likely to pass through Newry, and it does make a possible base for exploring Slieve Gullion and the south Armagh district, but you're unlikely to be tempted to stay.

One thing you'll notice as you wander around is that there seem to be dozens of lawyers practising here, with whole streets full of their offices. Perhaps the most interesting building in town, however, is the **Catholic Cathedral** on Hill Street, in the pedestrian precinct. Despite an unpromising exterior, the rich mosaic pattern along its walls gives an eastern feel to the interior, which also has a striking vaulted ceiling of decorative sweeping plaster arcs and vivid stained-glass windows. Not far away the **Town Hall** is remarkable mainly because it's built on a bridge over the Clanrye River – it's half in Down, half in Armagh. The **Newry and Mourne Arts Centre**, next door at 1a Bank Parade (with the classical facade; ☎0693/66232), has exhibitions of local artists' work, plays and all types of music in the auditorium: the new *O'Casey Theatre Company* is based here. There's a **tourist information centre** in Monaghan Row (☎0693/65411), but the Arts Centre may prove more helpful here too.

Newry has plenty of places serving cheap hot **meals**: the *Ambassador* restaurant, for example, at the start of the pedestrian precinct near to the Town Hall, will feed you well for under £3, or try the *Boulevard* on the same street, or in the

Town Hall Square *Friar Tuck's* (fast food) and *Little Italy* (good pizzas). A couple of good **pubs** are the *Brass Monkey* on Trevor Hill, which also does bar lunches, and *Squires*, off Hill Street. For livelier **nightlife** check out *JPS* in the central precinct square (9.30pm–1am; closed Tues), and *Cupid's* over the bridge, next to the cinema on Merchant's Quay.

There are a fair number of **B&Bs** should you want to stay – they include *Oisín House*, 4a Canal Street (☎0693/65715; £11); *Ashton Farm*, 37 Fathom Road (☎0693/62120; £10); *Hillside*, 1 Rock Road (☎0693/65484; £10); and *Millvale House*, 8 Millvale Road (☎0693/63789; £9). The *Mourne Country Hotel*, 52 Belfast Road (☎0693/67922; £25) is luxurious but characterless.

Heading south **towards Dundalk** in the Republic, you'll be struck by the multitude of petrol stations crammed in along the route to the border – people stock up here before hitting the more expensive South.

Southwest of Belfast: Hillsborough

Heading west from Belfast, the M1 motorway offers very rapid access to Armagh and Tyrone, while the A1 cuts south towards Newry. On the former route there's little to stop for until you're in County Armagh; on the latter the historic village of **HILLSBOROUGH**, just a mile off the main road, merits a quick detour. Named after Sir Arthur Hill, who built the castle in the park on the south side of town during the reign of Charles I, it hit the headlines in 1985 when the controversial **Anglo-Irish Agreement** was signed here. The main street is perhaps a bit too quaint, with a distinct rural-England ambience and a sprinkling of tea and antique shops: the real attractions of Hillsborough are its architecture and, above all, the surrounding belt of woodland.

To best appreciate these, start from the **war memorial** and head up the magnificent approach to the (rather spooky) parish church. Here bear to your right for the main entrance to Hillsborough's elegant **fort**, whose ruins you can freely inspect. Beyond this a deciduous forest opens up, set around a lake with brown and rainbow trout. Footpaths crisscross through the trees in all directions, popular with locals and day-trippers from Belfast – a circuit of the lake takes around an hour and is well worth the effort. Exiting via the car park, a driveway brings you out near the *White Gables Hotel*, beyond which you'll notice a statue on a raised column, master of all it beholds – the third Marquis of Downshire, in case you're interested.

A right turn at the end of the drive brings you back into town, with **Hillsborough Castle** on your left. Frankly the ornate gates are the best part, but it was here that the governor of Northern Ireland used to have his official residence, and here too that the Anglo-Irish Agreement was signed. You'll also notice the court building in front of the main gates, and the town hall at the head of the main street, proudly raising its Union Jack over the village.

By this time you'll be in need of **refreshment**, for which the *Ploughman's Lounge*, just ahead of you on your right, is recommended. A little further down, the *Hillside Restaurant and Wine Bar* (1777) has more substantial fare. Best of all, however, is the *Red Fox* tea shop at the bottom of the hill, through an arch and behind a boutique of the same name. When you've finished here, you'll be back where you began, at the war memorial. From here a regular *Ulsterbus* service runs to Newry and Belfast.

ARMAGH

Armagh has a history as rich as any county in Ireland, especially in Armagh City with its associations with Saint Patrick and early Christianity. The county town still has a few reminders of this, but the county as a whole is quiet and rural, with little evidence that anything of significance occurred here before this century. What has happened in recent years has hardly heightened the appeal for tourists, since south Armagh, especially, is now best known for its leading part in the Troubles and for cross-border incursions. Although it's peaceful enough most of the time – and you can travel entirely freely – the constant army presence does little to encourage peace of mind.

From Belfast the motorway cuts across the north of the county, below **Lough Neagh**, giving easy access to the industrial towns in the north of the county, LURGAN, CRAIGAVON and PORTADOWN. Virtually joined now by a single strip of development, these three offer little reason to stop and you're far better off pushing on down to Armagh City instead, pretty much at the centre of the county. If you do want to stop – and coarse anglers might be tempted by the River Bann, which teems with roach – then **Peatlands Park**, well signposted off the M1 and telling something of the social and industrial history of peat, and the nature reserve at **Oxford Islan**d near Craigavon offer the best excuses.

Armagh City and around

ARMAGH's small size disappoints some people, and certainly the city doesn't immediately present a greatly exciting prospect – but, rich in history at least, Armagh and its surroundings have plenty to keep you occupied for a day or two. The city offers cathedrals, museums and a planetarium set in handsome Georgian streets, while the ancient site of once-grand Navan Fort and two stately homes, Ardress and the Argory, are features of the excellent cycling country roundabout. Armagh has been the site of the Catholic primacy of all Ireland since Saint Patrick established his church here (it's also the seat of the Protestant Church of Ireland Archbishop of Armagh) and has rather ambitiously adopted the title the "Irish Rome" for itself – like Rome, it's positioned among seven small hills.

Historical background

Armagh (*Ard Mhacha*, the height of Mhacha) was first named after Queen Mhacha, wife of Nevry, who is said to have arrived in Ireland 608 years after the biblical flood. She's supposed to be buried somewhere in the side of the main hill, where the Protestant Cathedral now stands. If this is true, it confirms Armagh as one of the oldest settlements in Ireland, a theory supported by the city's position on one of the most ancient roads in the land, the Moyry Pass, which once stretched from the extreme south of Ireland, through Tara, to the north. In about 300 BC, the centre of power shifted westward across the Callan River to where another Queen (of the same name, Mhacha) built the legendary **Navan Fort**.

After nearly seven hundred years, the ruling dynasty at Navan was defeated by the Collas brothers, and the new rulers re-established their main base back on the hill of Armagh. A hundred years later, in 445 AD, **Saint Patrick** declared the

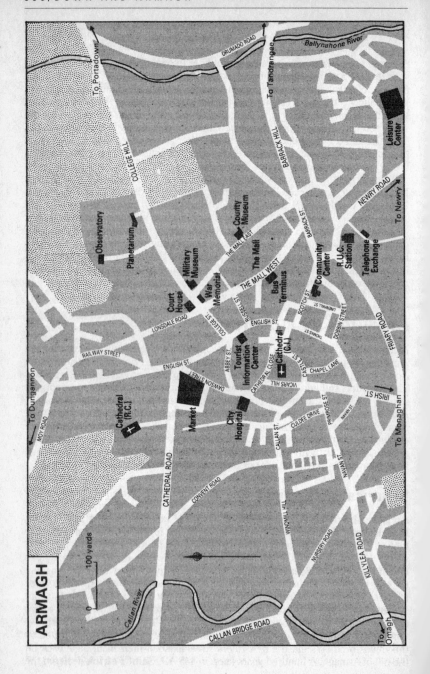

ARMAGH

To Portadown
DRUMADO ROAD
To Tandragee
Ballynahone River
BARRACK HILL
COLLEGE HILL
Leisure Center
NEWRY ROAD
To Newry
Observatory
Planetarium
County Museum
THE MALL EAST
The Mall
BARRACK ST.
Community Center
R.U.C. Station
Telephone Exchange
Military Museum
War Memorial
THE MALL WEST
Bus Terminus
RUSSELL ST.
SCOTCH ST.
LINENHALL ST.
Court House
COLLEGE ST.
COLLEGE ST.
LONSDALE ROAD
ENGLISH ST.
THOMAS ST.
DOBBIN STREET
FRIARY ROAD
RAILWAY STREET
ENGLISH ST.
ABBEY ST.
Tourist Information Center
CATHEDRAL CLOSE
Cathedral (C.I.)
CASTLE ST.
CHAPEL LANE
To Dungannon
MOY ROAD
DAWSON STREET
VICARS HILL
IRISH ST.
To Monaghan
Cathedral (R.C.)
Market
City Hospital
CALLAN ST.
CULDEE DRIVE
PRIMROSE ST.
NAVAN ST.
CATHEDRAL ROAD
CONVENT ROAD
WINDMILL HILL
NURSERY ROAD
KILLYLEA ROAD
100 yards
0
Callan River
CALLAN BRIDGE ROAD
To Omagh

hill the site of his Primacy and first Bishopric, and built his cathedral here (having first converted the local chieftain, Daire, a descendant of the Collas brothers). Other churches grew up around the cathedral and Armagh became *the* great centre of learning during the Dark Ages, the period when Ireland was known as the "Isle of Saints and Scholars". Armagh strongly challenges Downpatrick's claim to be the burial place of Saint Patrick; they argue that since the relics of Patrick's book, bell and staff are here, his body must be too (though the burial site, somewhere on the main hill, is not identified).

Between the ninth and the eleventh centuries, the city was constantly pillaged by the **Vikings**, mainly from the Norse settlements at Lough Neagh. The Irish king who claimed final victory over the Norsemen, **Brian Boru**, is buried in Armagh Cathedral. Armagh's ecclesiastical power weakened in the Middle Ages, and its history ran in line with the rest of the North for the next several hundred years, with no lengthy periods of peace until the eighteenth and nineteenth centuries, when there was a final flourish of building, much of which survives today. Modern Armagh is a predominantly Catholic city – it's strong on Gaelic sports – and although physically it has borne up well to the Troubles (certainly in comparison to Newry and Derry), it has not avoided them. One local to fall victim to the IRA was the moderate Protestant Chairman of the Council, Charlie Armstrong.

The City

The Mall, an elegant tree-lined promenade, is as good a place as any to begin looking around, and strongly sets the tone of the place. The handsome Georgian street architecture is by the early-nineteenth-century Armagh-born architect Francis Johnson, and you'll come across more of his work in many of the central streets that lead off The Mall (Johnson also designed many of Dublin's best Georgian buildings). In its late-eighteenth-century heyday The Mall was used as a racecourse; nowadays there's nothing more athletic than the occasional Sunday cricket game. A former schoolhouse on the east side of The Mall houses the **County Museum** (Mon–Sat 10am–1pm & 2–5pm; free; ☎0861/523070) with all the usual local miscellanea plus a little art gallery tucked away on the second floor. Here there are several mystical pastels, oils and cartoon sketches by the Irish turn-of-the-century poet **George Russell** (alias *AE*, and a much neglected companion to Yeats); a local painter, J.B. Vallely, is also represented with a superb oil showing five musicians having a session – Vallely currently runs the town's *Armagh Pipers' Club*. There's also a permanent exhibition of stuffed wildlife, alarmingly vivid. Further along The Mall, beside the Classical Courthouse, the **Royal Irish Fusiliers Museum** (Mon–Fri 10am–1pm & 2–4pm, but unreliable, so check with tourist office; ☎0861/522911) is pretty much as you'd expect: tons of weaponry, uniforms, medallions and regimental silverware.

Observatory and Planetarium

College Hill, the road that leaves The Mall by the Fusiliers Museum, will take you to the **Observatory** (not open to the public) and the **Planetarium** (Mon–Fri 2–4.45pm, Sat 1.30–4.45pm; *Star Shows* Sat 2pm & 3pm; £2; ☎0861/523689), which are linked by a short woodland path round the back. The Observatory is an ancient one – it celebrated its second centenary in 1990 – but it's still at the forefront of astronomical research. The Planetarium is much more recent (1968) and its best feature is a sophisticated video projection of a multitude of skies round the world onto its hemispherical ceiling, while you sit back on reclinable seats. It also has various antique astronomical instruments from the earliest days of the Observatory on display.

Cathedrals and Friary

St Patrick's Church of Ireland Cathedral lays claim to the summit of the principal hillock, where Saint Patrick founded his first church, commanding a distinctive Armagh view across to the other hills and down over the shambles of gable walls and pitched roofing on its own slopes. The church is more spartan inside than you might expect from its noble past; there have been a string of buildings on the site, and although the core is medieval, a nineteenth-century restoration coated the thirteenth-century outer walls in a sandstone plastercast, and robbed the interior of many of its ancient decorations. Just as you enter from the highly distinctive timber porch, there are a few remnants of an eleventh-century Celtic cross and a startling statue of Thomas Molyneux. Inside, high up, you should be able to sight the medieval carved heads of men, women and monsters. One other unusual feature is the tilt of the chancel, a medieval building practice meant to represent the slumping head of the dying Jesus. The **chapter house** has a small collection of stone statues (mostly gathered from elsewhere), the most noticeable of which is a *sheila-na-gig* with ass's ears – some reckon it's King Midas but most people guess it represents one of the Queen Mhachas.

The **public library** down the hill from the cathedral (Mon–Fri 10am–12.30pm & 2–4pm; ☎0861/523142) has a copy of *Gulliver's Travels* annotated by Swift himself, and an early edition of Raleigh's *History of the World* (1614) amongst many other rare tomes, as well as a collection of etchings including some by Hogarth.

The **Catholic St Patrick's Cathedral**, on another hillrise, is more recent, and at first sight little different to the many other nineteenth-century Gothic Revival Catholic cathedrals across the country. But it is impressively large and airy and inside, as befits the seat of the Cardinal Archbishop, every inch of wall glistens with mosaics, in colours ranging from marine- and sky-blue to terracotta pinks and oranges. Other striking pieces include the white granite "pincer-claw" tabernacle holder, reflected in a highly polished marble floor, and a statue of the Crucifixion which looks (deliberately or otherwise) like a CND symbol.

Moving on, the final piece of ecclesiastical interest, the ruins of **Armagh Friary**, lie within easy walking distance of the city centre, just off Friary Road in the grounds of the Archbishop's Palace (now the District Council Offices). This was a Franciscan Friary, dating from around 1263; the Franciscans, known as Grey Friars because of the colour of their robes, arrived in Ireland as soon as six years after Saint Francis' death in Italy, and spread their sect like wildfire through the country. The ruins here are those of the church alone – and the site is an unfortunate example of how atmosphere can be destroyed when a noisy major road runs alongside.

Practicalities

Armagh does not offer a great deal of choice if you want to stay. Your best bet is to ask first at the helpful **tourist information office** at 40 English Street (☎0861/ 527808). **B&Bs** are scarce, but they include two on Cathedral Road – *Desart* (no. 99; ☎0861/522387) and *Padua House* (no. 63; ☎0861/523584) – plus Susan

McParland, 1 Alexander Gardens (☎0861/525289) and *Clonhugh House* on College Hill (☎0861/522693) – all around £10. The nearest **camping** is at *Gosford Forest Park* (☎0861/551277), seven miles along the A28 near Markethill, with fine facilities set in wooded grounds around a castle.

Many of the **pubs** will serve bar food at lunchtime, but **eating** in the evening can be more problematic. Of the pubs, one of the best is *Calvert's Tavern*, 3 Scotch Street (☎0861/524186), or you can always get a reasonably priced full meal at the *Drumsill Hotel* (25 Moy Road; ☎0861/522009). An excellent new place with healthy food is *Jodies*, upstairs at 37 Scotch Street: other possibilities are mostly on English and Scotch streets: *Hester's Place* (English Street) and *The Lantern* (40 Scotch Street) both serve good value lunches, or you can pick up picnic supplies at *Armagh Fine Foods* (Scotch Street). Finally the best place for coffee and snacks is *The Archway*, through an arch off the east side of The Mall.

Armagh has a big **market**, *Shambles*, which takes place on Tuesdays and Fridays on Market Street with a variety of stalls, but mainly clothes. The **Ulsterbus station** (☎0861/522266) is on the west side of The Mall.

Navan Fort

Navan Fort is the Irish Camelot, with the one difference that the Irish have kept better track of their ancient capital. For nearly seven hundred years this was the great seat of Northern power, the rival of Tara. It was here that the Kings of Ulster ruled and that the court of the **Knights of the Red Branch**, Ireland's most prestigious order of chivalry, was based. The knights, like those of the Round Table, are historical figures who have been entirely subsumed into legend, their greatest champion the legendary defender of Ulster, **Cúchulainn**. The stories of these warriors' deeds are recited and sung in what's now known as the *Ulster Cycle*. Their dynasty was finally vanquished in 332 AD, when three brothers (the Collas), in a conquest known as the Black Pig's Dyke, destroyed Navan Fort, razing it to the ground and leaving only the earthen mounds you see today. The defeated Red Branch Knights were driven eastwards into Down and Antrim, but their glories withered away soon afterwards.

THE GAME OF BULLET

On the roads just north of Armagh City, you may be lucky enough to witness an ancient road game by the name of **Bullet**, played by local men. It's played here and in County Cork – and virtually nowhere else in the world. The game consists of throwing an iron ball (the size of a cricket ball but 28oz in weight) along about two and a half miles of winding road, and the aim is to know your road well and get the ball to the end with the least number of throws – it takes approximately twenty. The game draws big local crowds and there's even some betting along the way. Oncoming cars are hastily stopped, and the crowd has to scatter as the ball hurtles along cutting corners or clearing the heights of hedges. Roads where you're likely to catch sight of the game include Napper Road, Blackwater Town Road, Rock Road, Tassa Road, Keady Road, Newtonhamilton Road and Madden Road, usually on Sunday afternoons. The most reliable information on coming games is probably in local pubs. The "World Championship" takes place on the first Sunday in August in Armagh and the last Sunday in August in Cork: the Armagh world champion to look out for is Aiden McVeigh.

It's as well to keep the old stories in mind, as when you arrive at the site (just a couple of miles west of Armagh on the A28) there's nothing more than an earthen mound to be seen. Excavation of the mound took place over a ten-year period (1961–71) and revealed a peculiar structure, apparently unique in the Celtic world. Archaeologists reckon that around 100 BC the buildings that had existed since the Neolithic period were cleared, and a huge structure 36 yards in diameter was constructed. An outer wall of timber surrounded five concentric rings of large posts, 275 in all, with a massive post at the very centre. This was then filled with limestone boulders – and set on fire, creating a mountain of ashes that was then covered with sods of clay to make a high mound. It is anybody's guess what the purpose of the structure was; a temple, or maybe a momentous funeral pyre.

Loughgall, Ardress House and The Argory

LOUGHGALL, about five miles north of Armagh along the B27 in the middle of apple orchard country, beautiful in the spring, is worth visiting mainly for its **Orange Museum**. It was in Loughgall that the first Protestant Orange Order was founded in 1795, and today the little village, like many others in Armagh's rural north, is a strongly Protestant enclave. The museum occupies a terraced house at the northern end of the main street (key next door with Mrs Vallary) and includes such Orange paraphernalia as sashes, flags and the banner from the Dolly Brae victory, and the first Orange Order warrant signed on a Catholic after the battle of the Diamond. It was this fight just outside town, when the Protestant *Peep O' Day Boys* gave the Catholic *Defenders* a thrashing, that led to the foundation of the first Orange group: in its early days a crude organisation whose aim was to drive Catholics from their homes by threats or actual violence, condemned by most Protestant landowners and politicians. Nowadays the village is deceptively quiet – in 1988, however, it was the scene of a British Army ambush in which eight IRA men died. The main street is lined with antique shops and there's a nice tea-house parlour, *Emily's Cottage*; the *Famous Grouse Inn* on Ballyhegan Road (☎076/891778) is rather livelier, a bar/restaurant with regular live music. There's B&B **accommodation** at the McKeever's, 63 Main Street (☎076/891604) and at *Hillview*, 28 Grange Blundel Road (☎076/289679).

A further five miles or so north, and only a few miles apart, are two National Trust properties worth visiting if you've more than a day in the area. **Ardress House** (April, May & Sept weekends 2–6pm; June Fri–Mon 2–6pm; July & Aug Tues–Sun 2–7pm; ☎0762/851236) is a seventeenth-century manor house with ornate plasterwork, a good collection of paintings, a sizeable working farmyard and wooded grounds. **The Argory** (same hours, except July & Aug Wed–Mon 2–7pm; ☎08687/84753), built in 1820, is a fine Neoclassical building, containing the original furniture and lit by an original acetylene gas plant in the stable yard.

South Armagh

South Armagh is a tiny area, but a well-defined one, stretching from the border to a line drawn roughly between Newry and Monaghan. It's a completely different proposition from the more populated northern slice of the county. Today it's known to outsiders, if at all, primarily from news reports, and even locally it's often referred to as Bandit Country or The Killing Fields. Its towns, from

Bessbrook through Newtownhamilton to Keady, are heavily defended with electronic barriers and manned by army or RUC billets. These are Protestant-dominated bastions, forced into a kind of internal exile, and their Union Jack flags fly defiantly in an area where the countryside is heavily Catholic. The IRA are waging a campaign here aimed at driving out the remaining Protestant landowners (their sons are favourite targets), in the long-term hope that they'll pack up and leave the land to the Catholics. The British Army seem equally hell-bent on using the territory as a trainee war zone, much better preparation than the German bases in the event of another Falklands.

With both forces now firmly locked into this combat, the innocent majority of the Armagh people have to carry on with their lives in as normal a way as they can, and it's incredible to see, from the outside, with what little fuss the people view the situation. It's this continuation of normal everyday life that you'll come across as a passer-through, and probably little else. If you're cycling the country roads, you'll sooner or later round a corner and come up against an army foot patrol, who nine times out of ten couldn't be more polite; if they immediately recognise you as a tourist they won't even bother you for identification. If you're moving round in a vehicle you might suddenly get the shock of a *Chinook* helicopter swooping down across the road right in front of your windscreen. Once again, it's nothing to get bothered about – the sooner you run into the army, and the more often, the better, for then they'll be fully aware of your activity and purpose in the region and release you from any suspicion. It may not sound an attractive prospect, but in fact this is one of the most scenically beautiful parts of the North, where even the army encampments on the hill summits can come to seem weirdly atmospheric.

Around Slieve Gullion

Slieve Gullion (*sliabh gCuilinn*, the mountain of Culainn), which dominates the southeast corner of Armagh, is one of the most mysteriously beautiful mountains in the country. A store of romantic legends are attached to the mountain, especially concerning **Cúchulainn**, who took his name here after slaying the hound (*Cú*) of his chief, *Culainn*; and **Fionn Mac Cumhaill***, who founded the *Fianna*, a mythical National Militia whose adventures are told in the *Fenian Cycle*. Slieve Gullion itself is surrounded by a far-flung circular rampart of smaller hills that make up what is known as the **Gullion Ring Dyke**, which rises to no more than a thousand feet and encloses some of the most beautiful countryside of these two northern counties.

Approaching the mountain from the north, you'll pass BESSBROOK, where the Union Jack flies, and then CAMLOUGH, where the Tricolour flutters. As you turn off the main road to go down by the eastern slopes of Camlough mountain, you'll see a beautiful lake, inset like a jewel into its green sides. A little further on, between Camlough Mountain and Slieve Gullion, are the **Killevy churches**. Two churches of different periods, they share the same gable wall: the west church is pre-Romanesque, and one of the most important survivors of its kind in the

---

*One of the Fionn Mac Cumhaill legends refers to the little lake on the top of Slieve Gullion. A magic drinking-horn once disappeared here, near the "growth of slender twigs", and if you manage to look at the right area in the morning, having previously fasted, you'll instantly know everything that's going to happen that day.

country; the other, larger church dates from the thirteenth century. The grave of Saint Blinne, the founder of a fifth-century nunnery, is here, and there's a holy well dedicated to her a little further up the slopes of Slieve Gullion; pilgrims visit it on her feast day (the Sunday nearest July 6).

The official, tarmacked entrance up into Slieve Gullion is on the mountain's afforested southern face, after you've passed through the village of KILLEVY. Here there's a small forest park with a winding drive up to the summit, where various vertiginous viewpoints offer spectacular views over the Ring of Gullion and the surrounding countryside for miles around.

The border

JONESBOROUGH, east of the mountain, is the venue each Sunday for a vast **market**, with traders and customers coming from north and south of the border to buy and sell a wide range of wares (11am–5pm, up at the school). If you're around, it's well worth experiencing. Two miles south of Jonesborough is the **Pillar Stone of Kilnasaggart**, a beautifully inscribed Christian monument and one of the earliest of its kind (700 AD). Several small crosses are marked within circles on its back face, and the defaced markings on its edges are possibly ogham writing. It's surrounded by several other tiny stones with similar cross markings, all held within a pentagonal enclosure three fields away from the roadside, behind a farmhouse. Less than a mile west of here, on the other side of the railway line, you should be able to see **Moyry Castle** on the hill. It's a timid affair and not really worth even this slight detour; but amongst its interesting features are several musket loopholes – it was built by Lord Mountjoy, Queen Elizabeth I's deputy, in 1601 as the defence for the Gap to the North.

To get to FORKHILL, barely five miles west of Jonesborough, you'll have to take a long way round, back to the main Forkhill–Newry road: the obvious and quickest route passes along unapproved border roads. The more legitimate route will bring you to the **Three Steps Inn**, on the corner as you reach the main road. It's an ordinary looking pub, but was the site of the abduction of an undercover British Army Captain, **Robert Nairac**. Nairac was a regular visitor to pubs in the area during the mid-Seventies; it was well known that he was in the army, and no one could understand what he was up to. When handed the microphone in a singing pub, he once started singing a Republican song; at closing time, he was heard singing the Irish National anthem in Gaelic – while in uniform. It was also well known that when someone local was arrested and taken down to the army camp, Nairac aways tried to intervene for their release. What Nairac was in fact up to was a long-term intelligence survey, a phenomenally daring (not to say crazy) exercise. His luck ran out on May 14, 1977, when he was in the the *Three Steps Inn* with a large local crowd. That night he sang two songs on stage and the last anyone saw of him was when he left the pub. It's assumed that he was kidnapped in the car park outside and later executed by the IRA. His body has never been found.

Forkhill and Crossmaglen

FORKHILL is a tiny village right up by the border in the southwest foothills of Slieve Gullion, a simple, quiet and remote looking place – but for the massive army encampment stacked upon the crown of its hill, which entirely dominates everything else in sight. The village is strong on **traditional culture**; O'Neill's *Welcome Inn* has a storyteller, John Campbell, on a Tuesday night (check first on ☎0693/

888552) and a singalong on Thursday night. There's *céilí* dancing in the INF hall most Tuesday nights, and a two-day festival of singing (unaccompanied by instruments) takes place in late July; there's a lively musical tradition both here and in MULLAGHBANE further north up the road. If you want to **stay** in Forkhill there are a couple of B&Bs: *Ard Mhuire Guesthouse*, 27 Carrickasticken Road (☎0693/888316; £10), and *Green Gables*, 2 Tifferum Road (☎0693/888589; £10).

Passing through Mullaghbane, you get back to the main Newry–Crossmaglen road, on which there's a small **Cottage Folk Museum**, a little up towards the Newry end. **CROSSMAGLEN**, however, dominates the southwestern corner of Armagh. Its reputation in print looks frightening – seventeen soldiers have died in its main square alone, and it's seen by all as the eye of the storm in south Armagh. It has been a hotspot for so long largely because it's militantly Republican (note the very powerful Republican sculpture in the square) and only a couple of minutes away from the border; the army have therefore positioned one of their stronger encampments on the main square. Helicopters are continually flying in and out, and their approach path is only feet above the players on the neighbouring Gaelic football field – which, if you see it, is one of the most bewildering scenes you're ever likely to encounter here. All this said, on arrival you'll find the pubs much friendlier than you've been forewarned, and you're hardly likely to brush up against any trouble. Should you want to stay there's a tiny **B&B** at 6 Newry Street (☎0693/861630; £10) and another, *Lima Country House*, at 16 Drumalt Road, Ummericam, Silverbridge (☎0693/861944; £10).

Darkley

There's little to lure you up the western side of Armagh except for the natural beauty of the run. Up near KEADY, the small village of **DARKLEY** is, tragically, worth mentioning because in November 1983 it was the victim of one of the most brutal attacks of the Troubles. The INLA arrived at the *Mountain Lodge Pentecostal Assembly* while a Sunday prayer meeting was in progress and shot three men who were standing outside the main door, killing them all. They fired more shots through the door, then walked round the outside of the church, shooting low through its wooden walls in the hope of killing many more. In the event, they managed only to wound a number of the congregation.

travel details

Trains
From Bangor: to Belfast (2 an hour; 30min); Lisburn (2 an hour; 55min); Lurgan (every hour; 1hr); Portadown (every hour; 1hr).

Ulsterbuses
From Armagh: to Belfast (2 daily; 50min), Dublin (1; 2hr 20min)

CHAPTER SEVENTEEN

TYRONE AND FERMANAGH

C ounties Tyrone and Fermanagh form the bulk of inland Northern Ireland. Though these neighbouring counties are both predominantly rural, essentially their characters are quite different. **County Tyrone** is largely dull farming country; the chief scenic attractions are to be found in the wild and desolate **Sperrin Mountains**, to the north. It's remote country, and thinly served by the local bus network; if you don't have a car it's very much a region for determined hikers and cyclists only. In the lowlands the occasional castles, archaeological sites, and heritage centres are frustratingly scattered and difficult to get to – with the exception, luckily enough, of the Ulster American Folk Park north of the county town of **Omagh**. Overall it's an area where small villages dominate – none of enormous fascination, but most retaining an historical quirk or two which enliven the journey.

In contrast, **County Fermanagh** attracts plenty of visitors – chiefly for the watersports and fishing that are widely available. It has at its core the great **Lough Erne**, a huge lake complex dotted with islands and surrounded by richly beautiful countryside. Its county town of **Enniskillen** is resonant with history, while the remnants of the medieval past along with those of the seventeenth and eighteenth centuries are found all over the region, on islands and mainland alike. As in Tyrone, sights of interest are dispersed and the public bus service again only serves the main routes, but the key to getting the most from Fermanagh is to get out onto the water – and this is easy enough from Enniskillen, and a number of the villages that rest on the lakes' shores.

COUNTY TYRONE

Stretching from the shores of the vast Lough Neagh in the east to the border of the Republic and Donegal in the west, County Tyrone lies bang in the middle of Northern Ireland. Its northern limits are high in the desolate and beautiful Sperrin Mountains, and in the south it meets the lakes of County Fermanagh. It's a large and mainly featureless county, and if you are here at all the chances are you're heading elsewhere. The towns of Tyrone are not much of a draw. **Omagh** is the county's capital, agreeable enough, but with little to warrant a stop. **Cookstown** and **Dungannon** in the east, and **Strabane** on the border with Donegal are similarly places to pass through, with minimal points of interest scattered around. It's first and foremost farming country, with little evidence of industrialisation apart from the starchily neat planters' villages that grew up with the linen industry. Perhaps the nearest the county's settlements get to being picturesque are the villages to the northwest of Omagh: Castlederg, Newtownstewart, Sion Mills, and the tiny hamlets of the Sperrins.

The major scenic attractions are in the **Sperrin Mountains**, rich in wildlife, and an excellent target for determined, lonesome walking. For this, **Gortin**, a village on the **Ulster Way** footpath, is the place to head – and the only easily accessible overnight stop in the area. Tyrone also has no shortage of archaeological remains, the most remarkable being the **Beaghmore stone circles**, in the southeast of the Sperrins. There's little to detain the visitor in the way of sights beyond the **heritage centres** dotted around the county which celebrate the historic connections between Ulster and the USA. Of these the **Ulster American Folk Park** near Omagh is by far the best.

The only **local transport** in the region is *Ulsterbus* – reliable along main routes, and not as infrequent as you might expect in such a rural area; nonetheless, if this is your only way of getting around, it makes sense to pick up a timetable in a major bus station before you head off into the country. However, so scattered are the attractions of this largely empty county, you're likely to see little of the most interesting parts without a car or a bike. The one exception, of course, is in the Sperrins, where **hiking** is the best way to get around.

Some history

Tyrone is the land of the O'Neills, an heroic clan celebrated in legend as the sons of "Niall of the nine hostages", who became chiefs of Ulster, ruling from Omagh, Dungannon, and Cookstown. The county was a key source of Gaelic resistance to English rule. It was in Dungannon that the first Gaelic Bible was printed in 1567, and Hugh O'Neill, Earl of Tyrone, and his ally the Earl of Tyrconnell were the last of the great Gaelic chiefs to fight against Tudor control. Their continual wars with Elizabeth I inspired revolts throughout Ireland but, despite their Spanish Catholic allies, they were finally defeated at Kinsale in 1601. The Earls' departure for Europe in 1607 has been enshrined in folk memory as "The Flight of the Earls", the final departure of the Gaelic aristocracy. The subsequent Plantation of Ulster during the reign of James I established the hegemony of the Crown, giving control of Tyrone to the Protestant immigrants from England and Scotland.

But this was not the end of Gaelic resistance, and it was again from this part of Ulster that the next serious threat to English control came. The **Great Rebellion of 1641** began in Tyrone with Phelim O'Neill's capture of Dungannon and Charlemont. The rising spread throughout the country as Catholics all over Ireland joined together to claim their religious and civic rights. The rebellion was inevitably accompanied by considerable brutality, but horror stories grew to such an extent that settlers came to believe there was a concerted plan to massacre the entire Protestant population, and the alleged scale of the violence gave Cromwell his justification for the massacre at Drogheda ten years later. Ulster remained in the hands of the planters, and it was they who introduced linen manufacture in the eighteenth century – the county's only experience of industry.

The first significant emigration from Ireland to America was that of Ulster men and women in the early eighteenth century, many of whom were of Scottish Protestant origin. Of all the immigrant communities, it was the Irish who most quickly – and profoundly – made their mark: the three first-generation-American presidents were all of Ulster stock, and a further nine presidents could trace their roots here. Sit in any bar in Tyrone long enough and someone will tell you with pride that these men and women emigrated because they had ambition and vision, and that they were not, unlike later emigrants, forced out by famine and eviction.

Omagh

Tyrone's county town, and the most likeable place of any size, is **OMAGH** – *Ómaigh* in Irish, meaning "the seat of the chiefs" or "the virgin plain". The glory days are gone now, though, and there's no trace of the fortress from which the O'Neill clan once ruled Ulster, which once overlooked the river. Instead, Omagh's main street leads up to a fine classical courthouse and the irregular twin spires of the Sacred Heart Catholic Church. Pleasant enough, but the only reason you'll spend time here is for a breather if you're on your way to or from the west coast, or heading north into the Sperrins.

Tourism in the region is generally geared to those with cars out for scenery, and the **tourist office** in the main street (May–Sept Mon–Sat 9am–1pm & 1.30–5pm; Oct–April Mon–Fri 9am–1pm & 2–5pm; ☎0662/247831) promotes a very large area. Ask for **camping** and you'll be pointed toward the *Gortin Forest Park*, which is as pretty as is claimed, but lies six miles north of Omagh up the

Newtownstewart road (6 buses daily). Better to ask a farmer if you can use a field. Alternatively several **B&B**s are registered with the tourist office. Mrs McCann's, 12 Tamlaght Road (☎0662/243381; £11) is the nearest to the town centre: from the tourist office walk up the main street, take the left fork in front of the Sacred Heart up to James Street, and Tamlaght Road is the second on your right. Also near the centre is Mrs B. Cuddihy, 1 Georgian Villas, Hospital Road (☎0662/245254; £12): walk down the main street away from the courthouse, cross the river, and Hospital Road is to your right. The *Silver Birches Hotel* on Gortin Road offers more luxurious accommodation (from £20) plus regular entertainment.

The town is a good place to stop for **food**, particularly during the daytime. *Woodlanders*, on Gortin Road, is an excellent new restaurant and bar, with entertainment most nights. The *Pink Elephant* in the High Street is a local favourite, serving traditional daytime dinners in huge helpings. Almost as popular is the *Libbi Eating House*, open daytime, Monday to Saturday. The *Royal Arms Hotel* in the High Street serves excellent pub grub at midday, and limited hot snacks in the evening. There's no shortage of cafés and fast food either.

In the unlikely event of you spending time here, *Bogan's*, in Mountjoy Road, churns out traditional Irish **music** on Saturdays, as does *Kelly's Bar* in Abercorn Street, on Fridays and Saturdays. The *Clock Bar*, off Main Street, draws a young crowd with entertainment to match, and *Sally O'Briens* has traditional, folk and country-and-western sessions. Occasional jazz sessions are to be found at *McElroy's* in Castle Street, though at weekends the place is generally given over to discos. The *Royal Arms Hotel* has jazz and blues sessions for free on a Thursday, and again discos at weekends. Despite this apparently promising list of options, there is no tangible "scene" here and what you get is very much the luck of the draw.

Omagh's *Ulsterbus* **bus depot** (☎0662/242711), for all country-wide and local connections, is just across the river in Mountjoy Road (north off the High Street).

The Ulster American Folk Park

About five miles north of Omagh, and a short ride on the Omagh–Newtownstewart bus, is the **Ulster American Folk Park**, Camphill, the most successful of the American heritage projects dotted around the country (Easter to early Sept Mon–Sat 11am–6pm, Sun & public holidays 11.30am–6.30pm; mid-Sept to Easter Mon–Fri 10.30am–4.30pm; last admission 1hr before closing; £2). It makes a good afternoon out from Omagh, and is also on the **Ulster Way**, which to the northeast enters the scenic GORTIN area at the start of the Sperrins. Mrs Fulton, next door to the Folk Park's farm, does **B&B**.

The Folk Park tells the story of early emigrants: the first half is a typical eighteenth-century **Ulster village**; the second shows the communities they went on to build in America. The Ulster village is reconstructed around original buildings that include cottages, a school house and an austere Presbyterian meeting house. A full-size ship depicts the gruelling passage to America, forming a link with the **American settlement**. The buildings of the Irish village are modest, but the multi-purpose log barns of the Pennsylvanian settlers are massive. Again the attention to authenticity is excellent, and captures a sense of the ambition and hope these emigrants must have felt on their arrival in the New World. Whatever your feelings on the Ulster Presbyterian work ethic, this propagandist Folk Park does powerfully recreate something of the Ulster emigrants' experience. In the accompanying **museum** there's a comprehensive exhibition on the American War of Independence, the making of the Constitution, and more on the lives of the early pioneers.

Northwest from Omagh

Northwest Tyrone has some of the county's most attractive towns and countryside. The fastest route west – and the only feasible one if you're hitching – is the A5 through Newtownstewart, Sion Mills and Strabane. Far quieter is the route via Castlederg along minor country roads west to Castlefinn, County Donegal, which takes you through a much more remote and isolated border crossing point; it's only really possible by car or bike.

The friendly village of **CASTLEDERG** sits around a spruced-up square beside the River Derg, apparently trying to ignore its police barracks bristling with barbed wire. Across the river are the ruins of a Plantation castle, built in 1609, and not long after destroyed by Sir Phelim O'Neill: today it sits in picturesque innocence, as though it had nothing to do with the current state of affairs. Castlederg retains something of its traditional flavour as a staging post for travellers and wateringhole for pilgrims on their way to Lough Derg – its bars and cafés make this a good place to stop for food. If you're taking the fastest route west from Omagh you will pass through **NEWTOWNSTEWART**, settled in rich farmland, with its **castle** – another fourteenth-century O'Neill stronghold – looking clean and lonely on a hill to the south. There is a **tourist office** in the main street, next to the Church of Ireland church (mid-June to Sept Mon–Fri 9.30am–5pm; ☎06626/61560).

The linen industry of the eighteenth century made a big impact in Tyrone, as it did all over Ulster, but its traces are mostly faint ones – such as the disused mills along the Ballinderry River near Cookstown. **SION MILLS**, a planned linen village just two miles south of Strabane, is the glaring exception. Here simple millworkers' cottages are neatly laid out around the mill, the quaintness of the village today belying the gruesome conditions of nineteenth-century factory work. The **tourist office** at Sion Mills (mid-June to Sept daily 9.30am–5.30pm; ☎06626/58027) is geared towards the motoring traveller.

Strabane

Grim and congested, **Strabane** seems to glower over the River Foyle. Its recent history has been troubled, which is hardly surprising: not only does the town sit right on the border, but it's a small Catholic enclave uncomfortably surrounded by largely Protestant-owned farmland.

In the eighteenth century Strabane was an important printing and publishing centre. John Dunlap emigrated from here and went on to print the broadsheets of the American Declaration of Independence in 1776, as well as the *Pennsylvanian Packet*, America's first daily paper. All that is left in Strabane of these times is the cute, Georgian bow-windowed shopfront of *Gray's* printing shop, which is now owned by the National Trust; there's a small printing **museum** upstairs (April–Sept noon–6pm; closed Thurs & Sun; 50p). Sadly the shop's interior has been ripped out to provide maximum space for cards, completely destroying the scale and atmosphere the place must have once had.

Head east of Strabane two miles down the Plumbridge road, and you run into another tourist-product of the Ulster-American connection: the **President Woodrow Wilson ancestral home** at DERGALT (open any reasonable hour – ask at the adjacent farm). The President's father, who was a printer in Strabane, lived in this small, traditional farmer's cottage. Stuffed with furniture and effects belonging to the family, it's now a target for American tourists, who dutifully meander through the hallowed rooms.

The Sperrins

The huge, undulating **Sperrin Mountains** form the northern limits of County Tyrone. Wild, empty and beautiful, they reach 2240 feet at their highest, yet the smooth and gradually curving slopes give them a deceptively low appearance. The covering of bog and heather adds to this effect, suggesting nothing more than high, open moorland. For all this, views from the summits are panoramic, and the evenness of texture can make these mountains sumptuous when bathed in evening light. Once in the mountains it's impossible not to catch sight of the **wildlife**. Sparrow hawks and kestrels hover above, and you might see buzzards or the far rarer hen harrier. They're attracted by rich prey in a landscape undisturbed by development – the mountains teem with assorted rodents, rabbits, stoats and badgers, even the Irish hare. One threat to this delicately balanced ecosystem has been the recent rediscovery of gold in the mountains. Their future is in the balance, but for the moment at least, the Sperrins offer a wilderness to be enjoyed.

For local sheep-farming communities, however, the underpopulation of the Sperrins is a real problem, and their traditional way of life is now slowly dying. The sparseness of the population and the lack of focal centres makes it difficult for an outsider to key into this culture. For the same reason, hitching isn't easy, and walkers should bear in mind that there's a shortage of places to buy food, so thinking ahead is essential. Rely only on large villages for provisions of any sort; hamlets often have nothing.

The **Sperrin Centre**, between CRANAGH and SPERRIN, five miles east of Plumbridge (see below), enables you to explore the area's environmental and cultural issues without getting your feet wet (June–Sept Mon–Fri 11am–6pm, Sat 11.30am–6pm, Sun 2–7pm; Oct–May Mon–Sat 11am–5pm, Sun 1–6pm; £1). The video games and audio-visuals of this interpretive centre are of a decidedly educational bent – though they also organise gold-panning expeditions. It's tricky to get to without transport, but worth bearing in mind for its very pleasant tea room if you are walking in the area.

Walking

The Sperrins offer good long-distance **walking**, without necessarily involving steep inclines. You can ramble wherever you like, but remember that despite appearances these *are* high mountains, and changeable weather makes them potentially dangerous. A map and compass are essential for serious walking. For those not equipped for the high ground, the **Glenelly** and **Owenkillen** river valleys run through the heart of this stunning countryside from Plumbridge and Gortin respectively (see below), and are particularly enjoyable for cyclists.

The signposted **Ulster Way** can be picked up three and a half miles east of SPERRIN as the road leaves the Goles Forest, and will take you into the heart of the mountains. The problem is that you'll probably have to walk that distance to join it, since this valley is almost impossible to hitch through. From the forest the Way climbs Crockbrack (526m), to fine, wide views, and then heads north through the Glenshane Forest to the A6 main road, four miles south of DUNGIVEN, County Derry – a walk of around twelve miles. Route guides to the *Ulster Way* can be bought from the *Sports Council of Northern Ireland* (see "Information and Maps" in *Basics*) or from tourist offices.

Plumbridge and Gortin

Once in the mountains, settlements are mere specks of houses, and if you're tackling the Sperrins from Tyrone, there are really only two places that'll offer you any amenities at all. And even these are comatose for much of the year.

The first, **PLUMBRIDGE**, doesn't look like it's changed much over the years, beyond encouraging the fishing fraternity to down rods and drink in its bars. Apocryphally, it gets its name from the building of the village bridge. The engineer in charge didn't have a plumb line and so, from his scaffolding, spat in the water, using his phlegm to take the perpendicular. Nearby **GORTIN**, three and a half miles south, though greatly promoted as a tourist centre, is a one-horse town with a café and a pub. Mrs Kelly offers **B&B** for £10 at 34 Main Street (☎06626/48241), and you'll find a **campsite** at *Gortin Forest Park* (☎06626/48217). The **Ulster Way** passes through the village, though for now the signposting which should connect it with Goles Forest is incomplete, and stops at Craignaddy (300m), two and a half miles north. However, the signposted Way does continue to the south of Gortin through the pretty forest park, with its little loughs and wild deer, before swinging west to low farmland and the Ulster American Folk Park (see above).

Three and a half miles east of Gortin (on the B46 CREGGAN road) is the tiny village of **Rouskey**, with the ruins of a "sweat house" – a sort of early sauna. After the steam treatment, the luckless invalid was plunged into the icy stream nearby. The use of sweat houses died out after the Famine years, possibly because the experience of typhoid which accompanied the Famine dealt a severe blow to people's confidence in traditional medicinal treatments.

Prehistoric remains and the Beaghmore Stone Circles

County Tyrone is peppered with archaeological remains, the Sperrins themselves having their fair share – including over a thousand standing stones – and the county as a whole having numerous chambered graves. The **Lough Macrory** area, just east of MOUNTFIELD on the A505 (Omagh–Cookstown road), is particularly rich in dolmens and megaliths, though many of these are hard to find and of specialist interest only.

The uninitiated will get most out of the Bronze Age **Beaghmore Stone Circles**, in the southeast of the Sperrins; they're well signposted seven miles west of Cookstown, and are just three and a half miles off the A505. Although most of the stones on this lonely site are no more than three feet high, the complexity of the ritual they suggest is impressive: there are seven stone circles, ten stone rows, and a dozen round cairns (burial mounds, some containing cremated human remains). All of the circles stand in pairs, except for one, which is unique in that it is filled with over 800 upright stones, known as Dragon's Teeth. The alignments correlate to movements of sun, moon and stars. Two of the rows point to sunrise at the summer solstice, another may point to moonrise at the same period.

East Tyrone

The east of Tyrone is low-lying and uninspiring, and it seems even the legendary Fionn Mac Cumhaill was unimpressed. The tale goes that he took a massive lump of land from Ulster and hurled it across the Irish Sea. It landed and became the Isle of Man, and the hole it left behind became **Lough Neagh**. The lough's shores form the county's huge eastern boundary and provide excellent fishing and plenty of birdlife, but, beyond this, both land and lake are almost featureless. Small settlements house eel fishermen, whose catches go to the Toome Eel Fishery at Toomebridge (at the northern tip of the lake), the largest eel fishery in Europe.

Slight relief is to be found at ARDBOE, ten miles east of Cookstown, where there's a tenth-century **High Cross** heavily carved with Biblical scenes. Its size is exceptional – eighteen feet high – yet it lacks impact: so dull is this shore the cross stands devoid of spatial context.

Mountjoy Castle lurks behind a farm eight miles south of here on the road towards Dungannon. Built in 1602 as part of the English campaign against Hugh O'Neill, it was strategically important, but again the setting is disappointing.

Cookstown, Dungannon and around

The only places in the east of the county that could be described as anything more than villages are Cookstown and Dungannon. A planned planters' town, **COOKSTOWN** boasts the longest main street in Ireland, which in effect means the community now clings for dear life to the sides of a dual carriageway. There are a couple of places to **eat**: *The Royal Hotel*, Coagh Street, and *The Central Inn* in William Street. But the main attraction for the visitor is the *Edergole Riding School*, 70 Moneymore Road (☎06487/62924), whose one-hour to three-day treks wind up the slopes of Slieve Gallion and into the Sperrins. They can also arrange **canoeing** for you, and the school is attached to a friendly **B&B**.

Two miles out of Cookstown on the B520 is **Tullyhoge Fort**, the site of the inaugural ceremonies of the O'Neills. From the road it looks like nothing more than a copse of beech and scots pine on the top of a very gentle hill, but in fact these are very clear, comprehensible earthworks of the early Christian period – a circular outer bank with an inner oval enclosure. Ulster chiefs were crowned here from the twelfth to the seventeenth century, and it was in Tullyhoge forest that O'Neill tribesmen hid after the Flight of the Earls.

More recent history is on display three and a half miles west of Cookstown, at the National Trust-owned **Wellbrook Beetling Mill**, an eighteenth-century water-powered linen mill (Easter, May, Sept & Oct Sat, Sun & bank holidays 2–6pm; June–Aug Wed–Mon 2–6pm; Sun 2–7pm in July & Aug; 50p). "Beetling" is a process whereby linen is given a sheen and smoothness by hammering with wooden "beetles". The mill is very well preserved, and all the engines still work. As you hurry through dreary **DUNGANNON** pause and briefly reflect on its illustrious history as the hilltop seat of the O'Neills, from which they ruled Ulster for over five centuries. Heading west by car you might want to visit the **Simpson-Grant Farm** (3 miles east of BALLYGAWLEY, signposted off the A4 road; Oct–April Mon–Fri 10.30am–4.30pm; May–Sept Mon–Sat 10.30am–6.30pm & Sun 12.30–7pm; 60p). Based around the nineteenth-century homestead of the maternal ancestors of President Ulysses S. Grant, it's of interest chiefly for the traditional livestock of the working farm.

COUNTY FERMANAGH

It is for the intense beauty of its lakes that Fermanagh is famous. A third of the county is water, the great **Lough Erne** complex swinging right across the region from Lower Lough Erne in the northwest to Upper Lough Erne in the southeast. Surrounding hills are wooded with oak, ash and beech, producing a scene of fresh, verdant greens in spring, and rich and rusty colours in autumn. The water's rippling surface reflects whatever light there is, mirroring the palest of skies through to the ruddiest of magenta sunsets. It's a breathtaking landscape, where land and water complement one another in a fine, stately harmony.

The **Lower Lough** in winter has the character of an inland sea, dangerous waves making even the locals wary of sailing. Fabulous vistas reach across to the mostly uninhabited shores of richly wooded islands, on which are scattered early Christian ruins and evidence of earlier pagan cultures. The **Upper Lough** is quieter and less spectacular. The waterway here is a delightful muddle of little inlets and islands, where waters are shallower and shorelines reedy. Fields have shocks of bristly marsh-grasses; definitions between land and water are blurred.

The county town of **Enniskillen** sits at the point where the Upper and Lower loughs meet, long an important bridging point; it's still the only real town in Fermanagh, and a good base for exploring the region. If you want hostel accommodation, you'll have to stay out in the country at Castle Archdale, ten miles north of Enniskillen, or in the extreme west at Garrison – both good options, set in magnificent scenery. If you've transport, there are historical tracks to cover touring Fermanagh's impressive series of **planters' castles**, while the county's two stately houses – **Florence Court** and **Castlecoole** – are both open to the public.

There are plenty of opportunities for **watersports**, and the less energetic can get out onto the lakes by hiring a **boat** or taking one of the lough cruises. Surrounding hills are accessible to **walkers** along the *Ulster Way*, while **cyclists** will find the road surfaces smooth and empty. Boats aside, this last is perhaps the best way to get around the county, since **transport** is limited to *Ulsterbus* – reliable enough, but only main routes from Enniskillen are served with any frequency. If you look like a foreign tourist, then **hitching** along main roads is possible during the summer months, though never easy: County Fermanagh is as friendly as anywhere in the North, but people tend to be cautious because of the border.

History

The region's early history was dictated by the difficulties of the Lough Erne waterways, in earlier times even more confused and forested than today. Recorded history begins with the early Christians, who slowly permeated the culture and established religious foundations. They appreciated the seclusion of the lakes, and ruins of **medieval monasteries** remain. Centres of ecclesiastical power and learning were dotted on islands in the lough, and it is likely they were visited by pilgrims on their way to St Patrick's Purgatory, the shrine on Lough Derg. More brutal invaders found the lough complex difficult to infiltrate. Neither Vikings nor **Normans** ever managed to control the region, and throughout the medieval and Tudor period the English similarly failed to subdue it. The surrounding land was unruly and hard to govern even for the Irish. The

Maguires, who ruled the west of the kingdom of Oriel (Fermanagh, Monaghan, South Tyrone and Louth) from 1250 until 1600, were originally based at Lisnaskea, but the cattle raids of neighbouring chiefs forced them to move to Enniskillen in the early fifteenth century. The town was to become strategically crucial as the determination of the English to dominate Ireland increased during the sixteenth century. As the crossing point through the waterways it was one of only three land routes into Ulster available to the invaders, the others being over the river near Ballyshannon and the Moyry Pass between Dundalk and Newry. So Enniskillen and the Maguire castle became focal to the Irish resistance to the Tudors. It was taken in 1600, and in 1607, after the Flight of the Earls, the **Planters** arrived.

The usurpers were obliged to build a ring of **castles** around the Lough in order to maintain control: Crom, Portora, Tully, Castle Archdale, Crevenish, Caldwell and, most important of all, the old Maguire castle at Enniskillen. Given sizeable grants from the English crown, the planters of Enniskillen built an Established Church, a fort, and a royal school, turning the place into a British colonial town. It became a Loyalist stronghold, which successfully defended itself against the Irish during the Great Rebellion of 1641, and against an attack by James's troops in 1689. The Loyalists of Enniskillen formed a regiment which William of Orange chose as his personal guard at the Boyne. In the late eighteenth century Enniskillen proved to be of key military importance, with the threat of a French invasion through the northwest of Ireland. By now the town had two royal regiments – a unique phenomenon.

At **Partition** Fermanagh became a part of the state of Northern Ireland, despite its predominantly Catholic population, and despite this majority's cultural affinities with Cavan in the Republic, with whom it shares the tail end of the Lough Erne complex. In 1921 the county returned a Nationalist majority in local government elections, an undesirable state of affairs for the British. The abolition of proportional representation in 1922 and the gerrymandering which followed ensured the subsequent Loyalist majority. With a history of such blatant injustices, a large Catholic population, and a lengthy border with the Republic, Fermanagh is a nucleus of Nationalist activity, and today has strong Sinn Féin sympathies. It was Fermanagh and South Tyrone that in April 1981 returned **Bobby Sands** as Westminster MP. At the time of the election Sands was serving a fourteen-year prison sentence for possession of weapons, and was leading a hunger strike for political status for IRA prisoners. His death from starvation after 66 days made him one of the most famous IRA heroes.

Enniskillen

Amid the innumerable atrocities that have scarred Northern Ireland in recent years, the name **ENNISKILLEN** has a special capacity to shock, after the IRA bomb attack on Remembrance Day 1987, which killed 11 and injured 61 people as they gathered to commemorate the dead of the two world wars. In a town of only 10,500, the bombing profoundly affected the lives of every citizen, and at once gave Enniskillen a reputation for sectarian violence that bears no relation to its true nature. In fact, this is a pleasant, conservative little town, rather relaxed and very friendly. Central to both Fermanagh and the lakes, Enniskillen is a focus for visitors and locals alike. It's the only place of any size in the county, and although you can see all that it has to offer in a day, if you're using B&Bs it makes a good base from which to explore the lakes.

The town

The town sits on an island like an ornamental buckle, two narrow ribbons of water passing each side, connecting the Lower and Upper Lough complexes. The water loops its way around the core of the town, its glassy surface imbuing Enniskillen with a pervasive sense of calm, and reflecting the mini-turrets of the **Watergate**, so making a toy image of the military presence. Rebuilt by William Cole, the man to whom the British gave Enniskillen in 1609, the Watergate stands on the site of the old Maguire castle, next to the island's westerly bridges. Cole's additions show obvious Scottish characteristics in the turrets corbelled out from the angles of the main wall. It houses the **Fermanagh County Museum** (Mon–Fri 10am–1pm & 2–5pm; also May–Sept Sat 2–5pm, July & Aug Sun 2–5pm; free), a typical local collection, and **The Regimental Museum of the Royal Enniskillen Fusiliers** (same times), a proud and polished display of the uniforms, flags and paraphernalia of the town's two historic regiments. A new **History and Heritage Centre** should also be open.

Much of Enniskillen's character comes from a wealth based on the care of a colonial presence. Evidence of British influence is widespread: on a hill to the west the stately Portora Royal School overlooks the town, discreetly reminding one of the continued elitism in the social order. It was founded by Charles I in 1626, though the present building dates from 1777; old boys include Oscar Wilde and Samuel Beckett. Over on a hill to the east a Wellingtonian statue – **Cole's Monument** – keeps an eye on the town from a very British-style park; a small charge lets you ascend to the viewing gallery for a bird's eye view of town. Immediately below is the war memorial, scene of the bombing. The centre invites strolling: the main street undulates gently, lined with confident Victorian and Edwardian town houses, thriving shops and smart pub fronts. This street changes its name no less than six times between the bridges at either end, running from Anne Street to East Bridge Street: lanes fall to either side down towards the water, and calmly sitting next to one another are three fine church buildings, Church of Ireland, Catholic and Methodist.

On Queen Elizabeth Road, just off the main street, the **Buttermarket** is a new craft and design centre with the full range of craftsmen working on site. The original buildings date from 1835, and you'll find displays of art, music and drama, as well as craftwork and design. Here too is the excellent *Boston Quay* coffee shop.

Castlecoole

Evidence of how the richest of the colonists lived is found on the outskirts of town at **Castlecoole**, the eighteenth-century home of the Earls of Belmore (June–Aug daily except Thurs 2–6pm; April, May & Sept Sat & Sun 2–6pm; £2.20; grounds open April–Sept, free). A perfect Palladian building of Portland stone, with an interior of fine plasterwork and superb furnishings, it sits in a beautiful landscaped garden, whose cultivated naturalness reinforced its owners' belief that the harmony of God's creation mirrored that of society. Castlecoole can be walked to either from the Dublin road (signposted close to the *Ardhowen Theatre*), or across the golf course from Castlecoole road.

Practicalities

The very efficient **tourist office** is housed in the *Lakeland Visitor Centre*, on Shore Road, south of the main street (July & Aug Mon–Fri 9am–7pm, Sat 10am–5pm, Sun 10am–2pm; May, June & Oct Mon–Fri 9am–5pm, Sat 10am–5pm, Sun 2–5pm; Nov–April Mon–Fri 9am–5pm; ☎0365/323110, 325050). The "Round O" jetty for **lough cruises** is signposted off the Derrygonnelly road. Enniskillen's **bus station** is next to the tourist office – buses to Belfast, Dublin, Dungannon, Sligo, Derry, Omagh, and local services.

Accommodation

The tourist office has comprehensive accommodation lists and will book for you (50p charge). Alternatively, **B&B** is easily found across the town's western bridges, along the A46 Derrygonnelly road and along the Sligo road. On the former, try *Willoughby Guest House*, 24 Willoughby Place (☎0365/325275; £12); along the latter there's *Carraig Aonrai*, 19 Sligo Road (☎0365/324889; £8.50), *Rossole House*, 85 Sligo Road (☎0365/323462; £11), and *Mountview*, Irvinestown Road (☎0365/323147; £12.50; with snooker room). More upmarket, try the family-run *Railway Hotel*, conveniently central at 34 Fort Hill Street (☎0365/322084; £22). The nearest **hostel** is at Castle Archdale, ten miles north of town, and all local **campsites** are well out of town. *Florence Court Park* is off the A32, six miles south; *Blaney Caravan Park* (☎0365/364634; £3.50) is seven miles to the northwest, off the A46, directly behind the BLANEY service station – a beautifully situated and well-equipped site.

Eating, drinking and entertainment

Enniskillen has a handful of good cheap places to **eat**. Currently everybody's favourite is *Franco's* in Queen Elizabeth Road, the northerly road that runs into East Bridge; open daily from noon till late, it has delicious pizza, pasta, and seafood. *Peppercorn*, on the main street by the post office, is also good. A lot of the bars along the central main street do decent pub grub, particularly *The Vintage* and *Pat's Bar*: upstairs from the latter is *Melvin's Restaurant*, for lunches, grills and dinners. The restaurant at the *Ardhowen Theatre* is worth visiting for the setting, should you be hungry after a traipse around Castlecoole.

Enniskillen is also well served for **cafés**, many of which do good cheap meals. The most popular of these are *Leslie's*, in the main street, with good ice cream, and *Home and Away*, Head Street (off Queen Street), which serves plenty of delicious homemade dishes, including salads and vegetarian meals. *Johnson's Coffee Lounge*, on Townhall Street, and *The Barbizon*, Main Street, are also worth a try.

There's no shortage of cheerful **pubs** in Enniskillen, although there's little by way of entertainment. Musically, this is Country country: bands play at *The Watergate* on Friday and Saturday, at *The Tipplers Brook*, at the west end of town, and at *The Railway Hotel* in Fort Hill Street. As ever **discos** are in the hotels, in particular *The Fort Lodge Hotel*, Fort Hill Street, which also occasionally has local bands. *The Vintage*, on the main street, is a popular disco bar with video jukebox, while nearby *Blakes of the Hollow* is a traditional Victorian bar with original fittings. Others worth trying for traditional music are the *White Star Bar*, opposite *Blakes*, and the *Bush Bar* and the *Crow's Nest*; all on the main street.

The hub of Enniskillen's **arts scene** is *The Ardhowen Theatre* (☎0365/325440), in a wonderful setting overlooking the lough a mile out of town on the Dublin road (you can enjoy the view from an excellent bar). It has a year-round programme of top-quality drama, film and ballet, and hosts a great range of music events – traditional Irish, jazz, opera, country, classical – as well as productions by local community groups. Its annual **film festival** runs for a fortnight from the last week in August.

Listings

Bike hire Mr C. Stevenson, 31 Charterhill Road (☎0365/323597).

Boat hire Mr A. Birrell, Round "O" Jetty (☎0365/322882) – see the "Lough Erne" section below for more boat hire details.

Bureau de Change In the post office on Main Street.

Car hire *Lochside Garages* (☎0365/324366), Tempo Road; *Modern Motors* (☎0365/322974), 74 Fort Hill Street.

Early closing day Wednesday.

Fishing Licences, permits and info from the *Lakeland Visitor Centre*.

Hospital *Erne Hospital* (☎0365/324711), Corngrade Road.

Launderettes *The Wash Tub*, East Bridge Street, Enniskillen; and in Castle Street, Irvinestown (see below).

Taxis *West End Taxis* (☎0365/325999)

Travel Agency *Erne Travel* (☎0365/324477), Paget Square; youth/student tickets available.

Lough Erne: islands and idols

Lough Erne has had a profound effect on the history of Fermanagh. The earliest people to settle in the region lived on and around the two lakes; many of the islands here are in fact *crannógs* – early Celtic artificial islands. Its myriad connecting waterways were impenetrable to outsiders, protecting the settlers from invaders, and creating an enduring cultural isolation. Evidence from stone carving suggests that Christianity was accepted far more slowly here than elsewhere: several pagan idols have been found on Christian sites, and the early Christian remains to be found on the islands show strongly the influence of pagan culture. Here Christian carving has something of the stark symmetry and vacancy of expression found in pagan statues. Particularly suggestive of earlier cults is the persistence of the human head motif in stone carving – in pagan times a symbol of divinity and the most important of religious symbols.

The most popular of the Erne's ancient sites – **White Island** and **Devenish Island** – are on the **Lower Lough**, as is **Boa Island** in the far north, which is linked to the mainland by a bridge at each end. The **Upper Lough** is less rewarding, but it too has spots of interest which repay a leisurely dawdle. Whichever you choose, the easiest way to go is on one of the **cruises** or **ferries** that operate from Enniskillen (see box), the *Castle Archdale* hostel, and surrounding villages (see below); sailings two or three times daily in season, prices start from £3. **Hiring your own boat** – again from Enniskillen, Kesh or Belleek (see below) – will cost around £45 a day, including fuel, and you should let the owner know where you're going and ask to borrow navigation charts: this lough can be dangerous, and outside the summer months, not even the locals venture out. Larger **cruisers** are generally available for a minimum of a week, though you may be lucky and find someone prepared to offer a weekend deal.

LOUGH ERNE FERRIES

To White Island Boat from *Castle Archdale* jetty June–Aug Tues–Sat 10am–7pm, Sun 2–7pm, less frequently during Sept. ☎0365/322711 ext 40. £1.

To Devenish Island *Devenish Island Ferry Service* (☎0365/322711 ext 40) operates a continual service to Devenish from TRORY, 4 miles north of Enniskillen (April–Sept Tues–Sat 10am–7pm, Sun 2–7pm. £1.

A two-hour **cruise** of Lough Erne, stopping at Devenish for half an hour, operates from the "Round O" pier, Enniskillen. The *Kestrel*, operated by *Erne Tours* (☎0365/322882), sails May & June Sun 2.30pm; July & Aug Mon–Fri 10.30am, 2.15pm & 4.15pm, Tues & Thurs 7pm, Sun 11am, 3pm & 7.15pm; first two weeks Sept Tues, Sat & Sun 2.30pm. £3.

Devenish Island

The easiest place to visit from Enniskillen, certainly if you don't have transport of your own, is **Devenish Island**, in the south of the Lower Lough. A monastic settlement was founded here by Saint Molaise in the sixth century, and became so important during the early Christian period that it had 1500 novices attached to it. The foundation was plundered by Vikings in the ninth century and again in the twelfth, but continued to be an important religious centre up until the Plantations. It's a delightful setting, not far from the lough shore, and the ruins are considerable, spanning the entire medieval period. Most impressive are the sturdy oratory and perfect round tower, both from the twelfth century; Saint Molaise's church, a century older; and the ruined Augustinian priory, a fifteenth-century reconstruction of an earlier abbey. The priory has a fine Gothic sacristy door decorated with birds and vines; to the south is one of Ireland's finest high crosses, with highly complex, delicate carving. Other treasures found here – such as an early-eleventh-century book shrine, the *Soiscel Molaise* – are now kept in the National Museum in Dublin.

Killadeas, Irvinestown and Castle Archdale

In **KILLADEAS** churchyard, seven miles north of Enniskillen on the B82, stands the **Bishop's Stone**, carved some time between the ninth and eleventh centuries. It's one of the most striking examples of the appearance of pre-Christian images in early Christian culture, having a startled paganistic face on one side, and a bishop with bell and crozier on the other. There are other interesting carved stones in the graveyard too, including two cross-slabs and a rounded pillar, possibly a pagan phallic stone. If you want to get out onto the water, Manor House Marine, Killadeas (☎03656/21561), rents out **motor boats** from £45.

A few miles inland, in **IRVINESTOWN**, a head idol found in Enniskillen has been set in the wall of the lounge of *Mahon's Hotel*. It has an unusually long neck, long narrow face, wide slit mouth and two holes for eyes – almost certainly pre-Christian. If you want to stay in Irvinestown, there are a couple of **B&Bs** in the village: Mrs Hudson's *Roseville*, on the Dromore road (☎03656/21055; £10.50) or Mrs Allen's *Leraine*, Kesh Road (☎03656/21627; £10); there's also lakeside dormitory accommodation available at the *Extern Killadeas Pavilion* on the Kesh Road (☎03656/28202; £4.50).

To thoroughly immerse yourself in the beauty of the lough scenery, however, you could hardly do better than stay in the **hostel** of **Castle Archdale** (☎03656/

28118; £5.95; closed Dec 19 to Jan 19), set in a forest park near LISNARRICK, around five miles west of Irvinestown. It makes sense to arrive here in daylight – look out for a small sign beside a church for the turn-off from the main road. It's a *YHANI* hostel, with the attendant curfew restrictions, and three miles from the nearest shop, but the hostel warden sells milk, eggs and potatoes, and it's a perfect place for getting out onto the lough. The ferry to White Island (see below) leaves from nearby, and you can also **rent boats**.

White Island

Mounted on the wall of a ruined abbey, the seven early Christian carvings of **White Island** look eerily pagan. Found earlier this century, they are thought to be caryatics – carved supporting columns – from a monastic church of the ninth to eleventh centuries.

The most disconcerting statue is the lewd female figure known as a *sheila na gig*, with bulging cheeks, a big grin, open legs, and arms pointing to her genitals. This could be a female fertility figure, a warning to monks of the sins of the flesh, or an expression of the demoniacal power of women, designed to ward off evil. (In the epic *Táin Bó Cuailnge*, Cúchulainn was stopped by an army of 150 women led by their female chieftain Scannlach. Their only weapon was their display of nakedness, from which the boy Cúchulainn had to avert his face.) Less equivocal figures continue left to right: a seated Christ figure holding the Gospel on his knees; a hooded figure with bell and crozier, possibly Saint Anthony; David carrying a shepherd's staff, his hand towards his mouth showing his role as author and singer; Christ the Warrior holding two griffins by the scruff of their necks; and another Christ figure with a fringe of curly hair wearing a brooch on his left shoulder and carrying a sword and shield – here he is the King of Glory at his Second Coming. There is an unfinished seventh stone, and on the far right, a carved head with a downturned mouth which is probably later than the other statues. The church of White Island also contains eleventh-century gravestones; the large earthworks round the outside date from an earlier monastery.

Boa Island and Kesh

One of the most evocative of the carvings of Lough Erne is the double-faced Janus figure of **Boa Island**, at the northern end of the Lower Lough – barely an island at all these days, as it's connected to the mainland by bridges. The place to look out for is CALDRAGH cemetery, poorly signposted off the A47, about a mile and a half from the eastern bridge.

Down by the lake shore is an ancient Christian burial ground of broken, moss-covered tombstones, where low, encircling hazel trees enhance an almost druidic setting. Here you'll find the **Janus figure**, an idol of yellow stone with very bold symmetrical features. It has the phallus on one side, a belt and crossed limbs on the other. The figure was probably an invocation of fertility and a depiction of a god-hero – the belt being a reference to the bearing of weapons. Alongside it stands the smaller "Lusty Man", so called since it was moved here from nearby Lustymore Island. This idol has only one eye fully carved, which may be to indicate blindness – Cúchulainn had a number of encounters with war goddesses, divine hags described as blind in the left eye. There are chalets to rent, and a restaurant, on Lusty Beg Island just off Boa – a small ferry will take you across (☎03656/31342 for details).

The nearest village, **KESH**, four and a half miles to the east, is a possible overnight stop, having some cheapish **B&B** accommodation. Try Mrs Lee, *Ernevale*, 26 Main St (☎03656/31668; £12), or Mrs Stronge, *Alaise*, Kesh Road (☎03656/31096; £12). If you've transport there's also the option of staying in the *Ardess Craft Centre* (☎03656/31267; B&B £12), housed in a fine Georgian rectory, which offers residential courses in spinning, weaving and natural dyeing (courses start from £5 a half day). To find the centre take the Enniskillen road out of Kesh, turn left just before police barracks, take a hard right, then follow the road for one and a half miles.

The chief recommendation of Kesh itself is its position on the lough. You can hire **motor boats** here from Mr R. A. Graham, Manville House (☎03656/31668; £24 a day). If you want to combine **camping** with **watersports** it makes sense to stay at the *Lakeland Caravan Park*, Boa Island Road (☎03656/31025), which offers windsurfing, canoeing and waterskiing. Alternatively, away from the lough shore, there's also *Clonelly Forest Campsite*, three miles north of Kesh on the A35.

Upper Lough Erne

Upper Lough Erne holds nothing like the interest of the Lower Lough, nor the scenic splendour. The most you're really likely to do is disturb the fishermen or get lost amongst its crazy causeways and waterways – fun on a boat, but frustrating on dry land. Should you be tempted to venture further into the maze of reed and water, a "Viking longship" runs **cruises** daily in summer from the Shore Centre at Smith's Strand (☎03657/22122), where they also offer water-based activity holidays with facilities for disabled travellers, and B&B from £15.50. Boat trips may also be available from the National Trust **Crom Estate**, four miles west of NEWTOWNBUTLER. If you have transport, the elegantly chiselled gravestones on Galoon Island, with their chilly reliefs of skull and crossbones, hourglass and coffin are worth a detour. *Ports House*, right by the waterside at PORTS, not far from Newtownbutler, offers eccentric **B&B** (☎03657/53528; £11).

Around the county

Around the islands and waterways there are innumerable stunning routes for both walkers and cyclists, and as the county as a whole is geared towards fishing and boating, there's no problem finding somewhere to eat and sleep in villages around the lough. **Walkers** will find the countryside to be mostly gentle hills and woods, which rise to small mountains in the south and west of the county. For **cyclists**, there are well-surfaced (and empty) roads around the Lower Lough, though routes around the Upper Lough are harder to negotiate, with little lanes often leading to nowhere but some empty reed-infested shore.

Immediately around the entire lough complex is a ring of defensive planters' **castles**, while the most assured achievement of the colonists, 150 years on, is evident in the magnificent eighteenth-century house of **Florence Court**, southwest of Enniskillen. If you've transport, a visit to the house can be combined with an hour or so at the **Marble Arch Caves** – the finest cave-system in Ulster. Throughout the county, there's a wealth of **wildlife** (particularly waterfowl), and the lough, forest parks and **Ulster Way** all make access to the riches of the countryside very easy.

The planter castles

The Lough Erne complex was ringed by a series of planter castles early in the seventeenth century – a crucial part in the settlers' bid to control the region – and many of these are worth dropping in on as you travel around the county.

Monea Castle, on the west side of the Lower Lough, less than a mile off the B81, is a particularly fine ruin in a beautiful setting at the end of a beech-lined lane. Built around 1618, it bears the signs of Scottish influence in its design, with similar features to the reworked Maguire castle in Enniskillen. It was destroyed by fire in the Great Rebellion of 1641, and by Jacobite armies in 1689, and was eventually abandoned in 1750 after another fire. There's a **campsite** (☎0365/389609; £5 per tent) here, on the Derrygonnelly road, or you can ask at the *Castle Inn*, right by the castle. Five miles further north, beyond DERRYGONNELLY, the fortified house and bawn of **Tully Castle** sits down by the lough shore. Both castles are freely accessible at all times.

The best of the planter castles on the Upper Lough is **Castle Balfour** at **LISNASKEA**, twelve miles southeast of Enniskillen. Again, strong Scottish characteristics are clear in the turrets and parapets, high-pitched gables and tall chimneys. Lisnaskea itself is one of Fermanagh's few towns – and a small one at that. Its tiny nineteenth-century cornmarket yard has an early Christian carved cross depicting Adam and Eve beneath a tree, and the library contains a diminutive but interesting **folk museum** (Mon–Wed & Fri 9.15am–5pm, Sat 9.15am–12.30pm), with displays on local Gaelic traditions and festivals, including plenty of detail on the making of *poitín*. If you're **camping**, there are two campsites within three miles of Lisnaskea; one at Mullynascarthy, the other on the Derrylin road.

The Marble Arch Caves and Florence Court

Fermanagh's caves are renowned, and while some are for experts only, the most spectacular system of all – the **Marble Arch Caves**, south of Belcoo – is accessible to anyone. A tour of the system lasts around an hour and a half, taking you through brilliantly lit chambers dripping with stalactites and fragile mineral veils. **Tours** of the caves are sometimes booked out by parties, so it makes sense to ring ahead to check that your journey there will not be wasted (open last two weeks of June Mon–Sat 11am–4.30pm, Sun 11am–5pm; July & Aug Mon–Sat 11am–5pm, Sun 11am–6pm; Sept & Oct Mon–Sat 11am–4.30pm, Sun 11am–5pm; ☎0365/828855).

The caves are around eleven miles from Enniskillen, but there's no bus service. From Enniskillen follow the A4 Sligo road for three miles, branching off on the A32 Swalinbar road; the caves are well signposted from then on. Walkers can reach them along the *Ulster Way*, which from the A4 runs four miles south to the caves, past Lower Lough Macnean.

If you have transport, the magnificent **Florence Court** (April–Sept noon–6pm, closed Tues; £2.20; grounds free and open all day), eight miles southwest of Enniskillen and five from the caves, is worth a visit. A three-storey mansion built in 1764, and joined by long arcades to small pavilions, it was owned by the Coles, descendants of the planters of Enniskillen. It is notable for its lavish Rococo plasterwork and rare furnishings.

The Ulster Way

The **Ulster Way** provides a signposted, long-distance path across the county – in theory, indeed, around the whole of Northern Ireland, though it's extremely difficult to follow in places. In the southwest of Fermanagh it takes you through the bog and granite heights of the Cuilcagh mountains and Ballintempo Forest, offering fabulous views over the Lough. The Way then continues north, through the **Lough Navar Forest**, a well-groomed conifer plantation with tarmacked roads and shorter trails. Although a great deal of fir plantation walking is dark and frustrating, this forest does, at points, provide some of the most spectacular views in Fermanagh, looking over Lower Lough Erne and the mountains of Tyrone, Donegal, Leitrim and Sligo. The Lough Navar Forest also sustains a small herd of red deer, as well as wild goats, foxes, badgers, hares and red squirrels.

It is advisable to follow the signposting rather than design your own route where the Way runs close to the border with the Republic. Route sheets on the Navar Forest and Big Dog Forest trails are available from local tourist offices; and you can get a route guide for the southwest section of the Way from The Sports Council for Northern Ireland (see *Basics*).

Accommodation possibilities along the Way are limited. There are a couple of B&B places near BELCOO, two and a half miles west from the trail's ascent to the Ballintempo Forest: try Mr and Mrs Thornton, *Fir Grove*, Enniskillen Road (☎036586/387; £11) or Mr and Mrs Catterall, *Corralea Forest Lodge* (☎036586/ 325; £10). There's a **campsite** in the Lough Navar Forest, five miles west of Derrygonnelly, off the A46.

Castle Caldwell and Belleek

The forest of **Castle Caldwell**, near the western extremity of Lower Lough Erne, is the main breeding site in the British Isles for the common scoter (a species of duck), and a habitat of rarities such as the hen harrier, peregrine falcon and pine marten. A commercial, state-owned forest of spruce, pine and larch, it's protected as an area of wildlife conservation. At the entrance look out for the giant stone fiddle in front of the gate lodge, the sobering memorial to Denis McCabe, a local musician who in 1770 tumbled from the Caldwells' barge while drunk, and drowned.

BELLEEK itself, situated 24 miles from Enniskillen, has **B&B** accommodation – at Mrs McDonnell's, Main Street (☎036565/491; £11) – and several places from where you can **hire boats**. For rowing boats call at Carlton Cottages (☎036565/8181; £22 a day). *Belleek Pottery* offers interesting tours of the famous **pottery**, and a chance to buy the rather fussy products. There's a **fiddle festival** here in summer.

Five miles south of Belleek, at **GARRISON**, the *Lough Melvin Holiday Centre* is a residential **outdoor pursuits** centre (☎0365/3658142; prior arrangement essential), offering caving, canoeing, windsurfing and hill walking – prices from £5 a half day, £55 a weekend. The centre has **hostel** accommodation open to all comers, from £4.50 per person, camping £5 per tent – though you should ring ahead to check on space if you want to stop here.

travel details

Ulsterbus

From Strabane three buses daily to Omagh (1hr 5min); Monaghan (2hr 5min); Dublin (4hr 40min); two daily to Derry (50min).

From Enniskillen to Belfast (1 daily, 2 in summer; 2hr 35min); Dublin (3; 3hr 35min).

Private buses

Funtrek (☎01/730852) serves Omagh and Strabane on its daily Dublin–Letterkenny and Dublin–Derry routes.

PART THREE

THE

CONTEXTS

THE HISTORICAL FRAMEWORK

An understanding of Ireland's history is essential in order to make sense of its troubled present. In these few pages we cannot do more than provide a brief outline of that history, in the hope that it will serve as a starting point for further reading and discussion, and encourage the visitor to become familiar with the patterns of the past.

EARLIEST INHABITANTS

It is generally believed that the first settled inhabitants of Ireland were the **Mesolithic** hunters and fishers who arrived in the north-east of the country from Scotland some time around 6000 BC. They probably crossed the water in skin coracles, and they lived close to the sea, rivers and lakes; their flintwork has been found in Antrim, Down, Louth and Dublin. In about 3000 BC the Neolithic people arrived. With skills in animal husbandry, weaving, pottery, and farming they used their stone axes to clear the forests for cultivation.

These were the people responsible for the vast assortment of **megalithic remains** still to be seen throughout Ireland. Such sites can be found all along the Atlantic seaboard of Europe; not just the huge sites such as Carnac in Brittany, Stonehenge in England, and the Ring of Brodgar in the Orkneys, but also smaller examples from Galicia in Spain up to

Scandinavia. It used to be thought that the culture that produced them originated around the Mediterranean – many similar sites exist in Malta and Sardinia – and spread to the "barbaric outposts" of Europe, but radio-carbon dating techniques show that the progression was not so simple. The inhabitants of prehistoric Ireland are better considered as equal participants in a sophisticated and continent-wide culture, even at this early stage intimately connected with the peoples of Britain and Brittany.

Nonetheless, each area of Europe had its own distinct styles and traditions, and Ireland's contribution is exemplified by the great **passage tombs** such as Knowth and Newgrange in County Meath, with their elaborate spiral engravings, cut into the stone entirely without the use of metal tools.

Little is known of the people themselves, although their civilisation was long-lasting, with several thousand years separating the earliest and the latest megalithic constructions. Only rarely have skeletons been found in the graves, but what few there have been seem to indicate a short, dark, hairy race with a life expectancy of no more than the mid-30s. Legends call them the **Fir Bolg**, and speak of shambling subhuman giants who served as their slaves on such projects as the building of the Giant's Causeway on the coast of Antrim. The perpetual rivals of the Fir Bolg were the *Tuatha Dé Danann* (the Tribes of the Goddess Danu), who feature heavily in storytelling from this time on as the underground fairy people.

THE CELTS

The semi-mythical Fir Bolg were eventually supplanted by the **Celts**, an Indo-European group called *Keltoi* by the Greeks and *Galli* by the Romans, who had spread from Central Europe south into Italy and Spain and west through France and Britain into Ireland. The main Celtic arrivals in Ireland probably happened during the late Bronze Age, around 700 BC, although dating is complicated by the fact that the Celtic tribes continued to use bronze for weaponry long after the appearance of iron.

It is hard to separate the truth about the Celts from the stories they told of themselves. Theirs was an oral culture, very much in the mould of the *Iliad*, in which the immortality to be gained from starring in an epic tale was prized above all else. With an enthusiasm for war little short of bloodthirsty, they celebrated battles decided by the single combat of great champions, guided and aided by the unpredictable whims of the gods. They swiftly appropriated the religion and beliefs already current in Ireland; the *Tuatha* were transmuted into Celtic gods, and although the Celts had nothing to do with the building of the megaliths, the sites continued to have great symbolic significance.

The Atlantic seaboard of Europe in the first centuries AD was largely populated by independent tribes who had been driven westwards by the Romans. At a time when communications were much easier by sea than by land, a loose pan-Celtic trading confederation came into being. In Ireland itself, Celtic settlements took the form of ring forts, with the island consisting of about one hundred small **kingdoms** or *Tuatha*, each with its own king. The *Tuatha* were grouped into the *Five Fifths* or provinces, which were Ulster (*Ulaid*), Meath (*Midhe*), Leinster (*Laigin*), Munster (*Muma*) and Connaught (*Connacht*). In theory, the High King (*Ard Rí*) ruled over all from his throne on the Hill of Tara – a place long associated with mysterious power – although only rarely did any one figure of sufficient strength emerge to lay undisputed claim to that title.

The two greatest heroes of the epics, **Cúchulainn** and **Fionn Mac Cumhaill**, have been tentatively identified with warrior champions of the second and third centuries, transformed by legend into semi-divinities in much the same way as King Arthur was in England.

THE COMING OF CHRISTIANITY

The **Christianisation** of Ireland began as early as the third century AD, well before the arrival of Saint Patrick (assuming he existed at all). Vestiges did survive of the previous religion of the Celts, but after the collapse of the Roman empire Ireland assumed a position at the very forefront of European Christianity. Partly due to the sheer impassability of the landscape, the country became a haven for religious orders, which were the only sources of learning at this time. Many of the great Irish monasteries, such as St Enda's on the Aran Islands, Clonmacnoise in County Offaly and Clonard in County Meath

date from this period. **Ogham**, the Celtic line-based writing system seen on standing stones, was rapidly supplanted by the religious scholars, who introduced Latin to a people distrustful of the written word. The first – and best known – of their richly illuminated Latin manuscripts, the **Book of Kells**, can be seen in Trinity College, Dublin.

The traditional view of these as "Dark Ages" of terror and chaos throughout Europe bears little relation to what was happening in Ireland. Stable diplomatic and trading contact continued along the Atlantic seaboard, while Irish missionaries spread the Gospel onto the continent. Saint Columba's proselytising took him to Germany and to Italy, where he founded a monastery at Bobbio, and Irish bishops were responsible for the virtual colonisation of Brittany.

INVASION: VIKINGS AND NORMANS

Ireland itself, however, was increasingly plagued by destructive pirate raids, in which many of the great monasteries were plundered and burned – hence the invention of the Round Towers, which were used as look-out posts and places of sanctuary. The raids culminated in the full-scale **Viking invasion** of 795. The invaders then set about founding walled cities, usually at the mouths of rivers, such as Dublin, Wexford, Waterford, Youghal, Cork, Bantry and Limerick. The decisive defeat of the Danes by the High King Brian Boru at the Battle of **Clontarf** in 1014 at least spared Ireland from the threat of becoming a colony. However, the murder of Brian Boru immediately afterwards, and the subsequent fragmentation of his chieftains, meant that his victory was never consolidated by the formation of a strong unified kingdom. The Vikings that remained soon merged fully into the native Irish population.

From the time of the Norman Conquest onwards, the Norman kings of England coveted Ireland. The first of the **Anglo-Normans** to cross over to Ireland was something of a free lance adventurer, Richard FitzGilbert de Clare (**Strongbow**). He came in 1169 at the invitation of Dermot MacMurrough, the exiled king of Munster, who sought help to regain his throne. Henry II, however, was concerned that Strongbow might establish himself in an ineradicable power base and therefore went person ally to Ireland as overlord. He had earlier secured papal support and authorisation over all powers – native, Norse and Norman – from, ironically, the only English pope in history, Adrian IV.

In 1172, Pope Alexander III re-affirmed Henry II's lordship. This seemed to open the prospect of an Anglo-Norman conquest in which Gaelic tribal kingdoms would be reshaped into a strong feudal system, but the native Irish resisted so effectively that royal authority outside the "English Pale" was little more than nominal.

THE STATUTES OF KILKENNY

By the fourteenth century, this wave of Anglo-Norman settlers had integrated with the native Irish population to such an extent that the crown, eager to regain control, sought to drive a permanent wedge between the natives and the colonists with the introduction of **The Statutes of Kilkenny** (1366). This legislation prohibited intermarriage with the Irish, forbade the Irish from entering walled cities, and made the adoption of Irish names, dress, customs or speech illegal. Despite these measures, Gaelic influence continued to grow until, by the end of the fifteenth century, the "Pale" had been reduced to a narrow strip of land around Dublin.

THE TUDORS: HENRY VIII

The continued isolation of Irish politics from English and continental influence during the fifteenth century, and England's preoccupation with the Wars of the Roses, helped Ireland's most powerful Anglo-Norman family – The **FitzGeralds** of Kildare – to establish and consolidate control of the east and southeast of the country. For the most part, their growing authority was left unchallenged by the early Tudor monarchy, whose policy towards Ireland was based mainly on considerations of economy (it was cheaper to accept Kildare's rule than establish an English deputy who would need expensive military backing) and security; Irish discontent with English rule should not be allowed to take forms which might be exploited by England's foreign enemies.

THE REFORMATION

Henry VIII was able to retain this attitude of expedient caution until his break with Rome introduced several new factors: the clergy began to preach the necessity of rebellion against the schismatical king, while Henry was able to reward his supporters with the spoils from the dissolution of religious houses. Kildare's son, Lord Offaly ("Silken Thomas"), convinced that the family power was under threat, staged an insurrection in the summer of 1534. Aid from the Pope – who for the first time was seen as a potential supporter of opposition to England – was hoped for, but never came. Henry, inevitably, reacted forcibly, and changed his policy of prudence for one of aggression. War dragged on until 1540, by which time Kildare and his supporters, their power all but crushed, were forced to submit to the crown.

The Dublin Parliament enacted legislation accepting Henry's **Act of Supremacy**, which made the king head of the church. At least three distinct factions emerged in Ireland: the "Old English", who were loyal to the king but denied him spiritual primacy, the independent-minded and staunchly Catholic Gaelic Irish, and the new Protestants, many of whom had benefitted materially by acquiring church property. (At this stage, those "recusants" who refused to swear the oath acknowledging Henry as head of the church were not yet subject to discrimination.) The crown, in an attempt to bind the chiefs and nobles of Ireland more closely to its authority, forced them to surrender their lands only to return them again with the reduced status of landlords. This was central to Henry's policy – the wish to rule Ireland cheaply, with least risk of foreign intervention through Irish-born "deputies" whose loyalty was assured. But, of course, such loyalty could not be counted on and after Henry's death the authority of the English crown was again challenged.

ELIZABETH I

During the reign of **Queen Elizabeth I** (1558–1603), a growing number of "adventurers" (mainly younger sons of the aristocracy) arrived from Protestant England to pillage Ireland. For the first time, the supposed moral imperative to turn the Gaelic Irish away from the papacy was used as an excuse to invade and dispossess. This justification for the suppression of Irish culture, religion and language was to be the trademark of English occupation of Ireland for many years to come.

Elizabeth's aim was to establish an English colony. This policy of "**plantation**" had been started, albeit unsuccessfully, some thirty years earlier in the reign of Mary I, when Laois – renamed "Queen's County" – and Offaly – "King's County" – were confiscated from their native Irish owners and given into the possession of loyal Old English. Elizabeth's first attempt, in the 1570's, to "plant" northeast Ulster, which was then the most Gaelic area of the country, failed miserably. Nonetheless, the colonisation process, when eventually achieved, was to be instrumental in subjugating the entire country.

HUGH O'NEILL AND THE FLIGHT OF THE EARLS

At least three major Irish **rebellions** were prompted by Elizabeth's policies. Two, led by the Desmonds of Munster, were easily put down, and their lands were confiscated and given to English settlers. The third, last, and most serious was in Ulster, led by **Hugh O'Neill**. O'Neill was originally a protegé of the English court, instrumental in crushing the revolt of the Desmonds, and had long been groomed to become chief of Ulster. He'd always imagined the role to be that of an autonomous Gaelic chieftain; he turned against his Queen in 1595 when he began to appreciate the extent to which he would be the pawn of English Protestantism. His forces won one major victory over the English at the battle of the Yellow Ford in 1598, but were defeated in September 1601 when the Spanish reinforcements they were expecting at Kinsale failed to arrive in time.

The Tudor conquest of Ireland was completed when O'Neill signed the **Treaty of Mellifont** in 1603, ignorant of the death of Elizabeth just a few days before. Half a million acres of land were confiscated from the native Irish, including all the estates of O'Neill and O'Donnell. English plans to redistribute the land supposedly included generous endowments to the "natives". However, an abortive and unplanned insurrection in 1608 was enough to frighten them into abandoning any such idea, and English and Scottish "planters", many of whom were ex-soldiers, were instead brought over, to be ensconced in fortified enclosures known as "bawns". Chiefs such as O'Neill were still nominally landlords, but unable to accept the loss of their ancient authority, and living

under constant suspicion that they were plotting against the crown, many chose instead to leave their country as exiles. Their mass departure to continental Europe in 1607 became known as the **Flight of the Earls**.

It was at this time that the character of **Ulster** began to change. James VI of Scotland had just become James I of England, encouraging many Scots to emigrate the short distance to Ulster where so much newly confiscated land awaited them. There was a great deal of bitterness on the part of the dispossessed native people, and little intermarriage with the planters, so that the whole country, and above all Ulster, became divided along Catholic and Protestant lines.

CHARLES I AND THE ENGLISH CIVIL WAR

The widespread belief in England and Ireland that James' successor, **Charles I**, harboured pro-Catholic sympathies was one of the spurs for the armed rebellion in Ulster in 1641. Terrifying stories circulated in England of the torture and murder of Protestant planters, and the rebels' (bogus) claim that they were acting with Charles's blessing did much to provoke the **English Civil War**. The origins of the current situation in the six northeast counties of Ulster can in many respects be traced to the policy and events of this period.

During the Civil War, the "Old English" in Ireland allied with the native Irish in the **Confederation of Kilkenny**, supporting the Royalist cause in the hope of bringing about the restoration of Catholicism. It was an uneasy alliance, characterised by inadequate leadership and personal rivalries, in which the Irish felt they had nothing to lose in pursuit of liberty whereas the Old English lived in fear of a Protestant invasion should the forces of **Oliver Cromwell** achieve victory. The war did indeed end with the establishment of Cromwell's Protectorate and the execution of the King, and the conquest of Ireland became Cromwell's most immediate priority.

CROMWELL IN IRELAND

Cromwell's ruthless campaign in Ireland remains a source of great bitterness to this day. He arrived in Dublin with 3000 Ironsides in August 1649, and was soon joined by a larger force under General Ireton. **Drogheda** was stormed in September, and thousands, including civilians and children, were slaughtered. Cromwell continued south and quickly took Wexford and New Ross, whereupon the towns of Cork, Youghal and Kinsale in the southeast (all in the hands of Royalists) swiftly capitulated. Although Waterford held out valiantly for several months, it was not long before Cromwell's forces had overrun the entire country and broken the backbone of resistance.

THE ACT OF SETTLEMENT

By the time the struggle was over, almost two years on, one quarter of the Catholic population was dead, and those found wandering the country orphaned or dispossessed were sold into slavery in the West Indies. The **Act of Settlement** drawn up in 1652 confiscated land from the native Irish on a massive scale. All "transplantable persons" were ordered to move west of the River Shannon by May 1, 1654 on pain of death; in the famous phrase, it was a matter of indifference whether they went to "Hell or Connaught". The mass exodus continued for months, with many of the old and sick dying on the journey. Cromwell's soldiers were paid off with gifts of appropriated land, and, remaining as settlers, constituted a permanent reminder of English injustice.

KING JAMES AND KING BILLY

Irish hopes were raised once more by the **Restoration** of Charles II in 1660. He had regained the English throne, however, only as the result of lengthy negotiations with the Protestant parliamentarians of London and Dublin, and was in no position to give expression to any Catholic sympathies which he may have held.

Things only changed when Charles' brother James II succeeded him in 1685. He appointed a Catholic Viceroy in Ireland, and actually got as far as repealing the Act of Settlement. Had this had time to take effect, the land confiscated by Cromwell would have been returned to its former (Catholic) owners. However, the Whigs and the Tories in England united to invite the Protestant William of Orange to take the throne. James fled and was soon raising an army in Ireland. He was successful until he came to lay siege to the city of **Derry** in Ulster, where his forces were held at bay by the young trade apprentices of the city (known thereafter as the "**Apprentice Boys**") – a victory of Protestant over Catholic which is still celebrated annually.

In July 1690 the armies of James and William met at the **Battle of the Boyne**, and James was defeated. The repeal of the Act of Settlement was therefore never implemented; but the very idea that the Catholics still had claims to their old property which they might one day be able to reassert became established in the Protestant consciousness. As William's victory was consolidated, measures were taken to ensure irreversible Protestant control of the country.

THE PENAL LAWS

In 1641 59 percent of the land in Ireland was owned by Catholics. In 1688 the figure was 22 percent and by 1703, 14 percent. The Protestant population, about one tenth of the total, lived in fear of an uprising by the vast majority of dispossessed and embittered Catholics. In order to keep the native Catholics in a position of powerlessness, a number of acts were passed, collectively known as the **Penal Code**. Not only were Catholics forbidden to vote or join the army or navy, but it became illegal to educate a child in the Catholic faith; they could not teach, open their own schools or send their children to be educated abroad. Catholics could neither buy land, nor inherit it other than by the equal division of estates between all sons. There were vast rewards for turning Protestant; a male convert was entitled to all his brothers' inheritance, a female to her husband's property. Irish language, music and literature were banned, as was the saying of the Mass. The intention was to crush the identity of the Irish people through the suppression of their culture but it had, in fact, the opposite effect. Clandestine "hedge schools" developed where outlawed Catholic teachers taught Irish language and music, Mass was said in secret, often at night in the open countryside, and the culture remained as strong as ever.

GRATTAN'S PARLIAMENT

The next turning point in Irish history came in the late **eighteenth century**, when the increasingly prosperous merchant class ceased to identify its own interests exclusively with those of the English crown. The British, in their turn, were forced to realise that the best guarantee of stability was the country's economic strength. This was an age of bourgeois revolution, and the events of the **American War of Independence** attracted much Irish attention. As early as 1771, Benjamin Franklin was in Dublin suggesting future transatlantic cooperation. Although the rebellion of the American colonies threatened Irish commercial interests, opposition to the war did not mean opposition to the American cause. Thus far, the bulk of Irish emigrants to the American colonies had been Ulster Presbyterians, Catholic emigration being subject to legal restrictions, and the Protestants of Ireland felt a deep sympathy with Washington's campaign. The demand for "no taxation without representation" struck an emotional chord with the parliamentarians of Henry Grattan's Patriot Party – not that Ireland was directly taxed by the British Parliament, but the relationship between Dublin and London was sufficiently inequitable for that to seem a possibility.

Protestant and Catholics in Ireland made common cause to the extent that Grattan declared "the Irish Protestant could never be free till the Irish Catholic had ceased to be a slave". Its resources stretched to the limit by war, the British government was sufficiently intimidated by the thought of Irish rebellion to be in the mood for concessions. The land stipulations of the Penal Code were repealed in 1778, and in 1782 **Grattan's Parliament** achieved what was felt at the time to be constitutional independence for Ireland, beyond the interference of the London parliament although still subject to the veto of the king. In the "**Renunciation Act**" of 1783, the British parliament declared that the executive and judicial independence of Ireland should be "established and ascertained forever, and . . . at no time hereafter be questioned or questionable".

As it turned out, the independence of the Dublin parliament lasted for just eighteen years, and even those were long on dissent and short on achievement. Economic measures certainly benefited the merchants, but such issues as the extension of voting rights to Catholics – despite Grattan's personal support – were barely addressed. A major reason for this disappointing performance was the influence of the **French Revolution** in 1789.

WOLFE TONE AND THE UNITED IRISHMEN

In the 1770s, the threat of French invasion, coupled with the obvious inadequacy of the few British soldiers stationed in the country, had led to the formation throughout Ireland of bands of **Volunteers**. These were exclusively Protestant groups, at their strongest in Ulster and particularly Belfast, which rapidly acquired a political significance way beyond their supposed role as a sort of Home Guard.

The French Revolution transformed French invasion from a menace to be feared to a prospective means of national liberation. Wolfe Tone's **United Irishmen**, built on the foundations of the Protestant Volunteers but attracting, if anything, more support from Catholics, rallied to the call of Liberty, Equality and Fraternity. Tone himself was a Protestant barrister, who saw equal rights for Protestants and Catholics in Ireland as the only route to independence from England. The United Irishmen were originally disposed towards nonviolence, but for Tone the possibility of French aid was too appealing to resist. The British, and the majority of Ulster Protestants, were by contrast so alarmed by tales of the bloodshed in France, that they too prepared for war; it was at this juncture that the Protestant Orange Society, later the **Orange Order**, was established, with the aim of maintaining Protestant power.

The uprising came in **1798**; disorganised fighting broke out in different parts of the island well before the French fleet – and Tone himself – arrived, and the scattered rebels were swiftly and bloodily suppressed. Tone was sentenced to be hanged, drawn and quartered, but before he could be executed he was found with his throat cut in his cell. (See p.338 for more details.) The limited advances which Henry Grattan had won for Catholics were withdrawn as a result of the rebellion.

THE ACT OF UNION

The destiny of Ireland during the period following the uprising was largely subject to the whim of political factions in England, ever ready to make an emotional cause célèbre of the latest developments. The rebellion of 179? provoked Prime Minister William Pitt into support for the complete legislative union of Britain and Ireland, and the dissolution of the

Dublin parliament. Pitt argued that this offered the most hopeful road towards Catholic Emancipation while also ensuring the perpetuation of the Protestant ascendancy. In 1801 the **Act of Union** was therefore passed in London, and Ireland legally became a part of Britain.

All hopes of independence seemed crushed. Ireland itself housed an utterly divided people, a minority Protestant ruling class and a politically powerless Catholic majority. Robert Emmet, a romantic figure in Irish history, inspired by Wolfe Tone, made one last stand for independence, and attempted a rising in 1803. His followers however, were small in number and disorganised. The rising failed, and Emmet was executed.

DANIEL O'CONNELL

The quest for **Catholic Emancipation** by peaceful constitutional means was the life's work of Daniel O'Connell (1775–1847), the lawyer who became known as "The Liberator", and whom Gladstone called "the greatest popular leader the world has ever seen". He founded the Catholic Association in 1823, which attracted a mass following in Ireland with its campaign for full political rights for Catholics. O'Connell himself was elected to the British House of Commons as the member for Ennis, County Clare in 1828. As a Catholic, he was forbidden to take his seat in Westminster; but the moral force of his victory was such that a change in the law had to be conceded. Royal assent was given to the Catholic Emancipation Bill on April 13, 1829, granting voting rights to some Catholics. Stringent property qualifications, however, ensured that the Catholic vote remained a small one.

At the height of his success, O'Connell's popularity was phenomenal. He was elected Lord Mayor of (Protestant) Dublin for the year of 1841, and two years later embarked on an ambitious campaign for the **Repeal of the Union** with England. O'Connell addressed a series of vast "monster meetings" throughout Ireland; according to the conservative estimate of *The Times*, over a million people – one eighth of the Irish population – attended the meeting symbolically held at the Hill of Tara.

The climax of O'Connell's campaign was to be a meeting at **Clontarf** (where Brian Boru had defeated the Danes) on October 8, 1843. All Ireland was poised and waiting, conscious of the sympathy which O'Connell's profoundly peaceful movement had won from around the world. The pacifism which had led him to say that "no political change is worth the shedding of a single drop of human blood", and his determination always to act within the law, were, however, exploited by the British. One day before the Clontarf meeting, it was declared to be an illegal gathering; and O'Connell, remarkably, obliged by calling it off. The crowds which had already gathered, and the population at large, were baffled that O'Connell backed down from direct confrontation. His moment passed, and the stage was left to those who, having seen pacifism fail to secure independence, believed that armed struggle would prove the only way forward. The **Young Ireland movement**, once aligned with O'Connell, attempted an armed uprising in 1848, but by then there was little chance of mass support. The country was already undergoing a national disaster.

THE FAMINE

The failure of the Irish potato crop from 1845 to 1848 plunged the island into appalling **famine**. Elsewhere in Europe the blight was a resolvable problem, but Irish subsistence farmers were utterly dependent on the crop, as all other foodstuffs had to be sold to pay exorbitant rents to English landowners. No disease affected grain, cattle, dairy produce or corn, and throughout the disaster Irish produce that could have fed the hungry continued to be exported overseas. Millions were kept alive by charitable soup kitchens, and certain individual landlords were supportive to their tenants; for millions more, the only choice lay between starvation and escape.

In the space of a decade, the population of Ireland was reduced by two million. Half of them died, the other half – over a quarter of the population – left the country for good. Many were too ill to survive the journey on what became known as "coffin ships", some drowned when overcrowded ships sank, and still more died on arrival in the United States, Canada, Britain, Australia and New Zealand.

One consequence of **mass emigration** was the creation of large Irish communities abroad, which henceforth added an international dimension to the struggle for Irish independence. Financial support from the Irish overseas became crucial to such nationalist organisations as the Irish Republican Brotherhood, also known as the **Fenians**. Their attempted uprisings in 1865 and 1867 were little short of fiascos, but they nonetheless retained a loyal following both in the States and in England (where a number of bombings were carried out in their name).

The legacy of the Famine was such that the long-standing bitterness instilled by the English connection now deepened to a new level of emotional intensity. Resentment focused on the failure of the British government to intervene, and more specifically on the **absentee English landlords** who had continued to profit while remaining indifferent to the suffering of their tenants. Such landlords had little or no contact with the realities of life on their estates; rents were far higher than most tenants could pay and evictions became widespread.

PARNELL AND HOME RULE

The second half of the nineteenth century was characterised by a complex interplay of political and economic factors, which contributed towards the exacerbation of religious differences. The most important of these was the struggle for land, and for the rights of tenants. A coherent nationalist movement with modest aims began to emerge, operating within the setting of British parliamentary democracy.

Charles Stuart Parnell (1846–91), a Protestant who was elected to Westminster in 1875 and became leader of the **Home Rule Party** two years later, was the tenants' champion. He insisted that only a parliament meeting in Dublin could be responsive to the needs of the people, and to that end consistently disrupted the business of the Britsh House of Commons.

Parnell also organised the Irish peasantry in defiance of particularly offensive landlords, adding a new word to the English language when the first such target was a Captain Boycott.

A breakthrough seemed to be approaching when Parnell won the support of the Prime Minister, Gladstone, but the **Phoenix Park murders** in Dublin in 1882 (see p.63) again hardened English opinion against the Irish. Three Home Rule Bills were defeated in the space of ten years; instead the Prevention of Crimes Act (temporarily) abolished trial by jury and increased police powers. The transparent

honesty of Parnell's denials of complicity in the murders for a while served to boost his career, but public opinion finally swung against him in 1890, when he was cited in the divorce case of his colleague Captain O'Shea.

The attitude of many Irish Protestants to the agitation for Home Rule was summed up by the equation "Home Rule = Rome Rule"; such a threat was enough to unite the Anglican (broadly speaking, conservative gentry) and Presbyterian (liberal tradesmen) communities. These were certainly the people who were doing best from a modest boom in Ireland's economic fortunes, with Ulster, and specifically Belfast, having been the main beneficiary when the Industrial Revolution finally arrived in the country. Large-scale **industrialisation**, in export industries such as ship-building, linen manufacture and engineering gave the region an additional dependence on the British connection, while the fact that these industries were firmly under Protestant ownership increased social tensions.

The end of the nineteenth century saw a burst of activity aimed at the revival of interest in all aspects of Irish culture and identity. Ostensibly non-political organisations such as the **Gaelic League** and the Gaelic Athletic Association were founded to promote Irish language, music, and traditional sports, and these inevitably tended to attract the support of politically minded nationalists. As well as those who sought to encourage the use of Gaelic, a body of writers, with **W. B. Yeats** in the forefront, embarked on an attempt to create a national literature in English.

In 1898, Arthur Griffith, a printer in Dublin founded a newspaper called the *United Irishman*, in which he expounded the philosophy of **Sinn Féin**, meaning "We, Ourselves". His was a non-violent and essentially capitalist vision, arguing that the Irish MPs should simply abandon Westminster and set up their own parliament in Dublin, where, with or without the permission of the British, they would be able to govern Ireland by virtue of their unassailable moral authority. Such political freedom was a prerequisite for Ireland to achieve significant economic development. Sinn Féin incorporated itself into a political party in 1905. Meanwhile socialist analyses of the situation in Ireland were appearing in the *Workers' Republic*, the newspaper of **James Connolly**'s Irish Social-

Republican Party, pointing out that Ireland's frail prosperity rested on a basis of malnutrition, bad housing, and social deprivation.

REACTION AND COUNTER-REACTION

In reaction to the declared intentions of Asquith's Liberal government in Britain in 1911 to see through the passage of yet another (exceptionally tame) Home Rule Bill, the Protestants of Ulster mobilised themselves under the leadership of **Sir Edward Carson**. A Dublin barrister who at first glance had little in common with the people of Ulster, a region he barely knew, his one great aim was to preserve the Union, in the face of the "nefarious conspiracy" hatched by the British government itself. To that end he declared that, should the Home Rule Bill become law, the unionists would defy it and set up their own parliament. In preparation for that eventuality, they organised their own militia, the Ulster Volunteers.

James Connolly, who had spent the years from 1903 to 1910 in disillusionment in the United States, found himself on less fertile ground when he tried to convert the workers of Belfast to socialism. He was impressed, however, by the example of the Ulster Volunteers, and the brutal police suppression of a protracted and bitter strike in Dublin, organised by James Larkin's Irish Transport Workers Union, gave him the opportunity to form the **Irish Citizen Army**. Other militant Republicans had also resolved to create an armed force in the south to parallel the Ulster Volunteers, and almost simultaneously, in November 1913, the **Irish Volunteers** came into being. The Gaelic League and Gaelic Athletic association acted as prime recruiting places, and provided such leaders as Pádraig Pearse. The movement should not, however, be seen in strictly sectarian terms; at least two of its most prominent leaders were Ulster Protestant nationalists.

REVOLUTION AND CIVIL WAR

The British Parliament did eventually pass the **Home Rule Bill** of 1912, and for a while the conditions appeared to exist for Ireland to erupt into civil war. Before this could happen, however, the outbreak of World War I dramatically altered the situation. An immediate consequence of war was that implementation of the Bill was indefinitely postponed.

For the majority of the Irish Volunteers, the primary aim of their movement was to safeguard the postwar introduction of Home Rule. Not simply to that end, but also out of loyalty to the British Crown, many of them joined the British Army. Some, however, led by Owen MacNeil, in part supported the British war effort but were reluctant to commit too much of their strength towards defending Britain without a pledge of concrete rewards. These in turn fell under the domination of a small and secret militant faction, the revived **Irish Republican Brotherhood**, to whom "England's difficulty was Ireland's opportunity". They made tentative overtures for German support (and even contemplated installing a German prince as King of Ireland) but went ahead with preparations for armed insurrection regardless of whether or not they received foreign aid – indeed all but regardless of the virtual certainty of defeat.

THE EASTER RISING

The outbreak of fighting on the streets of Dublin on Easter Monday in 1916 was expected by neither the English nor the Irish Army, and was a source of bemusement to the Dubliners themselves. Republican forces swiftly took over a number of key buildings, although they missed an easy opportunity to capture the Castle itself.

The leaders of the Rising made their base in the General Post Office in O'Connell Street, and it was from there that Pádraig Pearse emerged to read the "Proclamation from The Provisional Government of the Irish Republic to the People of Ireland":

"Ireland, through us, summons her children to the flag and strikes for her freedom . . . The Irish Republic is entitled to, and hereby claims, the allegiance of every Irishman and Irishwoman. The Republic guarantees religious and civil liberty, equal rights and equal opportunities to all its citizens . . . cherishing all the children of the nation equally, and oblivious of the differences carefully fostered by an alien Government, which have divided a minority from the majority in the past".

To these fine democratic sentiments Pearse in particular added a quasi-mystical emphasis on the necessity for blood sacrifice; although potential allies such as Owen MacNeil declined to join them with so little prospect of success, these were men prepared to give their lives as inspiration to others.

So weak was the rebel position that they only held out five days; at the time of their surrender they were even less popular with the mass of the nation than when they began, as a result of the terrible physical damage Dublin had suffered.

And yet, as the leaders of the Rising were systematically and unceremoniously executed by the British – the crippled James Connolly was shot tied to a chair – sympathy did indeed grow for the Republicans and their cause. In the words of Yeats's *Easter 1916*,

> "All changed, changed utterly:
> A terrible beauty is born."

WAR WITH ENGLAND

When the British government felt able once again to turn their minds to Irish affairs, it found a dramatically altered situation. Sinn Féin won a resounding victory in the elections of 1917, refused to take their seats at Westminster, and met instead in Dublin as the Dáil Éireann (Assembly of Ireland). Leadership had passed to **Eamonn de Valera**, the sole surviving leader of the Easter Rising, whose sentence of death had been commuted. Ireland and England were therefore at war.

The main instrument of British power in Ireland, the Royal Irish Constabulary, experienced severe difficulties in recruiting sufficient new members (other than from Ulster). Newly demobilised British soldiers were therefore brought over from England, and by virtue of their distinctive uniforms became known as the **Black and Tans**. The Irish Republicans, fighting on home territory, were well able to hold their own in guerrilla fighting across the country, while the Black and Tans acquired an infamous reputation which endures.

The **Government of Ireland Act** of 1920 created separate parliaments for "Northern Ireland" (Derry, Antrim, Fermanagh, Down, Tyrone, and Armagh) and "Southern Ireland" (the twenty-six counties of the present-day Republic), to remain under the nominal authority of the British crown. Elections were held for the two bodies in 1921, but the members elected to the Southern Parliament constituted themselves instead as the **Dáil Éireann**, with De Valera as their President. With the Protestants of Ulster still firmly pledged to the Union, a negotiated settlement seemed the only way out. De Valera sent emissaries to

London, including Arthur Griffith and Michael Collins, but Lloyd George somehow persuaded them to think of the Act as merely a stopgap solution until a Boundary Commission could draw new borders – borders which he strongly suggested would be so small as to to preclude the North from being a viable entity. (That this never occurred is largely attributable to the pressure from Edward Carson.)

CIVIL WAR

The **Anglo-Irish Treaty** was signed on December 6, 1921, hailed by Lloyd George as "one of the greatest days in the history of the British Empire". Griffith and Collins had, however, allowed their exhaustion after endless negotiation to override the need to secure de Valera's agreement in Dublin. De Valera's refusal to accept the Treaty – he resigned from office and left the Dáil – plunged Ireland into a squalid and sectarian Civil War.

Men who had been fighting alongside each other the year before were now pitched into a bitter conflict with the "Free Staters" who supported the Treaty against the Republicans who could not. In the North, the understandably alarmed Protestant community created the Ulster Special Constabulary, including the "B Specials" drawn from Carson's Ulster Volunteers, ostensibly to control the rioting which persistently broke out in response to events south of the border.

De Valera and his supporters were eventually forced to capitulate; as he put it "military victory must be allowed to rest for the moment with those who have destroyed the Republic". The way was clear for a new constitution, approved by both the Dáil and Westminster, formally creating the **Irish Free State**.

THE IRISH FREE STATE

The Irish Free State's first government, under William T. Cosgrave, got on with the business of re-creating Ireland as an independent nation. A civil service was set up, along with a police force and the hydroelectric scheme on the River Shannon which was to lead to the establishment of the ESB (Electricity Supply Board).

Meanwhile Eamonn de Valera, still an important political force, abandoned Sinn Féin's postwar policy of boycotting the Dáil to form his own political party in 1926. This took the explicitly mythological name of **Fianna**

Fáil – Soldiers of Destiny – and was victorious in the 1932 general election. Under de Valera other state bodies were set up including *Coras Iompair Éireann* (road and rail transport), *Aer Lingus* (air transport) and *Bord na Mona* (peat production). In 1933 the rival **Fine Gael** (Tribes of Gaels) party was founded.

The recession of the Thirties was made considerably worse for Ireland by the **Economic War**. De Valera had withheld repayments to England of loans made to tenants to buy their holdings; the British responded by imposing heavy duties on Irish goods.

In 1938 a new **constitution** came into effect, which finally declared Ireland's complete independence by renouncing British sovereignty. The Free State, under the name of **Eire**, was to be governed by a two chamber parliament (the Dáil and the Seanad), with a president (the Uachtarán), and a prime minister (the Taoiseach).

Ireland remained officially neutral during **World War II**, although considerable informal help was given to the Allies. De Valera, on the other hand, was the only government leader in the world to offer his commiserations to the Reichstag on the suicide of Adolf Hitler.

POSTWAR PROSPERITY

It took Ireland twenty years to recover from the economic stagnation brought on by the war. Vast numbers, disproportionately drawn from the young and talented, moved across to fill Britain's labour shortage. Not until a break was made with the past, with the accession to the premiership in 1959 of the vigorous and expansionist **Sean Lemass**, was a sufficient level of prosperity achieved to slow down the process of chronic emigration. Foreign enterprises began investing heavily in Ireland, unemployment fell by a third, and the way was paved for the country's successful application to join the European Economic Community in 1972. The immediate benefits were enjoyed by those employed in agriculture (twenty percent of the working population), although Irish fishing waters had now to be shared with other EEC members.

Ireland's and Britain's membership of the EC did not, however, bring Southern and Northern Ireland closer together. Their membership was made official on January 22, 1972; eight days later came Bloody Sunday (see below), and on February 2 the British Embassy in Dublin was destroyed by an angry mob.

The international recession hit Ireland very severely in the Eighties. Emigration rocketed once again and unemployment remained consistently high. Referendums on abortion in 1983 and divorce in 1986 reflected the Catholic Church's considerable influence, and both abortion and divorce remain illegal in the Republic. The 1987 general election, fought principally on the issues of taxation and unemployment, resulted in the Fianna Fáil party coming to power, led by the resilient and wily **Charles Haughey**. In the summer of 1989, Mr. Haughey called another election with the intention of increasing his majority. The result, however, was a Fianna Fáil/Progressive Democrat alliance, in which Haughey's hold on power always seemed tenuous.

The presidential election of 1991 yielded a surprise result when **Mary Robinson**, an independent candidate supported by Labour and Workers' parties, was elected. Some in Haughey's party (and outside) accused the Taoiseach of sabotaging the campaign of his own party's candidate, Brian Lenihan (an old rival), but whatever the causes of her success, there can be no doubt that the new president has breathed new life into the office and into Irish politics in general: as a woman; and as a representative of causes outside the old two-party stalemate. In particular her election gave hope to many that a new era of greater integrity and liberalism in politics, and perhaps some easing of positions on the intractable problems of the North, was about to dawn.

Whether this is the case remains to be seen – and certainly the post of president is not designed as a very active or powerful one. Nonetheless further changes have followed, and in particular the resignation early in 1992 of Charles Haughey, whose government was finally weighed down by constant (though unproven) allegations of financial mismanagement and even corruption. The final straw came when Sean Doherty, speaker of the Seanad and a former minister under Haughey, claimed that he personally had delivered tapes of tapped phone calls, made by journalists unfriendly to Fiana Fáil, to Mr Haughey in 1982. Although Haughey denied any knowledge of such tapes, the threat of his coalition falling apart finally forced him to resign.

The new Taoiseach, **Albert Reynolds**, has taken over the leadership of a seemingly exhausted Fianna Fáil party and is prepared to continue the uneasy alliance with the Progressive Democrats. He, too, seems a politician in a more modern mould – a tough character certainly, but likely to offer more flexibility on the issues of the North, and on the moral affairs that seem to play so large a part in Irish politics. One such case almost immediately reared its head: that of the 14-year-old rape victim whom the Irish High Court at first refused to allow to go to Britain to seek an abortion (see "Women").

NORTHERN IRELAND

On June 22, 1921, the new political entity of Northern Ireland came into existence with the opening of the **Northern Irish Parliament** in Belfast's City Hall. In order to understand the present situation in the North it is necessary to grasp the political background to this development. Since the settlements of the seventeenth century, the Protestant descendants of the settlers had been concentrated in the northern part of the island; they rarely intermarried with the local people or assimilated the native culture, feeling both superior to and threatened by the Catholics, who formed the vast majority of the population of Ireland as a whole. The economically dominant group in the northern counties was essentially Protestant, and when an industrial base developed in this part of the island, the prosperity of the region was inextricably tied to the trading power of Britain. In negotiating for their exclusion from the new Irish state, Carson and the Unionist Council decided to accept just six counties of Ulster out of a possible nine, because only in this way could a safe Protestant majority be guaranteed. Thus Westminster gave political power into the hands of those whose pro-British sympathies were certain.

The Unionists were not slow to exploit their supremacy: a Protestant police force and military were set up, and "gerrymandering" (the redrawing of boundary lines in order to control the outcome of elections) was commonplace, so securing Protestant control even in areas with Catholic majorities. Thus Derry City, with a two-thirds Catholic majority, returned a two-thirds Protestant council. Nothing was done to rectify the situation for several decades. The Catholic community was to benefit from the British welfare state, but they were discriminated against in innumerable ways, most notoriously in jobs, and in housing, an area controlled by Protestant local authorities.

CIVIL RIGHTS

In 1967, inspired by the Civil Rights movement in America, the Northern Irish **Civil Rights Movement** was born, a non-sectarian organisation demanding equality of rights for all. Massively supported by the Catholic community, the campaign led to huge protest marches, some of which were viciously attacked by loyalist mobs. The **RUC** (Royal Ulster Constabulary) rarely intervened, and when they did take action, it was generally not to protect the Catholics. The Apprentice Boys' march of 1969 proved to be the flashpoint. Taking their name from the apprentices who shut the gates of Derry in the face of James II's troops in 1689, this loyalist order commemorates the city's siege with an annual march on August 12, a triumphal procession that goes through Derry's Catholic areas. The 1969 march provoked rioting that ended in the Catholic community barricading themselves in and Jack Lynch, the Irish prime minister, mobilising Irish troops and setting up field hospitals on the border.

On August 14, British troops were sent to Derry to protect the besieged minority, and at first they were welcomed by the Catholics, who were relieved to see the troops pushing back the RUC and B Specials. Belief in the neutrality of the British army did not last long, however. Escalating violence between the two communities across the North forced the army into a more interventionist role, but confusion arose as to whether **Stormont** (the Northern Parliament) or Westminster was giving the orders. Before long the army was acting not as a protective force but as a retaliatory one, and it was clear that retaliation against the Catholics was far harsher than measures taken against the Protestants. With the Catholic again vulnerable, the resurgent IRA quickly assumed the role of defenders of the ghetto areas of Derry and Belfast. Within a few months the **Provisional IRA**, now stronger than the less militant **Official** wing of the organisation, had launched an intensive bombing and shooting campaign across the North.

At the request of Brian Faulkner, prime minister of Northern Ireland, **internment without trial** was introduced in 1971, a measure which was used as an indiscriminate weapon against the minority population. Then, on Sunday, January 30 1972, thirteen unarmed civil rights demonstrators were shot dead by British paratroopers in Derry, an event that shocked the world and was to become known as **Bloody Sunday**. The Irish government declared February 2 a national day of mourning; on the same day an angry crowd in Dublin burned down the British embassy. Stormont was suspended and direct rule from Westminster imposed.

POWER SHARING AND ITS AFTERMATH

In 1973 a conference was held at **Sunningdale** between representatives of the British and Irish governments and both sections of the community in Northern Ireland, a meeting that led to the creation of a power-sharing executive representing both unionists and nationalists. An elected executive took office in November 1973, but in May of the next year the United Ulster Unionist Council responded by organising a massive strike which, enforced by the roadblocks of the UDA, crippled the power-stations and other essential services run by a strongly unionist workforce. In the same week as the strike, three car bombs planted by the UDA exploded in Dublin, without warning, at rush-hour – 33 people were killed, the highest death toll since 1969. By the end of the month, the Sunningdale executive – the first ever to have Catholic representation – was disbanded, and direct rule from Westminster has continued to the present day.

Almost immediately a bombing campaign was launched in Britain by the IRA, aimed at destabilising the government by provoking public revulsion. Twenty-one people were killed in a pub bombing in **Birmingham** in 1974, and in the same month seven people died in simultaneous pub bombings in Woolwich and Guildford. The British response was to introduce the **Prevention of Terrorism Act**, permitting lengthy detention without charge. Four people were arrested for the Guildford bombings, and convicted on the basis of confessions which even at the time were thought by many people to be unreliable. After fifteen years of imprisonment, all four were released when the judiciary finally conceded, with no hint of regret for the injustice, that they were indeed innocent. Six Irish people were given life sentences for the Birmingham attack, and their convictions, too, were finally overthrown in 1991.

In 1976 Special Category Status was abolished for future prisoners in Northern Ireland (previously those arrested for offences connected with "The Troubles" enjoyed the status of political prisoners), and when Republican prisoners refused to wear prison uniforms in accordance with their change in status, prisoners were locked naked in their cells in Long Kesh – the beginning of the famous "**Blanket Protest**" (see p.476). In 1978 Britain was found guilty by the European Court of Human Rights of "inhuman and degrading treatment" of republican prisoners. Soon afterwards in Northern Ireland the "Dirty Protest" began in Long Kesh and Armagh women's prison, with Republican prisoners forcing the issue of political status by refusing to wear criminal uniform or slop out their cells. In late 1980 a hunger strike for the same demands was called off when one of the strikers was close to death. The following March a **hunger strike** was begun by **Bobby Sands**, who on April 11 was elected as MP for Fermanagh and South Tyrone. By the day of his election, nine other Republicans had joined the hunger strike. All ten died, an outcome that brought widespread condemnation of British intransigence.

THE ANGLO-IRISH AGREEMENT

1982 saw the British government make a timid attempt to break the impasse, introducing the **Northern Ireland Assembly**, a power-sharing body with some legislative but no executive powers. It was boycotted by the nationalists, and survived only until 1985, by which time the final stages had been reached in the negotiations over the **Anglo-Irish Agreement**. Largely drafted by John Hume, the leader of the moderate nationalist SDLP, and signed in 1986, it instituted official cooperation between Dublin and Westminster on security and other issues, and strengthened the consultative part played by Dublin in Northern affairs.

Unfortunately the Anglo-Irish Agreement, for all its laudable intentions, has not proved much of an advance; above all because of the refusal of the Ulster Unionists to cooperate in any way.

There seems little prospect of progress towards a peaceful solution while two opposing groups remain entrenched in their positions, and ready to resort to violence in support of their views. In the final analysis – and in the light of a 1992 which opened with a fresh wave of horrific tit-for-tat sectarian killings – little seems to have changed in the past twenty years; and innocent people continue to die in a battle which has no clear rules of engagement nor any realistic definition of success. Perhaps closer relations between Dublin and Westminster, which genuinely do seem to be developing, offer some hope for the future, but in the face of the hardened divisions in Northern Ireland, it can be hard to believe.

WOMEN IN IRELAND

No account of the role of women in Ireland can omit reference to the **Catholic Church**. Doctrinally, the Church has a curious and ambivalent position on women. It unequivocally denies them the priesthood, thereby distancing itself sharply from recent developments in the Anglican Church. In the Catholic liturgy, women are allowed only to assist the celebrant in tasks which the hierarchy glorifies, but which are, in reality, menial. Like the rest of the laity, women are denied any voice in decision- or policy-making. Simultaneously, the Catholic Church promotes the veneration of Mary, virgin mother of Christ, as a model for women, claiming that this degree of veneration elevates the status of all women. It is significant, however, that Mary is wife, mother, and faithful follower, but completely asexual. This is seen as an essential aspect both of her complete sinlessness and her complete selflessness.

This role model may also reflect something of the strong position of women in traditional Irish society, which continues almost unchanged in many rural areas. For many Irishwomen, however, it is a barrier to fulfilment: not only do they have to learn to assert and enjoy their sexuality in the face of the Catholic Church's overt prohibition of sexual activity except within the bounds of marriage, but also in the face of their religion's loftiest model – an insidious pressure.

Ireland is unique among the countries of Europe in having no civil **divorce** – another example of the influence of the Catholic Church but not, it must be said, attributable solely to this. As recently as 1986, the Irish people voted in a referendum on divorce legislation: of the 64 percent turnout, 63 percent voted against divorce.

Contraception is now easily available, at least in theory, although the only free contraceptive available is the Pill. Despite the dangers of Aids, condoms are available only from licensed clinics and chemists: in 1990 the Irish Family Planning Association was fined in a Dublin District Court for selling condoms in the Virgin Megastore in central Dublin.

A 1983 referendum inserted a clause into the constitution guaranteeing the equal right of the unborn child to life. **Abortion**, therefore, remains illegal in Ireland, as does pregnancy counselling that includes information on abortion, although in practice some 4000 Irish women cross the Irish Sea every year to seek terminations in Britain. In February 1992, Irish abortion legislation was highlighted by the case of a 14-year-old Dublin girl who was raped by the father of her best friend and became pregnant. Planning to obtain an abortion for their daughter in England, the girl's parents reported the rape to the police, offering to provide foetal material to help in positive identification of the father. The result was a ruling by the High Court forbidding the girl to travel to Britain for an abortion. With time rapidly running out, the girl's family took the case to the Irish Supreme Court, which, amid calls for another referendum, overturned the High Court ruling. The Supreme Court ruling came as a relief to everyone, including the Church (which had refrained from using the case to take up the anti-abortion issue again), and seemed to open the road for a healthy secularisation of Irish society.

An unexpected new development in Irish politics was the election of a woman, **Mary Robinson**, as President in 1991. An ex-barrister and expert in European law, the new President is regarded as progressive and outward-looking. Before becoming President, she headed the Irish single parent association "Cherish" and she still strongly supports the liberalisation of the divorce law. In a country whose political life remains almost entirely dominated by men, and whose major parties, still defined by the antagonisms of the civil war, range from centre right to far right, the presence of a liberal, female voice at the heart of Irish politics has been a welcome one.

Changes in the status of women have not yet, however, resulted in significant change in the decision-making areas of Irish life. There are very few women members of the Dáil, and only one cabinet minister. Nor is the record any better in industry – women who succeed in the commercial world tend to make the headlines. In academic life, there are scarcely any female professors; though girls out-achieve boys in school and as college undergraduates, they are outstripped at post-graduate and research level.

This issue of the dearth of female representation is often aired in the liberal media, but change is very slow. As elsewhere, women in Ireland dominate the "caring" professions – teaching, nursing and social work – and make up the bulk of the lowest-paid and temporary workers.

Women's **economic situation** remains weak: women in the south earn 60 percent of the male average wage, while in the north, where the situation has traditionally been a little better, the figure is 73.5 percent. Equal employment and statutory maternity leave legislation exist on both sides of the border. Although politics in the north are almost as ossified as in the south, the situation for women there is generally a little less repressive: contraception is generally available, although abortions are difficult to obtain. The politicisation brought about by the British military presence has led to a more general feminist activism, with a proliferation of women's centres and Ireland's only women's magazine, the *Irish Women's News* (Winetavern Street, Belfast).

ENVIRONMENT AND WILDLIFE

Ireland conjures up images of a romantic wild territory unscarred by human activity – a somewhat rosy picture, but with more than a little truth to it. Genuine wilderness may be scarce, but centuries of economic deprivation have ensured that most of Ireland is a rural landscape in which the only intervention has come from generations of farmers.

IRISH LANDSCAPES AND HABITATS

The topography of Ireland is fairly homogenous: there are few high mountain ranges and most of the centre of the country is covered by a flat boggy plain. And with only four degrees of latitude from north to south, it lacks extremes of weather, the enveloping Atlantic Ocean producing a mild, damp climate. Summers are rarely hot, winters rarely cold, and in parts of the west it rains on two days out of three.

In these conditions you'd expect to find broad-leaved woodland, but intensive pressure on the landscape during the centuries leading up to the Great Famine of 1845 denuded the country of its original tree cover. It has been replaced mostly by a patchwork of small grass fields divided by wild untidy hedgerows – these long lines of trees acting as refuges for the former woodland community of plants and animals. (In common with many islands, Ireland has a limited number of animal species – there are no snakes, no moles, and no woodpeckers,

for instance.) The low population in Ireland today means that over much of the country the intensity of land use is lower than in many other European countries. Mixed farms are still more common than specialised intensive units. Visitor numbers in the countryside are still small and it is possible to find long sandy beaches that are completely deserted even in summer.

Natural habitats such as peat bogs, dunes and wetlands still survive here, having all but disappeared elsewhere under the relentless pace of modern development. However, the pressures are growing. The great midland bogs are being rapidly stripped for fuel; mountainsides are disappearing under blankets of exotic conifers; and shoals of dead fish are becoming all too frequent a sight in Irish waterways.

THE COASTS

With over 2000 miles of shoreline and hundreds of islands, there is plenty of variety along the Irish coast. There are spectacular cliffs, especially in the west and southwest, which hold large **bird colonies**. Razorbills, guillemots, kittiwakes, shags and gulls (seven different types) are among the commonest species, and a few of the larger colonies hold puffins, gannets and cormorants. After dark, some of the uninhabited islands are filled with the sounds of Manx shearwaters and storm petrels. The best time to see breeding seabirds is in early summer (May & June), but later in the year you can watch large flocks on the move by positioning yourself on a prominent headland. In the right weather conditions, some rare seabirds, such as great shearwaters, which normally feed well offshore, will come within sight of the land. Patient seawatching from a western headland may also be rewarded with a school of **dolphins** or porpoises or the occasional **whale** feeding in the rich inshore waters.

The remoteness of the western **islands** makes them ideal habitats, and several of their deserted villages are now tenanted only by seabirds. Grey **seals** breed on island beaches and in caves during the autumn months. Due to lack of disturbance, nocturnal animals like otters can be seen here during daylight, hunting for food among rocks and pools. Beachcombing can be a rewarding experience in the west of Ireland, where the waters of the Gulf Stream may yield up anything from tropical seeds to a massive turtle.

DIRECTORY OF WILD PLACES

The abbreviation **NNR** signifies "National Nature Reserve"

East

North Bull Island, Dublin Bay; NNR. Sand dunes, saltmarsh and mudflats. Large flocks of ducks, waders and brent geese in winter. Dune flowers and ferns in summer. Hares common on dunes and saltmarsh. Best months Nov–June. Interpretive centre with free entry. Three miles northeast of Dublin city centre on coast road to Howth.

Pollardstown Fen, Co. Kildare; NNR. Largest remaining limestone fen in Ireland. Open water surrounded by sedge and marsh vegetation. Best months June–July. No visitor facilities. Two miles northeast of Newbridge near Curragh racecourse.

Glendalough, Co. Wicklow; part NNR. Dramatic glaciated valley with two lakes and oak woodland. Rich in breeding birds. Best months April–June. Famous monastic remains. Visitor centre in car park. Eleven miles west of Wicklow. *St Kevin's* private coach from Dublin.

Wexford Wildfowl Reserve, Co. Wexford; NNR. Flat farmland reclaimed from sea. Large flocks of Greenland white-fronted and brent geese in winter. Best months Nov–April. Visitor centre with free entry open all year. Observation tower and bird-watching hides. Two miles north of Wexford town on Gorey road.

South

Ballycotton, Co. Cork. Two coastal lakes with marshland. Famous for rare migrant birds especially North American waders in autumn. Wintering ducks and swans. Best months Sept–Oct. No visitor facilities. Southeast of Cork city.

Cape Clear Island, Co. Cork. Rocky offshore island. Famous bird observatory known for rare migrant songbirds. Good place to watch seabirds' passage and occasional whales. Best months Sept–Oct. Booking necessary to stay at observatory. Daily ferry boat from Baltimore.

Skelligs, Co. Kerry; NNR. Two rocky islands. Large and spectacular seabird colonies containing mainly gannets, storm petrels, shearwaters and puffins. Best months May–July. No landing on Little Skellig but regular boat trips to Great Skellig to see early Christian monastic ruins from Portmagee and Valentia. Cost varies according to boat.

Killarney National Park, Co. Kerry. Extensive area of native woodland and bog surrounding famous lakes. Spectacular Torc waterfall and surrounding mountain ranges hold Ireland's only native herd of red deer. Best months April–May and Sept–Oct. Visitor centre and nature trails. One mile south of Killarney town.

In some counties, notably Donegal, Mayo, Kerry and Wexford, there are extensive **sand dunes**. In summer these are clothed in a profusion of **wild flowers** such as the yellow bird's-foot trefoil and pink sea bindweed. The exotic-looking bee orchid is one of the rarities sometimes to be found in the dunes. The absence of tree cover means few breeding birds, but **cuckoos** are a special feature of Irish sand dunes, as they exploit the nests of the ubiquitous meadow pipits. The **chough**, a comparatively rare crow, breeds extensively on the south and west coasts and can be seen in large flocks feeding in sand dune systems. The low sandy coasts of the northwest, particularly where they adjoin small lakes or marshes, are populated by breeding **waders** such as dunlin and lapwing.

The low coasts, especially on the east and south, are punctuated by **estuaries**, some with vast, lonely mudflats. Despite their bare appearance, below the surface they harbour uncountable shellfish and other burrowing animals, attracting feeding waders and wildfowl. From October to April the estuaries are alive with the calls of curlews, redshanks, godwits, widgeon, teal and shoveler. Virtually all the pale-bellied brent geese to be seen in Europe are on Irish estuaries in winter, having travelled from their breeding grounds in northern Canada. The estuaries and inlets of the west coast are wider and sandier; at low tide herds of common seals often bask on the sand banks.

LAKELANDS AND GRASSLANDS

Travellers in the midlands and west of Ireland will encounter numerous small **lakes** and reed-fringed **marshes**. High rainfall and poor drainage ensure plentiful surface water, especially in winter, and breeding **water birds** are extremely common as a result. Every waterway has its resident pair of swans, moorhens and herons. The lakes have a unique assemblage of plants and animals, but many of these special habitats have already been drained.

Limestone grassland, a special feature of the west of Ireland, is best exemplified by the

West

Burren, Co. Clare. Large area of limestone pavement famous for wild flowers. Many rare species of arctic-alpine and Mediterranean plants. Includes several turloughs (seasonal lakes). Best month May. Burren Display Centre at Kilfenora. Easiest access from coast road between Ballyvaughan and Lisdoonvarna.

Cliffs of Moher, Co. Clare. Sheer limestone cliffs, spectacular in cl. ar weather. Large colony of nesting seabirds– guillemots, razorbills, puffins and kittiwakes. Best months May–June. Visitor centre in car park near the cliffs is a good starting point for a walk. Six miles west of Lahinch.

Connemara, Co. Galway. Extensive area of mountain, bog and lakes surrounded by deeply indented coastline. Interesting plant communities. High numbers of nesting herons. Mountains heavily overgrazed. Best months June–July. Visitor centre and nature trails at National Park near Letterfrack, six miles north of Clifden. Oughterard–Clifden road gives good views of mountains and bogs.

Mullet Peninsula, Co. Mayo. Low, sandy spit of land linked by narow bridge to mainland. Low intensity farming supports wild flower meadows, corncrakes and breeding waders. Wintering barnacle geese and waders around shoreline. Best months May–June. No visitor facilities. Access via Belmullet, 38 miles west of Ballina.

North

Glenveagh National Park, Co. Donegal. Deep glaciated valley with lake surrounded by high mountain range and native woodland. Good for mountain birds and red deer. Best months April–June. Visitor centre and minibus tours of park available. Twelve miles northwest of Letterkenny.

Horn Head, Co. Donegal. High sea cliffs topped by heather moorland. Large seabird colonies especially razorbill, guillemot and kittiwake. First landfall for migrant birds from Iceland. Best months May–June. No visitor facilities. Three miles north of Dunfanaghy.

Rathlin Island, Co. Antrim; part NNR. Populated offshore island formed of chalk and basalt. Large seabird colony at western end. Good numbers of feeding buzzards. Best months May–July. No visitor facilities. Access by ferry from Ballycastle.

Strangford Lough, Co. Down; part NNR. Large landlocked inlet with numerous islands and shallows. Mudflats hold large winter flocks of waders, ducks and brent geese. Breeding terns and common seals easily seen. Very rich marine life studies by research station at Portaferry. Best months Oct–Dec. Visitor facilities at Castleward (National Trust) six miles west of Downpatrick. Regular ferry from Strangford to Portaferry.

Central Ireland

River Shannon Callows, Athlone–Portumna. Most extensive flood plain in Ireland. Hay meadow flowers, breeding waders and corncrakes. Wintering waders and wildfowl. Best months May–June & Nov–March. Birdwatching hide four miles west of Birr, Co. Offaly. Best access points at Banagher, Shannonbridge or Clonmacnoise.

Clara Bog, Co. Offaly; NNR. One of largest remaining raised bogs in Ireland, with well-developed wet areas and hummock and hollow surface. Interesting plant communities. Best months June–July. No visitor facilities at present. One mile from Clara town.

Books

Watching Birds in Ireland, Clive Hutchinson (Country House, 1986).

IPCC Guide to Irish Peatlands, Catharine O'Connell (Irish Peatland Conservation Council, 1987).

Bellamy's Ireland: The Wild Boglands, David Bellamy (Country House, 1986).

Nature in its Place, Stephen Mills (Bodley Head).

The Personality of Ireland, E. Evans (Cambridge University Press).

A Connaught Journey, Desmond Fennell (Gill & Macmillan).

Burren area in north Clare. Its main attraction is the wealth of wild flowers, which include a mixture of arctic-alpine species such as the mountain avens and Mediterranean species such as maidenhair fern – all found at or near sea level. Perhaps the most striking feature here is the large amount of bare rock, whose cracks and fissures give shelter to delicate plants.

THE BOGLANDS

Ten thousand years ago, when glaciers and ice sheets had stripped the soil from the Burren and retreated to the north, their melting ice left central Ireland covered by shallow lakes. As time went by, the lakeside vegetation grew, died and partly decomposed, in a cycle which changed these lakes to fens, and then the fens to bogs. Ireland now boasts the finest selection of **peatlands** in Europe, but it's a terrain at risk. At one time there were 850,000 acres of raised bog in the country; by 1974 there were 175,000 acres, and by 1985 that area had shrunk to just 54,000 acres. Ireland's bogs are disappearing at a rate of 8000 acres per year, and it's only recently that environmentalists have secured protection for a few of the finest.

The exploitation of the boglands has been going on for centuries. Dried peat sods have always been used for fuel; the top layer of matted vegetation was once used to insulate thatched roofs; and preserved timbers dug from the bog — some of them 5000 years old — provided stout beams for lintels. The lime-rich marl below the peat was used to fertilise the land. In World War I, sphagnum moss from the bogs was used for wound dressings, and extract of the carnivorous sundew was a traditional remedy for warts.

Because the bog preserves so well, it provides botanists with a calendar of plant history over the past 9000 years, and the archaeologist with a wealth of objects: dug-out canoes, gold and silver artefacts, shoes, spears and axe heads, amber beads, wooden vessels and, of course, bodies — in an extraordinarily good state.

The best introduction to this landscape is to visit the **Peatland Interpretation Centre** in Lullymore, County Kildare; nearby is a fine expanse of **fenland – Pollardstown Fen**, two miles northeast of Newbridge. To see a **raised bog** of international importance, go to **Mongan Bog** in County Offaly. The bog is part of the Clonmacnoise Heritage Zone, which includes one of Ireland's most important monastic sites, situated on the banks of the Shannon. Ask at the tourist office at Clonmacnoise about the Shannon Callows, a wetland area of great importance to wildfowl, sadly now threatened by drainage schemes. If you are in this area in late summer and the evening is calm and fine, then go to the bridge in **Banagher** and listen for the corncrakes as they search for mates.

For the finest example of relatively undamaged **blanket bog** you must go to the **Slieve Bloom** mountains, which straddle the counties of Laois and Offaly. The two mountain roads that divide the range rise to 1300 feet, with wonderful views in every direction across the flat plains to the distant horizons of Wicklow, Galway, Roscommon and Waterford.

ENVIRONMENTAL ISSUES

Several of the areas of Ireland renowned for their rugged beauty — Kerry and the Dingle peninsula, Connemara and Donegal — are now the scene of intense **gold prospecting**. The gold finds at Croagh Patrick and Doo Lough (County Mayo) and Cornamona (County Galway) have brought an influx of mining companies. Local communities fear the economic impact of the new mines, which could damage the existing industries of farming, fishing and tourism.

The ecological consequences are a contentious issue as well. Gold mining is generally an activity of arid areas, and it is not clear how the technology will translate to an area of watery landscape with high rainfall. Local populations dependent on surface water for their water supply compound the problem. Of great concern is the risk of cyanide spillage and overflow, and long-term pollution from heavy metals released by mining and milling the ore. A coalition of concerned groups is now trying to raise the money to commission an independent environmental impact assessment (EIA).

Other environmental issues in the Republic include the **drainage of wetlands** and the consequential loss of wildfowl habitat, the **expansion of forestry**, both state and private, and the growth of the **chemical** and **pharmaceutical** industries. Over the past couple of years, attention has turned to the damage being done to the country's **waterways**. A ridiculous situation had evolved whereby it was cheaper for a farmer to empty his tanks, pollute a waterway and pay the statutory fine, than to dispose of his effluent properly. Numerous fish kills were reported, and many rivers were poisoned by effluent from silage pits and slurry tanks. A national outcry led to an increase in fines for such actions, and this, coupled with a campaign to educate the farming community to the effects of pollution, should improve the situation.

Tom Joyce and Richard Nairn

ARCHITECTURE

BEGINNINGS

Although Ireland has a rich heritage of prehistoric remains, little of it can be discussed as "architecture", as the wealth of dolmens, burial chambers and passage graves are too remote to be fully understood in terms of construction, function and use. Irish prehistoric remains do, however, attest to a highly sophisticated culture capable of astounding engineering feats. The passage grave at **Newgrange** stands within a circle of large standing stones – similar to Stonehenge but now believed to be about 1000 years earlier. On the shortest day of the year, December 21, a shaft of light from the rising sun penetrates the tomb. In other words, the people who constructed this tomb were sufficiently sophisticated to have possessed an annual calendar.

The Bronze Age in Ireland (c. 2000–500 BC) is remembered more for its craft and decorative artistry (jewellery, tools and pottery) than for its building. Little is known of domestic structures, which seem to have been constructed of wood and daub. Towards the end of this period a new type of fortified enclosure known as a hill-fort began to emerge. The great fortress of **Dún Aengus** on the Aran Island of Inishmore is the most impressive piece of Iron Age architecture, and dates possibly from the first century AD.

From the fifth century, when the island was Christianised, up to the Viking invasions of the ninth century, Ireland lived in relative peace compared with the rest of Europe. The country

was divided into a series of bishoprics, which resulted in a system of scattered monasteries. As with domestic building of this period, the first churches were constructed of wood and daub, none of which has survived. The stone churches you now see when visiting early monastic sites are of a later date. **Early Christian** monastic complexes often included round towers, a specifically Irish phenomenon. Sometimes as high as 100 metres, these towers were traditionally believed to have functioned as fortresses in times of danger, as the door was several metres off the ground. It now seems that these buildings were used as bell-towers and that the doorways were positioned high in the wall for structural purposes. One of the best-preserved towers is **Devenish**, on an island in the southeast corner of Lower Lough Erne, near Enniskillen, County Fermanagh.

FROM ROMANESQUE TO THE SEVENTEENTH CENTURY

By the twelfth century the Romanesque style, imported from England and continental Europe, had begun to have an effect on Irish ecclesiastical building. **Cormac's Chapel** in Cashel, County Tipperary, erected between 1127 and 1134, is the earliest and best surviving example of an Irish church built in the Romanesque style, although very much a miniature version of its counterparts elsewhere. It was not until this century that Irish church builders stopped using the simple box design in favour of the basilica style – characterised by a nave, side-aisles and a round apse at the eastern end. The religious orders such as the Cistercians, Augustinians and Benedictines did much to propagate this change in taste. Monastic settlements such as the one at **Boyle**, County Roscommon, are very European in their layout of a cloister surrounded by church, chapter-house and dormitories. A wing of government called the Board of Works is the body responsible for most of the country's early and medieval remains; although chronically underfunded, it has achieved some major restorations.

By the end of the twelfth century much of Ireland had been brought under the control of the Normans. The Anglo-Normans, as they came to be known, introduced to Ireland the mighty stone castle of the European tradition. Good examples of the genre survive throughout the country, for example at **Trim** in County

Meath and **Athenry** in County Galway. The Anglo-Normans also introduced the Gothic style to Ireland. In Dublin, both **St Patrick's** and **Christchurch** are good examples of the early Gothic style.

Fortified dwellings of the fifteenth and sixteenth centuries tended to be smaller than their earlier prototypes. A good sixteenth-century example is **Dunguaire**, County Galway, which has been restored and is now open to the public. **Bunratty Castle**, which dates from the middle of the fifteenth century, has also been fully restored and can be visited by the public.

Rothe House in Kilkenny town, was erected in 1594, and is one of the very few examples of domestic architecture to survive from the period before 1600. It's now open as a museum. Nearly all domestic architecture of the seventeenth century has some provision for defence, reflecting the political unrest resulting from a succession of land confiscations, plantations of English settlers and religious suppression. While tower houses were still the favoured domestic building type, towards the end of the century a small number of unfortified, purely domestic houses were built. **Beaulieu**, County Louth, is the best surviving example of this type. Built in red brick, Beaulieu reflects the influence of Dutch prototypes popular in England at this time.

At about the same period, the **vernacular thatched cottage** came into being. These dwellings were usually built of clay with only one or two rooms in total. Windows were small and whitewash was used both inside and out. As a type it is perfectly suited to the damp Irish climate. Its simple, humble design did, however, reflect a repressive social system based on the rights of the landlord. Often viewed as picturesque by tourists, the thatched cottage has fallen into disuse during the latter half of this century because of these unpleasant connotations.

THE EIGHTEENTH CENTURY

In the 1680s the **Royal Hospital at Kilmainham**, Dublin, was built. Modelled on Les Invalides in Paris, the hospital catered for retired soldiers and consists of ranges around four sides of a courtyard. It is the first great classical building in Ireland and has recently been fully restored.

The eighteenth century in Ireland produced an unparalleled spate of building, both public and domestic. The ascendancy, having consolidated their claim to the lands granted to them in the previous century, began to build unfortified dwellings. A parliament independent of, but subject to, Westminster sat in Dublin, the city often subsequently referred to as the second capital of the Empire. It is still possible to get some idea of the great prosperity and confidence which emanated from this parliament by simply walking round Dublin and looking at the many splendid public buildings and elegant squares. This prosperity and confidence, however, was based on a repressive regime weighted very much in favour of the Protestant ascendancy. The Penal Laws, as they were known, sought to prevent Catholics from holding public office, owning property and practising their religion.

In the first half of the century the Palladian style (derived from the work of the sixteenth-century Italian architect Andrea Palladio) was favoured by the Irish ruling classes, as it was by the aristocracy in England. The great **Parliament House** in Dublin (now the Bank of Ireland) was built to a design by Sir Edward Lovett Pearce between 1729 and 1739. It is the earliest large-scale Palladian public building in all Ireland or England, and the model, a century later, for the British Museum building in London. Palladianism was also the style favoured for country house architecture in the first half of the century. As a style it was extremely adaptable, producing, on the one hand, splendid houses that bear comparison with any in Europe, such as **Castletown**, County Kildare, or **Russborough**, County Wicklow, and on the other, simpler houses built as much for utility as for ostentation, such as **Hazelwood**, County Sligo, and **Ledwithstown**, County Longford.

Towards the end of the century the Neoclassical style, based on Roman and Greek prototypes, became popular. **Marino Casino** just outside Dublin was built by Sir William Chambers for Lord Charlemont during the 1760s. Intended as a country villa, the Casino is one of the most refined architectural creations in the city and is well worth a visit. **Castlecoole**, County Fermanagh, is arguably the finest Neoclassical house in Ireland. Designed by James Wyatt, it is now owned by the British National Trust and has recently been lavishly, if controversially, restored – the National Trust's new colour scheme involves a shade that the previous owner, who still lives there, calls "Germolene pink".

Much of Ireland's Georgian architecture has disappeared. Thirty years ago Dublin was still one of the most perfectly intact eighteenth-century cities in Europe. Today, because of bad planning and inadequate legislation, much has been lost. This century has witnessed a decline in the fortunes of the Anglo-Irish ascendancy with the consequent selling-off of estates and houses, many of which are now in ruin. Because of their unsavoury associations, many of these houses were destroyed by the people who for so long had been held in check by a political system completely identified with the houses. The Anglo-Irish, and their estates and mansions, were viewed as alien to the country, and since independence in 1922 much has been done to erase their trace. Happily, this situation is now changing and the Anglo-Irish heritage is beginning to be seen as something inherently Irish. A good example of this change can be seen at **Strokestown**, County Roscommon, where an outstanding Palladian house is being carefully restored by a small local garage business. The house is now open to the public.

Surviving eighteenth-century church architecture is not all that common. Rarest of all are eighteenth-century Catholic churches, a notable survivor being the **South Parish Church** in Cork, built in 1766.

THE NINETEENTH CENTURY

In spite of the Act of Union (1800), which dissolved Ireland's independent government, building work flourished throughout the nineteenth century. An increasing number of Irish-born architects enjoyed patronage although, as in the previous century, many English architects also enjoyed considerable Irish practices. The Anglo-Irish ascendancy, perhaps feeling further isolated from their English contemporaries after Dublin ceased to be a centre of power, embarked on vast building programmes. In 1860, **Temple House**, County Sligo, originally a modest late Georgian residence, was turned into an enormous 100-room mansion which is now being run as a guest house.

Throughout the century, and in line with developments in England, the revival of styles as diverse as Gothic, Tudor, Greek and Oriental enjoyed great popularity. Much public architecture was undertaken throughout the country, such as jails, courthouses, and buildings to accommodate the fast developing railway system. With the advent of Catholic emancipation in 1829, church architecture flourished. Although predating emancipation, the **Pro-Cathedral** in Dublin is worth mentioning. Catholic church design usually took as its inspiration Baroque French or Italian models. In the Pro-Cathedral a graceful but severe Greek revival influence is evident, a style more often associated with large-scale public building. The Victorian period, characterised by an unrestrained eclecticism, flourished all over the country and is particularly evident in much urban public and suburban building.

The Celtic Revival was also reflected in architecture, particularly church architecture. Hiberno-Romanesque was the style favoured, and its influence can be seen in **Spiddal Church**, County Galway, and **St Honan's Chapel**, University College Cork.

THE PRESENT

Because of the low density of population, Irish cities still possess low skylines; even today, Dublin can be said to have just one skyscraper. During the 1930s and 1940s a restrained Art Deco style made itself evident in the design of many hospitals, dance halls and factories – for instance, the **Kodak building** in Rathmines, Dublin. Perhaps too often architects have opted to revive or invoke elements from earlier periods rather than embrace truly modern techniques, although this can also be the best option in certain cases. Two sides of Georgian **Mountjoy Square** in north Dublin is at present being completely rebuilt so that the street facades will at least have the proper appearance. A good example of the blending of old and new is **New Square** at Trinity College, Dublin, where modern buildings have been juxtaposed with existing ones. Perhaps the worst example of modern building is the recently erected **Civic Offices** at Wood Quay in Dublin. Commonly known as "the Bunkers", these offensive structures are doubly horrible in that they were constructed on the most important early Viking archaeological site in Europe before it could be properly excavated.

Luke Dodd

THE ART OF IRELAND

THE STONE, BRONZE AND IRON AGES

Sunrise at the time of the winter solstice on the passage grave at **Newgrange** illuminates the deep recesses of a burial chamber some 6000 years old. At this tomb can be seen the dawn of Irish art. The simple and poorly understood motifs consist of whorls and spirals, zigzags and rectangles which are cut into the stone in and around this great mound. The most impressive is the decorated entrance stone to the tumulus which is repeated again within. While these are the most impressive survivors of an obviously highly sophisticated culture the sites have also yielded stone balls and beads as well as some poor contemporary pottery.

The **Bronze Age** in Ireland began around 2000 BC and lasted about 1500 years. Some decorative work is found on stone but the most striking pieces are in the applied arts of gold. The Gleninsheen gorget and the gold plated lead pendant from the central Bog of Allen are perhaps the finest examples – both can be seen in the National Museum in Dublin. Much surviving bronze work consists of axe-heads and the like which, like most prehistoric art from this country, are abstractly decorated.

From the **Iron Age**, with its great fortresses of Dún Aengus on Inishmore and the Grianán of Aileach in Donegal, are a number of fine examples of carving in stone. These are scattered around the country and take a bit of a hike to get to but are well worth the effort. Two conjoined figures carved back-to-back at **Boa Island** in County Fermanagh and the **Tandragee Idol**, which is now in the cathedral in Armagh, are among the best examples of figurative stone art from this period. Another is the three-faced stone in the National Museum. At about this time Celtic linear designs of flowing tendrils typical of the **La Tène** style of Celtic art were becoming more common in Ireland. They can be seen on the well-known **Turoe stone** in County Galway (see p.346). If you only have time to spend in Dublin then good examples of this style can be seen in the National Museum where you should look at the **Somerset box-lid** (also from Galway) and the so-called **Petrie Crown** in bronze. A fine gold torc or neck-ornament in this manner was unearthed in Broighter, County Derry, in 1896 as part of a hoard which included a small but extraordinary model of a boat.

EARLY CHRISTIAN ART

In Ireland the early Christian era (432–1170 AD) is often described as the **Golden Age**. It reached its pinnacle with justifiably famous manuscripts such as the **Book of Kells**. Although these illuminated texts may be the best known, however, there are other wonderful artefacts – especially those in metal – and the magnificent **High Crosses** will take you to some of the most beautiful parts of the country.

ILLUMINATED MANUSCRIPTS

The first of the surviving books, **the Cathach** (pronounced Kohok), from the early seventh century, is a book of psalms that is now in the Royal Irish Academy. The decorative features are confined to the first letters of the paragraphs of Latin text and consist of scrolls and animals. These motifs set the style for the greater books.

The **Book of Durrow,** written about the same time, is the first of the really great illuminated manuscripts and, together with the Book of Kells, is kept in the Long Room in Trinity College, Dublin. In this book of the Four Gospels the three major stylistic components of spirals, animals and interlacing bands which are typical of the great books can be seen. The last of these, like the dots which surround some of the initial letters in the Cathach, may provide a stylistic link with Coptic or other Middle Eastern sources. Some of the pages, called carpet-pages, are given over entirely to ornament or to a depiction of the saint whose gospel follows.

For about a hundred and fifty years other books were written; some, such as the **Book of Dimma** (also at Trinity College), are in a smaller pocket format designed to be carried around. Similar manuscripts can be found in museums and libraries abroad, reflecting the travels of many of the monks of the period. Saint Colmcille, for example, spread the Gospels and founded monasteries around Britain and Europe.

But without a doubt the culmination of this art form in Ireland was the **Book of Kells**. This magnificent manuscript, also a copy of the Four Gospels in Latin, is a perfect synthesis of all the motifs and styles which had either been imported or developed locally and which had been used in previous books. Completed about the year 800, it takes its name from the Columban monastery at Kells, County Meath where it was kept for many years although its precise origin is still a matter of conjecture. If you can see the contemporary Book of St Gall (Library of St Gall), the Book of Lichfield (Lichfield Cathedral) or the Book of Lindisfarne (British Library), which are stylistically similar, then these should whet your appetite. Words without illustrations will do this book no justice and you should really try to see it for yourself.

METALWORK AND JEWELLERY

The style of the books is echoed in metalwork, the most impressive examples of which are the **Ardagh and Derrynaflan Chalices**. Some 20cm in height they are similar in shape, with a rounded cup and a conical base. The ninth century Derrynaflan Chalice has neither medallions on the bowl nor engravings and is technically less fine than the Ardagh chalice which is a century older. But not all was holy art. The bronze **Tara Brooch**, covered with gold and decorated with amber, glass and fine metalwork (c 700) is perhaps the finest piece of secular metalwork of the period, and clearly related in design to the religious pieces.

As metal working continued, influences from Romanesque and Viking styles became apparent. The **Crucifixion Plaque** from County Offaly and the magnificent **Cross of Cong** show these influences best. The Cross was made around 1123 and originally contained a chip from the True Cross, pieces of which were in demand as relics. The Pope presented one to Turlough O'Connor, then King of Connacht, who had the Cross made as a shrine. It is made of wood covered with gilt bronze and the arms are decorated with fine gold filigree. There is a central bronze boss into which is set a polished crystal.

HIGH CROSSES

This cross is a useful point at which to introduce another great, but also relatively short-lived, genre of Irish art, the **High Crosses**, which began in this period.

It is in **Ahenny**, County Tipperary, that the prototypes are to be found. The pyramidal base of these massive decorated crosses are surmounted by a cross, the arms of which are joined by a circle. This is the standard format for most subsequent crosses. The figures on the bases are, however, dissimilar to the more native design on the uprights.

The Ahenny crosses, although similar in style, antedate the **Scriptural Crosses**, the best of which rank with the finest artistic endeavours on this island. One of the earliest is at **Moone**, County Kildare. The setting is, perhaps, not as picturesque as that of some of the others but the long, narrowly proportioned cross with its almost naive flat figures depicting biblical scenes has an instantly appealing charm.

More striking examples are to be found at the beautiful locations of **Clonmacnoise**, County Offaly, and at **Monasterboice**, County Louth, where, in spite of a thousand years of the inclemencies of Irish weather, Eve still tempts Adam, Cain slays Abel and the Magi come to see the newborn Saviour. Others can be seen in **Kells**, County Meath and also in the north at **Donaghmore** and **Arboe** in County Tyrone. Many of these crosses were carved from local sandstone which has, sadly, perished or faded, but the granite **Castledermot Crosses**, in County Carlow, have done better than many and are also worth a look.

Although production of the scriptural crosses ceased early in the tenth century, crosses were still carved in stone almost two hundred years later. The later style is very different as can be seen in **Dysert O'Dea**, County Clare, where the biblical panels have been replaced by large figures on the shaft and the characteristic circle no longer links the arms of the cross.

NORMAN AND MEDIEVAL ART

From the twelfth to the sixteenth centuries, the church remained the premier focus and patron of the arts. The earliest of the stone figure carvings in the period following the Norman invasion of Ireland were of bishops; some of these can be seen at the great Norman cathedrals of **St Patrick** and **Christchurch** in Dublin. Not to be outdone, some Norman knights also had effigies carved of themselves – that of **Strongbow** in Christchurch is one of the best.

There are fine cloister carvings, probably from around 1400, in the important Cistercian monastery at **Jerpoint**, near Thomastown, County Kilkenny. This was the work of the nearby Callan carvers, who were also responsible for the tomb of Piers Fitz Oge Butler in **Kilcooly Abbey**, County Tipperary. The beautiful black marble effigies of Piers Butler and Lady Margaret Fitzgerald, his countess, can be seen in **St Canices Cathedral**, Kilkenny.

The Kilcorban Madonna (thirteenth-century) and Saint Catherine carvings in the **Diocesan Museum**, **Loughrea**, the Saint Molaise of Inishmurray and God the Father from Fethard, County Tipperary, both in the **National Museum**, are worth a look but few other figures in wood have survived. The misericords in **St Mary's Cathedral, Limerick** are perhaps the finest carvings still extant from this period. While in Limerick try also to see the Crozier and Mitre in **St John's Cathedral** as these are the finest religious artefacts of the Middle Ages in Ireland – unfortunately they may not currently be on public view.

Protective shrines or casings in metalwork have survived from the first millennium and a number of these were reworked in medieval style. **The Cathach Shrine**, for example, has work dating from about 1050, but the most impressive panels are possibly fifteenth-century. This, the **Breac Maodhóg** (Brack Mwee-ogue) and the **Domhnach Airgid** (Downock Arriggid) shrines can be seen in the National Museum. All are lavishly decorated with bronze or silver gilt illustrations of the Crucifixion, the saints or other religious themes.

SEVENTEENTH- TO NINETEENTH-CENTURY ART

Despite traces of frescoes in the Middle Ages and some portraits from the late sixteenth and seventeenth centuries, Irish painting really only developed from the eighteenth century onwards – the time of Swift and Berkeley. Much was portraiture in a Neoclassical style and landscape painting developed alongside this.

Garrett Morphey (fl 1680–1716) may have been the first Irish-born painter and portraitist of stature but the Antwerp-trained **James Latham** (1696–1747) was more important. His grand subjects, with elegant robes and modestly bejewelled women, were the best portraits of the day. The Englishman Stephen Slaughter, who also worked in Ireland at about this time, produced similarly magnificent pictures of lavishly costumed subjects. **Nathaniel Hone** (1718–84), ancestor of the later Nathaniel Hone and Evie Hone, was a painter of children and a miniaturist of note. His most famous work, *The Conjurer*, is now in the National Gallery, Dublin. This was a satire of Joshua Reynolds derivative approaches from Old Masters, and was rejected for exhibition by the Royal Academy in London in 1775. Not to be bullied, Hone, apparently, went off to hold a one-man show instead.

When the Dublin Society's Drawing Schools were founded around 1740 many artists such as **Robert Healy** received training in black-and-white chalk techniques. His work and that of the pastellist **Hugh Hamilton** can be seen in the National Gallery. Hamilton also achieved distinction as a painter in the Neoclassical mode which came into vogue later in the eighteenth century, much of it inspired by antique sculpture. In 1782, **James Barry** of Cork (1741–1806) became Professor of Painting at London's Royal Academy. His *Self Portrait* and *Adam and Eve* in the National Gallery are typical of this style. In yet another example of Anglo-Irish discord he was sacked in 1795 because of altercations with his colleagues and died in poverty at the age of 65.

The earlier landscapists of the eighteenth century such as **Robert Carver** and **George Barrett** (1732–84) were often romantic in flavour but there was also a Classical school which owes much to the Frenchman Claude Lorraine: both **Thomas Roberts** and **William Ashford** painted in this style. The green and brown foreground, green middle-distance and the lighter, blue background often with Gothic-style ruins in the distance are characteristic. Glimpses of contemporary Dublin architecture can be seen in the work of topographical painters such as **James Malton**, whose *Views of Dublin* were drawn in 1790–91.

APPLIED ARTS

Classical and Rococo styles were also seen in the applied arts in the eighteenth century particularly in stucco work. **Powerscourt Town House** in Dublin, now an imaginatively designed shopping centre, has a magnificent ceiling by **Michael Stapleton** and staircase by **James McCullagh** and **Michael Reynolds** which have been decorated with motifs of urns, scrolls and heads. The rich Baroque ceiling of the **Chapel** in the Rotunda Hospital by **Bartholomew Cramillion** is unlike anything else in the country. Life-size figures by the **Francini Brothers** and detailed birds and musical instruments by **Robert West** decorate **Newman House** at 85/86 St Stephen's Green.

The extraordinary beauty of these make it all the more poignant that heartless town "planners" and "developers" have allowed the wanton destruction or neglect of many equally fine interiors in Ireland's principal city.

The eighteenth century was also noted for heavy, deepcut glasswork and for high-quality silverware some of which, such as three-legged sugar bowls, were made in characteristically Irish shapes. Sculpture in Classical and Neoclassical styles can be seen on a number of buildings such as the **Custom House**, **the City Hall** and the **Casino in Marino**, Dublin.

THE NINETEENTH CENTURY

James Arthur O'Connor's (1792–1841) *Homeward Bound* and **Edwin Hayes**' seascape, *The Emigrant Ship*, reflect the persistence of Classical and Romantic painting into the nineteenth century. **George Petrie**, also distinguished as an antiquarian and music-

collector, produced many topographical pictures to illustrate travel books which became quite fashionable for a time. Portraiture continued although the style, less promising than a hundred years before, was sometimes a little sentimental and sweet as in **Richard Rothwell**'s *The Young Mother's Pastime*.

Daniel Maclise (1808–70), born in Cork, was noted for genre scenes such as *Merry Christmas in the Baron's Hall* and also composed numerous historical works. Filled with sometimes overpowering detail, his *Marriage of Eva and Strongbow*, like **Frederick Burton**'s touching medieval *Meeting on the Turret Stair*, depicts a life of earlier centuries.

The bust, in Classical style, of Mrs Prendergast by **John Foley** (1818–74) shows one aspect of **sculpture** from the Victorian period. He was also responsible for major public monuments to Henry Grattan, Oliver Goldsmith and Edmund Burke now in College Green. There is some fine stucco work from this time such as in the Hall of Ballyfin House, County Laois, by **Richard Morrison**.

IMPRESSIONISM AND THE TWENTIETH CENTURY

Continental painting of the French Realists influenced the late nineteenth-century landscapist **Nathaniel Hone**, the great-grandnephew of his namesake, and **Walter Osborne** also shows the mark of the realist Jules Bastien Lepage. Osborne, however, is better-known for more Impressionistic work, such as *Tea in the Garden* and for his depiction of the grime of the poorer areas of Dublin as in his *St Patrick's Close*. He was also much in demand as a portraitist. The influence of Post-Impressionists can be seen in **Roderic O'Conor**'s *Ferme de Lezaver* and his *Field of Corn* in the Ulster Museum is reminiscent of Cezanne and even Van Gogh.

William Orpen, a prodigious draughtsman, began at the Metropolitan School of Art at the age of eleven but spent much of his professional life in England. While an instructor at the School he painted some wonderful coastal scenes with figures near Howth. There are some studies which date from just before the 1916 Rising which illustrate dormant feelings for the country which he left. The early period of **John Lavery** of Belfast, like Osborne, shows the influence of Lepage but in the 1920's he became involved in Irish political life by portraying many of the leading figures of the day including Carson and Collins. Lady Lavery, his wife, was depicted on Irish paper money until 1976 when the design was changed in favour of motifs of figures from Irish cultural history.

The beginning of the twentieth century in Ireland was an awakening time for poet, playwright and patriot. It is odd that this period, seminal in literary, theatrical and political affairs, never gave birth to a true national school of painting. Social scenes and landscapes were, however, depicted by many including **Jack B Yeats** (1871–1957), the brother of WB Yeats, **William Conor**, **Seán Keating** and **Paul Henry**. The early social paintings of Yeats, also a fine portraitist, have great character in a strong, rugged style although his later period was wilder and more expressionistic. Henry's western landscapes of mountains and lakes with their large, flat areas of purple and blue are now almost a formula but are no less beautiful for that.

Abstract art arrived relatively late in Ireland and the Cubists **Mainie Jellett** and **Evie Hone** were among the most important. Evie Hone was best known as a distinguished member of a school for stained glass – *An Túr Gloine* – founded by the painter Sarah Purser.

The late **Séamus Murphy** of Cork was a noted stonemason, and active sculptors include **Clíona Cussen** and **Oisín Kelly** , whose *Children of Lir* in Parnell Square, inspired by the Celtic legend, is one of a number of public monuments placed around the capital by Dublin Corporation. The tradition of religious art work has been continued by **Imogen Stuart** and **Niall O'Neill**. Abstract painting is represented by **Louis le Brocquy**, among others, and an interesting school of primitives has emerged on

> ### IRELAND'S LEADING GALLERIES
>
> **Dublin**: National Gallery of Ireland, Merrion Square. The National Museum, Kildare Street. The Hugh Lane Gallery of Modern Art, Parnell Square. The Irish Museum of Modern Art, Kilmainham. The Long Room, Trinity College (manuscripts). The Royal Irish Academy, Dawson Street (manuscripts).
>
> **Belfast**: The Ulster Museum, Dundonald.
>
> **Cork**: The Crawford Municipal Gallery. The Triskel.
>
> **Galway**: Kenny's Gallery.
>
> **Limerick**: The City Gallery, Pery Square. The Belltable.

the Irish-speaking Tory Island off the coast of Donegal.

Over the past 25 years, partly due to government patronage introduced under the last Taoiseach, Charles Haughey, the visual arts, traditionally never very strong in Ireland, have flourished with, among other things, a vibrant private art gallery scene in Dublin, a lively Irish art magazine, Circa, and some imaginative placing of sculptural work in public places. The Irish Museum of Modern Art, opened in the Royal Hospital, Kilmainham in 1991, is likely to provide another focus for modern art in Ireland. Names to watch out for include the painter James Coleman, the sculptor Dorothy Corss and the performance artist Nigel Rolfe. In a country whose culture is so very verbal in its expression, it's no surprise to find that much of the conceptualist/minimalist work now being produced in Ireland, by artists such as Coleman and the New York-based Patrick Ireland, refers explicitly to the literary tradition.

Killian Robinson

THE MUSIC
OF IRELAND

Ireland is a very musical nation offering plenty of opportunities to enjoy any one of its many different musical strands. The radio stations, clubs and halls pump out an endless stream of derivatives of the country and western style whose popularity is increasing. Céilí (ceilidh) bands are hired in for the village weekend dances to bang out the boisterous rhythms of the set-dance tunes, and the pubs host raucous ballad-singing, the repertoire ranging from heartfelt love songs through to equally heartfelt rebel songs. (Some of the greatest date from the 1798 revolution – for example, "The Croppy Boy" and "The Wearing of the Green".) However, it is what is termed the **traditional music** culture that is by far the most intriguing and characteristic musical aspect of Ireland.

The turn-of-the-century English composer Arnold Bax said of the traditional music that "of all the antiquities in the world Ireland possesses the most varied and beautiful music", yet of all countries Ireland is the worst in appreciating and looking after its tradition. But a great revival of the tradition did take place in the Sixties at the instigation of the Irish composer **Seán Ó Riada**, when "sessions" (an *ad hoc* group of players improvising together) took place in pubs all over the country. Interest has now waned once again, as publicans attend to more commercial interests. In fact the pub is not a very good environment in which to appreciate the full brilliance of the music, but it seems there is no alternative to the pub session on offer at the moment.

Some places hold "open sessions", which are open to outsiders – make sure you gauge the class of performers before joining in. If you're there to listen, you shouldn't sit right by the players, for it's probable that space is being kept for late arrivals.

THE FORMS AND STATE OF IRISH MUSIC

Although Ireland is part of Western Europe, its music is much more akin to oriental forms. European classical music develops a very broad structure beginning with one idea (or two) that is taken through a crescendo eventually to arrive at a climax, which then resolves into a catharsis. Irish traditional music, on the other hand, unfolds in a cyclical pattern: the basic element of a song or tune remains the same in each repetition, with minuscule events of ornamentation and variation giving the music its distinctive texture (and testing the mettle of the player). Unlike the European tradition, there are no dynamics in the Irish tradition and you'll see this physically reflected in the emotionally uninvolved posture that most musicians assume whilst playing.

Unfortunately, the European dimension of modern Irish society has now all but suffocated the source of this culture, and most of the young players are unable to resist the influences of both European classical and popular musics. This diagnosis may at first seem baseless, because you'll find plenty of lively looking sessions on the midwest coast, especially around Clare. Yet enjoyable though these may be, few represent what was once the best of Ireland's musical culture. To begin with, the music is best heard from an individual musician, and groups of more than three cannot preserve the clarity of the pieces. Bands such as the *Chieftains*, the *Bothy Band* and *Clannad* have produced interesting material spun off from the tradition, but the genuine product is more likely to come from a single musician playing in South Sligo, Wexford or Clare.

THE STYLE OF SINGING

The heart of the Irish traditional music ethic lies in the **sean nós** style of singing, in which the singer is not allowed to sing any two verses of a song in the same way – tantamount to asking him to act as a composer as well as performer. Some songs have only two lines, presenting the ultimate challenge to the interpreter's skill.

The variations must be distinctly audible and yet small enough to maintain the basic structure of the song. Singers instinctively call upon a variety of improvisational techniques: glottal stopping or clicking to shut off the voice in mid-phrase; drawing attention to a single note or group of notes by nasalising the voice (but this should be used very sparingly); melisma; lengthening and shortening of intervals and notes; and changing stresses and speeds. Each region has its distinctive devices: the Connemara style, for instance, is traditionally very melismatic with a compressed vocal range, while the Munster style has a wider range and is slightly more nasal. These regional differences are becoming less marked; the older the singer, the more obvious they'll be. Sadly, it's not often that you'll come across *sean nós* singers, as they tend to perform in small social groups rather then public places. *Róisín Dubh* and *Eileinn Aroon* are among the most popular songs in the tradition.

THE UILLEANN PIPES

The instrument best able to emulate the voice is the **uilleann pipes** (elbow pipes). The pipes came into being during the seventeenth or eighteenth century, but only took on their present shape in the nineteenth. Nearly every country in the world has some form of bagpipe, but very few are as complex as these. The nine-holed wooden tube held in the player's hands is known as the *chanter*; players cover the holes an inch down from the fingertip, a technique that enables the tone to be varied. The chanter is capable of a two-octaves range, with the silver keys to the side of the holes creating extra semitone notes within the basic scale of D major. As for the mechanics of it – the double reed within the metal tubing is vibrated by dry air from the leather bag squeezed by the left elbow, which itself is fed from the bellows being squeezed by the right elbow. Notice how the chanter is sometimes pushed down on a *popping pad*, a piece of leather wrapped around the player's thigh. This produces the upper octave but is also used to great effect for clipping the notes, which is superb for the rhythm of the faster tunes.

This basic assembly of bag, bellows and chanter is called a *half set*. The virtuoso instrument has an extra set of tubes providing *regulators* (keys for making up harmonic chords) and *drones* (offering three octaves of the fundamental note D). The stylistic flourishes to listen out for are *cranning* (a repeated note preceded by a fast grace note) and the *roll* (dipping to a lower note to approach the main note from below). The mark of a great piper is the judicious but imaginative use of the regulators, not too much popping and an ability to emulate the *sean nós* style – especially in the slow airs, for which the naturally plaintive sound of the instrument is so suitable. One of the finest players ever was Johnny Doran; today both **Davy Spillane** and **Paddy Maloney** are excellent pipers.

THE FIDDLE

The violin in Irish music, commonly called the **fiddle**, differs from the classical instrument only in the way it's played. It is often held resting on the shoulder without chin support; only a small section of the bow is used (necessary for articulating the rapid notes); and the player stays mainly on the middle two strings, with the bottom G string sometimes used as an intermittent drone or chord maker.

As with *sean nós* singing, nearly every cultural area of the country has its own approach to the instrument and its repertoire. (Although, similarly, there's a growing uniformity.) For instance, the Donegal style is characterised by a relatively smooth and slick sound, and a heavy leaning of the bow producing a louder volume. The Sligo style, only a little further south in the country, is more flamboyant, with a liberal use of ornaments and a lightly pronounced tick-over in the rhythm. (The greatest fiddler Ireland ever had was a Sligoman, **Michael Coleman**.) In Clare the rhythmic component is much stronger than in any other area, the normal run of quaver notes nearly becoming a regular long–short, long–short sequence.

The fiddle should be heard on its own and certainly never with a piano vamping out chords to accompany it.

THE FLUTE AND THE WHISTLE

The Irish **flute** is a wooden instrument, descended from the German model of a hundred years ago. Again it's pitched in the key of D with a range of a couple of octaves, producing a really mellow sound even in the fast tunes. Again there are regional styles of approach, the Sligo and Leitrim one being the best known. A native Sligo player tends to break up the phrases but also extend the phrase length, using little ornamentation – unlike the fiddle playing in the region. Clare, in comparison, uses gentle rolling ornamentation and is not as emphatic with its rhythm, but makes an interesting rhythmical peculiarity by accenting the offbeats.

The **tin whistle** is regarded as the toy of Irish instruments only by those who have never heard a good player. Many pipers are also whistle players, as both possess a sharp upper-frequency quality and permit the same types of rapid ornamentation. If you're buying a whistle to learn, the D whistle is the one to get, for most of Irish music is in this key. Before buying, give the instrument a try to make sure the plastic top allows a clear and unfuzzy tone – some don't. The higher octave is obtained by just blowing harder, and lots of in-between notes can be produced with cross-fingerings and half-covering. This latter technique is now used a lot to create little slides up to the main notes, especially for laments and slow airs.

THE ACCORDION AND CONCERTINA

Two types of accordion are used for Irish music. The **piano accordion** is not highly thought of, because of the virtually complete lack of control the player has over its tone production and rhythmic articulation. However, it's size of tone is used to great advantage as a "filler-in" sound for the céilí bands. Articulation on the **button accordion** is a little bit better, as the bellows produce a different note when being compressed from the one produced during extension. It's getting much more popular now with the young musicians and is a delight to listen to at first. Its limited musical scope soon becomes obvious, though. To get out of these inherent difficulties many players revert to excessive, sugary ornamentation.

The **concertina**, also popular with the younger players, has a lightness of tone that makes it far more suitable for delivering the brittle bareness that is the predominant characteristic of most Irish tunes. The Anglo-German concertina is the preferred instrument (and much played in Clare, especially), its push-pull bellows style making it much more suitable for Irish music than the English version.

THE BODHRÁN, BONES AND SPOONS

The most ancient of all Irish instruments is the **bodhrán**, which may date from the Bronze Age. It's a small, shallow circular drum with a skin on one side, usually goatskin, and is often played with a small stick that has beaters at both ends to facilitate double and triple rhythms. Sometimes the skin is played with the bare hand, producing a more subtle scale of sounds. Sounds are also struck on the wooden rim, and for pitch variation the left hand can be used to bend the tuning of the skin by pressing into it. The best of players will use the instrument sparingly to augment or rub against the rhythms of the pitched instruments rather than cloud everything with a continuous roll of beats.

The **bones** (rib-bones of a sheep, goat or cow) make another purely rhythmical instrument and are ideal for traditional music. Two bones are held between the thumb, index and middle fingers and are played in a castenet style – usually using the left hand as a ceiling and the thigh as a base about nine inches below. **Spoons** are also used nowadays in a similar fashion, but they interfere with the timbre of the other instruments.

THE HARP

The normal-sized **harp** rarely appears as part of an ensemble, owing to its weaker voice and its sheer size. (There's a smaller version, the *clarseach*, which appears at the odd session.) Yet the harp began traditional music as we know it today. From 1100 to 1600 the harpists and the poets provided the "art music" for the Gaelic Chieftains, and it is not often acknowledged how intimately connected are the familiar tunes to those early Gaelic metres. With the demise of the Gaelic courts after the Battle of Kinsale in 1601 the native music became diluted by an influx of British tunes. The skill of the harpist flourished for a further hundred years, but eventually perished in the mid-nineteenth century, leaving few details of performance styles.

The harpist of the seventeenth and eighteenth centuries would have travelled the new Anglo-Irish households with his freshly

composed tunes, compositions that acknowledged the master's acquaintance with the mainstream European musical tradition. **O'Carolan**
was the most famous of all the harpists and his
love of the Italian composer Corelli is obvious in
the hundred or so melodies left us.

DANCING

Irish dancing is inextricably linked to the
music tradition, but nowadays it has become
either too loose and uncreative – as at most
céilís (although they are great fun all the same)
– or too formal, largely through the competitive
festivals (although they are better than nothing
at all). Gone is the old tradition when a
musician would have taken up a place at the
village corner and couples would have arrived
in ordinary dress to dance. The costumes you'll
see today at every *feis* – green dress, embroidered Celtic designs, black stockings, white
apron – only arrived on the scene at the time of
the Gaelic revival at the end of the last century.
In the opinion of the purists, the complexity and
rigidity of movement seen in supposedly
authentic performances is throttling the
creative development of the art.

IRISH LITERATURE

Samuel Beckett, in an interesting turn of phrase, maintained that Irish writers had been "buggered into existence by the English army and the Roman pope." Oscar Wilde sighed to Yeats that "we Irish have done nothing, but we are the greatest talkers since the Greeks." Both were right. Politics, religion and literature in Ireland have always been inextricably linked, sometimes in a futile attempt to escape from each other. And the suppression of the Irish language did give rise to a fresh and vital use of colloquial English that somehow retained the musical rhythms of the dying tongue. But it's a more complex story than that, and any outline of Ireland's vast canon of very different literatures has to go back a long way.

THE GAELS

Irish writing first appeared in the fifth century AD when monastic settlers brought classical culture into contact with a Gaelic civilisation that had a long and sophisticated oral tradition. Faced with the resistance of the pagan bards, the newcomers set about incorporating the Celtic sagas into the comparatively young system of Christian belief. These ancient tales told of war and famine, madness and love, death and magical rebirth – story sequences from deep in the folk memory. One of the earliest of these, the *Táin Bó Cuailnge*, deals with a rumpus between **Cúchulainn**, a prototypical Celtic superman, and the mighty Queen Medb over the theft of a prize bull.

Later Irish artists made much of the early tales, sometimes with less than proper reverence – in Beckett's novel *Murphy*, for instance, a character attempts suicide by banging his head repeatedly against the buttocks of the statue of Cúchulainn which still adorns the lobby of Dublin's GPO. New versions still appear from time to time, Seamus Heaney's translation of the mythical wanderings of the mad king *Sweeney Astray* being particularly brilliant.

Fairy tales from this Celtic era reveal a world of witches, imps and banshees, all jolly-ing around in a manichaean struggle with the forces of love, wisdom and goodness – which, refreshingly, do not always triumph. Check out Kevin Danaher's *Folk Tales of the Irish Countryside* for full-blooded retellings.

In the eighth century **Fionn Mac Cumhaill** toppled Cúchulainn from the top of the folk hero charts, and stories of his exploits with his posse, the Fianna, began to appear. Fionn was a more disturbing and sophisticated figure, and his antics can be read in various modern translations.

A LITERATURE OF RESISTANCE

The first of many incursions from England took place in the twelfth century, when gangs of Norman adventurers invaded at the invitation of an Irish high king. But it wasn't until five centuries later that the English presence found its way into the literature, when the excesses of English rule began finally to provoke an early literature of resistance.

The high point of this Gaelic tradition is the 1773 long poem by **Eibhlín Dhubh Ní Chonaill** (1748–1800), *Caoineadh Airt Uí Laoghaire*. (In English, *A Lament for Art O'Leary*.) A traditional *caoineadh* or lament infused with a new political awareness, it deals with the execution of the poet's lover, who had refused to sell his prized white horse to the local redcoat and was therefore hunted down and killed. Even in translation it has a sparse and chilling beauty.

Other marvellous laments include the anonymous *Donal Óg*, Lady Gregory's translation of which was included with cheeky but effective licence in the 1985 John Huston film of Joyce's short story, *The Dead*. But the early written tradition wasn't all tears, and some pieces harked back to a pre-Christian earthiness. One such text from the later Gaelic era is **Brian Merriman**'s satirical *aisling* (vision poem), *Cúirt an Mheán Oíche* (*The Midnight Court*), a trenchant attack on the sexual inadequacy of the Irish male. One translation which preserves the raunch of the original is by Frank O'Connor, in *Kings, Lords and Commons*.

Despite persecution the Irish language persisted well into the last century and Thomas Kinsella's book of translations, *An Duanaire: Poems of the Dispossessed*, records the voices of those marginalised by foreign rule and famine. But thanks to the ineptitude of successive Irish governments, the Irish language is now in an advanced state of decay. Despite occasional revivals, contemporary Gaelic literature has been almost completely wiped out. Urban Irish schoolchildren are forced into reading **Peig Sayers** (1873–1958), a miserable native of the Blaskets whose sentences usually start with "God between us and all harm" or "Ah sure, life, what can you do?" Arguably the finest of modern Gaelic writers is **Pádraig Ó Conaire** (1883–1928), whose statue stands in Eyre Square, Galway. His *Scothscéalta* reads like Maupassant, capturing the stark cruelty of the Irish landscape and the petty malices of rural life. But unless you want to know about turf cutting, hill farming and getting up at five in the morning to milk your one mangy cow, recent Gaelic literature is generally unrewarding.

THE START OF A LITERARY TRADITION

Between the 1690s and the 1720s the hated "Penal Laws" were passed, denying Catholics rights to property, education, political activity and religious practice. British misrule created widespread poverty which devastated the countryside and ravaged the population. It's in this period that **Anglo-Irish literature** began.

One of the most prominent of the early pamphleteers and agitators was **John Toland** (1670–1722) whom the authorities gave the dubious distinction of being the first Irish writer to have his work publicly burned. But the first big-league player arrived in the angry little shape of **Jonathan Swift** (1667–1745), Dean of Saint Patrick's Cathedral, Dublin. Swift was a cantankerous but basically compassionate man who used his pen to expose viciousness, hypocrisy and corruption whenever he saw it, which in eighteenth-century Dublin, was pretty often. In one of his seventy-five pamphlets he proposed that the children of the poor should be cooked to feed the rich, thereby getting rid of poverty and increasing affluence. His masterpiece is *Gulliver's Travels* (1726), a satire as terrifying now as it ever was. Following a life of unrequited love he died a bitter man, and in his will he left an endowment to build Dublin's first lunatic asylum, adding in a pithy codicil that if he'd had enough money he would have arranged for a 20-foot-high wall to be built around the entire island. He is buried in the vault of Saint Patrick's, where, as his epitaph says, "Savage indignation can rend his heart no more."

The elegant prose of **Edmund Burke** (1729–97) – graduate of Trinity College, philosopher, journalist and MP – argued for order in all things, decrying the French Revolution for its destruction of humanity's basic need for faith. He is a complex and difficult figure, and his ideas are claimed in Ireland both by the civil-liberties-trampling Right and by elements of the progressive Left.

1780–1880: THE CELTIC REVIVAL

Towards the end of the eighteenth century, a new interest in the Scottish and Welsh Celtic tradition was exported to Ireland, prompting a renaissance in Irish music and an interest in all things Celtic, vague and misty. A couple of important books appeared, including **Joseph Cooper Walker**'s *Historical Memoirs of the Irish Bards* (1786) and **Edward Bunting**'s *General Collection of Irish Music* (1796).

Dublin at the time of the Act of Union with Britain (1801) had long been a truly European city, frequently visited by French, German and Italian composers. Indeed, Handel's *Messiah* was first performed in Dublin's Fishamble Street. One Irish composer and writer who thrived under the European influence was the harpist **Turlough O'Carolan**, (1670–1738), who met and traded riffs with the Italian composer Geminiani.

At the turn of the century a series of Irish harp festivals began, their purpose being to recover the rapidly disappearing ancient music. With their evocation of the bardic tradition they became a focus not just for nifty fingerwork but for political agitation. The harpers continued on into the nineteenth century until **Thomas Moore** (1779–1852) finally stole many of their traditional airs, wrote words for them, published them as *Moore's Irish Melodies* and made a lot of money.

The concomitant literary revival entailed a resurrection of the Irish language too, and although few went so far as to learn it, it became a vague symbol of an heroic literary past that implied a fundamentally nationalist worldview. **John Mitchell**'s Fenian movement, provoked by Britain's callous response to the Famine, was at least as influenced by the

Celtic rvival as it was by the new revolutionary ideas being imported all the time from Europe. Particularly in their impact on Yeats, the Fenians were to provide a bridge between the heroic past and the demands of modernism. One of their supporters, **James Clarence Mangan** (1803–49), inaugurated in *My Dark Rosaleen* the image of suffering Ireland as a brutalised woman, awaiting defence by an heroic man. In a country where visual and literary imagery of the Virgin Mary is ubiquitous, the symbolism escaped nobody.

THE NINETEENTH-CENTURY NOVEL

The unease generated among the aristocracy by the growth of Irish Nationalism and the Fenian Rebellion of 1848 found expression in novels showing the peasantry plotting away in their cottages against their masters up in the mansion – the "Big House" sub-genre of Anglo-Irish writing, represented by such writers as **Lady Morgan** (1775–1859). Typically, such a book will involve an evil-smelling Irish hoodlum inheriting the mansion and either turning it into a barn or burning it to the ground. *Castle Rackrent* by **Maria Edgeworth** (1776–1849) is one of the few good "Big House" novels, its craftily resourceful narrator telling the story of the great family's demise with a subtle glee.

The Irish fought back, appropriating the well-made novel for themselves. **Gerald Griffin** (1803–40), **John Banim** (1796–1874), **William Carleton** (1794–1869) and **Charles Lever** (1806–72) emerged as the voice of the new middle class, protesting at the stereotyping of the Irish as savages, and demanding political and economic rights.

Meanwhile **Bram Stoker** (1847–1912) was busily writing his way into the history books with a novel that would enter modern popular culture in all its forms, from the movies to the comic book. *Dracula* is a wonderful book, more of a psychological Gothic thriller than a schlock horror bloodbath, and its concerns – the nature of the soul versus the bestial allure of the body, for instance – are curiously Irish. But even this had its political implications. With its pseudo-folkloric style and its pitting of the noble peasants against the aristocratic monster debauching away in his castle, its symbolism is inescapably revolutionary and romantic.

E. O. Somerville (1858–1949) and **Violet** (alias **Martin**) **Ross** (1861–1915) close the century with *Some Recollections of an Irish RM*. The partnership's work is imbued with a genuine love of Ireland and the ways of the Irish peasantry, yet occasionally there's a chilling sense of things not being quite right. The Irish had invaded English literature. Previously marginalised in the tradition, the peasants now seem to keep intruding, sneaking into the upstairs rooms, interrupting their betters, conspiring behind the bushes in the well-kept gardens. And we see them, in ominous prophecy of things to come, wielding ploughshares and scythes which slowly begin, in the grey light of Galway which the two genteel old ladies capture so well, to look like weapons.

THE STORY OF THE STAGE IRISHMAN

It's one of the delicious twists of fate which seem to beset Irish literary history that the country's most important early dramatist only took up writing by mistake. One evening a young Derry actor named **George Farquhar** was playing a bit part in the duel scene of Dryden's *Indian Emperor* at the Dublin Smock Alley theatre when, in a moment of tragic enthusiasm, he accidentaly stabbed a fellow actor, almost killing him. Understandably shaken, Farquhar gave up the stage for good and went off to London to write plays instead.

Farquhar (1677–1707) is often credited, if that is the word, with the invention of the stage Irishman, the descendants of whom can still be seen on many of the programmes euphemistically referred to as "situation comedies" on British television. Effusive in his own way, but basically sly, stupid and violent, this stock character stumbled through the dramas of **Steele** (1672–1729), **Chaigneau** (1709–81), **Goldsmith** (1728–74) and **Sheridan** (1751–1816), tugging his forelock, bumping into the furniture and going "bejayzus" at every available moment. In fact Irish stereotypes had existed in the British tradition for many centuries before these dramatists had at least the good sense to make some money out of them. The stage Irishman was brought to his ultimate idiocy by **Dion Boucicault** (1820–90), whose leprechaunic characters seemed to have staggered straight out of the "Big House" novel and onto the London stage.

Boucicault's chum, **George Bernard Shaw** (1856–1950) turned out to be the kind of stage Irishman the English couldn't patronise out of existence. A radical socialist and feminist, he championed all kinds of cranky causes and some very admirable ones, and lived long enough to be a founder member of CND. His cerebral and often polemical plays – of which *Saint Joan* is perhaps the best – have remained a mainstay of theatre repertoire.

Yet even Shaw paled in comparison to the ultimate king of the one-line put-down, **Oscar Wilde** (1856–1900). After a brilliant career at Oxford – during which he lost both his virginity and his Irish accent – Wilde went on to set literary London alight, creating the smiling resentment that would finally destroy him. In *The Picture of Dorian Gray* he expanded on the Gothic tradition of Stoker and Sheridan Le Fanu (1814–73) to explore the fundamental duality of the romantic hero. But it was in his satirical plays, particularly *The Importance of Being Earnest*, that he was at his most acerbic. A brilliant and gentle man, he poured scorn on his critics, openly espoused home rule for Ireland and lived with consummate style until the debacle of his affair with Lord Alfred Douglas. This self-obsessed bimbo persuaded Wilde into a foolish libel action against his thuggish father, the Marquess of Queensbury, which Wilde lost. Immediately afterwards he was arrested for homosexuality, publicly disgraced and privately condemned by his many fair-weather friends. He served two years in prison where he wrote his finest works, *The Ballad of Reading Gaol* and *De Profundis*. In early 1900 Ireland's greatest, and saddest, comedian died alone and distraught in Paris. "I will never live into the new century," he declared. "The English would just not allow it."

IRISH MODERNISM: POETRY AND DRAMA

Shortly before Wilde's death, the myth of the fallen hero had entered the vocabulary of Irish literature with the demise of Charles Stuart Parnell, Protestant hero of the Irish nationalist community. Savaged from the pulpit and the editorial page for his adulterous involvement with Kitty O'Shea, Parnell had resigned in disgrace, defended by only a few lonely voices in the literary world. He died shortly afterwards and Irish constitutional politics died with him.

The changed atmosphere of Irish life is caught in the work of **J. M. Synge** (1871–1909) and **George Moore** (1852–1933), who wrestled to accommodate a tradition they now saw rapidly slipping into the hands of the priests. Synge's *The Playboy of the Western World*, with its parricidal hero, is the last and perhaps the most brilliant attempt at a fundamentally English view of Irish peasant life, and was greeted by riots when it opened at the Abbey. His friend George Moore identified Catholicism as a life-denying and authoritarian creed, and his extraordinary volume *The Untilled Field* in many ways anticipates much later writers.

Meanwhile the separatist Sinn Féin party made great advances, and in 1916, led by the poet **Pádraig Pearse** (1879–1916) and **James Connolly** (1868–1916), an important socialist figure and powerful writer, there was an armed insurrection in Dublin. It was crushed savagely. Connolly and all the other leaders were court-martialled and shot, thereby becoming heroes overnight, and leading Yeats to observe that everything had been "changed utterly" and that "a terrible beauty" had been born.

William Butler Yeats (1865–1939) is one of the most written-about but most elusive characters in Irish literature. A Protestant aristocrat who argued for Irish independence, he helped found the world's first national theatre, *The Abbey*, before the nation even existed. He wrote early lyrical ballads about gossamer fairies and stunning sunsets until, stricken with desire for the beautiful Maude Gonne, he began reaming out some of the century's greatest works of unrequited love. Much of the work of his middle period lambasts Dublin middle class for its moneygrubbing complacency – *September 1913* is well worth a read if white-lipped rage is your thing. The late period is more problematic, producing a series of spare, lucid but complex meditations on the artist's task, but also some dodgy marching songs for the fascist Blueshirt movement.

Until the 1920s Yeats kept up a friendship with **Sean O'Casey** (1884–1964), who was that rarest of things, a working-class Irish writer. The Dublin slums in which he was born were later immortalised in his trilogy: *Shadow of a Gunman*, *Juno and the Paycock* and *The Plough and the Stars*. As with Synge, O'Casey's first nights were occasions for rioting and his plays were usually attended by more policemen than punters. Indeed one night, in one of the more unusual moments in Irish literary history, Yeats had to lead the coppers' charge into the stalls to break up the fracas. Later he harangued the audience, screeching that the very fact they had broken up his play meant that O'Casey was a genius, and that "this was his apotheosis." O'Casey's journal records that while he smiled nervously and twiddled his thumbs backstage he couldn't wait to get home so that he could look up the word "apotheosis" in the dictionary. O'Casey is currently the subject of a misplaced revisionism which condemns his plays as sentimental and preachy.

MODERN IRISH FICTION

As the tide of history turned towards national-ism and republicanism, and Yeats wondered glumly whether the tradition would die with the aristocracy, one of the seminal figures of literary modernism was emerging in Dublin. While still a student at the new University College – founded in 1908 by Cardinal John Henry Newman to provide a college for Catholic middle-class youth – **James Joyce** (1882–1941) set himself against the world of politics and religion, and announced that he would become, in his own phrase, "a high priest of art". His subsequent career was to be the epitome of obsessive dedication.

Dubliners, his first book, continued where George Moore had left off, evoking the city as a deathly place, its citizens quietly atrophying in a state of emotional paralysis. *A Portrait of the Artist as a Young Man* is largely autobio-graphical and deals with Stephen Dedalus' decision to leave Ireland, criticising the country as a priest-ridden and superstitious dump. After ten years of trying to get it published, Joyce finally had the bad luck to get it printed in 1916, year of the Easter Rising. Perhaps understandably, lack of patriotism was not fashionable. Joyce was condemned by just about everyone who mattered and quite a few people who didn't.

His next novel, *Ulysses*, came out in 1922, another flashpoint in Irish history, as the new Irish government turned its guns on its former supporters. Modelled on Homer's *Odyssey*, the book follows Stephen Dedalus and Leopold Bloom through one day and one night of Dublin life, recording their experiences with a relish and precision that repulsed the critics, including Virginia Woolf and D. H. Lawrence. The book was widely banned and its self-exiled author was condemned as a pornographer. *Ulysses* is a kaleidoscope of narrative techniques; Joyce's last work, the vast *Finnegans Wake*, is the only true polyglot novel, a bewitching – and often impenetrable – stew of languages, representing the history of the world as dreamed by its hero, Humphrey Chimpden Earwicker (alias "Here Comes Everybody", "Haveth Childers Everywhere" etc). Critics of different persuasions see it as either the pinnacle of literary modernism, or the greatest folly in the history of the novel.

The other great Irish modernist, **Samuel Beckett** (1906–89), emigrated to Paris and became Joyce's secretary in 1932. One writer has remarked that while Joyce tried to include everything in his work Beckett tried to leave everything out, and that's a pretty good summary. Beckett is bleak, pared down, exploring the fundamental paradox of the futility of speech and its absolute necessity. A modernist in his devotion to verbal precision, Beckett is on the other hand a dominant figure in what has been termed the postmodern "literature of exhaustion". As he said shortly before his death – "I have never been on my way anywhere, but simply on my way." Despite his reputation for terseness, Beckett was a prolific writer – the best places to start are the trilogy of novels (*Molloy*, *Malone Dies* and *The Unnamable*), and the play *Waiting for Godot*.

The absurdity of **Flann O'Brien** (1912–66) goes a little easier on the desperation. His comic vision of Purgatory, *The Third Policeman*, includes the famous molecular theory, which proposes that excessive riding of a bicycle can lead to the mixing of the molecules of rider and machine – hence a character who is half-man, half-bike. O'Brien's other great book, *At Swim-Two-Birds*, is a weird melange of mythology and pastiche that plays around with the notion that fictional characters might have a life inde-pendent of their creators. Under one of his several pseudonyms, Myles Na Gopaleen (Myles of the Little Horses), he wrote a daily column for the *Irish Times* for many years, and his hilarious journalism is collected in *The Best of Myles* and *Myles Away to Dublin*.

Traditional fiction continued, of course – for instance, **Brinsley MacNamara** (1890–1963) devastatingly portrayed small-town life *The Valley of the Squinting Windows*. But many writers had moved away from social observation and into a kind of modernist fantasy that had its roots way back in the Celtic twilight. **James Stephens** (1882–1950), a writer with an unjustly insignificant international reputation, used absurdity as a route to high lyricism. His *The Crock of Gold* is a profoundly moving fantasy on the Irish mythological tradition, part fairy story and part post-Joycean satire – in a sense, a precursor of "Magic Realism".

POSTWAR LITERATURE

Ireland in the late Forties and Fifties suffered severe economic recession and another wave of emigration began. Added to this, the people had in 1937 passed a Constitution – still operational today – which enshrined the Catholic Church's teachings in the laws of the land. Intolerance and xenophobia were bolstered by an economic war against Britain and a campaign of state censorship which was truly Stalinist in its vigour. Books which had never been read were snipped, shredded and scorched by committees of pious civil servants. No history of postwar Irish literature would be complete without at least a mention of *The Bell*, a highly influential but now defunct literary magazine. In the mid-Fifties it was a forum for writers like **Frank O'Connor** (1903–1966), **Seán Ó Faoláin** (1900–91) and **Liam O'Flaherty** (1897–1984), all of whom were veterans of the Independence War, and all of whom became outstanding short-story writers. They chronicled the raging betrayal they felt at state censorship and social intolerance – O'Connor's *Guests of the Nation* is perhaps the most eloquent epitaph for Ireland's revolutionary generation, a terrifying tale of the execution of two British soldiers by the IRA that influenced Brendan Behan's *The Hostage* enormously. *The Bell* also opened its pages to writers like **Peadar O'Donnell** (1893–1985), a radical socialist who, only six months before he died in 1985, publicly burned his honorary degree from the National University of Ireland on the occasion of a similar honour being conferred on Ronald Reagan.

In an infamous speech President Eamonn de Valera envisaged a new rural Ireland full of "comely maidens dancing at the crossroads and the laughter of athletic youths." But writers such as **Denis Devlin** (1908–59), **Francis Stuart** (1902–90), **Mary Lavin** (b. 1912) and **Brian Moore** (b. 1921) took up the fight for truth against propaganda. Their youths and maidens didn't dance. They were too busy packing their bags, or wandering in bewilderment across the desolate pages of an Ireland that had failed to live up to its possibilities. In their poetry **Austin Clarke** (1896–1974) and **Thomas Kinsella** (b. 1928) mourned the passing of hope into despair and fragmentation.

Patrick Kavanagh (1906–67) was an exception to all the rules. His poetry is almost entirely parochial, celebrating what he called "the spirit-shocking wonder of a black slanting Ulster hill", and his contemplative celebrations of the ordinary made him perhaps Ireland's best-loved poet. But as time went on, the harshness of reality began to press in on his work. His long poem *The Great Hunger* portrays rural Ireland – the same Ireland that Kavanagh had extolled – as physically barren, with the blasted landscape an incisive metaphor for sexual repression. Its publication was widely condemned and the writer was even questioned by the police, an event he discussed with customary venom in his own newspaper, *Kavanagh's Weekly*.

The forces of reaction were again about to wage war on Irish literature. O'Casey's anti-clerical play *The Drums of Father Ned* was produced in Dublin in 1955 and received aggressive reviews. Three years later there was a proposal to revive it for the new Dublin Theatre Festival. The Catholic Archbishop of Dublin, John Charles McQuaid, insisted that the plans be dropped, and when the Trade Unions stepped into the fray on his behalf, he succeeded. The year before, the young director Alan Simpson had been arrested and his entire cast threatened with imprisonment for indecency following the first night in Dublin of Tennessee Williams's play *The Rose Tattoo*. The important novelist **John McGahern** (b. 1935) lost his teaching job in a Catholic school in 1966 following the publication of his second book *The Dark*. It's a marvellous novel, dealing tenderly with adolescence and clerical celibacy, and was immediately banned.

A more celebrated literary victim – in this case a self-destructive one – was **Brendan Behan**, who died in 1964, only six years after the publication of his first book, *Borstal Boy*. He spent the last years of his life as a minor celebrity, reciting his books into tape recorders in Dublin pubs, drunk and surrounded by equally drunk admirers, some of whom sobered up for long enough to try and save him from becoming the victim of his own myth.

CONTEMPORARY WRITING

It was only in the Seventies that the climate of repression began to lift, and a sophisticated and largely progressive generation began to publish. **Seamus Heaney** (b. 1939) came to prominence as the unofficial leader of an unofficial group of Northern Irish poets who combine a sophistication of technique with a thoughtful political commitment. **John Banville** (b. 1945) brought out his first book, *Long Lankin*, in 1970 – a precocious debut that has been followed by a string of extraordinarily inventive novels.

The *Irish Writers' Co Op* produced novelists such as **Desmond Hogan** (b. 1951), **Ronan Sheehan** (b. 1953) and **Neil Jordan** (b. 1951), the last of whom has gone on to major international acclaim as a film director (*Company of Wolves, Mona Lisa*). Courageous young publishing companies founded by writers began to appear, of which Peter Fallon's *Gallery*, Dermot Bolger's *Raven Arts Press*, and Steve McDonogh's *Brandon* are still going from strength to strength.

At the end of the decade **Paul Durcan** (b. 1944) emerged as the inheritor of Kavanagh's mantle. He is a quirkily witty and profoundly religious poet, whose work encompasses social issues such as IRA bombings and Ireland's prohibition of divorce and abortion, but always addresses them in personal terms.

Other important poets include **Richard Murphy** (b. 1927), **Brendan Kennelly** (b. 1936), **Michael Hartnett** (b. 1941), **Padraic Fiacc** (b. 1924), **Derek Mahon** (b. 1941), **Michael Longley** (b. 1939), **Medbh McGuckian** (b. 1950) and **Eavan Boland** (b. 1944). Even more recently **Christopher Nolan** (b. 1965), a severely disabled writer, has proved to be an amazing talent, employing a rich language reminiscent of Dylan Thomas. His first book of poetry, *Damburst of Dreams*, received great acclaim and he later won the Whitbread Prize for his autobiographical novel *Under The Eye of The Clock*.

Drama has undergone a resurgence too, with Galway's *Druid Theatre* doing groundbreaking reinterpretations of Irish classics under the guidance of its brilliant director Garry Hynes. Roddy Doyle and Paul Mercier's *Passion Machine* theatre company offers plays about urban working-class experience in the manner of Stephen Berkoff or John Godber. Two other good young companies whose work is political and challenging, if more international in scope, are *Co-Motion* and *Rough Magic*. A more established and successful company is *Field Day*, a northern-based team founded by poets **Seamus Deane** (b. 1940) and **Tom Paulin** (b. 1949), and playwright **Brian Friel** (b. 1929). In addition to producing plays, *Field Day* publishes an excellent series of cultural and critical journalism pamphlets.

Any list of Ireland's innovative theatre writers must include **Thomas Murphy** (b. 1936) and **Thomas Kilroy** (b. 1934), but in the opinion of many the most important dramatist to emerge in the last few decades is **Frank McGuinness** (b. 1953). His play *Observe the Sons of Ulster Marching Towards the Somme*, staged in Dublin as talks began on the Anglo-Irish Agreement, focuses on the participation of a group of Northern loyalists in the Battle of the Somme. Its imagery exploits the symbolism of the whole Irish tradition, permitting a range of readings, in which the Somme represents the current situation in the North, or the battlefield of the Boyne, or the slaughters of the early sagas. It was his 1987 piece, *Carthaginians*, a play set in his native Derry, which thrust him into the major league of Irish writers. The play found a vocabulary in which to explore ancient Irish themes – the nature of political allegiance, death and resurrection, the relationship between Britain, Ireland and the North, sexuality, religion – in a way that seems to sum up the whole tradition while simultaneously threatening to demolish it. His work provides, if not some hope of unifying the various strands of Ireland's long cultural histories, at least an analysis of what divides them.

Joe O'Connor

BOOKS

This list is short by necessity, but anything you don't find here will be included in Maurice Harmon, *Select Bibliography for the Study of Anglo-Irish Literature* (Dublin 1977). Dates given below are those for most recent publication, not original publication. All these books are in paperback unless otherwise stated.

HISTORY AND POLITICS

J. C. Beckett *The Making of Modern Ireland 1603–1923* (Faber). Concise and elegant, this is probably the best introduction to the complexities of Irish history.

David Beresford *Ten Men Dead* (Grafton). Revelatory account of the 1981 hunger strike, using the prison correspondence as its basic material; a powerful refutation of the demonologies of the British press.

Peter Beresford Ellis *Hell or Connaught* and *The Boyne Water* (both Blackstaff). Vivid popular histories of Cromwell's rampage and the pivotal Battle of the Boyne.

Terence Brown, *Ireland: A Social and Cultural History 1922–1985* (Fontana). Brilliantly perceptive survey of writers' responses to the dog's breakfast made of post-revolutionary Ireland by its leaders.

James Connolly, *Selected Writings* (Pluto). Classic texts from the father of modern Irish socialism.

Tim Pat Coogan *The IRA* (Fontana). Substantially revised since its first publication in 1970, this well-researched and even-handed study remains the authoritative book on the subject.

Liz Curtis, *Ireland: the Propaganda War* (Pluto). An unanswerable indictment of the truth-bending of the British media.

John Devoy, *Recollections of an Irish Rebel* (Irish University Press). Pricey but excellent personal account from an old Fenian troublemaker.

Myles Dillon (ed.), *Lebor Na Cert: The Book of Rights* (Irish Texts Society). Fascinating and literary explanation of the early Brehon laws.

Michael Farrell, *Arming the Protestants: The Formation of the Ulster Special Constabulary and the Royal Ulster Constabulary, 1920–1927* (Pluto). Farrell is a fine journalist and veteran of Northern Ireland's civil rights campaigns. Argues, as the title implies, from a republican standpoint.

Michael Farrell *Northern Ireland: The Orange State* (Pluto). Occasionally tendentious but extremely persuasive political account of the development of Northern Ireland.

Roy Foster, *Modern Ireland 1600–1972* (Allen Lane). Superb and provocative new book, generally reckoned to be unrivalled in its scholarship and acuity, although it has been criticised for what some feel to be an excessive sympathy towards the Anglo-Irish. Not recommended for beginners.

Robert Kee, *The Green Flag* (Penguin; 3 vols). Scrupulous history of Irish Nationalism from the first plantations to the creation of the Free State. Masterful as narrative and as analysis.

Joseph Lee, *The Modernisation of Irish Society* (Gill & Macmillan). Collection of learned but refreshingly jargon-free articles.

F. S. L. Lyons, *Ireland Since the Famine* (Fontana). The most complete overview of recent Irish history, either iconoclastic or revisionist, depending on your point of view.

T. W. Moody and **F. X. Martin**, *The Course of Irish History* (Mercier Press). Shows its age a bit, but still very good on early Irish history.

Cecil Woodham Smith, *The Great Hunger* (Hamish Hamilton). Definitive, harrowing history of the Famine.

A. T. Q. Stewart, *The Narrow Ground* (Pretari). A Unionist overview of the history of the North from 1609 to the 1960s, providing an essential background to the current situation.

GAELIC TALES AND MUSIC

Brendan Behan, *An Giall*; in English, *The Hostage* (Methuen). Behan's play is better in Gaelic, but still pretty good in English. The best work from an overrated writer.

Breandán Breathnach, *Folk Music and Dances of Ireland* (Mercier Press). All the diddley-eye you could want, and in one volume.

Kevin Danaher, *Folk Tales of the Irish Countryside* (Mercier Press). The best available volume on fairy and folk tales, recorded with a civil servant's meticulousness and a novelist's literary style.

Myles Dillon (ed.), *Irish Sagas* (Mercier Press). A good examination of Cúchulainn, Fionn Mac Cumhaill etc, in literary and socio-psychological terms.

Myles Dillon, *Children's Book of Irish Folktales* (Mercier Press). Fairies, will o' the wisps, puck-oons and nasty hags with pointy noses.

Seamus Heaney, *Buile Suibhne*; in English, *Sweeney Astray* (Faber). A modern translation of the ancient Irish saga of the mad king Sweeney.

Thomas Kinsella and Seán Ó Tuama, *An Duanaire: Poems of the Dispossessed* (Dolmen Press). Excellent translations of stark Gaelic poems on famine and death. See also Kinsella's translation of one of the earliest sagas, the *Táin Bó Cuailnge* (Dolmen Press, 1985; £4.95)

Thomas Moore, *Irish Melodies*, edited by Seán Ó Faoláin (Irish University Press). All the prettied-up tunes Moore stole from the harpers, along with lyrics of mind-numbingly perfect rhythm. Moore is an important historical figure, who expressed the nationalism of the emerging middle class and brought revolution into the parlour.

Pádraig Ó Conaire, *Finest Stories* (Poolbeg Press). Ó Conaire's dispassionate eye roams over the cruelties of peasant life.

Tomás Ó Criomhtháin (sometimes Thomas O'Crohan), *An tOileánach*; in English, *The Islandman* (Oxford University Press). Similar to Ó Conaire but non-fiction and, if possible, even more raw.

George Petrie, *The Native Music of Ireland* (Gregg International Books). One of the most important cultural documents in Irish history.

Mark J. Prendergast, *Irish Rock: History, Roots and Perspectives* (The O'Brien Press). The only decent book on Irish rock music.

Peig Sayers, *An Old Woman's Reflections* (Oxford University Press). Unfortunately, Sayers's complacent acceptance of her own powerlessness is still held up as an example to Irish schoolchidren. Still, in spite of itself, a frightening insight into the eradication of the Gaelic language through emigration, poverty and political failure. A funny deconstruction of the Sayers style is Flann O'Brien's *An Béal Bocht*; in English, *The Poor Mouth* (Paladin).

William Butler Yeats, *Fairy and Folk Tales of Ireland* (Pan). Yeats gets all misty eyed about an Ireland that never existed.

FICTION

John Banville, *Birchwood* (Paladin); *The Newton Letter* (Panther); *The Book of Evidence* (Secker and Warburg). Three novels from the most important Irish novelist since McGahern, including his 1989 Booker Prize nomination, a sleazy tale of a weird Dublin murder.

Leland Bardwell, *The House* (Brandon Books). Quirky, bleak prose, often dealing with domestic violence, male cruelty, drink and poverty. But funny too, in a black way.

Samuel Beckett, *Molloy/Malone Dies/The Unnamable* (Picador). A wonderful trilogy of breakdown and glum humour.

Brendan Behan, *Borstal Boy* (Black Swan Press). Behan's gutsy *roman à clef* about his early life in the IRA and in jail.

Elizabeth Bowen *The Death of the Heart* (Penguin). Finely tuned tale of the anguish of unrequited love; generally rated as the masterpiece of this obliquely stylish writer.

Clare Boylan, *Concerning Virgins* (Penguin, 1991) Thirteen short stories from an emerging star of contemporary fiction, her first book since the novel *Nail on the Head* (Penguin, 1985).

Maria Edgeworth, *Castle Rackrent* (Oxford University Press). Best of the "Big House" books, in which Edgeworth displays a subversively subtle sympathy with her peasant narrator. Would have shocked her fellow aristos if they'd been able to figure it out.

Desmond Hogan, *A Curious Street* (Picador); *A New Shirt* (Faber). Closet gays, small town runaways, IRA bombers holed up in London bedsits, Hogan's characters are always outsiders in a hostile world. One of the country's most lyrical and rhapsodic prose writers.

Neil Jordan, *A Night in Tunisia and Other Stories* (Chatto). Jordan's Ireland is one where everything is implied and never said. The title story weaves together a painful evocation of lost innocence with the healing power of great music. See also his filmscript, with David Leland, for *Mona Lisa* (Faber, 1986).

James Joyce, *Dubliners* (Paladin); *Portrait of the Artist as a Young Man* (Grafton); *Ulysses* (Penguin); *Finnegans Wake* (Faber). No novel written in English this century can match the linguistic verve of *Ulysses*, Joyce's monumental evocation of twenty-four hours in the life of Dublin. From the time of its completion until shortly before his death – a period of 16 years – he laboured at *Finnegans Wake*, a dream-language recapitulation of the cycles of world history. Though indigestible as a whole, it contains passages of incomparable lyricism and wit: try the "Anna Livia Plurabelle" section, and you could be hooked.

Molly Keane, *Good Behaviour* (Sphere). Highly successful comic reworking of the "Big House" novel.

Mary Lavin, *The House in Clew Street* (Virago); *Stories* (Constable; 3 vols). Until her classic work, *Tales from Bective Bridge*, gets reprinted, the best available works by this much-lauded writer.

John McGahern, *The Dark*; *The Barracks*; *Amongst Women* (all Faber). *The Barracks* is classic McGahern; stark, murderous and not a spare adjective in sight. *Amongst Women*, an excellent tale of an old Republican and the oppression of rural and family life, won the *Irish Times* literature prize in 1990.

Bernard MacLaverty, *Cal* (Penguin); *Lamb* (Penguin). Both novels of love beset by crisis, the first deals with an unwilling IRA man and widow of one of his victims. *Lamb* is the disturbing tale of a Christian Brother who absconds from a borstal with a young boy.

Brinsley MacNamara, *The Valley of the Squinting Windows* (Anvil Books). A brilliant title for a brilliant book, set in the author's Westmeath birthplace.

Deirdre Madden, *Hidden Symptoms* and *The Birds of the Innocent Wood* (both Faber). Evocatively grim novel of life in the North.

Brian Moore, *The Lonely Passion of Judith Hearne* (Paladin). Moore's early novels are rooted in the landscape of his native Belfast; this was his first, a poignant tale of emotional blight and the possibilities of late redemption by love.

Christopher Nolan, *Under the Eye of the Clock* (Weidenfeld). Extraordinary and explosive fiction debut, won Whitbread Prize in 1987. Largely autobiographical story of a handicapped boy's celebration of the power of language.

Edna O'Brien, *Johnnie I Hardly Knew You* (Weidenfeld); *The Country Girls* (Penguin). Sensitively wrought novels from a top-class writer sometimes accused, unjustly, of wavering too much towards Mills and Boon.

Flann O'Brien, *At Swim-Two-Birds* (Penguin); *The Third Policeman* (Paladin). Enter the world of Ireland's master of the ominously absurd; *At Swim-Two-Birds*, O'Brien's first novel is an exhilarating blend of Gaelic fable and surrealism.

Frank O'Connor, *Guests of the Nation* (Poolbeg Press). The best Irish political fiction this century.

Joseph O'Connor, *True Believers* (Sinclair-Stevenson, 1991); *Cowboys and Indians* (Sinclair-Stevenson, 1991). Life on the peripheries in Ireland and London: love and loss, madness and redemption.

Peadar O'Donnell, *Islanders* (Mercier Press). Evocative, mesmerising prose from important republican figure.

Julia O'Faolain, *No Country for Young Men* (Penguin). Spanning four generations, this ambitious novel traces the personal repercussions of the Civil War.

Seán Ó Faoláin, *Bird Alone* (Oxford University Press); *Collected Stories* (Constable). A master of the short story form and the juiciness of rural dialect.

Liam O'Flaherty, *The Pedlar's Revenge and Other Stories* (Wolfhound Press). Best of the postwar generation of former IRA men turned writers.

E. O. Somerville and (Violet) Martin Ross, *Some Recollections and Further Experiences of an Irish RM* (Dent). The needle pushes the begorrah factor a little too heavily here and there, but Somerville and Ross write with witty flair and are very significant for what they reveal, accidentally, about a dying class.

James Stephens, *The Crock of Gold* (Picador); *The Charwoman's Daughter* (Gill & Macmillan). Two fabulous masterpieces from the country's most underrated genius.

Bram Stoker, *Dracula* (Penguin). Stoker woke up after a nightmare brought on by a hefty lobster supper, and proceeded to write his way into the nightmares of the twentieth century.

Jonathan Swift, *Gulliver's Travels* (Penguin); *The Tale of a Tub and Other Stories* (Oxford University Press). Surrealism and satire from the only writer in the English language with as sharp a pen as Voltaire.

Colm Toibin, *The South* (Serpent's Tail) A woman turns her back on Ireland for Spain and returns 30 years later to resolve her life, and to die. Powerful first novel. *Walking along the border* (Queen Anne Press) is a more straightforward account of a (real) journey along the line that divides Northern Ireland from the rest of the island.

William Trevor, *Stories* (Penguin). Five of Trevor's short-story collections in one volume, revealing more about Ireland than many a turgid sociological thesis. Often desperately moving, Trevor is one of the true giants of Irish fiction. *Reading Turgenev* (Viking), a sensitive account of an unhappy marriage, was shortlisted for the 1991 Booker Prize.

Oscar Wilde, *The Picture of Dorian Gray* (Penguin). Wilde's exploration of moral schizophrenia. A debauched socialite maintains his youthful good looks while his portrait in the attic slowly disintegrates into a vision of evil.

POETRY

Eavan Boland, *The Journey* (Carcanet). Thoughtful, spare and elegant verse from one of Ireland's most significant women poets.

Austin Clarke, *Selected Poems* (Dolmen Press). Clarke's tender work evokes the same stark grandeur as the paintings of Jack Yeats.

Anthony Cronin, *The End of the Modern World* (Raven Arts Press). Interesting attempt to sum up hundreds of years of history in one long poem series, Cronin's latest work is ambitious and skilful.

Seamus Deane, *History Lessons* and *Selected Poems* (both Gallery). Tersely precise poems about assassination victims, slowly fragmenting relationships and the petty disasters of daily life in a divided island.

Denis Devlin. Amazingly, no collected volume of Devlin's work exists. But he's such an important poet that he must be mentioned. Selections from his work are included in most anthologies of modern Irish poetry.

Paul Durcan, *The Berlin Wall Café* (Blackstaff). A lament for a broken marriage, recounted with agonising honesty, dignity and ultimately, forgiveness. See also his *Selected Paul Durcan* (Blackstaff, 1988; £4.95).

Padraic Fiacc, *Missa Terribilis* (Blackstaff). Fiacc's work is informed by the political and social tribalisms of Northern Ireland, and explores personal relationships in these contexts.

Seamus Heaney, *Death of a Naturalist* (Faber); *Selected Poems* (Faber); *Station Island* (Faber); *Seeing Things* (Faber). The most important Irish poet since Yeats. His poems are immediate and passionate, even when dealing with complex intellectual problems and radical social divisions.

Patrick Kavanagh, *Collected Poems* (Martin Brien & O'Keefe). Joyfully mystic exploration of the rural countryside and the lives of its inhabitants by Ireland's most popular poet. See also his autobiographical novel, *Tarry Flynn* (Penguin).

Brendan Kennelly, *Cromwell* (Bloodaxe). Speculative meditation on the role of the conqueror in Irish history.

Thomas Kinsella, *Poems: 1956–1973* (Dolmen Press). See also his translations from the Irish (above) and his first-rate anthology *The Oxford Book of Irish Verse* (Oxford University Press).

Patrick MacGill, *The Navvy Poet: The Collected Poetry of Patrick MacGill* (Brandon, in Ireland; Caliban in Britain). Not exactly what modern audiences would call poetry, but MacGill's ballad-style verses are important social texts, recording with quiet outrage a migrant labourer's life of poverty and loneliness.

Shane MacGowan, *Poguetry* (Faber). Rock-solid debut by the Pogues' bardperson. Not for Yeats fans.

Medbh McGuckian, *Venus in the Rain* (Oxford University Press). Trawling the subconscious for their imagery, McGuckian's sensuous and elusive poems are highly demanding and equally rewarding.

Louis MacNeice, *Collected Poems*, (Faber). Good chum of Auden, Spender and the rest of the "Thirties' generation", Carrickfergus-born MacNeice achieves a fruitier texture and an even more detached tone.

John Montague, *Dead Kingdom* (Dolmen). Terse poetry concerned with history, community and social decay. See also his anthology, *The Faber Book of Irish Verse* (1978).

Eileán Ní Chuilleanáin, *The Rose Geranium* (Gallery). A promising and constantly surprising young poet. Joint editor of *Cyphers*, a good Dublin literary magazine.

Nuala Ní Dhomhnaill, *An Dealg Droighin* (Mercier) is published in Irish only, but haunting translations of her modern erotic verse by the fine poet Michael Hartnett are included in *Raven Introductions 3* (Raven Arts Press) and in Frank Ormsby's anthology (see below).

Frank Ormsby (ed.), *The Long Embrace: Twentieth Century Irish Love Poems* (Blackstaff). Excellent anthology with major chunks from the work of almost every important twentieth-century Irish poet from Yeats to the present day. See also his *Poets from the North of Ireland* anthology (Blackstaff, 1979).

Tom Paulin, *Fivemiletown* and *The Strange Museum* (Faber). Often called "dry" both in praise and accusation, Paulin's work reverberates with thoughtful political commitment and a sophisticated irony.

Oscar Wilde, *The Ballad of Reading Gaol* (Journeyman). The great comedian achieves his greatest success, in tragedy.

William Butler Yeats, *Collected Poems* (Papermac). They're all here, poems of rhapsody, love, revolution and eventual rage at a disconnected and failed Ireland "fumbling in the greasy till."

DRAMA

Samuel Beckett, *Complete Dramatic Works; Collected Shorter Plays; Waiting for Godot* (all Faber). Bleak hilarity from the laureate of the void. All essential for swanning around Dublin coffee shops.

Brendan Behan, *The Complete Plays* (Methuen). Flashes of brilliance from a talent destroyed by alcoholism. His *The Quare Fellow* takes up where Wilde's *Ballad of Reading Gaol* leaves off.

George Farquhar, *The Recruiting Officer* (Manchester University Press). The usual helping of cross-dressing and mistaken identity, yet this goes beyond the implications of most restoration comedy, even flirting with feminism before finally marrying everyone off in the last scene.

Brian Friel, *Dancing at Lughnasa* (Faber) Family drama by Derry playwright examines the co-existence of Catholicism and paganism in Irish society, and the tension between them.

Oliver Goldsmith, *She Stoops to Conquer* (Collins). Sparky dialogue, with a more English sheen than Farquhar. Included in the same volume is Goldsmith's novel *The Vicar of Wakefield*, an affecting celebration of simple virtue.

Augusta, Lady Gregory, *Collected Plays* (Coole Press; 3 vols). The Anglo-Irish writer who understood most about the cadences of the Irish language. This gives not only her translations, but also her original drama, an authenticity lacking in the work of others.

Frank McGuinness, *Observe the Sons of Ulster Marching Towards the Somme* (Faber); *Carthaginians* and *Baglady* (Faber). Three major works from Ireland's most important contemporary dramatist.

Sean O'Casey, *Three Plays* (Pan). Contains his powerful Dublin trilogy, *Juno and the Paycock*, *Shadow of a Gunman*, and *The Plough and the Stars*, set against the backdrop of the Civil War.

John Millington Synge, *The Complete Plays* (Methuen). Lots of begorrahs and mavourneens and other dialogue kindly invented for the Irish peasantry by Synge; but *The Playboy of the Western World* is a brilliant and unique work, greeted in Dublin by riots, threats and moral outrage.

Oscar Wilde, *Complete Works* (Collins). Bittersweet satire, subversive one-liners and profound existentialist philosophy all masquerading as well-made, drawing-room farce.

William Butler Yeats, *Collected Plays* (Papermac). Long-haired hunky Celts and gorgeous princesses, as Yeats inaugurates the Finian's Rainbow school of Irish History. Stick to the poems.

OTHER NON-FICTION

Sally Belfrage, *The Crack* (Grafton). Readable if romanticised anecdotes and impressions of an American journalist, covering the spectrum of Belfast communities.

A. M. Brady and Brian Cleeve, (eds.), *Biographical Dictionary of Irish Writers* (Lilliput). Succinct entries on all the greats, better used as a magical mystery tour through the lost byways of Irish literature.

Seamus Deane, *Short History of Irish Literature* (Hutchinson). Deane brings a poet's sensitivity to a massive and sometimes unwieldy tradition, with skill and a profound sense of socio-political context.

Richard Ellmann, *James Joyce* (Oxford University Press); *Oscar Wilde* (Penguin). Ellman's *Joyce* is a major literary work in itself, a massive and brilliant book. His *Oscar Wilde* is at least its equal, an eloquent corrective to the image of Wilde as an intellectual mayfly.

Myles na Gopaleen, (aka Flann O'Brien), *Myles Away From Dublin* (Grafton). Hilarious journalism, pillorying petty bureaucracy, snobbery and pretension.

C. Desmond Greaves, *The Life and Times of James Connolly* (Lawrence & Wishart). Slightly folksy biography of major Irish socialist in which Greaves makes no secret of his unqualified admiration for his subject.

Michael Holroyd, *The Search for Love; The Pursuit of Power; The Lure of Fantasy, 1918–50* (all Chatto). Holroyd's three-part biography of Shaw has been unfairly slammed by the critics, but is actually a pretty successful stab at understanding one of the most difficult and complex authors in the whole Anglo-Irish canon.

Field Day Pamphlets, especially: **Seamus Deane**, *Heroic Styles: The Tradition of an Idea*; **Declan Kiberd**, *Anglo-Irish Attitudes*; **Michael Farrell**, *Apparatus of Repression in Ireland*; and **Seamus Heaney**, *An Open Letter*. Other pamphlets by Robert McCartney (a northern Unionist lawyer), Tom Paulin and other leading lights of the Irish cultural scene. *The Field Day Anthology of Irish Writing* (Field Day/Faber; general editor Seamus Deane) is a book to visit rather than buy: running to more than 4000 pages (in three volumes), and covering everything from early Celtic literature to the present, it costs £150. This insanely ambitious project aims to examine the nature of Irish writing - emphatically not just literature: as well as plays, poems, novels, it includes political speeches, pamphlets, analyses and essays, a fine record of a primarily literary culture.

Brenda Maddox, *Nora: A Biography of Nora Joyce* (Minerva). Eminently readable story of the funny, irreverent and formidable Nora Barnacle and her life with James Joyce – an interesting complement to Ellmann's Joyce biography.

T. Augustine Martin, *Anglo-Irish Literature* (Irish Department of Foreign Affairs). Readable scholarship and precise insight from the country's foremost Yeatsian scholar.

Nell McCafferty, *The Best of Nell* (Attic Press). Along with: *Magill* magazine's Gene Kerrigan, Nell McCafferty is Ireland's best journalist. Read the article *The Accusing Finger of Raymond Gilmour* in this volume. It will tell you more about Northern Ireland's divisions than anything you've read before.

Niall McCullough & Valerie Mulvin, *A Lost Tradition: The Nature of Architecture in Ireland* (Gandon Editions) A sensitive account of the common buildings of Ireland, making sense of structures from bawns and barracks to churches and country houses.

Tim Robinson, *The Stones of Aran* (Viking). Said by some to be the most perceptive book on Ireland yet produced by an English travel writer.

LANGUAGE

Irish is a Celtic language, evolved from a linguistic base of which ancient Gaulish is the sole written record.

The Celtic settlement of Ireland probably began in the seventh century BC; the later migration of Irish tribes to the Isle of Man and to Scotland established Irish-speaking kingdoms in those areas. With the rise of Rome the Celtic languages survived only in the peripheral western areas – today, Celtic languages are limited to parts of Scotland, Wales and Brittany in addition to Ireland. Cornish, another Celtic derivative, died out in the eighteenth century and this century Manx ceased to be a community language. In Ireland a succession of invaders speaking Norse, French and English were assimilated into the population, with resulting cross-fertilisation of languages. The first Anglo-Norman aristocracy became thoroughly Gaelicised, and even as late as 1578, the Lord Chancellor could report that "all English, and most part with delight, even in Dublin, speak Irish and greatly are spotted in manners, habit and conditions with Irish stains".

This situation soon changed, however. The Tudor and Stuart wars, Cromwell's campaign, the Orange invasion and the subsequent Penal Laws, resulted in the virtual elimination of the Irish aristocratic and learned classes and replaced them with English-speaking landowning middle classes.

Immediately after independence in 1921, Irish was installed as the first national language and steps were taken to revive it as a community tongue. It's now estimated that in the designated Irish-speaking (*Gaeltacht*) areas – in County Donegal, Galway and north Mayo, and in Counties Kerry, Cork and Waterford – there are around 66,000 speakers of the language, which is 77 percent of the *Gaeltacht* population. The use of Irish is widespread in Irish society, on public notices and documents, on television and radio, and in newspapers, books and magazines. Irish has been compulsory in Irish schools since independence, and until recently a qualification in Irish was required for university matriculation and for entrance to the civil service.

Yet figures show that only 30 percent of the population is competent in the language, and that the native speaker category is still declining, paralleling the population decline in the Gaeltacht areas. Only half of Irish children are introduced to the language before they attend school. The modernisation of Irish society is accelerating the decline of the native tongue, which has become associated with an economic status lower than that implied by the use of the international English language. The new social structures being introduced to these are threatening the existence of the tightly knit family communities on which the survival of Irish as a living language depends.

PHRASE BOOKS AND PRIMERS

Teach Yourself Irish, Miles Dillon/Donncha Ó Cróinín (Hodder, £2.50).
Archaic teaching methods, student needs to be a saint, southern dialects favoured.

Learning Irish Mícheál Ó Siadháil (Yale University Press, £10.95)
Modern guide to language through speaking. Cassettes available. Strong on grammar. Connaught dialect preferred.

The Pocket Irish Phrase Book (Apple Tree, £1.95)
Excellent introduction with useful background information. Brief on grammar but good on pronunciation. Dialect differences taken into consideration. Not possible to learn the language from this booklet but it is a valuable aid to any learner.

A GAELIC PRIMER

Although virtually everyone in Ireland speaks English, in the strong Gaeltacht areas you might hear almost no English at all. Obviously, people will speak with you in English when you arrive, but the greeting will be a lot warmer if you show even the most basic interest in the language. Should you take things a bit further and attend a college céilí, bear in mind that any student caught speaking English to you could face expulsion. Below are listed the most basic vocabulary and phrases you may like to try and use, and a bibliography of text books is on the facing page if you're intent on taking it any further.

Vocabulary

Yes	*Tá (ta)*	school	*scoil (scoyle)*
No	*Níl (neel)*	hospital	*ospidéal (oss-pe-jall)*
I am not	*Nílim (neelim)*	she	*sí (she)*
Hello	*Dia duit (jeea ditch)*	dry	*tirim (chirrim)*
Hello (in return)	*Dia's muire duit (jeea smoora ditch)*	cheers	*sláinte (slahncha)*
		Mass	*Aifreann (aff-rin)*
How are you doing?	*Cad é mar atá tú (ka jay mar a ta too)*	ocean	*aigéan (ag-ay-an)*
		money	*airgead (are-eh-gidge)*
Welcome	*Fáilte romhat (fal-cha row-at)*	weather	*aimsir (am-sheer)*
Goodbye (to the person leaving)	*Slán leat (slann lat)*	beautiful	*aoibhinn (even)*
		brown	*donn (don)*
Goodbye (to the person staying)	*Slán agat (slann ugget)*	black	*dubh (doo)*
		blue	*gorm (gawrim)*
I would like..	*Ba mhaith liom..(ba wo lum)*	red	*dearg (jarrug)*
Would you like..	*Ar maith leat..(air wo lat)*	fort	*dún (doon)*
the	*an (an)*	two	*dó (daw)*
who?	*cé?(kay)*	bright	*geal (gal)*
where?	*cén áit? (kane átch)*	also	*freisin (freshin)*
which?	*cé acu? (kay awkoo)*	another	*eile (ella)*
morning	*maidin (mojeen)*	I listen	*éistim (ayshcheem)*
day	*lá(laa)*	flute	*feadóg mhór (fadhawg wore)*
here	*anseo (on-shuh)*	fiddle	*fidil (fíjill)*
work	*obair (ubber)*	perhaps	*b'fhéidir (bayjir)*
quick	*luath/beo (looa/byaw)*	meat	*feoil (foil)*
OK	*ceart go leor (kyart go lower)*	hotel	*ostán (o-stan)*
food	*bia (bee-a)*	airport	*aerfort (air-fawrt)*
the famine	*an gorta mór (an gawrta more)*	street	*sráid (sroidj)*
big	*mór (more)*	town	*baile (bolya)*
small	*beag (bug)*	house	*teach (choch, rhymes with loch)*
island	*inis (innish)*	pub	*teach tábhairne (chachh taw-wir-na)*
centre	*lár (lahr)*		
milk	*bainne (bonya)*	poet	*file (filla)*
but	*ach (och)*	a romantic tale	*finscéal (feenscale)*
to	*do (daw)*	traditional music	*ceol traidisiúnta ¦cyawl traa-dish-oonta)*
at	*ag (eg)*		
from	*ó (aw)*	story	*scéal (scale)*
he	*sé (shay)*	tired	*tuirseach (tirshock)*
old	*sean (shan)*	thirsty	*tart (tart)*
young	*óg (ogue, rhymes with brogue)*	water	*uisce (ishka)*
tea	*tae (tay)*	whisky	*uisce beatha (ishka baha)*
cold	*fuar (foo-ar)*	station	*stáisiún ¦sta-shoon)*
pound	*punt (punt)*	post office	*oifig an phoist (iffig-on-fwisht)*
accordion	*bosca ceoil (boxa kyoil)*	song	*amhrán (hour-run)*
monastery	*mainistir (mon-ish-tcher)*	ten	*deich (jeh)*

Some Useful Phrases

It's a nice morning	*Tá an mhaidin go deas (ta an wojeen go jass)*	I'm hungry	*Tá ocras orm (ta aw-crus aw-rim)*
How much is that?	*Cá mheád sin? (Ka vayad shin)*	I'd like a room	*Ba mhaith liom seomra (bah wwych lum shawm-ra)*
It's a warm day	*Tá an lá te (ta an laa chay)*	Can you play the fiddle?	*An féidir leat an fidil a seinnm? (an fay-jure lat an fijil a shennim)*
Does the train stop at Derry?	*An stadann an traein ag Doire? (an sta-dan an train eg derrah)*		
Where is the man?	*Ca bhfuil an fear? (ka will an far)*	A pint of beer	*Pionta leanna (peenta lanna)*
Good night	*Oíche mhaith (ee woh)*	Would you like to dance?	*Ar mhaith leat damhsa? (ar mwaîch lat douse-ah)*
I understand	*Tuigim (tiggim)*	Will there be any music tonight?	*An mbeidh aon cheol ann anocht? (an may ayn kyole unn anocht)*
I don't understand	*Ní thuigim (nee higgim)*		
What's your name?	*Cad é an t-ainm atá ort? (ka jay an tan-nym a ta awrt)*	Do you speak Irish?	*An bhfuil Gaeilge agat? (an will gail-i-geh uggat)*
My name is Mary	*Máire an t-ainm atá orm (my-ra an tan-nym a ta aw-rim)*	I don't speak English	*Níl Béarla agam (neil Bare-lah sawg-um)*
		I don't know	*Níl a fhios agam (neil iss sawg-um)*
Excuse me	*Gabh mo leithscéal (gum awh lesh-kill)*	What time is it now?	*cad é an t-am é anois (ka jay an tam ay a-nish)*
		Where do you live?	*Cá bhfuil tú i do chónaí? (ka will too eh daw chon-nay)*

AN IRISH GLOSSARY

BAWN A castle enclosure or castlefold.

BODHRÁN (pronounced "bore-run") A hand-held, shallow, goatskin drum.

B-SPECIALS Auxiliary police force of the Stormont government, disbanded 1971.

CASHEL A kind of rath (see below), distinguished by a circular outer stone wall instead of earthern ramparts.

CLOCHÁN A beehive-shaped, weather-proof hut built of tightly fitted stone without mortar. Clocháns date from the early Christian period.

"THE CRACK" Good conversation, a good time, often accompanying drinking. "What's the crack?" meaning "what's the gossip?"

CURRACH/CURRAGH Small fishing vessel used off the west coast; traditionally made of leather stretched over a light wood frame, modern currachs are of tar-coated canvas.

THE DÁIL Lower house of the Irish Parliament.

DOLMEN (or "portal tomb") A chamber formed by standing stones that support a massive capstone. The capstone often slopes to form the entrance of the chamber. Date from the Copper Age (2000 BC – 1750 BC).

DRUMLIN Small, oval, hummocky hill formed from the detritus of a retreating glacier.

DUP Democratic Unionist Party, a loyalist political party founded by Ian Paisley and Desmond Boal (Shankill MP) in 1971. The party appeals to the hard-line loyalist section of the Protestant community, staunchly defends the Union with Britain, and is typified by intense hostility towards Catholicism.

ÉIRE Gaelic name for Ireland, but officially indicates the twenty-six counties.

FIANNA FÁIL The largest and most successful of Ireland's two main political parties since Independence. Essentially a conservative party, it has its origins in the republican faction of Sinn Féin, and fought against pro-Treaty forces in the civil war. During the Thirties the party did much to assert Ireland's separateness from Britain, and has always claimed a united Ireland. Despite a continuing nationalist stance calling for British withdrawal, Fianna Fáil co-operates with British military cross-border operations, and when in power Haughey worked with Britain on the issue of the future of the North.

FINE GAEL Ireland's second largest political party, Fine Gael sprang from the pro-Treaty faction of Sinn Féin which formed the first Free State government in 1921. Since that time it has not been able to gain a strong majority, and short periods in office have been in coalitions – last time with the Labour party. It advocates more liberal policies than Fianna Fáil in terms of social welfare, but in fact there is very little to distinguish the two main parties.

FIR Men (sign on men's public toilets).

GALLERY GRAVE A simple burial chamber of squared stones, generally found under a long mound.

GARDAÍ The police force of the Republic of Ireland.

INLA Irish National Liberation Army. Extreme splinter group of the IRA.

IRA Irish Republican Army.

LOYALIST A person loyal to the British Crown, usually a Northern Irish Protestant.

MNÁ Women (sign on women's public toilets).

MOTTE A circular mound, flat on top, which the Normans used as a fortification.

NATIONALIST Those who wish to see a united Ireland.

THE NORTH Term refering to Northern Ireland used by most people, except Loyalists.

OGHAM (rhyming with "poem") The earliest form of writing used by the Irish (fourth to seventh century), and found on the edge of standing stones. Employing a twenty-character alphabet derived from Latin, the letters were represented by varying strokes and notches, and read from the bottom upwards.

ORANGE ORDER A loyalist Protestant organisation, found throughout Northern Ireland, which promotes the Union with Britain. The name comes from William of Orange ("King Billy"), the Protestant king who defeated the Catholic James II at the Battle of the Boyne (1690) and at the Battle of Aughrim (1691). Most Unionist MPs are Orangemen, and outside of Northern Ireland, Orange Lodges (branches) are found amongst loyalist ex-pats.

OUP Official Unionist Party, the largest elected Protestant party.

PASSAGE GRAVE A megalithic tomb from the Neolithic period. A simple corridor of large, square, vertical stones lead to a burial chamber, and the whole tomb is covered with earth. The stones are decorated with simple patterns: double spirals, triangles, zigzag lines, and the sun symbol.

POTEEN/POITÍN (pronounced "potcheen") Highly alcoholic (and often toxic) and illegal spirit distilled from potatoes.

RATH or RINGFORT A farmstead dating from the first millennium AD. A circular timber enclosure banked by earth and surrounded by a ditch formed the outer walls, within which roofed dwellings were built and, in times of danger, cattle were herded. Today raths are visible as circular earthworks.

REPUBLICAN An Irish nationalist.

ROUND TOWER Narrow, tall (65–110 feet), and circular tower, tapering to a conical roof. Built from the ninth century onwards, they are unique to Ireland. They are found on the sites of early monasteries, and served to call the monks to prayer. The entrance is usually a doorway 10–15 feet above the ground, which was reached by a wooden or rope ladder that could be pulled up for safety.

RUC Royal Ulster Constabulary. Northern Ireland's regular, but armed, police force.

SDLP Social Democratic and Labour Party; a moderate nationalist party in the North.

SNUG Small room within a pub.

SOUTERRAIN Underground passage that served as a hiding place in times of danger; also used to store food and valuables.

TAOISEACH Irish prime minister.

TD, Teachta Dála. Member of the Irish Parliament

TRICOLOUR The green, white and orange flag of the Republic.

THE TWENTY-SIX COUNTIES The Republic of Ireland.

UDA Ulster Defence Association. A legal Protestant paramilitary organisation, the largest in Northern Ireland.

UDF Ulster Defence Force. Illegal paramilitary Protestant organisation.

UDR Ulster Defence Regiment. A regular regiment of the British army recruited in Northern Ireland.

UFF Ulster Freedom Fighters. Another illegal Protestant paramilitary faction.

UNIONISTS Those (predominantly Protestant) who wish to keep Northern Ireland in union with the rest of the United Kingdom.

UVF Ulster Volunteer Force. Yet another illegal Protestant paramilitary organisation.

INDEX

HELP US UPDATE

We've gone to considerable effort to ensure that this edition of the **Rough Guide: Ireland** is up-to-date and accurate. However, things do change, and any suggestions, comments, or corrections you can offer for the next edition would be much appreciated. We'll credit all contributions, and send a copy of the new book (or any other Rough Guide, if you prefer) for the best letters. Send them along to:
John Fisher, The Rough Guides, 1 Mercer Street, London WC2H 9QJ.

THE ROUGH GUIDES

The complete series of Rough Guides are available from all good bookshops but can be obtained directly from Penguin by writing to: *Penguin Direct, Penguin Books Ltd, Bath Road, Harmondsworth, West Drayton, Middlesex UB7 ODA; or telephone our credit line on 081 899 4036 (9am - 5pm)* and ask for Penguin Direct. Visa, Access and Amex accepted. Delivery will normally be within 14 working days.

Title	ISBN	Price
Amsterdam	1858280184	£6.99
Barcelona and Catalunya	0747102716	£7.99
Berlin	1858280338	£8.99
Brazil	0747101272	£7.95
Brittany & Normandy	1858280192	£7.99
Bulgaria	1858280478	£8.99
California	1858280575	£9.99
Canada	185828001X	£10.99
Crete	1858280494	£6.99
Cyprus	185828032X	£8.99
Czech and Slovak Republics	185828029X	£8.99
Egypt	1858280028	£9.99
Europe	1858280273	£12.99
Florida	1858280109	£7.99
France	1858280508	£9.99
Germany	1858280257	£11.99
Greece	1858280206	£9.99
Guatemala & Belize	1858280117	£7.99
Holland, Belgium, Luxembourg	1858280036	£8.99
Hong Kong & Macau	1858280761	£6.99
Hungary	1858280214	£7.99
Ireland	1858280516	£8.99
Italy	1858280311	£12.99
Kenya	185828063X	£7.99
Mediterranean Wildlife	0747100993	£7.95
Mexico	0747101493	£6.95
Morocco	1858280648	£7.99
New York	1858280737	£6.99
Nothing Ventured	0747102082	£7.99
Paris	1858280389	£7.99
Peru	0747102546	£7.95
Poland	1858280346	£9.99
Portugal	1858280222	£7.99
Prague	185828015X	£7.99
Provence/Cote d'Azur	1858280230	£8.99
Pyrenees	1858280524	£7.99
San Francisco	0747102589	£5.99
Scandinavia	1858280397	£10.99
Sicily	1858280370	£8.99
Spain	1858280079	£8.99
St. Petersburg	1858280303	£8.99
Thailand	1858280168	£8.99
Tunisia	074710249X	£8.99
Turkey	1858280133	£8.99
Tuscany and Umbria	1858280559	£8.99
U.S.A.	1858280281	£12.99
Venice	1858280362	£8.99
West Africa	1858280141	£12.99
Women Travel	1858280710	£7.99
Zimbabwe & Botswana	1858280060	£8.99

The availability and published prices quoted are correct at the time of going to press but are subject to alteration without prior notice.

Penguin Direct ordering facilities are only available in the UK.

You are
A STUDENT

You travel
THE WORLD

You want TO SAVE MONEY

Here's how

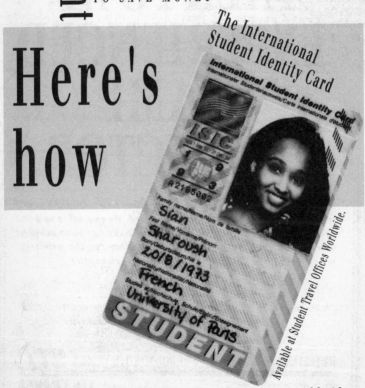

The International
Student Identity Card

Available at Student Travel Offices Worldwide.

Entitles you to discounts and special services worldwide.

BEFORE YOU TRAVEL THE WORLD, TALK TO AN EXPERIENCED STAMP COLLECTOR.

At STA Travel we're all seasoned travellers so we should know a thing or two about where you're headed. We can offer you the best deals on fares with the flexibility to change your mind as you go – without having to pay over the top for the privilege. We operate from 120 offices worldwide. So call in soon.

74 and 86 Old Brompton Road, SW7, 117 Euston Road, NW1. London.
Manchester. Leeds. Oxford. Cambridge. Bristol.
North America **071-937 9971**. Europe **071-937 9921**. Rest of World **071-937 9962**
(incl. Sundays 10am-2pm). **OR 061-834 0668 (Manchester)**
Africa Desk 071-465 0486.

WHEREVER YOU'RE BOUND, WE'RE BOUND TO HAVE BEEN.

 Retail Agents for ATOL Holders

STA TRAVEL